A FIRST BOOK OF C++

From Here to There

Second Edition

Gary J. Bronson
Fairleigh Dickinson University

Brooks/Cole Publishing Company

I(T)P® *An International Thomson Publishing Company*

Pacific Grove • Albany • Belmont • Boston • Cincinnati • Johannesburg • London • Madrid
Melbourne • Mexico City • New York • Scottsdale • Singapore • Tokyo • Toronto

Publisher: *Bill Stenquist*
Sponsoring Editor: *Kallie Swanson*
Product Developmental Editor: *Suzanne Jeans*
Marketing Manager: *Nathan Wilbur*
Editorial Assistant: *Grace Fujimoto*
Production Editor: *Kelsey McGee*
Manuscript Editor: *Connie Day*
Cover Design: *Denise Davidson*
Cover Photo: *Joseph Drivas/Image Bank*
Typesetting: *Mary Austin/Alexander Teshin Associates*
Cover Printing: *Webcom*
Printing and Binding: *Webcom*

For more information, contact:

BROOKS/COLE PUBLISHING COMPANY
511 Forest Lodge Road
Pacific Grove, CA 93950
USA

International Thomson Publishing Europe
Berkshire House 168-173
High Holborn
London WC1V 7AA
England

Thomas Nelson Australia
102 Dodds Street
South Melbourne 3205
Victoria, Australia

Nelson Canada
1120 Birchmount Road
Scarborough, Ontario
Canada M1K 5G4

International Thomson Editores
Seneca 53
Col. Polanco
11560 México, D. F., México

International Thomson Publishing GmbH
Königswinterer Strasse 418
53227 Bonn
Germany

International Thomson Publishing Asia
60 Albert Street
#15-01 Albert Complex
Singapore 189969

International Thomson Publishing Japan
Palaceside Bulding, 5F
1-1-1 Hitotsubashi
Chiyoda-ku, Tokyo 100-0003
Japan

Printed in Canada

10 9 8 7 6 5 4 3

Library of Congress Cataloging-in-Publication Data

Bronson, Gary J.
A first book of C++: from here to there
/ Gary J. Bronson. – 2nd ed.
p. cd.
ISBN 0-534-36801-8 (text)
1. C++ (Computer program language) I Title.
QA76.73.C153B76 1999 99-14647
005.13'3—dc21

Contents

Preface

". . . in the long term to get the most out of something like C++ you will need to use it in an object-oriented manner. You need to use object-oriented programming and to do object-oriented design. However, you also have to get from here to there." [1]

Object-oriented software development has been credited with many benefits, among which are reduced software development times and significant code reuse. Within the programming community, however, there has been serious debate as to how best to move to a complete object-oriented environment. The reason for this is that such an environment requires the integration of three interrelated areas: object-oriented requirements analysis (OOR), object-oriented design (OOD), and object-oriented programming (OOP).

One approach maintains that first, before any programming is attempted, object-oriented concepts should be learned. Adopting this approach means that students initially design within an object-oriented framework and only then implement a design with an object-oriented programming language.

A second approach, the one taken by this text, reverses this process: object-oriented programming (OOP) is learned first and becomes the entry point for further study into object-oriented design and requirements analysis. I believe that this approach is especially relevant to learning C++ because C++ is not a "pure" object-oriented programming language, but a hybrid that has all of the features of its procedural ancestor, C.

---

1 "Interview with Bjarne Stoustrup," *C++ Journal*, Vol. I, No. 3, pp. 16–25, 1991.

Specifically, my own experience is that it is much easier and more rewarding to work from C++ into object-oriented programming and then learn to design rather than the other way around. Doing so permits one to master the syntax and features of the language more easily and then move on, in a natural progression, to a proficiency in object-oriented programming. The text does this in two distinct steps:

- First, C++ is introduced as a language in its own right, not as an add-on to C, but as a better version of C. Thus, the procedural elements of C++ are stressed initially, with object concepts touched on for input (`cin`) and output (`cout`).
- Only after the syntax and semantics of C++ are learned are classes introduced. Proficiency in creating and using objects—including encapsulation and simple inheritance features—is then developed.

The first edition of this text was written to achieve these two objectives in recognition of C++'s growing importance in the applications and teaching areas. The success of the first edition and the many comments we received from both students and faculty stating that the book really did help them to learn and to teach C++, respectively, have been extremely gratifying.

Based on suggestions and more in-depth responses from adopters, a number of new pedagogical features and material appear in this second edition. The most extensive change has been to incorporate ANSI specifications for C++ into the text. From the standpoint of an introductory text, the actual language features affected by the new ANSI standard are not substantial. The most noticeable of these changes is that, in all program examples, `main`'s header line has been changed from `void main(void)` to `int main()`, and that the `main` function always returns a value to the operating system. Additional changes to this edition include the following:

- New material has been included on the Standard Template Library
- New material has been included on Namespaces
- New material has been added on function templates
- New "Point of Information" boxes have been added
- Information on using Visual C (versions 5.0 and 6.0) and C++ Builder have been added
- The `Date` class has been changed to store a 4-digit year to explicitly handle the Y2K problem

The basic requirement of this second edition, however, remains the same as the first edition: that all topics be presented in a clear, unambiguous, and accessible manner to beginning students. Toward this end, the central elements of the first edition remain essentially unchanged in the second edition. Thus, this new edition includes all of the topics, examples, explanations, and figures from the first edition updated to ANSI standards.

Distinctive Features of This Book

Writing Style. I firmly believe that introductory texts do not teach students—professors teach students. An introductory textbook, if it is to be useful, must be the primary "supporting actor" to the "leading role" of the professor. Once the professor sets the stage, however, the textbook must encourage, nurture, and assist the student in acquiring and "owning" the material presented in class. To do this the text must be written in a manner that makes sense to the student. My primary concern, and one of the distinctive features of this book, is that it has been written for the student. Thus, I feel the writing style used to convey the concepts presented is an important aspect of the text.

Software Engineering. Rather than simply introduce students to programming in C++, this text introduces students to the fundamentals of software engineering from both a procedural and object-oriented viewpoint. This begins with a discussion of these two programming approaches in Section 1.1, and is reinforced throughout the text.

Introduction to References and Pointers. One of the unique features of my previous text, *A First Book of C,* was the early introduction of pointer concepts. This was done by displaying the addresses of variables and then using other variables to store these addresses. This approach always seemed a more logical and intuitive method of understanding pointers than the indirection description in vogue at the time *A First Book of C* was released. I have since been pleased to see that the use of an output function to display addresses has become a standard way of introducing pointers. Although this approach, therefore, is no longer a unique feature of this book, I am very proud of its presentation, and continue to use it in this text. References are also introduced early, in Chapter 2.

Program Testing. Every C++ program in this text has been successfully compiled and run under Microsoft Corporation's Version 6.0 C++ Compiler. Source code for all program examples used in the text is available on-line. This will permit students to both experiment with and extend the existing programs and more easily modify them as required by a number of end-of-section exercises.

Pedagogical Features

To facilitate the goal of making C++ accessible as a first level course, the text includes the following pedagogical features:

Point of Information Boxes. These shaded boxes highlight important concepts, useful technical points, programming tips, and programming tricks used by professional programmers.

Chapter Supplements. Given the many different emphases that can be applied in teaching C++, these enrichment sections provide additional material that can be used—or not—to fit the needs of different students and courses.

C++ Quick Reference Card. This detachable reference card summarizes C++'s keywords, operators, statement syntax, and class structures for easy and quick reference purposes.

Function and Header File Reference. This is a quick reference of C++'s commonly used header files, library functions, and format flags.

End of Section Exercises. Almost every section in the book contains numerous and diverse skill-builder and programming exercises. Additionally, an appendix provides solutions to selected odd-numbered exercises.

Pseudocode Descriptions. The text stresses pseudocode throughout. Although the text presents flowchart symbols, it uses them only to visually demonstrate flow-of-control constructs.

Common Programming Errors and Chapter Review. Each chapter ends with a section on common programming errors and a review of the main topics covered in the chapter.

Appendices and Supplements. An expanded set of appendices includes appendices on operator precedence, ASCII codes, using the various new Visual C++ compilers, bit operations, and linked list examples using classes.

A final appendix offers solutions to selected odd-numbered problems. Source code for all program examples used in the text as well as an on-line series of supporting Microsoft® PowerPoint® slides are available at **http://www.brookscole.com/compsci/bronson/cpp**.

An instructor's manual including chapter outlines, answers to questions from the text, and a testbank of examination questions is available.

Acknowledgments

The writing of this second edition is a direct result of the success (and limitations) of the first edition. In this regard, my most heartfelt acknowledgment and appreciation is to the instructors and students who found the first edition to be of service to them in their respective quests to teach and learn C++.

Once a second edition was planned, its completion depended on the encouragement, skills, and efforts of many people. I especially want to thank the staff of Brooks/Cole Publishing Company for their many contributions. First, these include my product developmental editor, Suzanne Jeans, and acquisitions editor, Kallie Swanson. Each has become what all authors wish for, a truly skilled editor who becomes a working partner. Additionally, I am very grateful to editorial assistants Grace Fujimoto and Meg Weist for handling numerous scheduling and review details that permitted me to concentrate on the actual writing of the text.

I also wish to express my gratitude to the individual reviewers: Allan Berreitter, Fox Valley Technical College; Lee D. Cornell, Mankato State University; Barry Kolb, Ocean County College; Joe Kozlevcar, Lakeland Community College; Marlene Nudo, Youngstown State University; Art Shindhelm, Western Kentucky University; Charlotte Turner, DeVry Institute/Phoenix; Ka-Wing Wong, Eastern Kentucky University; Bob Blucher, Chemeketa College; Gerald Adkins, Georgia College and State University; and Catherine Wyman, DeVry Institute/Phoenix.

Each supplied extremely detailed and constructive reviews of the original manuscript and a number of revisions. Their suggestions and comments were extraordinarily helpful as the manuscript evolved and matured through the editorial process.

Finally, the task of turning the final manuscript into a textbook again required a dedicated production staff. I especially want to thank copy editor Connie Day, production editor Kelsey McGee, and compositor Mary Austin of Teshin Associates. Their dedication, their attention to detail, and their high standards have helped immensely to improve the quality of this edition. From the moment the book moved to the production stage they seemed to take personal ownership of the text, and I am very grateful to them.

Special thanks go to Janie Schwark, Academic Product Manager of Developer Tools at Microsoft Corporation, for providing invaluable support and product information. I greatly appreciate the priceless help and meticulous attention to detail provided by both Lea Mullikin and Lindsay Minnaar, two of my students at Fairleigh Dickinson University, in the preparation of the index. I also gratefully acknowledge the direct encouragement and support provided by Peter Falley, Fairleigh Dickinson University Provost; Paul Lerman, my dean; Ron Heim, my associate dean, and Joel Harmon, my chairperson. Without their support, this text could not have been written.

Finally, I deeply appreciate the patience, understanding, and love provided by my wife, friend, and partner, Rochelle.

Gary Bronson
1999

dedicated to

Rochelle,
Jeremy,
David,
and
Matthew Bronson

Fundamentals

Part I

Getting Started

Chapter One

1.1 Introduction to Programming

A computer is a machine, and like other machines, such as automobiles and lawn mowers, it must be turned on and then driven, or controlled, to do the task it was meant to do. In an automobile, control is provided by the driver, who sits inside of and directs the car. In a computer, control is provided by a computer program. More formally, a *computer program* is a structured combination of data and instructions that is used to operate a computer. Another term for a computer program is *software,* and we will use both terms interchangeably throughout the text.[1]

Programming is the process of writing a computer program in a language that the computer can respond to and that other programmers can understand. The set of instructions, data, and rules that can be used to construct a program is called a *programming language.*

Programming languages are usefully classified by level and orientation. Languages that use instructions resembling written languages, such as English, are referred to as *high-level languages.* Pascal, Visual Basic, C, and C++ are all examples of high-level languages.[2] The final program written in such languages can be run on a variety of computer types, such as computers manufactured by IBM, Apple, and DEC. In contrast, *low-level languages* use instructions that are directly tied to one type of computer.[3] Although programs written in low-level languages are limited in that they can be run only on the type of computer they were written for, they do permit using special features of the computer that are different from other machines. They can also be written to execute faster than programs written in high-level languages.

A second way of classifying programming languages makes use of the distinction between procedure-oriented and object-oriented languages. In a *procedure-oriented language,* the available instructions are used to create a logically consistent set of directions, called a procedure, that is meant to produce a specific result from the data. For example, consider Table 1–1, which lists the fundamental sets of instructions provided in Pascal, Visual Basic, C, and C++. Note that the instructions all resemble English words, a feature that is indicative

---

[1] More inclusively, the term *software* is also used to denote both the programs and the data that the programs will operate on.

[2] C++ is sometimes classified as a middle-level language to convey the fact that although C++ is written as a high-level language, it can also take advantage of machine features that historically could be accessed only with low-level languages.

[3] In actuality, the low-level language is defined for the processor around which the computer is constructed. These processors include the Intel microprocessor chip for IBM-type personal computers, Motorola chips for Apple-based computers, and alpha chips for many DEC-supported computers.

TABLE 1–1 Summary of Instructions in Several High-Level Programming Languages

Operation	Pascal	Visual Basic	C	C++
INPUT (Get the data)	READ READLN	INPUT	scanf() gets() getchar()	cin cin.get cin.getline
PROCESSING (Use the data)	:= IF/ELSE FOR WHILE REPEAT + - * / **	LET IF/ELSE FOR WHILE UNTIL + - * / ^	= if/else for while do +, =+, ++ -, =-, -- *, =* /, =/ pow()	= if/else for while do +, =+, ++ -, =-, -- *, =* /, =/ pow()
OUTPUT (Display the data)	WRITE WRITELN	PRINT	printf() puts() putchar()	cout

of high-level languages, and that the instructions can be conveniently grouped into input, processing, and output operations. These groupings are characteristic of a procedure-oriented approach, because they support the processing typically associated with a procedure-based program, which, as illustrated in Figure 1–1, is to accept data (input), to manipulate the data (process), and to produce a result (output).

For the last 25 years, all programming languages have been predominantly procedure-oriented. Within the past few years, a second orientation, referred to as object-oriented, has evolved to become a second major form for programming application.

One of the motivations for *object-oriented languages* has been the development of graphical screens capable of displaying multiple windows. In such an environment, each window on the screen can conveniently be considered as an object, with associated characteristics, such as color, position, and size. Under an object orientation, a program must first define the objects it will be

FIGURE 1–1 Procedure-Oriented Program Operations

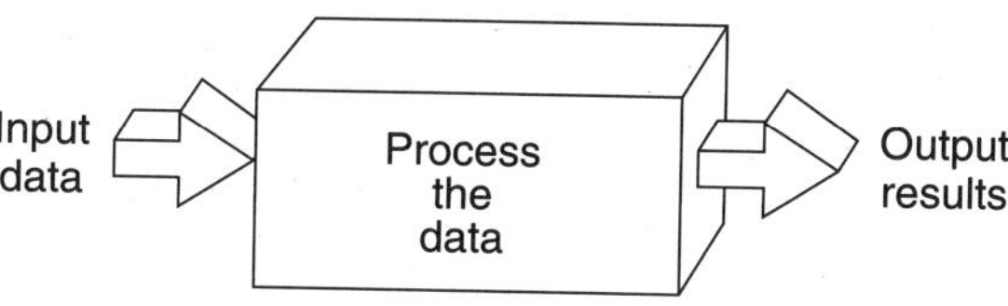

manipulating; this includes describing both the characteristics of the object and the procedures that can be used to manipulate and alter these characteristics. The remaining parts of the program are then concerned with activating each object as required. This is accomplished by passing information, called messages, to each object. As a message is passed to an object, the object responds and alters its characteristics by using its previously defined procedures. For now, it is sufficient to understand that these two distinct approaches to programming currently exist. This is because C++ contains features found in both procedure-oriented and object-oriented languages.

The reason for C++'s dual nature is that it began as an extension to C, which is a procedure-oriented language developed in the 1970s at AT&T Bell Laboratories. In the early 1980s, Bjarne Stroustrup (also at AT&T) used his background in simulation languages to develop C++. A central feature of simulation languages is that they model real-life situations as objects that respond to stimuli in well-defined ways. This object orientation, along with other procedure-oriented improvements, was combined with existing C language features to form the C++ language.

Algorithms and Procedures

Because algorithms are central to C++'s procedure-oriented side, it will serve us well to understand what an algorithm is. From a procedural point of view, before writing a program, a programmer must clearly understand what data is to be used, the desired result, and the procedure to be used to produce this result. The procedure to be used is referred to as an algorithm. More precisely defined, an *algorithm* is a step-by-step sequence of instructions that describes how a computation is to be performed.

Only after we clearly understand the data that we will be using and the algorithm (the specific steps required to produce the desired result) can we write the program. Seen in this light, procedure-oriented programming is the translation of a selected algorithm into a language that the computer can use.

To illustrate an algorithm, we shall consider a simple problem. Assume that a program must calculate the sum of all whole numbers from 1 through 100. Figure 1–2 illustrates three methods we could use to find the required sum. Each method constitutes an algorithm.

Most people would not bother to list the possible alternatives in a detailed step-by-step manner, as we did in Figure 1–2, and then select one of the algorithms to solve the problem. But then, most people do not think algorithmically; they tend to think intuitively. For example, if you had to change a flat tire on your car, you would not think of all the steps required—you would simply change the tire or call someone else to do the job. This is an example of intuitive thinking.

Method 1. *Columns:* Arrange the numbers from 1 to 100 in a column and add them:

$$\begin{array}{r} 1 \\ 2 \\ 3 \\ 4 \\ . \\ . \\ . \\ 98 \\ 99 \\ +100 \\ \hline 5050 \end{array}$$

Method 2. *Groups:* Arrange the numbers in convenient groups that sum to 100. Multiply the number of groups by 100 and add any unused numbers to the total:

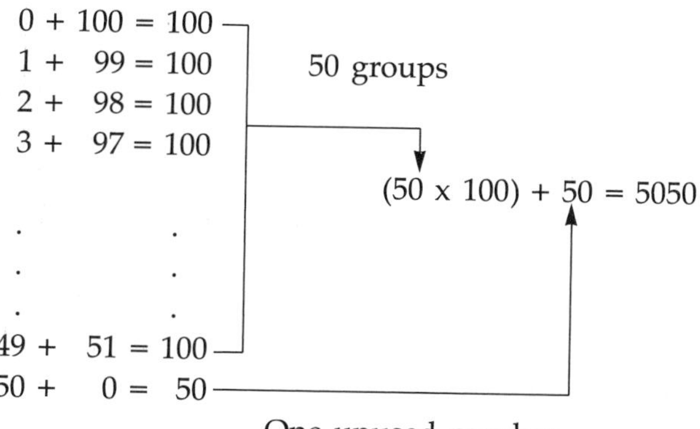

Method 3. *Formula:* Use the formula

$$\text{Sum} = \frac{n(a+b)}{2}$$

where

n = number of terms to be added (100)
a = first number to be added (1)
b = last number to be added (100)

$$\text{Sum} = \frac{100(1+100)}{2} = 5050$$

FIGURE 1–2 Summing the Numbers from 1 through 100

Unfortunately, computers do not respond to intuitive commands. A general statement such as "Add the numbers from 1 through 100" means nothing to a computer, because the computer can respond only to algorithmic commands written in an acceptable language such as C++. To program a computer successfully, you must clearly understand this difference between algorithmic and intuitive commands. A computer is an "algorithm-responding" machine; it is not an "intuition-responding" machine. You cannot tell a computer to change a tire or to add the numbers from 1 through 100. Instead, you must give the computer a detailed, step-by-step sequence of instructions that, collectively, forms an algorithm. For example, the sequence of instructions

Set n *equal to 100*
Set a = *1*
Set b *equal to 100*
Calculate sum = $\frac{n * (a + b)}{2}$

constitutes a detailed method, or algorithm, for determining the sum of the numbers from 1 through 100. Note that these instructions are not a computer program. Unlike a program, which must be written in a language the computer can respond to, an algorithm can be written or described in various ways. When English-like phrases are used to describe the algorithm (the processing steps), as in this example, the description is called *pseudocode*. When mathematical equations are used, the description is called a *formula*. When diagrams that employ the symbols shown in Figure 1–3 are used, the description is referred to as a *flowchart*. Figure 1–4 illustrates the use of these symbols in depicting an algorithm for determining the average of three numbers.

Because flowcharts are cumbersome to revise and can easily support unstructured programming practices, they have fallen out of favor among professional programmers, except for visually describing extremely simple program structures. In their place, pseudocode has gained increasing acceptance. In describing an algorithm with pseudocode, we use short English phrases. For example, acceptable pseudocode for describing the steps needed to compute the average of three numbers is

Input the three numbers into the computer
Calculate the average by adding the numbers and
  dividing the sum by 3
Display the average

Only after an algorithm has been selected and the programmer understands the steps required can the algorithm be written using computer-language statements. The writing of an algorithm using computer-language statements is called *coding* the algorithm (see Figure 1–5).

FIGURE 1–3 Flowchart Symbols

SYMBOL	NAME	DESCRIPTION
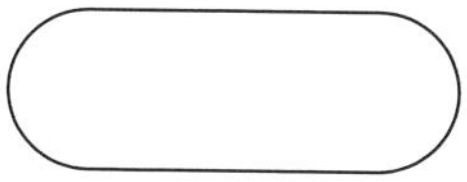	Terminal	Indicates the beginning or end of an algorithm
	Input/output	Indicates an input or output operation
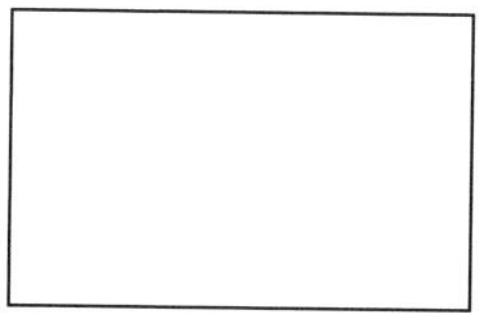	Process	Indicates computation or data manipulation
	Flow lines	Used to connect the flowchart symbols and indicates the logic flow
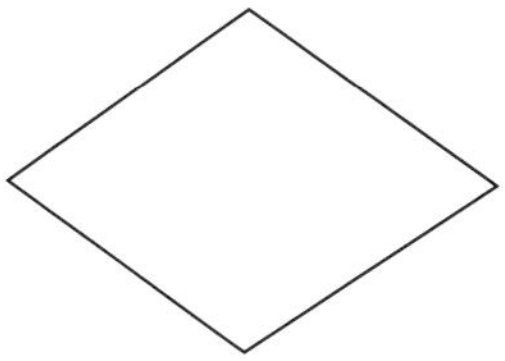	Decision	Indicates a decision point in the algorithm
	Loop	Indicates the initial, final, and increment values of a loop
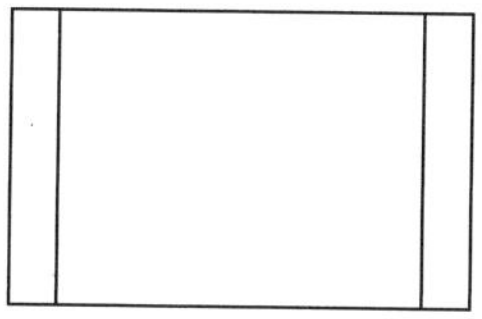	Predefined process	Indicates a predefined process, as in calling a sorting process
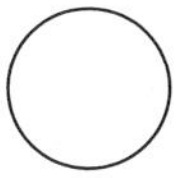	Connector	Indicates an entry to, or exit from another part of the flowchart

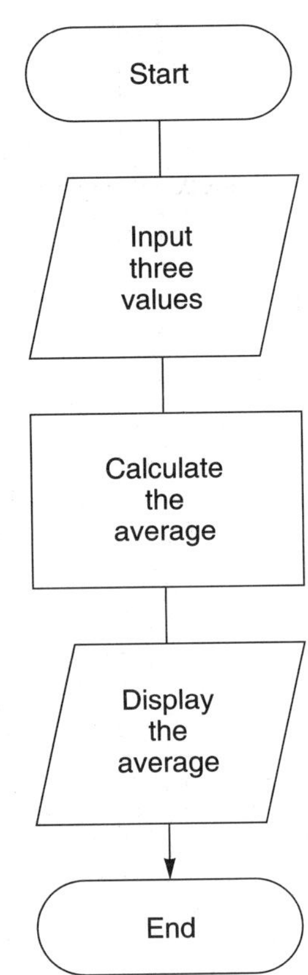

FIGURE 1–4 Flowchart for Calculating the Average of Three Numbers

Classes and Objects

Just as algorithms are central to procedure-oriented languages, classes are central to object-oriented languages, because objects are created from classes. As illustrated in Figure 1–6, an object consists of both data and the specific procedures that can be applied to the data within the object. These procedures are also referred to as methods, and we will use these terms interchangeably when talking about classes and objects.

Classes are broad categories that define both the characteristics of the data that an object can contain and the methods that can be applied to these data.

FIGURE 1–5 Coding an Algorithm

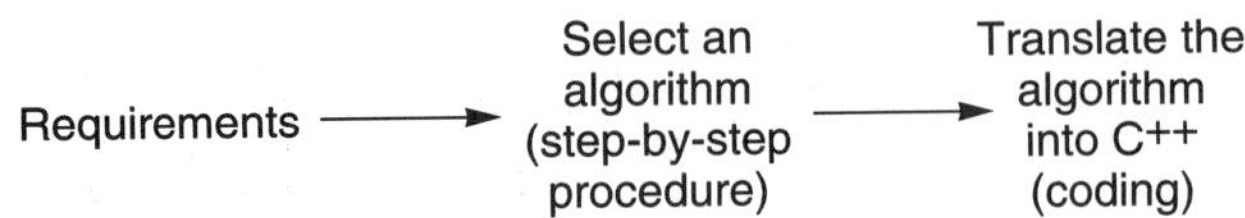

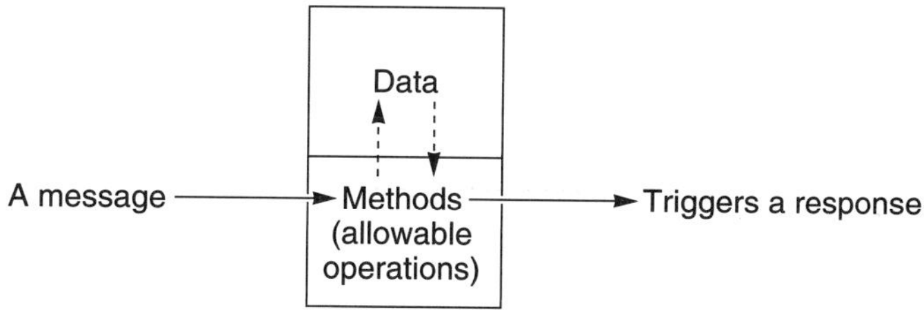

FIGURE 1–6 An Object Consists of Data and Methods

An *object* is a specific item from a class. The relationship of an object to a class is similar to the relationship of a specific geometric shape to a class of shapes. For example, if we define `Rectangles` as a class of four-sided shapes whose opposite sides are equal in length and whose adjacent sides are perpendicular, then a specific rectangle—for example, one that measures 2 inches by 3 inches—is an object of the class `Rectangles`. This particular object is a specific case, or instance, of the defined class `Rectangles`.

As a further example, consider the type of data that we call integers. If we expand the definition of integers to "all whole numbers plus the allowable methods that can be applied to integers" (the operations of addition, subtraction, multiplication, and so on), then we have, in object-oriented terms, defined a class. A number such as 5 that is a specific item from this class, in object-oriented terminology, is called an object. Again, an object is simply a particular instance of a class.

Note that a true class includes not only a data type but also the methods, or operations, that can be applied to the data in the class. A particular method is activated, or invoked, by sending the object a message (see Figure 1–6). For example, in object-oriented terms, the plus sign in an expression such as 5 + 2 is considered not an addition operation but a message: a message to the 2 object that it is to be added to the 5 object.

The important aspect of objects for our current purposes is that a message to an object triggers a well-defined response. Although we will create our own classes and objects as we become more fluent in C++, we can use any objects that are provided with C++ as long as we know the correct messages to trigger the appropriate responses. We will see shortly that two objects, named `cin` and `cout`, have been provided in C++ for the input and output, respectively, of data values. We will use these two objects extensively in our early work.

Program Translation

Once an algorithm or class is written in C++, it still cannot be executed on a computer without further translation. This is because the internal language of

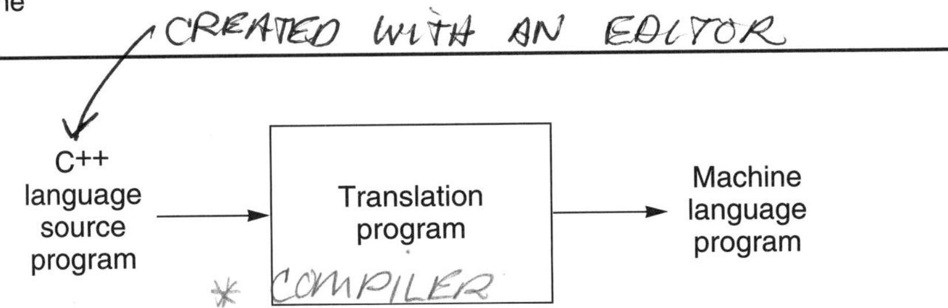

FIGURE 1–7 Source Programs Must Be Translated

all computers consists of a series of 1s and 0s, called the computer's *machine language.* To generate a machine-language program that can be executed by the computer requires that the C++ program, which is referred to as a *source program,* be translated into the computer's machine language (see Figure 1–7).

The translation into machine language can be accomplished in two ways. When each statement in the source program is translated individually and executed immediately, the programming language used is called an *interpreted language,* and the program doing the translation is called an *interpreter.*

When all of the statements in a source program are translated before any one statement is executed, the programming language used is called a *compiled language.* In this case, the program doing the translation is called a *compiler.* C++ is a compiled language. Here, the source program is translated as a unit into machine language. The output produced by the compiler is called an object program. An *object program* is simply a translated version of the source program that can be executed by the computer system with one more processing step. Let us see why this is so.

Most C++ programs contain statements that use preprogrammed routines for input and output and for finding such quantities as square roots, absolute values, and other commonly encountered mathematical calculations. Additionally, a large C++ program may be stored in two separate program files. In such a case, each file can be compiled separately. However, both files must be combined to form a single program before the program can be executed. In both of these cases, it is the task of a linker program, which is often called automatically by the compiler, to combine all of the preprogrammed routines and individual object files into a single program ready for execution. This final program is called an *executable program.*

Exercises 1.1

1. Define the following terms:
   a. computer program
   b. programming language

c. programming
d. algorithm
e. pseudocode
f. flowchart
g. procedure
h. object
i. method
j. message language
k. response
l. class
m. source program
n. compiler
o. object program
p. executable program
q. interpreter

2. Determine a step-by-step procedure (list the steps) to do each of the following tasks. ***Note:*** There is no one single correct answer for each task. The exercise is designed to give you practice in converting intuitive commands into equivalent algorithms and understanding the differences among the thought processes involved.
a. Fix a flat tire.
b. Make a telephone call.
c. Go to the store and purchase a loaf of bread.
d. Roast a turkey.

3. Determine and write an algorithm (list the steps) to interchange the contents of two cups of liquid. Assume that a third cup is available to hold the contents of either cup temporarily. Each cup should be rinsed before any new liquid is poured into it.

4. Write a detailed set of instructions, in English, to calculate the dollar amount of money in a piggybank that contains *h* half-dollars, *q* quarters, *n* nickels, *d* dimes, and *p* pennies.

5. Write a set of detailed, step-by-step instructions, in English, to find the smallest number in a group of three integer numbers.

6. *a.* Write a set of detailed, step-by-step instructions, in English, to calculate the least number of dollar bills needed to pay a bill of amount TOTAL. For example, if TOTAL were $98, the bills would consist of one $50 bill, two $20 bills, one $5 bill, and three $1 bills. For this exercise assume that only $100, $50, $20, $10, $5, and $1 bills are available.
b. Repeat Exercise 6a, but assume the bill is to be paid only in $1 bills.

7. *a.* Write an algorithm to locate the first occurrence of the name JEANS in a list of names arranged in random order.
b. Discuss how you could improve your algorithm for Exercise 7a if the list of names were arranged in alphabetical order.

8. Determine and write an algorithm to sort three numbers in ascending (from lowest to highest) order. How would you do this problem intuitively?

9. Define an appropriate class for each of the following specific objects:
a. the number 5
b. a square that measures 4 inches by 4 inches

- *c.* this C++ textbook
- *d.* a 1995 Ford Thunderbird car
- *e.* the last ballpoint pen that you used

10. *a.* What operations should the following objects be capable of doing?
   - *i.* a 1955 Ford Thunderbird car
   - *ii.* the last ballpoint pen that you used

b. Do the operations determined for Exercise 10a apply only to the particular object listed, or are they more general and applicable to all objects of the type listed?

1.2 Function and Class Names

A well-designed program is constructed by using a design philosophy similar to that used in constructing a well-designed building; it doesn't just happen but depends on careful planning and execution for the final design to accomplish its intended purpose. Just as an integral part of the design of a building is its structure, the same is true for a program.

Programs whose structure consists of interrelated segments arranged in a logical order to form an integrated and complete unit are referred to as *modular programs* (Figure 1–8). Modular programs are easier to develop, correct, and modify than programs constructed otherwise. In general programming terminology, the smaller segments used to construct a modular program are referred to as *modules.* In C++ the modules can be either classes or functions. We have already encountered classes. More formally, we can define a class as a unit containing a data structure and the procedures that can be applied to the data structure. A *function* is a simpler unit that contains only a sequence of operations.

FIGURE 1–8 A Well-Designed Program Is Built Using Modules

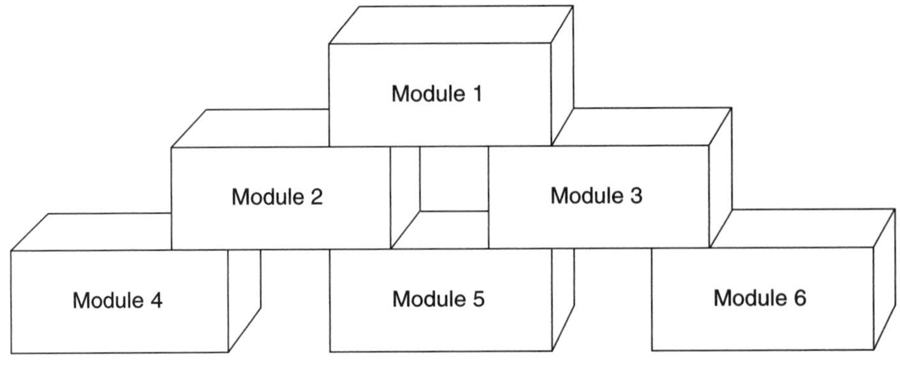

It helps to think of a function as a small machine that transforms the data it receives into a finished product. For example, Figure 1–9 illustrates a function that accepts two numbers as inputs and multiplies the two numbers to produce a result.

As illustrated in Figure 1–9, the interface to the function is its inputs and results. How the inputs are converted to results is both encapsulated and hidden within the function. In this regard, the function can be thought of as a single unit providing a special-purpose operation. A similar analogy is appropriate for a class. A class, which encapsulates both data and operations, can be thought of as a small dedicated computer. Thus each class contains all the elements required for the input, output, and processing of its objects.

One important requirement for designing a good function or class is to give it a name that conveys to the reader some idea about what the function or class does. The names permissible for functions and classes are also used to name other elements of the C++ language, and they are collectively referred to as identifiers. *Identifiers* can be made up of any combination of letters, digits, and underscores (_) selected according to the following rules:

1. The first character of an identifier must be a letter or underscore (_).
2. Only a letter, digit, or underscore may follow the initial letter. Blank spaces are not allowed; separate words in an identifier consisting of multiple words are indicated by capitalizing the first letter of one or more of the words. (Although underscores may also be used for this purpose, they are increasingly being used only for compiler-dependent identifiers.)
3. An identifier cannot be one of the keywords listed in Table 1–2. (A *keyword* is a word that is set aside by the language for a special purpose and should only be used in a specified manner.)[4]

NAMING

FIGURE 1–9 A Multiplying Function

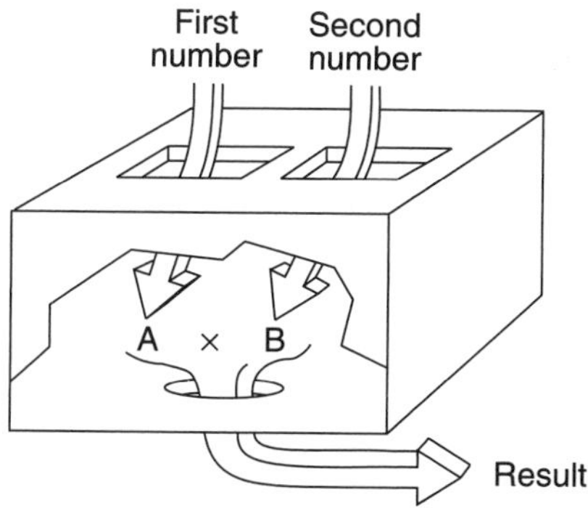

[4] Keywords in C++ are also reserved words, which means they must be used only for their specified purpose. Attempting to use them for any other purpose will generate an error message.

TABLE 1–2 C++ Keywords

auto	default	goto	public	this
break	do	if	register	template
case	double	inline	return	typedef
catch	else	int	short	union
char	enum	long	signed	unsigned
class	extern	new	sizeof	virtual
const	float	overload	static	void
continue	for	private	struct	volatile
delete	friend	protected	switch	while

4. The maximum number of characters in an identifier name is 255.[5] On some compilers, only the first 31 characters of an identifier are actually used.

Examples of valid C++ identifiers are

```
grosspay     taxCalc     addNums     degToRad
multByTwo    salestax    netpay      bessel
```

Examples of invalid identifiers are

`4ab3` (begins with a number, which violates Rule 1)
`e*6` (contains a special character, which violates Rule 2)
`while` (is a keyword, which violates Rule 3)

Besides conforming to C++'s identifier rules, a good function or class name should also be a mnemonic. A *mnemonic* is a word or name designed as a memory aid. For example, the name `degToRad` would be a mnemonic if it were the name of a function that converts degrees to radians. Here, the name itself helps to identify what is being done.

Examples of valid identifiers that are not mnemonics are

```
easy     c3po     r2d2     theForce     mike
```

Nonmnemonic identifiers should not be used, because they convey no information about their purpose.

[5] This feature is compiler-specific.

Note that all identifiers have been typed almost exclusively in lowercase letters. This is traditional in C++, although it is not absolutely necessary. Initial capitals and the use of all uppercase letters are usually reserved for symbolic constants, a topic covered in Chapter 3, and intermediate capitals are used for distinguishing words in multiword identifiers such as `degToRad`. Furthermore, C++ is a *case-sensitive* language. This means that the compiler distinguishes between uppercase and lowercase letters. In C++, therefore, `TOTAL`, `total`, and `TotaL` represent three distinct and different names.

The `main` Function

A distinct advantage of using functions and classes in C++ is that the overall structure of the program, in general, and of individual modules, in particular, can be planned in advance; this includes provision for testing and verifying each module's operation. Each function and class can then be written to meet its intended objective.

To provide for the orderly placement and execution of modules, each C++ program must have one and only one function named `main`. The `main` function is referred to as a *driver function* because it drives the other modules, or tells them the sequence in which they are to execute (Figure 1–10).[6]

Figure 1–11 illustrates a structure for the `main` function. The first line of the function, in this case `int main()`, is referred to as a function header line. A *function header line,* which is always the first line of a function, contains three pieces of information:[7]

1. What type of data, if any, is returned from the function
2. The name of the function
3. What type of data, if any, is sent into the function

The keyword before the function name defines the type of value the function returns when it has completed operation. When placed before the function's name, the keyword `int` (see Table 1–2) indicates that the function will return an integer value. Similarly, when the parentheses following the function name are empty, it signifies that no data will be transmitted into the function when it is run. (Data transmitted into a function at run time are referred to as *arguments* of the function.) The braces, `{` and `}`, determine the beginning and

[6] Modules executed from `main` may, in turn, execute other modules. Each module, however, always returns to the module that initiated its execution. This is true even for `main`, which returns control to the operating system that was in effect when `main` was initiated.

[7] As we will see in Chapter 11, a class must also begin with a header line that adheres to these same rules.

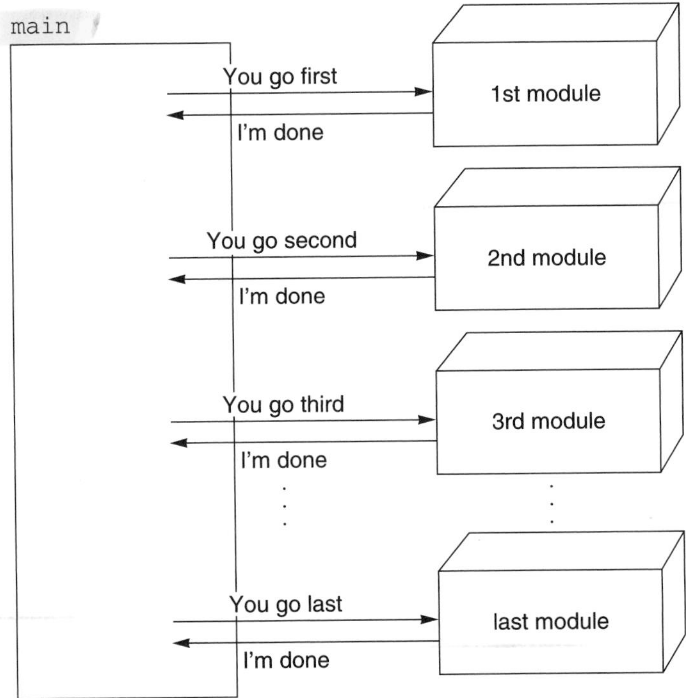

FIGURE 1–10 The `main` Function Directs All Other Modules

end of the function body and enclose the statements making up the function. The statements inside the braces determine what the function does. Each statement inside the function must end with a semicolon (`;`).

You will be naming and writing many of your own C++ functions. In fact, the rest of this book is primarily about the statements required to construct useful functions and how to combine functions and data into useful classes and programs. Each program, however, must have one and only one `main` function. Until we learn how to pass data into a function and return data from a function (the topics of Chapter 6), the header line illustrated in Figure 1–11 will serve

FIGURE 1–11 The Structure of a `main()` Function

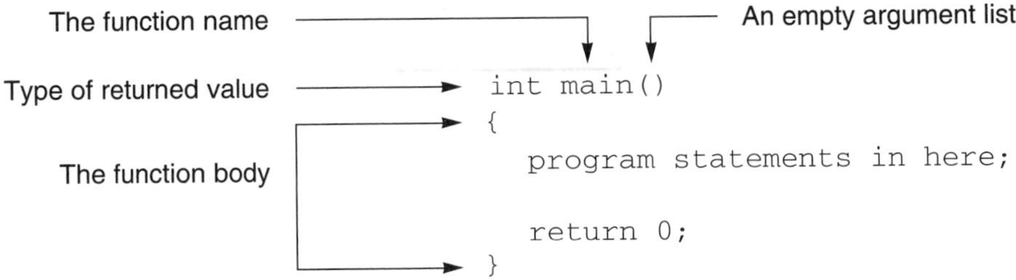

us for all the programs we need to write. Until they are explained more fully, it is useful simply to regard the first two lines

```
int main()
{
```

as indicating that "the program begins here" and to regard the last two lines

```
  return 0;
}
```

as designating the end of the program. Fortunately, many useful functions and classes have already been written for us. We will now see how to use an object created from one of these classes to create our first working C++ program.

Exercises 1.2

1. State whether the following are valid identifiers. For each that is valid, state whether it is a mnemonic name. A mnemonic identifier conveys some idea about its intended purpose. For each invalid identifier, state why it is invalid.

```
1m1234       newBal     abcd       A12345   1A2345
power        absVal     invoices   do       while
add5         taxes      netPay     12345    int
newBalance   a2b3c4d5   salesTax   amount   $taxes
```

2. Assume that functions with the following names have been written.

```
retrieveOldBal  enterSoldAmt  calcNewBal  report
```

a. From the functions' names, what do you think each function might do?
b. In what order do you think a `main` function might execute these functions (based on their names)?

3. Assume that the following functions have been written.

```
inputBill  calcSalestax  calcBalance
```

a. From the functions' names, what do you think each function might do?

b. In what order do you think a `main` function might execute these functions (based on their names)?

4. Determine names for functions that
   a. find the maximum value in a set of numbers
   b. find the minimum value in a set of numbers
   c. convert a lowercase letter to an uppercase letter
   d. convert an uppercase letter to a lowercase letter
   e. sort a set of numbers from lowest to highest
   f. alphabetize a set of names

5. Just as the keyword `int` can be used to signify that a function will return an integer, the keywords `void`, `char`, `float`, and `double` can be used to signify that a function will return no value, a character, a floating-point number, and a double-precision number, respectively. Using this information, write header lines for a `main` function that will receive no arguments but will return
   a. no value
   b. a character
   c. a floating-point number
   d. a double-precision number

1.3 The cout Object

One of the most versatile and commonly used objects provided in C++ is `cout` (pronounced "see out"). This object, whose name was derived from Console OUTput, is an output object that sends data given to it to the standard output display device. For most systems this display device is a video screen. The `cout` object displays, on the monitor, whatever is passed to it. For example, if the data `Hello there world!` is passed to `cout`, this data is printed (or displayed) on the terminal screen. The data `Hello there world!` is passed to the `cout` object by simply putting the insertion ("put to") symbol, <<, before the message and after the object's name, as shown in Figure 1–12.

Now let's put all this together into a working C++ program that can be run on your computer. Consider Program 1-1.

FIGURE 1–12 Passing a Message to `cout`

```
cout << "Hello there world!";
```

Program 1-1

```
#include <iostream.h>

int main()
{
  cout << "Hello there world!";

  return 0;
}
```

The first line of the program,

```
#include <iostream.h>
```

is a preprocessor command. *Preprocessor commands* begin with a pound sign (#) and perform some action before the compiler translates the source program into machine code. Specifically, the `#include` preprocessor command causes the contents of the named file, in this case `iostream.h`, to be inserted where the `#include` command appears.[8] The file `iostream.h` is referred to as a *header file* because it is placed at the top, or head, of a C++ program by using the `#include` command. In particular, the `iostream.h` file provides descriptions of two classes, *istream* and *ostream*. These two classes contain the actual data definitions and operations used for data input and output.[9] This header file must be included in all programs that use `cout`. As also indicated in Program 1-1, preprocessor commands do not end with a semicolon.

The preprocessor command is followed by the start of the program's `main()` function. The `main()` function begins with the header line developed in the previous section, and the body of the function, enclosed in braces, consists of only one statement. Remember that all statements end with a semicolon (`;`). The statement in `main()` passes one message to the `cout` object. The message is the string `Hello there world!`.

Because `cout` is an object of a prewritten class, we do not have to write it; it is available for use, and all we need to do is activate it correctly. Like all C++ objects, `cout` can perform only certain well-defined actions. For `cout`, that

---

8 Two other alternatives that use the `iostream` designation without the `.h` suffix are explained in Appendix H.

9 Formally, `cout` is an object of the class `ostream`, which is described in Chapter 14.

```
Hello there world!
```

FIGURE 1–13 The Output from Program 1-1

action is to assemble data for output display. When a string of characters is passed to `cout`, the object sees to it that the string is correctly displayed on the monitor, as shown in Figure 1–13.

Strings in C++ are any combination of letters, numbers, and special characters enclosed in double quotes (`"string in here"`). The double quotes are used to delimit (mark) the beginning and ending of the string; they are not considered part of the string. Thus the string of characters making up the message sent to `cout` must be enclosed in double quotes, as we have done in Program 1-1.

Let us write another program to illustrate `cout`'s versatility. Read Program 1-2 to determine what it does.

Program 1-2

```
#include <iostream.h>

int main()
{
  cout << "Computers, computers everywhere";
  cout << "\n   as far as I can C";

  return 0;
}
```

When Program 1-2 is run, the following is displayed:

```
Computers, computers everywhere
   as far as I can C
```

You might be wondering why the `\n` did not appear in the output. The two characters `\` and `n`, when used together, are called a *newline escape sequence*. They tell `cout` to instruct the display device to move to a new line. In C++, the backslash (\) character provides an "escape" from the normal interpretation of the character that follows it by altering the meaning of the next character. If

POINT OF INFORMATION

What Is Syntax?

A programming language's *syntax* is the set of rules for formulating grammatically correct language statements. In practice, this means that a C++ statement with correct syntax has the proper form specified for the compiler. Accordingly, the compiler will accept the statement and not generate an error message.

It should be noted that an individual statement or program can be syntactically correct and still be logically incorrect. Such a statement or program would be correctly structured but would produce an incorrect result. This is similar to an English statement that is grammatically correct but makes no sense. For example, although the sentence "The tree is a ragged cat" is grammatically correct, it makes no sense.

the backslash were omitted from the second cout statement in Program 1-2, the n would be printed as the letter n, and the program would print

```
Computers, computers everywheren   as far as I can C
```

Newline escape sequences can be placed anywhere within the message passed to cout. See whether you can determine what display Program 1-3 produces.

Program 1-3

```
#include <iostream.h>

int main()
{
  cout << "Computers everywhere\n as far as\n\nI can see";

  return 0;
}
```

The output for Program 1-3 is

```
Computers everywhere
 as far as

I can see
```

Exercises 1.3

1. *a.* Using `cout`, write a C++ program that prints your name on one line, your street address on a second line, and your city, state, and zip code on the third line.
   b. Run the program you wrote for Exercise 1a on a computer. (***Note:*** You must understand the procedures for entering and running a C++ program on the particular computer installation you are using.)
2. *a.* Write a C++ program to print out the following verse:

```
Computers, computers everywhere
  as far as I can see
I really, really like these things,
  Oh joy, Oh joy for me!
```

   b. Run the program you wrote for Exercise 2a on a computer.
3. *a.* Indicate how many `cout` statements you would use to print out the following:

PART NO.	PRICE
T1267	$6.34
T1300	$8.92
T2401	$65.40
T4482	$36.99

   b. What is the minimum number of `cout` statements that could be used to print the table in Exercise 3a?
   c. Write a complete C++ program to produce the output illustrated in Exercise 3a.
   d. Run the program you wrote for Exercise 3c on a computer.
4. In response to a newline escape sequence, `cout` positions the next displayed character at the beginning of a new line. This positioning of the next character actually represents two distinct operations. What are they?
5. *a.* Most computer operating systems allow the operator to redirect the output produced by `cout` either to a printer or directly to a floppy or hard disk file. Read the first part of Appendix D for a description of this redirection capability.
   b. If your computer supports output redirection, run the program written for Exercise 2a using this feature. Have your program's display redirected to a file named `poem`.
   c. If your computer supports output redirection to a printer, run the program you wrote for Exercise 2a using this feature.

1.4 Programming Style DO ON OWN

C++ programs start execution at the beginning of the `main()` function. Because a program can have only one starting point, every C++ language program must contain one and only one `main()` function. As we have seen, all of the statements that make up the main() function are then included within the braces { } following the function name. Although the main() function must be present in every C++ program, C++ does not require that the word main, the parentheses ( ), or the braces { } be placed in any particular form. The form used in the last section,

```
int main()
{
  program statements in here;

  return 0;
}
```

was chosen strictly for clarity and ease in reading the program.[10] For example, the following general form of a main() function would also work.

```
int main
 (
 ) { first statement;second statement;
          third statement;fourth
statement;
return 0;}
```

Note that more than one statement can be put on a line, or one statement can be written across lines. Except for strings, double quotes, identifiers, and keywords, C++ ignores all white space (white space is any combination of one or more blank spaces, tabs, or new lines). For example, changing the white space in Program 1-1 and making sure not to split the string Hello there world! across two lines results in the following valid program:

```
#include <iostream.h>

 int main
 (
 ){
 cout <<
 "Hello there world!";
  return 0;
}
```

10 If one of the program statements uses cout, the #include <iostream.h> preprocessor command is also required.

Although this version of `main()` does work, it is an example of extremely poor programming style. It is difficult to read and understand. For readability, the `main()` function should always be written in standard form:

```
int main()
{
  program statements in here;

  return 0;
}
```

In this standard form, the function name starts in column 1 and is placed, with the required parentheses, on a line by itself. The opening brace of the function body follows on the next line and is placed under the first letter of the line that contains the function name. Similarly, the closing function brace is placed by itself in column 1 as the last line of the function. This structure serves to highlight the function as a single unit.

Within the function itself, all program statements are indented at least two spaces. Indentation is another sign of good programming practice, especially if the same indentation is used for similar groups of statements. Review Program 1-2 and note that the same indentation was used for both `cout` object calls.

As you progress in your understanding and mastery of C++, you will develop your own indentation standards. Just keep in mind that the final form of your programs should be consistent and should always serve as an aid to the reading and understanding of your programs.

Comments

Comments are explanatory remarks made within a program. When used carefully, comments can be helpful in clarifying what the complete program is about, what a specific group of statements is meant to accomplish, or what one line is intended to do. C++ supports two types of comments: line and block. Both types of comments can be placed anywhere within a program, and neither has any effect on program execution. The computer ignores all comments—they are there strictly for the convenience of anyone reading the program.

A line comment begins with two slashes (`//`) and continues to the end of the line. For example, the following lines are all line comments.

```
// this is a comment
// this program prints out a message
// this program calculates a square root
```

The symbols `//`, with no white space between them, designate the start of the line comment. The end of the line on which the comment is written designates the end of the comment.

A line comment can be written either on a line by itself or at the end of the same line that contains a program statement. Program 1-4 illustrates the use of line comments within a program.

Program 1-4

```
// this program displays a message
#include <iostream.h>

int main()
{
  cout << "Hello there world!"; // this produces the display

  return 0;
}
```

The first comment appears on a line by itself at the top of the program and describes what the program does. This is generally a good place to put a short comment describing the program's purpose. If more comments are required, they can be added, one per line. When a comment is too long to be contained on one line, it can be separated into two or more line comments, with each separate comment preceded by the double-slash symbol set (//). The comment

```
// this comment is invalid because it
   extends over two lines
```

will result in a C++ error message on your computer. This comment is correct when written as follows:

```
// this comment is used to illustrate a
// comment that extends across two lines
```

Comments that span across two or more lines are, however, more conveniently written as block comments than as multiple-line comments. Such comments begin with the symbols `/*` and end with the symbols `*/`. For example,

```
/* This is a block comment that
   spans
   across three lines */
```

In C++, a program's structure is intended to make the program readable and understandable, rendering the use of extensive comments unnecessary. This is reinforced if function, class, and variable names, described in the next chapter, are carefully selected to convey their meaning to anyone reading the program. However, if the purpose of a function, class, or statement is still not clear from its structure, name, or context, it is important to include additional comments where clarification is needed. Obscure code with no comments is a sure sign of bad programming. Excessive comments are also a sign of bad programming, because they imply that insufficient thought was given to making the code self-explanatory. Typically, any program that you write should begin with a set of initial program comments that includes a short program description, your name, and the date that the program was last modified. To save space, and because all programs in this text were written by the author, initial comments will be used for short program descriptions only when they are not provided as part of the accompanying descriptive text.

Exercises 1.4

1. *a.* Will the following program work?

```
#include <iostream.h>
int main(){cout << "Hello there world!"; return 0;}
```

b. Why is the program given in Exercise 1a not a good program?

2. Rewrite the following programs to conform to good programming practice.

a.
```
#include <iostream.h>
int main(
){
cout            <<
"The time has come"
; return 0;}
```

b.
```
#include <iostream.h>
int main
(    ){cout << "Newark is a city\n";cout <<
"In New Jersey\n"; cout <<
"It is also a city\n"
; cout << "In Delaware\n"
; return 0;}
```

c.
```
#include <iostream.h>
int main(){cout << Reading a program\n";cout <<
"is much easier\n"
;cout << "if a standard form for main is used\n")
;cout
<<"and each statement is written\n";cout
<<           "on a line by itself\n")
; return 0;}
```

d.
```
#include <iostream.h>
int main
(   ){cout << "Every C++ program"
;cout
<<"\nmust have one and only one"
;
cout << "main function"
;
cout <<
"\n the escape sequence of characters")
;cout <<
 "\nfor a newline can be placed anywhere"
;cout
<<"\n within the message passed to cout"
; return 0;}
```

3. *a.* When used in a message, the backslash character alters the meaning of the character immediately following it. If we wanted to print the backslash character, we would have to tell `cout` to escape from the way it normally interprets the backslash. What character do you think is used to alter the way a single backslash character is interpreted?

b. Using your answer to Exercise 3a, write the escape sequence for printing a backslash.

4. *a.* A *token* of a computer language is any sequence of characters that as a unit, with no intervening characters or white space, has a unique meaning. Using this definition of a token, determine whether escape sequences, function names, and the keywords listed in Table 1–2 are tokens of the C++ language.

b. Discuss whether adding white space to a message alters the message. Discuss whether messages can be considered tokens of C++.

c. Using the definition of a token given in Exercise 4a, determine whether the following statement is true: "Except for tokens of the language, C++ ignores all white space."

1.5 Common Programming Errors

Part of learning any programming language is making the elementary mistakes commonly encountered as you begin to use the language. These mistakes tend to be frustrating, because each language has its own set of common programming errors lying in wait for the unwary. The errors commonly made when initially programming in C++ include

1. Omitting the parentheses after `main`
2. Omitting or incorrectly typing the opening brace `{` that signifies the start of a function body
3. Omitting or incorrectly typing the closing brace `}` that signifies the end of a function
4. Misspelling the name of an object or function—for example, typing `cot` instead of `cout`
5. Forgetting to close a string sent to `cout` with a double-quote symbol
6. Omitting the semicolon at the end of each statement
7. Forgetting the `\n` to indicate a new line

Our experience is that the third, fifth, sixth, and seventh errors in this list tend to be the most common. We suggest that you write a program and specifically introduce each of these errors, one at a time, to see what error messages your compiler produces. Then, when these error messages appear as a result of inadvertent errors, you will have had experience in understanding the messages and correcting the errors.

1.6 Chapter Summary

1. A C++ program consists of one or more modules. One of these modules must be the function `main()`. The `main()` function identifies the starting point of a C++ program.
2. The simplest C++ program consists of the single function `main` and has the form

```
#include <iostream.h>
int main()
{
  program statements in here;

  return 0;
}
```

This program consists of a preprocessor #include statement, a header line for the main() function, and the body of the main() function. The body of the function begins with the opening left-facing brace, {, and ends with the terminating right-facing brace, }.

3. All C++ statements within a function body must be terminated by a semicolon.
4. Many functions and classes are supplied in a standard library provided with each C++ compiler. One such set of classes, which are used to create input and output capabilities, is defined in the header file <iostream.h>.
5. The cout object is used to display text or numerical results. A stream of characters can be sent to cout by enclosing the characters in double quotes and using the insertion ("put to") operator, <<, as in the statement cout << "Hello World!";. The text in the string is displayed directly on the screen and may include newline escape sequences for format control.

Data Types, Declarations, and Displays

Chapter Two

C++ programs can process different types of data in different ways. For example, calculating the bacteria growth in a polluted pond requires mathematical operations on numerical data, whereas sorting a list of names requires comparison operations using alphabetical data. In this chapter we introduce C++'s elementary data types and the operations that can be performed on them. We also show how to use the `cout` object to display the results of these operations.

2.1 Data Types

Tradititionally, there were three basic data types used in C++: integers, floating-point numbers, and character values. A fourth type, Boolean, was introduced by the new ANSI/ISO standard. Each of these data values is described in the subsections that follow.[1]

Integer Values

An *integer value* is zero or any positive or negative number without a decimal point. Examples of valid integer values are

0   5   –10   +25   1000   253   –26351   +36

As these examples illustrate, integers may be signed (a leading + or – sign) or unsigned (no leading + or – sign). No commas, decimal points, or special symbols, such as a dollar sign, are allowed. Examples of invalid integer values are

$255.62   2,523   3.   6,243,892   1,492.89   +6.0

Different computer types have their own internal limit on the largest (most positive) and smallest (most negative) integer values that can be used in a program. These limits depend on the amount of storage each computer sets aside for an integer; thus they are said to be implementation-dependent. The more commonly used storage allocations are listed in Table 2–1. (Review Section 2.8 if you are unfamiliar with the concept of a byte.) By referring to your computer's reference manual or by using the `sizeof` operator introduced in Section 2.5, you can determine the actual number of bytes allocated by your computer for an integer value.[2] To store integer values greater than those

[1] ANSI is an acronym for American National Standards Institute. ISO stands for International Standards Organization.

[2] The limits imposed by the compiler can also be found in the `limits.h` header file. The values listed are in hexadecimal notation and are defined as the constants `INT_MAX` and `INT_MIN`.

TABLE 2–1 Integer Values and Word Size[3]

Word Size	Minimum Integer Value	Maximum Integer Value
1 byte	–128	127
2 bytes	–32768	32767
4 bytes	–2147483648	2147483647

supported by the memory allocation shown in Table 2–1 requires using integer qualifiers. These qualifiers are described in Section 2.5.

Floating-Point Numbers

A *floating-point number,* which is also called a *real number,* is any signed or unsigned number that has a decimal point. Examples of floating-point numbers are

+10.625 5. –6.2 3251.92 0.0 0.33 –6.67 +2.

Note that the numbers 5., 0.0, and +2. are classified as floating-point numbers, whereas the same numbers written without a decimal point (5, 0, and +2) are integer values. As with integer values, special symbols, such as the dollar sign and the comma, are not permitted in real numbers. Examples of invalid real numbers are

5,326.25 24 123 6,459 $10.29

C++ supports three different categories of floating-point numbers: float, double, and long double. The difference among these numbers is the amount of storage that a compiler allocates for each type. Most compilers use twice as much storage for doubles as for floats, which allows a double to have approximately twice the precision of a float (for this reason, floats are sometimes referred to as *single-precision* numbers and doubles as *double-precision* numbers). Similarly, long double numbers typically use twice the storage used for doubles, with a consequent increase in precision. The actual storage allocation for each data type, however, depends on the particular compiler. In compilers that allocate the same amount of storage for double- and single-precision numbers,

[3] It is interesting to note that in all cases the magnitude of the most negative integer allowed is always one more than the magnitude of the most positive integer. This is due to the method commonly used to represent integers, called twos complement representation. For an explanation of twos complement representation, see the supplement (Section 2.8) at the end of this chapter.

these two data types become identical. The same is true for long doubles, and the `sizeof` operator introduced in Section 2.5 will enable you to determine the amount of storage your compiler reserves for each of these data types. A float number is indicated to the compiler by appending either F or f to the number, and a double is created by appending either L or l to the number. In the absence of these suffixes, a floating-point number is considered a double. For example,

9.234 indicates a double
9.234f indicates a float
9.234L indicates a long double

The only difference among these numbers is the amount of storage the computer may use to store them. For numbers having more than six significant digits to the right of the decimal point, this storage becomes important. Appendix F describes the binary storage format typically used for real values and explains its impact on number precision. The exact difference, if any, in allocated storage is compiler-dependent. The only requirement imposed by C++ is that a long double must provide at least the same precision as a double and that a double must provide at least the same precision as a float.

Exponential Notation

Floating-point numbers can be written in exponential notation, which is similar to scientific notation and is commonly used to express both very large and very small numbers in a compact form. The following examples illustrate how numbers with decimals can be expressed in exponential and scientific notation.

Decimal Notation	Exponential Notation	Scientific Notation
1625.	1.625*e*3	1.625×10^3
63421.	6.3421*e*4	6.3421×10^4
.00731	7.31*e*–3	7.31×10^{-3}
.000625	6.25*e*–4	6.25×10^{-4}

In exponential notation the letter *e* stands for exponent. The number following the *e* represents a power of 10 and indicates the number of places the decimal point should be moved to obtain the standard decimal value. The decimal point is moved to the right if the number after the *e* is positive or is moved to the left if the number after the *e* is negative. For example, the *e*3 in the number 1.625*e*3 means to move the decimal place three places to the right, so that the number becomes 1625. The *e*–3 in the number 7.31*e*–3 means to move the decimal point three places to the left, so that 7.31*e*–3 becomes .00731.

POINT OF INFORMATION

What Is Precision?

In number theory, a statement such as "This computation is precise to the fifth decimal place" is used to mean that the fifth digit after the decimal point has been rounded and that the number is accurate to within $\pm \frac{1}{2} 10^{-5}$.

In computer programming, *precision* refers to the number of significant digits in the number, where the number of *significant digits* is defined as the number of clearly correct digits plus one. For example, if the number 12.6874 has been rounded to the fourth decimal place, it is correct to say that this number is precise to the fourth decimal place. This statement means that all the digits in the number are accurate except for the fourth digit, which has been rounded. Similarly, it can be said that the number has a precision of six digits, which means that the first five digits are correct and the sixth digit has been rounded. Another way of saying this is that the number 12.6874 has six significant digits.

Note that the significant digits in a number need not have any relation to the number of displayed digits. For example, if the number 687.45678921 has five significant digits, then it is precise only to the value 687.46, where the last digit is assumed to be rounded. In a similar manner, dollar values in many large financial applications are frequently rounded to the nearest hundred thousand dollars. In such applications a displayed dollar value of $12,400,000, for example, is not precise to the closest dollar. Because this value has only three significant digits, it is precise only to the 10^5, or hundred thousands, digit. In C++ the digits displayed to the left of the decimal point are assumed to be significant.

Character Values

The third basic type of data recognized by C++ consists of characters. Characters include the letters of the alphabet (both uppercase and lowercase letters), the ten digits 0 through 9, and special symbols such as + $. , – !. A single *character value* is any one letter, digit, or special symbol enclosed by single quotes. Examples of valid character values are

'A'   '$'   'b'   '7'   'y'   '!'   'M'   'q'

Character values are typically stored in a computer using either the ASCII or the ANSI codes. *ASCII,* pronounced AS-KEY, is an acronym for American Standard Code for Information Interchange and consists of 128 codes. *ANSI,* pronounced ANN-SEE, is an acronym for American National Standards Institute and is an extended set of 256 codes, the first 128 of which are the same as the ASCII codes. Each of these codes assigns individual characters to a specific pattern of 0s and 1s. Table 2–2 lists the correspondence between bit patterns and the uppercase and lowercase letters of the alphabet used by both the ASCII and the ANSI codes.

POINT OF INFORMATION

Boolean Data

Boolean data are restricted to one of two values, either `true` or `false`. Traditionally, neither C nor C++ supported built-in Boolean data.

As specified by the ANSI/ISO C++ standard, C++ will now incorporate a Boolean data type and permit the use of two Boolean values, `true` and `false`. In C++ compilers currently implementing a Boolean data type, the actual values represented by the two Boolean values, `true` and `false`, are the integer values `1` and `0`, respectively.

In actual practice, Boolean data are most useful when we are examining a specific condition and, on the basis of whether the condition is `true` or `false`, taking a prescribed course of action. We will encounter Boolean data once again in Chapter 4 as we consider the examination of conditions.

TABLE 2–2 The ASCII and ANSI Letter Codes

Letter	Code	Letter	Code	Letter	Code	Letter	Code
a	01100001	n	01101110	A	01000001	N	01001110
b	01100010	o	01101111	B	01000010	O	01001111
c	01100011	p	01110000	C	01000011	P	01010000
d	01100100	q	01110001	D	01000100	Q	01010001
e	01100101	r	01110010	E	01000101	R	01010010
f	01100110	s	01110011	F	01000110	S	01010011
g	01100111	t	01110100	G	01000111	T	01010100
h	01101000	u	01110101	H	01001000	U	01010101
i	01101001	v	01110110	I	01001001	V	01010110
j	01101010	w	01110111	J	01001010	W	01010111
k	01101011	x	01111000	K	01001011	X	01011000
l	01101100	y	01111001	L	01001100	Y	01011001
m	01101101	z	01111010	M	01001101	Z	01011010

Using Table 2–2, we can determine how the characters 'J', 'E', 'A', 'N', and 'S', for example, are stored inside a computer that uses the ASCII character code. Using the ASCII code, this sequence of characters requires five bytes of storage (one byte for each letter) and would be stored as illustrated in Figure 2–1.

TABLE 2–3 **Escape Sequences**

Escape Sequence	Meaning
`\b`	move back one space
`\f`	move to next page
`\n`	move to next line
`\r`	carriage return
`\t`	move to next tab setting
`\\`	backslash character
`\'`	single quote
`\"`	double quote
`\nnn`	treat `nnn` as an octal number

Escape Sequences

When a backslash (\) is used directly in front of a select group of characters, the backslash tells the compiler to escape from the way these characters would normally be interpreted. For this reason, combinations of a backslash and these specific characters are called *escape sequences*. We have already encountered an example of this in the newline escape sequence `\n`. Table 2–3 lists C++'s most commonly used escape sequences.

Although each escape sequence listed in Table 2–3 is made up of two distinct characters, the combination of the two characters with no intervening white space causes the computer to store one character code. Table 2–4 lists the ASCII code byte patterns for the escape sequences given in Table 2–3.

Exercises 2.1

1. Determine data types appropriate for the following data.
   a. the average of four grades
   b. the number of days in a month

FIGURE 2–1 The Letters JEANS Stored Inside a Computer

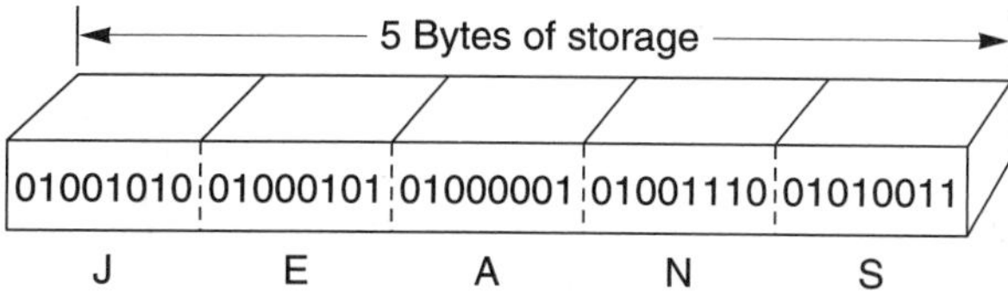

TABLE 2–4 The ASCII Escape Sequence Codes

C++ Escape Sequence	Meaning	Computer Code
`\b`	backspace	00001000
`\f`	form feed	00001100
`\n`	newline	00001010
`\r`	carriage return	00001101
`\\`	backslash	01011100
`\'`	single quote	00100111
`\"`	double quote	00100010

c. the length of the Golden Gate Bridge
d. the numbers in a state lottery
e. the distance from Brooklyn, NY, to Newark, NJ

2. Convert the following numbers into standard decimal form.

6.34*e*5 1.95162*e*2 8.395*e*1 2.95*e*–3 4.623*e*–4

3. Convert the following decimal numbers into exponential notation.

126. 656.23 3426.95 4893.2 .321 .0123 .006789

4. Using the system reference manuals for your computer, determine what character code your computer uses.

5. *a.* Using the ASCII codes, determine the number of bytes required to store the letters KINGSLEY.
b. Show how the letters KINGSLEY would be stored inside a computer that uses the ASCII codes. That is, draw a figure similar to Figure 2–1 for the letters KINGSLEY.

6. *a.* Repeat Exercise 5a using lowercase ANSI letter codes.
b. Repeat Exercise 5b using lowercase ANSI letter codes.

7. *a.* Repeat Exercise 6a using the letters of your own last name.
b. Repeat Exercise 6b using the letters of your own last name.

8. Because most computers use different amounts of storage for integers, floating-point numbers, double-precision numbers, and character values, discuss how a program might alert the computer to the amount of storage needed for the various data types in the program.

Note: *For the following exercise, the reader should understand basic computer storage concepts. Specifically, if you are unfamiliar with the concept of a byte, refer to Section 2.8 before doing the next exercise.*

9. Although the total number of bytes varies from computer to computer, memory sizes of 65,536 to more than several million bytes are not uncommon. In computer language,

the letter K is used to represent the number 1024, which is 2 raised to the 10th power, and M is used to represent the number 1,048,576, which is 2 raised to the 20th power. Thus a memory size of 640K is really 640 times 1024, or 655,360 bytes, and a memory size of 4M is really 4 times 1,048,576, which is 4,194,304 bytes. Using this information, calculate the actual number of bytes in

a. a memory containing 8M bytes
b. a memory containing 16M bytes
c. a memory containing 32M bytes
d. a memory containing 96M bytes
e. a memory containing 8M words, where each word consists of 2 bytes
f. a memory containing 16M words, where each word consists of 4 bytes
g. a floppy diskette that can store 1.44M bytes

2.2 Arithmetic Operators

Integers and real numbers may be added, subtracted, divided, and multiplied. Although it is usually better not to mix integers and real numbers when performing arithmetic operations, predictable results are obtained when different data types are used in the same arithmetic expression. Somewhat surprising is the fact that character data can also be added to and subtracted from both character and integer data to produce useful results.

The operators used for arithmetic operations are called arithmetic operators. The operators are:

Operation	Operator
Addition	+
Subtraction	-
Multiplication	*
Division	/
Modulus	%

A *simple arithmetic expression* consists of an arithmetic operator connecting two operands:

3 + 7
`operand` `operator` `operand`

Examples of simple arithmetic expressions are

3 + 7
18 – 3
12.62 + 9.8
.08 * 12.2
12.6 / 2.

The spaces around the arithmetic operators in these examples are inserted strictly for clarity and may be omitted without affecting the value of the expression. When evaluating simple arithmetic expressions, we determine the data type of the result by applying the following rules:

1. If both operands are integers, the result is an integer.
2. If any operand is a floating-point value, the result is a floating-point value.

An expression that contains only integer operands is called an *integer expression,* and the result of the expression is an integer value (Rule 1). Similarly, an expression that contains only floating-point operands is called a *floating-point expression,* or *real expression,* and the result of the expression is a floating-point value (Rule 2). An arithmetic expression that contains both integer and non-integer operands is called a *mixed-mode expression.* The result of a mixed-mode expression is always a floating-point value (Rule 2).

It is worth noting that the arithmetic operations of addition, subtraction, multiplication, and division are implemented differently for integer and floating-point values. Specifically, whether an integer or a floating-point arithmetic operation is performed depends on what types of operands (integer or floating-point) are contained in the arithmetic expression. In this sense, the arithmetic operators are considered to be overloaded. More formally, an *overloaded operator* is a symbol that represents more than one operation and whose execution depends on the types of operands encountered. Although the overloaded nature of the arithmetic operators is rather simple, we will encounter the concept of overloading many more times in our journey through C++.

Integer Division

The division of two integers can produce results that seem rather strange to the unwary. For example, dividing the integer 15 by the integer 2 yields an integer result. Because integers cannot contain a fractional part, a result such as 7.5 cannot be obtained. In C++, the fractional part of the result obtained when two integers are divided is dropped (truncated). Thus the value of 15/2 is 7, the value of 9/4 is 2, and the value of 17/5 is 3.

There are times when we would like to retain the remainder of an integer division. To make this possible, C++ provides a nonoverloaded arithmetic operator that is implemented only for integers. This operator, called the modulus operator, has the symbol % and is used to capture the remainder when two integers are divided. For example,

9 % 4 is 1
17 % 3 is 2
14 % 2 is 0

TABLE 2–5 Summary of Arithmetic Operators

Operation	Operator	Type	Operand	Result
Addition	+	Binary	Both integers	Integer
			One operand not an integer	Double-precision
Subtraction	–	Binary	Both integers	Integer
			One operand not an integer	Double-precision
Multiplication	*	Binary	Both integers	Integer
			One operand not an integer	Double-precision
Division	/	Binary	Both integers	Integer
			One operand not an integer	Double-precision
Remainder	%	Binary	Both integers	Integer
Negation	–	Unary	Integer	Integer
			Floating-point	Double-precision

Negation

Besides the binary operators for addition, subtraction, multiplication, and division, C++ also provides unary operators. One of these unary operators uses the same symbol that is used for binary subtraction (–). The minus sign used in front of a single numerical operand negates (reverses the sign of) the number.

Table 2–5 summarizes the six arithmetic operations we have described so far and lists the data type of the result produced by each operator on the basis of the data type of the operands involved.

Operator Precedence and Associativity

Besides such simple expressions as 5 + 12 and .08 * 26.2, we frequently need to create more complex arithmetic expressions. C++, like most other programming languages, requires that we follow certain rules when writing expressions that contain more than one arithmetic operator. These rules are:

1. Two binary arithmetic operator symbols must never be placed side by side.
   For example, 5 * % 6 is invalid because the two operators * and % are placed next to each other.

2. Parentheses may be used to form groupings, and all expressions enclosed within parentheses are evaluated first.

   For example, in the expression (6 + 4) / (2 + 3), the 6 + 4 and 2 + 3 are evaluated first to yield 10 / 5. The 10 / 5 is then evaluated to yield 2.

   Sets of parentheses may also be enclosed by other parentheses. For example, the expression (2 * (3 + 7)) / 5 is valid. When parentheses are used within parentheses, the expressions in the innermost parentheses are always evaluated first. The evaluation continues from innermost to outermost parentheses until the expressions in all the parentheses have been evaluated. The number of right-facing parentheses, (, must always equal the number of left-facing parentheses,) , so that there are no unpaired sets.

3. Parentheses cannot be used to indicate multiplication; the multiplication operator, *, must be used.

   For example, the expression (3 + 4) (5 + 1) is invalid. The correct expression is (3 + 4) * (5 + 1).

Parentheses should be used to specify logical groupings of operands and to indicate clearly, both to the computer and to programmers, the intended order of arithmetic operations. In the absence of parentheses, expressions containing multiple operators are evaluated by the priority, or precedence, of the operators. Table 2–6 lists both the precedence and the associativity of the operators considered in this section.

The precedence of an operator establishes its priority relative to all other operators. Operators at the top of Table 2–6 have a higher priority than operators at the bottom of the table. In expressions with multiple operators, an operator with a higher precedence is used before an operator with a lower precedence. For example, in the expression 6 + 4 / 2 + 3, the division is done before the addition, yielding an intermediate result of 6 + 2 + 3. The additions are then performed to yield a final result of 11.

Expressions that contain operators with the same precedence are evaluated according to their associativity. This means that evaluation is either from left to right or from right to left as each operator is encountered. For example, in the expression 8 + 5 * 7 % 2 * 4, the multiplication and modulus operators are of

TABLE 2–6 Operator Precedence and Associativity

Operator	Associativity
unary –	right to left
* / %	left to right
+ –	left to right

higher precedence than the addition operator and hence are evaluated first. Both of these operators, however, are of equal priority. Therefore, these operators are evaluated according to their left-to-right associativity, which yields

$$\begin{aligned} 8 + 5 * 7 \% 2 * 4 &= \\ 8 + 35 \% 2 * 4 &= \\ 8 + 1 * 4 &= \\ 8 + 4 &= 12 \end{aligned}$$

Exercises 2.2

1. Following are algebraic expressions and incorrect C++ expressions corresponding to them. Find the errors and write corrected C++ expressions.

	Algebra	*C++ Expression*
a.	(2)(3) + (4)(5)	(2)(3) + (4)(5)
b.	$\dfrac{6 + 18}{2}$	6 + 18 / 2
c.	$\dfrac{4.5}{12.2 - 3.1}$	4.5 / 12.2 – 3.1
d.	4.6(3.0 + 14.9)	4.6(3.0 + 14.9)
e.	(12.1 + 18.9)(15.3 – 3.8)	(12.1 + 18.9)(15.3 – 3.8)

2. Assuming that amount = 1, $m = 50$, $n = 10$, and $p = 5$, evaluate the following expressions.

a. n / p + 3
b. m / p + n – 10 * amount
c. m – 3 * n + 4 * amount
d. amount / 5
e. 18 / p
f. 18 % p
g. –p * n
h. –m / 20
i. –m % 20
j. (m + n) / (p + amount)
k. m + n / p + amount

3. Repeat Exercise 2, assuming that amount = 1.0, $m = 50.0$, $n = 10.0$, and $p = 5.0$.

4. Determine the value of the following integer expressions.

a. 3 + 4 * 6
b. 3 * 4 / 6 + 6
c. 2 * 3 / 12 * 8 / 4
d. 10 * (1 + 7 * 3)
e. 20 – 2 / 6 + 3
f. 20 – 2 / (6 + 3)
g. (20 – 2) / 6 + 3
h. (20 – 2) / (6 + 3)

5. Determine the value of the following floating-point expressions.

a. 3.0 + 4.0 * 6.0
b. 3.0 * 4.0 / 6.0 + 6.0
c. 2.0 * 3.0 / 12.0 * 8.0 / 4.0
d. 10.0 * (1.0 + 7.0 * 3.0)
e. 20.0 – 2.0 / 6.0 + 3.0
f. 20.0 – 2.0 / (6.0 + 3.0)
g. (20.0 – 2.0) / 6.0 + 3.0
h. (20.0 – 2.0) / (6.0 + 3.0)

6. Evaluate each of the following expressions and list the data type of the result. In evaluating the expressions, be aware of the data types of all intermediate calculations.

a. 10.0 + 15 / 2 + 4.3
b. 10.0 + 15 % 2 + 4.3
c. 10.0 + 15.0 / 2 + 4.3
d. 3.0 * 4 / 6 + 6
e. 3.0 * 4 % 6 + 6
f. 3 * 4.0 / 6 + 6
g. 20.0 – 2 / 6 + 3
h. 10 + 17 % 3 + 4
i. 10 + 17 % 3 + 4.
j. 10 + 17 / 3. + 4

2.3 Numerical Output Using cout

In addition to displaying strings, the `cout` object allows us to display, on the standard output device, the numerical result of an expression. To do this we must pass the desired value to `cout`. For example, the statement

```
cout << (6 + 15);
```

yields the display `21`. Strictly speaking, the parentheses surrounding the expression `6 + 15` are necessary to indicate that it is the value of the expression, which is `21`, that is being placed on the output stream.[4]

In addition to displaying a numerical value, a string identifying the output can also be displayed by passing the string to `cout` as we did in Chapter 1. For example, the statement

```
cout << "The total of 6 and 15 is " << (6 + 15);
```

causes two pieces of data to be sent to `cout`: a string and a value. Individually, each set of data is sent to the `cout` preceded by its own insertion symbol (<<). Here the first data sent to the stream is the string `"The total of 6 and 15 is "`, and the second item stream is the value of the expression `6 + 15`. The display produced by this statement is

```
The total of 6 and 15 is 21
```

Note that the space between the word `is` and the number `21` is caused by the space placed within the string passed to `cout`. As far as `cout` is concerned, its input is simply a set of characters that are then sent on to be displayed in the order in which they are received. Characters from the input are queued, one behind the other, and sent to an output stream for display. Placing a space in

[4] This is because the + operator has a higher precedence than the << operator.

the input causes this space to be part of the output stream that is ultimately displayed. For example, the statement

```
cout << "The sum of 12.2 and 15.754 is " << (12.2 + 15.754);
```

yields the display

```
The sum of 12.2 and 15.754 is 27.954
```

Note that insertion of data into the output stream can be made over multiple lines and is terminated only by a semicolon. Thus the prior display is also produced by the statement

```
cout << "The sum of 12.2 and 15.754 is "
     <<  (12.2 + 15.754);
```

The requirements for using multiple lines are that a string contained within double quotes cannot be split across lines and that the terminating semicolon must appear only on the last line. Within a line, multiple insertion symbols can be used.

As the last display indicates, floating-point numbers are displayed with sufficient digits to the right of the decimal place to accommodate the fractional part of the number. This is true if the number has six or fewer significant digits. If the number has more than six significant digits, the fractional part is rounded to six significant digits, and if the number has no decimal digits, neither a decimal point nor any decimal digits are displayed.[5]

Character data can also be displayed using cout. For example, the statement

```
cout << "The first letter of the alphabet is an " << 'a';
```

results in the display

```
The first letter of the alphabet is an a
```

Program 2-1 illustrates using cout to display the results of an expression within the statements of a complete program. In reviewing this program, note the use of the term endl as the last item to be inserted into the output stream. The keyword endl is an example of a *C++ manipulator,* which is an item used to manipulate how the output stream of characters is displayed. In particular, the

[5] Note that none of this output is defined as part of the C++ language. Rather, it is defined by a set of classes and routines provided with each C++ compiler.

endl manipulator first causes a newline character ('\n') to be added to the output stream and then forces an immediate flushing of the output stream. When used with the cout object, this has the effect of ensuring an immediate display of the stream on the terminal. (Additional manipulators are listed in Table 2–7.)

Program 2-1

```
#include <iostream.h>
int main()
{
  cout << "15.0 plus 2.0 equals " << (15.0 + 2.0) << endl
       << "15.0 minus 2.0 equals " << (15.0 - 2.0) << endl
       << "15.0 times 2.0 equals " << (15.0 * 2.0) << endl
       << "15.0 divided by 2.0 equals " << (15.0 / 2.0) << endl;

  return 0;
}
```

The output of Program 2-1 is

```
15.0 plus 2.0 equals 17
15.0 minus 2.0 equals 13
15.0 times 2.00 equals 30
15.0 divided by 2.0 equals 7.5
```

Formatted Output

Besides displaying correct results, it is extremely important for a program to present its results attractively. Most programs are judged, in fact, on the perceived ease of data entry and the style and presentation of their output. For example, displaying a monetary result as 1.897000 is not in keeping with accepted report conventions. The display should be either $1.90 or $1.89, depending on whether rounding or truncation is used.

The format of numbers displayed by cout can be controlled by field width manipulators included in each output stream. Table 2-7 lists the most commonly used manipulators available for this purpose.[6]

[6] As was noted previously, the endl manipulator inserts a newline and then flushes the stream.

TABLE 2–7 Commonly Used Stream Manipulators

Manipulator	Action
`setw(n)`	Set the field width to *n*
`setprecision(n)`	Set the floating-point precision to *n* places
`setiosflags(flags)`	Set the format flags (see Table 2–9 for flag settings)
`dec`	Set output for decimal display
`hex`	Set output for hexadecimal display
`oct`	Set output for octal display

For example, the statement

```
cout << "The sum of 6 and 15 is" << setw(3) << 21;
```

causes the printout

```
The sum of 6 and 15 is 21
```

The `setw(3)` field width manipulator included in the stream of data passed to `cout` is used to set the displayed field width. The `3` in this manipulator sets the default field width for the next number in the stream to be three spaces wide. This field width setting causes the `21` to be printed in a field of three spaces, which includes one blank and the number 21. As illustrated, integers are right-justified within the specified field.

Field width manipulators are useful in printing columns of numbers so that the numbers in each column align correctly. For example, Program 2-2 illustrates how a column of integers would align in the absence of field width manipulators.

Program 2-2

```
#include <iostream.h>

int main()
{
  cout << 6 << endl
       << 18 << endl
       << 124 << endl
       << "---\n"
       << (6+18+124) << endl;

  return 0;
}
```

The output of Program 2-2 is

```
6
18
124
---
148
```

Because no field width manipulators are given, the `cout` object allocates enough space for each number as it is received. To force the numbers to align on the units digit requires a field width great enough for the largest displayed number. For Program 2-2, a width of three spaces is enough. The use of this field width is illustrated in Program 2-3.

Program 2-3

```
#include <iostream.h>
#include <iomanip.h>

int main()
{
  cout << setw(3) << 6 << endl
       << setw(3) << 18 << endl
       << setw(3) << 124 << endl
       << "---\n"
       << (6+18+124) << endl;

  return 0;
}
```

The output of Program 2-3 is

```
  6
 18
124
---
148
```

Note that the field width manipulator must be included for each occurrence of a number inserted into the data stream sent to `cout` and that the manipulator applies only to the next insertion of data immediately following it. Also note that if manipulators are to be included within an output display, the iomanip.h header file must be included as part of the program. This is accomplished by the preprocessor command #include <iomanip.h>.[7]

Formatted floating-point numbers require the use of three field width manipulators. The first manipulator sets the total width of the display, including the decimal point; the second manipulator sets the output type (exponential or conventional decimal display); and the third manipulator determines how many digits can be printed to the right of the decimal point. For example, the statement

```
cout << '|' << setw(10) << setiosflags(ios:: fixed) << setprecision(3) << 25.67 << '|';
```

causes the printout

```
|    25.670|
```

The bar symbol, |, in the example is used to delimit (mark) the beginning and end of the display field. The setw manipulator tells cout to display the number in a total field of 10, and the setprecision manipulator tells cout to display three digits to the right of the decimal point. The setiosflags manipulator using the ios::fixed flag ensures that the output is displayed in conventional decimal format—that is, as a fixed-point rather than an exponential number.

For all numbers (integer, floating-point, and double-precision), cout ignores the setw manipulator specification if the total specified field width is too small and allocates enough space for the integer part of the number to be printed. The fractional part of both floating-point and double-precision numbers is displayed up to the precision set with the setprecision manipulator (in the absence of a setprecision manipulator, the default precision is set to six decimal places). If the fractional part of the number to be displayed contains more digits than are called for in the setprecision manipulator, the number is rounded to the indicated number of decimal places; if the fractional part contains fewer digits than specified, the number is displayed with the fewer digits. Table 2–8 illustrates the effect of various combinations of format manipulators. Again, for clarity, the bar symbol, |, is used to indicate the beginning and end of the output fields.

In addition to the setw and setprecision manipulators, a field justification manipulator is also available. As we have seen, numbers sent to cout are normally displayed right-justified in the display field, whereas strings are

---

[7] Because the iomanip.h header file will include the iostream.h header file if it has not already been included, the #include statement for iostream.h can be omitted.

TABLE 2–8 Effect of Format Manipulators[8]

Manipulators	Number	Display	Comments
`setw(2)`	3	`| 3|`	Number fits in field
`setw(2)`	43	`|43|`	Number fits in field
`setw(2)`	143	`|143|`	Field width ignored
`setw(2)`	2.3	`|2.3|`	Field width ignored
`setw(5)` `setiosflags(ios::fixed)` `setprecision(2)`	2.366	`| 2.37|`	Field width of three spaces with two decimal digits
`setw(5)` `setiosflags(ios::fixed)` `setprecision(2)`	42.3	`|42.3|`	Number fits in field
`setw(5)` `setiosflags(ios::fixed)` `setprecision(2)`	142.364	`|142.36|`	Field width ignored but precision specification used
`setw(5)` `setiosflags(ios::fixed)` `setprecision(2)`	142.366	`|142.37|`	Field width ignored but precision specification used
`setw(5)` `setiosflags(ios::fixed)` `setprecision(2)`	142	`| 142|`	Field width used, precision irrelevant

displayed left-justified. To alter the default justification for a stream of data, the `setiosflags` manipulator can be used. For example, the statement

```
cout << '|' << setw(10) << setiosflags(ios::left) << 142 << '|';
```

causes the following left-justified display:

```
|142       |
```

As we have previously seen, because data passed to `cout` may be continued across multiple lines, the previous display would also be produced by the statement

```
cout << '|' << setw(10)
     << setiosflags(ios::left)
     << 142 << '|';
```

[8] If neither the manipulator flag `ios::fixed` nor the flag `ios::scientific` is in effect, the `setprecision` value indicates the total number of significant digits displayed rather than the number of digits after the decimal point.

As always, the field width manipulator is in effect only for the next single set of data passed to cout. Right-justification for strings in a stream is obtained by the manipulator setiosflags(ios::right). The symbols ios in both the function name and the ios::right argument come from the first letters of the words *input output stream.*

In addition to the left and right flags that can be used with the setiosflags() manipulator, other flags may also be used to affect the output. The most commonly used flags for this manipulator are listed in Table 2–9.

Note that all of the flags in Table 2–9 are used as arguments to the setiosflags() manipulator function. Another name for a manipulator function that uses arguments is *parameterized manipulator.* As an example of using parameterized manipulator functions, consider the statement

```
cout << setiosflags(ios::fixed)
     << setiosflags(ios::showpoint)
     << setprecision(4);
```

TABLE 2–9 Format Flags for Use with setiosflags()

Flag	Meaning
ios::showpoint	Always display a decimal point. In the absence of the ios::fixed flag, a numerical value with a decimal point is displayed with a default of six significant digits. If the integer part of the number requires more than six digits, the display will be in exponential notation, unless the ios::fixed flag is in effect. For example, the value 1234567. is displayed as 1.23457e0 unless the ios::fixed flag is in effect. This flag has no effect on integer values.
ios::showpos	Display a leading + sign when the number is positive.
ios::fixed	Display the number in conventional fixed-point decimal notation (that is, with an integer and fractional part separated by a decimal point), not in exponential notation.
ios::scientific	Use exponential notation on output.
ios::dec	Display as a decimal number (this is the default).
ios::oct	Display as an octal number.
ios::hex	Display as a hexadecimal number.
ios::left	Left-justify output.
ios::right	Right-justify output.

POINT OF INFORMATION

What Is a Flag?

In current programming usage, the term *flag* refers to an item, such as a variable or argument, that sets a condition usually considered as either active or nonactive. Although the exact origin of this term in programming is not known, it probably derives from the use of real flags to signal a condition, such as the Stop, Go, Caution, and Winner flags used at car races.

In a similar manner, each flag argument to the `setiosflags()` manipulator function activates a specific condition. For example, the `ios::dec` flag sets the display format to decimal, and the flag `ios::oct` activates the octal display format. These conditions are mutually exclusive, which means that only one condition can be active at a time, so activating one such flag automatically deactivates the others.

Flags that are not mutually exclusive, such as `ios::dec`, `ios::showpoint`, and `ios::fixed`, can all be activated at the same time. This can be done by using three individual `setiosflag()` calls or by combining all arguments into one call as follows:

```
cout << setiosflags(ios::dec || ios::showpoint || ios::fixed);
```

This forces all subsequent floating-point numbers sent to the output stream to be displayed with a decimal point and four decimal digits. If the number has fewer than four decimal digits, it will be padded with trailing zeros.

In addition to outputting integers in decimal notation, the `ios::oct` and `ios::hex` flags permit conversions to octal and hexadecimal, respectively. Program 2-4 illustrates the use of these flags. Because decimal is the default display, an `ios::dec` flag is not required in the first output stream.

Program 2-4

```
// a program to illustrate output conversions
#include <iostream.h>
#include <iomanip.h>

int main()
{
  cout << "The decimal (base 10) value of 15 is " << 15 << endl
       << "The octal (base 8) value of 15 is "
       << setiosflags(ios::oct) << 15 << endl
       << The hexadecimal (base 16) value of 15 is "
       << setiosflags(ios::hex) << 15 << endl;

  return 0;
}
```

POINT OF INFORMATION

Formatting cout Stream Data

The data in a cout output stream can be formatted in precise ways. One of the most common format requirements is to display numbers in a monetary format by always displaying two digits after the decimal point, such as 123.45. This can be done with the following statement:

```
cout << setiosflags(ios::fixed)
     << setiosflags(ios::showpoint)
     << setprecision(2);
```

The first manipulator flag, ios::fixed, forces all numbers placed on the cout stream to be placed in conventional decimal point notation. The next flag, ios::showpoint, tells the stream always to display a decimal point. Thus a value such as 1.0 will appear as 1.0 and not as a 1 with no displayed decimal value. Finally, the setprecision manipulator tells the stream always to display two decimal values after the decimal point. Thus the number 1.0 will appear as 1.00.

Instead of using manipulators, you can also use the cout stream functions setf() and precision(). For example, the previous formatting can also be accomplished using the code

```
cout.setf(ios::fixed);
cout.setf(ios::showpoint);
cout.precision(2);
```

Note the syntax here: The name of the object, cout, is separated from the function by a period. As we shall see in Chapter 6, this is the standard way of specifying a function and connecting it to a specific object.

Which style you select is a matter of preference. In both cases the formats need only be specified once. They then remain in effect for every number subsequently inserted into the cout stream.

The output produced by Program 2-4 is:

```
The decimal (base 10) value of 15 is 15
The octal (base 8) value of 15 is 17
The hexadecimal (base 16) value of 15 is f
```

In place of the conversion flags ios::dec, ios::oct, and ios::hex, three simpler manipulators, dec, oct, and hex, are provided in <iostream.h>. Unlike their longer counterparts, these simpler manipulators leave the conversion base set for all subsequent output streams. Using these simpler manipulators, we can rewrite Program 2-4 as

```
#include <iostream.h>

int main()  // a program to illustrate output conversions
{
  cout << "The decimal (base 10) value of 15 is " << 15 << endl
       << "The octal (base 8) value of 15 is " << oct << 15 << endl
       << "The hexadecimal (base 16) value of 15 is " << hex << 15 << endl;

  return 0;
}
```

The display of integer values in one of the three possible number systems (decimal, octal, and hexadecimal) does not affect how the number is actually stored inside a computer. All numbers are stored via the computer's own internal codes. The manipulators sent to `cout` simply tell the object how to convert the internal code for output display purposes.

Besides displaying integers in octal or hexadecimal form, integer constants can also be written in a program in these forms. To designate an octal integer constant, the number must have a leading zero. The number 023, for example, is an octal number in C++. Hexadecimal numbers are denoted using a leading 0x. The use of octal and hexadecimal integer constants is illustrated in Program 2-5.

Program 2-5

```
#include <iostream.h>

int main()
{
  cout << "The decimal value of 025 is " << 025 << endl
       << "The decimal value of 0x37 is "<< 0x37 << endl;

  return 0;
}
```

When Program 2-5 is run, the following output is obtained:

```
The decimal value of 025 is 21
The decimal value of 0x37 is 55
```

The way the input, storage, and display of integers are related is illustrated in Figure 2–2.

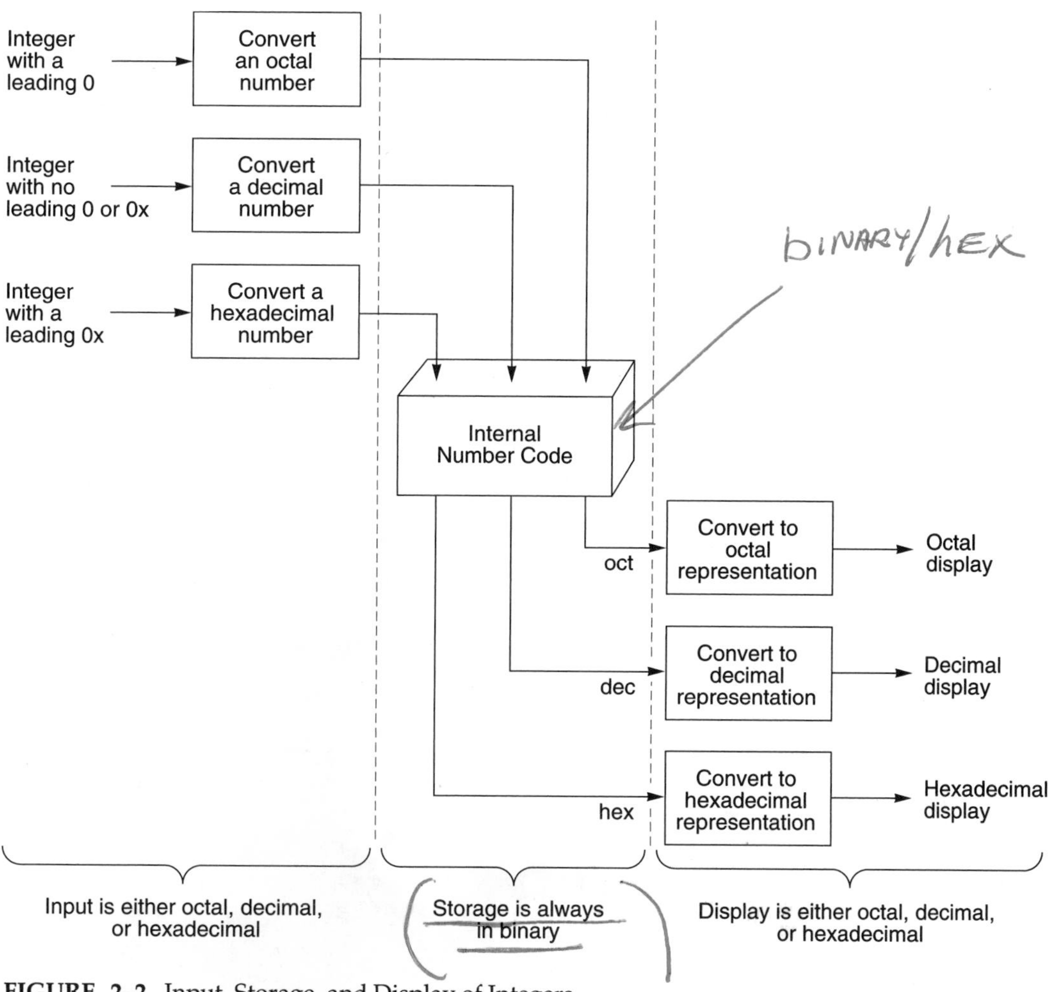

FIGURE 2–2 Input, Storage, and Display of Integers

Exercises 2.3

1. Determine the output of the following program.

```
#include <iostream.h>
int main()  // a program illustrating integer truncation
{
  cout << "answer1 is the integer " << 9/4
       << "answer2 is the integer " << 17/3 << endl;

  return 0;
}
```

2. Determine the output of the following program.

```
#include <iostream.h>
int main()   // a program illustrating the % operator
{
  cout << "The remainder of 9 divided by 4 is " << 9 % 4
       << "\nThe remainder of 17 divided by 3 is " << 17 % 3
       << endl;

  return 0;
}
```

3. Write a C++ program that displays the results of the expressions 3.0 * 5.0, 7.1 * 8.3 – 2.2, and 3.2 / (6.1 * 5). Calculate the value of each expression manually to verify that the displayed values are correct.

4. Write a C++ program that displays the results of the expressions 15 / 4, 15 % 4, and 5 * 3 – (6 * 4). Calculate the value of these expressions manually to verify that the display produced by your program is correct.

5. Determine the errors in each of the following statements.

a. `cout << "\n << " 15)`

b. `cout << "setw(4)" << 33;`

c. `cout << "setprecision(5)" << 526.768;`

d. `"Hello World!" >> cout;`

e. `cout << 47 << setw(6);`

f. `cout << set(10) << 526.768 << setprecision(2);`

6. Determine and write out the display produced by the following statements.

a. `cout << "|" << 5 <<"|";`

b. `cout << "|" << setw(4) << 5 << "|";`

c. `cout << "|" << setw(4) << 56829 << "|";`

d.
```
cout << "|" << setw(5) << setiosflags(ios::fixed)
     << setprecision(2) << 5.26 << "|";
```

e.
```
cout << "|" << setw(5) << setiosflags(ios::fixed)
     << setprecision(2) << 5.267 << "|";
```

f.
```
cout << "|" << setw(5) << setiosflags(ios::fixed)
     << setprecision(2) << 53.264 << "|";
```

g.
```
cout << "|" << setw(5) << setiosflags(ios::fixed)
     << setprecision(2) << 534.264 << "|";
```

h.
```
cout << "|" << setw(5) << setiosflags(ios::fixed)
     << setprecision(2) << 534. << "|";
```

7. Write out the display produced by the following statements.

a.
```
cout << "The number is " << setw(6) << setiosflags(ios::fixed)
     << setprecision(2) << 26.27 << endl;
cout << "The number is " << setw(6) << setiosflags(ios::fixed)
     << setprecision(2) << 682.3 << endl;
cout << "The number is " << setw(6) << setiosflags(ios::fixed)
     << setprecision(2) << 1.968 << endl;
```

b.
```
cout << setw(6) << setiosflags(ios::fixed)
     << setprecision(2) << 26.27 << endl;
cout << setw(6) << setiosflags(ios::fixed)
     << setprecision(2) << 682.3 << endl;
cout << setw(6) << setiosflags(ios::fixed)
     << setprecision(2) << 1.968 << endl;
cout << "------\n";
cout << setw(6) << setiosflags(ios::fixed)
     << setprecision(2) << 27.27 + 682.3 + 1.968 << endl;
```

c.
```
cout << setw(5) << setiosflags(ios::fixed)
     << setprecision(2) << 26.27 << endl;
cout << setw(5) << setiosflags(ios::fixed)
     << setprecision(2) << 682.3 << endl;
cout << setw(5) << setiosflags(ios::fixed)
     << setprecision(2) << 1.968 << endl;
cout << "-----\n";
cout << setw(5) << setiosflags(ios::fixed)
     << setprecision(2) << 27.27 + 682.3 + 1.968 << endl;
```

d.
```
cout << setw(5) << setiosflags(ios::fixed)
     << setprecision(2) << 36.164 << endl;
cout << setw(5) << setiosflags(ios::fixed)
     << setprecision(2) << 10.003 << endl;
cout << "-----" << endl;
```

8. The following table lists the correspondence between the decimal numbers 1 through 15 and their octal and hexadecimal representations.

Decimal:	1	2	3	4	5	6	7	8	9	10	11	12	13	14	15
Octal:	1	2	3	4	5	6	7	10	11	12	13	14	15	16	17
Hexadecimal:	1	2	3	4	5	6	7	8	9	a	b	c	d	e	f

Using this table, determine the output of the following program.

```
#include <iostream.h>
#include <iomanip.h>

int main()
{
  cout << "\nThe value of 14 in octal is " << oct << 14
       << "\nThe value of 14 in hexadecimal is " << hex << 14
       << "\nThe value of 0xA in decimal is " << dec << 0xA
       << "\nThe value of 0xA in octal is " << oct << 0xA
       << endl;

  return 0;
}
```

2.4 Variables and Declarations

All integer, floating-point, and other values used in a computer program are stored in and retrieved from the computer's memory unit. Conceptually, individual memory locations in the memory unit are arranged like the rooms in a large hotel. Like hotel rooms, each memory location has a unique address ("room number"). Before high-level languages such as C++ existed, memory locations were referenced by their addresses. For example, to store the integer values 45 and 12 in the memory locations 1652 and 2548 (see Figure 2–3), respectively, required instructions equivalent to

Put a 45 in location 1652
Put a 12 in location 2548

To add the two numbers just stored and save the result in another memory location—for example, at location 3000—required a statement comparable to

Add the contents of location 1652
to the contents of location 2548
and store the result into location 3000

Clearly this method of storage and retrieval is a cumbersome process. In high-level languages like C++, symbolic names are used in place of actual memory addresses. These symbolic names are called *variables*. A variable is simply a name the programmer uses to refer to computer storage locations. The term *variable* is used because the value stored in the variable can change, or *vary*. The computer keeps track of the actual memory address that corresponds to each name the programmer assigns. In our hotel room analogy, this is equivalent to putting a name on the door of a room and referring to the room by this name, such as the Blue Room, rather than using the actual room number.

FIGURE 2–3 Enough Storage for Two Integers.

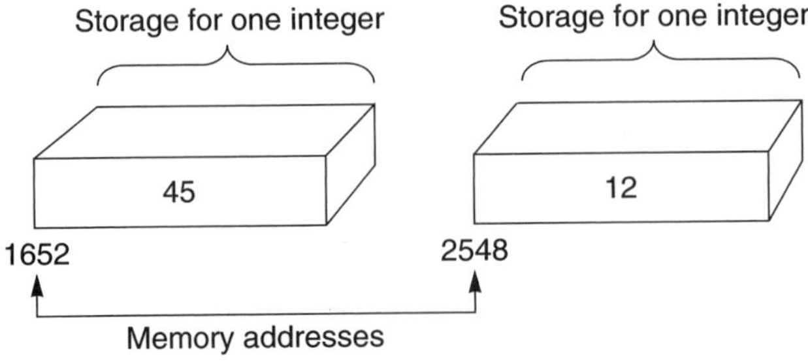

In C++ the selection of variable names is left to the programmer, as long as the following rules are observed.

1. The variable name must begin with a letter or underscore (_) and may contain only letters, underscores, or digits. It cannot contain any blanks, special symbols such as `()&$#.!\?`, or commas. It uses initial capital letters to separate names that consist of multiple words.
2. A variable name cannot be a keyword (see Table 1–2).
3. The variable name cannot consist of more than 31 characters. The number of characters is compiler-dependent.

These rules are similar to those used for selecting function names. Like function names, variable names should be mnemonics that give some indication of the variable's use. For example, a good name for a variable used to store a value that is the total of some other values would be `sum` or `total`. Variable names that give no clue to the type of value stored, such as `r2d2`, `linda`, `bill`, and `getum`, should not be selected. Like function names, variable names can be typed in uppercase and lowercase letters.

Now assume that the first memory location illustrated in Figure 2–3, which has address 1652, is given the name `num1`. Also assume that memory location 2548 is given the variable name `num2` and that memory location 3000 is given the variable name `total`, as illustrated in Figure 2–4.

With these variable names, the operation of storing 45 in location 1652, storing 12 in location 2548, and adding the contents of these two locations is accomplished by the C++ statements

```
num1 = 45;
num2 = 12;
total = num1 + num2;
```

FIGURE 2–4 Naming Storage Locations

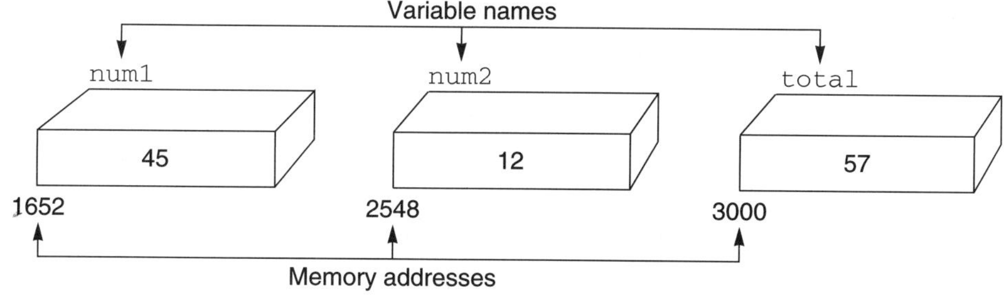

Each of these three statements is called an *assignment statement* because it tells the computer to assign a value to (store it in) a variable. Assignment statements always have an equals (=) sign and one variable name immediately to the left of this sign. The value on the right of the equals sign is determined first, and this value is assigned to the variable on the left of the equals sign. The blank spaces in the assignment statements are inserted for readability. We will have much more to say about assignment statements in the next chapter, but for now we will just use them to store values in variables.

A variable name is useful because it frees the programmer from concern over where data are physically stored inside the computer. We simply use the variable name and let the compiler worry about where the data are actually stored in memory. However, C++ requires that before we store a value in a variable, we clearly declare the type of data that is to be stored in it. We must tell the compiler, in advance, the names of the variables that will be used for characters, the names that will be used for integers, and the names that will be used to store the other C++ data types.

Declaration Statements

Naming a variable and specifying the data type that can be stored in it are accomplished by using *declaration statements*. A declaration statement has the general form

```
data-type variable-name;
```

where `data-type` designates a valid C++ data type and `variable-name` is a user-selected variable name. For example, variables used to hold integer values are declared using the keyword `int` to specify the data type and have the form

```
int variable-name;
```

Thus the declaration statement

```
int sum;
```

declares `sum` as the name of a variable capable of storing an integer value.

In addition to the reserved word `int` used to specify an integer, the reserved word `long`, which is considered a data type qualifier, is used to specify a long integer.[9] For example, the statement

```
long int datenum;
```

[9] Additionally, the reserved words `unsigned int` are used to specify an integer that can store only nonnegative numbers, and the reserved words `short int` are used to specify a short integer.

POINT OF INFORMATION

Atomic Data

The variables we have declared have all been used to store atomic data values. An atomic data value is a value that is considered a complete entity by itself and is not decomposable into a smaller data type supported by the language. For example, although an integer can be decomposed into individual digits, C++ does not have a numerical digit type. Rather, each integer is regarded as a complete value by itself and, as such, is considered an atomic data value. Similarly, because the integer data type supports only atomic data values, it is said to be an atomic data type. As you might expect, floating-point characters and Boolean data types are atomic data types also.

declares `datenum` as a variable that will be used to store a long integer. When using the long qualifier, we can omit the keyword `int`. Thus the previous declaration can be written as

```
long datenum;
```

Variables used to hold single-precision floating-point values are declared using the keyword `float`, whereas variables that will be used to hold double-precision values are declared using the keyword `double`. For example, the statement

```
float firstnum;
```

declares `firstnum` as a variable that will be used to store a floating-point number. Similarly, the statement

```
double secnum;
```

declares that the variable `secnum` will be used to store a double-precision number.

Although declaration statements may be placed anywhere within a function, most declarations are typically grouped together and placed immediately after the function's opening brace. In all cases, however, a variable must be declared before it can be used, and like all C++ statements, declaration statements must end with a semicolon. If the declaration statements are placed after the opening function brace, a simple `main()` function containing declaration statements would have the general form

```
#include <iostream.h>

int main()
{
  declaration statements;

  other statements;

  return 0;
}
```

Program 2-6 illustrates this form in declaring and using four floating-point variables, with the `cout` object used to display the contents of one of the variables.

Program 2-6

```
#include <iostream.h>

int main()
{
  float grade1;  // declare grade1 as a float variable
  float grade2;  // declare grade2 as a float variable
  float total;   // declare total as a float variable
  float average; // declare average as a float variable

  grade1 = 85.5;
  grade2 = 97.0;
  total = grade1 + grade2;
  average = total/2.0;  // divide the total by 2.0
  cout << "The average grade is " << average << endl;

  return 0;
}
```

The placement of the declaration statements in Program 2-6 is straightforward, although we will see that the four individual declarations can be combined into a single declaration. When Program 2-6 is run, the following output is displayed:

```
The average grade is 91.25
```

Note that when a variable name is sent to `cout`, the value stored in the variable is placed on the output stream and displayed.

Just as integer and real (floating-point, double-precision, and long-double) variables must be declared before they can be used, a variable used to store a single character must also be declared. Character variables are declared by using the reserved word `char`. For example, the declaration

```
char ch;
```

declares `ch` to be a character variable. Program 2-7 illustrates this declaration and the use of `cout` to display the value stored in a character variable.

Program 2-7

```
#include <iostream.h>

int main()
{
  char ch;      // this declares a character variable

  ch = 'a';    // store the letter a into ch
  cout << "The character stored in ch is " << ch << endl;
  ch = 'm';    // now store the letter m into ch
  cout << "The character now stored in ch is "<< ch << endl;

  return 0;
}
```

When Program 2-7 is run, the output produced is

```
The character stored in ch is a
The character now stored in ch is m
```

Note in Program 2-7 that the first letter stored in the variable `ch` is `a` and the second letter stored is `m`. Because a variable can be used to store only one value at a time, the assignment of `m` to the variable automatically causes `a` to be overwritten.

Multiple Declarations

Variables that have the same data type can always be grouped together and declared by using a single declaration statement. The common form of such a declaration is

```
data-type variable list;
```

For example, the four separate declarations used in Program 2-6,

```
float grade1;
float grade2;
float total;
float average;
```

can be replaced by the single declaration statement

```
float grade1, grade2, total, average;
```

Similarly, the two character declarations

```
char ch;
char key;
```

can be replaced by the single declaration statement

```
char ch, key;
```

Note that declaring multiple variables in a single declaration requires that the data type of the variables be given only once, that all the variables' names be separated by commas, and that only one semicolon be used to terminate the declaration. The space after each comma is inserted for readability and is not required.

Declaration statements can also be used to store an initial value in declared variables. For example, the declaration statement

```
int num1 = 15;
```

both declares the variable `num1` as an integer variable and sets the value of `15` in the variable. When a declaration statement is used to store a value in a variable, the variable is said to be *initialized*. Thus, in this example, it is correct to say that the variable `num1` has been initialized to `15`. Similarly, the declaration statements

```
float grade1 = 87.0;
float grade2 = 93.5;
float total;
```

declare three floating-point variables and initialize two of them. Good programming practice dictates that when initializations are used, each initialized variable be declared on a line by itself. Constants, expressions using only constants (such as 87.0 + 12 – 2), and expressions using constants and previously initialized variables can all be used as initializers within a function. For example, Program 2-6 with declaration initialization becomes Program 2-6a.

Program 2-6a

```
#include <iostream.h>

int main()
{
  float grade1 = 85.5;
  float grade2 = 97.0;
  float total, average;

  total = grade1 + grade2;
  average = total/2.0;  // divide the total by 2.0
  cout << "The average grade is " << average << endl;

  return 0;
}
```

Note the blank line after the declaration statement. Inserting a blank line after the variable declarations placed at the top of a function body is good programming practice. It improves both a program's appearance and its readability.

An interesting feature of C++ is that variable declarations may be freely intermixed and even contained within other statements; the only requirement is that a variable must be declared prior to its use. For example, the variable `float` in Program 2-6a could have been declared when it was first used by using the statement `float total = grade1 + grade2`. In very restricted situations (such as debugging, described in Section 4.7, or in a `for` loop, described in Section 5.3), declaring a variable at its point of use can be helpful. In general, it is preferable not to disperse declarations but rather to group them, in as concise and clear a manner as possible, at the top of each function.

Reference Variables[10]

Once a variable has been declared, it may be given additional names. This is accomplished by using a reference declaration, which has the form

```
data-type &new_name = existing_name;
```

For example, the reference declaration

```
float &sum = total;
```

equates the name `sum` to the name `total`—both now refer to the same variable, as illustrated in Figure 2–5.[11]

Once another name has been established for a variable by using a reference declaration, the new name, which is referred to as an alias, can be used in place of the original name. For example, consider Program 2-8.

Program 2-8

```
#include <iostream.h>
int main()
{
  float total = 20.5;     // declare and initialize total
  float &sum = total;     // declare another name for total

  cout << "sum = " << sum << endl;
  sum = 18.6;             // this changes the value in total
  cout << "total = " << total << endl;
  return 0;
}
```

The following output is produced by Program 2-8:

```
sum = 20.5
total = 18.6
```

[10] This section may be omitted on first reading without loss of subject continuity.

[11] Knowledgeable C programmers should not confuse the use of the ampersand symbol, &, in a reference declaration with the address operator or with the use of a reference variable as a pointer. A reference variable simply equates two variable names.

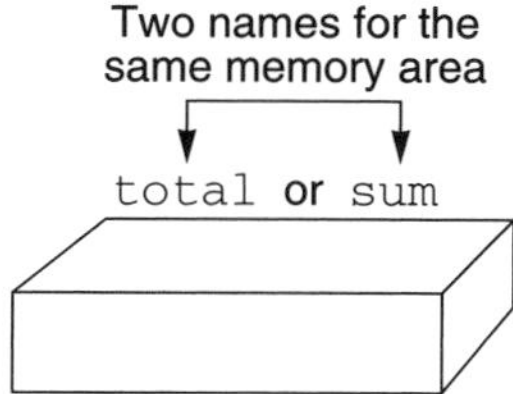

FIGURE 2–5 `sum` Is an Alternative Name for `total`

Because the variable `sum` is simply another reference to the variable `total`, it is the value stored in `total` that is obtained by the first call to `cout` in Program 2-8. Changing the value in `sum` then changes the value in `total`, which is displayed by the second call to `cout` in Program 2-8.

In constructing references, remember that the reference should be of the same data type as the variable it refers to. For example, the sequence of declarations

```
int num = 5;
double &numref = num;
```

does not equate `numref` to `num`; they are not of the same data type. Rather, because the compiler cannot correctly associate the reference with a variable, it creates an unnamed variable of the reference type first and then references this unnamed variable with the reference variable. Such unnamed variables are called *anonymous variables*. For example, consider Program 2-9, which illustrates the effect of creating an anonymous variable.

Program 2-9

```
#include <iostream.h>
int main()
{
  int num = 10;
  float &numref = num;// this does not equate numref to num
                      // instead, it equates numref to an
                      // anonymous floating-point variable

  numref = 23.6;
  cout << "The value of num is " << num
       << "\nThe value of numref is " << numref << endl;
  return 0;
}
```

The output produced by Program 2-9 is

```
The value of num is 10
The value of numref is 23.6
```

Note that the value of num is not affected by the value stored in numref. This is because numref could not be created as a reference for num; rather, it is another name for an unnamed (anonymous) floating-point variable that can be reached only by using the reference name numref.

Just as declaring a reference to an incorrect data type produces an anonymous variable, so does equating a reference to a constant. For example, the declaration

```
int &val = 5;  // an anonymous variable is created
```

creates an anonymous variable with the number 5 stored in it. The only way to access this variable is by the reference name. Clearly, creating references to anonymous variables should be avoided. Once a reference name has been equated to either a legal variable or an anonymous one, the reference cannot be changed to refer to another variable.

As with all declaration statements, multiple references may be declared in a single statement as long as each reference name is preceded by the ampersand symbol. Thus the declaration

```
float &sum = total, &mean = average;
```

creates two reference variables named sum and average.[12]

As we learn more about C++, we will have occasion to use reference variables in more detail, primarily as function arguments or as a function return type. Reference variables used in this manner are described in Section 6.3.

Specifying Storage Allocation

The declaration statements we have introduced perform both software and hardware tasks. From a software perspective, declaration statements always provide a list of all variables and their data types. In this software role, variable declarations also help to control an otherwise common and troublesome error caused by the misspelling of a variable's name within a program. For example,

[12] Reference declarations may also be written in the form data-type& new_name = existing name;, where a space is placed between the ampersand symbol and the reference variable name. This form, however, becomes prone to error when multiple references are declared in the same declaration statement and the ampersand symbol is inadvertently omitted after the first reference name is declared. In order to accommodate multiple references in the same declaration more easily and mark a variable clearly as a reference, we will adhere to the convention of placing the ampersand directly in front of each reference variable name.

assume that a variable named `distance` is declared and initialized using the statement

```
int distance = 26;
```

Now assume that this variable is inadvertently misspelled in the statement

```
mpg = distnce / gallons;
```

In languages that do not require variable declarations, the program would treat `distnce` as a new variable and either assign an initial value of zero to the variable or use whatever value happened to be in the variable's storage area. In either case, a value would be calculated and assigned to `mpg`, and finding the error could be extremely troublesome (one might not even be aware that an error had occurred). Such errors are impossible in C++, because the compiler would flag `distnce` as an undeclared variable. The compiler cannot, of course, detect when one declared variable is typed in place of another declared variable.

In addition to their software role, declaration statements can also perform a distinct hardware task. Because each data type has its own storage requirements, the computer can allocate sufficient storage for a variable only after it knows the variable's data type. Variable declarations provide this information, so they can be used to force the compiler to reserve enough physical memory storage for each variable. Declaration statements used for this hardware purpose are also called *definition statements* because they define, or tell the compiler, how much memory is needed for data storage.

All the declaration statements that we have encountered so far have also been definition statements. Later, we will see cases of declaration statements that do not cause any new storage to be allocated and are used simply to declare, or alert the program to, the data types of variables that are created elsewhere in the program.

Figures 2–6(a–d) illustrate the series of operations set in motion by declaration statements that also perform a definition role. The figures show that definition statements (or, if you prefer, declaration statements that also cause memory to be allocated) "tag" the first byte of each set of reserved bytes with a name. This name is, of course, the variable's name and is used by the computer to locate correctly the starting point of each variable's reserved memory area.

Within a program, after a variable has been declared it is typically used by a programmer to refer to the contents of the variable (that is, the variable's value). Where in memory this value is stored generally matters little to the programmer. The compiler, however, must be concerned with where each value is stored and with correctly locating each variable. In this task the computer uses the variable name to locate the first byte of storage previously allocated to the variable. Knowing the variable's data type then allows the compiler to store or retrieve the correct number of bytes.

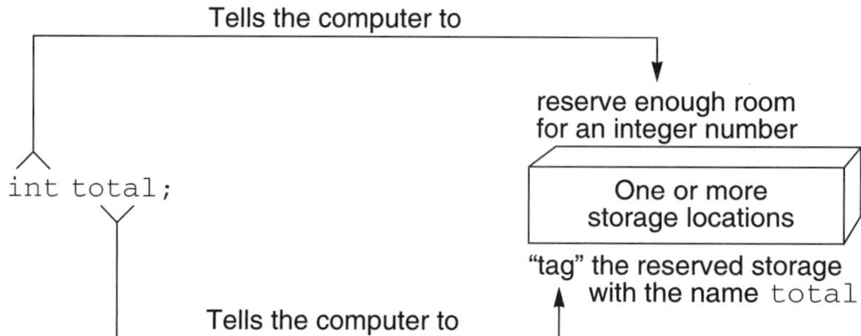

FIGURE 2–6a Defining the Integer Variable Named `total`

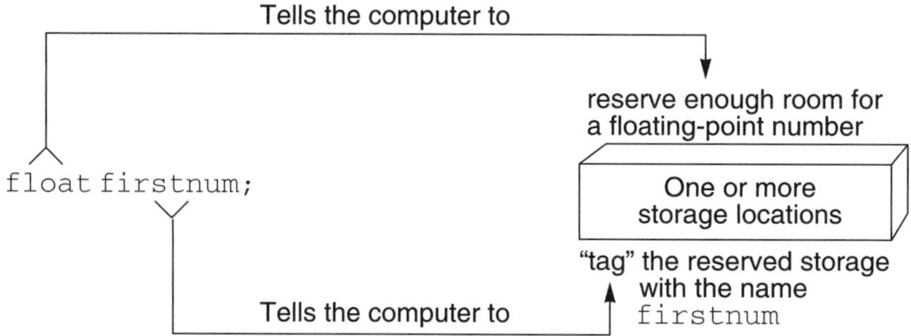

FIGURE 2–6b Defining the Floating-Point Variable Named `firstnum`

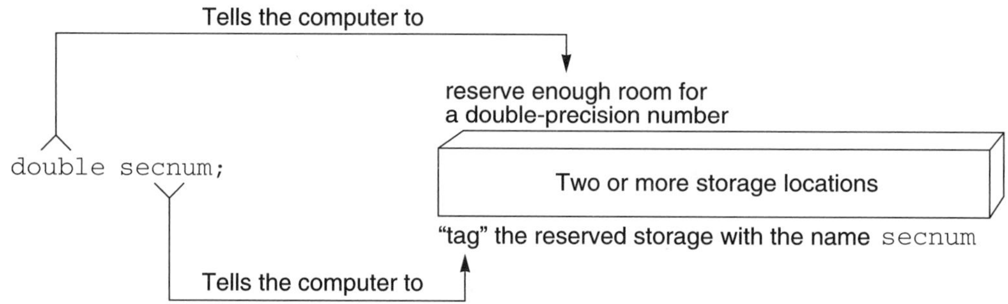

FIGURE 2–6c Defining the Double-Precision Variable Named `secnum`

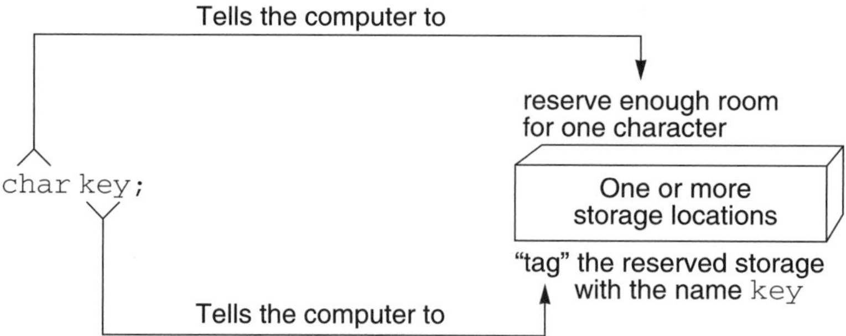

FIGURE 2–6d Defining the Character Variable Named `key`

Exercises 2.4

1. State whether each of the following variable names is valid. For those that are invalid, give the reason why.

```
prod_a      c1234      abcd       -c3        12345
newbal      while      $total     new bal    a1b2c3d4
9ab6        sum.of     average    grade1     finGrad
```

2. State whether each of the following variable names is valid. For those that are invalid, give the reason why. Also indicate which of the valid variable names should not be used because they convey no information about the variable.

```
salestax    a243    r2d2     firstNum   cca1
harry       sue     c3p0     average    sum
maximum     okay    a        awesome    goforit
3sum        for     tot.a1   c$five     netpay
```

3. *a.* Write a declaration statement to declare that the variable `count` will be used to store an integer.
   b. Write a declaration statement to declare that the variable `grade` will be used to store a floating-point number.
   c. Write a declaration statement to declare that the variable `yield` will be used to store a double-precision number.
   d. Write a declaration statement to declare that the variable `initial` will be used to store a character.

4. Write declaration statements for the following variables.
   a. `num1`, `num2`, and `num3` used to store integer numbers
   b. `grade1`, `grade2`, `grade3`, and `grade4` used to store floating-point numbers
   c. `tempa`, `tempb`, and `tempc` used to store double-precision numbers
   d. `ch`, `let1`, `let2`, `let3`, and `let4` used to store character types

5. Write declaration statements for the following variables.
   a. `firstnum` and `secnum` used to store integers
   b. `price`, `yield`, and `coupon` used to store floating-point numbers
   c. `maturity` used to store a double-precision number

6. Rewrite each of these declaration statements as three individual declarations.
   a. `int month, day = 30, year;`
   b. `double hours, rate, otime = 15.62;`
   c. `float price, amount, taxes;`
   d. `char in_key, ch, choice = 'f';`

7. *a.* Determine what each statement causes to happen in the following program.

```
#include <iostream.h>
int main()
{
  int num1, num2, total;

  num1 = 25;
  num2 = 35;
  total = num1 + num2;
  cout << "The total of" << num1 << " and "
       << num2 << " is " << total << endl;
  return 0;
}
```

b. What is the output that will be printed when the program listed in Exercise 7a is run?

8. Write a C++ program that stores the sum of the integer numbers 12 and 33 in a variable named `sum`. Have your program display the value stored in `sum`.

9. Write a C++ program that stores the integer value 16 in the variable `length` and the integer value 18 in the variable `width`. Have your program calculate the value assigned to the variable `perimeter`, using the assignment statement

```
perimeter = 2 * length + 2 * width;
```

and print out the value stored in the variable `perimeter`. Be sure to declare all the variables as integers at the beginning of the `main()` function.

10. Write a C++ program that stores the integer value 16 in the variable `num1` and the integer value 18 in the variable `num2`. (Be sure to declare the variables as integers.) Have your program calculate the total of these numbers and their average. Store the total in an integer variable named `total` and the average in an integer variable named `average`. (Use the statement `average = total/2.0;` to calculate the average.) Use the `cout` object to display the total and average.

11. Repeat Exercise 10, but store the number 15 in `num1` instead of 16. With a pencil, write down the average of `num1` and `num2`. What do you think your program will store in the integer variable that you used for the average of these two numbers? How can you ensure that the correct answer will be printed for the average?

12. Write a C++ program that stores the number 105.62 in the variable `firstnum`, 89.352 in the variable `secnum`, and 98.67 in the variable `thirdnum`. (Be sure to declare the variables first as either float or double.) Have your program calculate the total of the three numbers and their average. The total should be stored in the variable `total` and the average in the variable `average`. (Use the statement `average = total /3.0;` to calculate the average.) Use the `cout` object to display the total and average.

13. Every variable has at least two items associated with it. What are these two items?

14. *a.* A statement used to clarify the relationship between squares and rectangles is "All squares are rectangles but not all rectangles are squares." Write a similar statement that describes the relationship between definition and declaration statements.

b. Why must a variable be defined before any other C++ statement that uses the variable?

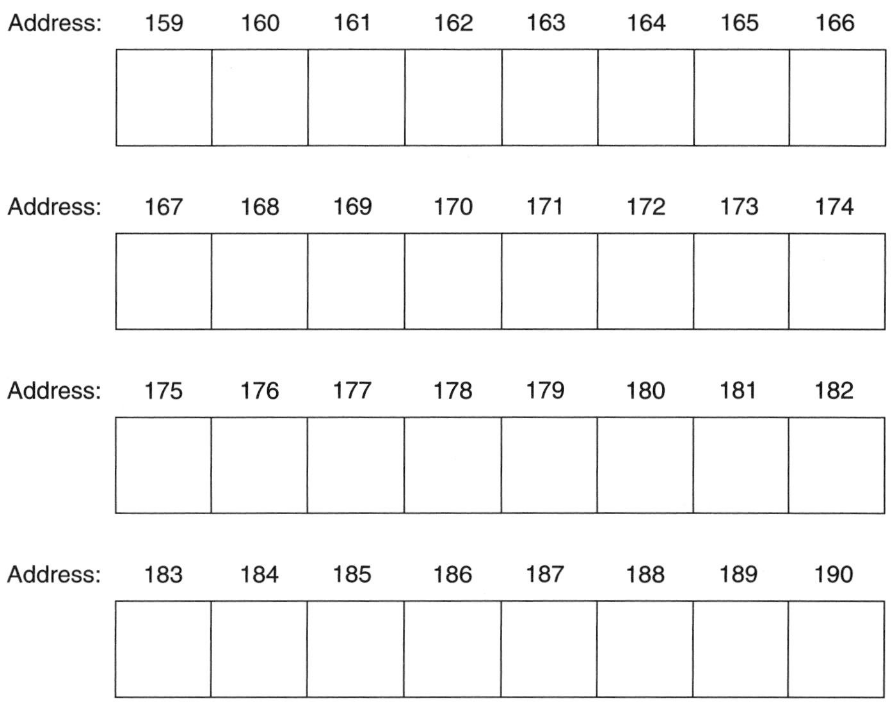

FIGURE 2–7 Memory Bytes for Exercises 15, 16, and 17

Note for Exercises 15 through 17: *Assume that a character requires one byte of storage, an integer two bytes, a floating-point number four bytes, and a double-precision number eight bytes and that variables are assigned storage in the order in which they are declared (review Section 2.8 if you are unfamiliar with the concept of a byte).*

15. a. Using Figure 2–7 and assuming that the variable named `rate` is assigned to the byte that has memory address 159, determine the address that corresponds to each variable declared in the following statements. Also fill in the appropriate bytes with the initialization data included in the declaration statements (use letters for the characters, not the computer codes that would actually be stored).

```
float rate;

char ch1 = 'w', ch2 = 'o', ch3 = 'w', ch4 = '!';

double taxes;

int num, count = 0;
```

b. Repeat Exercise 15a, but substitute the actual byte patterns that a computer employing the ASCII code would use to store the characters in the variables `ch1`, `ch2`, `ch3`, and `ch4`. (*Hint:* Use Table 2–2.)

16. a. Using Figure 2–7 and assuming that the variable named `cn1` is assigned to the byte at memory address 159, determine the address that corresponds to each variable declared in the following statements. Also, fill in the appropriate bytes with the initialization data included in the declaration statements (use letters for the characters, not the computer codes that would actually be stored).

```
char cn1 = 'a', cn2 = ' ', cn3 = 'b', cn4 = 'u', cn5 = 'n';

char cn6 = 'c', cn7 = 'h', key = '\\', sch = '\'', inc = 'o';

char inc1 = 'f';
```

b. Repeat Exercise 16a, but substitute the actual byte patterns that a computer employing the ASCII code would use to store the characters in each of the declared variables. (*Hint:* Use Table 2–2.)

17. Using Figure 2–7 and assuming that the variable named `miles` is assigned to the byte at memory address 159, determine the address that corresponds to each variable declared in the following statements.

```
float miles;

int count, num;

double dist, temp;
```

2.5 Integer Qualifiers

Integer numbers are generally used in programs as counters to keep track of the number of times something has occurred. For most applications, the counts needed are less than 32,767, which is the greatest signed-integer value that can be stored in two bytes. Because most computers allocate at least two bytes for integers, there is usually no problem.

Cases do arise, however, where larger integer numbers are needed. In financial applications, for example, dates such as 7/12/89 are typically converted to the number of days since the turn of the century. This conversion makes it possible to store and sort dates by using a single number for each date. Unfortunately, for dates after 1987, the number of days since the turn of the century is larger than the 32,767 allowed when only two bytes are allocated for each integer variable. For financial programs dealing with mortgages or bonds maturing after 1987 that are run on computers allocating only two bytes per integer (PCs, for example), the limitation on the maximum integer value must be overcome.

To accommodate the requirements of real applications such as this, C++ provides long-integer, short-integer, and unsigned-integer data types. These three additional integer data types are obtained by adding the qualifiers `long`, `short`, and `unsigned`, respectively, to the normal integer declaration statements. For example, the declaration statement

```
long int days;
```

declares the variable `days` to be a long integer. The word `int` in a long-integer declaration statement is optional, so the previous declaration statement can also be written as `long days;`. The amount of storage allocated for a long integer depends on the computer being used. Although you would expect that a long-integer variable would be allocated more space than a standard integer, this may not be the case. About all we can say for certain is that long integers will provide no less space than regular integers. You should check the actual amount of storage allocated by your computer by using the `sizeof` operator described at the end of this section.

Once a variable is declared as a long integer, integer values may be assigned as usual for standard integers, or an optional letter `L` (either uppercase or lowercase, with no space between the number and letter) may be appended to the integer. For example, the declaration statement

```
long days = 38276L;
```

declares `days` to be of type long integer and assigns the long-integer constant `38276` to the variable `days`.

In addition to the long qualifier, C++ also provides for a short qualifier. Although you would expect a short integer to conserve computer storage by reserving fewer bytes than are used for an integer, this is not always the case. Some computers use the same amount of storage for both integers and short integers. Again, the amount of memory space allocated for a short-integer data type depends on your computer and can be checked by using the `sizeof` operator (described at the end of this section). As with long integers, short integers may be declared by using the term `short` or `short int` in a declaration statement. Once a variable is declared as a short integer, values are assigned as is normally done with integers.

The final integer data type is the unsigned integer. This data type is obtained by prefixing the reserved word `int` with the qualifier `unsigned`. For example, the declaration statement

```
unsigned int days;
```

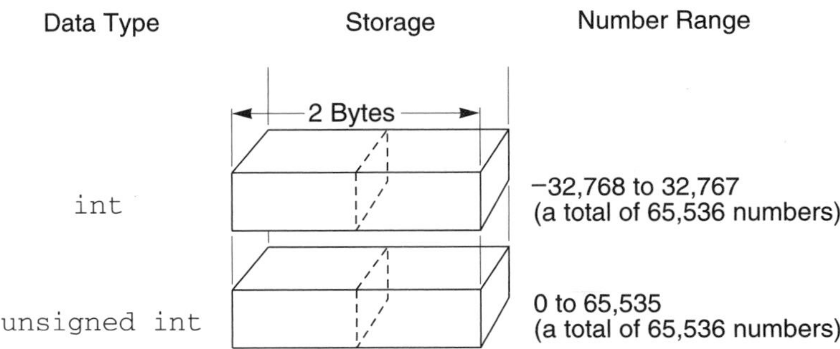

FIGURE 2–8 Unsigned Integer Storage Using Two Bytes

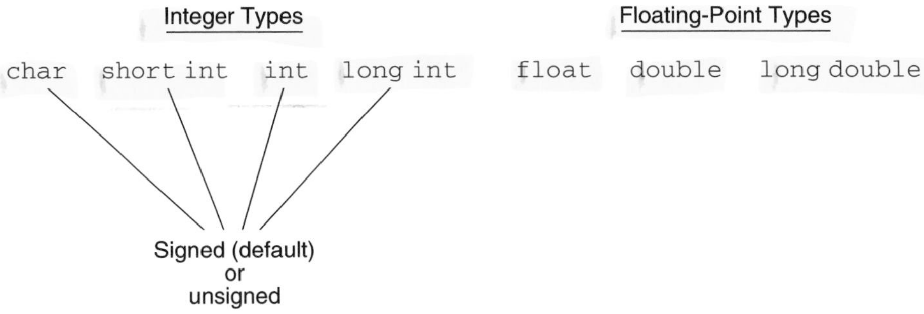

FIGURE 2–9 C++'s Fundamental Data Types

declares the variable `days` to be of type `unsigned`. Unsigned integers are generally used only for positive integers, and they have the effect of doubling the positive value that can be stored without increasing the number of bytes allocated to an integer. This is accomplished by effectively treating all unsigned integers as positive numbers, as illustrated in Figure 2–8.

Figure 2–9 illustrates all of C++'s fundamental data types and their relationships to each other.

Converting Among Data Types

The general rules for converting integer and floating-point operands in mixed-mode arithmetic expressions were presented in Section 2.2. A more detailed set of conversion rules for arithmetic operators, which includes character, short-integer, and long-integer operands, is provided in Table 2–10, where the rules are applied in order, starting with Rule 1.

TABLE 2–10 Conversion Rules for Arithmetic Operators

1. If both operands are either character or integer operands, then: ***a.*** when both operands are character, short-integer, or long-integer data types, the result of the expression is an integer value. ***b.*** when one of the operands is a long integer, the result is a long integer, unless one of the operands is an unsigned integer. In this case the other operand is converted to an unsigned integer value, and the resulting value of the expression is an unsigned value.
2. If any one operand is a floating-point value, then: ***a.*** when one or both operands are floats, the result of the operation is a float value. ***b.*** when one or both operands are doubles, the result of the operation is a double value. ***c.*** when one or both operands are long doubles, the result is a long-double value.

Note that the rules in Table 2–10 apply to each individual arithmetic operation in their correct order of evaluation. For example, in the expression `14.78F - 4 * 3L`, the multiplication, which has a higher precedence than the subtraction, is performed first. For this multiplication of two integer operands, the integer 4 is converted to a long-integer value, and the result of the expression is `12L` (Rule 1b). The result of the next operation, `14.78F - 12L`, is the single-precision (float) value 2.78 (Rule 2a).

Determining Storage Size[13]

C++ provides an operator for determining the amount of storage your compiler allocates for each data type. This operator, called the `sizeof()` operator, returns the number of bytes of the variable or data type included in the parentheses. Unlike a function, which itself is made up of C++ statements, the `sizeof()` operator is an integral part of the C++ language itself. Examples using the `sizeof()` operator are

```
sizeof(num1)     sizeof(int)     sizeof(float)
```

If the item in parentheses is a variable, as in the example `sizeof(num1)`, then `sizeof()` returns the number of bytes of storage that the computer reserved for the variable. If the item following the word `sizeof` is a data type, such as `int` or `char`, then `sizeof` returns the number of bytes of storage that the computer uses for the given data type. With either approach, we can use `sizeof()` to determine the amount of storage used by different data types. Consider Program 2-10.

---

[13] This section assumes a basic understanding of concepts and terms related to computer storage. If you are not familiar with these concepts, please read the supplement at the end of this chapter.

Program 2-10

```
#include <iostream.h>
int main()
{
  char ch;
  int num1;

  cout << "Bytes of storage used by a character: "
       << sizeof(ch) << endl
       << "Bytes of storage used by an integer: "
       << sizeof(num1) << endl;

  return 0;
}
```

Program 2-10 declares that the variable `ch` is used to store a character and that the variable `num1` is used to store an integer. From our discussion in the last section, we know that each of these declaration statements is also a definition statement. Accordingly, the first declaration statement instructs the compiler to reserve enough storage for a character, and the second declaration statement instructs it to reserve enough storage for an integer. The `sizeof()` operator is then used to tell us how much room the computer really set aside for these two variables. The `sizeof()` operator itself is used as an argument to the `cout` object. When Program 2-10 is run on an IBM personal computer, the following output is obtained:

```
Bytes of storage used by a character: 1
Bytes of storage used by an integer: 2
```

Exercises 2.5

1. *a.* Run Program 2-10 to determine how many bytes your computer uses to store character and integer data types.
   b. Expand Program 2-10 to determine how many bytes your computer uses for short integers, long integers, and unsigned integers.
2. After running the program written for Exercise 1, use Table 2–1 (see Section 2.1) to determine the maximum and minimum numbers that can be stored in integer, short-integer, and long-integer variables for your computer.
3. Program 2-10 did not actually store any values in the variables `ch` and `num1`. Why was this not necessary?

4. *a.* Expand Program 2-10 to determine how many bytes your computer uses to store floating-point and double-precision numbers.
b. Although there is no long-float data class, double-precision numbers are sometimes considered the equivalent long form for floating-point numbers. Why is this so? Does the output of the program written for Exercise 4a support this statement?

2.6 Common Programming Errors

The common programming errors associated with the material presented in this chapter are

1. Forgetting to declare all the variables used in a program. This error is detected by the compiler, and an error message is generated for all undeclared variables.
2. Attempting to store one data type in a variable declared for a different type. This error is not detected by the compiler. Here, the value is converted to the data type of the variable it is assigned to.
3. Using a variable in an expression before a value has been assigned to the variable. Here, whatever value happens to be in the variable will be used when the expression is evaluated, and the result will be meaningless.
4. Dividing integer values incorrectly. This error is usually disguised within a larger expression and can be troublesome to detect. For example, the expression

   ```
   3.425 + 2/3 + 7.9
   ```

   yields the same result as the expression

   ```
   3.425 + 7.9
   ```

   because the integer division of `2/3` is `0`.
5. Mixing data types in the same expression without clearly understanding the effect produced. C++ allows mixed-mode expressions, so it is important to be clear about the order of evaluation and the data type of all intermediate calculations. The rules for evaluating the result of a numeric expression follow:
   a. If all operands are integers, the result is an integer.
   b. If any operand is a floating-point value, the result is a floating-point value.

   As a general rule, it is better not to mix data types in an expression unless a specific effect is desired.
6. Forgetting to separate individual data streams passed to `cout` with an insertion ("put to") symbol, <<.

2.7 Chapter Summary

1. The four basic types of data recognized by C++ are integer, floating-point, character, and Boolean data. Each of these types of data is typically stored in a computer using different amounts of memory.
2. The `cout` object can be used to display all of C++'s data types.
3. Every variable in a C++ program must be declared as to the type of value it can store. Declarations within a function may be placed anywhere within the function, although a variable can be used only after it is declared. Variables may also be initialized when they are declared. Additionally, variables of the same type may be declared by using a single declaration statement. Variable declaration statements have the general form

```
data-type variable-name(s);
```

4. Reference variables can be declared that associate a second name to an existing variable. The reference variable, which is also called an alias, is simply another name for the existing variable. Reference declarations have the form

```
data_type &reference_name = existing_name;
```

5. A simple C++ program containing declaration statements typically has the following form:

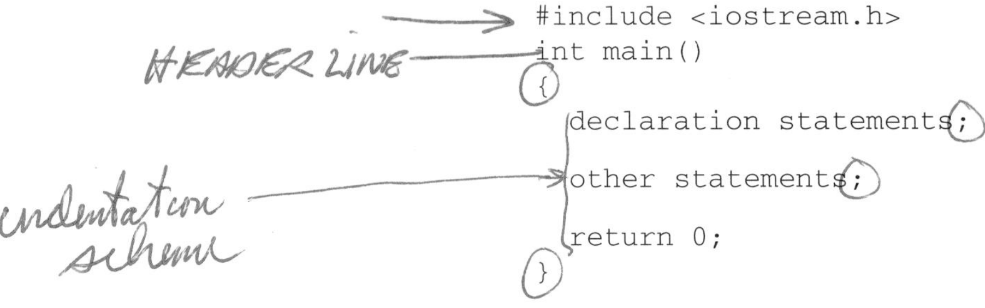

```
#include <iostream.h>
int main()
{
  declaration statements;

  other statements;

  return 0;
}
```

Although declaration statements may be placed anywhere within the function's body, a variable may be used only after it is declared.

6. Declaration statements always play a software role, informing the compiler of a function's valid variable names. When a variable declaration also causes the computer to set aside memory locations for the variable, the declaration statement is also called a definition statement. (All the declarations we have used in this chapter have also been definition statements.)
7. The `sizeof()` operator can be used to determine the amount of storage reserved for variables.

2.8 Chapter Supplement: Bits, Bytes, Addresses, and Number Codes

The physical components used in manufacturing a computer require that the numbers and letters inside its memory unit are not stored using the same symbols that people use. The number 126, for example, would not be stored using the symbols 1, 2, and 6. Nor is the letter that we recognize as A stored using this symbol. In this section, we will see why this is so and how computers store numbers.

The smallest and most basic data item in a computer is called a *bit*. Physically, a bit is really a switch that can be either open or closed. The convention we will follow is that the open and closed positions of each switch are represented as 0 and 1, respectively.[14]

A single bit that can represent the values 0 and 1, by itself, has limited usefulness. All computers, therefore, group a set number of bits together, both for storage and for transmission. The grouping of eight bits to form a larger unit is an almost universal computer standard. Such groups are commonly referred to as *bytes*. A single byte consisting of eight bits, where each bit is either 0 or 1, can represent any one of 256 distinct patterns. These consist of the pattern 00000000 (all eight switches open), the pattern 11111111 (all eight switches closed), and all possible combinations of 0s and 1s in between. Each of these patterns can be used to represent a letter of the alphabet, other single characters (such as a dollar sign, a comma, or a single digit), or numbers containing more than one digit. The patterns consisting of 0s and 1s used to represent letters, single digits, and other single characters are called *character codes* (two such codes, the ASCII and ANSI codes, were presented in Section 2.1). The patterns used to store numbers are called *number codes,* one of which is presented at the end of this section.

Words and Addresses

One or more bytes may themselves be grouped into larger units, called *words,* which facilitate faster and more extensive data access. For example, retrieving from a computer's memory a word that consists of four bytes results in more information than retrieving a word that consists of a single byte. Such a retrieval is also considerably faster than four individual byte retrievals. This increase

[14] This convention, unfortunately, is rather arbitrary, and you frequently will encounter the reverse correspondence, where the open and closed positions are represented as 1 and 0, respectively.

$-(2^7)$	(2^6)	(2^5)	(2^4)	(2^3)	(2^2)	(2^1)	(2^0)
−128	64	32	16	8	4	2	1

FIGURE 2–10 An Eight-Bit Value Box

in speed and capacity, however, is achieved by increasing the computer's cost and complexity.

Early personal computers, such as the Apple IIe and Commodore machines, internally stored and transmitted words consisting of single bytes. The first IBM-PCs used word sizes consisting of two bytes, and more current Pentium-based PCs store and process words consisting of four bytes each.

The arrangement of words in a computer's memory can be compared to the arrangement of suites in a large hotel, where each suite is made up of rooms of the same size. Just as each suite has a unique room number to locate and identify it, each word has a unique numeric address. In computers that allow each byte to be individually accessed, each byte has its own address. Like room numbers, word and byte addresses are always unsigned whole numbers that are used for location and identification purposes. And like hotel rooms with connecting doors for forming larger suites, words can be combined to form larger units for the accommodation of different-sized data types.

Twos Complement Numbers

The most common number code for storing integer values inside a computer is called the *twos complement* representation. With this code, the integer equivalent of any bit pattern, such as 10001101, is easy to determine and can be found for either positive or negative integers with no change in the conversion method. For convenience, we will assume byte-sized bit patterns consisting of a set of eight bits each, although the procedure carries directly over to bit patterns of larger sizes.

The easiest way to determine the integer represented by each bit pattern is first to construct a simple device called a value box. Figure 2–10 illustrates such a box for a single byte. Mathematically, each value in the box illustrated in Figure 2–10 represents an increasing power of 2. Because twos complement numbers must be capable of representing both positive and negative integers, the leftmost position, in addition to having the largest absolute magnitude, also has a negative sign.

Conversion of any binary number—for example, 10001101—simply requires inserting the bit pattern in the value box and adding the values that have 1s under them. Thus, as illustrated in Figure 2–11, the bit pattern 10001101 represents the integer number −115.

–128	64	32	16	8	4	2	1
1	0	0	0	1	1	0	1

–128 + 0 + 0 + 0 + 8 + 4 + 0 + 1 = –115

FIGURE 2–11 Converting 10001101 to a Base-10 Number

The value box can also be used in reverse, to convert a base-10 integer number into its equivalent binary bit pattern. Some conversions, in fact, can be made by inspection. For example, the base-10 number –125 is obtained by adding 3 to –128. Thus the binary representation of –125 is 10000011, which equals –128 + 2 + 1. Similarly, the twos complement representation of the number 40 is 00101000, which is 32 plus 8.

Although the value box conversion method is deceptively simple, the method is directly related to the underlying mathematical basis of twos complement binary numbers. The twos complement code was originally called the weighted-sign code, which correlates directly with the value box. As the name *weighted sign* implies, each bit position has a weight, or value, of 2 raised to a power and a sign. The signs of all bits except the leftmost bit are positive, and the sign of the leftmost bit is negative.

In reviewing the value box, it becomes evident that any twos complement binary number with a leading 1 represents a negative number and that any bit pattern with a leading 0 represents a positive number. Using the value box, it is easy to determine the most positive and the most negative values capable of being stored. The most negative value that can be stored in a single byte is the decimal number –128, which has the bit pattern 10000000. Any other nonzero bit will simply add a positive amount to the number. It is also clear that a positive number must have 0 as its leftmost bit. From this you can see that the largest positive eight-bit twos complement number is 01111111, or 127.

Assignment and Interactive Input

Chapter Three

In the last chapter we introduced the concept of data storage, variables, and their associated declaration statements. We also presented the use of `cout` for formatted output. This chapter completes our introduction to C++ by discussing the proper use of both constants and variables in constructing expressions and statements and the use of the `cin` object for entering data interactively while a program is running.

3.1 Assignment Operators

We have already encountered simple assignment statements. In Chapter 2, we saw that assignment statements are the most basic C++ statements for both assigning values to variables and performing computations. This statement has the syntax

```
variable = expression;
```

The simplest expression in C++ is a single constant. In each of the following assignment statements, the operand to the right of the equals sign is a constant.

```
length = 25;

width = 17.5;
```

In each of these assignment statements, the value of the constant to the right of the equals sign is assigned to the variable to the left of the equals sign. It is important to note that the equals sign in C++ does not have the same meaning as an equals sign in algebra. The equals sign in an assignment statement tells the computer first to determine the value of the operand to the right of the equals sign and then to store (or assign) that value in the locations associated with the variable to the left of the equals sign. In this regard, the C++ statement `length = 25;` is read "length is assigned the value 25." The blank spaces in the assignment statement are inserted for readability only.

Recall that a variable can be initialized when it is declared. If an initialization is not done within the declaration statement, the variable should be assigned a value with an assignment statement before it is used in any computation. Subsequent assignment statements can, of course, be used to change the value assigned to a variable. For example, assume that the following statements are executed one after another and that `total` was not initialized when it was declared.

```
total = 3.7;

total = 6.28;
```

The first assignment statement assigns the value of 3.7 to the variable named `total`.[1] The next assignment statement causes the computer to assign a value of 6.28 to `total`. The 3.7 that was in `total` is overwritten with the new value of 6.28 because a variable can store only one value at a time. It is sometimes useful to think of the variable to the left of the equals sign as a temporary parking spot in a huge parking lot. Just as an individual parking spot can be used by only one car at a time, each variable can store only one value at a time. The "parking" of a new value in a variable automatically causes the computer to remove any value that has previously been parked there.

In addition to being a constant, the operand to the right of the equals sign in an assignment statement can be a variable or any other valid C++ expression. An *expression* is any combination of constants and variables that can be evaluated to yield a result. Thus the expression in an assignment statement can be used to perform calculations via the arithmetic operators introduced in Section 2.2. Here are some examples of assignment statements using expressions that contain these operators:

```
sum = 3 + 7;
diff = 15 - 6;
product = .05 * 14.6;
tally = count + 1;
newtotal = 18.3 + total;
taxes = .06 * amount;
totalWeight = factor * weight;
average = sum / items;
slope = (y2 - y1) / (x2 - x1);
```

As always in an assignment statement, the computer first calculates the value of the expression to the right of the equals sign and then stores this value in the variable to the left of the equals sign. For example, in the assignment statement `totalWeight = factor * weight;` the arithmetic expression

---

[1] Because this is the first time a value is explicitly assigned to this variable, it is frequently referred to as an initialization. This stems from historical usage that said a variable was initialized the first time a value was assigned to it. Under this usage, it is correct to say that "`total` is initialized to 3.7." From an implementation viewpoint, however, this later statement is incorrect. This is because the assignment operation is handled differently by the C++ compiler than an initialization performed when a variable is created by a declaration statement. This difference is important only when we are using C++'s class features and is explained in detail in Section 12.1.

factor * weight is first evaluated to yield a result. This result, which is a number, is then stored in the variable totalWeight.

In writing assignment expressions, you must be aware of two important considerations. The expression to the right of the equals sign is evaluated first, so all variables used in the expression must previously have been given valid values if the result is to make sense. For example, the assignment statement totalWeight = factor * weight; causes a valid number to be stored in totalWeight only if the programmer first takes care to assign valid numbers to factor and weight. Thus the sequence of statements

```
factor = 1.06;
weight = 155.0;
totalWeight = factor * weight;
```

ensures that we know the values being used to obtain the result that will be stored in totalWeight.

The second consideration to keep in mind is that because the value of an expression is stored in the variable to the left of the equals sign, there must be a variable listed immediately to the left of the equals sign. For example, the assignment statement

```
amount + 1892 = 1000 + 10 * 5
```

is invalid. The expression on the right-hand side of the equals sign evaluates to the integer 1050, which can be stored only in a variable. Because amount + 1892 is not a valid variable name, the computer does not know where to store the calculated value. Program 3-1 illustrates the use of assignment statements in calculating the area of a rectangle.

When Program 3-1 is run, the output obtained is

```
The length of the rectangle is 27.2
The width of the rectangle is 13.6
The area of the rectangle is 369.92
```

Consider the flow of control that the computer uses in executing Program 3-1. Program execution begins with the first statement and continues sequentially, statement by statement, until the closing brace of main() is encountered. This flow of control is true for all programs. The computer works on one statement at a time, executing that statement with no knowledge of what the next statement will be. This explains why all operands used in an expression must have values assigned to them before the expression is evaluated.

Program 3-1

```
// this program calculates the area of a rectangle
//    given its length and width

#include <iostream.h>

int main()
{
  float length, width, area;

  length = 27.2;
  width = 13.6;
  area = length * width;
  cout << "The length of the rectangle is " << length << endl;
  cout << "The width of the rectangle is " << width << endl;
  cout << "The area of the rectangle is " << area << endl;

  return 0;
}
```

When the computer executes the statement `area = length * width;` in Program 3-1, it uses whatever values are stored in the variables `length` and `width` at the time the assignment is executed. If no values have been specifically assigned to these variables before they are used in the expression `length * width`, the computer uses whatever values happen to occupy these variables when they are referenced. The computer does not "look ahead" to see that you might assign values to these variables later in the program.

It is important to realize that in C++ the equals sign, `=`, used in assignment statements is itself an operator, *which differs from the way most other high-level languages process this symbol*. In C++ (as in C), the `=` symbol is called the *assignment operator,* and an expression using this operator, such as `interest = principal * rate`, is an assignment expression. Because the assignment operator has a lower precedence than any other arithmetic operator, the value of any expression to the right of the equals sign is evaluated first, prior to assignment.

Like all expressions, assignment expressions themselves have a value. The value of the complete assignment expression is the value assigned to the variable on the left of the assignment operator. For example, the expression `a = 5` both assigns a value of 5 to the variable `a` and results in the expression itself having a value of 5. The value of the expression can always be verified by using a statement such as

```
cout << "The value of the expression is " << (a = 5);
```

Here, the value of the expression itself is displayed, not the contents of the variable a. Although both the contents of the variable and the expression have the same value, it is worthwhile to realize that we are dealing with two distinct entities.

From a programming perspective, it is the actual assignment of a value to a variable that is significant in an assignment expression; the final value of the assignment expression itself is of little consequence. However, the fact that assignment expressions have a value has implications that must be considered when C++'s relational operators are presented.

Any expression that is terminated by a semicolon becomes a C++ statement. The most common example of this is the assignment statement, which is simply an assignment expression terminated with a semicolon. For example, terminating the assignment expression a = 33 with a semicolon results in the assignment statement a = 33; which can be used in a program on a line by itself.

Because the equals sign is an operator in C++, multiple assignments are possible in the same expression or in its equivalent statement. For example, in the expression a = b = c = 25, all the assignment operators have the same precedence. The assignment operator has a right-to-left associativity, so the final evaluation proceeds in the sequence

```
c = 25
b = c
a = b
```

In this case, this has the effect of assigning the number 25 to each of the variables individually, and it can be represented as

```
a = (b = (c = 25))
```

Appending a semicolon to the original expression results in the multiple assignment statement

```
a = b = c = 25;
```

This latter statement assigns the value 25 to the three individual variables equivalent to the following order:

```
c = 25;
b = 25;
a = 25;
```

It should be noted that conversions of data type can take place across assignment operators; that is, the value of the expression on the right-hand side of the assignment operator is converted to the data type of the variable to the left of the assignment operator. Thus, assigning an integer value to a real variable causes the integer to be converted to a real value. Similarly, assigning a real value to an integer variable forces conversion of the real value to an integer, which always results in the loss of the fractional part of the number because of truncation. For example, if `temp` is an integer variable, the assignment `temp = 25.89` causes the integer value 25 to be stored in the integer variable `temp`.[2]

Another example of data type conversions, which includes both mixed-mode and assignment conversion, is the evaluation of the expression

```
a = b * d
```

where `a` and `b` are integer variables and `d` is a floating-point variable. When the mixed-mode expression `b * d` is evaluated,[3] the value of `d` used in the expression is converted to a double-precision number for purposes of computation (it is important to note that the value stored in `d` remains a floating-point number). Because one of the operands is a double-precision variable, the value of the integer variable `b` is converted to a double-precision number for the computation (again, the value stored in `b` remains an integer), and the resulting value of the expression `b * d` is a double-precision number. Finally, data type conversion across the assignment operator comes into play. The left side of the assignment operator is an integer variable, so the double-precision value of the expression (`b * d`) is truncated to an integer value and stored in the variable `a`.

Assignment Variations

Although only one variable is allowed immediately to the left of the equals sign in an assignment expression, the variable to the left of the equals sign can also be used to the right of the equals sign. For example, the assignment expression `sum = sum + 10` is valid. Clearly, if this were an algebra equation, `sum` could never be equal to itself plus 10. But in C++, the expression `sum = sum + 10` is not an equation—it is an expression that is evaluated in two major steps. The first step is to calculate the value of `sum + 10`. The second step is to store the computed value in `sum`. See whether you can determine the output of Program 3-2.

---

[2] Clearly, the correct integer portion is retained only when it is within the range of integers allowed by the compiler.

[3] Review the rules given in Table 2–10 (Section 2.5) for the evaluation of mixed-mode expressions, if necessary.

POINT OF INFORMATION

lvalues and rvalues

The terms lvalue and rvalue are used often in programming technology. Both of these terms are language-independent, and their meanings are as follows: An lvalue can have a value assigned to it, whereas an rvalue cannot.

In both C and C++ this means that an lvalue can appear on both the left side and the right side of an assignment operator, whereas an rvalue can appear only on the right side of an assignment operator. For example, each variable we have encountered can be either an lvalue or an rvalue, but a number can be only an rvalue. Not all variables, however, can be lvalues and rvalues. For example, an array type, which is introduced in Chapter 7, cannot be an lvalue or an rvalue, whereas individual array elements can be both.

Program 3-2

```
#include <iostream.h>

int main()
{
  int sum;

  sum = 25;
  cout << "The number stored in sum is " << sum << endl;
  sum = sum + 10;
  cout << "The number now stored in sum is " << sum << endl;

  return 0;
}
```

The assignment statement `sum = 25;` tells the computer to store the number 25 in `sum`, as shown in Figure 3–1.

The first `cout` statement causes the value stored in `sum` to be displayed by the message `The number stored in sum is 25`. The second assignment statement in Program 3-2, (`sum = sum + 10;`) causes the program to retrieve the 25 stored in `sum` and add 10 to this number, yielding the number 35. The

FIGURE 3–1 The Integer 25 Is Stored in sum

sum	25

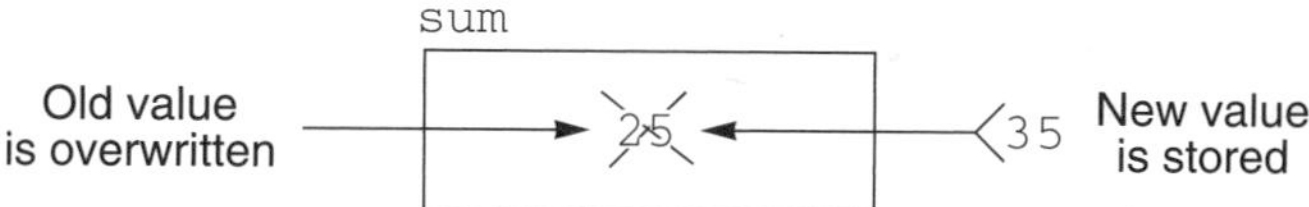

FIGURE 3–2 `sum = sum + 10;` Causes a New Value to Be Stored in `sum`.

number 35 is then stored in the variable on the left side of the equals sign, which is the variable `sum`. The 25 that was in `sum` is simply overwritten with the new value of 35, as shown in Figure 3–2.

Assignment expressions such as `sum = sum + 25`, which use the same variable on both sides of the assignment operator, can be written by using the following shortcut *assignment operators*:

```
+=     -=     *=     /=     %=
```

For example, the expression `sum = sum + 10` can be written as `sum += 10`. Similarly, the expression `price *= rate` is equivalent to the expression `price = price * rate`.

In using these new assignment operators it is important to note that the variable to the left of the assignment operator is applied to the *complete* expression on the right. For example, the expression `price *= rate + 1` is equivalent to the expression

`price = price * (rate + 1)`, not to `price = price * rate + 1`

Accumulating

Assignment expressions like `sum += 10` or its equivalent, `sum = sum + 10`, are very common in programming. These expressions are required in accumulating subtotals when data is entered one number at a time. For example, if we want to add the numbers 96, 70, 85, and 60 in calculator fashion, we could use the following statements:

Statement	Value in sum
`sum = 0;`	0
`sum = sum + 96;`	96
`sum = sum + 70;`	166
`sum = sum + 85;`	251
`sum = sum + 60;`	311

The first statement initializes `sum` to 0. This removes any number ("garbage value") stored in `sum` that would invalidate the final total. As each number is added, the value stored in `sum` is increased accordingly. After completion of the last statement, `sum` contains the total of all the added numbers.

Program 3-3 illustrates the effect of these statements by displaying `sum`'s contents after each addition is made.

Program 3-3

```
#include <iostream.h>

int main()
{
  int sum;

  sum = 0;
  cout << "The value of sum is initially set to " << sum << endl;
  sum = sum + 96;
  cout << "  sum is now " << sum << endl;
  sum = sum + 70;
  cout << "  sum is now " << sum << endl;
  sum = sum + 85;
  cout << "  sum is now " << sum << endl;
  sum = sum + 60;
  cout << "  The final sum is " << sum << endl;

  return 0;
}
```

The output displayed by Program 3-3 is

```
The value of sum is initially set to 0
  sum is now 96
  sum is now 166
  sum is now 251
  The final sum is 311
```

Although Program 3-3 is not a practical program (it is easier to add the numbers by hand), it does illustrate the subtotaling effect of the repeated use of statements that have the form

```
variable = variable + newValue;
```

We will find many uses for this type of statement when we become more familiar with the repetition statements introduced in Chapter 5.

Counting

An assignment statement that is very similar to the accumulating statement is the counting statement. Counting statements have the form

```
variable = variable + fixedNumber;
```

Here are some examples of counting statements:

```
i = i + 1;
n = n + 1;
count = count + 1;
j = j + 2;
m = m + 2;
kk = kk + 3;
```

In each of these examples, the same variable is used on both sides of the equals sign. After the statement is executed, the value of the respective variable is increased by a fixed amount. In the first three examples, the variables `i`, `n`, and `count` have all been increased by 1. In the next two examples, the respective variables have been increased by 2, and in the final example, the variable `kk` has been increased by 3.

For the special case in which a variable is either increased or decreased by 1, C++ provides two unary operators. Using the *increment operator*,[4] `++`, we can replace the expression `variable = variable + 1` by either the expression `variable++` or the expression `++variable`. Examples of the increment operator follow.

Expression	**Alternative**
`i = i + 1`	`i++` or `++i`
`n = n + 1`	`n++` or `++n`
`count = count + 1`	`count++` or `++count`

Program 3-4 illustrates the use of the increment operator. The output displayed by Program 3-4 is:

```
The initial value of count is 0
  count is now 1
  count is now 2
  count is now 3
  count is now 4
```

[4] As an historical note, the ++ in C++ was inspired by the increment operator symbol. It was used to indicate that C++ was the next increment to the C language.

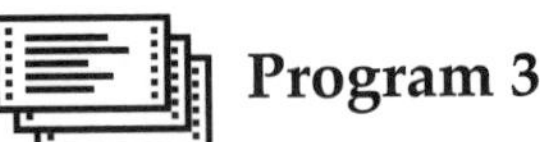

Program 3-4

```
#include <iostream.h>

int main()
{
  int count;

  count = 0;
  cout << "The initial value of count is " << count << endl;
  count++;
  cout << "   count is now " << count << endl;
  count++;
  cout << "   count is now " << count << endl;
  count++;
  cout << "   count is now " << count << endl;
  count++;
  cout << "   count is now " << count << endl;

  return 0;
}
```

When the `++` operator appears before a variable, it is called a *prefix increment operator;* when it appears after a variable, it is called a *postfix increment operator.* The distinction between a prefix increment operator and a postfix increment operator is important when the variable being incremented is used in an assignment expression. For example, the expression `k = ++n` does two things in one expression. Initially the value of `n` is incremented by 1, and then the new value of `n` is assigned to the variable `k`. Thus the statement `k = ++n;` is equivalent to the two statements

```
n = n + 1;   // increment n first
k = n;       // assign n's value to k
```

The assignment expression `k = n++`, which uses a postfix increment operator, reverses this procedure. A postfix increment operates after the assignment is completed. Thus the statement `k = n++;` first assigns the current value of `n` to `k` and then increments the value of `n` by 1. This is equivalent to the two statements

```
k = n;          // assign n's value to k
n = n + 1;      // and then increment n
```

In addition to the increment operator, C++ also provides a *decrement operator*, `--`. As you might expect, the expressions `variable--` and `--variable` are both equivalent to the expression `variable = variable - 1`.

Examples of the decrement operator are

Expression	**Alternative**
`i = i - 1`	`i--` or `--i`
`n = n - 1`	`n--` or `--n`
`count = count - 1`	`count--` or `--count`

When the `--` operator appears before a variable, it is called a *prefix decrement operator.* When the decrement appears after a variable, it is called a *postfix decrement operator*. For example, the expressions `n--` and `--n` both reduce the value of `n` by 1. These expressions are equivalent to the longer expression `n = n - 1`. As with the increment operator, however, the prefix and postfix decrement operators produce different results when used in assignment expressions. For example, the expression `k = --n` first decrements the value of `n` by 1 before assigning the value of `n` to `k`, whereas the expression `k = n--` first assigns the current value of `n` to `k` and then reduces the value of `n` by 1.

The increment and decrement operators can often be used advantageously to reduce program storage requirements significantly and increase execution speed. For example, consider the following three statements:

```
count = count + 1;
count += 1;
count++;
```

All perform the same function; however, when these instructions are compiled for execution on an IBM personal computer, the storage requirements for the instructions are 9, 4, and 3 bytes, respectively.[5] Using the assignment operator, `=`, instead of the increment operator results in using three times as much storage space for the instruction, with an accompanying decrease in execution speed.

[5] This is obviously a compiler-dependent result.

Exercises 3.1

1. Determine and correct the errors in the following programs.

a.
```
#include <iostream.h>
int main()
{
  width = 15
  area = length * width;
  cout << "The area is " << area
 return 0;
}
```

b.
```
#include <iostream.h>
int main()
{
  int length, width, area;
  area = length * width;
  length = 20;
  width = 15;
  cout << "The area is " << area;
```

c.
```
#include <iostream.h>
int main()
{
  int length = 20; width = 15, area;
  length * width = area;
  cout << "The area is " , area;
 return 0;
}
```

2. a. Write a C++ program to calculate and display the average of the numbers 32.6, 55.2, 67.9, and 48.6.
   b. Run the program written for Exercise 2a on a computer.

3. a. Write a C++ program to calculate the circumference of a circle. The equation for determining the circumference of a circle is *circumference* = 2 * 3.1416 * *radius*. Assume that the circle has a radius of 3.3 inches.
   b. Run the program written for Exercise 3a on a computer.

4. a. Write a C++ program to calculate the area of a circle. The equation for determining the area of a circle is *area* = 3.1416 * *radius* * *radius*. Assume that the circle has a radius of 5 inches.
   b. Run the program written for Exercise 4a on a computer.

5. a. Write a C++ program to calculate the volume of a pool. The equation for determining the volume is *volume* = *length* * *width* * *depth*. Assume that the pool has a length of 25 feet, a width of 10 feet, and a depth of 6 feet.
   b. Run the program written for Exercise 5a on a computer.

6. a. Write a C++ program to convert temperature in degrees Fahrenheit to temperature in degrees Celsius. The equation for this conversion is *Celsius* = 5.0/9.0 * (*Fahrenheit* – 32.0).

Have your program convert and display the Celsius temperature corresponding to 98.6 degrees Fahrenheit.

b. Run the program written for Exercise 6a on a computer.

7. a. Write a C++ program to calculate the dollar amount contained in a piggy bank. The bank currently contains 12 half-dollars, 20 quarters, 32 dimes, 45 nickels, and 27 pennies.

b. Run the program written for Exercise 7a on a computer.

8. a. Write a C++ program to calculate the distance, in feet, of a trip that is 2.36 miles long. One mile is equal to 5280 feet.

b. Run the program written for Exercise 8a on a computer.

9. a. Write a C++ program to calculate the elapsed time it took to make a 183.67-mile trip. The equation for computing elapsed time is *elapsed time = total distance / average speed.* Assume that the average speed during the trip was 58 miles per hour.

b. Run the program written for Exercise 9a on a computer.

10. a. Write a C++ program to calculate the sum of the numbers from 1 to 100. The formula for calculating this sum is $sum = (n/2) * (2*a + (n - 1)*d)$, where n = number of terms to be added, a = the first number, and d = the difference between each number and the next.

b. Run the program written for Exercise 10a on a computer.

11. Determine why the expression `a - b = 25` is invalid but the expression `a - (b = 25)` is valid.

3.2 Mathematical Library Functions

As we have seen, assignment statements can be used to perform arithmetic computations. For example, the assignment statement

```
totalPrice = unitPrice * amount;
```

multiplies the value in `unitPrice` times the value in `amount` and assigns the resulting value to `totalPrice`. Although addition, subtraction, multiplication, and division are easily accomplished using C++'s arithmetic operators, no such operators exist for raising a number to a power, finding the square root of a number, or determining trigonometric values. To facilitate such calculations, C++ provides standard preprogrammed functions that can be included in a program.

Before using one of C++'s mathematical functions, you need to know

- The name of the desired mathematical function
- What the mathematical function does
- The type of data required by the mathematical function
- The data type of the result returned by the mathematical function

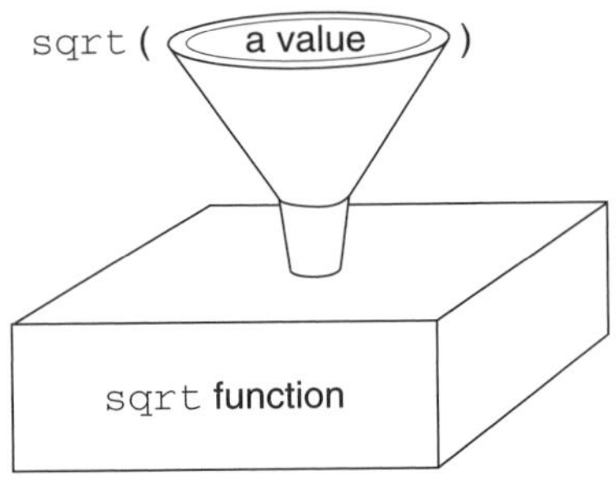

FIGURE 3–3 Passing Data to the `sqrt()` Function

To illustrate the use of C++'s mathematical functions, consider the mathematical function named `sqrt()`, which calculates the square root of a number. The square root of a number is computed using the expression

```
sqrt(number)
```

where the function's name, in this case `sqrt`, is followed by parentheses containing the number for which the square root is desired. The purpose of the parentheses after the function name is to provide a funnel through which data can be passed to the function (see Figure 3–3). The items that are passed to the function through the parentheses are called *arguments* of the function and constitute its input data. For example, the following expressions are used to compute the square root of the arguments 4, 17.0, 25, 1043.29, and 6.4516, respectively.

```
sqrt(4)
sqrt(17.0)
sqrt(25)
sqrt(1043.29)
sqrt(6.4516)
```

Note that the argument to the `sqrt` function can be either an integer or a real value. This is an example of C++'s overloading capabilities. Function overloading permits the same function name to be defined for different argument data types. In this case there are really five square root functions named `sqrt` —defined for `integer`, `long-integer`, `float`, `double`, and `long-double` arguments. The correct `sqrt` function is called, depending on the type of value given it. The `sqrt` function determines the square root of its argument and

TABLE 3–1 Common C++ Functions

Function Name	Description	Returned Value
`abs(x)`	absolute value	same data type as argument
`pow(x1,x2)`	`x1` raised to the `x2` power	data type of argument `x1`
`sqrt(x)`	square root of `x`	same data type as argument
`sin(x)`	sine of `x` (`x` in radians)	double
`cos(x)`	cosine of `x` (`x` in radians)	double
`tan(x)`	tangent of `x` (`x` in radians)	double
`log(x)`	natural logarithm of `x`	double
`log10(x)`	common log (base 10) of `x`	double
`exp(x)`	*e* raised to the `x` power	double

returns the result as a double. The values returned by the previous expressions are

Expression	Value Returned
`sqrt(4)`	2.0
`sqrt(17.0)`	4.123106
`sqrt(25)`	5.0
`sqrt(1043.29)`	32.3
`sqrt(6.4516)`	2.54

Table 3–1 lists the more commonly used mathematical functions provided in C++. To access these functions in a program requires that the mathematical header file named `math.h`, which contains appropriate declarations for the mathematical function, be included with the function. This is done by placing the following preprocessor statement at the top of any program using a mathematical function:

`#include <math.h>` ←——— no semicolon

Although some of the mathematical functions listed require more than one argument, all functions, by definition, can directly return at most one value. Furthermore, all of the functions listed are overloaded: This means the same function name can be used with integer and real arguments. Table 3–2 lists the values returned by selected functions in response to sample arguments.

Each time a mathematical function is used, it is called into action by giving the name of the function and passing any data to it within the parentheses following the function's name (see Figure 3–4).

TABLE 3–2 Selected Examples of Functions

Example	Returned Value
`abs(-7.362)`	7.362000
`abs(-3)`	3
`pow(2.0,5.0)`	32.000000
`pow(10,3)`	1000
`log(18.697)`	2.928363
`log10(18.697)`	1.271772
`exp(-3.2)`	0.040762

The arguments that are passed to a function need not be single constants. An expression can also be an argument, provided that the expression can be computed to yield a value of the required data type. For example, the following arguments are valid for the given functions:

```
sqrt(4.0 + 5.3 * 4.0)           abs(2.3 * 4.6)
sqrt(16.0 * 2.0 - 6.7)          sin(theta - phi)
sqrt(x * y - z/3.2)             cos(2.0 * omega)
```

The expressions in parentheses are first evaluated to yield a specific value. Thus, values would have to be assigned to the variables `theta`, `phi`, `x`, `y`, `z`, and `omega` before their use in the foregoing expressions. After the value of the argument is calculated, it is passed to the function.

Functions may be included as part of larger expressions, as in the following example:

```
4 * sqrt(4.5 * 10.0 - 9.0) - 2.0 =
            4 * sqrt(36.0) - 2.0 =
                   4 * 6.0 - 2.0 =
                      24.0 - 2.0 = 22.0
```

FIGURE 3–4 Using and Passing Data to a Function

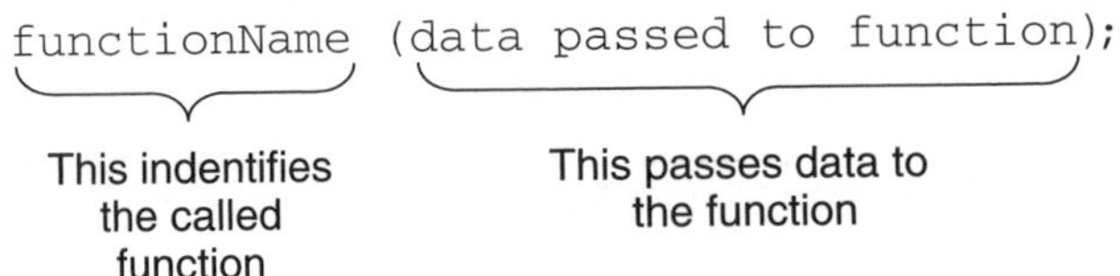

The step-by-step evaluation of an expression such as

```
3.0 * sqrt(5 * 33 - 13.71) / 5
```

is

Step	Result
1. Perform multiplication in argument	`3.0 * sqrt(165 - 13.71) / 5`
2. Complete argument calculation	`3.0 * sqrt(151.29) / 5`
3. Return a function value	`3.0 * 12.3 / 5`
4. Perform the multiplication	`36.9 / 5`
5. Perform the division	`7.38`

Program 3-5 illustrates the use of the `sqrt` function to determine the time it takes a ball to hit the ground after it has been dropped from an 800-foot tower. The mathematical formula used to calculate the time, in seconds, that it takes to fall a given distance, in feet, is

$$time = sqrt(2 * distance / g)$$

where g is the gravitational constant, which is equal to 32.2 ft/sec^2.

Program 3-5

```
#include <iostream.h>   // this line may be placed second instead of first
#include <math.h>       // this line may be placed first instead of second

int main()
{
  int height;
  double time;

  height = 800;
  time = sqrt(2 * height / 32.2);
  cout << "\nIt will take " << time << " seconds "
       << "to fall " << height << " feet.\n";

  return 0;
}
```

The output produced by Program 3-5 is:

```
It will take 7.049074 seconds to fall 800 feet.
```

As used in Program 3-5, the value returned by the `sqrt` function is assigned to the variable `time`. In addition to being assigned to a variable, a function's returned value may be included within a larger expression or even used as an argument to another function. For example, the expression

```
sqrt( pow( abs(num1),num2 ) )
```

is valid. Because parentheses are present, the computation proceeds from the inner pair of parentheses to the outer pair. Thus the absolute value of `num1` is computed first and used as an argument to the `pow()` function. The value returned by the `pow()` function is then used as an argument to the `sqrt()` function.

Casts

We have already seen the conversion of an operand's data type within mixed-mode arithmetic expressions (Sections 2.2 and 2.5) and across assignment operators (Section 3.1). In addition to these implicit data type conversions that are automatically made in mixed-mode arithmetic and assignment expressions, C++ also provides for explicit user-specified type conversions. The operator used to force the conversion of a value to another type is the cast operator. This is a unary operator that has the form *datatype (expression)*, where *datatype* is the desired data type of the expression following the cast. For example, the expression

```
int (a * b)
```

ensures that the value of the expression `a * b` is converted to an integer value.[6]

Exercises 3.2

1. Write function calls to determine each of the following:

a. the square root of 6.37
b. the square root of $x - y$
c. the sine of 30 degrees
d. the sine of 60 degrees
e. the absolute value of $a^2 - b^2$
f. the value of e raised to the third power

[6] The cast syntax used in C, in this case `(int)(a*b)`, where the parentheses are placed around the keyword `int`, also works in C++.

2. For $a = 10.6$, $b = 13.9$, and $c = -3.42$, determine the value of each of the following:

a. `int(a)`

b. `int(b)`

c. `int(c)`

d. `int(a + b)`

e. `int(a) + b + c`

f. `int(a + b) + c`

g. `int(a + b + c)`

h. `float(int (a)) + b`

i. `float(int (a + b))`

j. `abs(a) + abs(b)`

k. `sqrt(abs(a - b))`

3. Write C++ statements for the following:

a. $c = \sqrt{a^2 + b^2}$

b. $p = \sqrt{|m - n|}$

c. $\text{sum} = \dfrac{a(r^n - 1)}{r - 1}$

4. Write, compile, and execute a C++ program that calculates and returns the fourth root of the number 81, which is 3. When you have verified that your program works correctly, use it to determine the fourth root of 1,728.896400. Your program should make use of the `sqrt` function.

5. Write, compile, and execute a C++ program that calculates the distance between two points whose coordinates are (7, 12) and (3, 9). Use the fact that the distance between two points having coordinates ($x1$, $y1$) and ($x2$, $y2$) is $distance = sqrt([x1 - x2]^2 + [y1 - y2]^2)$. When you have verified that your program works correctly by calculating the distance between the two points manually, use your program to determine the distance between the points (–12, –15) and (22, 5).

6. A model of worldwide population after 1990, in billions of people, is given by the equation

$$\text{Population} = 5.5e^{.02\,[\text{Year} - 1990]}$$

Using this formula, write, compile, and execute a C++ program to estimate the worldwide population in the year 2002. Verify the result displayed by your program by calculating the answer manually. After you have verified that your program is working correctly, use it to estimate the world's population in the year 2012.

7. Although we have been concentrating on integer and real arithmetic, C++ allows characters and integers to be added or subtracted. This can be done because C++ always converts a character to an equivalent integer value whenever a character is used in an arithmetic expression (the decimal value of each character can be found in Appendix B). Thus characters and integers can be freely mixed in arithmetic expressions. For example, if your computer uses the ASCII code, the expression `'a' + 1` equals 98 and `'z' - 1` equals 121. These values can be converted back into characters by using the cast operator. Thus `char ('a' + 1) = 'b'` and `char ('z' - 1) = 'y'`. Similarly, `char('A' +1)` is `'B'` and `char('Z' - 1)` is `'Y'`. With this as background, determine the character results of the following expressions (assume that all characters are stored using the ASCII code).

a. `char ('m' - 5)`

b. `char ('m' + 5)`

c. `char ('G' + 6)`

d. `char ('G'- 6)`

e. `('b' - 'a')`

f. `('g' - 'a' + 1)`

g. `('G' -'A' + 1)`

8. *a.* The table in Appendix B lists the integer values corresponding to each letter stored using the ASCII code. Note that in this table, the uppercase letters consist of contiguous codes starting with an integer value of 65 for the letter A and ending with 90 for the letter Z. Similarly, the lowercase letters begin with the integer value of 97 for the letter a and end with 122 for the letter z. With this as background, determine the character value of the expressions `char ('A' + 32)` and `char ('Z' + 32)`.
b. Using Appendix B, determine the integer value of the expression `'a' - 'A'`.
c. Using the results of Exercises 8a and 8b, determine the character value of the following expression, where *uppercase letter* can be any uppercase letter from A to Z.

```
char (uppercase letter + 'a' - 'A')
```

3.3 Program Input Using the `cin` Object

Data for programs that are going to be executed only once may be included directly in the program. For example, if we wanted to multiply the numbers 30.0 and 0.05, we could use Program 3-6.

Program 3-6

```
#include <iostream.h>

int main()
{
  float num1, num2, product;

  num1 = 30.0;
  num2 = 0.05;
  product = num1 * num2;
  cout << "30.0 times 0.05 is " << product << endl;

  return 0;
}
```

The output displayed by Program 3-6 is

```
30.0 times 0.05 is 1.5
```

Program 3-6 can be shortened, as illustrated in Program 3-7. Both programs, however, suffer from the same basic problem: They must be rewritten in order to multiply different numbers. Neither program allows us to enter different numbers to be operated on.

Program 3-7

```
#include <iostream.h>

int main()
{
  cout << "30.0 times 0.05 is " << 30.0 * 0.05 << endl;

  return 0;
}
```

Except that they give the programmer practice in writing, entering, and running the program, programs that do the same calculation only once, on the same set of numbers, are clearly not very useful. After all, it is simpler to use a calculator to multiply two numbers than to enter and run either Program 3-6 or Program 3-7.

This section presents the `cin` object, which is used to enter data into a program while it is executing. Just as the `cout` object displays a copy of the value stored inside a variable, the `cin` object allows the user to enter a value at the terminal (see Figure 3–5). The value is then stored directly in a variable.

When a statement such as `cin >> num1;` is encountered, the computer stops program execution and accepts data from the keyboard. When a data item is typed, the `cin` object stores the item in the variable listed after the extraction ("get from") operator, `>>`. The program then continues execution with the next statement after the call to `cin`. To see this, consider Program 3-8.

FIGURE 3–5 `cin` Is Used to Enter Data; `cout` Is Used to Display Data

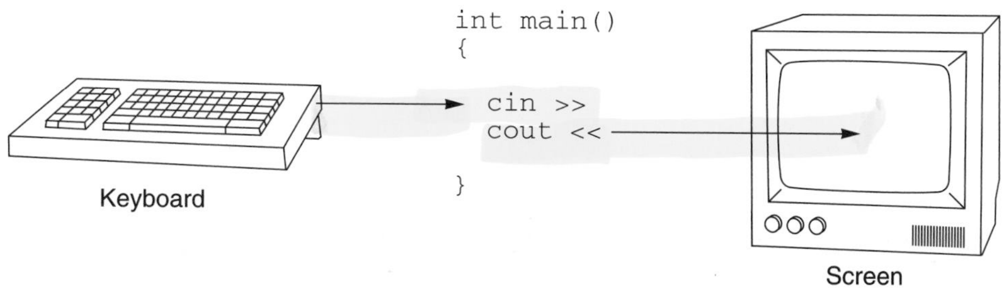

Program 3-8

```
#include <iostream.h>

int main()
{
  float num1, num2, product;

  cout << "Please type in a number: ";
  cin >> num1;
  cout << "Please type in another number: ";
  cin >> num2;
  product = num1 * num2;
  cout << num1 << " times " << num2 << " is " << product << endl;

  return 0;
}
```

The first `cout` statement in Program 3-8 prints a string that tells the person at the terminal what should be typed. When an output string is used in this manner, it is called a *prompt.* In this case the prompt tells the user to type a number. The computer then executes the next statement, which is a call to `cin`. The `cin` object puts the computer into a temporary pause (or wait) state for as long as it takes the user to type a value. Then the user signals the `cin` object that the data entry is finished by pressing the return key after the value has been typed. The entered value is stored in the variable to the right of the extraction symbol, and the computer is taken out of its paused state. Program execution then proceeds with the next statement, which in Program 3-8 is another `cout` activation. This call causes the next message to be displayed. The second `cin` statement again puts the computer into a temporary wait state while the user types a second value. This second number is stored in the variable `num2`.

The following sample run was made using Program 3-8.

```
Please type in a number: 30
Please type in another number: 0.05
30 times 0.05 is 1.5
```

In Program 3-8, each time `cin` is invoked, it is used to store one value in a variable. The `cin` object, however, can be used to enter and store as many values as there are extraction symbols, >>, and variables to hold the entered data. For example, the statement

```
cin >> num1 >> num2;
```

results in two values being read from the terminal and assigned to the variables num1 and num2. If the data entered at the terminal were

```
0.052  245.79
```

the variables num1 and num2 would contain the values 0.052 and 245.79, respectively. Note that when we are entering numbers such as 0.052 and 245.79, there must be at least one space between the numbers. The space between the entered numbers clearly indicates where one number ends and the next begins. Inserting more than one space between the numbers has no effect on cin.

The same spacing is applicable to entering character data; that is, the extraction operator, >>, will skip blank spaces and store the next nonblank character in a character variable. For example, in response to the statements

```
char ch1, ch2, ch3;   // declare three character variables
cin >> ch1 >> ch2 >> ch3;   // accept three characters
```

the input

```
a     b  c
```

causes the letter a to be stored in the variable ch1, the letter b to be stored in the variable ch2, and the variable c to be stored in the variable ch3. Because a character variable can be used only to store one character, the input

```
abc
```

can also be used.

Any number of statements using the cin object may be made in a program, and any number of values may be input using a single cin statement. Program 3-9 illustrates using the cin object to input three numbers from the keyboard. The program then calculates and displays the average of the numbers entered.

The following sample run was made using Program 3-9.

```
Enter three integer numbers: 22 56 73
The average of the numbers is 50.333333
```

Program 3-9

```
#include <iostream.h>

int main()
{
  int num1, num2, num3;
  float average;

  cout << "Enter three integer numbers: ";
  cin >> num1 >> num2 >> num3;
  average = (num1 + num2 + num3) / 3.0;
  cout << "The average of the numbers is " << average << endl;

  return 0;
}
```

Note that the data typed at the keyboard for this sample run consist of the input

```
22  56  73
```

In response to this stream of input, Program 3-9 stores the value 22 in the variable `num1`, the value 56 in the variable `num2`, and the value 73 in the variable `num3` (see Figure 3–6). Because the average of three integer numbers can be a floating-point number, the variable `average`, which is used to store the average, is declared as a floating-point variable. Note also that the parentheses are needed in the assignment statement `average = (num1 + num2 + num3) / 3.0;`. Without these parentheses, the only value that would be divided by 3 would be the integer in `num3` (because division has a higher precedence than addition).

The `cin` extraction operation, like the `cout` insertion operation, is "clever" enough to make a few data type conversions. For example, if an integer is entered in place of a floating-point or double-precision number, the integer will be converted to the correct data type.[7] Similarly, if a floating-point or double-precision number is entered when an integer is expected, only the integer part of the number will be used. For example, assume the following numbers are typed in response to the statement `cin >> num1 >> num2 >> num3;` where

---

[7] Strictly speaking, what comes in from the keyboard is not any data type, such as an `int` or a `float`, but is simply a sequence of characters. The extraction operation handles the conversion from the character sequence to a defined data type.

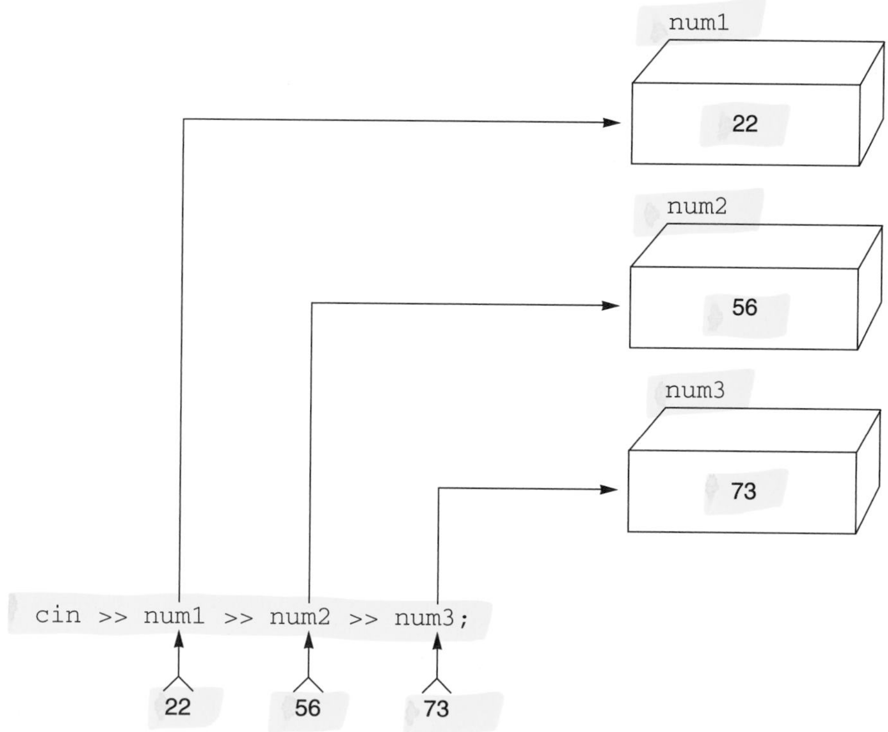

FIGURE 3–6 Inputting Data into the Variables num1, num2, and num3

num1 and num3 have been declared as floating-point variables and num2 is an integer variable.

```
56  22.879  33.923
```

The 56 will be converted to 56.0 and stored in the variable num1. The extraction operation continues extracting data from the input stream sent to it, expecting an integer value. As far as cin is concerned, the decimal point after the 22 in the number 22.879 indicates the end of an integer and the start of a decimal number. Thus the number 22 is assigned to num2. Continuing to process its input stream, cin takes the .879 as the next floating-point number and assigns it to num3. As far as cin is concerned, 33.923 is extra input and is ignored. If, though, you do not initially type enough data, the cin object will continue to make the computer pause until sufficient data have been entered.

Exercises 3.3

1. For the following declaration statements, write a statement using the cin object that will cause the computer to pause while the appropriate data are typed by the user.

a. `int firstnum;`
b. `float grade;`
c. `double secnum;`
d. `char keyval;`
e.
```
int month, years;
float average;
```
f.
```
char ch;
int num1,num2;
double grade1,grade2;
```
g.
```
float interest, principal, capital;
double price,yield;
```
h.
```
char ch,letter1,letter2;
int num1,num2,num3;
```
i.
```
float temp1,temp2,temp3;
double volts1,volts2;
```

2. Write, compile, and execute a C++ program that displays the following prompt:

```
Enter the radius of a circle:
```

After accepting a value for the radius, your program should calculate and display the area of the circle. (**Note:** $area = 3.1416 * radius^2$.) For testing purposes, verify your program by using a test input radius of 3 inches. After manually determining that the result produced by your program is correct, use your program to complete the following table:

Radius (in.)	Area (sq. in.)
1.0	
1.5	
2.0	
2.5	
3.0	
3.5	

3. *a.* Write a C++ program that first displays the following prompt:

```
Enter the temperature in degrees Celsius:
```

Have your program accept a value entered from the keyboard and convert the temperature entered to degrees Fahrenheit, using the formula $Fahrenheit = (9.0 / 5.0) * Celsius + 32.0$. Your program should then display the temperature in degrees Celsius, using an appropriate output message.

b. Compile and execute the program written for Exercise 3a. Verify your program by calculating, by hand and then using your program, the Fahrenheit equivalent of the following test data:

Test data set 1: 0 degrees Celsius
Test data set 2: 50 degrees Celsius
Test data set 3: 100 degrees Celsius

When you are sure your program is working correctly, use it to complete the following table:

Degrees Celsius	Degrees Fahrenheit
45	
50	
55	
60	
65	
70	

4. *a* Write a C++ program that displays the following prompts:

```
Enter the length of the room:
Enter the width of the room:
```

After each prompt is displayed, your program should use a `cin` object call to accept data from the keyboard for the displayed prompt. After the width of the room is entered, your program should calculate and display the area of the room. The area displayed should be calculated using the equation *area* = *length* * *width* and should be included in an appropriate message.

b. Check the area displayed by the program written for Exercise 4a by calculating the result manually.

5. *a.* Write, compile, and execute a C++ program that displays the following prompts:

```
Enter the miles driven:
Enter the gallons of gas used:
```

After each prompt is displayed, your program should use an input statement to accept data from the keyboard for the displayed prompt. After the "gallons of gas used" number has been entered, your program should calculate and display the miles per gallon obtained. This value should be calculated using the equation *miles per gallon* = *miles* / *gallons used* and should be included in an appropriate message. Verify your program using the following test data:

Test data set 1: Miles = 276, Gas = 10 gallons
Test data set 2: Miles = 200, Gas = 15.5 gallons

When you have completed your verification, use your program to complete the following table:

Miles Driven	Gallons Used	Miles per Gallon
250	16.00	
275	18.00	
312	19.54	
296	17.39	

b. For the program written for Exercise 5a, determine how many verification runs are required to ensure that the program is working correctly, and give a reason supporting your answer.

6. a. Write a C++ program that displays the following prompts:

```
Enter the length of the swimming pool:
Enter the width of the swimming pool:
Enter the average depth of the swimming pool:
```

After each prompt is displayed, your program should use a cin object call to accept data from the keyboard for the displayed prompt. After the depth of the swimming pool is entered, your program should calculate and display the volume of the pool. The volume should be calculated using the equation *volume = length * width * average depth* and should be included in an appropriate message.

b. Check the volume displayed by the program written for Exercise 6a by calculating the result manually.

7. a. Write a C++ program that displays the following prompts:

```
Enter a number:
Enter a second number:
Enter a third number:
Enter a fourth number:
```

After each prompt is displayed, your program should use a `cin` object call to accept a number from the keyboard for the displayed prompt. After the fourth number has been entered, your program should calculate and display the average of the numbers. The average should be included in an appropriate message.

b. Check the average displayed for the program written in Exercise 7a by calculating the result manually.

c. Repeat Exercise 7a, making sure that you use the same variable name, `number`, for each number input. Also use the variable `sum` for the sum of the numbers. (*Hint:* To do this, you must use the statement `sum = sum + number;` after each number is accepted. Review the material on accumulating presented in Section 3.1.)

8. Write a C++ program that prompts the user to type in a number. Have your program accept the number as an integer and immediately display the integer using a `cout` object call. Run your program three times. The first time you run the program enter a valid integer number, the second time enter a floating-point number, and the third time enter a character. Using the output display, see what number your program actually accepted from the data you entered.

9. Repeat Exercise 8, but have your program declare the variable used to store the number as a floating-point variable. Run the program four times. The first time enter an integer, the second time enter a decimal number that has fewer than six decimal places, the third time enter a number that has more than six decimal places, and the fourth time enter a character. Using the output display, keep track of what number your program actually accepted from the data you typed in. What happened, if anything, and why?

10. Repeat Exercise 8, but have your program declare the variable used to store the number as a double-precision variable. Run the program four times. The first time enter an integer, the second time enter a decimal number that has fewer than six decimal places, the third time enter a number that has more than six decimal places, and the fourth time enter a character. Using the output display, keep track of what number your program actually accepted from the data you typed in. What happened, if anything, and why?

11. *a.* Why do you think successful application programs contain extensive data input validity checks? (*Hint:* Review Exercises 8, 9, and 10.)
b. What do you think is the difference between a data type check and a data reasonableness check?
c. Assume that a program requests that a month, day, and year be entered by the user. What are some checks that could be made on the data entered?

12. Program 3-8 prompts the user to input two numbers, where the first value entered is stored in `num1` and the second value is stored in `num2`. Using this program as a starting point, write a program that swaps the values stored in the two variables.

3.4 The const Qualifier

Literal data are any data within a program that explicitly identify themselves. For example, the constants 2 and 3.1416 in the assignment statement

```
circum = 2 * 3.1416 * radius;
```

are also called literals because they are literally included directly in the statement. Additional examples of literals are contained in the following C++ assignment statements. See if you can identify them.

```
perimeter = 2 * length * width;
        y = (5 * p) / 7.2;
 salestax = 0.05 * purchase;
```

The literals are the numbers 2, 5 and 7.2, and 0.05 in the first, second, and third statements, respectively.

Quite frequently, literal data used within a program have a more general meaning that is recognized outside the context of the program. Examples of these types of constants include the number 3.1416, which is π accurate to four decimal places; 32.2 ft/sec^2, which is the gravitational constant; and the number 2.71828, which is Euler's number accurate to five decimal places.

The meanings of certain other constants that appear in a program are defined strictly in the context of the application being programmed. For example, in a program used to determine bank interest charges, the interest rate would typically appear in a number of different places throughout the program. Similarly, in a program used to calculate taxes, the tax rate might appear in many individual instructions. Programmers refer to numbers such as these as *magic numbers.* By themselves the numbers are ordinary, but in the context of a particular application they have a special ("magical") meaning. Frequently, the same magic number appears repeatedly within the same program. This recurrence of the same constant throughout a program is a potential source of error should the constant have to be changed. For example, if either the interest rate or the sales tax rate changed, as such rates are likely to do, the programmer would have the cumbersome task of changing the value everywhere it appeared in the program. Such multiple changes are subject to error: If just one rate value is overlooked and remains unchanged, the result obtained when the program is run will be incorrect, and the source of the error will be difficult to locate.

To avoid the problem of having a magic number spread throughout a program in many places, and to permit clear identification of more universal constants, such as π, C++ allows the programmer to give these constants their own symbolic names. Then, instead of the number being used throughout the program, the symbolic name is used instead. If the number ever has to be changed, the change need only be made once, at the point where the symbolic name is equated to the actual number value. Equating numbers to symbolic names is accomplished by means of a `const` declaration qualifier. The `const` qualifier specifies that the declared identifier can be read only after it is initialized; it cannot be changed. Here are three examples using this qualifier:

```
const float PI = 3.1416;
const double SALESTAX = 0.05;
const int MAXNUM = 100;
```

The first declaration statement creates a floating-point variable named `PI` and initializes it with the value 3.1416. The second declaration statement creates the double-precision constant named `SALESTAX` and initializes it to 0.05. Finally, the third declaration creates an integer constant named `MAXNUM` and initializes it with the value 100.

Once a `const` identifier is created and initialized, *the value stored in it cannot be changed.* Thus, for all practical purposes, the name of the constant and its value are linked together for the duration of the program that declares them.

Although we have typed the `const` identifiers in uppercase letters, lowercase letters could have been used. It is customary in C++, however, to use uppercase letters for `const` identifiers to make them easy to identify. Then, whenever a programmer sees uppercase letters in a program, he or she knows that the value of the constant cannot be changed within the program.

Once declared, a `const` identifier can be used in any C++ statement in place of the number it represents. For example, the assignment statements

```
circum = 2 * PI * radius;
amount = SALESTAX * purchase;
```

are both valid. These statements must, of course, appear after the declarations for all their variables and constants. Because a const declaration effectively equates a constant value to an identifier, and the identifier can be used as a direct replacement for its initializing constant, such identifiers are commonly referred to as *symbolic constants* or *named constants*. We shall use these terms interchangeably.

Placement of Statements

At this stage we have introduced a variety of statement types. The general rule in C++ for statement placement is simply that a variable or named constant must be declared before it can be used. Although this rule permits both preprocessor directives and declaration statements to be placed throughout a program, doing so results in a very poor program structure. As a matter of good programming form, the following statement order should be used:

```
preprocessor directives

int main()
{
  named constants
  variable declarations
  other executable statements

  return value
}
```

As new statement types are introduced, we will expand this placement structure to accommodate them. Note that comment statements can be freely intermixed anywhere within this basic structure.

Program 3-10 illustrates the use of a symbolic constant to calculate the sales tax due on a purchased item.

The following sample run was made using Program 3-10:

```
Enter the amount purchased: 36.00
The sales tax is 1.80
The total bill is 37.80
```

Although we have used the const qualifier to construct symbolic constants, we will encounter this data type once again in Chapter 12, where we will show that it is useful as a function argument in ensuring that the argument is not modified within the function.

Program 3-10

```
#include <iostream.h>
#include <iomanip.h>

int main()
{
  const float SALESTAX = 0.05;
  float amount, taxes, total;

  cout << "\nEnter the amount purchased: ";
  cin >> amount;
  taxes = SALESTAX * amount;
  total = amount + taxes;
  cout << setiosflags(ios::fixed)
       << setiosflags(ios::showpoint)
       << setprecision(2);
  cout << "The sales tax is " << setw(4) << taxes << endl;
  cout << "The total bill is " << setw(5) << total << endl;

  return 0;
}
```

Exercises 3.4

Determine the purpose of the programs given in Exercises 1 through 3. Then rewrite each program using a symbolic constant for the appropriate literals.

1.
```
#include <iostream.h>

int main()
{
  float radius, circum;

  cout << "Enter a radius: ";
  cin >> radius;
  circum = 2.0 * 3.1416 * radius;
  cout << "\nThe circumference of the circle is " << circum << endl;

  return 0;
}
```

2.
```
#include <iostream.h>

int main()
{
  float prime, amount, interest;

  prime = .08;       // prime interest rate
  cout << "Enter the amount: ";
  cin >> amount;
  interest = prime * amount;
  cout << "The interest earned is " << interest << endl;

  return 0;
}
```

3.
```
#include <iostream.h>

int main()
{
  float fahren, celsius;

  cout << "Enter a temperature in degrees Fahrenheit: ";
  cin >> fahren;
  celsius = (5.0/9.0) * (fahren - 32.0);
  cout << "The equivalent Celsius temperature is "
       << celsius << endl;

  return 0;
}
```

3.5 Common Programming Errors

In using the material presented in this chapter, be aware of the following possible errors.

1. Forgetting to assign or initialize values for all variables before the variables are used in an expression. Such values can be assigned by assignment statements, initialized within a declaration statement, or assigned interactively by entering values using the `cin` object.
2. Applying either the increment or the decrement operator to an expression. For example, the expression

```
(count + n)++
```

is incorrect. The increment and decrement operators can be applied only to individual variables.

3. Forgetting to separate all variables passed to `cin` with an extraction symbol, `>>`. A more exotic and less common error occurs when the increment and decrement operators are used with variables that appear more than once in the same expression. This error occurs because C++ does not specify the order in which operands are accessed within an expression. For example, the value assigned to `result` in the statement

```
result = i + i++;
```

is computer-dependent. If your computer accesses the first operand, `i`, first, this statement is equivalent to

```
result = 2 * i;
i++;
```

However, if your computer accesses the second operand, `i++`, first, the value of the first operand will be altered before it is used the second time, and the value `2i + 1` is assigned to `result`. As a general rule, therefore, do not use either the increment or the decrement operator in an expression when the variable it operates on appears more than once in the expression.

3.6 Chapter Summary

1. An *expression* is a sequence of one or more operands separated by operators. An *operand* is a constant, a variable, or another expression. A *value* is associated with an expression.
2. Expressions are evaluated according to the precedence and associativity of the operators used in the expression.
3. The assignment symbol, `=`, is an operator. Expressions using this operator assign a value to a variable, and the expression itself also takes on a value. Because assignment is an operation in C++, multiple uses of the assignment operator are possible in the same expression.
4. The increment operator, `++`, adds 1 to a variable, whereas the decrement operator, `--`, subtracts 1 from a variable. Both of these operators can be used as prefixes or postfixes. In prefix operation, the variable is incremented (or decremented) before its value is used. In postfix operation, the variable is incremented (or decremented) after its value is used.

5. C++ provides library functions for performing square root, logarithmic, and other mathematical computations. Each program that uses one of these mathematical functions must either include the statement `#include <math.h>` or have a function declaration for the mathematical function before it is called.
6. Every mathematical library function operates on its arguments to calculate a single value. To use a library function effectively, you must know what the function does, the name of the function, the number and data types of the arguments expected by the function, and the data type of the returned value.
7. Data passed to a function are called arguments of the function. Arguments are passed to a library function by including each argument, separated by commas, within the parentheses following the function's name. Each function has its own requirements for the number and data types of the arguments that must be provided.
8. Functions may be included within larger expressions.
9. The `cin` object is used for data input. This object accepts a stream of data from the keyboard and assigns the data to variables. The general form of a statement using `cin` is

   ```
   cin >> var1 >> var2 . . . >> varn;
   ```

   The extraction symbol, `>>`, must be used to separate the variable names.
10. When a `cin` statement is encountered, the computer temporarily suspends statement execution until sufficient data have been entered for the number of variables contained in the `cin` function.
11. It is good programming practice to display, prior to a `cin` statement, a message that alerts the user to the type and number of data items to be entered. Such a message is called a *prompt.*
12. Values can be equated to a single constant by using the `const` keyword. This creates a named constant that is read-only after it is initialized within the declaration statement. This declaration has the form

    ```
    const data-type constant-name = initial value;
    ```

    and permits the constant to be used instead of the initial value anywhere in the program after the declaration. Generally, such declarations are placed before a program's variable declarations.

Selection

Chapter Four

The term *flow of control* refers to the order in which a program's statements are executed. Unless directed otherwise, the normal flow of control for all programs is sequential. This means that the statements are executed in sequence, one after another, in the order in which they are placed within the program.

Both selection and repetition statements allow the programmer to alter the normal sequential flow of control. As their names imply, selection statements make it possible to select which statement, from a well-defined set, will be executed next, and repetition statements make it possible to go back and repeat a set of statements. In this chapter we present C++'s selection statements. Because selection requires choosing between alternatives, we begin this chapter with a description of C++'s selection criteria.

4.1 Relational Expressions

Besides providing addition, subtraction, multiplication, and division capabilities, all computers have the ability to compare numbers. Because many seemingly "intelligent" decision-making situations can be reduced to the level of choosing between two values, a computer's comparison capability can be used to create a remarkable intelligence-like facility.

The expressions used to compare operands are called *relational expressions*. A *simple relational expression* consists of a relational operator connecting two variable and/or constant operands, as shown in Figure 4–1. The relational operators available in C++ are given in Table 4–1. These relational operators may be used with integer, float, double, or character data, but they must be typed exactly as given in Table 4–1. Thus the following examples are all valid:

```
  age > 40      length <= 50        temp > 98.6
    3 < 4         flag == done     idNum == 682
 day != 5          2.0 > 3.3       hours > 40
```

FIGURE 4–1 Anatomy of a Simple Relational Expression

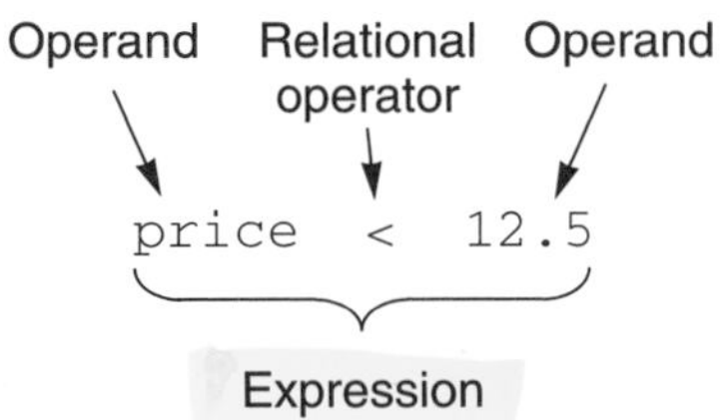

TABLE 4–1 Relational Operators in C++

Relational Operator	Meaning	Example
`<`	less than	`age < 30`
`>`	greater than	`height > 6.2`
`<=`	less than or equal to	`taxable <= 20000`
`>=`	greater than or equal to	`temp >= 98.6`
`==`	equal to	`grade == 100`
`!=`	not equal to	`number != 250`

The following are invalid:

```
length =< 50        // incorrect symbol
2.0 >> 3.3          // invalid relational operator
flag = = done       // spaces are not allowed
```

Relational expressions are sometimes called conditions, and we will use both terms to refer to these expressions. Like all C++ expressions, relational expressions are evaluated to yield a numerical result.[1] *A condition that we would interpret as true evaluates to an integer value of 1, and a false condition results in an integer value of 0.* For example, because the relationship 3 < 4 is always true, this expression has a value of 1, and because the relationship 2.0 > 3.3 is always false, the value of the expression itself is 0. This can be verified by using the statements

```
cout << "The value of 3 < 4 is " << (3 < 4);
cout << "\nThe value of 2.0 > 3.0 is " << (2.0 > 3.3);
```

which result in the display

```
The value of 3 < 4 is 1
The value of 2.0 > 3.0 is 0
```

The value of a relational expression such as `hours > 40` depends on the value stored in the variable `hours`.

---

1 In this regard, both C and C++ differ from other high-level programming languages that yield a Boolean (true, false) result.

In a C++ program, a relational expression's value is not so important as the interpretation C++ places on the value when the expression is used as part of a selection statement. In these statements, which are presented in the next section, we will see that a zero value is used by C++ to represent a false condition and that any nonzero value is used to represent a true condition. The selection of which statement to execute next is then based on the value obtained.

In addition to numerical operands, character data can also be compared by using relational operators. For example, in the ASCII code the letter `'A'` is stored using a code that has a lower numerical value than the letter `'B'`, the code for a `'B'` is lower in value than the code for a `'C'`, and so on. For character sets coded in this manner, the conditions listed in the following table are evaluated as shown.

Expression	Value	Interpretation
`'A' > 'C'`	0	False
`'D' <= 'Z'`	1	True
`'E' == 'F'`	0	False
`'G' >= 'M'`	0	False
`'B' != 'C'`	1	True

Comparing letters is essential in alphabetizing names or using characters to select a particular choice in decision-making situations.

Logical Operators

In addition to using simple relational expressions as conditions, we can create more complex conditions by using the logical operations AND, OR, and NOT. These operations are represented by the symbols `&&`, `||`, and `!`, respectively.

When the AND operator, `&&`, is used with two simple expressions, the condition is true only if both individual expressions are true by themselves. Thus the compound condition

```
(age > 40) && (term < 10)
```

is true (has a value of 1) only if `age` is greater than 40 and `term` is less than 10. Because relational operators have a higher precedence than logical operators, the parentheses in this logical expression could have been omitted.

The OR operator, ||, is also applied between two expressions. When using the logical OR operator, the condition is satisfied if either one of the two expressions is true or both are true. Thus the compound condition

```
(age > 40) || (term < 10)
```

is true if age is greater than 40, if term is less than 10, or if both conditions are true. Again, the parentheses around the relational expressions are included to make the expression easier to read. Because relational operators have a higher precedence than logical operators, the same evaluation would be made even if the parentheses were omitted.

For the declarations

```
int i,j;
float a,b,complete;
```

the following represent valid conditions:

```
a > b
(i == j) || (a < b) || complete
(a/b > 5) && (i <= 20)
```

Before these conditions can be evaluated, the values of a, b, i, j, and complete must be known. For the assignments

```
       a = 12.0;
       b = 2.0;
       i = 15;
       j = 30;
complete = 0.0;
```

the previous expressions yield the following results:

Expression	Value	Interpretation
`a > b`	1	True
`(i == j) || (a < b) || complete`	0	False
`(a/b > 5) && (i <= 20)`	1	True

The NOT operation is used to change an expression to its opposite state; that is, if the expression has any nonzero value (true), then !expression produces

TABLE 4–2 Precedence of Relational and Logical Operators

<table>
<tr><th>Operator</th><th>Associativity</th></tr>
<tr><td>! unary - ++ --</td><td>right to left</td></tr>
<tr><td>* / %</td><td>left to right</td></tr>
<tr><td>+ -</td><td>left to right</td></tr>
<tr><td>< <= > >=</td><td>left to right</td></tr>
<tr><td>== !=</td><td>left to right</td></tr>
<tr><td>&&</td><td>left to right</td></tr>
<tr><td>||</td><td>left to right</td></tr>
<tr><td>= += -= *= /=</td><td>right to left</td></tr>
</table>

a zero value (false). If an expression is false to begin with (has a zero value), then `!expression` is true and evaluates to 1. For example, if the number 26 is stored in the variable `age`, then the expression (`age > 40`) has a value of zero (it is false), and the expression `!(age > 40)` has a value of 1. Because the `NOT` operator is used with only one operand, it is a unary operator.

The relational and logical operators have a hierarchy of execution similar to that of the arithmetic operators. Table 4–2 shows the precedence of these operators in relation to the other operators we have used.

The following example illustrates the use of an operator's precedence and associativity to evaluate relational expressions, assuming these declarations:

```
char key = 'm';
int i = 5, j = 7, k = 12;
double x = 22.5;
```

Expression	Equivalent Expression	Value	Interpretation
i + 2 == k - 1	(i + 2) == (k - 1)	0	False
3 * i - j < 22	((3 * i) - j) < 22	1	True
i + 2 * j > k	(i + (2 * j)) > k	1	True
k + 3 <= -j + 3 * i	(k + 3) <= ((-j) + (3*i))	0	False
'a' + 1 == 'b'	('a' + 1) == 'b'	1	True
key - 1 > 'p'	(key - 1) > 'p'	0	False
key + 1 == 'n'	(key + 1) == 'n'	1	True
25 >= x + 1.0	25 >= (x + 1.0)	0	False

REMEMBER, CHARACTERS HAVE ASCII VALUES

As with all expressions, parentheses can be used to alter the assigned operator priority and to improve the readability of relational expressions. By evaluating the expressions within parentheses first, we find that the following compound condition is evaluated as shown.

```
(6 * 3 == 36 / 2) || (13 < 3 * 3 + 4)  && !(6 - 2 < 5)
      (18 == 18)  ||    (13 < 9 + 4)   && !(4 < 5)
               1  ||    (13 < 13)      && !1
               1  ||        0          &&  0
               1  ||        0
                  1
```

A Numerical Accuracy Problem

A subtle numerical accuracy problem related to floating-point and double-precision numbers can occur with C++'s relational expressions. Because of the way computers store these numbers, tests for equality of floating-point and double-precision values and variables using the relational operator `==` should be avoided.

The reason for this is that many decimal numbers, such as 0.1, cannot be represented exactly in binary using a finite number of bits. Thus, testing for exact equality for such numbers can fail. When equality of noninteger values is desired, it is better to require that the absolute value of the difference between operands be less than some extremely small value. Thus, for real operands, the general expression

```
operand_1 == operand_2
```

should be replaced by the condition

```
fabs(operand_1 - operand_2) < EPSILON
```

where `EPSILON` can be a named constant set to any acceptably small value, such as 0.0000001.[2] Thus, if the difference between the two operands is less than the value of `EPSILON`, the two operands are considered essentially equal. For example, if `x` and `y` are floating-point variables, a condition such as

```
x/y == 0.35
```

---

[2] Using the `fabs()` function requires inclusion of the `math.h` header file. This is done by placing the preprocessor statement `#include <math.h>` either immediately before or immediately after the `#include <iostream.h>` preprocessor statement. Unix-based systems also require specific inclusion of the math library at compile time with a `-lm` command line argument.

should be programmed as

```
fabs(x/y - 0.35) < EPSILON
```

This latter condition ensures that slight inaccuracies in representing noninteger numbers in binary do not affect evaluation of the tested condition.

Exercises 4.1

1. Determine the values of the following expressions. Assume `a` = 5, `b` = 2, `c` = 4, `d` = 6, and `e` = 3.

a. `a > b`
b. `a != b`
c. `d % b == c % b`
d. `a * c != d * b`
e. `d * b == c * e`
f. `a * b`
g. `a % b * c`
h. `c % b * a`
i. `b % c * a`

2. Using parentheses, rewrite the following expressions to indicate the correct order of evaluation. Then evaluate each expression, assuming `a` = 5, `b` = 2, and `c` = 4.

a. `a % b * c && c % b * a`
b. `a % b * c || c % b * a`
c. `b % c * a && a % c * b`
d. `b % c * a || a % c * b`

3. Write relational expressions to express the following conditions (use variable names of your own choosing).

a. A person's age is equal to 30.
b. A person's temperature is greater than 98.6.
c. A person's height is less than 6 feet.
d. The current month is 12 (December).
e. The letter input is m.
f. A person's age is equal to 30 and the person is taller than 6 feet.
g. The current day is the 15th day of the 1st month.
h. A person is older than 50 or has been employed at the company for at least 5 years.
i. A person's identification number is less than 500 and the person is older than 55.
j. A length is greater than 2 feet and less than 3 feet.

4. Determine the value of the following expressions, assuming `a` = 5, `b` = 2, `c` = 4, and `d` = 5.

a. `a == 5`
b. `b * d == c * c`
c. `d % b * c > 5 || c % b * d < 7`

4.2 The `if-else` Statement

The `if-else` statement directs the computer to select a sequence of one or more instructions on the basis of the result of a comparison. For example, if a New Jersey resident's income is less than $20,000, the applicable state tax rate is 2 percent. If the person's income is greater than $20,000, a different rate is applied to the amount over $20,000. The `if-else` statement can be used in this situation to determine the actual tax on the basis of whether the income is less than or equal to $20,000. The general form of the `if-else` statement is

```
if (expression) statement1;
else statement2;
```

The expression is evaluated first. If the value of the expression is nonzero, `statement1` is executed. If the value is zero, the statement after the keyword `else` is executed. Thus, one of the two statements (either `statement1` or `statement2`) is always executed, depending on the value of the expression. Note that the tested expression must be put in parentheses and that a semicolon is placed after each statement.

For clarity, we generally write the `if-else` statement on four lines, using the form

```
if (expression)   <----------  no semicolon here
  statement1;
else   <--------------------  no semicolon here
  statement2;
```

The form of the `if-else` statement that is selected typically depends on the lengths of statements 1 and 2. However, when using the second form, do not put a semicolon after the parentheses or the keyword `else`. The semicolons are placed only at the end of each statement.

As an example, let us write an income tax computation program containing an `if-else` statement. As previously described, a New Jersey state income tax is assessed at 2 percent of taxable income for incomes less than or equal to $20,000. For taxable incomes greater than $20,000, state taxes are 2.5 percent of the income that exceeds $20,000, plus a fixed amount of $400. The expression to be tested is whether taxable income is less than or equal to $20,000. An appropriate `if-else` statement for this situation follows.[3]

[3] Note that in actual practice, the numerical values in this statement would be defined as named constants.

```
if (taxable <= 20000.0)
  taxes = 0.02 * taxable;
else
  taxes = 0.025 * (taxable - 20000.0) + 400.0;
```

Here we have used the relational operator <= to represent the relation "is less than or equal to." If the value of `taxable` is less than or equal to 20000.0, the condition is true (has a value of 1) and the statement `taxes = 0.02 * taxable;` is executed. If the condition is not true, the value of the expression is zero, and the statement after the keyword `else` is executed. Program 4-1 illustrates the use of this statement in a complete program.

Program 4-1

```
#include <iostream.h>
#include <iomanip.h>

int main()
{
  float taxable, taxes;

  cout << "Please type in the taxable income: ";
  cin  >> taxable;

  if (taxable <= 20000.0)
    taxes = 0.02 * taxable;
  else
    taxes = 0.025 * (taxable - 20000.0) + 400.0;

  cout << setiosflags(ios::fixed)
       << setprecision(2)
       << "Taxes are $ " << taxes << endl;

  return 0;
}
```

Here we inserted a blank line before and after the `if-else` statement to highlight it in the complete program. We will continue to do this throughout the text to emphasize the statement being presented.

To illustrate selection in action, we ran Program 4-1 twice with different input data. The results were:

```
Please type in the taxable income: 10000.
Taxes are $ 200.00
```

and

```
Please type in the taxable income: 30000.
Taxes are $ 650.00
```

Observe that the taxable income input in the first run of the program was less than $20,000, and the tax was correctly calculated as 2 percent of the number entered. In the second run, the taxable income was more than $20,000, and the else part of the if-else statement was used to yield a correct tax computation of

$$0.025 * (\$30,000. - \$20,000.) + \$400. = \$650.$$

Although any expression can be tested by an if-else statement, only relational expressions are generally used. However, statements such as

```
if (num)
  cout << "Bingo!";
else
  cout << "You lose!";
```

are valid. Because num, by itself, is a valid expression, the message Bingo! is displayed if num has any nonzero value, and the message You lose! is displayed if num has a value of zero.

Compound Statements

Although only a single statement is permitted in both the if part and the else part of the if-else statement, this statement can be a single compound statement. A *compound statement* is any number of single statements contained between braces, as shown in Figure 4–2.

The use of braces to enclose a set of individual statements creates a single block of statements, which may be used anywhere in a C++ program in place of a single statement. The next example illustrates the use of a compound statement within the general form of an if-else statement.

```
{
  statement1;
  statement2;
  statement3;
      .
      .
      .
  last statement;
}
```

FIGURE 4–2 A Compound Statement Consists of Individual Statements Enclosed Within Braces

```
if (expression)
{
  statement1;     // as many statements as necessary
  statement2;     // can be put within the braces
  statement3;     // each statement must end with a ;
}
else
{
  statement4;
  statement5;
      .
      .
      .
  statementn;
}
```

Program 4-2 illustrates the use of a compound statement in an actual program. This checks whether the value in `tempType` is `f`. If the value is `f`, the compound statement that corresponds to the `if` part of the `if-else` statement is executed. Any other letter results in execution of the compound statement that corresponds to the `else` part. A sample run of Program 4-2 follows.

```
Enter the temperature to be converted: 212
Enter an f if the temperature is in Fahrenheit
or a c if the temperature is in Celsius: f

The equivalent Celsius temperature is 100.00
```

POINT OF INFORMATION

The Boolean Data Type

Traditionally, neither C nor C++ had a built-in Boolean data type with its two Boolean values *true* and *false*. Because this data type was not originally a part of the language, a tested expression could not evaluate to a Boolean value. Thus the syntax

```
if(boolean expression is true)
  execute this statement;
```

was also not built into either C or C++. Rather, both C and C++ use the more encompassing syntax

```
if(expression)
  execute this statement;
```

(continued on next page)

Program 4-2

```
#include <iostream.h>
#include <iomanip.h>

// a temperature conversion program
int main()
{
  char tempType;
  float temp, fahren, celsius;

  cout << "Enter the temperature to be converted: ";
  cin  >> temp;
  cout << "Enter an f if the temperature is in Fahrenheit";
  cout << "\n or a c if the temperature is in Celsius: ";
  cin  >> tempType;

    // set output formats
  cout << setiosflags (ios::fixed)
       << setiosflags (ios::showpoint)
       << setprecision(2);

  if (tempType == 'f')
  {
    celsius = (5.0 / 9.0) * (temp - 32.0);
    cout << "\nThe equivalent Celsius temperature is " << celsius << endl;
  }
  else
  {
    fahren = (9.0 / 5.0) * temp + 32.0;
    cout << "\nThe equivalent Fahrenheit temperature is " << fahren << endl;
  }

  return 0;
}
```

(continued from previous page)

where *expression* is any expression that evaluates to a numerical value. If the value of the tested expression is a nonzero value, it is considered as true, and only a zero value is considered as false.

As specified by the ANSI/ISO C++ standard, C++ will have a new Boolean data type containing the two values `true` and `false`. Boolean variables will be declared using the keyword `bool`. As currently implemented, the actual values represented by the two Boolean values `true` and `false` are the integer values 1 and 0, respectively. For example, consider the following program, which declares two Boolean variables.

```
#include <iostream.h>
int main()
{
  bool t1, t2;

  t1 = true;
  t2 = false;

  cout <<"The value of t1 is " << t1
       << "\n and the value of t2 is " << t2 << endl;
  return 0;
}
```

The output produced by this program is

```
The value of t1 is 1
 and the value of t2 is 0
```

As this output shows, the Boolean values `true` and `false` are represented by the integer values 1 and 0, respectively. The Boolean values `true` and `false` have the following relationships:

```
!true = false
!false = true
```

Additionally, applying either a postfix or a prefix `++` operator to a variable of type `bool` will set the Boolean value to `true`. The postfix and prefix `--` operators cannot be applied to a Boolean variable.

Boolean values can also be compared, as illustrated in the following code:

```
if (t1 == t2)
  cout << "The values are equal" << endl;
else
  cout << "The values are not equal" << endl;
```

Finally, assigning any nonzero value to a Boolean variable results in the variable being set to `true`—that is, to a value of 1—and assigning a zero value to a Boolean variable results in the variable being set to `false`—that is, to a value of 0.

Block Scope

All statements contained within a compound statement constitute a single block of code, and any variable declared within such a block has meaning only between its declaration and the closing braces that define the block. For example, consider the following section of code, which consists of two blocks of code.

```
{   // start of outer block
    int a = 25;
    int b = 17;

    cout << "The value of a is " << a << " and b is " << b << endl;

    {      // start of inner block
      float a = 46.25;
      int c = 10;

      cout << "a is now " << a
           << " b is now " << b
           << " and c is " << c << endl;
    }    // end of inner block

    cout << "a is now " << a << " and b is "<< b << endl;

}   // end of outer block
```

The output that is produced by this section of code is

```
The value of a is 25 and b is 17
a is now 46.25 b is now 17 and c is 10
a is now 25 and b is 17
```

This output is produced as follows: The first block of code defines two variables named a and b, which may be used anywhere within this block after their declaration, including within any block contained inside it. Within the inner block, two new variables named a and c have been declared. At this stage, then, we have created four different variables, two of which have the same name. Any referenced variable first results in an attempt to access a variable correctly declared within the block that contains the reference. If no variable is defined within the block, then an attempt is made to access a variable in the next immediate outside block, and so on until a valid access results.

Thus the values of the variables a and c referenced within the inner block use the values of the variables a and c declared in that block. Because no variable named b was declared inside the inner block, the value of b displayed

POINT OF INFORMATION

Placement of Braces in a Compound Statement

A common practice for some C++ programmers is to place the opening brace of a compound statement on the same line as the `if` and `else` statements. If this convention were used, the `if` statement in Program 4-2 would appear as shown below. (This placement is a matter of preference. Both styles are used, and both are acceptable.)

```
if (tempType == 'f') {
  celsius = (5.0 / 9.0) * (temp - 32.0);
  cout << "\nThe equivalent Celsius temperature is "
       << celsius << endl;
}
else {
  fahren = (9.0 / 5.0) * temp + 32.0;
  cout << "\nThe equivalent Fahrenheit temperature is "
       << fahren << endl;
}
```

from within the inner block is obtained from the outer block. Finally, the last `cout` object, which is outside the inner block, displays the value of the variable `a` declared in the outer block. If an attempt were made to display the value of `c` anywhere in the outer block, the compiler would issue an error message stating that `c` is an undefined symbol.

The location within a program where a variable can be used is formally referred to as the *scope* of the variable, and we will have much more to say on this subject in Chapter 6.[4]

One-Way Selection

A useful modification of the `if-else` statement involves omitting the `else` part of the statement altogether. In this case, the `if` statement takes the shortened and frequently useful form

```
if (expression)
  statement;
```

The statement following the *`if (expression)`* is executed only if the expression has a nonzero value (a true condition). As before, the statement may be a compound statement.

---

[4] Blocks that consist only of definition statements can be given explicit names. Such named blocks are referred to as *namespaces* and are described in Appendix F.

This modified form of the `if` statement is called a one-way `if` statement. It is illustrated in Program 4-3, which checks a car's mileage and prints a message if the car has been driven more than 3000.0 miles.

Program 4-3

```
#include <iostream.h>

int main()
{
  const float LIMIT = 3000.0;
  int idNum;
  float miles;

  cout << "Please type in car number and mileage: ";
  cin  >> idNum >> miles;

  if(miles > LIMIT)
    cout << "  Car " << idNum << " is over the limit." << endl;

  cout << "End of program output." << endl;

  return 0;
}
```

To illustrate the one-way selection criteria in action, Program 4-3 was run twice, each time with different input data. Only the input data for the first run causes the message `Car 256 is over the limit` to be displayed.

```
Please type in car number and mileage: 256 3562.8
  Car 256 is over the limit.
End of program output.
```

and

```
Please type in car number and mileage: 23 2562.3
End of program output.
```

Problems Associated with the `if-else` Statement

Two of the most common problems that programmers encounter when first using C++'s `if-else` statement are

1. Misunderstanding the full implications of what an expression is
2. Using the assignment operator, `=`, in place of the relational operator, `==`

Recall that an expression is any combination of operands and operators that yields a result. This definition is extremely broad and is more encompassing than is initially apparent. For example, all of the following are valid C++ expressions:

```
age + 5
age = 30
age == 40
```

Assuming that the variables are suitably declared, each of these expressions yields a result. The following section of code uses the `cout` object to display the value of these expressions when `age` is initially assigned the value 18.

```
age = 18;
cout << "The value of the first expression is " << (age + 5) << endl;
cout << "The value of the second expression is " << (age = 30) << endl;
cout << "The value of the third expression is " << (age == 40) << endl;
```

The display produced by this section of code is

```
The value of the first expression is 23
The value of the second expression is 30
The value of the third expression is 0
```

As this output illustrates, each expression, by itself, has a value associated with it. The value of the first expression is the sum of the variable `age` plus 5, which is 23. The value of the second expression is 30, which is also assigned to the variable `age`. The value of the third expression is zero, because `age` is not equal to 40, and a false condition is represented in C++ with a value of zero. If the value in `age` were 40, the relational expression `a == 40` would be true and would have a value of 1.

Now assume that the relational expression `age == 40` was intended to be used in the `if` statement

```
if (age == 40)
  cout << "Happy Birthday!";
```

but was mistyped as `age = 40`, resulting in

```
if (age = 40)
  cout << "Happy Birthday!";
```

Because the mistake results in a valid C++ expression, and any C++ expression can be tested by an `if` statement, the resulting `if` statement is valid and will cause the message Happy Birthday! to be printed regardless of what value was previously assigned to age. Can you see why?

The condition tested by the if statement does not compare the value in age to the number 40 but rather assigns the number 40 to age. That is, the expression age = 40 is not a relational expression at all, but an assignment expression. At the completion of the assignment, the expression itself has a value of 40. Because C++ treats any nonzero value as true, the cout statement is executed. Another way of looking at this is to realize that the if statement is equivalent to the following two statements:

```
age = 40;       // assign 40 to age
if (age)        // test the value of age
cout << "Happy Birthday!";
```

Because a C++ compiler has no means of knowing that the expression being tested is not the desired one, you must be especially careful when writing conditions.

Exercises 4.2

1. Rewrite Program 4-1 using the following statements:

```
const float LIMIT = 20000.0;
const float REGRATE = 0.02;
const float HIGHRATE = 0.025;
const float FIXED = 400.0;
```

(If necessary, review Section 3.4 for the use of named constants.)

2. a. If money is left in a particular bank for more than 5 years, interest is paid by the bank at a rate of 9.5 percent; otherwise, the interest rate is 5.4 percent. Write a C++ program that uses the cin object to accept the number of years into the variable numYears and display the appropriate interest rate, depending on the value input into numYears.

b. How many runs should you make for the program written in Exercise 2a to verify that it is operating correctly? What data should you input in each of the program runs?

3. a. In a pass/fail course, a student passes if the grade is greater than or equal to 70 and fails if the grade is lower. Write a C++ program that accepts a grade and prints the message A passing grade or A failing grade, as appropriate.

b. How many runs should you make for the program written in Exercise 3a to verify that it is operating correctly? What data should you input in each of the program runs?

4. a. Write a C++ program to compute and display a person's weekly salary as determined by the following expressions:

If the number of hours worked is less than or equal to 40, the person receives $8.00 per hour; otherwise, the person receives $320.00, plus $12.00 for each hour worked over 40 hours.

The program should request the hours worked as input and should display the salary as output.

b. How many runs should you make for the program written in Exercise 4a to verify that it is operating correctly? What data should you input in each of the program runs?

5. *a.* A senior salesperson is paid $400 a week, and a junior salesperson is paid $275 a week. Write a C++ program that accepts as input a salesperson's status in the character variable `status`. If status equals `'s'`, the senior person's salary should be displayed; otherwise, the junior person's salary should be output.

b. How many runs should you make for the program written in Exercise 5a to verify that it is operating correctly? What data should you input in each of the program runs?

6. *a.* Write a C++ program that displays either the message `I feel great today!` or `I feel down today #$*!` depending on the input. If the character `u` is entered in the variable `ch`, the first message should be displayed; otherwise, the second message should be displayed.

b. How many runs should you make for the program written in Exercise 6a to verify that it is operating correctly? What data should you input in each of the program runs?

7. *a.* Write a program to display the following two prompts:

```
Enter a month: (use a 1 for Jan, etc.)
Enter a day of the month:
```

Have your program accept and store a number in the variable `month` in response to the first prompt and, in response to the second prompt, accept and store a number in the variable `day`. If the month entered is not between 1 and 12, inclusive, print a message informing the user that an invalid month has been entered. If the day entered is not between 1 and 31, print a message informing the user that an invalid day has been entered.

b. What will your program do if the user types a number with a decimal point for the month? How can you ensure that your `if` statements check for an integer number?

8. Write a C++ program that accepts a character using the `cin` object and determines whether the character is a lowercase letter. A lowercase letter is any character that is greater than or equal to `'a'` and less than or equal to `'z'`. If the entered character is a lowercase letter, display the message `The character just entered is a lowercase letter.` If the entered letter is not lowercase, display the message `The character just entered is not a lowercase letter.`

9. Write a C++ program that first determines whether an entered character is a lowercase letter (see Exercise 8). If the letter is lowercase, determine and print out its position in the alphabet. For example, if the entered letter is `c`, the program should print out `3`, because `c` is the third letter in the alphabet. (*Hint:* If the entered character is in lowercase, its position can be determined by subtracting `'a'` from the letter and adding 1.)

10. Repeat Exercise 8 to determine whether the character entered is an uppercase letter. An uppercase letter is any character greater than or equal to `'A'` and less than or equal to `'Z'`.

11. Write a C++ program that first determines whether an entered character is an uppercase letter (see Exercise 10). If the letter is uppercase, determine and print its position in the alphabet. For example, if the entered letter is `g`, the program should print out `7`, because `g` is the seventh letter in the alphabet. (*Hint:* If the entered character is in uppercase, its position can be determined by subtracting `'A'` from the letter and adding 1.)

12. Write a C++ program that accepts a character using the `cin` object. If the character is a lowercase letter (see Exercise 8), convert the letter to uppercase and display the letter in its uppercase form. (*Hint:* Subtracting the integer value 32 from a lowercase letter yields the code for the equivalent uppercase letter. Thus, `'A' = (char) ('a' - 32)`.)

13. The following program displays the message `Hello there!` regardless of the letter input. Determine where the error is and, if possible, why the program always causes the message to be displayed.

```
#include <iostream.h>
int main()
{
  char letter;

  cout << "Enter a letter: ";
  cin  >> letter;
  if (letter = 'm')
    cout << "Hello there!" << endl;

  return 0;
}
```

14. Write a C++ program that asks the user to input two numbers. After your program accepts these numbers using one or more `cin` object calls, have your program check the numbers. If the first number entered is greater than the second number, print the message `The first number is greater`; otherwise, print the message `The first number is not greater than the second`. Test your program by entering the numbers 5 and 8 and then using the numbers 11 and 2. What will your program display if the two numbers entered are equal?

4.3 Nested `if` Statements

As we have seen, an `if-else` statement can contain simple or compound statements. Any valid C++ statement can be used, including another `if-else` statement. Thus, one or more `if-else` statements can be included within either part of an `if-else` statement. For example, substituting the one-way `if` statement

```
if (hours > 6)
  cout << "snap";
```

for `statement1` in the `if` statement

```
if (hours < 9)
  statement1;
else
  cout << "pop";
```

results in the nested `if` statement

```
if (hours < 9)
{
  if (hours > 6)
    cout << "snap";
}
  else
    cout << "pop";
```

The braces around the inner one-way `if` are essential, because in their absence, C++ associates an `else` with the closest unpaired `if`. Thus, without the braces, the foregoing statement is equivalent to

```
if (hours < 9)
  if (hours > 6)
    cout << "snap";
  else
    cout << "pop";
```

Here the `else` is paired with the inner `if`, which destroys the meaning of the original `if-else` statement. Note also that the indentation is irrelevant as far as the compiler is concerned. Whether the indentation exists or not, the statement is compiled by associating the last `else` with the closest unpaired `if`, unless braces are used to alter the default pairing.

The process of nesting `if` statements can be extended indefinitely, so the `cout << "snap";` statement could itself be replaced by either a complete `if-else` statement or another one-way `if` statement.

The `if-else` Chain

Generally, the case in which the statement in the `if` part of an `if-else` statement is another `if` statement tends to be confusing and is best avoided. However, an extremely useful construction occurs when the `else` part of an `if` statement contains another `if-else` statement. This takes the form

```
if (expression_1)
  statement1;
else
  if (expression_2)
    statement2;
  else
    statement3;
```

As with all C++ programs, the indentation we have used is not required. In fact, the foregoing construction is so common that it is typically written using the following arrangement:

```
if (expression_1)
  statement1;
else if (expression_2)
  statement2;
else
  statement3;
```

This construction is called an `if-else` chain and is used extensively in programming applications. The conditions are evaluated in order, and if any condition is true, the corresponding statement is executed and the remainder of the chain is terminated. The final `else` statement is executed only if none of the previous conditions is satisfied. This serves as a default or catch-all case that is useful for detecting an impossible or error condition.

The chain can be continued indefinitely by repeatedly making the last statement another `if-else` statement. Thus the general form of an `if-else` chain is

```
if (expression_1)
  statement1;
else if (expression_2)
  statement2;
else if (expression_3)
  statement3;
      .
      .
      .
else if (expression_n)
  statement_n;
else
  last_statement;
```

As with all C++ statements, each individual statement can be a compound statement bounded by the braces `{` and `}`. To illustrate the `if-else` chain, Program 4-4 displays a person's marital status corresponding to a letter input. The following letter codes are used:

Marital Status	Input Code
Married	M
Single	S
Divorced	D
Widowed	W

Program 4-4

```
#include <iostream.h>

int main()
{
  char marcode;

  cout << "Enter a marital code: ";
  cin  >> marcode;

  if (marcode == 'M')
    cout << "Individual is married." << endl;
  else if (marcode == 'S')
    cout << "Individual is single." << endl;
  else if (marcode == 'D')
    cout << "Individual is divorced." << endl;
  else if (marcode == 'W')
    cout << "Individual is widowed." << endl;
  else
    cout << "An invalid code was entered." << endl;

  return 0;
}
```

As a final example illustrating the `if-else` chain, let us calculate the monthly income of a salesperson by using the following commission schedule:

Monthly Sales	Income
greater than or equal to $50,000	$375 plus 16% of sales
less than $50,000 but greater than or equal to $40,000	$350 plus 14% of sales
less than $40,000 but greater than or equal to $30,000	$325 plus 12% of sales
less than $30,000 but greater than or equal to $20,000	$300 plus 9% of sales
less than $20,000 but greater than or equal to $10,000	$250 plus 5% of sales
less than $10,000	$200 plus 3% of sales

The following if-else chain can be used to determine the correct monthly income, where the variable monthlySales is used to store the salesperson's current monthly sales.

```
if (monthlySales >= 50000.00)
  income = 375.00 + .16 * monthlySales;
else if (monthlySales >= 40000.00)
  income = 350.00 + .14 * monthlySales;
else if (monthlySales >= 30000.00)
  income = 325.00 + .12 * monthlySales;
else if (monthlySales >= 20000.00)
  income = 300.00 + .09 * monthlySales;
else if (monthlySales >= 10000.00)
  income = 250.00 + .05 * monthlySales;
else
  income = 200.000 + .03 * monthlySales;
```

Note that this example makes use of the fact that the chain is stopped once a true condition is found. This is accomplished by checking for the highest monthly sales first. If the salesperson's monthly sales are less than $50,000, the if-else chain continues checking for the next highest sales amount until the correct category is obtained.

Program 4-5 uses this if-else chain to calculate and display the income that corresponds to the value of monthly sales that is input to the cin object.

Program 4-5

```
#include <iostream.h>
#include <iomanip.h>

int main()
{
  float monthlySales, income;

  cout << "Enter the value of monthly sales: ";
  cin  >> monthlySales;
```

(continued on next page)

(continued from previous page)

```
  if (monthlySales >= 50000.00)
    income = 375.00 + .16 * monthlySales;
  else if (monthlySales >= 40000.00)
    income = 350.00 + .14 * monthlySales;
  else if (monthlySales >= 30000.00)
    income = 325.00 + .12 * monthlySales;
  else if (monthlySales >= 20000.00)
    income = 300.00 + .09 * monthlySales;
  else if (monthlySales >= 10000.00)
    income = 250.00 + .05 * monthlySales;
  else
    income = 200.00 + .03 * monthlySales;

  cout << setiosflags(ios::showpoint)
       << setiosflags(ios:: fixed)
       << setprecision(2)
       << "The income is $" << income << endl;

  return 0;
}
```

A sample run using Program 4-5 follows.

```
Enter the value of monthly sales: 36243.89
The income is $4674.27
```

Exercises 4.3

1. A student's letter grade is calculated according to the following schedule:

Numerical Grade	Letter Grade
greater than or equal to 90	A
less than 90 but greater than or equal to 80	B
less than 80 but greater than or equal to 70	C
less than 70 but greater than or equal to 60	D
less than 60	F

Write a C++ program that accepts a student's numerical grade, converts the numerical grade to an equivalent letter grade, and displays the letter grade.

2. The interest rate paid on funds deposited in a bank is determined by the amount of time the money is left on deposit. For a particular bank, the following schedule is used:

Time on Deposit	Interest Rate
greater than or equal to 5 years	.095
less than 5 years but greater than or equal to 4 years	.09
less than 4 years but greater than or equal to 3 years	.085
less than 3 years but greater than or equal to 2 years	.075
less than 2 years but greater than or equal to 1 year	.065
less than 1 year	.058

Write a C++ program that accepts the time that funds are left on deposit and displays the interest rate that corresponds to the time entered.

3. Write a C++ program that accepts a number followed by one space and then a letter. If the letter following the number is `f`, the program is to treat the number entered as a temperature in degrees Fahrenheit, convert the number to the equivalent temperature in degrees Celsius, and print a suitable display message. If the letter following the number is `c`, the program is to consider the number entered as a Celsius temperature, convert the number to the equivalent Fahrenheit temperature, and print a suitable display message. If the letter is neither `f` nor `c`, the program is to print a message that the data entered is incorrect and then terminate. Use an `if-else` chain in your program and make use of the conversion formulas

```
Celsius = (5.0 / 9.0) * (Fahrenheit - 32.0)
Fahrenheit = (9.0 / 5.0) * Celsius + 32.0
```

4. Using the commission schedule from Program 4-5, the following program calculates monthly income.

```
#include <iostream.h>
#include <iomanip.h>

int main()
{
  float monthlySales, income;

  cout << "Enter the value of monthly sales: ";
  cin  >> monthlySales;
```

(continued on next page)

(continued from previous page)

```
   if (monthlySales >= 50000.00)
     income = 375.00 + .16 * monthlySales;
   if (monthlySales >= 40000.00 && monthlySales < 50000.00)
     income = 350.00 + .14 * monthlySales;
   if (monthlySales >= 30000.00 && monthlySales < 40000.00)
     income = 325.00 + .12 * monthlySales;
   if (monthlySales >= 20000.00 && monthlySales < 30000.00)
     income = 300.00 + .09 * monthlySales;
   if (monthlySales >= 10000.00 && monthlySales < 20000.00)
     income = 250.00 + .05 * monthlySales;
   if (monthlySales < 10000.00)
     income = 200.00 + .03 * monthlySales;

   cout << setiosflags(ios::showpoint)
        << setiosflags(ios:: fixed)
        << setprecision(2)
        << "\n\nThe income is $" << income << endl;

   return 0;
 }
```

a. Will this program produce the same output as Program 4-5?
b. Which program is better? Why?

5. The following program was written to produce the same result as Program 4-5.

```
#include <iostream.h>
#include <iomanip.h>
int main()
{
  float monthlySales, income;

  cout << "Enter the value of monthly sales: ";
  cin  >> monthlySales;

  if (monthlySales < 10000.00)
    income = 200.00 + .03 * monthlySales;
  else if (monthlySales >= 10000.00)
    income = 250.00 + .05 * monthlySales;
  else if (monthlySales >= 20000.00)
    income = 300.00 + .09 * monthlySales;
  else if (monthlySales >= 30000.00)
    income = 325.00 + .12 * monthlySales;
  else if (monthlySales >= 40000.00)
    income = 350.00 + .14 * monthlySales;
  else if (monthlySales >= 50000.00)
    income = 375.00 + .16 * monthlySales;
```

```
   cout << setiosflags(ios::showpoint)
        << setiosflags(ios:: fixed)
        << setprecision(2)
        << "The income is $" << income << endl;

   return 0;
}
```

a Will this program run?
b. What does this program do?
c. For what values of monthly sales does this program calculate the correct income?

4.4 The switch Statement

The `if-else` chain is used in programming applications where one set of instructions must be selected from many possible alternatives. The `switch` statement provides an alternative to the `if-else` chain for cases that compare the value of an integer expression to a specific value. The general form of a `switch` statement is

```
switch (expression)
{                              // start of compound statement
   case value_1:  <--------------- terminated with a colon
     statement1;
     statement2;
          .
          .
          .
     break;
   case value_2:  <--------------- terminated with a colon
     statementm;
     statementn;
          .
          .
          .
     break;
          .
          .
          .
   case value_n:  <--------------- terminated with a colon
     statementw;
     statementx;
          .
          .
          .
     break;
   default:  <-------------------- terminated with a colon
     statement_aa;
     statement_bb;
}                              // end of switch and compound statement
```

The `switch` statement uses four new keywords: `switch`, `case`, `default`, and `break`. Let's see what each of these words does.

The keyword `switch` identifies the start of the `switch` statement. The expression in parentheses following this word is evaluated, and the result of the expression is compared to various alternative values contained within the compound statement. The expression in the `switch` statement must evaluate to an integer result; otherwise, a compilation error results.

Internal to the `switch` statement, the keyword `case` is used to identify or label individual values that are compared to the value of the `switch` expression. The `switch` expression's value is compared to each of these `case` values, in the order in which these values are listed, until a match is found. When a match occurs, execution begins with the statement immediately following the match. Thus, as illustrated in Figure 4–3, the value of the expression determines where in the `switch` statement execution actually begins.

FIGURE 4–3 The Expression Determines an Entry Point

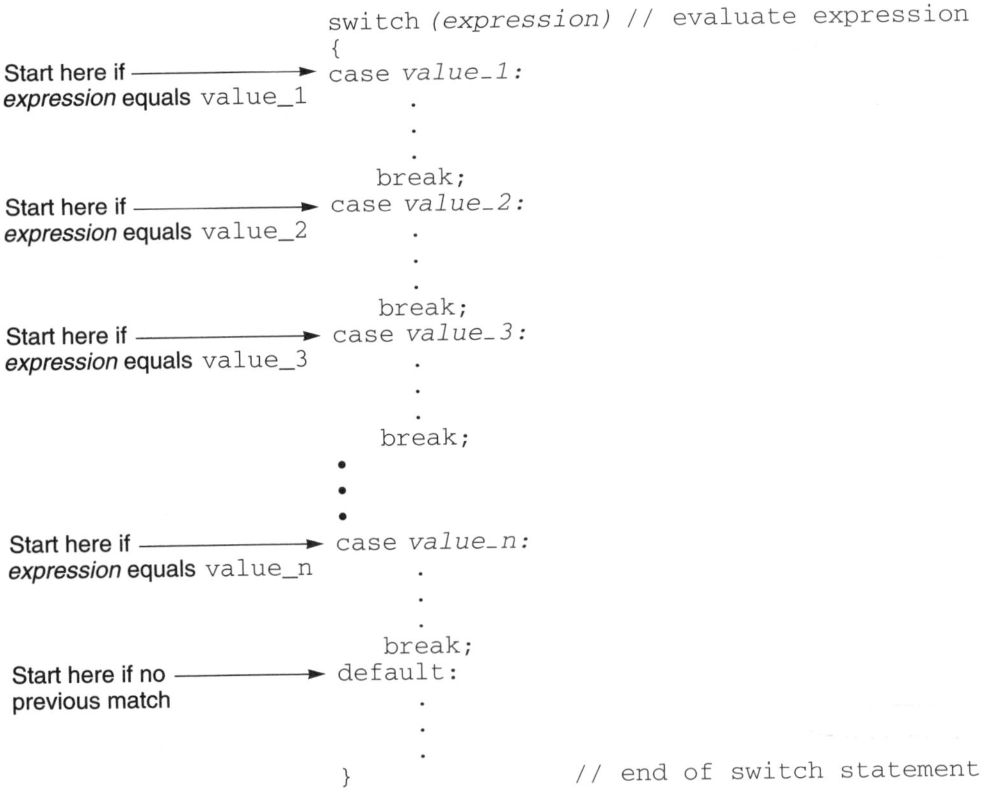

```
                                 switch (expression) // evaluate expression
                                 {
Start here if ---------------->  case value_1:
expression equals value_1            .
                                     .
                                     .
                                   break;
Start here if ---------------->  case value_2:
expression equals value_2            .
                                     .
                                     .
                                   break;
Start here if ---------------->  case value_3:
expression equals value_3            .
                                     .
                                     .
                                   break;
                                 •
                                 •
                                 •
Start here if ---------------->  case value_n:
expression equals value_n            .
                                     .
                                     .
                                   break;
Start here if no ------------->  default:
previous match                       .
                                     .
                                     .
                                 }              // end of switch statement
```

Any number of case labels may be contained within a switch statement, in any order. If the value of the expression does not match any of the case values, however, no statement is executed unless the keyword default is encountered. The keyword default is optional and operates the same as the last else in an if-else chain. If the value of the expression does not match any of the case values, program execution begins with the statement following the word default.

Once an entry point has been located by the switch statement, all further case evaluations are ignored, and execution continues through the end of the compound statement unless a break statement is encountered. This is the reason for the break statement, which identifies the end of a particular case and causes an immediate exit from the switch statement. Thus, just as the word case identifies possible starting points in the compound statement, the break statement determines terminating points. If the break statements are omitted, all cases following the matching case value, including the default case, are executed.

In writing a switch statement, we can use multiple case values to refer to the same set of statements; the default label is optional. For example, consider the following:

```
switch (number)
{
  case 1:
    cout << "Have a Good Morning" << endl;
    break;
  case 2:
    cout << "Have a Happy Day" << endl;
    break;
  case 3: case 4: case 5:
    cout << "Have a Nice Evening" << endl;
}
```

If the value stored in the variable number is 1, the message Have a Good Morning is displayed. Similarly, if the value of number is 2, the second message is displayed. Finally, if the value of number is 3 or 4 or 5, the last message is displayed. Because the statements to be executed for these last three cases are the same, the cases for these values can be "stacked together," as shown in the example. Also, because there is no default, no message is printed if the value of number is not one of the listed case values. Although it is good programming practice to list case values in increasing order, this is not required by the switch statement. A switch statement may have any number of case values, in any order; we need to list only the values being tested.

Program 4-6 uses a switch statement to select the arithmetic operation (addition, multiplication, or division) to be performed on two numbers, depending on the value of the variable opselect.

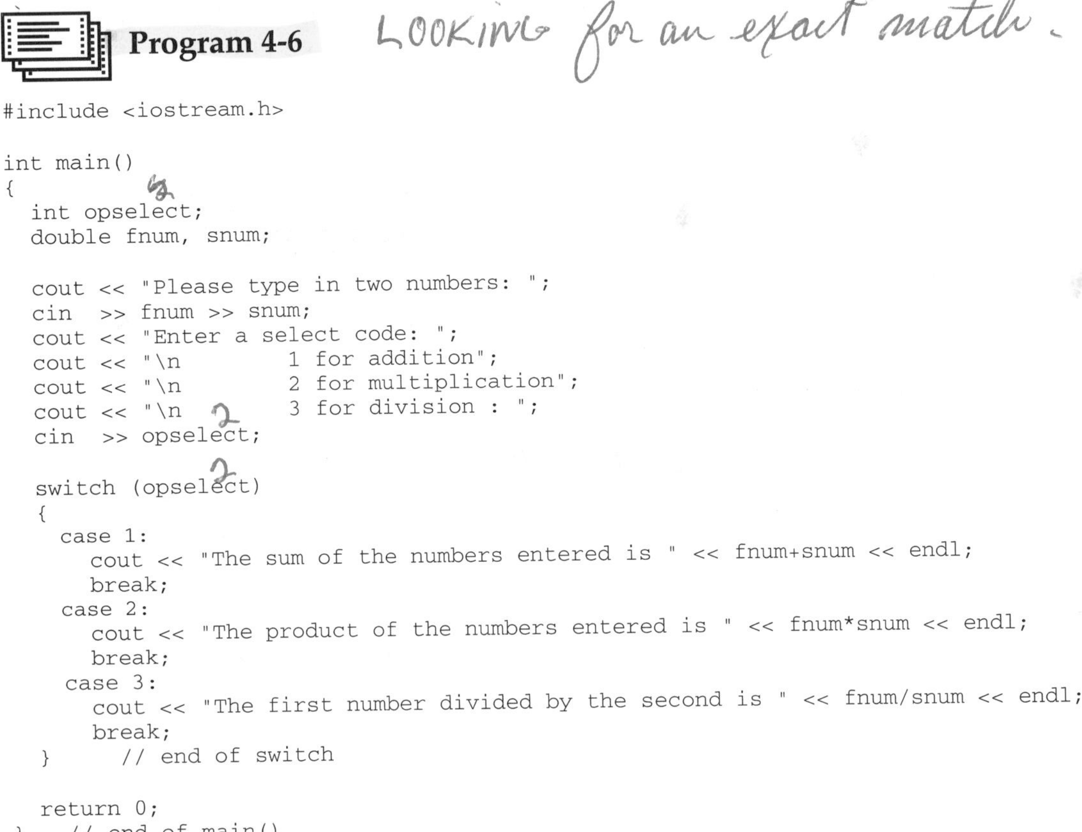

Program 4-6

```
#include <iostream.h>

int main()
{
  int opselect;
  double fnum, snum;

  cout << "Please type in two numbers: ";
  cin  >> fnum >> snum;
  cout << "Enter a select code: ";
  cout << "\n        1 for addition";
  cout << "\n        2 for multiplication";
  cout << "\n        3 for division : ";
  cin  >> opselect;

  switch (opselect)
  {
    case 1:
      cout << "The sum of the numbers entered is " << fnum+snum << endl;
      break;
    case 2:
      cout << "The product of the numbers entered is " << fnum*snum << endl;
      break;
    case 3:
      cout << "The first number divided by the second is " << fnum/snum << endl;
      break;
  }     // end of switch

  return 0;
}   // end of main()
```

Program 4-6 was run twice. The resulting display clearly identifies the case selected. The results were

```
Please type in two numbers: 12 3
Enter a select code:
        1 for addition
        2 for multiplication
        3 for division : 2
The product of the numbers entered is 36
```

and

```
Please type in two numbers: 12 3
Enter a select code:
          1 for addition
          2 for multiplication
          3 for division : 3

The first number divided by the second is 4
```

In reviewing Program 4-6, note the break statement in the last case. Although this break is not necessary, it is good practice to terminate the last case in a switch statement with a break. This prevents a possible program error later, if an additional case is subsequently added to the switch statement. With the addition of a new case, the break between cases becomes necessary; having the break in place ensures that you will not forget to include it at the time of the modification.

Because character data types are always converted to integers in an expression, a switch statement can also be used to "switch" on the basis of the value of a character expression. For example, assuming that choice is a character variable, the following switch statement is valid:

```
switch(choice)
{
  case 'a': case 'e': case 'i': case 'o': case 'u':
    cout << "\nThe character in choice is a vowel" << endl;
    break;
  default:
     cout << "\nThe character in choice is not a vowel" << endl;
     break;  // this break is optional
}   // end of switch statement
```

Exercises 4.4

1. Rewrite the following if-else chain using a switch statement:

```
if (letGrad == 'A')
  cout << "The numerical grade is between 90 and 100";
else if (letGrad == 'B')
  cout << "The numerical grade is between 80 and 89.9";
else if (letGrad == 'C')
  cout << "The numerical grade is between 70 and 79.9";
else if (letGrad == 'D')
  cout << "How are you going to explain this one" << endl;
else
{
  cout << "Of course I had nothing to do with my grade." << endl;
  cout << "\nThe professor was really off the wall." << endl;
}
```

convert 'if else', into a switch

2. Rewrite the following `if-else` chain using a `switch` statement:

```
if (bondType == 1)
{
  inData();
  check();
}
else if (bondType == 2)
{
  dates();
  leapYr();
}
else if (bondTyp == 3)
{
  yield();
  maturity();
}
else if (bondType == 4)
{
  price();
  roi();
}
else if (bondType == 5)
{
  files();
  save();
}
else if (bondType == 6)
{
  retrieve();
  screen();
}
```

3. Rewrite Program 4-4 in Section 4.3 using a `switch` statement.

4. Determine why the `if-else` chain in Program 4-5 cannot be replaced with a `switch` statement.

5. Repeat Exercise 3 in Section 4.3 using a `switch` statement instead of an `if-else` chain.

6. Rewrite Program 4-6 using a character variable for the select code.

7. Each disk drive in a shipment is stamped with a code from 1 to 4, where the codes indicate the following drive manufacturers:

Code	Disk Drive Manufacturer
1	3M Corporation
2	Maxell Corporation
3	Sony Corporation
4	Verbatim Corporation

Write a C++ program that accepts the code number as an input and, on the basis of the value entered, displays the correct disk drive manufacturer.

4.5 Common Programming Errors

There are three programming errors that are commonly made in C++'s selection statements. Let us briefly consider each.

1. Using the assignment operator, =, in place of the relational operator, ==. This can cause an enormous amount of frustration because any expression can be tested by an if-else statement. For example, the statement

```
if (opselect = 2)
  cout << "Happy Birthday";
else
  cout << "Good Day";
```

   always results in the message Happy Birthday being printed, regardless of the initial value in the variable opselect. This is because the assignment expression opselect = 2 has a value of 2, which is considered a true value in C++. The correct expression to determine the value in opselect is opselect == 2.

2. Assuming that the if-else statement is selecting an incorrect choice when the problem is really the values being tested. This is a typical debugging problem in which the programmer mistakenly concentrates on the tested condition as the source of the problem rather than on the values being tested. For example, assume that the following correct if-else statement is part of your program.

```
if (key == 'F')
{
  contemp = (5.0/9.0) * (intemp - 32.0);
  cout << "Conversion to Celsius was done";
}
else
{
  contemp = (9.0/5.0) * intemp + 32.0;
  cout << "Conversion to Fahrenheit was done";
}
```

   This statement will always display Conversion to Celsius was done when the variable key contains an F. Therefore, if this message is displayed when you believe key does not contain F, investigation of key's value is called for. As a general rule, whenever a selection statement does not act as you think it should, be sure to test your assumptions about the values assigned to the tested variables by displaying their values. If an unanticipated value is displayed, you have at least traced the source of the problem to the variables themselves, rather than the structure of the `if-else` statement. From there you will have to determine where and how the incorrect value was obtained.

3. Using nested `if` statements without including braces to indicate clearly the desired structure. Without braces, the compiler defaults to pairing `else`s with the closest unpaired `if`s, which sometimes destroys the original intent of the selection statement. To avoid this problem and to create code that is readily adaptable to change, it is useful to write all `if-else` statements as compound statements in the form

```
if (expression)
{
  one or more statements in here
}
else
{
  one or more statements in here
}
```

Using this form maintains the original integrity and intent of the `if` statement, no matter how many statements are added later.

4.6 Chapter Summary

1. Relational expressions, which are also called conditions, are used to compare operands. If a relational expression is true, the value of the expression is the integer 1. If the relational expression is false, it has an integer value of 0. Relational expressions are created by using the following relational operators:

Relational Operator	Meaning	Example
<	less than	`age < 30`
>	greater than	`height > 6.2`
<=	less than or equal to	`taxable <= 20000`
>=	greater than or equal to	`temp >= 98.6`
==	equal to	`grade == 100`
!=	not equal to	`number != 250`

2. More complex conditions can be constructed from relational expressions by using C++'s logical operators, `&&` (AND), `||` (OR), and `!` (NOT).
3. `if-else` statements are used to select between two alternative statements on the basis of the value of an expression. Although relational expressions are generally used for the tested expression, any valid expression can be used. In testing an expression, `if-else` statements interpret a nonzero value as true and a zero value as false. The most common form of an `if-else` statement is

```
if (expression)
  statement1;
else
  statement2;
```

   This is a two-way selection statement. If the expression has a nonzero value, it is considered as true, and `statement1` is executed; otherwise, `statement2` is executed.
4. `if-else` statements can contain other `if-else` statements. In the absence of braces, each `else` is associated with the closest unpaired `if`.
5. The `if-else` chain is a multiway selection statement that has the general form

```
if (expression_1)
  statement_1;
else if (expression_2)
  statement_2;
else if (expression_3)
  statement_3;
         .
         .
         .
else if (expression_m)
  statement_m;
else
  statement_n;
```

   The expressions are evaluated in the order in which they appear in the chain. Once an expression is true (has a nonzero value), only the statement between that expression and the next `else if` or `else` is executed, and no further expressions are tested. The final `else` is optional, and the statement corresponding to the final `else` is executed only if none of the previous expressions were true.

6. A compound statement consists of any number of individual statements enclosed within the brace pair { and }. Compound statements are treated as a single block and can be used anywhere a single statement is called for.
7. Variables have meaning only within the block where they are declared, which includes any inner blocks contained within the declaring block.
8. The `switch` statement is a multiway selection statement. The general form of a `switch` statement is

```
switch (expression)
{                              // start of compound statement
  case value_1: <----------------- terminated with a colon
    statement1;
    statement2;
        .
        .
        .
    break;
  case value_2: <----------------- terminated with a colon
    statementm;
    statementn;
        .
        .
        .
    break;
        .
        .
        .
  case value_n: <----------------- terminated with a colon
    statementw;
    statementx;
        .
        .
        .
    break;
  default: <---------------------- terminated with a colon
    statement_aa;
    statement_bb;
        .
        .
        .
}                    // end of switch and compound statement
```

For this statement, the value of an integer expression is compared to a number of integer or character constants or constant expressions. Program execution is transferred to the first matching `case` and continues through the end of the `switch` statement unless an optional `break` statement is encountered. `case`s in a `switch` statement can appear in any order, and an optional `default case` can be included. The `default` is executed if none of the other `case`s is matched.

4.7 Chapter Supplement: Errors, Testing, and Debugging

The ideal in programming is to produce readable, error-free programs that work correctly and that can be modified or changed with a minimum of testing required for reverification. In this regard, it is useful to know the different types of errors that can occur, when they are detected, and how to correct them.

Compile-Time and Run-Time Errors

A program error can be detected at a variety of times:

1. Before a program is compiled
2. While the program is being compiled
3. While the program is being run
4. After the program has been executed and the output is being examined
5. Not at all

Errors detected by the compiler are formally referred to as *compile-time errors,* and errors that occur while the program is being run are formally referred to as *run-time errors.*

Methods are available for detecting errors before a program is compiled and after it has been executed. The method for detecting errors after a program has been executed is called *program verification and testing*. The method for detecting errors before a program is compiled is called *desk checking.* Desk checking refers to the procedure of checking a program, by hand at a desk or table, for syntax and logic errors, which are described next.

Syntax and Logic Errors

Computer literature distinguishes between two primary types of errors, syntax errors and logic errors. A *syntax error* is an error in the structure or spelling of a statement. For example, the statements

```
if (a lt b
{
 cout << "There are five syntax errors here\n
  cout << " Can you find tem;
}
```

contain five syntax errors:

1. The relational operator in the first line is incorrect; it should be the symbol <.
2. The closing parenthesis is missing in the first line.
3. The object name `cout` is misspelled in the third line.
4. The third line is missing the terminating semicolon.
5. The string in the fourth line is not terminated with double quote marks.

All of these errors will be detected by the compiler when the program is compiled. This is true of all syntax errors. Because they violate the basic rules of C++, if they are not discovered by desk checking, the compiler will detect them and display an error message indicating that a syntax error exists.[5] In some cases, the error message is extremely clear and the error is obvious; in other cases, it takes a little detective work to understand the error message displayed by the compiler. All syntax errors are detected at compile time, so the terms *compile-time error* and *syntax error* are often used interchangeably. Strictly speaking, however, *compile-time* refers to when the error was detected and *syntax* refers to the type of error detected. Note that the misspelling of the word `tem` in the second `cout` statement is not a syntax error. Although this spelling error will result in an undesirable output line being displayed, it is not a violation of C++'s syntactical rules. It is a simple case of a typographical error, commonly referred to as a "typo."

Logic errors are characterized by erroneous, unexpected, or unintentional errors that are a direct result of some flaw in the program's logic. These errors, which are never caught by the compiler, may be detected by desk checking, by program testing, by accident when a user obtains an obviously erroneous output, while the program is executing, or not at all. If the error is detected while the program is executing, a run-time error occurs that results in an error message being generated and/or in abnormal and premature termination of the program.

Logic errors may not be detected by the computer, so they are always more difficult to detect than syntax errors. If not detected by desk checking, a logic error will reveal itself in one of two predominant ways. In one instance, the program executes to completion but produces incorrect results. Logic errors of this type include

No output: This is caused either by omission of a `cout` statement or by a sequence of statements that inadvertently bypass a `cout` statement.

---

5 They may not, however, all be detected at the same time. Frequently, one syntax error "masks" another error, and the second error is detected only after the first error is corrected.

Unappealing or misaligned output: This is caused by an error in a `cout` statement.

Incorrect numerical results: This is caused by incorrect values assigned to the variables used in an expression, by the use of an incorrect arithmetic expression, by the omission of a statement, by roundoff error, or by the use of an improper sequence of statements.

See whether you can detect the logic error in Program 4-7.

Program 4-7

```
#include <iostream.h>
#include <iomanip.h>
#include <math.h>

int main()  // a compound interest program
{
  float capital, amount, rate, nyrs;

  cout << "This program calculates the amount of money\n"
       << "in a bank account for an initial deposit\n"
       << "invested for n years at an interest rate r.\n\n"
       << "Enter the initial amount in the account: ";
  cin  >> amount;
  cout << "Enter the number of years: ";
  cin  >> nyrs;
  capital = amount * pow((1 + rate/100.0), nyrs);

    // set output formats
  cout << setiosflags(ios::fixed)
       << setiosflags(ios::showpoint)
       << setprecision(2);

  cout << "\nThe final amount of money is "
       << setw(8) << '$' << capital << endl;

  return 0;
}
```

A sample run of Program 4-7 follows.

```
This program calculates the amount of money
in a bank account for an initial deposit
invested for n years at an interest rate r.

Enter the initial amount in the account: 1000.
Enter the number of years: 5

The final amount of money is $ 1000.00
```

As indicated in the output, the final amount of money is identical to the initial amount that was input. Did you spot the error in Program 4-7 that produced this apparently erroneous output?

Unlike a misspelled output message, the error in Program 4-7 causes a mistake in a computation. Here, the error is that the program does not initialize the variable `rate` before this variable is used in the calculation of `capital`. When the assignment statement that calculates `capital` is executed, the program uses whatever value is stored in `rate`. On those systems that initialize all variables to zero, the value zero will be used for `rate`. However, on those systems that do not initialize all variables to zero, the program will use whatever "garbage" value happens to occupy the storage locations that correspond to the variable `rate`. (The manuals supplied with your compiler will indicate which of these two actions your compiler takes). In either case, an error is produced.

Although the logic error in this example program did not cause premature termination of the program, this type of faulty or incomplete program logic can cause run-time error. Attempts to divide by zero and attempts to take the square root of a negative number are examples of logic errors that will cause premature run-time program termination.

Testing and Debugging

In theory, a comprehensive set of test runs would reveal all logic errors and ensure that a program will work correctly for any and all combinations of input and computed data. In practice, this requires checking all possible combinations of statement executions. Because of the time and effort required, that is impossible for all but extremely simple programs. Let us see why this is so. Consider Program 4-8.

Program 4-8 has two paths that can be traversed from when the program is run to when the program reaches its closing brace. The first path, which is executed when the input number is 5, is in the sequence

```
cout << "Enter a number: ";
cin  >> num;
cout << "Bingo!" << endl;
```

Program 4-8

```
#include <iostream.h>

int main()
{
  int num;

  cout << "Enter a number: ";
  cin  >> num;

  if (num == 5)
    cout << "Bingo!" << endl;
  else
    cout << "Bongo!" << endl;

  return 0;
}
```

The second path, which is executed whenever any number except 5 is input, includes the sequence of instructions

```
cout << "Enter a number: ";
cin  >> num;
cout << "Bongo!" << endl;
```

To test each possible path through Program 4-8 requires two runs of the program, with a judicious selection of test input data to ensure that both paths of the `if` statement are exercised. The addition of one more `if` statement in the program increases the number of possible execution paths by a factor of 2 and requires four (2^2) runs of the program for complete testing. Similarly, two additional `if` statements increase the number of paths by a factor of 4 and require eight (2^3) runs for complete testing, and three additional `if` statements produce a program that requires sixteen (2^4) test runs.

Now consider a modest-size application program consisting of only ten modules, each module containing five `if` statements. Assuming that the modules are always called in the same sequence, there are 32 possible paths through each module (2 raised to the fifth power) and more than 1,000,000,000,000,000 (2 raised to the 50th power) possible paths through the complete program (all modules executed in sequence). The time needed to create individual test data to exercise each path and the actual computer run time required to check each path make the complete testing of such a program impossible.

Our inability to test fully all combinations of statement execution sequences has led to the programming proverb "There is no error-free program." It has also led to the realization that any testing that is done should be well thought out to maximize the chances of locating errors. An important corollary is that although a single test can reveal the presence of an error, it cannot verify the absence of an error. The fact that one error is revealed by testing does not ensure that no other error is lurking somewhere else in the program. And the fact that one test revealed no errors does not indicate that there really are none.

Once an error is discovered, however, the programmer must locate where the error occurs and then fix it. In computer jargon, a program error is referred to as a *bug*, and the process of isolating, correcting, and verifying the correction is called *debugging*.[6]

Although there are no hard-and-fast rules for isolating the cause of an error, some useful techniques can be applied. The first of these is a preventive technique. Many errors are introduced when a programmer rushes to code and run a program before fully understanding what is required and how the result is to be achieved. A symptom of this haste to get a program entered into the computer is the lack of an outline of the proposed program (pseudocode or flowcharts) or a handwritten program itself. Many errors can be eliminated simply by checking a copy of the program before it is ever entered or compiled—by *desk checking* the program. A second useful technique is to mimic the computer and execute each statement by hand, as the computer would. This means writing down each variable as it is encountered in the program and listing the value that should be stored in the variable as each input and assignment statement is encountered. Doing this also sharpens your programming skills, because it requires that you fully understand what each statement in your program causes to happen. Such a check is called *program tracing*.

A third and very powerful debugging technique is to use the `cout` object stream to display the values of selected variables. For example, again consider Program 4-7. Because this program produced an incorrect value for `capital`, it is worthwhile to place a `cout` statement immediately before the assignment statement for `capital` to display the value of all variables used in the computation. If the displayed values are correct, then the problem is in the assignment statement; if the values are incorrect, then we must determine where the incorrect values were actually obtained.

6 The derivation of this term is rather interesting. When a program stopped running on the MARK I computer at Harvard University in September 1945, the malfunction was traced to a dead insect that had gotten into the electrical circuits. The programmer, Grace Hopper, recorded the incident in her logbook as ". . . First actual case of bug being found."

Another use of the `cout` object stream in debugging is to display the values of all input data immediately. This technique, referred to as *echo printing,* is useful in establishing that the program is correctly receiving and interpreting the input data.

The most powerful of all debugging and tracing techniques is to use a program called a debugger. The debugger program controls the execution of a C++ program, can interrupt the C++ program at any point in its execution, and can display the values of all variables at the point of interruption.

Finally, no discussion of debugging is complete without mention of the primary ingredient needed for successful isolation and correction of errors. This is the attitude and spirit you bring to the task. You wrote the program, so you naturally assume that it is correct or you would have changed it before it was compiled. It is extremely difficult to back away and honestly test for, and find, errors in your own software. As a programmer, you must constantly remind yourself that merely being confident that your program is correct does not make it so. Finding errors in your own programs is a sobering experience, but one that will help you become a master programmer. It can also be exciting and fun if approached as a detection problem with you as the master detective.

Repetition

Chapter Five

The programs examined so far have been useful in illustrating the correct structure of C++ programs and in introducing fundamental C++ input, output, assignment, and selection capabilities. By now you should have gained enough experience to be comfortable with the concepts and mechanics of the C++ programming process. It is time to move up a level in our knowledge and abilities.

The real power of most computer programs resides in their ability to repeat the same calculation or sequence of instructions over and over, each time using different data, without the necessity of rerunning the program for each new set of data values. In this chapter we explore the C++ statements that make this possible. These statements are the `while`, `for`, and `do-while` statements.

5.1 The while Statement

The `while` statement is a general repetition statement that can be used in a variety of programming situations. The general form of the `while` statement is

```
while (expression)
  statement;
```

The expression contained within the parentheses is evaluated in exactly the same manner as an expression contained in an `if-else` statement; the difference is how the expression is used. As we have seen, when the expression is true (has a nonzero value) in an `if-else` statement, the statement following the expression is executed once. In a `while` statement, the statement following the expression is executed repeatedly as long as the expression retains a nonzero value. This naturally means that somewhere in the `while` statement there must be a statement that alters the value of the tested expression. As we will see, this is indeed the case. For now, however, when we consider just the expression and the statement following the parentheses, the process used by the computer in evaluating a `while` statement is

1. test the expression
2. `if` the expression has a nonzero (true) value
  ***a.* execute the statement following the parentheses**
  ***b.* go back to step 1**
 `else`
  exit the `while` statement

Note that step 2b forces program control to be transferred back to step 1. This transfer of control back to the start of a `while` statement in order to reevaluate the expression is what forms the program loop. The `while` statement literally loops back on itself to recheck the expression until it evaluates to zero (becomes false). This naturally means that somewhere in the loop, provision must be made for the value of the tested expression to be altered. As we will see, this is indeed the case.

This looping process produced by a `while` statement is illustrated in Figure 5–1. A diamond shape is used to show the entry and exit points required in the decision part of the `while` statement.

To make this a little more tangible, consider the relational expression `count <= 10` and the statement `cout << count;`. Using these, we can write the following valid `while` statement:

```
while (count <= 10)
  cout << count;
```

FIGURE 5–1 Anatomy of a `while` Loop

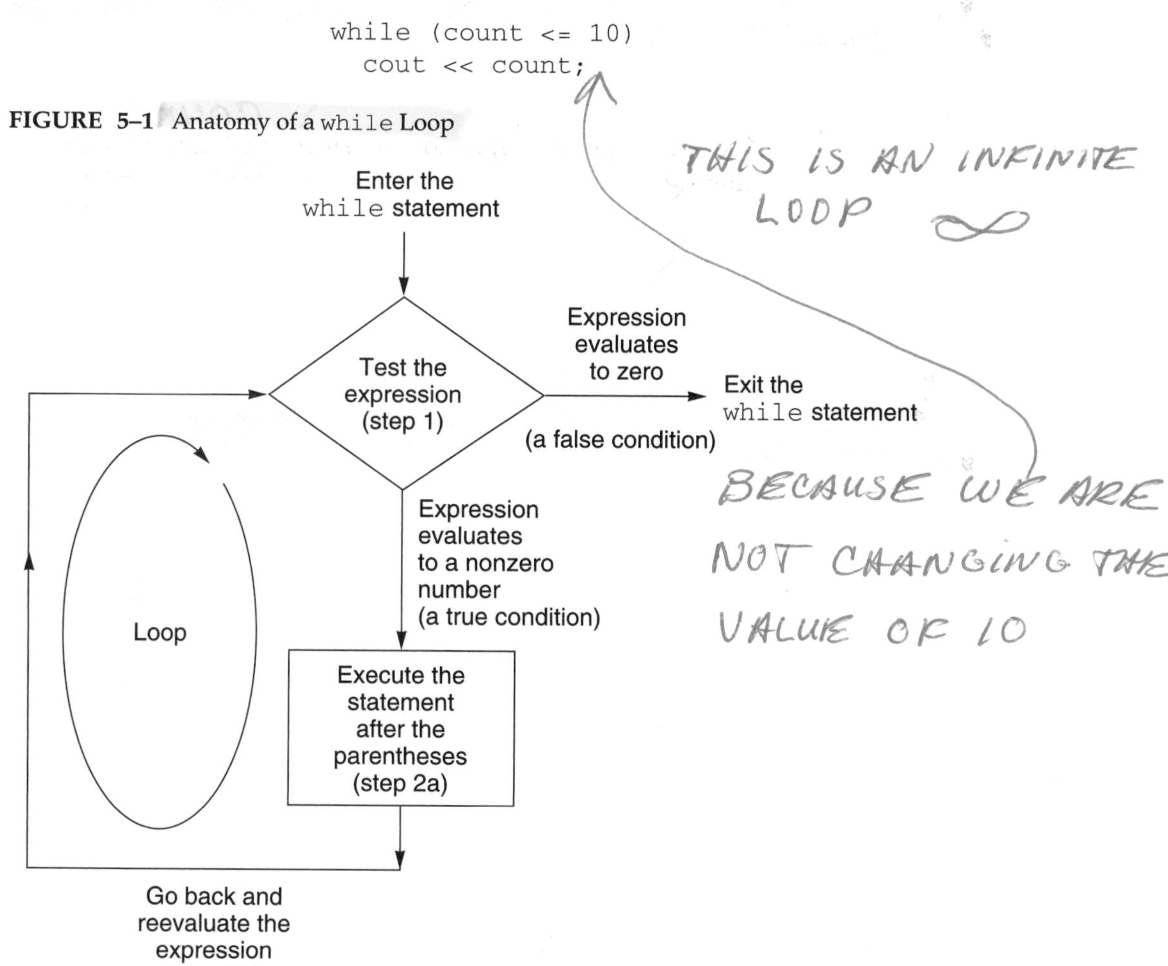

Although this statement is valid, the alert reader will realize that we have created a situation in which the cout object either is called forever (or until we stop the program) or is not called at all. Let us see why this happens.

If count has a value less than or equal to 10 when the expression is first evaluated, a call to cout is made. The while statement then automatically loops back on itself and retests the expression. Because we have not changed the value stored in count, the expression is still true and another call to cout is made. This process continues forever, or until the program containing this statement is prematurely stopped by the user. However, if count starts with a value greater than 10, the expression is false to begin with and the cout object call is never made.

How do we set an initial value in count to control what the while statement does the first time the expression is evaluated? The answer, of course, is to assign values to each variable in the tested expression before the while statement is encountered. For example, the following sequence of instructions is valid:

```
count = 1;
while (count <= 10)
  cout << count;
```

Using this sequence of instructions, we have ensured that count starts with a value of 1. We could assign any value to count in the assignment statement—the important thing is to assign *some* value. In practice, the assigned value depends on the application.

We must still change the value of count so that we can finally exit the while statement. To do this requires an expression such as count++ to increment the value of count each time the while statement is executed. The fact that a while statement provides for the repetition of a single statement does not prevent us from including an additional statement to change the value of count. All we have to do is replace the single statement with a compound statement. Here is an example:

```
count = 1;                  // initialize count
while (count <= 10)
{
  cout << count;
  count++;                  // increment count
}
```

Note that, for clarity, we have placed each statement in the compound statement on a separate line. This is consistent with the convention adopted for compound statements in the last chapter. Let us now analyze the foregoing sequence of instructions.

The first assignment statement sets `count` equal to 1. The `while` statement is then entered, and the expression is evaluated for the first time. The value of `count` is less than or equal to 10, so the expression is true and the compound statement is executed. The first statement in the compound statement is a call to the `cout` object to display the value of `count`. The next statement adds 1 to the value currently stored in `count`, making this value equal to 2. The `while` statement now loops back to retest the expression. Because `count` is still less than or equal to 10, the compound statement is executed again. This process continues until the value of `count` reaches 11. Program 5-1 illustrates these statements in an actual program.

Program 5-1

```
#include <iostream.h>

int main()
{
  int count;

  count = 1;                 // initialize count
  while (count <= 10)
  {
    cout << count << "   ";
    count++;                 // increment count
  }

  return 0;
}
```

The output produced by Program 5-1 is

```
1  2  3  4  5  6  7  8  9  10
```

There is nothing special about the name `count` used in Program 5-1. Any valid integer variable could have been used.

Before we consider other examples of the `while` statement, two comments concerning Program 5-1 are in order. First, the statement `count++` can be replaced with any statement that changes the value of `count`. A statement such as `count = count + 2`, for example, would cause every second integer to be displayed. Second, it is the programmer's responsibility to ensure that `count` is changed in a way that ultimately leads to a normal exit from the `while`. For example, if we replace the expression `count++` with the expression `count--`, the value of `count` will never reach 10, and an infinite loop will be created. An *infinite loop* is a loop that never ends. The computer will not tap you on the shoulder and say, "Excuse me, you have created an infinite loop." It just keeps displaying numbers until you realize that the program is not working as you expected.

Now that you have some familiarity with the `while` statement, see whether you can read and determine the output of Program 5-2.

Program 5-2

```
#include <iostream.h>

int main()
{
  int i;

  i = 10;
  while (i >= 1)
  {
    cout << i << "  ";
    i--;              // subtract 1 from i
  }

  return 0;
}
```

The assignment statement in Program 5-2 initially sets the `int` variable `i` to 10. The `while` statement then checks whether the value of `i` is greater than or equal to 1. While the expression is true, the value of `i` is displayed by the `cout` object and the value of `i` is decremented by 1. When `i` finally reaches zero, the expression is false and the program exits the `while` statement. Thus the following display is obtained when Program 5-2 is run:

```
10  9  8  7  6  5  4  3  2  1
```

To illustrate the power of the `while` statement, consider the task of printing a table of numbers from 1 to 10 with their squares and cubes. This can be done with a simple `while` statement, as illustrated by Program 5-3.

Program 5-3

```
#include <iostream.h>
#include <iomanip.h>

int main()
{
  int num;

  cout << "NUMBER    SQUARE    CUBE\n"
       << "------    ------    ----\n";

  num = 1;
  while (num < 11)
  {
    cout << setw(3) << num << "        "
         << setw(3) << num * num       << "       "
         << setw(4) << num * num * num << endl";
    num++;    // increment num
  }

  return 0;
}
```

When Program 5-3 is run, the following display is produced:

```
NUMBER    SQUARE    CUBE
------    ------    ----
     1         1       1
     2         4       8
     3         9      27
     4        16      64
     5        25     125
     6        36     216
     7        49     343
     8        64     512
     9        81     729
    10       100    1000
```

Note that the expression used in Program 5-3 is `num < 11`. For the integer variable `num`, this expression is exactly equivalent to the expression `num <= 10`. The choice of which to use is entirely up to you.

If we want to use Program 5-3 to produce a table of 1000 numbers, all we do is change the expression in the `while` statement from `i < 11` to `i < 1001`. Changing the 11 to 1001 produces a table of 1000 lines—not bad for a simple five-line `while` statement.

All the program examples illustrating the `while` statement are examples of fixed-count loops, because the tested condition is a counter that checks for a fixed number of repetitions. A variation on the fixed-count loop can be made where the counter is not incremented by 1 each time through the loop but is incremented by some other value. For example, consider the task of producing a Celsius-to-Fahrenheit temperature-conversion table. Assume that Fahrenheit temperatures corresponding to Celsius temperatures ranging from 5 to 50 degrees are to be displayed in increments of 5 degrees. The desired display can be obtained with the following series of statements:

```
celsius = 5;      // starting Celsius value
while (celsius <= 50)
{
  fahren = (9.0/5.0) * celsius + 32.0;
  cout << celsius
       << fahren;
  celsius = celsius + 5;
}
```

As before, the `while` statement consists of everything from the word `while` through the closing brace of the compound statement. Prior to entering the `while` loop, we have made sure to assign a value to the counter being evaluated, and there is a statement to alter the value of the counter within the loop (in increments of 5) to ensure an exit from the `while` loop. Program 5-4 illustrates the use of this code in a complete program.

The display obtained when Program 5-4 is executed is

```
DEGREES    DEGREES
CELSIUS   FAHRENHEIT
-------   ----------
   5        41.00
  10        50.00
  15        59.00
  20        68.00
  25        77.00
  30        86.00
  35        95.00
  40       104.00
  45       113.00
  50       122.00
```

Program 5-4

```
#include <iostream.h>
#include <iomanip.h>

// a program to convert Celsius to Fahrenheit
int main()
{

  const int MAXCELSIUS = 50;
  const int STARTVAL = 5;
  const int STEPSIZE = 5;
  int celsius;
  float fahren;

  cout << "DEGREES   DEGREES\n"
       << "CELSIUS  FAHRENHEIT\n"
       << "-------  ----------\n";

  celsius = STARTVAL;

    // set output formats for floating point numbers only
  cout << setiosflags(ios::showpoint)
       << setprecision(2);

  while (celsius <= MAXCELSIUS)
{
   fahren = (9.0/5.0) * celsius + 32.0;
    cout << setw(4) << celsius
         << setw(13) << fahren << endl;
    celsius = celsius + STEPSIZE;
  }

  return 0;
}
```

Exercises 5.1

1. Rewrite Program 5-1 to print the numbers 2 to 10 in increments of 2. The output of your program should be

```
2  4  6  8  10
```

2. Rewrite Program 5-4 to produce a table that starts at a Celsius value of –10 and ends with a Celsius value of 60, in increments of 10 degrees.

3. *a.* For the following program, determine the total number of items displayed. Also, determine the first and last numbers printed.

```
#include <iostream.h>

int main()
{
  int num = 0;

  while (num <= 20)
  {
    num++;
    cout << num << "  ";
  }

  return 0;
}
```

b. Enter and run the program from Exercise 3a on a computer to verify your answers to the exercise.

c. How would the output be affected if the two statements within the compound statement were reversed (that is, if the `cout` call were made before the `num++` statement)?

4. Write a C++ program that converts gallons to liters. The program should display gallons from 10 to 20 in 1-gallon increments and the corresponding liter equivalents. Use the relationship that 1 gallon of liquid is equivalent to 3.785 liters.

5. Write a C++ program that converts feet to meters. The program should display feet from 3 to 30 in 3-foot increments and the corresponding meter equivalents. Use the relationship that there are 3.28 feet to a meter.

6. A machine purchased for $28,000 is depreciated at a rate of $4,000 a year for 7 years. Write and run a C++ program that computes and displays a depreciation table for 7 years. The table should have the form

```
                                 END-OF-YEAR      ACCUMULATED
YEAR        DEPRECIATION            VALUE         DEPRECIATION
----        ------------         -----------      ------------
 1              4000                24000              4000
 2              4000                20000              8000
 3              4000                16000             12000
 4              4000                12000             16000
 5              4000                 8000             20000
 6              4000                 4000             24000
 7              4000                    0             28000
```

7. An automobile travels at an average speed of 55 miles per hour for 4 hours. Write a C++ program that displays the distance, in miles, that the car has traveled after 0.5, 1.0, 1.5, etc., hours until the end of the trip.

5.2 cin within a while Loop

Combining interactive data entry with the repetition capabilities of the while statement produces very adaptable and powerful programs. To understand the concept involved, consider Program 5-5, where a while statement is used to accept and then display four user-entered numbers, one at a time. Although it employs a very simple idea, the program highlights the flow-of-control concepts needed to produce more useful programs.

Program 5-5

```
#include <iostream.h>
#include <iomanip.h>

int main()
{
  const int MAXNUMS = 4;
  int count;
  float num;

  cout << "\nThis program will ask you to enter "
       << MAXNUMS << " numbers.\n";
  count = 1;

  while (count <= MAXNUMS)
  {
    cout << "\nEnter a number: ";
    cin  >> num;
    cout << "The number entered is " << num;
    count++;
  }
  cout << endl;

  return 0;
}
```

The following is a sample run of Program 5-5. The italicized items were input in response to the appropriate prompts.

```
This program will ask you to enter 4 numbers.

Enter a number: 26.2
The number entered is 26.2
Enter a number: 5
The number entered is 5
Enter a number: 103.456
The number entered is 103.456
Enter a number: 1267.89
The number entered is 1267.89
```

OBJECT

Let us review the program so that we clearly understand how the output was produced. The first message displayed is caused by execution of the first `cout` object call. This call is outside and before the `while` statement, so it is executed once before any statement in the `while` loop.

Once the `while` loop is entered, the statements within the compound statement are executed while the tested condition is true. The first time through the compound statement, the message `Enter a number:` is displayed. The program then calls `cin`, which forces the computer to wait for a number to be entered at the keyboard. Once a number is typed and the Return or Enter key is pressed, the `cout` object displays the number. The variable `count` is then incremented by 1. This process continues until four passes through the loop have been made and the value of `count` is 5. Each pass causes the message `Enter a number:` to be displayed, one call to `cin` to be made, and the message `The number entered is` to be displayed. Figure 5–2 illustrates this flow of control.

Rather than simply displaying the entered numbers, Program 5-5 can be modified to use the entered data. For example, let us add the numbers entered and display the total. To do this, we must be very careful about how we add the numbers. Because the same variable, `num`, is used for each number entered, the entry of a new number in Program 5-5 automatically causes the previous number stored in `num` to be lost. Thus each number entered must be added to the total before another number is entered. The required sequence is

Enter a number
Add the number to the total

How do we add a single number to a total? A statement such as `total = total + num` does the job perfectly. This is the accumulating statement introduced in Section 3.1. After each number is entered, the accumulating statement adds the number into the total, as illustrated in Figure 5–3. The

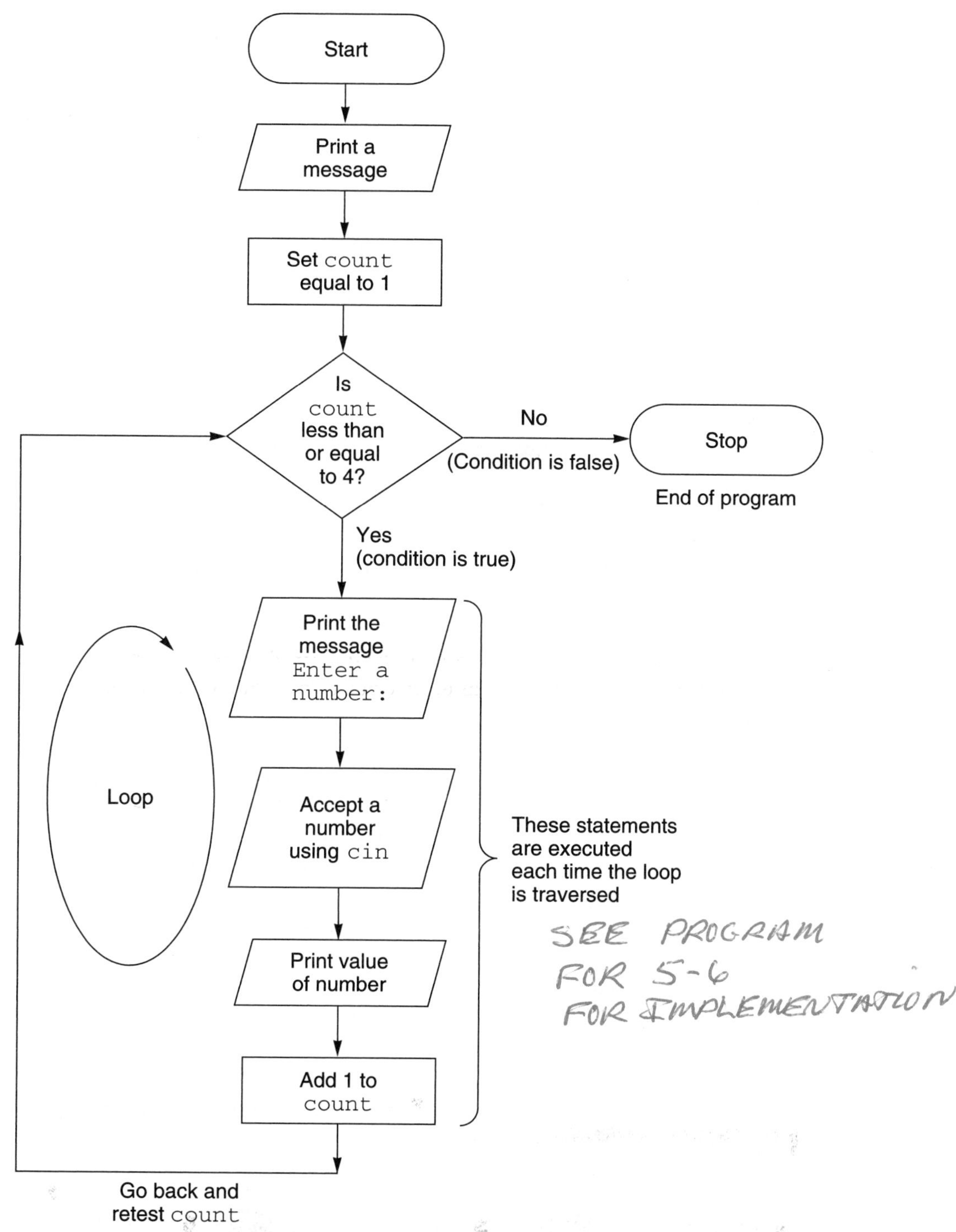

FIGURE 5–2 Flow-of-Control Diagram for Program 5-5

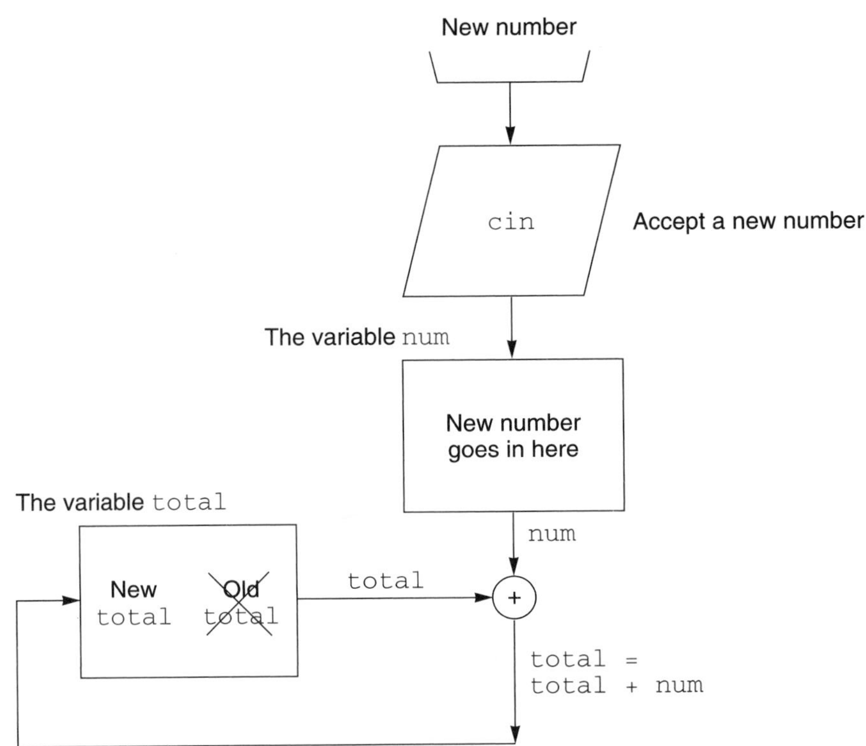

FIGURE 5–3 Accepting and Adding a Number to a Total

complete flow of control required for adding the numbers is illustrated in Figure 5–4.

In reviewing Figure 5–4, observe that we have made a provision for initially setting the total to zero before the `while` loop is entered. If we were to clear the total inside the `while` loop, it would be set to zero each time the loop was executed, and any value previously stored would be erased.

Program 5-6 incorporates the necessary modifications to Program 5-5 to total the numbers entered. As indicated in the flow diagram shown in Figure 5–4, the statement `total = total + num;` is placed immediately after the `cin` object statement. Putting the accumulating statement at this point in the program ensures that the entered number is immediately "captured" into the total.

Let us review Program 5-6. The variable `total` was created to store the total of the numbers entered. Prior to our entering the `while` statement, the value of `total` is set to zero. This ensures that any previous value present in the storage location(s) assigned to the variable `total` is erased. Within the `while` loop, the statement `total = total + num;` is used to add the value of the entered number into `total`. As each value is entered, it is added into the

VARIABLES ARE NAMES FOR DESIGNATED STORAGE LOCATIONS

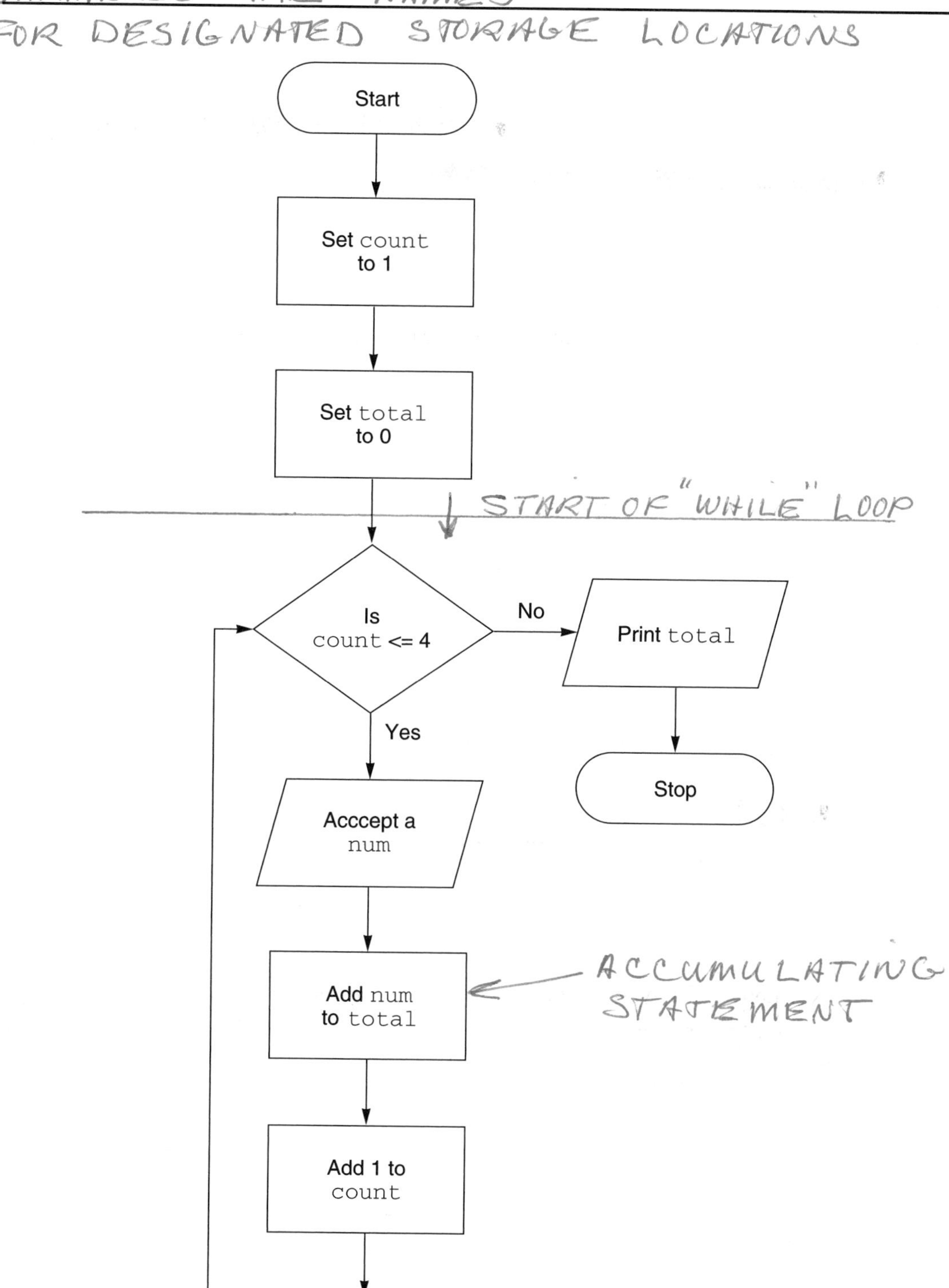

FIGURE 5–4 Accumulation Flow of Control

existing total to create a new total. Thus `total` becomes a running subtotal of all the values entered. Only when all numbers are entered does `total` contain the final sum of all the numbers. After the `while` loop is finished, the last `cout` object call is used to display this sum.

Program 5-6

```
#include <iostream.h>
#include <iomanip.h>

int main()
{
  const int MAXNUMS = 4;
  int count;
  float num, total;

  cout << "\nThis program will ask you to enter "
       << MAXNUMS << " numbers.\n";
  count = 1;
  total = 0;

  while (count <= MAXNUMS)
  {
    cout << "\nEnter a number:  ";
    cin  >> num;
    total = total + num;
    cout << "The total is now " << total;
    count++;
  }

  cout << "\nThe final total is " << total << endl;

  return 0;
}
```

We made the following sample run of Program 5-6 using the same data we entered in the sample run for Program 5-5.

```
This program will ask you to enter 4 numbers.

Enter a number: 26.2
The total is now 26.2
Enter a number: 5
The total is now 31.2
Enter a number: 103.456
The total is now 134.656
Enter a number: 1267.89
The total is now 1402.546

The final total is 1402.546
```

Having used an accumulating assignment statement to add the numbers entered, we can now go further and calculate the average of the numbers. Where do we calculate the average, within the while loop or outside of it?

In the case at hand, calculating an average requires that both a final sum and the number of items in that sum be available. The average is then computed by dividing the final sum by the number of items. Now we must ask, "At what point in the program is the correct sum available, and at what point is the number of items available?" In reviewing Program 5-6, we see that the correct sum needed for calculating the average is available after the while loop is finished. In fact, the whole purpose of the while loop is to ensure that the numbers are entered and added correctly to produce a correct sum. After the loop is finished, we also have a count of the number of items used in the sum. However, because of the way the while loop was constructed, the number in count (5) when the loop is finished is 1 more than the number of items (4) used to obtain the total. Knowing this, we simply subtract 1 from count before using it to determine the average. With this as background, see whether you can read and understand Program 5-7.

Program 5-7 is almost identical to Program 5-6, except for the calculation of the average. We have also removed the constant display of the total within and after the while loop. The loop in Program 5-7 is used to enter and add four numbers. Immediately after the loop is exited, the average is computed and displayed. A sample run of Program 5-7 follows.

```
This program will ask you to enter 4 numbers.

Enter a number: 26.2
Enter a number: 5
Enter a number: 103.456
Enter a number: 1267.89

The average of the numbers is 350.6365
```

Program 5-7

```
#include <iostream.h>
#include <iomanip.h>

int main()
{
  const int MAXNUMS = 4;
  int count;
  float num, total, average;

  cout << "\nThis program will ask you to enter "
       << MAXNUMS << " numbers.\n";
  count = 1;
  total = 0;

  while (count <= MAXNUMS)
  {
    cout << "Enter a number: ";
    cin  >> num;
    total = total + num;
    count++;
  }

  count--;
  average = total / count;
  cout << "The average of the numbers is " << average << endl;

  return 0;
}
```

Sentinels

All of the loops we have created thus far have been examples of fixed-count loops, where a counter has been used to control the number of loop iterations. By means of a `while` statement, variable-condition loops may also be constructed. For example, when entering grades, we may not want to count the number of grades that will be entered but may prefer to enter the grades continuously and, at the end, type in a special data value to signal the end of data input.

In computer programming, data values used to signal either the start or the end of a data series are called *sentinels.* The sentinel values must, of course, be selected so as not to conflict with legitimate data values. For example, if we were constructing a program to process a student's grades, and assuming that no extra credit is given that could produce a grade higher than 100, we could use any grade higher than 100 as a sentinel value. Program 5-8 illustrates this concept. In Program 5-8, data is continuously requested and accepted until a number larger than 100 is entered. Entry of a number higher than 100 alerts the program to exit the `while` loop and display the sum of the numbers entered.

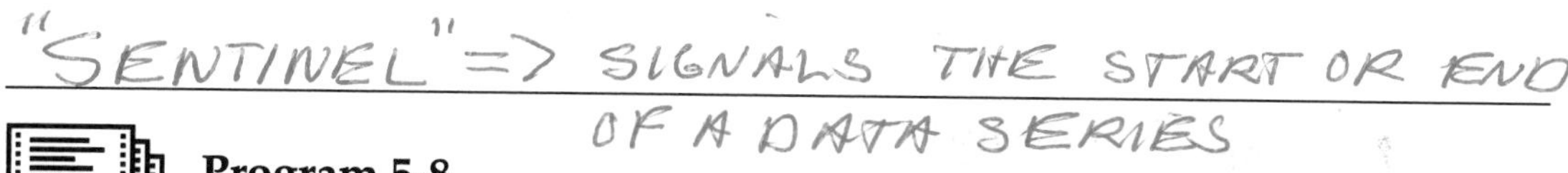

"SENTINEL" => SIGNALS THE START OR END
OF A DATA SERIES

Program 5-8

```
#include <iostream.h>

int main()
{
  const int HIGHGRADE = 100;
  float grade, total;

  grade = 0;
  total = 0;
  cout << "\nTo stop entering grades, type in any number";
  cout << "\n greater than 100.\n\n";

  while (grade <= HIGHGRADE)
  {
    total = total + grade;
    cout << "Enter a grade: ";
    cin  >> grade;
  }

  cout << "\nThe total of the grades is " << total << endl;

  return 0;
}
```

We show a sample run using Program 5-8 on the next page. As long as grades less than or equal to 100 are entered, the program continues to request and accept additional data. When a number less than or equal to 100 is entered, the program adds this number to the total. When a number greater than 100 is entered, the loop is exited and the sum of the grades that were entered is displayed.

```
To stop entering grades, type in any number
  greater than 100.

Enter a grade: 95
Enter a grade: 100
Enter a grade: 82
Enter a grade: 101

The total of the grades is 277
```

break and continue Statements

Two statements useful in connection with repetition statements are the `break` and `continue` statements. We have encountered the `break` statement in relation to the `switch` statement. The syntax of this statement is

```
break;
```

A `break` statement, as its name implies, forces an immediate break, or exit, from `switch`, `while`, and the `for` and `do-while` statements presented in the next sections.

For example, execution of the following `while` loop is immediately terminated if a number greater than 76 is entered.

```
while(count <= 10)
{
  cout << "Enter a number: ";
  cin  >> num;
  if (num > 76)
  {
    cout << "You lose!"\n;
    break;        // break out of the loop
  }
  else
    cout << "Keep on truckin!\n";
  count++;
}
// break jumps to here
```

The `break` statement violates pure structured programming principles because it provides a second, nonstandard exit from a loop. Nevertheless, the `break` statement is extremely useful and valuable for breaking out of loops when an unusual condition is detected. The `break` statement is also used to exit from a `switch` statement, but this is because the desired case has been detected and processed.

BREAK STATEMENT WILL IMMEDIATELY END THE LOOP

The continue statement is similar to the break statement but applies only to loops created with while, do-while, and for statements. The general format of a continue statement is

```
continue;
```

When continue is encountered in a loop, the next iteration of the loop is immediately begun. For while loops, this means that execution is automatically transferred to the top of the loop, and reevaluation of the tested expression is initiated. Although the continue statement has no direct effect on a switch statement, it can be included within a switch statement that itself is contained in a loop. Here the effect of continue is the same: The next loop iteration is begun.

As a general rule, the continue statement is less useful than the break statement, but it is convenient for skipping over data that should not be processed while remaining in a loop. For example, invalid grades are simply ignored in the following section of code, and only valid grades are added to the total.[1]

```
while (count < 30)
{
  cout << "Enter a grade: ";
  cin  >> grade;
  if(grade < 0 || grade > 100)
    continue;
  total = total + grade;
  count++;
}
```

The Null Statement

All statements must be terminated by a semicolon. A semicolon with nothing preceding it is also a valid statement, called the *null statement.* Thus the statement

```
;
```

NULL STATEMENT

[1] Although this section of code is useful in illustrating the flow of control provided by the continue statement, it is not the preferred way of achieving the desired result. Rather than using an if and a continue statement to *exclude* invalid data, a better method is to include valid data using the statement

```
if (grade >= 0 && grade <= 100)
{
  total = total + grade;
  count++;
}
```

is a null statement. This is a do-nothing statement that is used where a statement is syntactically required but no action is called for. Null statements typically are used with either `while` or `for` statements. An example of a `for` statement that uses a null statement is found in Program 5-9c in the next section.

Exercises 5.2

1. Rewrite Program 5-6 to compute the total of eight numbers.

2. Rewrite Program 5-6 to display the prompt

```
Please type in the total number of data values to be added:
```

In response to this prompt, the program should accept a user-entered number and then use this number to control the number of times the `while` loop is executed. Thus, if the user enters `5` in response to the prompt, the program should request the input of five numbers and display the total after five numbers have been entered.

3. ***a.*** Write a C++ program to convert Celsius degrees to Fahrenheit. The program should request the starting Celsius value, the number of conversions to be made, and the increment between Celsius values. The display should have appropriate headings and should list the Celsius value and the corresponding Fahrenheit value. Use the relationship *Fahrenheit = (9.0 / 5.0) * Celsius + 32.0.*

b. Run the program written in Exercise 3a on a computer. Verify that your program starts at the correct starting Celsius value and contains the exact number of conversions specified in your input data.

4. ***a.*** Modify the program written in Exercise 3 to request the starting Celsius value, the ending Celsius value, and the increment. Thus, instead of the condition checking for a fixed count, the condition will check for the ending Celsius value.

b. Run the program written in Exercise 4a on a computer. Verify that your output starts at the correct beginning value and ends at the correct ending value.

5. Rewrite Program 5-7 to compute the average of ten numbers.

6. Rewrite Program 5-7 to display the prompt

```
Please type in the total number of data values to be averaged:
```

In response to this prompt, the program should accept a user-entered number and then use this number to control the number of times the `while` loop is executed. Thus, if the user enters `6` in response to the prompt, the program should request the input of six numbers and display the average of the next six numbers entered.

7. By mistake, a programmer put the statement `average = total / count;` within the `while` loop immediately after the statement `total = total + num;` in Program 5-7. Thus the `while` loop became

```
while (count <= 4)
{
  cout << "\nEnter a number: ";
  cin  >> num;
  total = total + num;
  average = total / count;
  count++;
}
```

Will the program yield the correct result with this `while` loop? From a programming perspective, which `while` loop is better to use, and why?

8. a. Modify Program 5-8 to compute the average of the grades entered.

b. Run the program written in Exercise 8a on a computer and verify the results.

9. a. A bookstore summarizes its monthly transactions by keeping the following information for each book in stock:

Book identification number
Inventory balance at the beginning of the month
Number of copies received during the month
Number of copies sold during the month

Write a C++ program that accepts this data for each book and then displays the book identification number and an updated book inventory balance using the relationship

New balance = Inventory balance at the beginning of the month
+ Number of copies received during the month
– Number of copies sold during the month

Your program should use a `while` statement with a fixed-count condition so that information on only three books is requested.

b. Run the program written in Exercise 9a on a computer. Review the display produced by your program and verify that the output produced is correct.

10. Modify the program you wrote for Exercise 9 to keep requesting and displaying results until a sentinel identification value of 999 is entered. Run the program on a computer.

5.3 The for Statement

MOST IMPORTANT

The `for` statement performs the same functions as the `while` statement but uses a different form. In many situations, especially those with a fixed-count condition, the `for` statement format is easier to use than its `while` statement equivalent. The general form of the `for` statement is

```
for (initializing list; expression; altering list)
  statement;
```

Although the `for` statement looks a little complicated, it is really quite simple if we consider each of its parts separately. Within the parentheses of the `for` statement are three items separated by semicolons. Each of these items is optional and can be described individually, but the semicolons must be present. As we shall see, the items in parentheses correspond to the initialization, expression evaluation, and altering of expression values that we have already used with the `while` statement.

The middle item in the parentheses, the expression, is any valid C++ expression, and there is no difference in the way `for` and `while` statements use this expression. In both statements, as long as the expression has a nonzero (true) value, the statement following the parentheses is executed. This means that prior to the first check of the expression, initial values for the tested expression's variables must be assigned. It also means that before the expression is reevaluated there must be one or more statements that alter these values. Recall that the general placement of these statements using a `while` statement follows the pattern

```
initializing statements;
while (expression)
{
  loop statements;
        .
        .
        .
  expression-altering statements;
}
```

The need to initialize variables or make some other evaluations prior to entering a repetition loop is so common that the `for` statement allows all the initializing statements to be grouped together as the first set of items within the `for`'s parentheses. The items in this initializing list are executed only once, before the expression is evaluated for the first time.

The `for` statement also provides a single place for all expression-altering statements. These items can be placed in the altering list, which is the last list contained within the `for`'s parentheses. All items in the altering list are executed by the `for` statement at the end of the loop, just before the expression is reevaluated. Figure 5–5 shows the `for` statement's flow-of-control diagram.

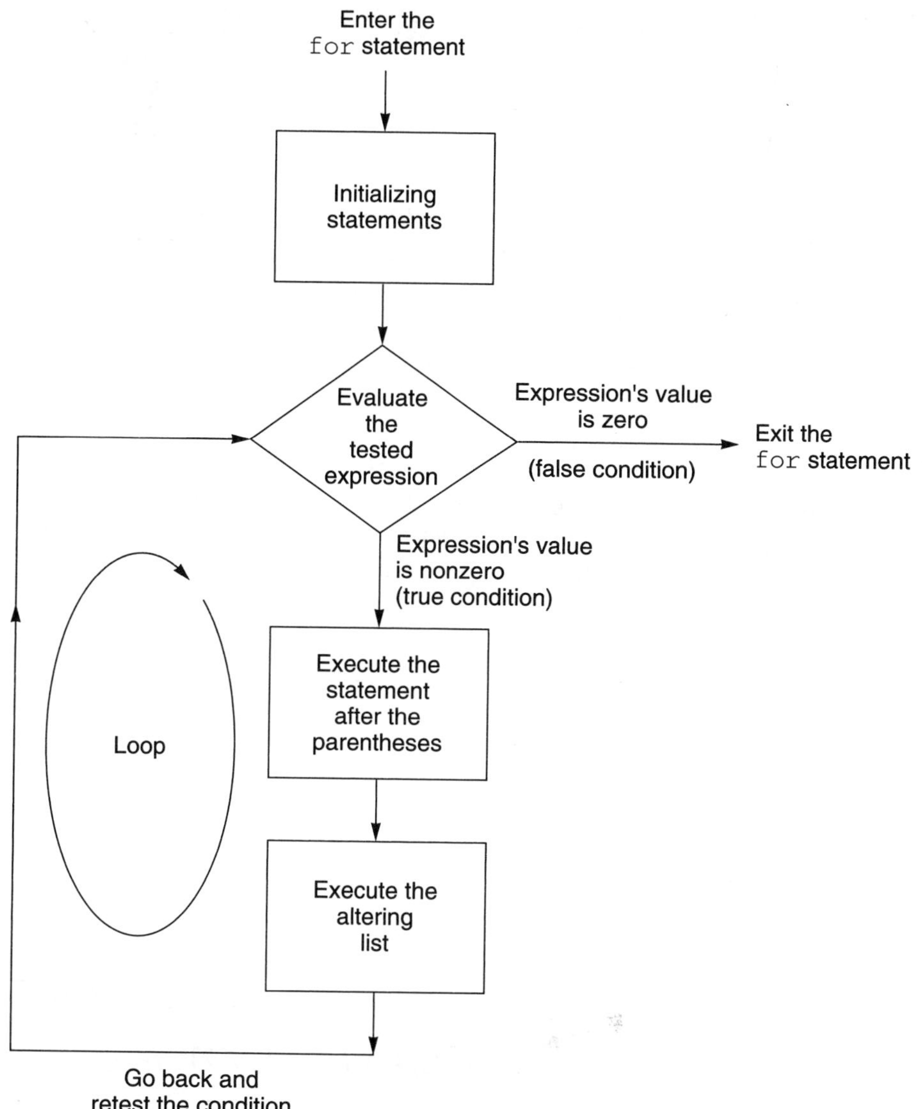

FIGURE 5–5 The `for` Statement's Flow of Control

The following section of code illustrates the correspondence between the `for` and `while` statements:

```
count = 1;
while (count <= 10)
{
  cout << count;
  count++;
}
```

WHILE STATEMENT

The for statement corresponding to this section of code is

```
for (count = 1; count <= 10; count++)
  cout << count;
```

As this example shows, the only difference between the for statement and the while statement is the placement of equivalent expressions. The grouping together of the initialization, expression test, and altering list in the for statement is very convenient, especially when they are used to create fixed-count loops. Consider the following for statement:

```
for (count = 2; count <= 20; count = count + 2)
  cout << count;
```

In this statement all the loop control information is contained within the parentheses. The loop starts with a count of 2, stops when the count exceeds 20, and increments the loop counter in steps of 2. Program 5-9 illustrates this for statement in an actual program. Two blanks are placed between output values for readability.

Program 5-9

```
#include <iostream.h>

int main()
{
  int count;

  for (count = 2; count <= 20; count = count + 2)
    cout << count << "  ";

  return 0;
}
```

The output of Program 5-9 is

```
2  4  6  8  10  12  14  16  18  20
```

The for statement does not require that any of the items in parentheses be present or that they be used for initializing or altering the values in the expression statements. However, the two semicolons must be present within the for's parentheses. For example, the construction for (; count <= 20 ;) is valid.

If the initializing list is missing, the initialization step is omitted when the `for` statement is executed. This, of course, means that the programmer must provide the required initializations before the `for` statement is encountered. Similarly, if the altering list is missing, any expressions needed to alter the evaluation of the tested expression must be included directly within the statement part of the loop. The `for` statement ensures only that all expressions in the initializing list are executed once, before evaluation of the tested expression, and that all expressions in the altering list are executed at the end of the loop before the tested expression is rechecked. Thus Program 5-9 can be rewritten in any of the three ways shown in Programs 5-9a, 5-9b, and 5-9c.

Program 5-9a

```
#include <iostream.h>

int main()
{
  int count;

  count = 2;     // initializer outside for statement
  for ( ; count <= 20; count = count + 2)
    cout << count << "   ";

  return 0;
}
```

Program 5-9b

```
#include <iostream.h>

int main()
{
  int count;

  count = 2;     // initializer outside for loop
  for( ; count <= 20; )
  {
    cout << count << "   ";
    count = count + 2;      // alteration statement
  }

  return 0;
}
```

Program 5-9c

```
#include <iostream.h>

int main()    // all expressions within the for's parentheses
{
  int count;

  for (count = 2; count <= 20; cout << count << "   ", count = count + 2);

  return 0;
}
```

In Program 5-9a, count is initialized outside the for statement, and the first list inside the parentheses is left blank. In Program 5-9b, both the initializing list and the altering list are removed from within the parentheses. Program 5-9b also uses a compound statement within the for loop, with the expression-altering statement included in the compound statement. Finally, Program 5-9c has included all items within the parentheses, so there is no need for any useful statement following the parentheses. Here the null statement satisfies the syntactical requirement of one statement to follow the for's parentheses. Observe also in Program 5-9c that the altering list (the last set of items in parentheses) consists of two items and that a comma has been used to separate these items. The use of commas to separate items in both the initializing list and the altering list is required if either of these two lists contains more than one item. Finally, note the fact that Programs 5-9a, 5-9b, and 5-9c are all inferior to Program 5-9. The for statement in Program 5-9 is much clearer, because all the expressions that pertain to the tested expression are grouped together within the parentheses.

Although the initializing and altering lists can be omitted from a for statement, omitting the tested expression results in an infinite loop. For example, such a loop is created by the statement

```
for (count = 2; ; count++)
  cout << count;
```

Like the while statement, both break and continue statements can be used within a for loop. The break forces an immediate exit from the for loop, as it does from the while loop. The continue, however, forces control to be passed to the altering list in a for statement, after which the tested expression is reevaluated. This differs from the action of a continue in a while

POINT OF INFORMATION

Where to Place the Opening Braces

Two styles of writing for loops are used by professional C++ programmers. These styles come into play only when the for loop contains a compound statement. The style illustrated and used in the text takes the form

```
for (expression)
{
  compound statement in here
}
```

An equally acceptable style that is used by many programmers places the initial brace of the compound statement on the first line. In this style, a for loop appears as

```
for (expression) {
  compound statement in here
}
```

The advantage of the first style is that the braces line up under one another, making it easier to locate brace pairs. The advantage of the second style is that it makes the code more compact and saves a line, permitting more code to be viewed in the same display area. Both styles are used, but they are almost never intermixed. As always, the indentation used within a compound statement (two or four spaces, or a tab) should also be consistent throughout all of your programs. If the choice is yours, select whichever style appeals to you and be consistent in its use. If a style is dictated by the company or course in which you are programming, find out what the style is and be consistent in following it.

statement, where control is passed directly to the reevaluation of the tested expression.

Finally, many programmers use the initializing list of a for statement to both declare and initialize the counter variable and any other variables used primarily within the for loop. For example, in the for statement

```
for(int count = 0; count < 10; count++)
  cout << count << endl;
```

the variable count is both declared and initialized from within the for statement. As always, having been declared, the variable count can now be used anywhere following its declaration within the body of the function that contains the declaration.

To understand the enormous power of the for statement, consider the task of printing a table of numbers from 1 to 10, including their squares and cubes, using this statement. In Program 5-3, we saw the use of a while statement to produce such a table. You may wish to review Program 5-3 and compare it to Program 5-10 to get a further sense of the equivalence between the `for` and `while` statements.

Program 5-10

```
#include <iostream.h>
#include <iomanip.h>

int main()
{
  const int MAXNUMS = 10;
  int num;

  cout << "NUMBER    SQUARE    CUBE\n"
       << "------    ------    ----\n";

  for (num = 1; num <= MAXNUMS; num++)
    cout << setw(3) << num << "         "
         << setw(3) << num * num << "       "
         << setw(4) << num * num * num << endl;

  return 0;
}
```

When Program 5-10 is run, the display produced is

```
NUMBER    SQUARE    CUBE
------    ------    ----
  1          1         1
  2          4         8
  3          9        27
  4         16        64
  5         25       125
  6         36       216
  7         49       343
  8         64       512
  9         81       729
 10        100      1000
```

Simply changing the number 10 in the `for` statement of Program 5-10 to 100 creates a loop that is executed 100 times and produces a table of numbers from 1 to 100. As with the `while` statement, this small change produces an immense increase in the processing and output provided by the program. Note also that the expression `num++` was used in the altering list in place of the equivalent `num = num + 1`.

`cin` within a `for` Loop

Using the `cin` object inside a `for` loop produces the same effect as using this object within a `while` loop. For example, in Program 5-11 a `cin` object is used to input a set of numbers. As each number is input, it is added to a total. When the `for` loop is exited, the average is calculated and displayed.

Program 5-11

```
#include <iostream.h>

// This program calculates the average
// of MAXCOUNT user-entered numbers
int main()
{
  const int MAXCOUNT = 5;
  int count;
  float num, total, average;

  total = 0.0;

  for (count = 0; count < 5; count++)
  {
    cout << "Enter a number: ";
    cin  >> num;
    total = total + num;
  }

  average = total / count;
  cout << "The average of the data entered is " << average << endl;

  return 0;
}
```

POINT OF INFORMATION

Do You Use a `for` or a `while` Loop?

Beginning programmers often ask whether they should use a `for` or a `while` loop. This is a good question, because both of these loop structures are pretest loops that, in C++, can be used to construct both fixed-count and variable-condition loops.

In nearly all other computer languages, including Visual Basic and Pascal, the answer is relatively straightforward because the `for` statement can be used only to construct fixed-count loops. Thus, in these languages, `for` statements are used to construct fixed-count loops and `while` statements are generally used only to construct variable-condition loops.

In C++, this easy distinction does not hold, inasmuch as each statement can be used to create each type of loop. The answer in C++, then, is that it's really a matter of style. Because `for` loops and `while` loops are interchangeable in C++, either loop is appropriate. Some professional programmers always use a `for` statement for every pretest loop they create and almost never use a `while` statement; others always use a `while` statement and rarely use a `for` statement. A third group tends to retain the convention used in other languages: A `for` loop is generally used to create fixed-count loops, and a `while` loop is used to create variable-condition loops. In C++ it is a matter of preference, and you will encounter all three styles in your programming career.

The `for` statement in Program 5-11 creates a loop that is executed five times. The user is prompted to enter a number each time through the loop. After each number is entered, it is immediately added to the total. Although `total` was initialized to zero before the `for` statement, this initialization could have been included with the initialization of `count`, as follows:

```
for (total = 0.0, count = 0; count < 5; count++)
```

Additionally, the declarations for both `total` and `count` could have been included with their initializations from within the initializing list, as follows:

```
for (float total = 0.0, int count = 0; count < 5; count++)
```

Any one of these `for` constructs represents good programming practice. Which one you choose is simply a matter of your own programming style.

LOOP WITHIN A LOOP

Nested Loops

In many situations it is very convenient to have a loop contained within another loop. Such loops are called *nested loops*. A simple example of a nested loop is

```
for(i = 1; i <= 5; i++)                  // start of outer loop <-------+
{                                              //                       |
  cout << "\ni is now " << i << endl;          //                       |
                                               //                       |
  for(j = 1; j <= 4; j++)                // start of inner loop          |
    cout << "  j = " << j;               // end of inner loop            |
}                                        // end of outer loop   <-------+
```

The first loop, controlled by the value of `i`, is called the *outer loop*. The second loop, controlled by the value of `j`, is called the *inner loop*. Note that all statements in the inner loop are contained within the boundaries of the outer loop and that we have used a different variable to control each loop. For each single trip through the outer loop, the inner loop runs through its entire sequence. Thus, each time the `i` counter increases by 1, the inner `for` loop executes completely. This situation is illustrated in Figure 5–6.

Program 5-12 includes the foregoing code in a working program.

Program 5-12

```
#include <iostream.h>

int main()
{
  int i,j;

  for(i = 1; i <= 5; i++)                  // start of outer loop <-------+
  {                                              //                       |
    cout << "\ni is now " << i << endl;          //                       |
                                                 //                       |
    for(j = 1; j <= 4; j++)                // start of inner loop          |
      cout << "  j = " << j;               // end of inner loop            |
  }                                        // end of outer loop   <-------+

  return 0;
}
```

Following is the output of a sample run of Program 5-12.

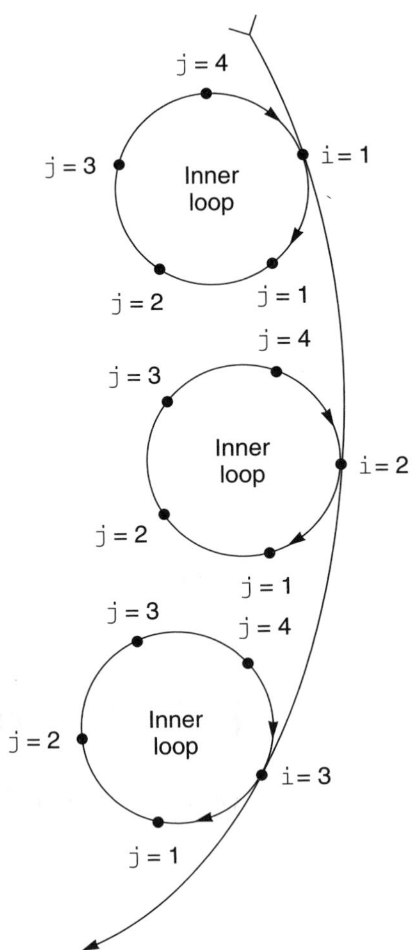

FIGURE 5–6 For Each i, j Loop

```
i is now 1
  j = 1  j = 2  j = 3  j = 4
i is now 2
  j = 1  j = 2  j = 3  j = 4
i is now 3
  j = 1  j = 2  j = 3  j = 4
i is now 4
  j = 1  j = 2  j = 3  j = 4
i is now 5
  j = 1  j = 2  j = 3  j = 4
```

Let us use a nested loop to compute the average grade for each student in a class of 20 students. Each student has taken four exams during the course of the semester. The final grade is calculated as the average of these examination grades.

The outer loop in our program will consist of 20 passes. Each pass through the outer loop is used to compute the average for one student. The inner loop will consist of 4 passes. One examination grade is entered in each inner-loop pass. As each grade is entered, it is added to the total for the student, and at the end of the loop, the average is calculated and displayed. Program 5-13 uses a nested loop to make the required calculations.

Program 5-13

```
#include <iostream.h>

int main()
{

  const int NUMGRADES = 4;
  const int NUMSTUDENTS = 20;
  int i,j;
  float grade, total, average;

  for (i = 1; i <= NUMSTUDENTS; i++)     // start of outer loop
  {
    total = 0;                          // clear the total for this student
    for (j = 1; j <= NUMGRADES; j++)    // start of inner loop
    {
      cout << "Enter an examination grade for this student: ";
      cin  >> grade;
      total = total + grade;    // add the grade into the total
    }                           // end of the inner for loop
    average = total / NUMGRADES;        // calculate the average
    cout << "\nThe average for student " << i
         << " is " << average << "\n\n";
  }                             // end of the outer for loop

  return 0;
}
```

In reviewing Program 5-13, pay particular attention to the initialization of `total` within the outer loop, before the inner loop is entered. `total` is initialized 20 times, once for each student. Also note that the average is calculated and displayed immediately after the inner loop is finished. Because the statements that compute and print the average are also contained within the outer loop, 20 averages are calculated and displayed. The entry and addition of each grade within the inner loop use techniques we have seen before, which should now be familiar to you.

Exercises 5.3

1. Determine the output of the following program:

```
#include <iostream.h>
int main()
{
  int i;

  for (i = 20; i >= 0; i -= 4)
    cout << i;

  return 0;
}
```

2. Modify Program 5-10 to produce a table of the numbers 0 through 20 in increments of 2, with their squares and cubes.

3. Modify Program 5-10 to produce a table of numbers from 10 to 1, instead of from 1 to 10 as it currently does.

4. Write and run a C++ program that displays a table of 20 temperature conversions from Fahrenheit to Celsius. The table should start with a Fahrenheit value of 20 degrees and should be incremented in values of 4 degrees. Recall that $Celsius = (5.0/9.0) * (Fahrenheit - 32.0)$.

5. Modify the program written for Exercise 4 to request initially the number of conversions to be displayed.

6. Write a C++ program that converts Fahrenheit to Celsius temperature in increments of 5 degrees. The initial value of Fahrenheit temperature and the total conversions to be made are to be requested as user input during program execution. Recall that $Celsius = (5.0/9.0) * (Fahrenheit - 32.0)$.

7. Write and run a C++ program that accepts six Fahrenheit temperatures, one at a time, and converts each value entered to its Celsius equivalent before the next value is requested. Use a `for` loop in your program. The conversion required is $Celsius = (5.0/9.0) * (Fahrenheit - 32.0)$.

8. Write and run a C++ program that accepts ten individual values of gallons, one at a time, and converts each value entered to its liter equivalent before the next value is requested. Use a `for` loop in your program. There are 3.785 liters in 1 gallon of liquid.

9. Modify the program written for Exercise 7 to request initially the number of data items that will be entered and converted.

10. Is the following program correct? If it is, determine its output. If it is not, determine the error and correct it so that the program will run.

```
#include <iostream.h>
int main()
{

  for(int i = 1; i < 10; i++)
   cout << i << '\n';

  for (int i = 1; i < 5; i++)
   cout << i << endl;

  return 0;
}
```

11. Write and run a C++ program that calculates and displays the amount of money available in a bank account that initially has $1000 deposited in it and that earns interest at the rate of 8 percent a year. Your program should display the amount available at the end of each year for a period of 10 years. Use the relationship that the money available at the end of each year equals the amount of money in the account at the start of the year plus .08 times the amount available at the start of the year.

12. a. Modify the program written for Exercise 11 to prompt the user for the amount of money initially deposited in the account.

b. Modify the program written for Exercise 11 to prompt the user for both the amount of money initially deposited and the number of years that should be displayed.

c. Modify the program written for Exercise 11 to prompt the user for the amount of money initially deposited, the interest rate to be used, and the number of years to be displayed.

13. A machine purchased for $28,000 is depreciated at a rate of $4,000 a year for 7 years. Write and run a C++ program that computes and displays a depreciation table for 7 years. The table should have the form

```
                  DEPRECIATION SCHEDULE
                  ---------------------

                              END-OF-YEAR       ACCUMULATED
YEAR      DEPRECIATION           VALUE          DEPRECIATION
----      ------------        -----------       ------------
1             4000               24000              4000
2             4000               20000              8000
3             4000               16000             12000
4             4000               12000             16000
5             4000                8000             20000
6             4000                4000             24000
7             4000                   0             28000
```

14. A well-regarded manufacturer of widgets has been losing 4 percent of its sales each year. The annual profit for the firm is 10 percent of sales. This year the firm has had $10 million in sales and a profit of $1 million. Determine the expected sales and profit for the next 10 years. Your program should complete and produce a display as follows:

```
                  SALES AND PROFIT PROJECTION
                  ---------------------------

YEAR          EXPECTED SALES            PROJECTED PROFIT
----          --------------            ----------------
  1            $10000000.00               $1000000.00
  2            $ 9600000.00               $ 960000.00
  3                  .                          .
  .                  .                          .
  .                  .                          .
  .                  .                          .
 10                  .                          .
-----------------------------------------------------
Totals:        $     .                    $     .
```

15. Four experiments are performed, each experiment consisting of six test results. The results for each experiment follow. Write a C++ program using a nested loop to compute and display the average of the test results for each experiment.

1st experiment results:	23.2	31.5	16.9	27.5	25.4	28.6
2nd experiment results:	34.8	45.2	27.9	36.8	33.4	39.4
3rd experiment results:	19.4	16.8	10.2	20.8	18.9	13.4
4th experiment results:	36.9	39.5	49.2	45.1	42.7	50.6

16. Modify the program written for Exercise 15 so that the number of test results for each experiment is entered by the user. Write your program so that a different number of test results can be entered for each experiment.

17. a. A bowling team consists of five players. Each player bowls three games. Write a C++ program that uses a nested loop to enter each player's individual scores and then computes and displays the average score for each bowler. Assume that each bowler has the following scores:

1st bowler:	286	252	265
2nd bowler:	212	186	215
3rd bowler:	252	232	216
4th bowler:	192	201	235
5th bowler:	186	236	272

b. Modify the program written for Exercise 17a to calculate and display the average team score. (*Hint:* Use a second variable to store the total of all the players' scores.)

18. Rewrite the program written for Exercise 17a to eliminate the inner loop. To do this, you will have to input three scores for each bowler rather than one at a time. Each score must be stored in its own variable name before the average is calculated.

19. Write a C++ program that calculates and displays the yearly amount available if $1000 is invested in a bank account for 10 years. Your program should display the amounts available for interest rates from 6 percent to 12 percent, inclusive, in 1 percent increments. Use a nested loop, with the outer loop having a fixed count of 7 and the inner loop a fixed count of 10. The first iteration of the outer loop should use an interest rate of 6 percent and display the amount of money available at the end of the first 10 years. In each subsequent pass through the outer loop, the interest rate should be increased by 1 percent. Use the relationship that the money available at the end of each year equals the amount of money in the account at the start of the year plus the interest rate times the amount available at the start of the year.

5.4 The do Statement

Both the `while` statement and the `for` statement evaluate an expression at the start of the repetition loop. In some cases, however, it is more convenient to test the expression at the end of the loop. For example, suppose we have constructed the following `while` loop to calculate sales taxes:

```
cout << "Enter a price: ";
cin  >> price;
while (price != SENTINEL)
{
  salestax = RATE * price;
  cout << "The sales tax is $" << salestax;
  cout << "\nEnter a price: ";
  cin  >> price;
}
```

Using this `while` statement requires either duplicating the prompt and `cin` object calls before the loop and then within the loop, as we have done, or resorting to some other artifice to force initial execution of the statements within the `while` loop.

The `do` statement, as its name implies, allows us to execute some statements before an expression is evaluated. In many situations, this approach can be used to eliminate the duplication illustrated in the previous example. The general form of the `do` statement is

```
do
  statement;
while (expression);   ← don't forget the final ;
```

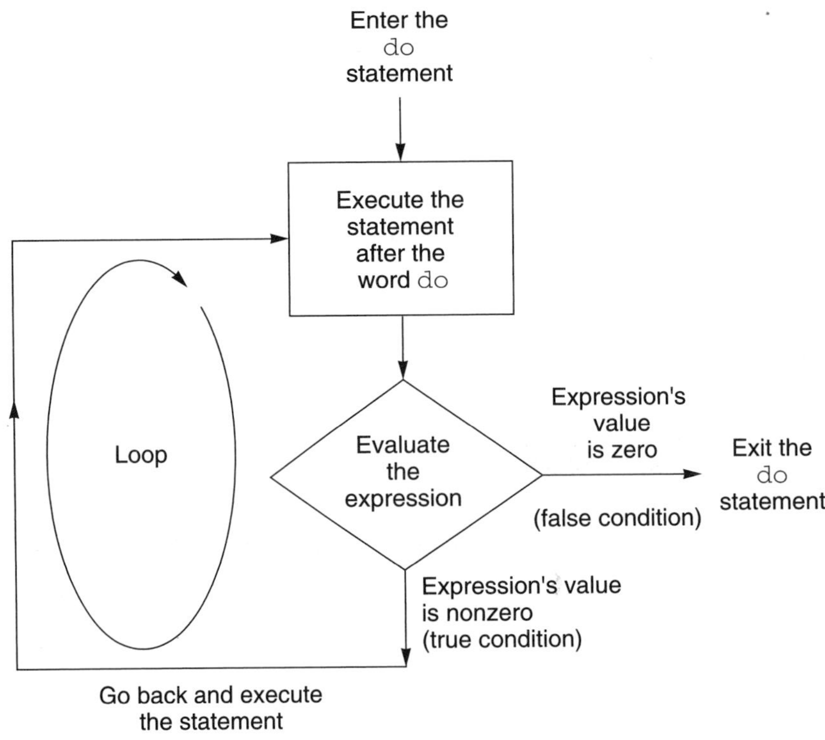

FIGURE 5–7 The do Statement's Flow of Control

As with all C++ programs, the single statement in the do may be replaced with a compound statement. Figure 5–7 is a flow-of-control diagram illustrating the operation of the do statement.

As shown in Figure 5–7, all statements within the do statement are executed at least once before the expression is evaluated. Then, if the expression has a nonzero value, the statements are executed again. This process continues until the expression evaluates to zero. For example, consider the following do statement:

```
do
{
  cout << "\nEnter a price: ";
  cin  >> price;
  if ( abs(price - SENTINEL) < 0.0001 ) break;
  salestax = RATE * price;
  cout << "The sales tax is $" << salestax;
}
while (price != SENTINEL);
```

Observe that only one prompt and cin statement are used here, because the tested expression is evaluated at the end of the loop.

As with all repetition statements, the do statement can always replace or be replaced by an equivalent while or for statement. The choice of which statement to use depends on the application and on the style the programmer prefers. In general, the while and for statements are preferred because they clearly let anyone reading the program know what is being tested "right up front" at the top of the program loop.

Validity Checks

The do statement is particularly useful in filtering user-entered input and providing data validity checks. For example, assume that an operator is required to enter a valid customer identification number between the numbers 100 and 1999. A number outside this range is to be rejected and a new request for a valid number made. The following section of code provides the necessary data filter to verify the entry of a valid identification number.

```
do
{
  cout << "\nEnter an identification number: ";
  cin  >> idNum;
}
while (idNum < 100 || idNum > 1999);
```

Here, a request for an identification number is repeated until a valid number is entered. This section of code is "bare bones" in that it neither alerts the operator to the cause of the new request for data nor allows premature exit from the loop if a valid identification number cannot be found. An alternative that removes the first drawback is

```
do
{
  cout << "\nEnter an identification number: ";
  cin  >> idNum;
  if (idNum < 100 || idNum > 1999)
  {
    cout << "\n An invalid number was just entered"
         << "\nPlease check the ID number and re-enter";
  }
  else
    break;     // break if a valid id num was entered
} while(1);    // this expression is always true
```

Here we have used a break statement to exit from the loop. Because the expression being evaluated by the do statement is always 1 (true), an infinite loop has been created that is exited only when the break statement is encountered.

Exercises 5.4

1. *a.* Using a do statement, write a C++ program to accept a grade. The program should request a grade continuously as long as an invalid grade is entered. An invalid grade is any grade less than 0 or greater than 100. After a valid grade has been entered, your program should display the value of the grade entered.
   b. Modify the program written for Exercise 1a so that the user is alerted when an invalid grade has been entered.
   c. Modify the program written for Exercise 1b so that it allows the user to exit the program by entering the number 999.
   d. Modify the program written for Exercise 1b so that it automatically terminates after five invalid grades are entered.
2. *a.* Write a C++ program that continuously requests a grade to be entered. If the grade is less than 0 or greater than 100, your program should print an appropriate message informing the user that an invalid grade has been entered; otherwise, the grade should be added to a total. When a grade of 999 is entered, the program should exit the repetition loop and compute and display the average of the valid grades entered.
   b. Run the program written in Exercise 2a on a computer and verify the program using appropriate test data.
3. *a.* Write a C++ program to reverse the digits of a positive integer number. For example, if the number 8735 is entered, the number displayed should be 5378. (*Hint:* Use a do statement and continuously strip off and display the units digit of the number. If the variable num initially contains the number entered, the units digit is obtained as (num % 10). After a units digit is displayed, dividing the number by 10 sets up the number for the next iteration. Thus (8735 % 10) is 5 and (8735 / 10) is 873. The do statement should continue as long as the remaining number is not zero.)
   b. Run the program written in Exercise 3a on a computer and verify the program using appropriate test data.
4. Repeat any of the exercises in Section 5.3 using a do statement rather than a for statement.

5.5 Common Programming Errors

Six errors are commonly made by beginning C++ programmers when they are using repetition statements. The most troublesome of these for new programmers is the "off by one" error, where the loop executes either one too many or one too few times than was intended. For example, the loop created by the statement for(i = 1; i < 11; i++) executes 10 times, not 11, even though the number 11 is used in the statement. Thus an equivalent loop can be constructed using the statement `for(i = 1; i <= 10; i++)`. However, if the loop is started with an initial value of `i = 0`, using the statement `for(i = 0; i < 11; i++)`, the loop will be traversed 11 times, as will a loop constructed with the statement `for(i = 0; i <= 10; i++)`. Thus, in constructing loops, you must pay particular attention to both initial and tested conditions used to control the loop to ensure that the number of loop traversals is not off by one, resulting in either one too many or one too few executions.

The next two errors pertain to the tested expression and have already been encountered with the `if` and `switch` statements. The first is the inadvertent use of the assignment operator, `=`, for the equality operator, `==`, in the tested expression. An example of this error is typing the assignment expression `a = 5` instead of the desired relational expression `a == 5`. Because the tested expression can be any valid C++ expression, including arithmetic and assignment expressions, this error is not detected by the compiler.

As with the `if` statement, repetition statements should not use the equality operator, `==`, when testing floating-point or double-precision operands. For example, the expression `fnum == 0.01` should be replaced by a test requiring that the absolute value of `fnum - 0.01` be less than an acceptable amount. The reason for this is that all numbers are stored in binary form. Given that we are limited to a finite number of bits, decimal numbers such as .01 have no exact binary equivalent, so tests requiring equality with such numbers can fail.

The next two errors are specific to the `for` statement. The more common is to place a semicolon at the end of the `for`'s parentheses, which frequently produces a do-nothing loop. For example, consider the statements

```
for(count = 0; count < 10; count++);
  total = total + num;
```

Here the semicolon at the end of the first line of code is a null statement. This has the effect of creating a loop that is executed ten times with nothing done except the incrementing and testing of `count`. This error tends to occur because C++ programmers are used to ending most lines with a semicolon.

The next error occurs when commas, instead of the required semicolons, are used to separate the items in a `for` statement. An example of this is the statement

```
for (count = 1, count < 10, count++)
```

Commas must be used to separate items within the initializing and altering lists, and semicolons must be used to separate these lists from the tested expression.

The last error we want to point out occurs when the final semicolon is omitted from the do statement. This error is usually made by programmers who have learned to omit the semicolon after the parentheses of a while statement and carry over this habit when the reserved word while is encountered at the end of a do statement.

5.6 Chapter Summary

1. The while, for, and do repetition statements create program loops. These statements evaluate an expression and, on the basis of the resulting expression value, either terminate the loop or continue with it. Each pass through the loop is referred to as a repetition or iteration. The tested condition must always be explicitly set prior to its first evaluation by the repetition statement. Within the loop there must always be a statement that permits altering of the condition so that the loop, once entered, can be exited.
2. The while statement checks its expression before any other statement in the loop. This requires that any variables in the tested expression have values assigned before the while is encountered. Within a while loop there must be a statement that either alters the tested expression's value or forces a break from the loop. The general form of a while statement is

```
while (expression)
  statement;
```

   If the statement contained within a while statement is a compound statement, the while statement takes the form

```
while(expression)
{
  any number of statements in here;
}
```

3. The for statement is extremely useful in creating loops that must be executed a fixed number of times. Initializing expressions (including declarations), the tested expression, and expressions that affect the tested expression can all be included in parentheses at the top of a for loop. Any other loop statement can also be included within the for's parentheses as part of its altering list. The general form of a for statement is

```
for(initialization; expression; altering-statements)
  statement;
```

If the statement contained within a `for` statement is a compound statement, the `for` statement takes the form

```
for(initialization; expression; altering-statements)
{
  any number of statements in here;
}
```

4. The `do` statement checks its expression at the end of the loop. This ensures that the body of a `do` loop is executed at least once. Within a `do` loop there must be at least one statement that either alters the tested expression's value or forces a break from the loop. The general form of a `do` statement is

```
do
  statement;
while (expression);
```

If the statement contained within a `do` statement is a compound statement, the `do` statement takes the form

```
do
{
  any number of statements in here;
}
while(expression);
```

Modularity Using Functions

Chapter Six

Professional programs are designed, coded, and tested very much like hardware, as a set of modules that are integrated to form a completed whole. A good analogy for this is an automobile, where one major module is the engine, another is the transmission, a third the braking system, a fourth the body, and so on. All of these modules are linked together and ultimately placed under the control of the driver, who is comparable to a supervisor or main program module. The whole now operates as a complete unit able to do useful work, such as driving to the store. During the assembly process, each module is individually constructed, tested, and found to be free of defects (bugs) before it is installed in the final product.

In this analogy, each of a car's major systems can be compared to a function. For example, the driver calls on the engine when the gas pedal is pressed. The engine accepts inputs of fuel, air, and electricity to turn the driver's request into a useful product—power—and then sends this output to the transmission for further processing. The transmission receives the output of the engine and converts it to a form that can be used by the drive axle. An additional input to the transmission is the driver's selection of gears (drive, reverse, neutral, and so on).

In each case, the engine, transmission, and other modules only "know" the universe bounded by their inputs and outputs. You, as the car's driver, need never know how the engine, transmission, air-conditioning, brakes, steering, and other modules work internally. You simply need to know what each system does and how to "call" on each system when that component's output is required. Communication between components is restricted to passing needed inputs to each module as that module is called on to perform its task, and each module operates internally in a relatively independent manner. Programmers employ this same modular approach to create and maintain reliable C++ programs using functions.

As we have seen, each C++ program must contain a `main()` function. In addition to this required function, C++ programs may also contain any number of additional functions. In this chapter we learn how to write these additional functions, pass data to them, process the passed data, and return a result.

6.1 Function and Parameter Declarations

In creating C++ functions we must be concerned with both the function itself and how it interacts with other functions, such as `main()`. This includes correctly passing data into a function when it is called and returning values from a function. In this section we describe the first part of the interface, passing

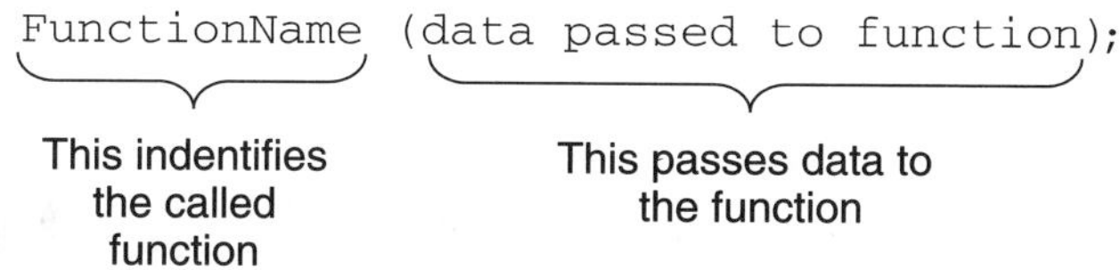

FIGURE 6–1 Calling and Passing Data to a Function

data to a function and having the function correctly receive, store, and process the transmitted data.

As we have already seen with mathematical functions, a function is called, or used, by giving the function's name and passing any data to it, as arguments, in the parentheses following the function name (see Figure 6–1).

The called function must be able to accept the data passed to it by the function doing the calling. Only after the called function successfully receives the data can the data be manipulated to produce a useful result.

To clarify the process of sending and receiving data, consider Program 6-1, which calls a function named `FindMax()`. The program, as shown, is not yet complete. Once the function `FindMax()` is written and included in Program 6-1, the completed program, consisting of the functions `main()` and `FindMax()`, can be compiled and executed.

Program 6-1

```
#include <iostream.h>

void FindMax(int, int); // the function declaration (prototype)

int main()
{
  int firstnum, secnum;

  cout << "\nEnter a number: ";
  cin  >> firstnum;
  cout << "Great! Please enter a second number: ";
  cin  >> secnum;

  FindMax(firstnum, secnum); // the function is called here

  return 0;
}
```

Let us examine the declaration and calling of the function `FindMax()` from `main()`. We will then write `FindMax()` to accept the data passed to it and determine the largest or maximum value of the two passed values.

The function `FindMax()` is referred to as the *called function* because it is called or summoned into action by its reference in `main()`. The function that does the calling, in this case `main()`, is referred to as the *calling function*. The terms *called* and *calling* come from standard telephone usage, where one party calls the other on a telephone. The party initiating the call is referred to as the calling party, and the party receiving the call is referred to as the called party. The same terms describe function calls. The called function, in this case `FindMax()`, is declared as a function that expects to receive two integer numbers and to return no value (a void) back to `main()`. This declaration is formally referred to as a function prototype. The function is then called by the last statement in the program.

Function Prototypes

Before a function can be called, it must be declared to the function that will do the calling. The declaration statement for a function is referred to as a *function prototype*. The function prototype tells the calling function the type of value that will be formally returned, if any, and the data type and order of the values that the calling function should transmit to the called function. For example, the function prototype used in Program 6-1,

```
void FindMax(int, int);
```

declares that the function `FindMax()` expects two integer values to be sent to it and that this particular function formally returns no value (`void`). Function prototypes may be placed with the variable declaration statements of the calling function, above the calling function name, as in Program 6-1, or in a separate header file that will be included using a `#include` preprocessor statement. Thus the function prototype for `FindMax()` could have been placed either before or after the statement `#include <iostream.h>`, prior to `main()`, or within `main()`. (The reasons for the choice of placement are presented in Section 6.3.) The general form of function prototype statements is

```
return-data-type function-name(list of parameter data types);
```

where the data-type refers to the data type of the value that will be formally returned by the function. Examples of function prototypes are

```
FindMax(firstnum,secnum);
```

This indentifies the `FindMax()` function

This causes two values to be passed to `FindMax()`

FIGURE 6–2 Calling and Passing Two Values to `FindMax()`

```
int fmax(int, int);
float swap(int, char, char, double);
void display(double, double);
```

In the first example, function prototype for `fmax()` declares that this function expects to receive two integer arguments and will formally return an integer value. The function prototype for `swap()` declares that this function requires four arguments, consisting of an integer, two characters, and a double-precision argument, in this order, and that it will formally return a floating-point number. Finally, the function prototype for `display()` declares that this function requires two double-precision arguments and does not return any value. Such a function might be used to display the results of a computation directly, without returning any value to the called function.

The use of function prototypes permits error checking of data types by the compiler. If the function prototype does not agree with data types defined when the function is written, an error message (typically `Undefined symbol`) will occur. The prototype also performs another task: It ensures conversion of all arguments passed to the function to the declared parameter data type when the function is called.

Calling a Function

Calling a function is a rather easy operation. The only requirements are that the name of the function be used and that any data passed to the function be enclosed within the parentheses following the function name, using the same order and type as declared in the function prototype. The items enclosed within the parentheses are called *arguments* of the called function (see Figure 6–2).

If a variable is one of the arguments in a function call, the called function receives a copy of the value stored in the variable. For example, the statement `FindMax(firstnum,secnum);` calls the function `FindMax()` and causes the values currently residing in the variables `firstnum` and `secnum` to be passed to `FindMax()`. The variable names in parentheses are arguments that provide values to the called function. After the values are passed, control is transferred to the called function.

As illustrated in Figure 6–3, the function `FindMax()` *does not receive the variables named* `firstnum` *and* `secnum` *and has no knowledge of these variable*

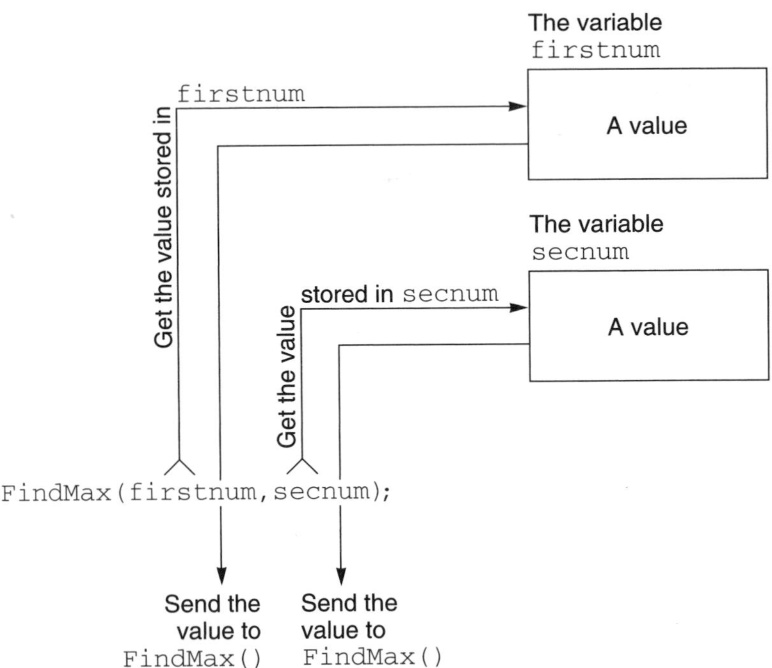

FIGURE 6–3 `FindMax()` Receives Actual Values

names.[1] The function simply receives the values in these variables and must itself determine where to store these values before it does anything else. Although this procedure for passing data to a function may seem surprising, it is really a safety procedure for ensuring that a called function does not inadvertently change data stored in a variable. The function gets a copy of the data to use. It may change its copy and, of course, change any variables declared inside itself. However, unless specific steps are taken to enable it to do so, a function is not allowed to change the contents of variables declared in other functions.

Now we will begin writing the function `FindMax()` to process the values passed to it.

Defining a Function

A function is defined when it is written. Each function is defined once (that is, written once) in a program and can then be used by any other function in the program that suitably declares it.

[1] This is significantly different from computer languages such as FORTRAN, where functions and subroutines receive access to these variables and can pass data back through them. In Section 6.3 we will see how C++, using reference variables, also permits direct access to the calling function's variables.

```
function header line   <—— Function header
{
  C++ statements;        } Function body
}
```

FIGURE 6–4 General Format of a Function

Like the `main()` function, every C++ function consists of two parts, a *function header* and a *function body*, as illustrated in Figure 6–4. The purpose of the function header is to identify the data type of the value returned by the function; provide the function with a name; and specify the number, order, and type of arguments expected by the function. The purpose of the function body is to operate on the passed data and directly return, at most, one value back to the calling function. (We will see, in Section 6.3, how a function can be made to return multiple values through the parameter list.)

The function header is always the first line of a function and contains the function's returned value type, its name, and the names and data types of its arguments. Because `FindMax()` will not formally return any value and is to receive two integer arguments, the following header line can be used:

```
void FindMax(int x, int y) <———— no semicolon
```

The argument names in the header are referred to as *formal parameters* of the function.[2] Thus the parameter `x` will be used to store the first value passed to `FindMax()`, and the parameter `y` will be used to store the second value passed at the time of the function call. The function does not know where the values come from when the call is made from `main()`. The first part of the call procedure executed by the computer involves going to the variables `firstnum` and `secnum` and retrieving the stored values. These values are then passed to `FindMax()` and ultimately stored in the parameters `x` and `y` (see Figure 6–5).

The function name and all parameter names in the header (in this case `FindMax`, `x`, and `y`) are chosen by the programmer. Any names selected according to the rules used to choose variable names can be used. All parameters listed in the function header line must be separated by commas and must have their individual data types declared separately.

Now that we have written the function header for the `FindMax()` function, we can construct its body. Let us assume that the `FindMax()` function selects and displays the larger of the two numbers passed to it.

As illustrated in Figure 6–6, a function body begins with an opening brace, `{`, contains any necessary declarations and other C++ statements, and ends with

---

2 The portion of the function header that contains the function name and parameters is formally referred to as a *function declarator*.

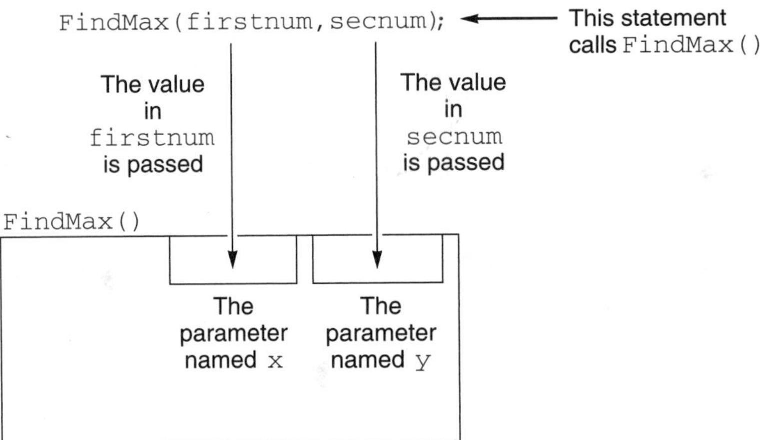

FIGURE 6–5 Storing Values into Parameters

a closing brace, }. This should be familiar to you because it is the same structure used in all the `main()` functions we have written. This should not be a surprise; `main()` is itself a function and must adhere to the rules that govern the construction of all legitimate functions.

In the body of the function `FindMax()`, we will declare one variable to store the maximum of the two numbers passed to it. We will then use an `if-else` statement to find the maximum of the two numbers. Finally, a `cout` object stream will be used to display the maximum. The complete function definition for the `FindMax()` function is

```
void FindMax(int x, int y)
{                         // start of function body
  int maxnum;             // variable declaration

  if (x >= y)             // find the maximum number
    maxnum = x;
  else
    maxnum = y;

  cout << "\nThe maximum of the two numbers is " << maxnum << endl;

}  // end of function body and end of function
```

FIGURE 6–6 Structure of a Function Body

```
{
  variable declarations and
  other C++ statements
}
```

POINT OF INFORMATION

Function Definitions and Function Prototypes

A *function definition* defines a function. Thus, when you write a function, you are really writing a function definition. Each definition begins with a header line that includes a parameter list, if any, enclosed in parentheses and ends with the closing brace that terminates the function's body. The parentheses are required whether or not the function uses any parameters. A commonly used syntax for a function definition is

```
return-data-type function-name(parameter list)
{
     constant declarations
     variable declarations

     other C++ statements

     return value
}
```

A *function prototype* declares a function. The syntax for a function prototype, which provides the return data type of the function, the function's name, and a list of parameter data types (parameter names are optional), is

```
return-data-type function-name(list of parameter data types);
```

Thus the prototype, along with precondition and postcondition comments (see the Point of Information box on page 227), should provide users with all the programming information they need to call the function successfully.

Generally, all function prototypes are placed at the top of the program, and all definitions are placed after the `main()` function. However, this placement can be changed. The only requirement in C++ is that a function cannot be called before it has been either declared or defined.

Note that the parameter declarations are made within the header line and that the variable declaration is made immediately after the opening brace of the function's body. This is in keeping with the concept that parameter values are passed to a function from outside the function and that variables are declared and assigned values from within the function body.

Program 6-2 includes the `FindMax()` function within the program code listed in Program 6-1.

Program 6-2

```
#include <iostream.h>

void FindMax(int, int);  // the function prototype

int main()
{
  int firstnum, secnum;

  cout << "\nEnter a number: ";
  cin  >> firstnum;
  cout << "Great! Please enter a second number: ";
  cin  >> secnum;

  FindMax(firstnum, secnum); // the function is called here

  return 0;
}

// following is the function FindMax()

void FindMax(int x, int y)
{                        // start of function body
  int maxnum;            // variable declaration

  if (x >= y)            // find the maximum number
    maxnum = x;
  else
    maxnum = y;

  cout << "\nThe maximum of the two numbers is " << maxnum << endl;

  return 0;
} // end of function body and end of function
```

Program 6-2 can be used to select and print the maximum of any two integer numbers entered by the user. A sample run using Program 6-2 follows.

```
Enter a number: 25
Great! Please enter a second number: 5

The maximum of the two numbers is 25
```

POINT OF INFORMATION

Preconditions and Postconditions

Preconditions are any set of conditions that a function requires to be true if it is to operate correctly. For example, if a function uses the named constant `MAXCHARS`, which must have a positive value, a precondition is that `MAXCHARS` must be declared with a positive value before the function is called.

Similarly, a postcondition is a condition that will be true after the function is executed, assuming that the preconditions are met.

Preconditions and postconditions are typically documented as user comments. For example, consider the following declaration and comments:

```
int leapyr(int)
// Preconditions: the integers must represent a year in a four
//              : digit form, such as 1999
// Postcondition: a 1 is returned if the year is a leap year;
//              : otherwise a 0 will be returned
```

Precondition and postcondition comments should be included with both function prototypes and function definitions whenever clarification is needed.

The placement of the `FindMax()` function after the `main()` function in Program 6-2 is a matter of choice. We will always list `main()` first, because it is the driver function that should give those who read the program an idea of what the complete program is about before they encounter the details of each function. However, in no case can the definition of `FindMax()` be placed inside `main()`. This is true for all C++ functions, which must be defined by themselves outside any other function. Each C++ function is a separate and independent entity with its own parameters and variables; nesting of functions is never permitted.

Placement of Statements

C++ does not impose a rigid statement-ordering structure on the programmer. The general rule for placing statements in a C++ program is simply that all preprocessor directives, named constants, variables, and functions must be either declared or defined before they can be used. As we have noted previously, although this rule permits both preprocessor directives and declaration statements to be placed throughout a program, doing so results in a very poor program structure.

As a matter of good programming practice, the following statement ordering should form the basic structure around which all of your C++ programs are constructed.

```
preprocessor directives

function prototypes

int main()
{
  named constants
  variable declarations

  other executable statements

  return value
}

function definitions
```

As always, comment statements can be freely intermixed anywhere within this basic structure.

Function Stubs

An alternative to completing each function required in a complete program is to write the `main()` function first and add the functions later, as they are developed. The problem that arises with this approach, however, is the same problem that occurred with Program 6-1—that is, the program cannot be run until all of the functions are included. For convenience, we have reproduced the code for Program 6-1 here.

```
#include <iostream.h>

void FindMax(int, int);  // the function declaration (prototype)

int main()
{
  int firstnum, secnum;

  cout << "\nEnter a number: ";
  cin  >> firstnum;
  cout << "Great! Please enter a second number: ";
  cin  >> secnum;

  FindMax(firstnum, secnum); // the function is called here

  return 0;
}
```

This program would be complete if there were a function definition for FindMax. But we really don't need a *correct* FindMax function to test and run what has been written; we just need a function that *acts* as though it is. A "fake" FindMax that accepts the proper number and types of parameters and returns values of the proper form for the function call is all we need for initial testing. This fake function is called a stub. A *stub* is the beginning of a final function that can be used as a placeholder for the final unit until the unit is completed. A stub for FindMax() follows.

```
void FindMax(int x, int y)
{
  cout << "In FindMax()\n";
  cout << "The value of x is " << x << endl;
  cout << "The value of y is " << y << endl;
}
```

We can now compile this stub function and link it with the previously completed code to obtain an executable program. The code for the function can then be further developed, with the "real" code, when it is completed, replacing the stub portion.

The minimum requirement of a stub function is that it compile and link with its calling module. In practice, it is a good idea to have a stub display a message that it has been entered successfully and the value(s) of its received parameters, as in the stub for FindMax().

As the function is refined, you let it do more and more, perhaps allowing it to return intermediate or incomplete results. This incremental, or stepwise, refinement is an important concept in efficient program development. It provides you with the means to run a program that does not yet meet all of its final requirements.

Functions with Empty Parameter Lists

Although useful functions that have an empty parameter list are extremely limited (one such function is provided in Exercise 10), they can occur. The function prototype for such a function requires writing either the keyword void or nothing at all between the parentheses following the function's name. For example, both prototypes

```
int display();
```

and

```
int display(void);
```

POINT OF INFORMATION

Isolation Testing

One of the most successful software-testing principles is always to embed the code being tested within an environment of working code. For example, assume you have two untested functions that are called in the order shown below, and the result returned by the second function is incorrect.

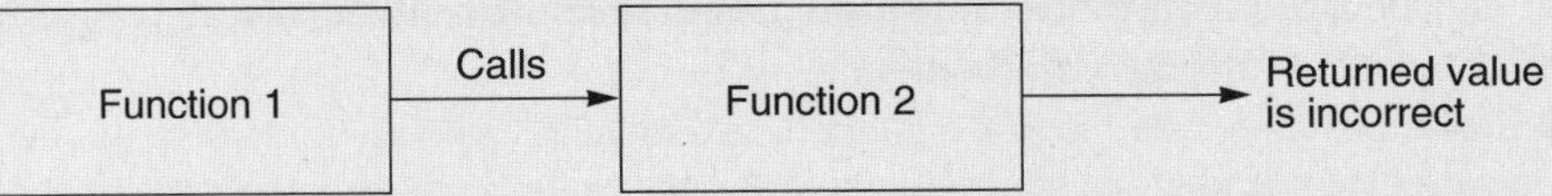

From the information shown in this figure, one or possibly both of the functions could be operating incorrectly. The first order of business is to isolate the problem to a specific function.

One of the most powerful methods of performing this code isolation is to decouple the functions. This is done either by testing each function individually or by testing one function first and then, when you know it is operating correctly, reconnecting it to the second function. Then, if an error occurs, you have isolated the error to either the transfer of data between functions or the internal operation of the second function.

This specific procedure is an example of the *basic rule of testing,* which states that each function should be tested only in a program in which all other functions are known to be correct. This means that one function must first be tested by itself, using stubs if necessary for any called functions, that a second tested function should be tested either by itself or with a previously tested function, and so on. This ensures that each new function is isolated within a test bed of correct functions, and the final program is effectively built up of tested function code.

indicate that the `display()` function takes no parameters and returns an integer. A function with an empty parameter list is called by its name with nothing written within the required parentheses following the function's name. For example, the statement `display();` correctly calls the `display()` function whose prototype is given above.

Default Arguments[3]

A convenient feature of C++ is its flexibility in providing default arguments in a function call. The primary use of default arguments is to extend the parameter list of existing functions without requiring any change in the calling argument lists already in place within a program.

Default argument values are listed in the function prototype and are automatically transmitted to the called function when the corresponding arguments are omitted from the function call. For example, the function prototype

---

3 This topic may be omitted on first reading with no loss of subject continuity.

```
void example(int, int = 5, float = 6.78);
```

provides default values for the last two arguments. If any of these arguments are omitted when the function is actually called, the C++ compiler will supply these default values. Thus all of the following function calls are valid:

```
example(7, 2, 9.3)   // no defaults used
example(7, 2)        // same as example(7, 2, 6.78)
example(7)           // same as example(7, 5, 6.78)
```

Four rules must be followed when using default parameters. The first is that default values should be assigned in the function prototype.[4] The second is that if any parameter is given a default value in the function prototype, all parameters following it must also be supplied with default values. The third rule is that if one argument is omitted in the actual function call, then all arguments to its right must also be omitted. The second and third rules make it clear to the C++ compiler which arguments are being omitted and enable the compiler to supply correct default values for the missing arguments, starting with the rightmost argument and working in toward the left. The last rule specifies that the default value used in the function prototype may be an expression consisting of both constants and previously declared variables. If such an expression is used, it must pass the compiler's check for validly declared variables, even though the actual value of the expression is evaluated and assigned at run time.

Default arguments are extremely useful when we are extending an existing function to include more features that require additional arguments. Adding the new arguments to the right of the existing arguments and providing each new argument with a default value permit all existing function calls to remain as they are. Thus the effect of the new changes is conveniently isolated from existing code in the program.

Function Templates[5]

In most high-level languages, including C++'s immediate predecessor, C, each function requires its own unique name. In theory this makes sense, but in practice it can lead to a profusion of function names, even for functions that perform essentially the same operations. For example, consider determining and displaying the absolute value of a number. If the number passed into the function can be an integer value, a floating-point value, or a double-precision value, three distinct functions must be written to handle each case correctly.

---

4 Some compilers accept default assignments in the function definition.

5 This topic may be omitted on first reading with no loss of subject continuity.

Certainly, we could give each of these functions a unique name, such as `abs()`, `fabs()`, and `dabs()`, respectively, having the function prototypes

```
void abs(int);
void fabs(long);
void dabs(double);
```

Clearly, each of these three functions performs essentially the same operation, but on different parameter data types. A much cleaner and more elegant solution is to write a general function that handles all cases, but whose parameters, variables, and even return type can be set by the compiler on the basis of the actual function call. This can be done in C++ by using function templates.

A *function template* is a single, complete function that serves as a model for a family of functions. Which function from the family is actually created depends on subsequent function calls. To make this more tangible, consider a function template that computes and displays the absolute value of a passed argument. An appropriate function template is

```
template <class T>
void showabs(T number)
{
  if (number < 0)
    number = -number;
  cout << "The absolute value of the number "
       << " is " << number << endl;

  return;
}
```

For the moment, ignore the first line `template <class T>` and look at the second line, which consists of the function header `void showabs(T number)`. Note that this header line has the same syntax that we have been using for all of our function definitions, except for the `T` where a data type is usually placed. For example, if the header line were `void showabs(int number)`, you should recognize this as a function named `showabs` that expects one integer argument to be passed to it and that returns no value. Similarly, if the header line were `void showabs(float number)`, you should recognize it as a function that expects one floating-point argument to be passed when the function is called.

The advantage in using the `T` within the function template header line is that it represents a general data type that is replaced by an actual data type, such as `int`, `float`, or `double`, when the compiler encounters an actual function call. For example, if a function call with an integer argument is encountered, the compiler will use the function template to construct the code for a function that expects an integer parameter. Similarly, if a call is made with a floating-point argument, the compiler will construct a function that expects a floating-point parameter. As a specific example of this, consider Program 6-3.

Program 6-3

```
#include <iostream.h>

template <class T>
void showabs(T number)
{
  if (number < 0)
    number = -number;
  cout << "The absolute value of the number is "
       << number << endl;

  return;
}

int main()
{
  int num1 = -4;
  float num2 = -4.23;
  double num3 = -4.23456;

  showabs(num1);
  showabs(num2);
  showabs(num3);

  return 0;
}
```

First note the three function calls made in the `main()` function shown in Program 6-3, which call the function `showabs()` with an integer, float, and double value, respectively. Now let's review the function template for `showabs()` and consider the first line `template <class T>`. This line, which is called a *template prefix,* is used to inform the compiler that the function immediately following is a template that uses a data type named `T`. Within the function template, the T is used in the same manner as any other data type, such as int, float, double, and so on. Then, when the compiler encounters an actual function call for showabs(), the data type of the argument passed in the call is substituted for T throughout the function. In effect, the compiler creates a specific function, using the template, that expects the argument type in the call. Because Program 6-3 makes three calls to showabs, each with a different argument data type, the compiler will create three separate showabs() functions. The compiler knows which function to use on the basis of the arguments passed at the time of the call. The output displayed when Program 6-3 is executed is

```
The absolute value of the number is 4
The absolute value of the number is 4.23
The absolute value of the number is 4.23456
```

The letter T used in the template prefix template <class T> is simply a placeholder for a data type that is defined when the function is actually invoked. Accordingly, any letter or non-keyword identifier can be used instead. Thus the showabs() function template could just as well have been defined as follows:

```
template <class DTYPE>
void showabs(DTYPE number)
{
  if (number < 0)
    number = -number;
  cout << "The absolute value of the number is "
       << number << endl;

  return;
}
```

In this regard, it is sometimes simpler and clearer to read the word *class* in the template prefix as the words *data type*. Thus, the template prefix template <class T> can be read as "We are defining a function template that has a data type named T." Then, within both the header line and the body of the defined function, the data type T (or any other letter or identifier defined in the prefix) is used in the same manner as any built-in data type, such as int, float, or double.

Now, suppose we would like to create a function template to include both a return type and an internally declared variable. For example, consider the following function template.

```
template <class T> // template prefix
T abs(T value)     // header line
{
  T absnum;  // variable declaration

  if (value < 0)
    absnum = -value;
  else
    absnum = value;

  return absnum;
}
```

In this template definition, we have used the data type `T` to declare three items: the return type of the function, the data type of a single function parameter named `value`, and one variable declared within the function. Program 6-4 illustrates how this function template could be used within the context of a complete program.

Program 6-4

```
#include <iostream.h>

template <class T> // template prefix
T abs(T value)     // header line
{
  T absnum;  // variable declaration

  if (value < 0)
    absnum = -value;
  else
    absnum = value;

  return absnum;
}
int main()
{
  int num1 = -4;
  float num2 = -4.23;
  double num3 = -4.23456;

  cout << "The absolute value of " << num1
       << " is " << abs(num1) << endl;
  cout << "The absolute value of " << num2
       << " is " << abs(num2) << endl;
  cout << "The absolute value of " << num3
       << " is " << abs(num3) << endl;

  return 0;
}
```

In the first call to abs() made within main(), an integer value is passed as an argument. In this case, the compiler substitutes an int data type for the T data type in the function template and creates the following function:

```
int showabs(int value) // header line
{
  int absnum;  // variable declaration

  if (value < 0)
    absnum = -value;
  else
    absnum = value;

  return (absnum);
}
```

Similarly, in the second and third function calls, the compiler creates two more functions, one in which the data type T is replaced by the keyword float, and one in which the data type T is replaced by the keyword double. The output produced by Program 6-4 is

```
The absolute value of -4 is 4
The absolute value of -4.23 is 4.23
The absolute value of -4.23456 is 4.23456
```

The value of using the function template is that one function definition has been used to create three different functions, all of which use the same logic and operations but operate on different data types.

Finally, although both Program 6-3 and Program 6-4 define a function template that uses a single placeholder data type, function templates with more than one data type can be defined. For example, the template prefix

```
template <class DTYPE1, class DTYPE2, class DTYPE3>
```

can be used to create a function template that requires three different data types. As before, within the header and body of the function template, the data types DTYPE1, DTYPE2, and DTYPE3 would be used in the same manner as any built-in data type, such as int, float, double, and so on. Additionally, as we noted before, the names DTYPE1, DTYPE2, and DTYPE3 can be any non-keyword identifier. Conventionally, the letter T followed by nothing or by a digit such as T, T1, T2, T3, etc. would be used.

Reusing Function Names (Overloading)[6]

C++ provides the capability of using the same function name for more than one function, which is referred to as *function overloading*. The only requirement in creating more than one function with the same name is that the compiler must be able to determine which function to use on the basis of the data types of the parameters (not the data type of the return value, if any). For example, consider the three following functions, all named `cdabs()`.

```
void cdabs(int x)   // compute and display the absolute value of an integer
{
  if ( x < 0 )
    x = -x;
  cout << "The absolute value of the integer is  " << x << endl;
}

void cdabs(float x)   // compute and display the absolute value of a float
{
  if ( x < 0 )
    x = -x;
  cout << "The absolute value of the float is  " << x << endl;
}

void cdabs(double x)   // compute and display the absolute value of a double
{
  if ( x < 0 )
   x = -x;
  cout << "The absolute value of the double is  " << x << endl;
}
```

Which of the three functions named `cdabs()` is actually called depends on the argument types supplied at the time of the call. Thus the function call `cdabs(10);` would cause the compiler to use the function named `cdabs()` that expects an integer argument, and the function call `cdabs(6.28f);` would cause the compiler to use the function named `cdabs()` that expects a floating-point argument.[7]

---

6 This topic may be omitted on first reading with no loss of subject continuity.

7 This is accomplished by a process referred to as *name mangling*. In name mangling, the function name actually generated by the C++ compiler differs from the function name used in the source code. The compiler appends information to the source code function name, depending on the type of data being passed, and the resulting name is said to be a mangled version of the source code name.

Note that overloading a function's name simply means using the same name for more than one function. Each function that uses the name must still be written, and each exists as a separate entity. The use of the same function name does not require that the code within the functions be similar, although good programming practice dictates that functions with the same name should perform essentially the same operations. All that is formally required in using the same function name is that the compiler be able to distinguish which function to select on the basis of the data types of the arguments when the function is called. Clearly, however, if all that is different about the overloaded functions is the argument types, a better programming solution is simply to create a function template. Employing overloaded functions, however, is extremely useful with constructor functions, a topic that is presented in Section 11.3.

Exercises 6.1

1. For the following function headers, determine the number, type, and order (sequence) of the values that must be passed to the function.
   a. `void factorial(int n)`
   b. `void price(int type, double yield, double maturity)`
   c. `void yield(int type, double price, double maturity)`
   d. `void interest(char flag, float price, float time)`
   e. `void total(float amount, float rate)`
   f. `void roi(int a, int b, char c, char d, float e, float f)`
   g. `void getVal(int item, int iter, char decflag, char delim)`
2. *a.* Write a function named `check` that has three arguments. The first argument should accept an integer number, the second argument a floating-point number, and the third argument a double-precision number. The body of the function should just display the values of the data passed to the function when it is called. (*Note:* When tracing errors in functions, it is helpful to have the function display the values it has been passed. Quite frequently, the error is not in what the body of the function does with the data but, rather, in the data received and stored.)
   b. Include the function written in Exercise 2a in a working program. Make sure your function is called from `main()`. Test the function by passing various data to it.
3. *a.* Write a function named `FindAbs()` that accepts a double-precision number passed to it, computes its absolute value, and displays the absolute value. The absolute value of a number is the number itself if the number is positive and is the negative of the number if the number is negative.
   b. Include the function written in Exercise 3a in a working program. Make sure your function is called from `main()`. Test the function by passing various data to it.
4. *a.* Write a function called `mult()` that accepts two floating-point numbers as arguments, multiplies these two numbers, and displays the result.

b. Include the function written in Exercise 4a in a working program. Make sure your function is called from `main()`. Test the function by passing various data to it.

5. a. Write a function named `square()` that computes the square of the value passed to it and displays the result. The function should be capable of squaring numbers with decimal points.

b. Include the function written in Exercise 5a in a working program. Make sure your function is called from `main()`. Test the function by passing various data to it.

6. a. Write a function named `powfun()` that raises an integer number passed to it to a positive integer power and displays the result. The positive integer should be the second value passed to the function. Declare the variable used to store the result as a long-integer data type to ensure sufficient storage for the result.

b. Include the function written in Exercise 6a in a working program. Make sure your function is called from `main()`. Test the function by passing various data to it.

7. a. Write a function that produces a table of the numbers from 1 to 10, their squares, and their cubes. The function should produce the same display as that produced by Program 5-10.

b. Include the function written in Exercise 7a in a working program. Make sure your function is called from `main()`. Test the function by passing various data to it.

8. a. Modify the function written for Exercise 7 to accept the starting value of the table, the number of values to be displayed, and the increment between values. If the increment is not explicitly sent, the function should use a default value of 1. Name your function `selTable()`. A call to `selTable(6,5,2);` should produce a table of five lines, the first line starting with the number 6 and each succeeding number increasing by 2.

b. Include the function written in Exercise 8a in a working program. Make sure your function is called from `main()`. Test the function by passing various data to it.

9. a. Write a C++ program that accepts an integer argument and determines whether the passed integer is even or odd. (*Hint:* Use the % operator.)

b. Enter, compile, and execute the program written for Exercise 9a.

10. A useful function that uses no parameters can be constructed to return a value for π that is accurate to the maximum number of decimal places allowed by your computer. This value is obtained by taking the arcsine of 1.0, which is $\pi/2$, and multiplying the result by 2. In C++, the required expression is *2.0 * asin(1.0)*, where the `asin()` function is provided in the standard C++ mathematics library (remember to include `math.h`). Using this expression, write a C++ function named `Pi()` that calculates and displays the value of π.

11. a. Write a function template named `display()` that displays the value of the single argument that is passed to it when the function is called.

b. Include the function template created in Exercise 11a within a complete C++ program that calls the function four times: once with a character argument, once with an integer argument, once with a floating-point argument, and once with a double-precision argument.

12. a. Write a function template named `whole()` that returns the integer value of any argument that is passed to it when the function is called.

b. Include the function template created in Exercise 12a within a complete C++ program that calls the function four times: once with a character argument, once with an integer argument, once with a floating-point argument, and once with a double-precision argument.

13. *a.* Write a function template named `maximum()` that returns the maximum value of three arguments that are passed to the function when it is called. Assume that all three arguments will be of the same data type.
b. Include the function template created for Exercise 13a within a complete C++ program that calls the function with three integers and then with three floating-point numbers.

14. *a.* Write a function template named `square()` that computes and returns the square of the single argument passed to the function when it is called.
b. Include the function template created for Exercise 14a within a complete C++ program.

6.2 Returning a Single Value

When the method of passing data into a function presented in the previous section is used, the called function receives copies only of the values contained in the arguments at the time of the call (review Figure 6–3 if this is unclear to you). When a value is passed to a called function in this manner, the passed argument is referred to as a *pass by value* argument and is a distinct advantage of C++.[8] Because the called function does not have direct access to the variables used as arguments by the calling function, it cannot inadvertently alter the value stored in one of these variables.

The function receiving the passed by value arguments may process the values sent to it in any fashion desired and may directly return at most one, and only one, "legitimate" value to the calling function (see Figure 6–7). In this section we see how such a value is returned to the calling function. As you might expect in view of C++'s flexibility, there is a way of returning more than a single value, but that is the topic of the next section.

As with the calling of a function, directly returning a value requires that the interface between the called and calling functions be handled correctly. From its side of the return transaction, the called function must provide

- The data type of the returned value
- The actual value being returned

[8] This is also referred to as a *call by value*. The term, however, does not refer to the function call as a whole but, rather, to how an individual argument is passed when the call to a function is made.

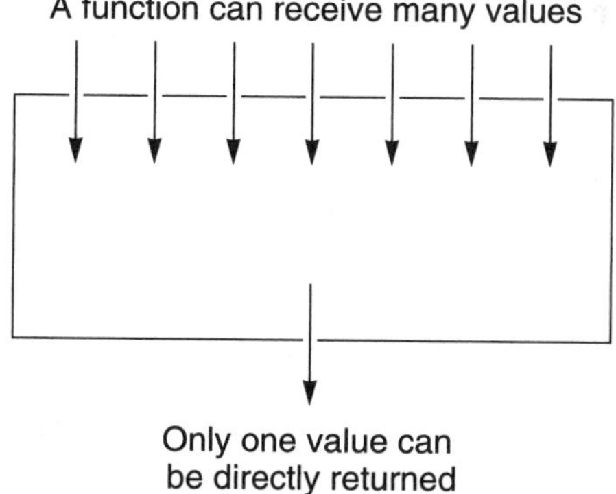
A function can receive many values
Only one value can
be directly returned

FIGURE 6–7 A Function Directly Returns at Most One Value

A function returning a value must specify, in its header line, the data type of the value that will be returned. Recall that the function header line is the first line of the function, which includes both the function's name and a list of parameter names. As an example, consider the `FindMax()` function written in the last section. It determined the maximum value of two numbers passed to the function. For convenience, we will list the `FindMax()` code again:

```
void FindMax(int x, int y)
{                          // start of function body
  int maxnum;              // variable declaration

  if (x >= y)              // find the maximum number
    maxnum = x;
  else
    maxnum = y;

  cout << "\nThe maximum of the two numbers is "
       << maxnum << endl;

}  // end of function body and end of function
```

As written, the function's header line is

```
void FindMax(int x, int y)
```

where `x` and `y` are the names chosen for the function's parameters.

If `FindMax()` is now to return a value, the function's header line must be amended to include the data type of the value being returned. For example, if an integer value is to be returned, the proper function header line is

```
int FindMax(int x, int y)
```

Similarly, if the function is to receive two floating-point values and return a floating-point value, the correct function header line is

```
float FindMax(float x, float y)
```

and if the function is to receive two double-precision values and return a double-precision value, the correct header line is[9]

```
double FindMax(double x, double y)
```

Let us now modify the function `FindMax()` to return the maximum value of the two numbers passed to it. To do this, we must first determine the data type of the value that is to be returned and include this data type in the function's header line.

The maximum value determined by `FindMax()` is stored in the integer variable `maxnum`, so it is the value of this variable that the function should return. Returning an integer value from `FindMax()` requires that the function declaration be

```
int FindMax(int x, int y)
```

Observe that this is the same as the original function header line for `FindMax()` with the substitution of the keyword `int` for the keyword `void`.

Having declared the data type that `FindMax()` will return, all we need to do is include a statement within the function to cause the return of the correct value. To return a value, a function must use a `return` statement, which has the form[10]

```
return expression;
```

When the `return` statement is encountered, the expression is evaluated first. The value of the expression is then automatically converted to the data type declared in the function header before being sent back to the calling function. After the value is returned, program control reverts to the calling function. Thus, to return the value stored in `maxnum`, all we need to do is add the statement `return maxnum;` before the closing brace of the `FindMax()` function. The complete function code is

---

[9] The return data type is related to the parameter data types only inasmuch as the returned value is computed from parameter values. In this case, because the function is used to return the maximum value of its parameters, it would make little sense to return a data type that did not match the function's parameter types.

[10] Many programmers place the expression within parentheses, yielding the statement `return (expression);`. Although either form can be used, for consistency only one should be adopted.

These should be the same data type.

```
int FindMax(int x, int y)   // function header line
{                           // start of function body
  int maxnum;               // variable declaration

  if (x >= y)
    maxnum = x;
  else
    maxnum = y;

  return maxnum;            // return statement
}
```

In this new code for the function `FindMax()`, note that the data type of the expression contained in the `return` statement correctly matches the data type in the function's header line. It is up to the programmer to ensure that this is so for every function that returns a value. Failure to match the `return` value exactly with the function's declared data type may not result in an error when your program is compiled, but it may lead to undesired results because the `return` value is always converted to the data type declared in the function declaration. Usually this is a problem only when the fractional part of a returned floating-point or double-precision number is truncated because the function was declared to return an integer value.

Having taken care of the sending side of the `return` transaction, we must now prepare the calling function to receive the value sent by the called function. On the calling (receiving) side, the calling function must

- Be alerted to the type of value to expect
- Properly use the returned value

Alerting the calling function to the type of `return` value to expect is properly taken care of by the function prototype. For example, including the function prototype

```
int FindMax(int, int);
```

before the `main()` function is sufficient to alert `main()` that `FindMax()` is a function that will return an integer value.

To actually use a returned value we must either provide a variable to store the value or use the value directly in an expression. Storing the returned value in a variable is accomplished by using a standard assignment statement. For example, the assignment statement

```
max = FindMax(firstnum, secnum);
```

can be used to store the value returned by `FindMax()` in the variable named `max`. This assignment statement does two things. First the right-hand side of the assignment statement calls `FindMax()`, and then the result returned by `FindMax` is stored in the variable `max`. The value returned by `FindMax()` is an integer, so the variable `max` must also be declared as an integer variable within the calling function's variable declarations.

The value returned by a function need not be stored directly in a variable but can be used wherever an expression is valid. For example, the expression `2 * FindMax(firstnum,secnum)` multiplies the value returned by `FindMax()` by 2, and the statement

```
cout << FindMax(firstnum, secnum);
```

displays the returned value.

Program 6-5 illustrates the inclusion of both prototype and assignment statements for `main()` to correctly call and store a returned value from `FindMax()`. As before, and in keeping with our convention of placing the `main()` function first, we have placed the `FindMax()` function after `main()`.

Program 6-5

```
#include <iostream.h>

int FindMax(int, int);  // the function prototype

int main()
{
  int firstnum, secnum, max;


  cout << "\nEnter a number: ";
  cin  >> firstnum;
  cout << "Great! Please enter a second number: ";
  cin  >> secnum;

  max = FindMax(firstnum, secnum); // the function is called here

  cout << "\nThe maximum of the two numbers is " << max << endl;

  return 0;
}
```

```
int FindMax(int x, int y)
{                          // start of function body
  int maxnum;              // variable declaration


  if (x >= y)              // find the maximum number
    maxnum = x;
  else
    maxnum = y;


  return maxnum;           // return statement
}
```

In reviewing Program 6-5, it is important to note the four items we have introduced in this section. The first item is the prototype for `FindMax()`. This statement, which ends with a semicolon as all declaration statements do, alerts `main()` and any subsequent functions that use `FindMax()` to the data type that `FindMax()` will be returning. The second item to notice in `main()` is the use of an assignment statement to store the returned value from the `FindMax()` call into the variable `max`. We have also made sure to declare `max` correctly as an integer within `main()`'s variable declarations so that it matches the data type of the returned value.

The last two items of note concern the coding of the `FindMax()` function. The first line of `FindMax()` declares that the function will return an integer value, and the expression in the `return` statement evaluates to a matching data type. Thus `FindMax()` is internally consistent in sending an integer value back to `main()`, and `main()` has been correctly alerted to receive and use the returned integer.

In writing your own functions, you must always keep these four items in mind. For another example, see whether you can identify these four items in Program 6-6.

In reviewing Program 6-6, let us first analyze the `tempvert()` function. The complete definition of the function begins with the function's header line and ends with the closing brace after the `return` statement. The function is declared as a double; this means the expression in the function's `return` statement must evaluate to a double-precision number, which it does. Because a function header line is not a statement but the start of the code defining the function, the function header line does not end with a semicolon.

Program 6-6

```
#include <iostream.h>

double tempvert(double);    // function prototype

int main()
{
  const CONVERTS = 4;       // number of conversions to be made
  int count;                // start of variable declarations
  double fahren;

  for(count = 1; count <= CONVERTS; count++)
  {
    cout << "\nEnter a Fahrenheit temperature: ";
    cin  >> fahren;
    cout << "The Celsius equivalent is "
         << tempvert(fahren) << endl;
  }

  return 0;
}

// convert fahrenheit to celsius
double tempvert(double inTemp)
{
  return (5.0/9.0) * (inTemp - 32.0);
}
```

For the receiving side, there is a prototype for the function `tempvert()` that agrees with `tempvert()`'s function definition. No variable is declared in `main()` to store the returned value from `tempvert()` because the returned value is immediately passed to `cout` for display.

One further point is worth mentioning here. One of the purposes of declarations, as we learned in Chapter 2, is to alert the compiler to the amount of internal storage to reserve for the data. The prototype for `tempvert()` performs this task and alerts the compiler to the type of storage needed for the returned value. Had we placed the `tempvert()` function definition before `main()`, the function's header line would serve the same purpose and the function prototype could be eliminated. We have chosen always to list `main()` as the first function in a file, so we must include function prototypes for all functions called by `main()` and any subsequent functions.

Inline Functions[11]

Calling a function places a certain amount of overhead on a computer. This consists of placing argument values in a reserved memory region that the function has access to (this memory region is referred to as the *stack*), passing control to the function, providing a reserved memory location for any returned value (again, the stack region of memory is used for this purpose), and finally returning to the proper point in the calling program. Paying this overhead is well justified when a function is called many times because it can significantly reduce the size of a program. Rather than the same code being repeated each time it is needed, the code is written once, as a function, and called whenever it is needed.

For small functions that are not called many times, however, paying the overhead for passing and returning values may not be warranted. It still would be convenient, though, to group repeating lines of code together under a common function name and have the compiler place this code directly into the program wherever the function is called. This capability is provided by *inline functions.*

Telling the C++ compiler that a function is *inline* causes a copy of the function code to be placed in the program at the point where the function is called. For example, consider the function `tempvert()` defined in Program 6-6. This relatively short function is an ideal candidate to be an inline function. To make this, or any other function, an inline one, we simply place the reserved word `inline` before the function name and define the function before any calls are made to it. This is done for the `tempvert()` function in Program 6-7.

Observe in Program 6-7 that the inline function is placed ahead of any calls to it. This is a requirement of all inline functions and obviates the need for a function prototype before any subsequent calling function. Because the function is now an inline one, its code will be expanded directly into the program wherever it is called.

The advantage of using an inline function is an increase in execution speed. The inline function is directly expanded and included in every expression or statement calling it, so no loss of execution time results from the call and return overhead required by a non-inline function. The disadvantage is the increase in program size when an inline function is called repeatedly. Each time an inline function is referenced, the complete function code is reproduced and stored as an integral part of the program. A non-inline function, however, is stored in memory only once. No matter how many times the function is called, the same code is used. Therefore, inline functions should be used only for small functions that are not extensively called in a program.

---

[11] This section is optional and may be omitted on first reading without loss of subject continuity.

Program 6-7

```
#include <iostream.h>

inline double tempvert(double inTemp)  // an inline function
{
  return( (5.0/9.0) * (inTemp - 32.0). );
}

int main()
{
  const CONVERTS = 4;         // number of conversions to be made
  int count;                  // start of variable declarations
  double fahren;

  for(count = 1; count <= CONVERTS; count++)
  {
    cout << "\nEnter a Fahrenheit temperature: ";
    cin  >> fahren;
    cout << "The Celsius equivalent is "
         << tempvert(fahren) << endl;
  }

  return 0;
}
```

Exercises 6.2

1. Rewrite Program 6-5 to have the function `FindMax()` accept two floating-point arguments and return a floating-point value to `main()`. Make sure to modify `main()` in order to pass two floating-point values to `FindMax()` and accept and store the floating-point value returned by `FindMax()`.

2. For the following function headers, determine the number, type, and order (sequence) of values that should be passed to the function when it is called and the data type of the value returned by the function.

a. `int factorial(int n)`
b. `double price(int type, double yield, double maturity)`
c. `double yield(int type, double price, double maturity)`
d. `char interest(char flag, float price, float time)`
e. `int total(float amount, float rate)`
f. `float roi(int a, int b, char c, char d, float e, float f)`
g. `void getVal(int item, int iter, char decflag)`

3. Write function headers for the following functions.

a. A function named `check()`, which has three parameters. The first parameter should accept an integer number, the second parameter a floating-point number, and the third parameter a double-precision number. The function returns no value.

b. A function named `FindAbs()` that accepts a double-precision number passed to it and returns that number's absolute value.

c. A function named `mult()` that accepts two floating-point numbers as parameters, multiplies these two numbers, and returns the result.

d. A function named `square()` that computes and returns the square of the integer value passed to it.

e. A function named `powfun()` that raises an integer number passed to it to a positive integer power (also passed as an argument) and returns the result as a long integer.

f. A function named `table()` that produces a table of the numbers from 1 to 10, their squares, and their cubes. No arguments are to be passed to the function, and the function returns no value.

4. *a.* Write a C++ function named `FindAbs()` that accepts a double-precision number passed to it, computes that number's absolute value, and returns the absolute value to the calling function. The absolute value of a number is the number itself if the number is positive or zero; it is the negative of the number if the number is negative.

b. Include the function written in Exercise 4a in a working program. Make sure your function is called from `main()` and correctly returns a value to `main()`. Have `main()` use `cout` to display the value returned. Test the function by passing various data to it.

5. *a.* Write a C++ function called `mult()` that accepts two double-precision numbers, multiplies these two numbers, and returns the result to the calling function.

b. Include the function written in Exercise 5a in a working program. Make sure your function is called from `main()` and correctly returns a value to `main()`. Have `main()` use `cout` to display the value returned. Test the function by passing various data to it.

6. *a.* Write a C++ function named `powfun()` that raises an integer number passed to it to a positive integer power (also passed as an argument) and returns the result to the calling function. Declare the variable used to return the result as a long-integer data type to ensure sufficient storage for the result.

b. Include the function written in Exercise 6a in a working program. Make sure your function is called from `main()` and correctly returns a value to `main()`. Have `main()` use `cout` to display the value returned. Test the function by passing various data to it.

7. A second-degree polynomial in x is given by the expression $ax^2 + bx + c$, where a, b, and c are known numbers, and a is not equal to zero. Write a C++ function named `polyTwo(a,b,c,x)` that computes and returns the value of a second-degree polynomial for any passed values of a, b, c, and x.

8. *a.* Rewrite the function `tempvert()` in Program 6-6 to accept a temperature and a character as parameters. If the character passed to the function is the letter `f`, the function should convert the passed temperature from Fahrenheit to Celsius; otherwise, the function should convert the passed temperature from Celsius to Fahrenheit.

b. Modify the `main()` function in Program 6-6 to call the function written for Exercise 8a. Your `main()` function should ask the user for the type of temperature being entered and pass the type (`f` or `c`) into `tempvert()`.

9. *a.* Write a function named `RightTriangle()` that accepts the lengths of two sides of a right triangle as the parameters `a` and `b`, respectively. The subroutine should determine and return the hypotenuse, `c`, of the triangle. (*Hint:* Use the Pythagorean theorem, $c^2 = a^2 + b^2$.)
   b. Include the function written for Exercise 9a in a working program. The `main()` function unit should correctly call `RightTriangle()` and display the value returned by the function.

10. *a.* Write a function named `totamt()` that uses four parameters named `quarters`, `dimes`, `nickels`, and `pennies`, which represent the number of quarters, dimes, nickels, and pennies in a piggybank. The function should determine the dollar value of the number of quarters, dimes, nickels, and pennies passed to it and return the calculated value.
   b. Include the function written in Exercise 10a in a working program. Make sure your function is called from `main()` and correctly returns a value to `main()`. Have `main()` use a `cout` statement to display the value returned. Test the function by passing various data to it.

11. *a.* The volume, v, of a cylinder is given by the formula

$$v = \pi r^2 l$$

   where r is the cylinder's radius and l is its length. Using this formula, write a C++ function named `cylvol()` that accepts the radius and length of a cylinder and returns its volume.
   b. Include the function written in Exercise 11a in a working program. Make sure your function is called from `main()` and correctly returns a value to `main()`. Have `main()` use a `cout` statement to display the value returned. Test the function by passing various data to it.

12. *a.* An extremely useful programming algorithm for rounding a real number to n decimal places is

   Step 1. Multiply the number by 10^n
   Step 2. Add .5
   Step 3. Delete the fractional part of the result
   Step 4. Divide by 10^n

   For example, using this algorithm to round the number 78.374625 to three decimal places yields

   Step 1: $78.374625 \times 10^3 = 78374.625$
   Step 2: $78374.625 + .5 = 78375.125$
   Step 3: Retaining the integer part = 78375
   Step 4: 78375 divided by $10^3 = 78.375$

   Using this algorithm, write a C++ function that accepts a user-entered value of money, multiplies the entered amount by an 8.675 percent interest rate, and displays the result rounded to two decimal places.
   b. Enter, compile, and execute the program written for Exercise 12a.

13. *a.* Write a C++ function named `whole()` that returns the integer part of any number passed to the function. (*Hint:* Assign the passed argument to an integer variable.)
b. Include the function written in Exercise 13a in a working program. Make sure your function is called from `main()` and correctly returns a value to `main()`. Have `main()` use `cout` to display the value returned. Test the function by passing various data to it.
c. Write a C++ function named `fracpart()` that returns the fractional part of any number passed to the function. For example, if the number 256.879 is passed to `fracpart()`, the number .879 should be returned. Have the function `fracpart()` call the function `whole()` that you wrote in Exercise 13a. The number returned can then be determined as the number passed to `fracpart()` less the returned value when the same argument is passed to `whole()`. The completed program should consist of `main()` followed by `fracpart()` followed by `whole()`.
d. Include the function written in Exercise 13c in a working program. Make sure your function is called from `main()` and correctly returns a value to `main()`. Have `main()` use `cout` to display the value returned. Test the function by passing various data to it.

6.3 Pass by Reference

In a typical function invocation, the called function receives values from its calling function, stores and manipulates the passed values, and directly returns at most one single value. When data is passed in this manner, it is referred to as a *pass by value.*

Calling a function and passing arguments by value is a distinct advantage of C++. It allows functions to be written as independent entities that can use any variable or parameter name without concern that other functions may also be using the same name. It also alleviates any concern that altering a parameter or variable in one function may inadvertently alter the value of a variable in another function. Under this approach, parameters can be considered as either initialized variables or variables that will be assigned values when the function is executed. However, at no time does the called function have direct access to any variable defined in the calling function, even if the variable is used as an argument in the function call.

There are times when it is necessary to alter this approach by giving a called function direct access to the variables of its calling function. This allows one function, which is the called function, to use and change the values of variables that have been defined in the calling function. To do this requires that the address of the variable be passed to the called function. Once the called function has the variable's address, it "knows where the variable lives," so to speak, and can directly access and change the value stored there.

Passing addresses is referred to as a function *pass by reference*[12] because the called function can reference, or access, the variable whose address has been passed. C++ provides two types of address parameters: references and pointers. In this section we describe the method that uses reference parameters.

Passing and Using Reference Parameters

As always, in exchanging data between two functions, we must be concerned with both the sending side and the receiving side of the data exchange. From the sending side, however, calling a function and passing an address as an argument that will be accepted as a reference parameter on the receiving side is exactly the same as calling a function and passing a value; the called function is summoned into action by giving its name and a list of arguments. For example, the statement `newval(firstnum, secnum);` both calls the function named `newval` and passes two arguments to it. Whether a value or an address is actually passed depends on the parameter types declared for `newval()`. Let us now write the `newval()` function and prototype so that it receives the addresses of the variables `firstnum` and `secnum`, which we will assume to be floating-point variables, rather than their values.

One of the first requirements in writing `newval()` is to declare two reference parameters for accepting passed addresses. In C++ a reference parameter is declared using the syntax

```
data-type& reference-name
```

For example, the reference declaration

```
float& num1;
```

declares that `num1` is a reference parameter that will be used to store the address of a `float`. Similarly, `int& secnum` declares that `secnum` is a reference to an integer, and `char& key` declares that `key` is a reference to a character.

Recall from Section 2.4 that the ampersand, `&`, symbol in C++ means "the address of." Additionally, when an `&` symbol is used within a declaration, it refers to "the address of" the preceding data type. Thus, declarations such as `float& num1` and `int& secnum` are sometimes more clearly understood if they are read backward. Reading the declaration `float& num1` in this manner yields the information that "`num1` is the address of a floating-point value."

---

12 It is also referred to as a *call by reference*, where again the term applies only to the arguments whose addresses have been passed.

Because we need to accept two addresses in the parameter list for `newval()`, the declarations `float& num1` and `float& num2` can be used. When we include these declarations within the parameter list for `newval()`, and assuming that the function returns no value (`void`), the function header for `newval()` becomes

```
void newval(float& num1, float& num2)
```

For this function header line, an appropriate function prototype is

```
void newval(float&, float&);
```

This prototype and header line are included in Program 6-8, which includes a completed `newval()` function body that both displays and directly alters the values stored in these reference parameters from within the called function.

Program 6-8

```
#include <iostream.h>

void newval(float&, float&);  // prototype with two reference parameters

int main()
{
  float firstnum, secnum;


  cout << "Enter two numbers: ";
  cin  >> firstnum >> secnum;
  cout << "\nThe value in firstnum is: " << firstnum << endl;
  cout << "The value in secnum is: " << secnum << "\n\n";

  newval(firstnum, secnum);   // call the function

  cout << "The value in firstnum is now: " << firstnum << endl;
  cout << "The value in secnum is now: " << secnum << endl;

  return 0;
}

void newval(float& xnum, float& ynum)
{
   cout << "The value in xnum is: " << xnum << endl;
   cout << "The value in ynum is: " << ynum << "\n\n";
   xnum = 89.5;
   ynum = 99.5;

   return;
}
```

In calling the `newval()` function within Program 6-8, it is important to understand the connection between the arguments, `firstnum` and `secnum`, used in the function call and the parameters, `xnum` and `ynum`, used in the function header. *Both refer to the same data items.* The significance of this is that the values in the arguments (`firstnum` and `secnum`) can now be altered from within `newval()` by using the parameter names (`xnum` and `ynum`). Thus the parameters `xnum` and `ynum` do not store copies of the values in `firstnum` and `secnum` but directly access the locations in memory set aside for these two arguments. The equivalence of argument and parameter names in Program 6-8, which is the essence of a pass by reference, is illustrated in Figure 6–8. As this figure shows, the argument names and their matching parameter names are simply different names referring to the same memory storage areas. In `main()` these memory locations are referenced by the names `firstnum` and `secnum`, respectively, whereas in `newval()` the same locations are referenced by the parameter names `xnum` and `ynum`, respectively.

The following sample run was obtained using Program 6-8:

```
Enter two numbers: 22.5 33.0

The value in firstnum is: 22.5
The value in secnum is:   33

The value in xnum is: 22.5
The value in ynum is: 33

The value in firstnum is now: 89.5
The value in secnum is now: 99.5
```

FIGURE 6–8 The Equivalence of Arguments and Parameters in Program 6-8.

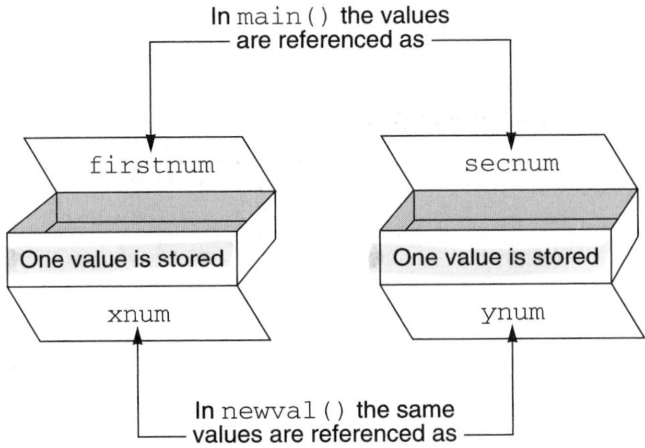

In reviewing this output, note that the values initially displayed for the parameters xnum and ynum are the same as those displayed for the arguments firstnum and secnum. Because xnum and ynum are reference parameters, however, newval() now has direct access to the arguments firstnum and secnum. Thus any change to xnum within newval() directly alters the value of firstnum in main(), and any change to ynum directly changes secnum's value. As illustrated by the final displayed values, the assignment of values to xnum and ynum within newval() is reflected in main() as the altering of firstnum's and secnum's values.

The equivalence between actual calling arguments and function parameters illustrated in Program 6-8 provides the basis for returning multiple values from within a function. For example, assume that a function is required to accept three values, compute these values' sum and product, and return these computed results to the calling routine. Naming the function calc() and providing five parameters (three for the input data and two references for the returned values) enables us to use the following function:

```
void calc(float num1, float num2, float num3, float& total, float& product)
{
  total = num1 + num2 + num3;
  product = num1 * num2 * num3;
  return;
}
```

This function has five parameters, named num1, num2, num3, total, and product, of which only the last two are declared as references. Thus the first three arguments are passed by value, and the last two arguments are passed by reference. Within the function, only the last two parameters are altered. The value of the fourth parameter, total, is calculated as the sum of the first three parameters, and the last parameter, product, is computed as the product of the parameters num1, num2, and num3. Program 6-9 includes this function in a complete program.

Within main(), the function calc() is called using the five arguments firstnum, secnum, thirdnum, sum, and product. As required, these arguments agree in number and data type with the parameters declared by calc(). Of the five arguments passed, only firstnum, secnum, and thirdnum have been assigned values when the call to calc() is made. The remaining two arguments have not been initialized and will be used to receive values back from calc(). Depending on the compiler used in compiling the program, these arguments will initially contain either zeros or "garbage" values. Figure 6–9 illustrates the relationship between actual and parameter names and the values they contain after the return from calc().

Program 6-9

```
#include <iostream.h>

void calc(float, float, float, float&, float&);  // prototype

int main()
{
  float firstnum, secnum, thirdnum, sum, product;

  cout << "Enter three numbers: ";
  cin  >> firstnum >> secnum >> thirdnum;

  calc(firstnum, secnum, thirdnum, sum, product);  // function call

  cout << "\nThe sum of the numbers is: " << sum << endl;
  cout << "The product of the numbers is: " << product << endl;

  return 0;
}

void calc(float num1, float num2, float num3, float& total, float& product)
{
  total = num1 + num2 + num3;
  product = num1 * num2 * num3;
  return;
}
```

Once `calc()` is called, it uses its first three parameters to calculate values for `total` and `product` and then returns control to `main()`. Because of the order of its actual calling arguments, `main()` knows the values calculated by `calc()` as `sum` and `product`, which are then displayed. Following is a sample run using Program 6-9:

```
Enter three numbers: 2.5 6.0 10.0

The sum of the entered numbers is: 18.5
The product of the entered numbers is: 150
```

As a final example illustrating the usefulness of passing references to a called function, we will construct a function named `swap()` that exchanges the values

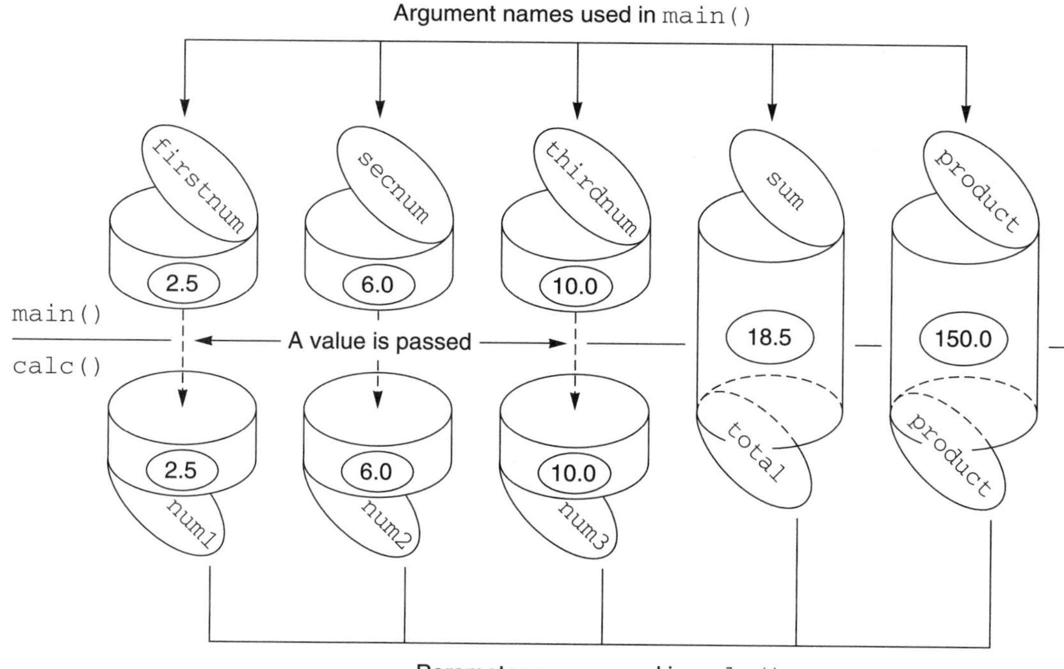

FIGURE 6–9 Relationship Between Argument and Parameter Names

of two of `main()`'s floating-point variables. Such a function is useful when we are sorting a list of numbers.

Because the value of more than a single variable is affected, `swap()` cannot be written as a pass by value function that returns a single value. The desired exchange of `main()`'s variables by `swap()` can be obtained only by giving `swap()` access to `main()`'s variables. One way of doing this is to use reference parameters.

We have already seen, in Program 6-8, how to pass references to two variables. We will now construct a function to exchange the values in the passed reference parameters. Exchanging values in two variables is accomplished by using the three-step exchange algorithm

1. Store the first parameter's value in a temporary location (see Figure 6–10a)
2. Store the second parameter's value in the first variable (see Figure 6–10b)
3. Store the temporary value in the second parameter (see Figure 6–10c)

Following is the function `swap()` written according to these specifications:

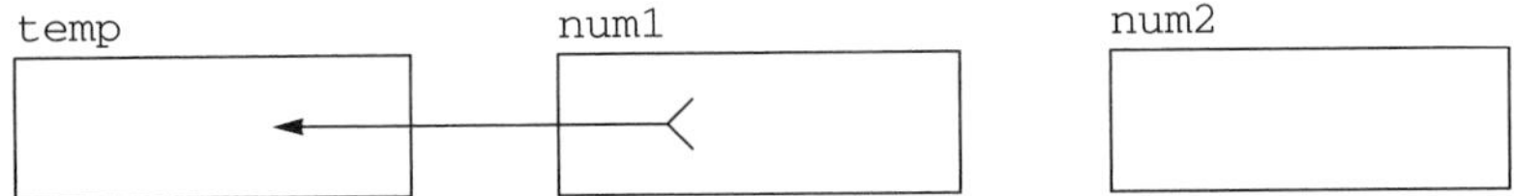

FIGURE 6–10a Save the First Value

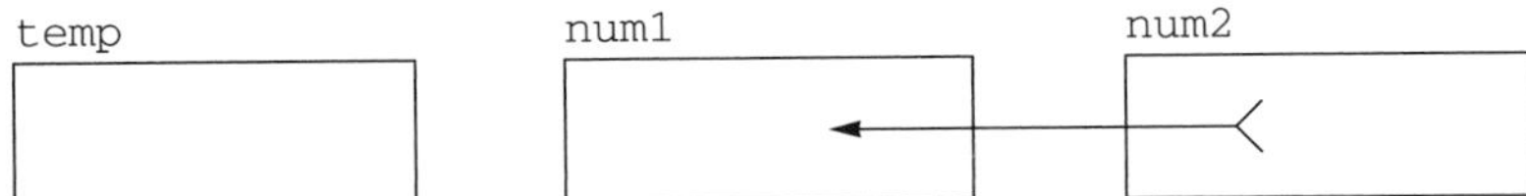

FIGURE 6–10b Replace the First Value with the Second Value

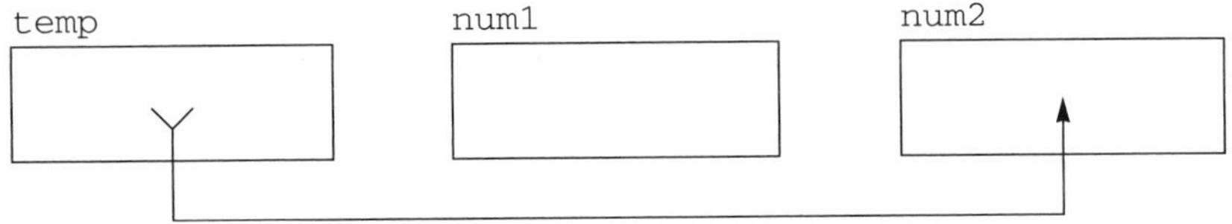

FIGURE 6–10c Change the Second Value

```
void swap(float& num1, float& num2)
{
  float temp;

  temp = num1;      // save num1's value
  num1 = num2;      // store num2's value in num1
  num2 = temp;      // change num2's value

  return;
}
```

Note that the use of references in `swap()`'s header line gives `swap()` access to the equivalent arguments in the calling function. Thus any changes to the two reference parameters in `swap()` automatically change the values in the calling function's arguments. Program 6-10 contains `swap()` in a complete program.

The following sample run was obtained using Program 6-10:

```
The value stored in firstnum is: 20.5
The value stored in secnum is: 6.25

The value stored in firstnum is now: 6.25
The value stored in secnum is now: 20.5
```

Program 6-10

```
#include <iostream.h>

void swap(float&, float&);    // function receives 2 references

int main()
{
  float firstnum = 20.5, secnum = 6.25;

  cout << "The value stored in firstnum is: " << firstnum << endl;
  cout << "The value stored in secnum is: "<< secnum << "\n\n";

  swap(firstnum, secnum);    // call the function with references

  cout << "The value stored in firstnum is now: " << firstnum << endl;
  cout << "The value stored in secnum is now: " << secnum << endl;

  return 0;
}

void swap(float& num1, float& num2)
{
  float temp;

  temp = num1;       // save num1's value
  num1 = num2;       // store num2's value in num1
  num2 = temp;       // change num2's value

  return;
}
```

As the output illustrates, the values stored in `main()`'s variables have been modified from within `swap()`, which was made possible by the use of reference parameters. If a pass by value had been used instead, the exchange within `swap()` would affect only `swap()`'s parameters and would accomplish nothing with respect to `main()`'s variables. Thus a function such as `swap()` can be written only using references or some other means that provides access to `main()`'s variables (this other means is by pointers, the topic of Chapter 8).

There are two cautions to keep in mind when using reference parameters. The first is that the equivalent arguments *must* be variables (that is, they cannot be used to change constants). For example, calling `swap()` with two constants, such as in the call `swap(20.5, 6.5)`, passes two constants to the function. Although `swap()` may execute, it will not change the values of these constants.[13]

The second caution is that a function call itself gives no indication that the called function will be using reference parameters. The default in C++ is to make passes by value rather than passes by reference, precisely to limit a called function's ability to alter variables in the calling function. This calling procedure should be adhered to whenever possible, which means that reference parameters should be used only in very restricted situations that actually require multiple return values, such as in the `swap()` function illustrated in Program 6-10. The `calc()` function, included in Program 6-9, though it is useful for illustrative purposes, could also be written as two separate functions, each returning a single value.

Exercises 6.3

1. Write parameter declarations for:
   a. A formal parameter named `amount` that will be a reference to a floating-point value
   b. A formal parameter named `price` that will be a reference to a double-precision number
   c. A formal parameter named `minutes` that will be a reference to an integer number
   d. A formal parameter named `key` that will be a reference to a character
   e. A formal parameter named `yield` that will be a reference to a double-precision number

2. Three integer arguments are to be used in a call to a function named `time()`. Write a suitable function header for `time()`, assuming that `time()` accepts these variables as the reference parameters `sec`, `min`, and `hours` and returns no value to its calling function.

3. Rewrite the `FindMax()` function in Program 6-5 so that the variable `max`, declared in `main()`, is used to store the maximum value of the two passed numbers. The value of `max` should be set directly from within `FindMax()`. (*Hint:* A reference to `max` will have to be accepted by `FindMax()`.)

4. Write a function named `change()` that has an integer parameter and six integer reference parameters named `hundreds`, `fifties`, `twenties`, `tens`, `fives`, and `ones`. The function is to consider the integer passed value as a dollar amount and convert the value into the least number of equivalent bills. Using the references, the function should directly alter the respective arguments in the calling function.

5. Write a function named `time()` that has an integer parameter named `seconds` and three integer reference parameters named `hours`, `min`, and `sec`. The function is to convert the passed number of seconds into an equivalent number of hours, minutes, and seconds. Using the references, the function should directly alter the respective actual arguments in the calling function.

---

[13] Most compilers will catch this error.

6. Write a function named `yrCalc()` that has a long-integer parameter representing the total number of days since the turn of the century (1/1/1900) and reference parameters named `year`, `month`, and `day`. The function is to calculate the current year, month, and day for the given number of days passed to it. Using the references, the function should directly alter the respective actual arguments in the calling function. For this problem, assume that each year has 365 days and each month has 30 days.

7. Write a function named `liquid()` that has an integer number parameter and reference parameters named `gallons`, `quarts`, `pints`, and `cups`. The passed integer represents the total number of cups, and the function is to determine the numbers of gallons, quarts, pints, and cups in the passed value. Using the references, the function should directly alter the respective actual arguments in the calling function. Use the relationships of 2 cups to a pint, 4 cups to a quart, and 16 cups to a gallon.

8. The following program uses the same argument and parameter names in both the calling function and the called function. Determine whether this causes any problem for the computer.

```
#include <iostream.h>

int main()
{
  int min, hour;
  void time(int &, int &);   // function prototype

  cout << "Enter two numbers :";
  cin  >> min >> hour;
  time(min, hour);

  return 0;
}

void time(int&min, int&hour)    // accept two references
{
  int sec;

  sec = (hour * 60 + min) * 60;
  cout << "The total number of seconds is " << sec << endl;

  return 0;
}
```

6.4 Variable Scope

Now that we have begun to write programs that contain more than one function, we can look more closely at the variables declared within each function and their relationship to variables in other functions.

By their very nature, C++ functions are constructed to be independent modules. As we have seen, values are passed to a function using the function's parameter list, and a value is returned from a function using a `return` statement. Seen in this light, a function can be thought of as a closed box, with slots at the top to receive values and a single slot at the bottom of the box to return a value (see Figure 6–11).

The metaphor of a closed box is useful because it emphasizes the fact that what goes on inside the function, including all variable declarations within the function's body, is hidden from the view of all other functions. Because the variables created inside a function are conventionally available only to the function itself, they are said to be local to the function, or *local variables*. This term refers to the scope of an identifier, where *scope* is defined as the section of the program where the identifier, such as a variable, is valid or "known." This section of the program is also referred to as where the variable is visible. A variable can have either a local scope or a global scope. A variable with a *local scope* is simply one that has had storage locations set aside for it by a declaration statement made within a function body. Local variables are meaningful only when used in expressions or statements inside the function that declared them. This means that the same variable name can be declared and used in more than one function. For each function that declares the variable, a separate and distinct variable is created.

All the variables that we have used until now have been local variables. This is a direct result of placing our declaration statements inside functions and using them as definition statements that cause the compiler to reserve storage for the declared variable. As we shall see, declaration statements can be placed outside functions, and they need not act as definitions that cause new storage areas to be reserved for the declared variable.

FIGURE 6–11 A Function Can Be Considered a Closed Box

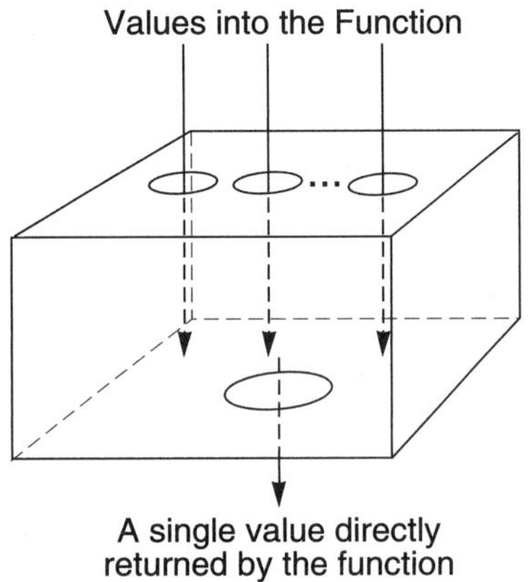

A variable with *global scope*, more commonly termed a *global variable*, is one whose storage has been created for it by a declaration statement located outside any function. These variables can be used by all functions that are physically placed after the global variable declaration. This is shown in Program 6-11, where we have purposely used the same variable name inside both functions contained in the program.

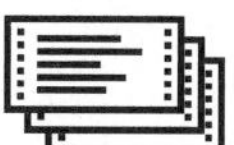

Program 6-11

```
#include <iostream.h>

int firstnum;          // create a global variable named firstnum

void valfun(void);     // function prototype (declaration)

int main()
{
  int secnum;          // create a local variable named secnum

  firstnum = 10;  // store a value into the global variable
  secnum = 20;    // store a value into the local variable

  cout << "From main(): firstnum = " << firstnum << endl;
  cout << "From main(): secnum =  " << secnum << endl;

  valfun();       // call the function valfun

  cout << "\nFrom main() again: firstnum = " << firstnum << endl;
  cout << "From main() again: secnum = " << secnum << endl;

  return 0;
}

void valfun(void)    // no values are passed to this function
{
  int secnum;   // create a second local variable named secnum

  secnum = 30;  // this only affects this local variable's value

  cout << "\nFrom valfun(): firstnum = " << firstnum << endl;
  cout << "From valfun(): secnum = " << secnum << endl;

  firstnum = 40;     // this changes firstnum for both functions

  return;
}
```

The variable `firstnum` in Program 6-11 is a global variable because its storage is created by a definition statement located outside a function. Because both functions, `main()` and `valfun()`, follow the definition of `firstnum`, both of these functions can use this global variable with no further declaration needed.

Program 6-11 also contains two separate local variables, both named `secnum`. Storage for the `secnum` variable named in `main()` is created by the definition statement located in `main()`. A different storage area for the `secnum` variable in `valfun()` is created by the definition statement located in the `valfun()` function. Figure 6–12 illustrates the three distinct storage areas reserved by the three definition statements found in Program 6-11.

All of the variables named `secnum` are local to the function in which their storage is created, and each of these variables can be used only from within the appropriate function. Thus when `secnum` is used in `main()`, the storage area reserved by `main()` for its `secnum` variable is accessed, and when `secnum` is used in `valfun()`, the storage area reserved by `valfun()` for its `secnum` variable is accessed. The following output is produced when Program 6-11 is run:

```
From main(): firstnum = 10
From main(): secnum = 20

From valfun(): firstnum = 10
From valfun(): secnum = 30

From main() again: firstnum = 40
From main() again: secnum = 20
```

FIGURE 6–12 The Three Storage Areas Created by Program 6-11

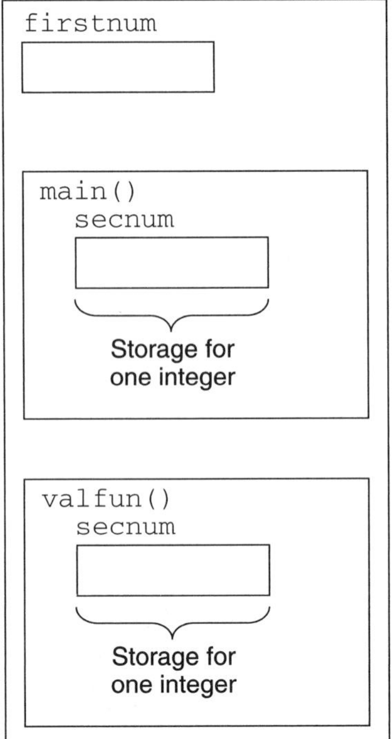

Let's analyze the output. Because `firstnum` is a global variable, both the `main()` function and the `valfun()` function can use and change its value. Initially, both functions print the value of 10 that `main()` stored in `firstnum`. Before returning, `valfun()` changes the value of `firstnum` to 40, which is the value displayed when the variable `firstnum` is next displayed from within `main()`.

Because each function "knows" only its own local variables, `main()` can send only the value of its `secnum` to the `cout` object, and `valfun()` can send only the value of its `secnum` to the `cout` object. Thus whenever `secnum` is obtained from `main()`, the value 20 is displayed, and whenever `secnum` is obtained from `valfun()`, the value 30 is displayed.

C++ does not confuse the two `secnum` variables because only one function can execute at a given moment. While a function is executing, only those variables and parameters that are "in scope" for that function (global and local) can be accessed.

The scope of a variable in no way influences or restricts the data type of the variable. Just as a local variable can be a character, integer, float, double, or any of the other data types (long/short) that we have introduced, so can global variables be of these data types, as illustrated in Figure 6–13. The scope of a variable is determined by the placement of the definition statement that reserves storage for it and optionally by a declaration statement that makes it visible, whereas the data type of the variable is determined by using the appropriate keyword (`char`, `int`, `float`, `double`, etc.) before the variable's name in a declaration statement.

Scope Resolution Operator

When a local variable has the same name as a global variable, all references to the variable name made within the scope of the local variable refer to the local variable. This situation is illustrated in Program 6-12, where the variable name `number` is defined as both a global and a local variable.

FIGURE 6–13 Relating the Scope and Type of a Variable

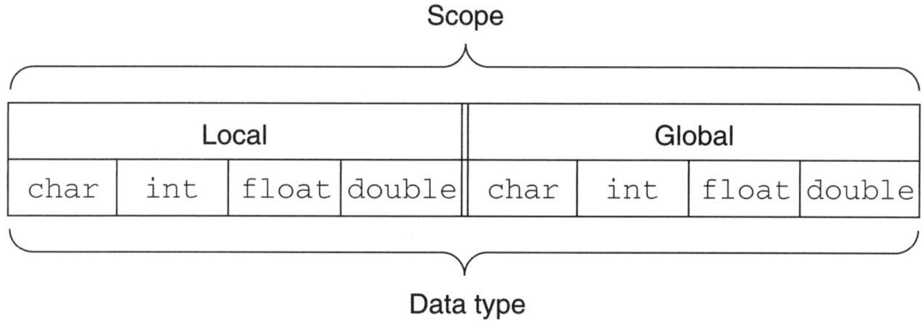

Program 6-12

```
#include <iostream.h>

float number = 42.8;        // a global variable named number

int main()
{
  float number = 26.4;      // a local variable named number

  cout << "The value of number is " << number << endl;

  return 0;
}
```

When Program 6-12 is executed, the following output is displayed:

```
The value of number is 26.4
```

As shown by this output, the local variable name takes precedence over the global variable. In such cases, we can still access the global variable by using C++'s scope resolution operator. This operator, which has the symbol `::`, must be placed immediately before the variable name, as in `::number`. When used in this manner, the `::` tells the compiler to use the global variable. As an example, the scope resolution operator is used in Program 6-12a.

Program 6-12a

```
#include <iostream.h>

float number = 42.5;        // a global variable named number

int main()
{
  float number = 26.4;      // a local variable named number

  cout << "The value of number is " << ::number << endl;

  return 0;
}
```

The output produced by Program 6-10a is

```
The value of number is 42.5
```

As indicated by this output, the scope resolution operator causes the global, rather than the local, variable to be accessed.

Misuse of Globals

Global variables allow the programmer to "jump around" the normal safeguards provided by functions. Rather than passing variables to a function, it is possible to make all variables global ones. **Do not do this**. By indiscriminately making all variables global, you instantly destroy the safeguards that C++ provides to make functions independent and insulated from each other, including the necessity of carefully designating the type of parameters a function needs, the variables used in the function, and the value returned.

Using only global variables can be especially disastrous in larger programs that have many user-created functions. Because all variables in a function must be declared, creating functions that use global variables requires that you remember to write the appropriate global declarations at the top of each program that uses the function; they no longer come along with the function. More devastating than this, however, is the horror of trying to track down an error in a large program using global variables. A global variable can be accessed and changed by any function following the global declaration, so it is a time-consuming and frustrating task to locate the origin of an erroneous value.

Global definitions, however, are sometimes useful in creating variables and named constants that must be shared among many functions. Rather than passing the same value to each function, it is easier to define the variable or constant once as a global. Doing so also notifies anyone reading the program that many functions use the variable. Most large programs nearly always make use of a few global variables and/or constants. Smaller programs containing a few functions, however, should almost never contain global variables.

The misuse of globals does not apply to function prototypes, which typically are global. Note that all of the function prototypes we have used have been of global scope, which declares the prototype to all subsequent functions. Placing a function prototype within a function makes the prototype a local declaration, available only to the function within which it is declared.

Exercises 6.4

1. a. For the following section of code, determine the data type and scope of all declared constants and variables. To do this, use a separate sheet of paper and list the three column headings that follow (we have filled in the entries for the first variable).

Identifier	Data Type	Scope
PRICE	integer	global to main(), roi(), and step()

```
#include <iostream.h>

const int PRICE;
const long YEARS;
const double YIELD;
int main()
{
  int bondtype;
  double interest, coupon;
     .
     .
     .
  return 0;
}
double roi(int mat1, int mat2)
{
  int count;
  double effectiveRate;
       .
       .
       .
  return effectiveRate;
}
int step(float first, float last)
{
  int numofyrs;
  float fracpart;
       .
       .
       .
  return(10*numofyrs);
}
```

b. Draw boxes around the appropriate section of the above code to enclose the scope of each variable.

c. Determine the data type of the parameters that the functions `roi()` and `step()` expect and the data type of the value returned by these functions.

2. *a.* For the following section of code, determine the data type and scope of all declared constants and variables. To do this, use a separate sheet of paper and list the three column headings that follow (we have filled in the entries for the first variable).

Identifier	Data Type	Scope
KEY	char	global to main(), func1(), and func2()

```
#include <iostream.h>

const char KEY;
const long NUMBER;
int func1(int, int);          // function prototype
double func2(float, float); // function prototype
int main()
{
  int a,b,c;
  double x,y;
      .
      .
      .
  return 0;
}

double secnum;
int func1(int num1, int num2)
{
  int o,p;
  float q;
      .
      .
      .
  return p;
}

double func2(float first, float last)
{
  int a,b,c,o,p;
  float r;
  double s,t,x;
      .
      .
      .
  return s * t;
}
```

b. Draw a box around the appropriate section of the above code to enclose the scope of the variables `key`, `secnum`, `y`, and `r`.

c. Determine the data type of the parameters for the functions `func1()` and `func2()` and the data type of the value returned by these functions.

3. Besides speaking about the scope of a variable, we can also apply the term to a function's parameters. What do you think is the scope of all function parameters?

4. Determine the values displayed by each `cout` statement in the following program:

```
#include <iostream.h>
int firstnum = 10;   // declare and initialize a global variable
void display(void);  // function prototype
int main()
{
  int firstnum = 20;   // declare and initialize a local variable

  cout << "\nThe value of firstnum is " << firstnum;
  display();

  return 0;
}
void display(void)
{
  cout << "\nThe value of firstnum is now " << firstnum;

  return;
}
```

6.5 Variable Storage Class

The scope of a variable defines the location within a program where that variable can be used. Given a program, you could take a pencil and draw a box around the section of the program where each variable is valid. The space inside the box would represent the scope of a variable. From this viewpoint, the scope of a variable can be thought of as the space within the program where the variable is valid.

In addition to the space dimension represented by its scope, variables also have a time dimension. The time dimension refers to the length of time that storage locations are reserved for a variable. This time dimension is referred to as the variable's "lifetime." For example, all variable storage locations are released back to the operating system when a program is finished running. However, while a program is still executing, interim variable storage areas also are reserved and subsequently released back to the operating system. Where and how long a variable's storage locations are kept before they are released can be determined by the *storage class* of the variable.

Besides having a data type and scope, every variable also has a storage class. The four available storage classes are called `auto`, `static`, `extern`, and `register`. If one of these class names is used, it must be placed before the variable's data type in a declaration statement. Examples of declaration statements that include a storage class designation are

```
auto int num;       // auto storage class and int data type
static int miles;   // static storage class and int data type
register int dist;  // register storage class and int data type
extern int volts;   // extern storage class and int data type
auto float coupon;  // auto storage class and float data type
static double yrs;  // static storage class and double data type
extern float yld;   // extern storage class and float data type
auto char inKey;    // auto storage class and char variable
```

To understand what the storage class of a variable means, we will consider first local variables (those variables created inside a function) and then global variables (those variables created outside a function).

Local Variable Storage Classes

Local variables can only be members of the `auto`, `static`, or `register` storage classes. If no class description is included in the declaration statement, the variable is automatically assigned to the `auto` class. Thus `auto` is the default class used by C++. Because the storage class designation was omitted, all the local variables that we have used have been `auto` variables.

The term `auto` is short for *automatic*. Storage for `auto` local variables is automatically reserved (that is, created) each time a function declaring `auto` variables is called. As long as the function has not returned control to its calling function, all `auto` variables local to the function are "alive"—that is, storage for the variables is available. When the function returns control to its calling function, its local `auto` variables "die"—that is, the storage for the variables is released back to the operating system. This process repeats itself each time a function is called. For example, consider Program 6-13, where the function `testauto()` is called three times from `main()`.

The output produced by Program 6-13 is

```
The value of the automatic variable num is 0
The value of the automatic variable num is 0
The value of the automatic variable num is 0
```

Each time `testauto()` is called, the `auto` variable `num` is created and initialized to zero. When the function returns control to `main()`, the variable `num` is destroyed, along with any value stored in `num`. Thus the effect of incrementing `num` in `testauto()`, before the function's `return` statement, is lost when control is returned to `main()`.

Program 6-13

```
#include <iostream.h>

void testauto(void);     // function prototype

int main()
{
  int count;                  // count is a local auto variable

  for(count = 1; count <= 3; count++)
    testauto();

  return 0;
}

void testauto(void)
{
  int num = 0;      // num is a local auto variable
                    // that is initialized to zero
  cout << "The value of the automatic variable num is "
       << num << endl;
  num++;

  return;
}
```

For most applications, the use of `auto` variables works just fine. There are cases, however, where we would like a function to remember values between function calls. This is the purpose of the `static` storage class. A local variable that is declared as `static` causes the program to keep the variable and its latest value, even when the function that declared it is finished executing. Examples of `static` variable declarations are

```
static int rate;
static float taxes;
static double amount;
static char inKey;
static long resistance;
```

A local `static` variable is not created and destroyed each time the function declaring the `static` variable is called. Once created, local `static` variables remain in existence for the life of the program. This means that the last value stored in the variable when the function is finished executing is available to the function the next time it is called.

Because local `static` variables retain their values, they are not initialized within a declaration statement in the same way as `auto` variables. To understand why, consider the automatic declaration `int num = 0;`, which causes the `auto` variable `num` to be created and set to zero each time the declaration is encountered. This is called a *run-time initialization* because initialization occurs each time the declaration statement is encountered. This type of initialization would be disastrous for a `static` variable because resetting the variable's value to zero each time the function is called would destroy the very value we are trying to save.

The initialization of `static` variables (both local and global) is done only once, when the program is first compiled. At compilation time, the variable is created and any initialization value is placed in it.[14] Thereafter, the value in the variable is kept without further initialization each time the function is called. To see how this works, consider Program 6-14.

Program 6-14

```
#include <iostream.h>

void teststat(void);     // function prototype

int main()
{
  int count;                 // count is a local auto variable

  for(count = 1; count <= 3; count++)
    teststat();

  return 0;
}

void teststat(void)
{
  static int num = 0;      // num is a local static variable
  cout << "The value of the static variable num is now "
       << num << endl;
  num++;

  return;
}
```

[14] Some compilers initialize `static` local variables the first time the definition statement is executed rather than when the program is compiled.

The output produced by Program 6-14 is

```
The value of the static variable num is now 0
The value of the static variable num is now 1
The value of the static variable num is now 2
```

As illustrated by this output, the `static` variable `num` is set to zero only once. The function `teststat()` then increments this variable just before returning control to `main()`. The value that `num` has when leaving the function `teststat()` is retained and displayed when the function is next called.

Unlike `auto` variables that can be initialized by either constants or expressions using both constants and previously initialized variables, `static` variables can be initialized only by using constants or constant expressions, such as `3.2 + 8.0`. Also, unlike `auto` variables, all `static` variables are set to zero when no explicit initialization is given. Thus the specific initialization of `num` to zero in Program 6-14 is not required.

The remaining storage class available to local variables, the `register` class, is not used as extensively as either `auto` or `static` variables. Examples of `register` variable declarations are

```
register int time;
register double diffren;
register float coupon;
```

`Register` variables have the same time duration as `auto` variables; that is, a local `register` variable is created when the function declaring it is entered, and it is destroyed when the function completes execution. The only difference between `register` and `auto` variables is in where the storage for the variable is located.

Storage for all variables (local and global), except `register` variables, is reserved in the computer's memory area. Most computers have a few additional high-speed storage areas located directly in the computer's processing unit that can also be used for variable storage. These special high-speed storage areas are called *registers*. Because registers are physically located in the computer's processing unit, they can be accessed faster than the normal memory storage areas located in the computer's memory unit. Also, computer instructions that access registers typically require less space than instructions that access memory locations because there are fewer registers that can be accessed than there are memory locations. When the compiler substitutes the location of a register for a variable during program compilation, less space in the instruction is needed than is required to address a memory that has millions of locations.

Besides decreasing the size of a compiled C++ program, using register variables can also increase the execution speed of a C++ program if the compiler you are using supports this data type. Variables declared with the register storage class are automatically switched to the auto storage class if your compiler does not support register variables or if the declared register variables exceed the computer's register capacity.

The only restriction in using the register storage class is that the address of a register variable, using the address operator &, cannot be taken. This is easily understood when you realize that registers do not have standard memory addresses.

Global Variable Storage Classes

Global variables are created by definition statements external to a function. By their nature, these externally defined variables do not come and go with the calling of any function. Once a global variable is created, it exists until the program in which it is declared is finished executing. Thus global variables cannot be declared as either auto or register variables that are created and destroyed as the program is executing. Global variables may additionally be declared as members of the static or the extern storage class (but not both). Examples of declaration statements including these two class descriptions are

```
extern int sum;
extern double volts;
static double current;
```

The static and extern classes affect only the scope, not the time duration, of global variables. Like static local variables, all global variables are initialized to zero at compile time.

The purpose of the extern storage class is to extend the scope of a global variable beyond its normal boundaries. To understand this, we must first note that all of the programs we have written so far have been contained together in one file. Thus, when you have saved or retrieved programs, you have only needed to give the computer a single name for your program. This is not required by C++.

Larger programs typically consist of many functions that are stored in multiple files. An example of this is shown in Figure 6–14, where the three functions main(), func1(), and func2() are stored in one file and the two functions func3() and func4() are stored in a second file.

For the files illustrated in Figure 6–14, the global variables volts, current, and power declared in file1 can be used only by the functions main(), func1(), and func2() in this file. The single global variable factor declared in file2 can be used only by the functions func3() and func4() in file2.

POINT OF INFORMATION

Storage Classes

Variables of the type auto and register are always local variables. Only non-static global variables may be externed, which extends the variable's scope into another file or function.

Making a global variable static makes the variable private to the file in which it is declared. Thus static variables cannot be externed. Except for static variables, all variables are initialized each time they come into scope.

Although the variable volts has been created in file1, we may want to use it in file2. Placing the declaration statement extern int volts; in file2, as shown in Figure 6–15, allows us to do this. Putting this statement at the top of file2 extends the scope of the variable volts into file2 so that it may be used by both func3() and func4(). Thus the extern designation simply declares a global variable that is defined in another file. So placing the statement extern float current; in func4() extends the scope of this global variable, created in file1, into func4(), and the scope of the global variable factor, created in file2, is extended into func1() and func2() by the declaration statement extern double factor; placed before func1(). Notice that factor is not available to main().

FIGURE 6–14 A Program May Extend Beyond One File

file1

```
int volts;
float current;
static double power;
int main()
{
  func1();
  func2();
  func3();
  func4();
}
int func1()
{
    .
    .
    .
}
int func2()
{
    .
    .
    .
}
```

file2

```
double factor;
int func3()
{
    .
    .
    .
}
int func4()
{
    .
    .
    .
}
```

file1

```
int volts;
float current;
static double power;
int main()
{
  func1();
  func2();
  func3();
  func4();
}
extern double factor;
int func1()
{
   .
   .
   .
}
int func2()
{
   .
   .
   .
}
```

file2

```
double factor;
extern int volts;
int func3()
{
   .
   .
   .
}
int func4()
{
  extern float current;
   .
   .
   .
}
```

FIGURE 6–15 Extending the Scope of Global Variables

A declaration statement that specifically contains the word `extern` is different from every other declaration statement in that it does not cause the creation of a new variable by reserving new storage for the variable. An `extern` declaration statement simply informs the compiler that a global variable already exists and can now be used. The actual storage for the variable must be created somewhere else in the program using one, and only one, global declaration statement in which the word `extern` has not been used. Initialization of the global variable can, of course, be made with the original declaration of the global variable. Initialization within an `extern` declaration statement is not allowed and will cause a compilation error.

The existence of the `extern` storage class is the reason we have been so careful to distinguish between the creation and the declaration of a variable. Declaration statements that contain the word `extern` do not create new storage areas; they only extend the scope of existing global variables.

The last global class, `static` global variables, is used to prevent the extension of a global variable into a second file. Global `static` variables are declared in the same way as local `static` variables, except that the declaration statement is placed outside any function.

The scope of a global `static` variable cannot be extended beyond the file in which it is declared. This provides a degree of privacy for `static` global variables. Because they are only "known" and can be used only in the file in which they are declared, other files cannot access or change their values. Thus `static` global variables cannot subsequently be extended to a second file by using an `extern` declaration statement. Trying to do so will result in a compilation error.

Exercises 6.5

1. *a.* List the storage classes available to local variables.
   b. List the storage classes available to global variables.
2. Describe the difference between a local `auto` variable and a local `static` variable.
3. What is the difference between the following functions?

```
void init1(void)
{
  static int yrs = 1;
  cout << "\nThe value of yrs is " << yrs;
  yrs = yrs + 2;

  return;
}

void init2(void)
{
  static int yrs;
  yrs = 1;
  cout << "\nThe value of yrs is " << yrs;
  yrs = yrs + 2;

  return;
}
```

4. *a.* Describe the difference between a `static` global variable and an `extern` global variable.
   b. If a variable is declared with an `extern` storage class, what other declaration statement must be present somewhere in the program?
5. The declaration statement `static double years;` can be used to create either a local or a global `static` variable. What determines the scope of the variable `years`?
6. For the function and variable declarations illustrated in Figure 6–16, place an `extern` declaration to individually accomplish each of the following:

file1

```
char choice;
int flag;
long date, time;
int main()
{
    .
    .
    .
}
double coupon;
int price()
{
    .
    .
    .
}
int yield()
{
    .
    .
    .
}
```

file2

```
char bondType;
double maturity;
int roi()
{
    .
    .
    .
}
int pduction()
{
    .
    .
    .
}
int bid()
{
    .
    .
    .
}
```

FIGURE 6–16 Files for Exercise 6

a. Extend the scope of the global variable `choice` into all of `file2`.
b. Extend the scope of the global variable `flag` into the function `pduction()` only.
c. Extend the scope of the global variable `date` into `pduction()` and `bid()`.
d. Extend the scope of the global variable `date` into `roi()` only.
e. Extend the scope of the global variable `coupon` into `roi()` only.
f. Extend the scope of the global variable `bondType` into all of `file1`.
g. Extend the scope of the global variable `maturity` into both `price()` and `yield()`.

6.6 Common Programming Errors

An extremely common programming error related to functions is passing incorrect data types. The values passed to a function must correspond to the data types of the parameters declared for the function. One way to verify that correct values have been received is to display all passed values within a function's body before any calculations are made. Once this verification has taken place, the display can be dispensed with.[15]

15 In practice, a good debugger program should be used.

Another common error can occur when the same variable is declared locally within both the calling function and the called function. Even though the variable name is the same, a change to one local variable *does not* alter the value in the other local variable.

Related to this error is the error that can occur when a local variable has the same name as a global variable. Within the function declaring it, the use of the variable's name affects only the local variable's contents unless the scope resolution operator, `::`, is used.

Another common error is omitting the called function's prototype either before or within the calling function. The called function must be alerted to the type of value that will be returned, and this information is provided by the function prototype. The prototype can be omitted if the called function is physically placed in a program before its calling function. Although it is also permissible to omit the prototype and return type for functions that return an integer, it is poor documenting practice to do so. The actual value returned by a function can be verified by displaying it both before and after it is returned.

The last two common errors are terminating a function's header line with a semicolon and forgetting to include the data type of a function's parameters within the function header line.

6.7 Chapter Summary

1. A function is called by giving its name and passing any data to it in the parentheses following the name. If a variable is one of the arguments in a function call, the called function receives a copy of the variable's value.
2. The commonly used form of a user-written function is

```
return-type function-name(parameter list)
{
  declarations and other C++ statements;
   return expression;
}
```

The first line of the function is called the *function header*. The opening and closing braces of the function and all statements in between these braces constitute the function's *body*. When no returned data type is specified, the returned data type is, by default, an integer. The parameter list is a comma-separated list of parameter declarations.

3. A function's return type is the data type of the value returned by the function. If no type is declared, the function is assumed to return an integer value. If the function does not return a value, it should be declared as a `void` type.
4. Functions can directly return at most a single data type value to their calling functions. This value is the value of the expression in the `return` statement.
5. Using reference parameters, a function can be passed the address of a variable. If a called function is passed an address, it has the capability of directly accessing the respective calling function's variable. Using passed addresses permits a called function effectively to return multiple values.
6. Functions can be declared to all calling functions by means of a *function prototype.* The prototype provides a declaration for a function that specifies the data type returned by the function, its name, and the data types of the arguments expected by the function. Like all declarations, a function prototype is terminated with a semicolon and may be included within local variable declarations or as a global declaration. The most common form of a function prototype is

```
data-type function-name(parameter data type list);
```

   If the called function is placed physically above the calling function, no further declaration is required because the function's definition serves as a global declaration to all following functions.
7. Every variable used in a program has a *scope,* which determines where in the program the variable can be used. The scope of a variable is either local or global and is determined by where the variable's definition statement is placed. A local variable is defined within a function and can be used only within its defining function or block. A global variable is defined outside a function and can be used in any function following the variable's definition. All global variables that are not specifically initialized by the user are initialized to zero by the compiler and can be shared between files by using the keyword `extern`.
8. Every variable has a *class.* The class of a variable determines how long the value in the variable will be retained: `auto` variables are local variables that exist only while their defining function is executing; `register` variables are similar to automatic variables but are stored in a computer's internal registers rather than in memory; `static` variables can be either global or local and retain their values for the duration of a program's execution. All `static` variables are set to zero when they are defined if they are not explicitly initialized by the user.

6.8 Chapter Supplement: Generating Random Numbers

There are many business and engineering simulation problems in which probability must be considered or statistical sampling techniques must be used. For example, statistical models are required in simulating automobile traffic flow or telephone usage patterns. Additionally, applications such as simple computer games and more involved gaming scenarios can be described only statistically. All of these statistical models require the generation of *random numbers*—that is, a series of numbers whose order cannot be predicted.

In practice, there are no truly random numbers. Dice are never perfect; cards are never shuffled completely randomly; the supposedly random motions of molecules are influenced by the environment; and digital computers can handle numbers only within a finite range and with limited precision. The best one can do is generate *pseudorandom* numbers, which are sufficiently random for the task at hand.

Some computer languages contain a library function that produces random numbers; others do not. All C++ compilers provide two functions for creating random numbers: `rand()` and `srand()`. The `rand()` function produces a series of random numbers in the range 0 ≤ `rand()` ≤ `RAND_MAX`, where the constant `RAND_MAX` is defined in the `stdlib.h` header file. The `srand()` function provides a starting "seed" value for `rand()`. If `srand()` or some other equivalent "seeding" technique is not used, `rand()` will always produce the same series of random numbers.

The general procedure for creating a series of *N* random numbers using C++'s library functions is illustrated by the following code:

```
srand(time(NULL));   // this generates the first "seed" value

for (int i = 1; i <= N; i++)   // this generates N random numbers
{
  rvalue = rand();
  cout << rvalue << endl;
}
```

Here, the argument to the `srand()` function is a call to the `time()` function with a `NULL` argument. With this argument, the `time()` function reads the computer's internal clock time, in seconds. The `srand()` function then uses this time, converted to an unsigned `int`, to initialize the random number generator function `rand()`.[16] Program 6-15 uses this code to generate a series of ten random numbers.

Program 6-15

```
#include <iostream.h>
#include <iomanip.h>
#include <stdlib.h>
#include <time.h>
// this program generates ten pseudo random numbers
// using C++'s rand() function

int main()
{
  const int NUMBERS = 10;

  float randvalue;
  int i;

  srand(time(NULL));
  for (i = 1; i <= NUMBERS; ++i)
  {
    randvalue = rand();
    cout << setw(20) << randvalue << endl;
  }

  return 0;
}
```

The following is the output produced by one run of Program 6-15:

```
20203
21400
15265
26935
 8369
10907
31299
15400
 5074
20663
```

[16] Alternatively, many C++ compilers have a `randomize()` routine that is defined using the `srand()` function. If this routine is available, the call `randomize()` can be used in place of the call `srand(time(NULL))`. In either case, the initializing "seed" routine is called only once, after which the `rand()` function is used to generate a series of random numbers.

Because of the `srand()` function call in Program 6-15, the series of ten random numbers will differ each time the program is executed. Without the randomizing "seeding" effect of this function, the same series of random numbers would always be produced. Note also the inclusion of the `stdlib.h` and `time.h` header files. The `stdlib.h` file contains the function prototypes for the `srand` and `rand()` functions, whereas the `time.h` header file contains the function prototype for the `time()` function.

Scaling

In practice, it is typically necessary to make one modification to the random numbers produced by the `rand()` function. In most applications, the random numbers are required to be either floating-point numbers within the range of 0.0 to 1.0 or integers within a specified range, such as 1 to 100. The method for adjusting the random numbers produced by a random number generator to reside within such ranges is called *scaling*.

Scaling random numbers to reside within the range of 0.0 to 1.0 is easily accomplished by dividing the returned value of `rand()` by `RAND_MAX`. Thus the expression `float(rand())/RAND_MAX` produces a floating-point random number between 0.0 and 1.0.

Scaling a random number as an integer value between 0 and *N* is accomplished using either the expression `rand() % (N+1)` or the expression `int((rand()/RAND_MAX) * N)`. For example, the expression

```
int(rand()/RAND_MAX * 100)
```

produces a random integer between 0 and 100.[17]

To produce an integer random number between 1 and *N*, we can use the expression `1 + rand() % N`. For example, in simulating the roll of a die, the expression `1 + rand() % 6` produces a random integer between 1 and 6. The more general scaling expression `a + rand() % (b + 1 - a)` can be used to produce a random integer between the numbers *a* and *b*.

[17] Many C++ compilers have a routine named `random()` that can be used to produce the same result. For example, if your compiler has the `random()` function, the call `random(100)` will produce a random integer between 0 and 100.

Data Structures

Part II

Arrays

Chapter Seven

The variables that we have used so far have all had a common characteristic: Each variable could be used to store only a single value at a time. For example, although the variables `key`, `count`, and `grade` declared in the statements

```
char key;
int count;
float grade;
```

are of different data types, each variable can store only one value of the declared data type. These types of variables are called atomic variables. An *atomic variable,* which is also referred to as a *scalar variable,* is a variable whose value cannot be further subdivided or separated into legitimate data types.

Frequently we may have a set of values, all of the same data type, that form a logical group. For example, Figure 7–1 illustrates three groups of items. The first group is a list of five integer grades, the second group is a list of four character codes, and the last group is a list of six floating-point prices.

A simple list containing individual items of the same data type is called a one-dimensional array. In this chapter we describe how one-dimensional arrays are declared, initialized, stored inside a computer, and used. We also explore the use of one-dimensional arrays with example programs and present the procedures for declaring and using multidimensional arrays.

7.1 One-Dimensional Arrays

A *one-dimensional array,* which may also be referred to as a *single-dimensional array,* or a *vector,* is a list of related values with the same data type that is stored using a single group name.[1] In C++, as in other computer languages, the group

FIGURE 7–1 Three Lists of Items

Grades	Codes	Prices
98	x	10.96
87	a	6.43
92	m	2.58
79	n	.86
85		12.27
		6.39

[1] Note that lists can be implemented in a variety of ways. An array is simply one implementation of a list in which all of the list elements are of the same type and each element is stored consecutively in a set of contiguous memory locations.

Grade
98
87
92
79
85

FIGURE 7–2 A List of Grades

name is referred to as the *array name.* For example, consider the list of grades shown in Figure 7–2.

All the grades in the list are integer numbers and must be declared as such. However, the individual items in the list do not have to be declared separately. The items in the list can be declared as a single unit and stored under a common variable name called the array name. For convenience, we will choose `grade` as the name for the list shown in Figure 7–2. To specify that `grade` is to store five individual floating-point values requires the declaration statement `float grade[5]`. Note that this declaration statement gives the array (or list) name, the data type of the items in the array, and the number of items in the array. It is a specific example of the general array declaration statement that has the syntax

```
data-type array-name[number-of-items]
```

Common programming practice requires defining the number of items in the array as a constant before declaring the array. This constant is extremely useful later for processing all the items in an array. Thus the previous array declaration for `grade` would, in practice, be declared by using two statements, such as

```
const int NUMELS = 5; // define a constant for the number of items
int grade[NUMELS];    // declare the array
```

Further examples of array declarations that use this two-line syntax are

```
const int ARRAYSIZE = 4;
char code[ARRAYSIZE];

const int NUMELS = 6;
float prices[NUMELS];

const int SIZE = 100;
double amount[SIZE];
```

In these declaration statements, each array is allocated sufficient memory to hold the number of data items given in the declaration statement. Thus the array named `code` has storage reserved for four characters, the array named `prices` has storage reserved for six floating-point numbers, and the array named `amount` has storage reserved for 100 floating-point numbers. The constant identifiers, `ARRAYSIZE`, `NUMELS`, and `SIZE`, are programmer-selected names.

Figure 7–3 illustrates the storage reserved for the `grade` and `code` arrays, assuming that an integer is stored using two bytes and a character is stored using one byte.

Each item in an array is called an *element* or *component* of the array. The individual elements stored in the arrays illustrated in Figure 7–3 are stored sequentially, the first array element being stored in the first reserved location, the second element in the second reserved location, and so on until the last element is stored in the last reserved location. This contiguous storage allocation for the list is a key feature of arrays; it provides a simple mechanism for easily locating any single element in the list.

Because elements in the array are stored sequentially, any individual element can be accessed by giving the name of the array and the element's position. This position is called the element's *index* or *subscript value* (the two terms are synonymous). For a single-dimensional array, the first element has an index of 0, the second element has an index of 1, and so on. In C++, the array name and index of the desired element are combined by listing the index in braces after the array name. For example, given the declaration `float grade[5]`,

FIGURE 7–3 The `grade` and `code` Arrays in Memory

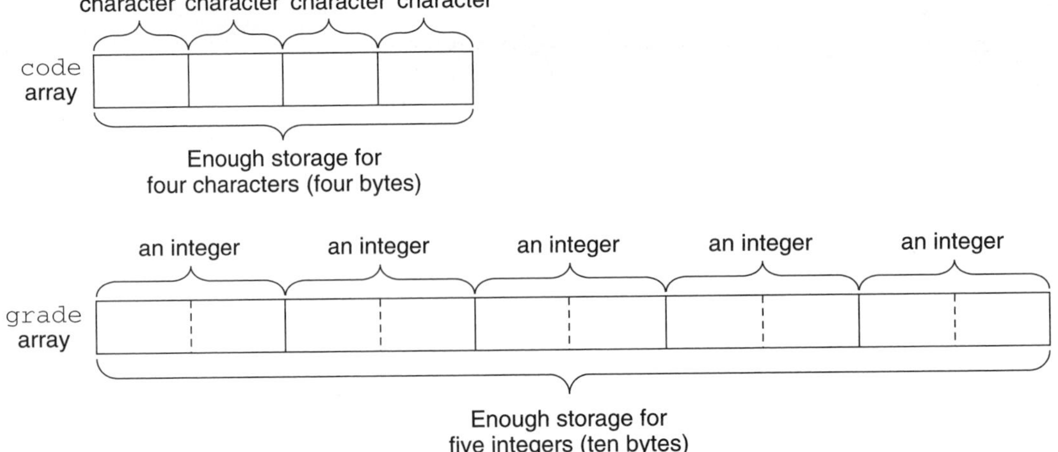

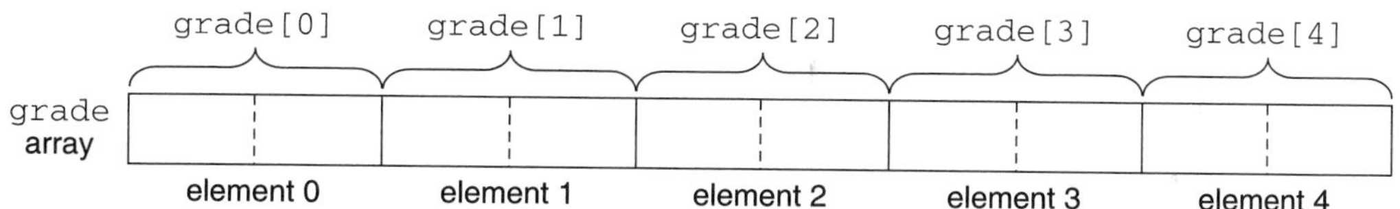

FIGURE 7–4 Identifying Individual Array Elements.

`grade[0]` refers to the first grade stored in the `grade` array
`grade[1]` refers to the second grade stored in the `grade` array
`grade[2]` refers to the third grade stored in the `grade` array
`grade[3]` refers to the fourth grade stored in the `grade` array
`grade[4]` refers to the fifth grade stored in the `grade` array

Figure 7–4 illustrates the `grade` array in memory with the correct designation for each array element. Each individual element is called an *indexed variable* or a *subscripted variable,* because both a variable name and an index or subscript value must be used to reference the element. Remember that the index or subscript value gives the *position* of the element in the array.

The subscripted variable `grade[0]` is read as "grade sub zero." This is a shortened way of saying "the grade array subscripted by zero" and distinguishes the first element in an array from an atomic variable that could be declared as `grade0`. Similarly, `grade[1]` is read as "grade sub one," `grade[2]` as "grade sub two," and so on.

Although it may seem unusual to reference the first element with an index of zero, doing so increases the computer's speed when it accesses array elements. Internally, unseen by the programmer, the computer uses the index as an offset from the array's starting position. As illustrated in Figure 7–5, the index tells the computer how many elements to skip, starting from the beginning of the array, to get to the desired element.

FIGURE 7–5 Accessing an Individual Array Element—Element 3

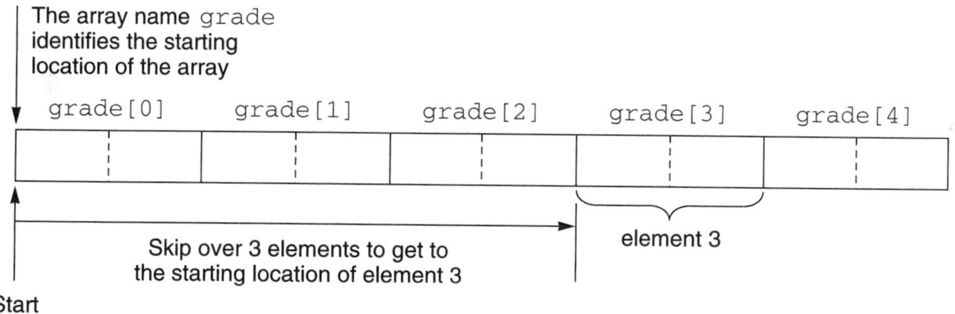

Subscripted variables can be used anywhere that scalar variables are valid. Here are some examples that use the elements of the `grade` array:

```
grade[0] = 95.75;
grade[1] = grade[0] - 11.0;
grade[2] = 5.0 * grade[0];
grade[3] = 79.0;
grade[4] = (grade[1] + grade[2] - 3.1) / 2.2;
sum = grade[0] + grade[1] + grade[2] + grade[3] + grade[4];
```

The subscript contained within brackets need not be an integer constant; any expression that evaluates to an integer may be used as a subscript.[2] In each case, of course, the value of the expression must be within the valid subscript range defined when the array is declared. For example, assuming that `i` and `j` are `int` variables, the following subscripted variables are valid:

```
grade[i]
grade[2*i]
grade[j-i]
```

One extremely important advantage of using integer expressions as subscripts is that it allows sequencing through an array by using a loop. This makes statements like

```
sum = grade[0] + grade[1] + grade[2] + grade[3] + grade[4];
```

unnecessary. The subscript values in this statement can be replaced by a `for` loop counter to access each element in the array sequentially. For example, the code

```
sum = 0;                          // initialize the sum to zero
for (i = 0; i < NUMELS; i++)
  sum = sum + grade[i];           // add in a grade
```

sequentially retrieves each array element and adds the element to `sum`. Here the variable `i` is used both as the counter in the `for` loop and as a subscript. As `i` increases by 1 each time through the loop, the next element in the array is referenced. This procedure for adding the array elements within the `for` loop is similar to the accumulation procedure we have used many times before.

---

2 Note: Some compilers permit floating-point variables as subscripts; in these cases, the floating-point value is truncated to an integer value.

The advantage of using a `for` loop to sequence through an array becomes apparent when we are working with larger arrays. For example, if the `grade` array contains 100 values rather than just 5, simply setting the constant `NUMELS` to 100 is sufficient both to create the larger array and to have the `for` statement sequence through the 100 elements and add each grade to the sum.

As another example of using a `for` loop to sequence through an array, assume that we want to locate the maximum value in an array of 1000 elements named `prices`. The procedure we will use to locate the maximum value is to assume initially that the first element in the array is the largest number. Then, as we sequence through the array, the maximum is compared to each element. When an element with a higher value is located, that element becomes the new maximum. The following code does the job:

```
const int NUMELS = 1000;

maximum = prices[0];                     // set the maximum to element zero
for (int i = 1; i < NUMELS; i++)   // cycle through the rest of the array
  if (prices[i] > maximum)              // compare each element to the maximum
        maximum = prices[i];             // capture the new high value
```

In this code the `for` statement consists of one `if` statement. The search for a new maximum value starts with the element 1 of the array and continues through the last element. In a 1000-element array, the last element is 999. Each element is compared to the current maximum, and when a higher value is encountered, it becomes the new maximum.

Input and Output of Array Values

Individual array elements can be assigned values interactively by using a `cin` stream object. Examples of individual data entry statements are

```
cin >> grade[0];
cin >> grade[1] >> grade[2] >> grade[3];
cin >> grade[4] >> prices[6];
```

In the first statement, a single value will be read and stored in the variable named `grade[0]`. The second statement causes three values to be read and stored in the variables `grade[1]`, `grade[2]`, and `grade[3]`, respectively. The last `cin` statement can be used to read values into the variables `grade[4]` and `prices[6]`.

Alternatively, a `for` loop can be used to cycle through the array for interactive data input. For example, the code

```
const int NUMELS = 5;

for (int i = 0; i < NUMELS; i++)
{
  cout << "Enter a grade: ";
  cin  >> grade[i];
}
```

prompts the user for five grades. The first grade entered is stored in `grade[0]`, the second in `grade[1]`, and so on until five grades have been input.

One caution should be mentioned about storing data or accessing in an array. Most implementations of C++ do not check the value of the index being used (called a *bounds check*). If an array has been declared as consisting of ten elements, for example, and you use an index of 12, which is outside the bounds of the array, C++ will not notify you of the error when the program is compiled. The program will attempt to access element 12 by skipping over the appropriate number of bytes from the start of the array. This usually results in a program crash—but not always. If the referenced location itself contains a data value, the program will simply access the value in the referenced memory locations. This leads to more errors, which are particularly troublesome to locate when the variable legitimately assigned to the storage location is used at a different point in the program. Using named constants as we have done helps to eliminate this problem.

During output, individual array elements can be displayed by using the `cout` object, or complete sections of the array can be displayed by including a `cout` statement within a `for` loop. Here are some examples where `cout` is used to display subscripted variables:

```
cout << prices[5];
```

and

```
cout << "The value of element " << i << " is " << grade[i];
```

and

```
const int NUMELS = 20;

for (int k = 5; k < NUMELS; k++)
  cout << k << "  " << amount[k];
```

The first `cout` statement displays the value of the subscripted variable `prices[5]`. The second `cout` statement displays the value of the subscript `i` and the value of `grade[i]`. Before this statement can be executed, `i` would have to have an assigned value. The last example includes a `cout` statement within a `for` loop. Both the value of the index and the value of the elements from 5 to 19 are displayed.

POINT OF INFORMATION

Aggregate Data Types

In contrast to atomic types, such as integer and floating-point data, there are aggregate types. An aggregate type, which is also referred to as a *structured type* and a *data structure,* is any type whose values can be decomposed and are related by some defined structure. Additionally, operations must be available for retrieving and updating individual values in the data structure.

Single-dimensional arrays are examples of a structured type. In a single-dimensional array, such as an array of integers, the array is composed of individual integer values where integers are related by their position in the list. Indexed variables provide the means of accessing and modifying values in the array.

Program 7-1 illustrates these input and output techniques using an array named `grade` that is defined to store five integer numbers. Included in the program are two `for` loops. The first `for` loop is used to cycle through each array element and allows the user to input individual array values. After five values have been entered, the second `for` loop is used to display the stored values.

Program 7-1

```
#include <iostream.h>

int main()
{
  const int NUMELS = 5;

  int i, grade[NUMELS];

  for (i = 0; i < NUMELS; i++)          // Enter the grades
  {
    cout << "Enter a grade: ";
    cin  >> grade[i];
  }

  cout << endl;

  for (i = 0; i < NUMELS; i++)          // Print the grades
    cout << "grade " << i << " is " << grade[i] << endl;

  return 0;
}
```

Following is a sample run using Program 7-1:

```
Enter a grade: 85
Enter a grade: 90
Enter a grade: 78
Enter a grade: 75
Enter a grade: 92

grade[0] is 85
grade[1] is 90
grade[2] is 78
grade[3] is 75
grade[4] is 92
```

In reviewing the output produced by Program 7-1, pay particular attention to the difference between the subscript value displayed and the numerical value stored in the corresponding array element. The subscript value refers to the *location* of the element in the array, whereas the subscripted variable refers to the *value* stored in the designated location.

In addition to simply displaying the values stored in each array element, the elements can also be processed by appropriately referencing the desired element. In Program 7-2, for example, the value of each element is accumulated in a total, which is displayed upon completion of the individual display of each array element.

Following is a sample run using Program 7-2:

```
Enter a grade: 85
Enter a grade: 90
Enter a grade: 78
Enter a grade: 75
Enter a grade: 92

The total of the grades  85  90  78  75  92  is  420
```

Note that in Program 7-2, unlike Program 7-1, only the values stored in each array element are displayed. Although the second `for` loop was used to accumulate the total of each element, the accumulation could also have been accomplished in the first loop by placing the statement `total = total + grade[i];` after the `cin` statement used to enter a value. Also note that the `cout` statement used to display the total is made outside the second `for` loop, so that the total is displayed only once, after all values have been added to the total. If this `cout` statement were placed inside the `for` loop, five totals would be displayed, with only the last displayed total containing the sum of all of the array values.

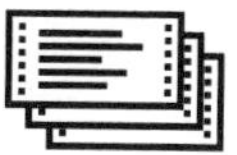

Program 7-2

```
#include <iostream.h>

int main()
{
  const int NUMELS = 5;

  int i, grade[NUMELS], total = 0;

  for (i = 0; i < NUMELS; i++)        // Enter the grades
  {
    cout << "Enter a grade: ";
    cin  >> grade[i];
  }

  cout << "\nThe total of the grades";

  for (i = 0; i < NUMELS; i++)     // Display and total the grades
  {
    cout << "   " << grade[i];
    total = total + grade[i];
  }

  cout << " is  " << total << endl;

  return 0;
}
```

Exercises 7.1

1. Write array declarations for the following:
   a. A list of 100 integer grades
   b. A list of 50 floating-point temperatures
   c. A list of 30 characters, each representing a code
   d. A list of 100 integer years
   e. A list of 32 floating-point velocities
   f. A list of 1000 floating-point distances
   g. A list of 6 integer code numbers

2. Write appropriate notation for the first, third, and seventh elements of the following arrays.

a. `int grades[20]`
b. `float prices[10]`
c. `float amps[16]`
d. `int dist[15]`
e. `float velocity[25]`
f. `float time[100]`

3. *a.* Using the `cin` object, write individual statements that can be used to enter values into the first, third, and seventh elements of each of the arrays declared in Exercises 2a through 2f.
b. Write a `for` loop that can be used to enter values for the complete array declared in Exercise 2a.

4. *a.* Write individual statements that can be used to display the values from the first, third, and seventh elements of each of the arrays declared in Exercises 2a through 2f.
b. Write a `for` loop that can be used to display values for the complete array declared in Exercise 2a.

5. List the elements that will be displayed by the following sections of code.

a.
```
for (m = 1; m <= 5; m++)
  cout << a[m] << "  ";
```
b.
```
for (k = 1; k <= 5; k = k + 2)
  cout << a[k] << "  ";
```
c.
```
for (j = 3; j <= 10; j++)
  cout << b[j] << "  ";
```
d.
```
for (k = 3; k <= 12; k = k + 3)
  cout << b[k] << "  ";
```
e.
```
for (i = 2; i < 11; i = i + 2)
  cout << c[i] << "  ";
```

6. *a.* Write a program to input the following values into an array named `prices`: 10.95, 16.32, 12.15, 8.22, 15.98, 26.22, 13.54, 6.45, 17.59. After the data have been entered, have your program output the values.
b. Repeat Exercise 6a, but after the data have been entered, have your program display them in the following form:

```
10.95    16.32    12.15
 8.22    15.98    26.22
13.54     6.45    17.59
```

7. Write a C++ program to input eight integer numbers into an array named `grade`. As each number is input, add the numbers into a total. After all numbers are input, display the numbers and their average.

8. *a.* Write a C++ program to input ten integer numbers into an array named `fmax` and determine the maximum value entered. Your program should contain only one loop, and the maximum should be determined as array element values are being input. (*Hint:* Set the maximum equal to the first array element, which should be input before the loop used to input the remaining array values.)

b. Repeat Exercise 8a, keeping track of both the maximum element in the array and the index number for the maximum. After displaying the numbers, display these two messages:

```
The maximum value is: ___
This is element number ___ in the list of numbers
```

Have your program display the correct values in place of the underlines in the messages.

c. Repeat Exercise 8b, but have your program locate the minimum value of the data entered.

9. a. Write a C++ program to input the following integer numbers into an array named `grades`: 89, 95, 72, 83, 99, 54, 86, 75, 92, 73, 79, 75, 82, 73. As each number is input, add the numbers to a total. After all numbers are input and the total is obtained, calculate the average of the numbers and use the average to determine the deviation of each value from the average. Store each deviation in an array named `deviation`. Each deviation is obtained as the element value less the average of all the data. Have your program display each deviation alongside its corresponding element from the `grades` array.

b. Calculate the variance of the data used in Exercise 9a. The variance is obtained by squaring each individual deviation and dividing the sum of the squared deviations by the number of deviations.

10. Write a C++ program that specifies three one-dimensional arrays named `price`, `amount`, and `total`. Each array should be capable of holding ten elements. Using a `for` loop, input values for the `price` and `amount` arrays. The entries in the `total` array should be the product of the corresponding values in the `price` and `amount` arrays (thus, `total[i] = price[i] * amount[i]`). After all the data have been entered, display the following output:

```
total        price        amount
-----        -----        ------
```

Under each column heading, display the appropriate value.

11. a. Write a program that inputs ten floating-point numbers into an array named `raw`. After ten user-input numbers are entered into the array, your program should cycle through `raw` ten times. During each pass through the array, your program should select the lowest value in `raw` and place the selected value in the next available slot in an array named `sorted`. Thus, when your program is complete, the `sorted` array should contain the numbers in `raw` in sorted order from lowest to highest. (*Hint:* Be sure to reset the lowest value selected during each pass to a very high number so that it is not selected again. You will need a second `for` loop within the first `for` loop to locate the minimum value for each pass.)

b. The method used in Exercise 11a to sort the values in the array is very inefficient. Can you determine why? What might be a better method of sorting the numbers in an array?

7.2 Array Initialization

Array elements can be initialized within their declaration statements in the same manner as scalar variables, except that the initializing elements must be included in braces. Examples of such initializations are

```
int grade[5] = {98, 87, 92, 79, 85};
char code[6] = {'s', 'a', 'm', 'p', 'l', 'e'};
double width[7] = {10.96, 6.43, 2.58, .86, 5.89, 7.56, 8.22};
```

Initializers are applied in the order in which they are written, with the first value used to initialize element 0, the second value used to initialize element 1, and so on, until all values have been used. Thus, in the declaration

```
const NUMELS = 5;
int grade[NUMELS] = {98, 87, 92, 79, 85};
```

`grade[0]` is initialized to 98, `grade[1]` is initialized to 87, `grade[2]` is initialized to 92, `grade[3]` is initialized to 79, and `grade[4]` is initialized to 85.

Because white space is ignored in C++, initializations may be continued across multiple lines. For example, the declaration for `gallons[]` in the set of declarations

```
const int NUMGALS = 20;
int gallons[NUMGALS] = {19, 16, 14, 19, 20, 18,   // initializing values
                        12, 10, 22, 15, 18, 17,   // may extend across
                        16, 14, 23, 19, 15, 18,   // multiple lines
                        21, 5};
```

uses four lines to initialize all of the array elements.

If the number of initializers is less than the declared number of elements listed in square brackets, the initializers are applied starting with array element zero. Thus, in the declarations

```
const int ARRAYSIZE = 7;
float length[ARRAYSIZE] = {7.8, 6.4, 4.9, 11.2};
```

only `length[0]`, `length[1]`, `length[2]`, and `length[3]` are initialized with the listed values. The other array elements are initialized to zero.

Unfortunately, there is no method of either indicating repetition of an initialization value or initializing later array elements without first specifying values for earlier elements.

A unique feature of initializers is that the size of an array may be omitted when initializing values are included in the declaration statement. For example, the declaration

```
int gallons[] = {16, 12, 10, 14, 11};
```

reserves enough storage room for five elements. Similarly, the following declarations are equivalent:

```
const int NUMCODES = 6;
char code[6] = {'s', 'a', 'm', 'p', 'l', 'e'};
```

and

```
char code[] = {'s', 'a', 'm', 'p', 'l', 'e'};
```

Both declarations set aside six character locations for an array named `code`. An interesting and useful simplification can also be used when initializing character arrays. For example, the declaration

```
char code[] = "sample";    // no braces or commas
```

uses the string `"sample"` to initialize the `code` array. Recall that a string is any sequence of characters enclosed in double quotes. This last declaration creates an array named `code` having seven elements and fills the array with the seven characters illustrated in Figure 7–6. The first six characters, as expected, are the letters `s`, `a`, `m`, `p`, `l`, and `e`. The last character, which is the escape sequence `\0`, is called the *null character*. The null character is automatically appended to all strings by the C++ compiler. This character has an internal storage code that is numerically equal to zero (the storage code for the zero character has a numerical value of decimal 48, so the two cannot be confused by the computer) and is used as a marker, or sentinel, to mark the end of a string. As we shall see in Chapter 9, this marker is invaluable when we are manipulating strings of characters.

FIGURE 7–6 A String Is Terminated with a Special Symbol

code[0]	code[1]	code[2]	code[3]	code[4]	code[5]	code[6]
s	a	m	p	l	e	\0

Once values have been assigned to array elements, either through initialization within the declaration statement or by using interactive input, the array elements can be processed as described in the previous section. For example, Program 7-3 illustrates element initialization within the declaration of the array and then uses a `for` loop to locate the maximum value stored in the array.

Program 7-3

```
#include <iostream.h>

int main()
{
  const int MAXELS = 5;

  int i, max, nums[MAXELS] = {2, 18, 1, 27, 16};

  max = nums[0];

  for (i = 1; i < MAXELS; i++)
    if (max < nums[i])
      max = nums[i];

  cout << "The maximum value is " << max << endl;

  return 0;
}
```

The output produced by Program 7-3 is

```
The maximum value is 27
```

Exercises 7.2

1. Write array declarations, including initializers, for the following:
   a. A list of ten integer grades: 89, 75, 82, 93, 78, 95, 81, 88, 77, 82
   b. A list of five double-precision amounts: 10.62, 13.98, 18.45, 12.68, 14.76
   c. A list of 100 double-precision interest rates; the first six rates are 6.29, 6.95, 7.25, 7.35, 7.40, 7.42

d. A list of 64 floating-point temperatures; the first ten temperatures are 78.2, 69.6, 68.5, 83.9, 55.4, 67.0, 49.8, 58.3, 62.5, 71.6

e. A list of 15 character codes; the first seven codes are f, j, m, q, t, w, z

2. Write an array declaration statement that stores the following values in an array named `prices`: 16.24, 18.98, 23.75, 16.29, 19.54, 14.22, 11.13, 15.39. Include these statements in a program that displays the values in the array.

3. Write a program that uses an array declaration statement to initialize the following numbers in an array named `slopes`: 17.24, 25.63, 5.94, 33.92, 3.71, 32.84, 35.93, 18.24, 6.92. Your program should locate and display both the maximum and the minimum values in the array.

4. Write a program that stores the following numbers in an array named `prices`: 9.92, 6.32, 12.63, 5.95, 10.29. Your program should also create two arrays named `units` and `amounts`, each capable of storing five double-precision numbers. Using a `for` loop and a `cin` object, have your program accept five user-input numbers into the `units` array when the program is run. Your program should store the product of the corresponding values in the `prices` and `units` arrays in the `amounts` array (for example, `amounts[1] = prices[1] * units[1]`) and should display the following output (fill in the table appropriately).

```
Price          Units          Amount
-----          -----          ------
 9.92            .               .
 6.32            .               .
12.63            .               .
 5.95            .               .
10.29            .               .
                              ------
Total:                           .
```

5. The string of characters `"Good Morning"` is to be stored in a character array named `goodstr1`. Write the declaration for this array in three different ways.

6. *a.* Write declaration statements to store the string of characters `"Input the Following Data"` in a character array named `message1`, the string `"------------------------"` in the array named `message2`, the string `"Enter the Date: "` in the array named `message3`, and the string `"Enter the Account Number: "` in the array named `message4`.

b. Include the array declarations written in Exercise 6a in a program that uses the `cout` object to display the messages. For example, the statement `cout << message1;` causes the string stored in the `message1` array to be displayed. Your program will require four such statements to display the four individual messages. Using the `cout` object to display a string requires that the end-of-string marker `\0` be present in the character array used to store the string.

7. *a.* Write a declaration to store the string `"This is a test"` into an array named `strtest`. Include the declaration in a program to display the message using the following loop:

```
for (int i = 0; i < NUMDISPLAY; i++)
  cout << strtest[i];
```

where `NUMDISPLAY` is a named constant for the number 15.

b. Modify the `for` statement in Exercise 7a to display only the array characters `t`, `e`, `s`, and `t`.

c. Include the array declaration written in Exercise 7a in a program that uses the `cout` object to display characters in the array. For example, the statement `cout << strtest;` will cause the string stored in the `strtest` array to be displayed. Using this statement requires that the last character in the array be the end-of-string marker `\0`.

d. Repeat Exercise 7a using a `while` loop. (*Hint:* Stop the loop when the `\0` escape sequence is detected. The expression `while (strtest[i] != '\0')` can be used.)

7.3 Arrays as Arguments

Individual array elements are passed to a called function in the same manner as individual scalar variables; they are simply included as subscripted variables when the function call is made. For example, the function call `FindMax(grades[2], grades[6]);` passes the values of the elements `grades[2]` and `grades[6]` to the function `FindMax()`.

Passing a complete array of values to a function is in many respects an easier operation than passing individual elements. The called function receives access to the actual array, rather than a copy of the values in the array. For example, if `grades` is an array, the function call `FindMax(grades);` makes the complete `grades` array available to the `FindMax()` function. This is different from passing a single variable to a function.

You will recall that when a single scalar argument is passed to a function, the called function receives only a *copy* of the passed value, which is stored in one of the function's parameters. If arrays were passed in this manner, a copy of the complete array would have to be created. For large arrays, making duplicate copies of the array for each function call would be wasteful of computer storage and would frustrate the effort to return multiple element changes made by the called program (remember that a function directly returns at most one value). To avoid these problems, the called function is given direct access to the original array. Thus any changes made by the called function are made directly to the array itself. For the following specific examples of function calls, assume that the arrays `nums`, `keys`, `units`, and `grades` are declared as

```
int nums[5];                       // an array of five integers
char keys[256];                    // an array of 256 characters
double units[500], grades[500];    // two arrays of 500 doubles
```

For these arrays, the following function calls can be made:

```
FindMax(nums);
FindCharacter(keys);
calcTotal(nums, units, grades);
```

In each case, the called function receives direct access to the named array.

On the receiving side, the called function must be alerted that an array is being made available. For example, suitable function header lines for the previous functions are

```
int FindMax(int vals[5])
char FindCharacter(char inKeys[256])
void calcTotal(int arr1[5], double arr2[500], double arr3[500])
```

In each of these function header lines, the names in the parameter list are chosen by the programmer. However, the parameter names used by the functions still refer to the original array created outside the function. This is made clear in Program 7-4.

Program 7-4

```
#include <iostream.h>

const int MAXELS = 5;
int FindMax(int [MAXELS]);      // function prototype

int main()
{
  int nums[MAXELS] = {2, 18, 1, 27, 16};

  cout << "The maximum value is " << FindMax(nums) << endl;

  return 0;
}

// find the maximum value
int FindMax(int vals[MAXELS])
{
  int i, max = vals[0];

  for (i = 1; i < MAXELS; i++)
    if (max < vals[i])
      max = vals[i];

  return max;
}
```

First, note that the named constant `MAXELS` has been declared globally, not within the `main()` function. This placement of the declaration means that this constant can be used in any subsequent declaration or within any subsequent function. Next, observe that the prototype for `FindMax()` uses this named constant and declares that the function will return an integer and expects an array of five integers as an argument. It is also important to know that only one array is created in Program 7-4. In `main()` this array is known as `nums`, and in `FindMax()` it is known as `vals`. As illustrated in Figure 7–7, both names refer to the same array. Thus in Figure 7–7, `vals[3]` is the same element as `nums[3]`.

The parameter declaration in both the `FindMax()` prototype and the function header line in Program 7-4 actually contains extra information that is not required by the function. All that `FindMax()` must know is that the parameter `vals` references an array of integers. Because the array has been created in `main()` and no additional storage space is needed in `FindMax()`, the declaration for `vals` can omit the size of the array. Thus an alternative function header line is

```
int FindMax(int vals[])
```

FIGURE 7–7 Only One Array Is Created

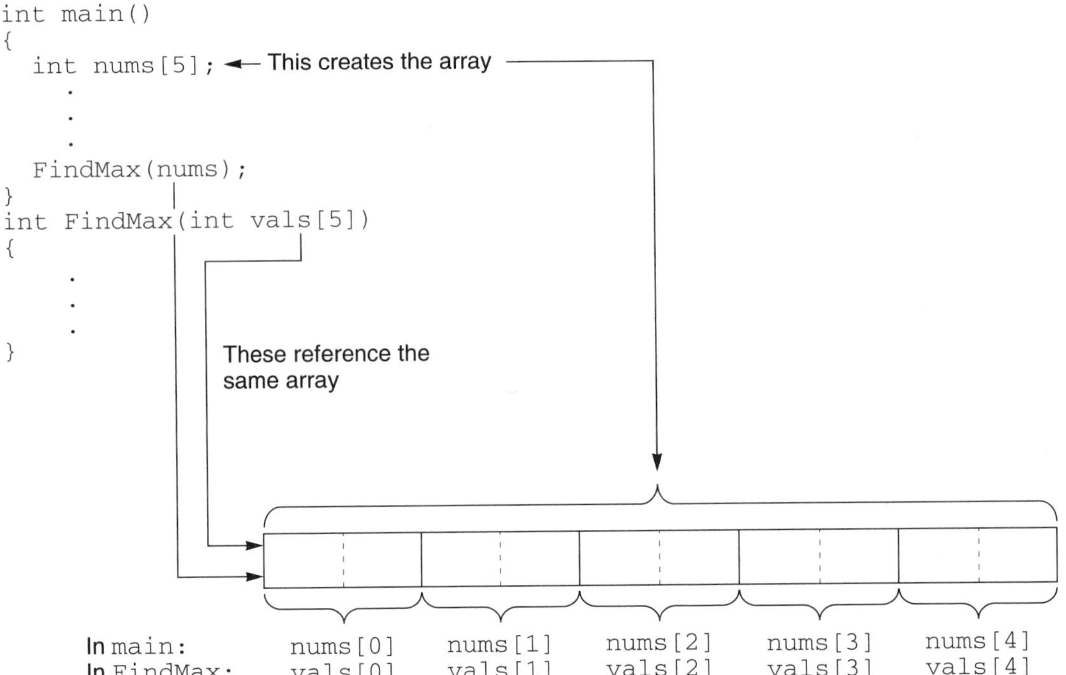
int main()
{
int nums[5]; ← This creates the array
FindMax(nums);
}
int FindMax(int vals[5])
{
}
These reference the same array
In main:
In FindMax:
nums[0] nums[1] nums[2] nums[3] nums[4]
vals[0] vals[1] vals[2] vals[3] vals[4]

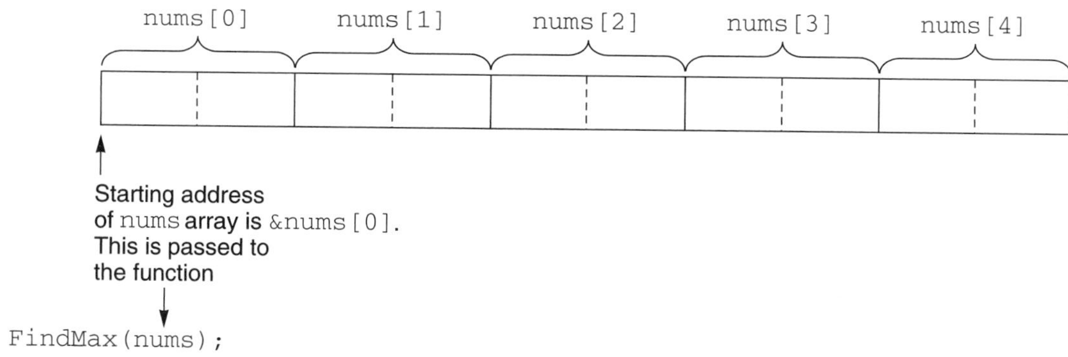

FIGURE 7–8 The Starting Address of the Array Is Passed

This form of the function header makes more sense when you realize that only one item is actually passed to `FindMax()` when the function is called, which is the starting address of the `num` array. This is illustrated in Figure 7–8.

Because only the starting address of `vals` is passed to `FindMax()`, the number of elements in the array need not be included in the declaration for `vals`.[3] In fact, it is generally advisable to omit the size of the array in the function header line. For example, consider the more general form of `FindMax()`, which can be used to find the maximum value of an integer array of arbitrary size:

```
int FindMax(int vals[], int numels)    // find the maximum value
{
  int i, max = vals[0];

  for (i = 1; i < numels; i++)
   if (max < vals[i])
     max = vals[i];

  return max;
}
```

The more general form of `FindMax()` declares that the function returns an integer value. The function expects the starting address of an integer array and the number of elements in the array as arguments. Then, using the number of elements as the boundary for its search, the function's `for` loop causes each array element to be examined in sequential order to locate the maximum value. Program 7-5 illustrates the use of `FindMax()` in a complete program.

---

[3] An important consequence of this is that `FindMax()` has direct access to the passed array. This means that any change to an element of the `vals` array actually is a change to the `nums` array. This is significantly different from the situation with scalar variables, where the called function does not receive direct access to the passed variable.

Program 7-5

```
#include <iostream.h>

int FindMax(int [], int);    // function prototype

int main()
{
  const int MAXELS = 5;
  int nums[MAXELS] = {2, 18, 1, 27, 16};

  cout << "The maximum value is " << FindMax(nums, MAXELS) << endl;

  return 0;
}

// find the maximum value
int FindMax(int vals[], int numels)
{
  int i, max = vals[0];

  for (i = 1; i < numels; i++)
    if (max < vals[i]) max = vals[i];

  return max;
}
```

The output displayed by both Program 7-4 and Program 7-5 is

```
The maximum value is 27
```

Exercises 7.3

1. The following declarations were used to create the `grades` array:

```
const int NUMGRADES = 500;
double grades[NUMGRADES];
```

Write two different function header lines for a function named `sortArray()` that accepts the `grades` array as a parameter named `inArray` and returns no value.

2. The following declarations were used to create the keys array:

```
const int NUMKEYS = 256;
char keys[NUMKEYS];
```

Write two different function header lines for a function named findKey() that accepts the keys array as a parameter named select and returns a character.

3. The following declarations were used to create the rates array:

```
const int NUMRATES = 256;
float rates[NUMRATES];
```

Write two different function header lines for a function named prime() that accepts the rates array as a parameter named rates and returns a floating-point number.

4. *a.* Modify the FindMax() function in Program 7-4 to locate the minimum value of the passed array.
   b. Include the function written in Exercise 4a in a complete program and run the program on a computer.

5. Write a program that has a declaration in main() to store the following numbers into an array named rates: 6.5, 7.2, 7.5, 8.3, 8.6, 9.4, 9.6, 9.8, 10.0. There should be a function call to show() that accepts the rates array as a parameter named rates and then displays the numbers in the array.

6. *a.* Write a program that has a declaration in main() to store the string "Vacation is near" into an array named message. There should be a function call to display() that accepts message in a parameter named strng and then displays the message.
   b. Modify the display() function written in Exercise 6a to display the first eight elements of the message array.

7. Write a program that declares three single-dimensional arrays named price, quantity, and amount. Each array should be declared in main() and should be capable of holding ten double-precision numbers. The numbers that should be stored in price are 10.62, 14.89, 13.21, 16.55, 18.62, 9.47, 6.58, 18.32, 12.15, 3.98. The numbers that should be stored in quantity are 4, 8.5, 6, 7.35, 9, 15.3, 3, 5.4, 2.9, 4.8. Your program should pass these three arrays to a function named extend(), which should calculate the elements in the amount array as the product of the corresponding elements in the price and quantity arrays (for example, amount[1] = price[1] * quantity[1]). After extend() has put values into the amount array, the values in the array should be displayed from within main().

8. Write a program that includes two functions named calcAverage() and variance(). The calcAverage() function should calculate and return the average of the values stored in an array named testvals. The array should be declared in main() and should include the values 89, 95, 72, 83, 99, 54, 86, 75, 92, 73, 79, 75, 82, 73. The variance() function should calculate and return the variance of the data. The variance is obtained by subtracting the average from each value in testvals, squaring the values obtained, adding them, and dividing by the number of elements in testvals. The values returned from calcAverage() and variance() should be displayed using cout statements activated from within main().

7.4 Two-Dimensional Arrays

A *two-dimensional array*, which is also referred to as a table, consists of both rows and columns of elements. For example, the array of numbers

8	16	9	52
3	15	27	6
14	25	2	10

is called a two-dimensional array of integers. This array consists of three rows and four columns and thus is called a 3-by-4 array. To reserve storage for this array, both the number of rows and the number of columns must be included in the array's declaration. If we call the array `val`, the correct specification for this two-dimensional array is

```
int val[3][4];
```

Similarly, the declarations

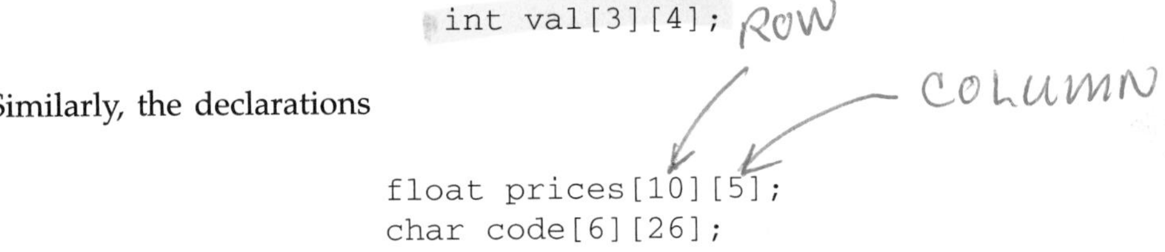

```
float prices[10][5];
char code[6][26];
```

declare that the array `prices` consists of 10 rows and 5 columns of floating-point numbers and that the array `code` consists of 6 rows and 26 columns, with each element capable of holding one character.

In order to locate each element in a two-dimensional array, we identify an element by its position in the array. As illustrated in Figure 7–9, the term `val[1][3]` uniquely identifies the element in row 1, column 3. As with single-dimensional array variables, double-dimensional array variables can be used anywhere scalar variables are valid. Examples using elements of the `val` array are

```
price = val[2][3];
val[0][0] = 62;
newnum = 4 * (val[1][0] - 5);
sumRow = val[0][0] + val[0][1] + val[0][2] + val[0][3];
```

The last statement causes the values of the four elements in row 0 to be added and the sum to be stored in the scalar variable `sumRow`.

As with single-dimensional arrays, two-dimensional arrays can be initialized from within their declaration statements. This is done by listing the initial values

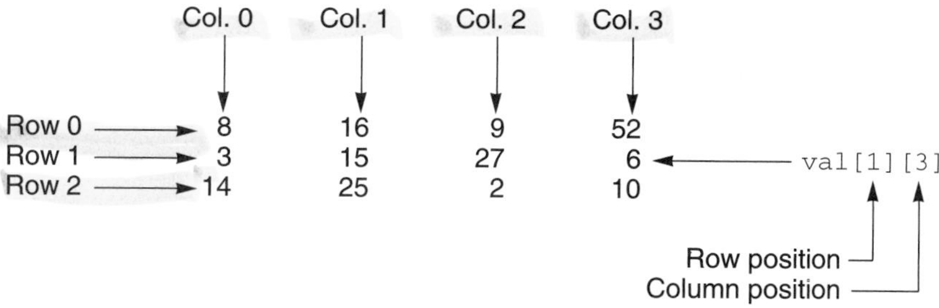

FIGURE 7–9 Each Array Element Is Identified by Its Row and Column Position

within braces and separating them by commas. Additionally, braces can be used to separate individual rows. For example, the declaration

```
int val[3][4] = { {8,16,9,52},
                  {3,15,27,6},
                  {14,25,2,10} };
```

declares `val` to be an array of integers with three rows and four columns, with the initial values given in the declaration. The first set of internal braces contains the values for row 0 of the array, the second set of braces the values for row 1, and the third set of braces the values for row 2.

Although the commas in the initialization braces are always required, the inner braces can be omitted. Thus the initialization for `val` may be written as

```
int val[3][4] = {8,16,9,52,
                  3,15,27,6,
                 14,25,2,10};
```

The separation of initial values into rows in the declaration statement is not necessary because the compiler assigns values beginning with the `[0][0]` element and proceeds row by row to fill in the remaining values. Thus the initialization

```
int val[3][4] = {8,16,9,52,3,15,27,6,14,25,2,10};
```

is equally valid but does not clearly tell another programmer where one row ends and another begins.

As illustrated in Figure 7–10, the initialization of a two-dimensional array is done in row order. First, the elements of the first row are initialized, then the elements of the second row are initialized, and so on, until the initializations are completed. This row ordering is also the same ordering used to store two-dimensional arrays. That is, array element `[0][0]` is stored first, followed by

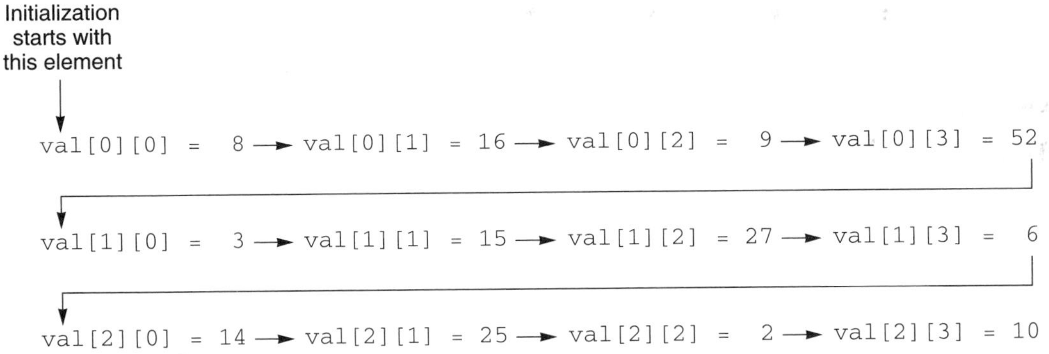

FIGURE 7–10 Storage and Initialization of the `val[]` Array

element `[0][1]`, followed by element `[0][2]`, and so on. Following the first row's elements are the second row's elements, and so on for all the rows in the array.

Like single-dimensional arrays, two-dimensional arrays may be displayed by individual element notation or by using loops (either `while` or `for`). This is illustrated by Program 7-6, which displays all the elements of a 3-by-4 two-dimensional array using two different techniques. Note in Program 7-6 that we have used named constants to define the array's rows and columns.

The display produced by Program 7-6 is

```
Display of val array by explicit element
    8   16    9   52
    3   15   27    6
   14   25    2   10

Display of val array using a nested for loop
    8   16    9   52
    3   15   27    6
   14   25    2   10
```

The first display of the `val` array produced by Program 7-6 is constructed by explicitly designating each array element. The second display of array element values, which is identical to the first, is produced by using a nested `for` loop. Nested loops are especially useful with two-dimensional arrays because they allow the programmer to designate and cycle through each element easily. In Program 7-6, the variable `i` controls the outer loop and the variable `j` controls the inner loop. Each pass through the outer loop corresponds to a single row, with the inner loop supplying the appropriate column elements. After a complete row is printed, a new line is started for the next row. The effect is a display of the array in a row-by-row fashion.

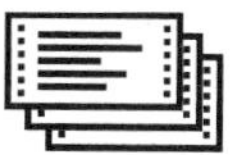

Program 7-6

```
#include <iostream.h>
#include <iomanip.h>

int main()
{

  const int NUMROWS = 3;
  const int NUMCOLS = 4;

  int i, j
  int val[NUMROWS][NUMCOLS] = {8,16,9,52,3,15,27,6,14,25,2,10};

  cout << "\nDisplay of val array by explicit element"
       << endl << setw(4) << val[0][0] << setw(4) << val[0][1]
       << setw(4) << val[0][2] << setw(4) << val[0][3]
       << endl << setw(4) << val[1][0] << setw(4) << val[1][1]
       << setw(4) << val[1][2] << setw(4) << val[1][3]
       << endl << setw(4) << val[2][0] << setw(4) << val[2][1]
       << setw(4) << val[2][2] << setw(4) << val[2][3];

  cout << "\n\nDisplay of val array using a nested for loop";

  for (i = 0; i < NUMROWS; i++)
  {
    cout << endl;       // print a new line for each row
    for (j = 0; j < NUMCOLS; j++)
      cout << setw(4) << val[i][j];
  }

  cout << endl;

  return 0;
}
```

Once two-dimensional array elements have been assigned values, array processing can begin. Typically, `for` loops are used to process two-dimensional arrays because, as we have noted, they make it easy to designate and cycle through each array element. For example, the nested `for` loop illustrated in Program 7-7 is used to multiply each element in the `val` array by the scalar number 10 and display the resulting value.

Program 7-7

```
#include <iostream.h>
#include <iomanip.h>

int main()
{
  const int NUMROWS = 3;
  const int NUMCOLS = 4;

  int i, j;
  int val[NUMROWS][NUMCOLS] = {8,16,9,52,
                               3,15,27,6,
                              14,25,2,10};

  // multiply each element by 10 and display it
  cout << "\nDisplay of multiplied elements";
  for (i = 0; i < NUMROWS; i++)
  {
    cout << endl;        // start each row on a new line
    for (j = 0; j < NUMCOLS; j++)
    {
      val[i][j] = val[i][j] * 10;
      cout << setw(5) << val[i][j];
    }  // end of inner loop
  }    // end of outer loop
  cout << endl;

  return 0;
}
```

Following is the output produced by Program 7-7:

```
Display of multiplied elements
   80  160   90  520
   30  150  270   60
  140  250   20  100
```

Passing two-dimensional arrays into functions is identical to passing single-dimensional arrays. The called function receives access to the entire array. For example, assuming that `val` is a two-dimensional array, the function call `display(val);` makes the complete `val` array available to the function named `display()`. Thus any changes made by `display()` will be made directly to the `val` array. As further examples, assume that the following two-dimensional arrays named `test`, `code`, and `stocks` are declared as

```
int test[7][9];
char code[26][10];
float stocks[256][52];
```

Then the following function calls are valid:

```
FindMax(test);
obtain(code);
price(stocks);
```

On the receiving side, the called function must be alerted that a two-dimensional array is being made available. For example, assuming that each of the previous functions returns an integer, suitable function header lines for these functions are

```
int FindMax(int nums[7][9])
int obtain(char key[26][10])
int price(float names[256][52])
```

In each of these function header lines, the parameter names chosen are local to the function. However, the internal local names used by the function still refer to the original array created outside the function. Program 7-8 illustrates passing a two-dimensional array into a function that displays the array's values.

Only one array is created in Program 7-8. This array is known as `val` in `main()` and as `nums` in `display()`. Thus `val[0][2]` refers to the same element as `nums[0][2]`.

Note the use of the nested `for` loop in Program 7-8 for cycling through each array element. In Program 7-8, the variable `rowNum` controls the outer loop, and the variable `colNum` controls the inner loop. For each pass through the outer loop, which corresponds to a single row, the inner loop makes one pass through the column elements. After a complete row is printed, a new line is started for the next row. The effect is a display of the array in a row-by-row fashion:

```
 8   16    9   52
 3   15   27    6
14   25    2   10
```

Program 7-8

```
#include <iostream.h>
#include <iomanip.h>

const int ROWS = 3;
const int COLS = 4;

void display(int [ROWS][COLS]);     // function prototype

int main()
{
  int val[ROWS][COLS] = {8,16,9,52,
                          3,15,27,6,
                         14,25,2,10};

  display(val);

  return 0;
}

void display(int nums[ROWS][COLS])
{
  int rowNum, colNum;
  for (rowNum = 0; rowNum < ROWS; rowNum++)
  {
    for(colNum = 0; colNum < COLS; colNum++)
      cout << setw(4) << nums[rowNum][colNum];
    cout << endl;
  }

  return;
}
```

The parameter declaration for `nums` in `display()` contains extra information that is not required by the function. The declaration for `nums` can omit the row size of the array. Thus an alternative function declaration is

```
display(int nums[][4]);
```

The reason the column size must be included, whereas the row size is optional, becomes obvious when you consider how the array elements are stored in

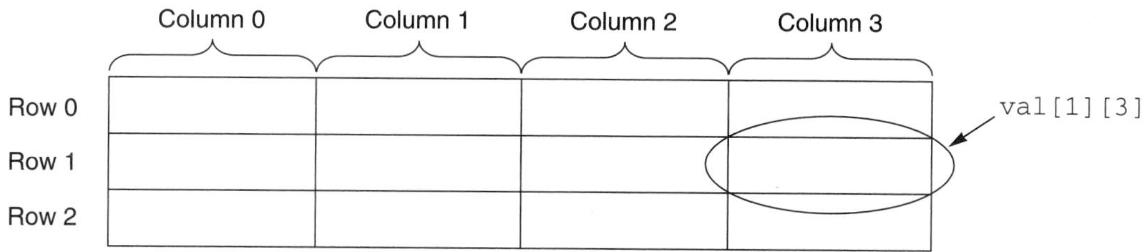

FIGURE 7–11 Storage of the `val[]` Array

memory. Starting with the element `val[0][0]`, the succeeding elements are stored consecutively, row by row, as `val[0][0]`, `val[0][1]`, `val[0][2]`, `val[0][3]`, `val[1][0]`, `val[1][1]`, and so on, as illustrated in Figure 7–11.

As with all array accesses, an individual element of the `val` array is obtained by adding an offset to the starting location of the array. For example, the element `val[1][3]` is located at an offset of 14 bytes from the start of the array (assuming two bytes for an `int`). Internally, the computer employs the row index, column index, and column size to determine this offset using the following calculation.

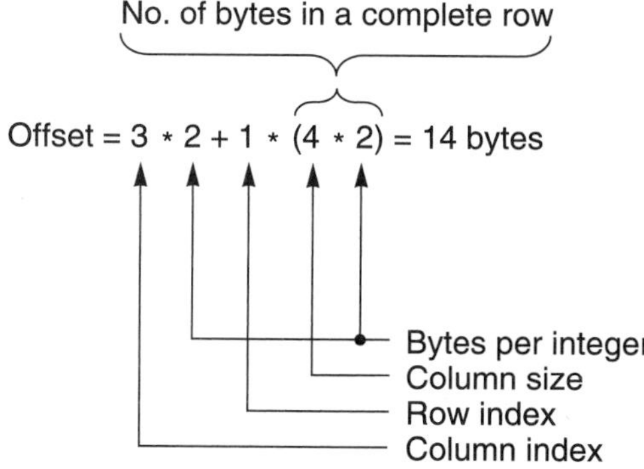

The number of columns is necessary in the offset calculation so that the computer can determine how many positions to skip over to get to the desired row.

Larger-Dimensional Arrays

Although arrays with more than two dimensions are not commonly used, C++ does allow any number of dimensions to be declared. This is done by listing the maximum size of all dimensions for the array. For example, the declaration `int response [4][10][6];` declares a three-dimensional array. The first element in the array is designated as `response [0][0][0]` and the last element as `response [3][9][5]`.

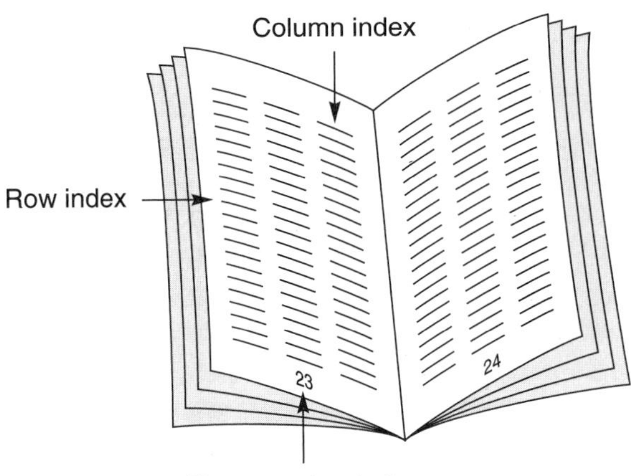

FIGURE 7–12 Representation of a Three-Dimensional Array

Conceptually, as illustrated in Figure 7–12, a three-dimensional array can be viewed as a book of data tables. Using this visualization, the first subscript, which is often called the "rank," can be thought of as the page number of the selected table, the second subscript value as the desired row in the table, and the third subscript value as the desired column.

Similarly, arrays of any dimension can be declared. Conceptually, a four-dimensional array can be represented as a shelf of books, where the first dimension is used to declare a desired book on the shelf, and a five-dimensional array can be viewed as a bookcase filled with books, where the first dimension refers to a selected shelf in the bookcase. Using the same analogy, a six-dimensional array can be considered as a single row of bookcases, where the first dimension references the desired bookcase in the row; a seven-dimensional array can be considered as multiple rows of bookcases, where the first dimension references the desired row, and so on. Alternatively, arrays of three-, four-, five-, and six-dimensional arrays can be viewed as mathematical *n*-tuples of order 3, 4, 5, and 6, respectively, and so on.

Exercises 7.4

1. Write appropriate specification statements for each of the following:
   a. An array of integers with 6 rows and 10 columns
   b. An array of integers with 2 rows and 5 columns
   c. An array of characters with 7 rows and 12 columns
   d. An array of characters with 15 rows and 7 columns
   e. An array of floating-point numbers with 10 rows and 25 columns
   f. An array of floating-point numbers with 16 rows and 8 columns

2. Determine the output produced by the following program:

```
#include <iostream.h>
int main()
{
 int i, j, val[3][4] = {8,16,9,52,3,15,27,6,14,25,2,10};

  for (i = 0; i < 3; i++)
    for (j = 0; j < 4; j++)
      cout << val[i][j] << "  ";

  return 0;
}
```

3. *a.* Write a C++ program that adds the values of all elements in the `val` array used in Exercise 2 and displays the total.
b. Modify the program written for Exercise 3a to display the total of each row separately.

4. Write a C++ program that adds equivalent elements of the two-dimensional arrays named `first` and `second`. Both arrays should have two rows and three columns. For example, element `[1][2]` of the resulting array should be the sum of `first[1][2]` and `second[1][2]`. The `first` and `second` arrays should be initialized as follows:

First			Second		
16	18	23	24	52	77
54	91	11	16	19	59

5. *a.* Write a C++ program that finds and displays the maximum value in a two-dimensional array of integers. The array should be declared as a 4-by-5 array of integers and initialized with these data: 16, 22, 99, 4, 18, –258, 4, 101, 5, 98, 105, 6, 15, 2, 45, 33, 88, 72, 16, 3.
b. Modify the program written in Exercise 5a so that it also displays the maximum value's row and column subscript values.

6. Write a C++ program to select the values in a 4-by-5 array of integers in increasing order, and store the selected values in the single-dimensional array named `sort`. Use the data given in Exercise 5a to initialize the two-dimensional array.

7. *a.* A professor has constructed a 3-by-5 two-dimensional array of float numbers. This array currently contains the test grades of the students in the professor's advanced compiler design class. Write a C++ program that reads 15 array values and then determines the total number of grades in the ranges less than 60, greater than or equal to 60 and less than 70, greater than or equal to 70 and less than 80, greater than or equal to 80 and less than 90, and greater than or equal to 90.
b. Entering 15 grades each time the program written for Exercise 7a is run is cumbersome. What method is appropriate for initializing the array during the testing phase?
c. How might the program you wrote for Exercise 7a be modified to include the case of no grade being present? That is, what grade could be used to indicate an invalid grade, and how would your program have to be modified to exclude counting such a grade?

8. a. Write a function named `FindMax()` that finds and displays the maximum value in a two-dimensional array of integers. The array should be declared as a 10-row-by-20-column array of integers in `main()`.
b. Modify the function written in Exercise 8a so that it also displays the row and column numbers of the element with the maximum value.
c. Can the function you wrote for Exercise 8a be generalized to handle a two-dimensional array of any size?

9. Write a function that can be used to sort the elements of a 10-by-20 two-dimensional array of integers. (*Hint:* Use the `swap()` function developed for Program 6-8 to exchange array elements.)

7.5 Common Programming Errors

Four common errors associated with using arrays are

1. Forgetting to declare the array. This error results in a compiler error message equivalent to "invalid indirection" each time a subscripted variable is encountered within a program.
2. Using a subscript that references a nonexistent array element—for example, declaring the array to be of size 20 and using a subscript value of 25. This error is not detected by most C++ compilers. It will, however, probably cause a run-time error that results in either a program "crash" or a value that has no relation to the intended element being accessed from memory. In either case, this is usually an extremely troublesome error to locate. The only solution to this problem is to make sure, either by specific programming statements or by careful coding, that each subscript references a valid array element. Using named constants for an array's size and for the maximum subscript value helps to eliminate this problem.
3. Not using a large enough counter value in a `for` loop counter to cycle through all the array elements. This error usually occurs when an array is initially specified to be of size `n` and there is a `for` loop within the program of the form `for (int i = 0; i < n; i++)`. The array size is then expanded, but the programmer forgets to change the interior `for` loop parameters. In practice, this error is eliminated by using the same `const` declaration for the array size and loop parameter.
4. Forgetting to initialize the array. Although many compilers automatically set all elements of integer-valued and real-valued arrays to zero and all elements of character arrays to blanks, it is up to the programmer to ensure that each array is correctly initialized before the processing of array elements begins.

7.6 Chapter Summary

1. A single-dimensional array is a data structure that can be used to store a list of values of the same data type. Such arrays must be declared by giving the data type of the values that are stored in the array and the array size. For example, the declaration

```
int num[100];
```

creates an array of 100 integers. A preferable approach is first to use a named constant to set the array size and then to use this constant in the definition of the array—for example,

```
const int MAXSIZE = 100;
```

and

```
int num[MAXSIZE];
```

2. Array elements are stored in contiguous locations in memory and referenced using the array name and a subscript—for example, `num[22]`. Any non-negative integer-value expression can be used as a subscript, and the subscript 0 always refers to the first element in an array.

3. A two-dimensional array is declared by listing both a row and a column size with the data type and name of the array. For example, the declaration

```
int mat[5][7];
```

creates a two-dimensional array consisting of five rows and seven columns of integer values.

4. Arrays may be initialized when they are declared. For two-dimensional arrays this is accomplished by listing the initial values, in a row-by-row manner, within braces and separating them with commas. For example, the declaration

```
int vals[3][2] = { {1, 2},
                   {3, 4},
                   {5, 6} };
```

produces the following 3-row-by-2-column array:

```
1 2
3 4
5 6
```

Because C++ uses the convention that initialization proceeds in rowwise order, the inner braces can be omitted. Thus an equivalent initialization is provided by the statement

```
int vals[3][2] = { 1, 2, 3, 4, 5, 6};
```

5. Arrays are passed to a function by passing the name of the array as an argument. The value actually passed is the address of the first array storage location. Thus the called function receives direct access to the original array, not a copy of the array elements. Within the called function, a parameter must be declared to receive the passed array name. The declaration of the parameter can omit the row size of the array.

7.7 Chapter Supplement: Searching and Sorting Methods

Most programmers encounter the need to both sort and search a list of data items at some time in their programming careers. For example, experimental results may have to be arranged in either increasing (ascending) or decreasing (descending) order for statistical analysis, lists of names may have to be sorted in alphabetical order, or a list of dates may have to be rearranged in ascending date order. Similarly, a list of names may have to be searched to find a particular name in the list, or a list of dates may have to be searched to locate a particular date. In this section we introduce the fundamentals of both sorting and searching lists. Note that it is not necessary to sort a list before searching it, although, as we shall see, much faster searches are possible if the list is in sorted order.

Search Algorithms

A common requirement of many programs is to search a list for a given element. For example, in a list of names and telephone numbers, we might search for a specific name so that the corresponding telephone number can be printed, or we might wish to search the list simply to determine whether a name is there. The two most common methods of performing such searches are the linear and binary search algorithms.

Linear Search

In a *linear search,* which is also known as a *sequential search,* each item in the list is examined in the order in which it occurs in the list until the desired item is found or the end of the list is reached. This is analogous to looking at every name in the phone directory, beginning with Aardvark, Aaron, until you find the one you want or until you reach Zzxgy, Zora. Obviously, this is not the most efficient way to search a long alphabetized list. However, a linear search has these advantages:

1. The algorithm is simple.
2. The list need not be in any particular order.

In a linear search, the search begins with the first item in the list and continues sequentially, item by item, through the list. The pseudocode for a function performing a linear search is

For all the items in the list
  Compare the item with the desired item
  If the item was found
    Return the index value of the current item
  EndIf
EndFor
Return –1 because the item was not found

Note that the function's return value indicates whether the item was found or not. If the return value is –1, the item was not in the list; otherwise, the return value within the `for` loop provides the index of where the item is located within the list.

The function `LinearSearch()` illustrates this procedure as a C++ function:

```
// this function returns the location of key in the list
// a -1 is returned if the value is not found
int LinearSearch(int list[], int size, int key)
{
  int i;

  for (i = 0; i < size; i++)
  {
    if (list[i] == key)
      return i;
  }

  return -1;
}
```

In reviewing `LinearSearch()`, note that the `for` loop is used simply to access each element in the list, from first element to last, until a match is found with the desired item. If the desired item is located, the index value of the current item is returned, which causes the loop to terminate; otherwise, the search continues until the end of the list is encountered.

To test this function, we have written a `main()` driver function to call it and display the results returned by `LinearSearch()`. The complete test program is illustrated in Program 7-9.

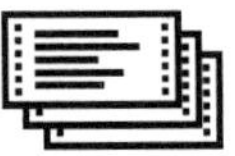

Program 7-9

```
#include <iostream.h>

int LinearSearch(int [], int, int);

int main()
{
  const int NUMEL = 10;
  int nums[NUMEL] = {5,10,22,32,45,67,73,98,99,101};
  int item, location;

  cout << "Enter the item you are searching for: ";
  cin  >> item;

  location = LinearSearch(nums, NUMEL, item);

  if (location > -1)
    cout << "The item was found at index location " << location
         << endl;
  else
    cout << "The item was not found in the list\n";

  return 0;
}

// this function returns the location of key in the list
// a -1 is returned if the value is not found
int LinearSearch(int list[], int size, int key)
{
  int i;

  for (i = 0; i < size; i++)
  {
    if (list[i] == key)
      return i;
  }

  return -1;
}
```

Sample runs of Program 7-9 follow.

```
Enter the item you are searching for: 101
The item was found at index location 9
```

and

```
Enter the item you are searching for: 65
The item was not found in the list
```

As has already been pointed out, an advantage of linear searches is that the list does not have to be in sorted order to perform the search. Another advantage is that if the desired item is toward the front of the list, only a small number of comparisons will be done. The worst case, of course, occurs when the desired item is at the end of the list. On average, however, and assuming that the desired item is equally likely to be anywhere within the list, the number of required comparisons will be $N/2$, where N is the list's size. Thus, for a 10-element list, the average number of comparisons needed for a linear search is 5, and for a 10,000-element list, the average number of comparisons needed is 5000. As we show next, this number can be significantly reduced by using a binary search algorithm.

Binary Search

In a *binary search,* the list must be in sorted order. Starting with an ordered list, the desired item is first compared to the element in the middle of the list (for lists with an even number of elements, either of the two middle elements can be used). Three possibilities present themselves once the comparison is made: The desired item may be equal to the middle element, it may be greater than the middle element, or it may be less than the middle element.

In the first case the search has been successful, and no further searches are required. In the second case, because the desired item is greater than the middle element, if it is found at all it must be in the second half of the list. This means that the front part of the list, consisting of all elements from the first to the midpoint element, can be discarded from any further search. In the third case, because the desired item is less than the middle element, if it is found at all it must be in the first half of the list. For this case the second half of the list, containing all elements from the midpoint element to the last element, can be discarded from any further search.

The algorithm for implementing this search strategy is illustrated in Figure 7–13 and defined by the following pseudocode:

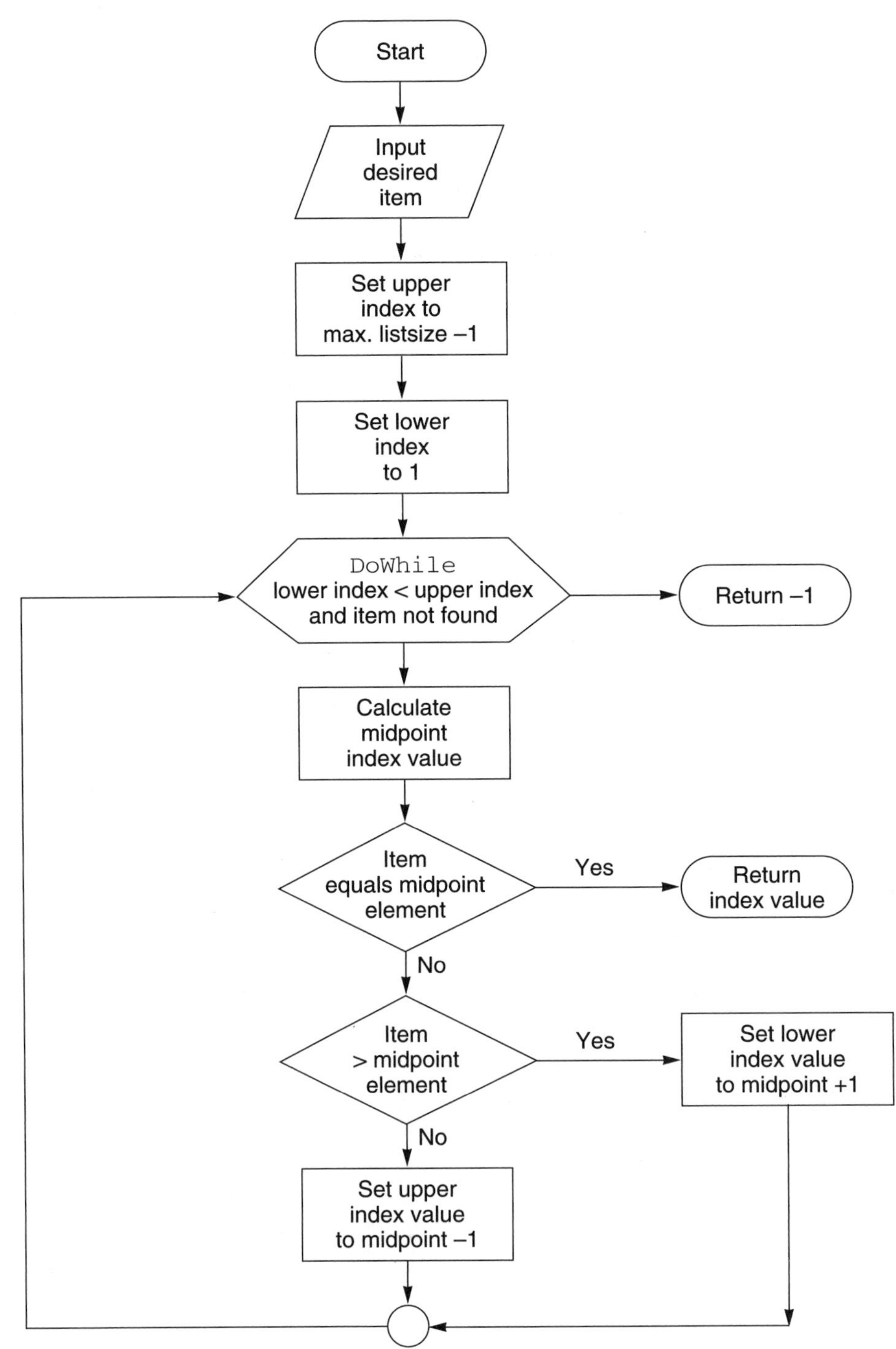

FIGURE 7-13 The Binary Search Algorithm

Set the lower index to 0
Set the upper index to one less than the size of the list
Begin with the first item in the list
While the lower index is less than or equal to the upper index
    Set the midpoint index to the integer average of the lower and upper index values
    Compare the desired item to the midpoint element
        If the desired element equals the midpoint element
            Return the index value of the current item
      Else if the desired element is greater than the midpoint element
            Set the lower index value to the midpoint value plus 1
      Else if the desired element is less than the midpoint element
            Set the upper index value to the midpoint value less 1
      Endif
EndWhile
Return –1 because the item was not found

As illustrated by both the pseudocode and the flowchart of Figure 7–13, a `while` loop is used to control the search. The initial list is defined by setting the left index value to 0 and the right index value to one less than the number of elements in the list. The midpoint element is then taken as the integerized average of the left and right values. Once the comparison to the midpoint element is made, the search is subsequently restricted either by moving the left index to one integer value above the midpoint or by moving the right index to one integer value below the midpoint. This process is continued until the desired element is found or the left and right index values become equal. The function `BinarySearch()` presents the C++ version of this algorithm.

```
// this function returns the location of key in the list
// a -1 is returned if the value is not found
int BinarySearch(int list[], int size, int key)
{
  int left, right, midpt;

  left = 0;
  right = size - 1;

  while (left <= right)
  {
    midpt = (int) ((left + right) / 2);
    if (key == list[midpt])
    {
      return midpt;
    }
```

(continued on next page)

(continued from previous page)

```
       else if (key > list[midpt])
          left = midpt + 1;
        else
          right = midpt - 1;
    }

    return -1;
  }
```

For purposes of testing this function, Program 7-10 is used.

Program 7-10

```
#include <iostream.h>

int BinarySearch(int [], int, int);

int main()
{
  const int NUMEL = 10;
  int nums[NUMEL] = {5,10,22,32,45,67,73,98,99,101};
  int item, location;

  cout << "Enter the item you are searching for: ";
  cin >> item;
  location = BinarySearch(nums, NUMEL, item);
  if (location > -1)
    cout << "The item was found at index location "
         << location << endl;
  else
    cout << "The item was not found in the array\n";
  return 0;
}

// this function returns the location of key in the list
// a -1 is returned if the value is not found
int BinarySearch(int list[], int size, int key)
{
  int left, right, midpt;

  left = 0;
  right = size -1;
```

```
    while (left <= right)
    {
      midpt = (int) ((left + right) / 2);
      if (key == list[midpt])
      {
        return midpt;
      }
      else if (key > list[midpt])
        left = midpt + 1;
      else
        right = midpt - 1;
    }

    return -1;
  }
```

A sample run using Program 7-10 yielded the following:

```
Enter the item you are searching for: 101
The item was found at index location 9
```

The beauty of using a binary search algorithm is that the number of elements that must be searched is cut in half each time through the `while` loop. Thus, the first time through the loop, N elements must be searched; the second time through the loop, $N/2$ of the elements have been eliminated and only $N/2$ remain. The third time through the loop, half of the remaining elements have been eliminated, and so on.

In general, after p passes through the loop, the number of values remaining to be searched is $N/(2^p)$. In the worst case, the search can continue until there is less than or equal to one element remaining to be searched. Mathematically, this can be expressed as $N/(2^p) \leq 1$. Alternatively, this may be rephrased as "p is the smallest integer such that $2^p \geq N$. For example, for a 1000-element array, N is 1000, and the maximum number of passes, p, required for a binary search is 10. Table 7–1 shows the numbers of loop passes needed for a linear and a binary search for various list sizes.

As illustrated, the maximum number of loop passes for a 50-item list is almost 10 times more for a linear search than for a binary search, and the difference is even more spectacular for larger lists. As a rule of thumb, 50 elements are usually taken as the switchover point: For lists smaller than 50 elements, linear searches are acceptable; for larger lists, a binary search algorithm should be used.

TABLE 7–1 A Comparison of `while` Loop Pass for Linear and Binary Searches

Array size	10	50	500	5,000	50,000	500,000	5,000,000	50,000,000
Average linear search passes	5	25	250	2,500	25,000	250,000	2,500,000	25,000,000
Maximum linear search passes	10	50	500	5,000	50,000	500,000	5,000,000	50,000,000
Maximum binary search passes	4	6	9	13	16	19	23	26

Big O Notation

On average, over a large number of linear searches with N items in a list, we would expect to examine half ($N/2$) of the items before locating the desired item. In a binary search, the maximum number of passes, p, occurs when $N/2^p = 1$. This relationship can be algebraically manipulated to $2^p = N$, which yields $p = \log_2 N$, which approximately equals $3.33 \log_{10} N$.

For example, finding a particular name in an alphabetical directory with $N = 1000$ names would require an average of 500 ($= N/2$) comparisons with a linear search. With a binary search, only about 10 ($\approx 3.33 \times \log_{10} 1000$) comparisons would be required.

A common way to express the number of comparisons required in any search algorithm using a list of N items is to give the order of magnitude of the number of comparisons required, on average, to locate a desired item. Thus the linear search is said to be of order N, the binary search of order $\log_2 N$. Notationally, this is expressed as $O(N)$ and $O(\log_2 N)$, where the O is read as "the order of."

Sort Algorithms

For sorting data, there are two major categories of sorting techniques. *Internal sorts* are used when the data list is not too large and the complete list can be stored within the computer's memory, usually in an array. *External sorts* are used for much larger data sets that are stored in large external disk or tape files and cannot be accommodated within the computer's memory as a complete unit. Here we present two internal sort algorithms that can be used effectively when sorting lists with less than approximately 50 elements. For larger lists, more sophisticated sorting algorithms are typically employed.

Selection Sort

One of the simplest sorting techniques is the selection sort. In a *selection sort,* the smallest value is initially selected from the complete list of data and exchanged with the first element in the list. After this first selection and exchange, the next smallest element in the revised list is selected and exchanged with the second element in the list. Because the smallest element is already in the first position in the list, this second pass need consider only the second

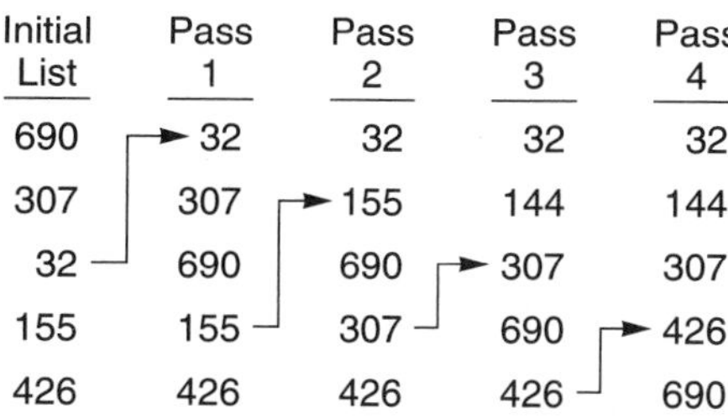

Initial List
Pass 1
Pass 2
Pass 3
Pass 4
690 307 32 155 426
32 307 690 155 426
32 155 690 307 426
32 144 307 690 426
32 144 307 426 690

FIGURE 7-14 A Sample Selection Sort

through the last elements. For a list consisting of N elements, this process is repeated $N - 1$ times, with each pass through the list requiring one less comparison than the previous pass.

For example, consider the list of numbers shown in Figure 7–14. The first pass through the initial list results in the number 32 being selected and exchanged with the first element in the list. The second pass, made on the reordered list, results in the number 155 being selected from the second through the fifth elements. This value is then exchanged with the second element in the list. The third pass selects the number 307 from the third through the fifth elements in the list and exchanges this value with the third element. Finally, the fourth and last pass through the list selects the remaining minimum value and exchanges it with the fourth element. Although each pass in this example resulted in an exchange, no exchange would have been made in a pass if the smallest value had already been in the correct location.

In pseudocode, the selection sort is described as follows:

```
Set interchange count to zero (not required, but done just to keep track of the interchanges)
For each element in the list from first to next-to-last
  Find the smallest element from the current element being referenced to the last element by:
    Setting the minimum value equal to the current element
    Saving (storing) the index of the current element
   For each element in the list from the current element + 1 to the last element in the list
     If element[inner loop index] < minimum value
       Set the minimum value = element[inner loop index]
       Save the index of the new found minimum value
     EndIf
   EndFor
   Swap the current value with the new minimum value
   Increment the interchange count
EndFor
Return the interchange count
```

The function `SelectionSort()` incorporates this procedure into a C++ function.

```
int SelectionSort(int num[], int numel)
{
  int i, j, min, minidx, temp, moves = 0;

  for ( i = 0; i < (numel - 1); i++)
  {
    min = num[i];    // assume minimum is the first array element
    minidx = i;      // index of minimum element
    for(j = i + 1; j < numel; j++)
    {
      if (num[j] < min)    // if we've located a lower value
      {                    // capture it
        min = num[j];
        minidx = j;
      }
    }
    if (min < num[i])   // check if we have a new minimum
    {                   // and if we do, swap values
      temp = num[i];
      num[i] = min;
      num[minidx] = temp;
      moves++;
    }
  }

  return moves;
}
```

The `SelectionSort()` function expects two arguments, the list to be sorted and the number of elements in the list. As specified by the pseudocode, a nested set of `for` loops performs the sort. The outer `for` loop causes one less pass through the list than the total number of data items in the list. For each pass, the variable `min` is initially assigned the value `num[i]`, where `i` is the outer `for` loop's counter variable. Because `i` begins at 0 and ends at one less than `numel`, each element in the list, except the last, is successively designated as the current element.

The inner loop cycles through the elements below the current element and is used to select the next smallest value. Thus this loop begins at the index value `i+1` and continues through the end of the list. When a new minimum is found, its value and position in the list are stored in the variables named `min` and `minidx`, respectively. Upon completion of the inner loop, an exchange is made only if a value less than that in the current position was found.

For purposes of testing `SelectionSort()`, Program 7-11 was constructed. This program implements a selection sort for the same list of ten numbers that was previously used to test our search algorithms. For later comparison to the other sorting algorithms that will be presented, the number of actual moves made by the program to get the data into sorted order is counted and displayed.

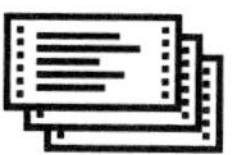

Program 7-11

```
#include <iostream.h>

int SelectionSort(int [], int);

int main()
{
  const int NUMEL = 10;
  int nums[NUMEL] = {22,5,67,98,45,32,101,99,73,10};
  int i, moves;

  moves = SelectionSort(nums, NUMEL);

  cout << "The sorted list, in ascending order, is:\n";
  for (i = 0; i < NUMEL; i++)
    cout << "   " << nums[i];

  cout << '\n' << moves << " moves were made to sort this list\n";

  return 0;
}

int SelectionSort(int num[], int numel)
{
  int i, j, min, minidx, temp, moves = 0;

  for ( i = 0; i < (numel - 1); i++)
  {
    min = num[i];    // assume minimum is the first array element
    minidx = i;      // index of minimum element
    for(j = i + 1; j < numel; j++)
    {
      if (num[j] < min)    // if we've located a lower value
      {                    // capture it
        min = num[j];
        minidx = j;
      }
    }
    if (min < num[i])  // check if we have a new minimum
    {                  // and if we do, swap values
      temp = num[i];
      num[i] = min;
      num[minidx] = temp;
      moves++;
    }
  }

  return moves;
}
```

The output produced by Program 7-11 is

```
The sorted list, in ascending order, is:
  5  10  22  32  45  67  73  98  99  101
8 moves were made to sort this list
```

Clearly, the number of moves displayed depends on the initial order of the values in the list. An advantage of the selection sort is that the maximum number of moves that must be made is $N - 1$, where N is the number of items in the list. Further, each move is a final move that results in an element residing in its final location in the sorted list.

A disadvantage of the selection sort is that $N(N - 1)/2$ comparisons are always required, regardless of the initial arrangement of the data. This number of comparisons is obtained as follows: The last pass always requires one comparison, the next-to-last pass requires two comparisons, and so on, to the first pass, which requires $N - 1$ comparisons. Thus the total number of comparisons is

$$1 + 2 + 3 + \cdots + N - 1 = N(N - 1)/2 = N^2/2 - N/2$$

For large values of N, the N^2 dominates, and the order of the selection sort is $O(N^2)$.

Exchange ("Bubble") Sort

In an *exchange sort,* or *bubble sort,* adjacent elements of the list are exchanged with one another in such a manner that the list becomes sorted. One example of such a sequence of exchanges is provided by the bubble sort, where successive values in the list are compared, beginning with the first two elements. If the list is to be sorted in ascending (from smallest to largest) order, the smaller value of the two being compared is always placed before the larger value. For lists sorted in descending (from largest to smallest) order, the smaller of the two values being compared is always placed after the larger value.

For example, assuming that a list of values is to be sorted in ascending order, if the first element in the list is larger than the second, the two elements are interchanged. Then the second and third elements are compared. Again, if the second element is larger than the third, these two elements are interchanged. This process continues until the last two elements have been compared and exchanged, if necessary. If no exchanges were made during this initial pass through the data, the data is in the correct order and the process is finished; otherwise, a second pass is made through the data, starting from the first element and stopping at the next-to-last element. The reason for stopping at the

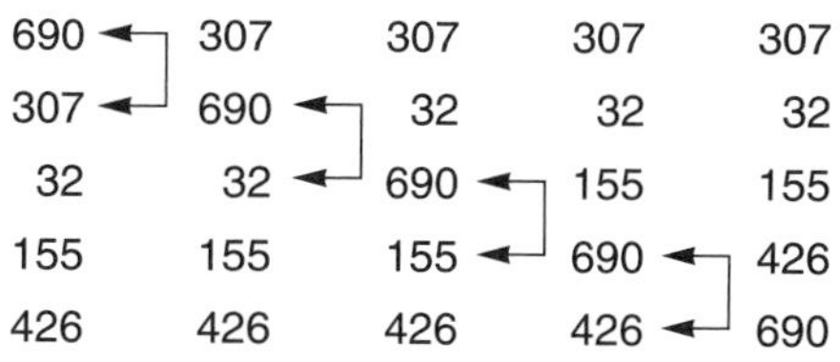

690	307	307	307	307
307	690	32	32	32
32	32	690	155	155
155	155	155	690	426
426	426	426	426	690

FIGURE 7–15 The First Pass of an Exchange Sort

next-to-last element on the second pass is that the first pass always results in the most positive value "sinking" to the bottom of the list.

As a specific example of this process, consider the list of numbers shown in Figure 7–15. The first comparison results in the interchange of the first two element values, 690 and 307. The next comparison, between elements two and three in the revised list, results in the interchange of values between the second and third elements, 690 and 32. This comparison and possible switching of adjacent values is continued until the last two elements have been compared and possibly switched. This process completes the first pass through the data and results in the largest number moving to the bottom of the list. As the largest value sinks to its resting place at the bottom of the list, the smaller elements slowly rise, or "bubble," to the top of the list. This bubbling effect of the smaller elements is what gave rise to the name *bubble sort* for this sorting algorithm.

Because the first pass through the list ensures that the largest value always moves to the bottom of the list, the second pass stops at the next-to-last element. This process continues, each pass stopping at one higher element than the previous pass, until either $N - 1$ passes through the list have been completed or no exchanges are necessary in any single pass. In both cases, the resulting list is in sorted order. The pseudocode describing this sort is

```
Set interchange count to zero (not required, but done just to keep track of the interchanges)
For the first element in the list to one less than the last element (i index)
  For the second element in the list to the last element (j index)
    If num[j] < num[j – 1]
    {
      swap num[j] with num[j – 1]
      increment interchange count
    }
  EndFor
EndFor
Return interchange count
```

This sort algorithm is coded in C++ as the function `BubbleSort()`, which in included within Program 7-12 for testing purposes. This program tests `BubbleSort()` with the same list of ten numbers used in Program 7-11 to test `SelectionSort()`. For comparison to the earlier selection sort, the number of adjacent moves (exchanges) made by `BubbleSort()` is also counted and displayed.

Program 7-12

```
#include <iostream.h>

int BubbleSort(int [], int);

int main()
{
  const int NUMEL = 10;
  int nums[NUMEL] = {22,5,67,98,45,32,101,99,73,10};
  int i, moves;

  moves = BubbleSort(nums, NUMEL);

  cout << "The sorted list, in ascending order, is:\n";
  for (i = 0; i < NUMEL; i++)
    cout << "  " << nums[i];

  cout << '\n' << moves << " were made to sort this list\n";

  return 0;
}

int BubbleSort(int num[], int numel)
{
  int i, j, temp, moves = 0;

  for ( i = 0; i < (numel - 1); i++)
  {
    for(j = 1; j < numel; j++)
    {
      if (num[j] < num[j-1])
      {
        temp = num[j];
        num[j] = num[j-1];
        num[j-1] = temp;
        moves++;
      }
    }
  }

  return moves;
}
```

Here is the output produced by Program 7-12:

```
The sorted list, in ascending order, is:
  5  10  22  32  45  67  73  98  99  101
18 moves were made to sort this list
```

As with the selection sort, the number of comparisons using a bubble sort is $O(N^2)$, and the number of required moves depends on the initial order of the values in the list. In the worst case, when the data is in reverse sorted order, the selection sort performs better than the bubble sort. Here both sorts require $N(N - 1)/2$ comparisons, but the selection sort needs only $N - 1$ moves, whereas the bubble sort needs $N(N - 1)/2$ moves. The additional moves required by the bubble sort result from the intermediate exchanges between adjacent elements to "settle" each element into its final position. In this regard the selection sort is superior, because no intermediate moves are necessary. For random data, such as that used in Programs 7-11 and 7-12, the selection sort generally performs as well as or better than the bubble sort.

Pointers

Chapter Eight

A fact not generally known to most programmers of high-level languages other than C and C++ is that memory addresses of variables are used extensively throughout the executable versions of their programs. The computer uses these addresses to keep track of where data and instructions are physically located inside of the computer.

One of C++'s advantages is that it provides the programmer access to the addresses of variables used in a program. This access enables a programmer to enter directly into the computer's inner workings and manipulate the computer's basic storage structure. It provides the C++ programmer with capabilities and programming power that are not typically available in other high-level languages.

This chapter presents the basics of declaring variables to store addresses. Such variables are referred to as *pointer variables*, or simply *pointers*. We also discuss methods of using pointer variables to access and use their stored addresses in meaningful ways.

8.1 Addresses and Pointers

Every variable has three major items associated with it: its data type, the actual value stored in the variable, and the address of the variable. As we have already seen, a variable's data type is declared with a declaration statement, and a value is stored in a variable by initialization when the variable is declared, by assignment, or by input. For the majority of applications, the variable's name is a simple and sufficient means of locating the variable's contents, and the translation of a variable's name to actual memory storage location is done by the computer each time the variable is referenced in a program.

Figure 8–1 illustrates the relationship among these three variable attributes (type, contents, and location). As this figure shows, the data type determines the number of memory bytes set aside for the variable, and the variable's name is a stand-in for the variable's actual memory address.

Programmers are usually concerned only with the value assigned to a variable (its contents) and pay little attention to where the value is stored (its address). For example, consider Program 8-1.

The output displayed when Program 8-1 is run is

```
The value stored in num is 22
2 bytes are used to store this value
```

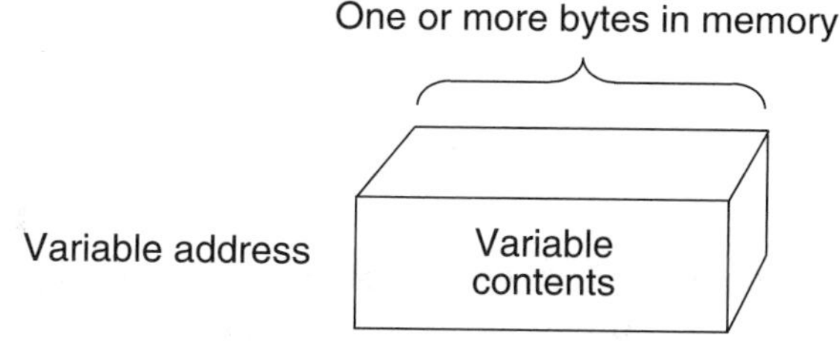

FIGURE 8–1 A Typical Variable

Program 8-1

```
#include <iostream.h>
int main()
{
  int num;

  num = 22;
  cout << "The value stored in num is " << num << endl;
  cout << sizeof(num) << " bytes are used to store this value" << endl;

  return 0;
}
```

Program 8-1 displays both the number 22, which is the value stored in the integer variable `num`, and the amount of storage used for this number.[1] The information provided by Program 8-1 is illustrated in Figure 8–2.

FIGURE 8–2 Somewhere in Memory

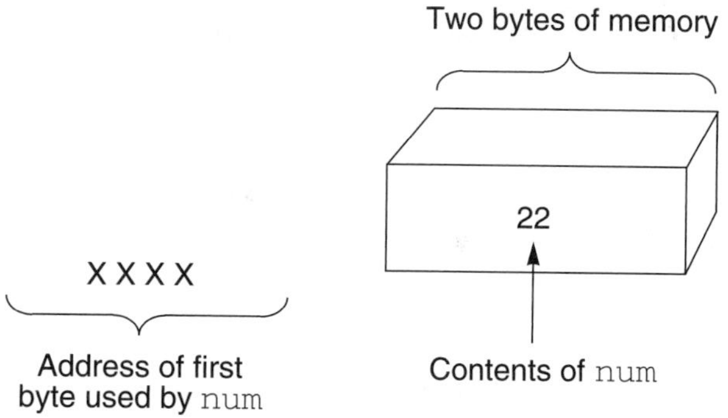

[1] The amount of storage allocated for each data type is compiler-dependent.

We can go further and obtain the address corresponding to the variable `num`. The address that is displayed corresponds to the address of the first byte set aside in the computer's memory for the variable.

To determine the address of `num`, we must use the address operator, `&`. We have seen this symbol before in declaring reference variables. Here it means *the address of* and when placed in front of a variable name is translated as *the address of the variable.*[2] For example, `&num` means *the address of* `num`, `&total` means *the address of* `total`, and `&price` means *the address of* `price`. Program 8-2 uses the address operator to display the address of the variable `num`.

Program 8-2

```
#include <iostream.h>
int main()
{
  int num;

  num = 22;
  cout << "num = " << num << endl;
  cout << "The address of num = " << &num << endl;

  return 0;
}
```

The output of Program 8-2 is

```
num = 22
The address of num = 0x0064FDF4
```

Figure 8–3 illustrates the additional address information provided by the output of Program 8-2.

Clearly, the address output by Program 8-2 depends on the computer used to run the program. Every time Program 8-2 is executed, however, it displays the address of the first memory location used to store the variable `num`. As

---

[2] When used in the declaration of a reference variable, the `&` symbol has a similar meaning. For example, the declaration `int &num = factor;` can also be read as "`num` is the address of an `int`" (though it is more often read as "`num` is a reference to an `int`"). Because `num` is a reference variable, the compiler automatically assigns the address of `factor` to the address of `num`; both variables have the same memory address, so they both refer to the same variable.

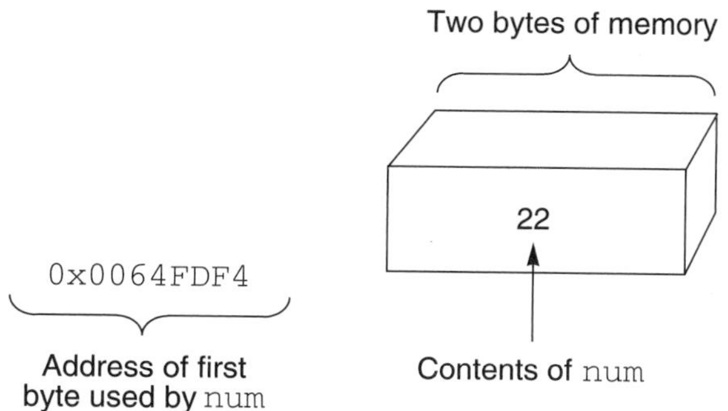

FIGURE 8–3 A More Comprehensive Picture of the Variable `num`

illustrated by the output of Program 8-2, the display of addresses is in hexadecimal notation. This display has no effect on how addresses are used within the program; it merely provides us with a means of displaying addresses that is helpful in understanding them. As we shall see, using addresses (as opposed to only displaying them) provides the C++ programmer with an extremely powerful programming tool.

Storing Addresses

Besides displaying the address of a variable, as was done in Program 8-2, we can also store addresses in suitably declared variables. For example, the statement

```
numAddr = &num;
```

stores the address that corresponds to the variable `num` in the variable `numAddr`, as illustrated in Figure 8–4. Similarly, the statements

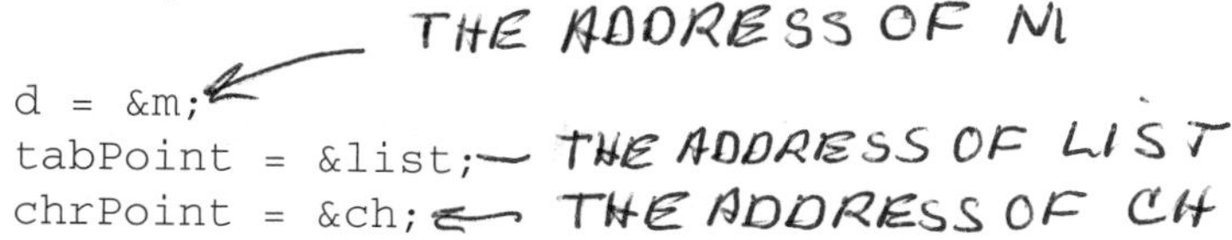

```
d = &m;
tabPoint = &list;
chrPoint = &ch;
```

FIGURE 8–4 Storing `num`'s Address in `numAddr`

Variable name	Contents
`numAddr`	Address of `num`

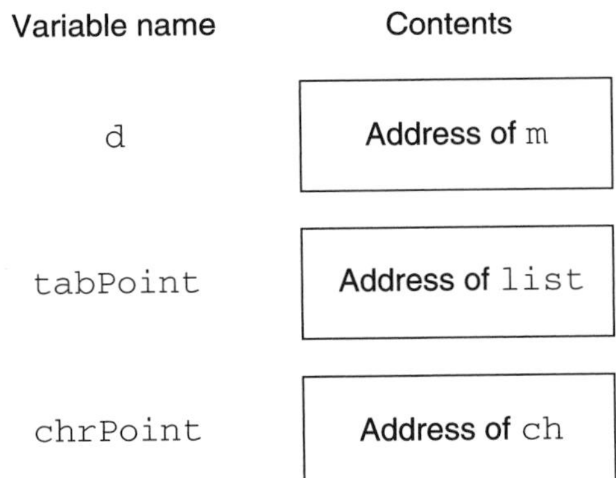

FIGURE 8–5 Storing More Addresses

store the addresses of the variables `m`, `list`, and `ch` in the variables `d`, `tabPoint`, and `chrPoint`, respectively, as illustrated in Figure 8–5.

The variables `numAddr`, `d`, `tabPoint`, and `chrPoint` are formally called *pointer variables*, or *pointers* for short. Pointers are simply variables that are used to store the addresses of other variables.

Using Addresses

To use a stored address, C++ provides us with an *indirection operator*, `*`. The `*` symbol, when followed by a pointer, means *the variable whose address is stored in*. Thus, if `numAddr` is a pointer (remember that a pointer is a variable that stores an address), then `*numAddr` means *the variable whose address is stored in* `numAddr`. Similarly, `*tabPoint` means *the variable whose address is stored in* `tabPoint`, and `*chrPoint` means *the variable whose address is stored in* `chrPoint`. Figure 8–6 shows the relationship between the address contained in a pointer variable and the variable ultimately addressed.

Although `*d` literally means *the variable whose address is stored in* `d`, this is commonly shortened to the statement *the variable pointed to by* `d`. Similarly, referring to Figure 8–6, `*y` can be read as *the variable pointed to by* `y`. The value ultimately obtained, as shown in Figure 8–6, is `qqqq`.

When we are using a pointer variable, the value that is finally obtained is always found by first going to the pointer variable (or pointer, for short) for an address. The address contained in the pointer is then used to get the desired contents. Certainly, this is a rather indirect way of getting to the final value, and not unexpectedly, the term *indirect addressing* is used to describe this procedure.

Because using a pointer requires the computer to do a double lookup (first the address is retrieved, and then the address is used to retrieve the actual data),

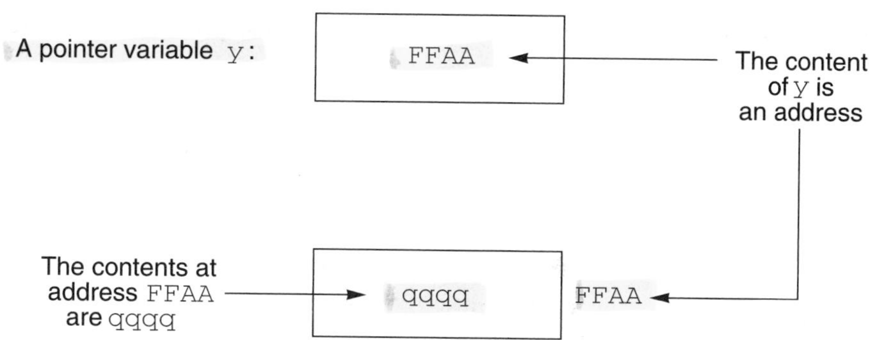

FIGURE 8–6 Using a Pointer Variable

a worthwhile question is, why would we want to store an address in the first place? The answer to this question rests on the intimate relationship between pointers and arrays and the ability of pointers to create and delete new variable storage locations dynamically, as a program is running. Both of these topics are presented later in this chapter. For now, however, given that each variable has a memory address associated with it, the idea of actually storing an address should not seem overly strange.

Declaring Pointers

Like all variables, pointers must be declared before they can be used to store an address. C++ requires that when we declare a pointer variable, we also specify the type of variable that is pointed to. For example, if the address in the pointer `numAddr` is the address of an integer, the correct declaration for the pointer is

```
int *numAddr;
```

This declaration is read as *the variable pointed to by* `numAddr` (from the `*numAddr` in the declaration) *is an integer.*[3]

---

[3] Pointer declarations may also be written in the form `data-type* pointer-name;`, where a space is placed between the indirection operator symbol and the pointer variable name. This form, however, becomes error-prone when multiple pointer variables are declared in the same declaration statement and the asterisk symbol is inadvertently omitted after the first pointer name is declared. For example, the declaration `int* num1, num2;` declares `num1` as a pointer variable and `num2` as an integer variable. In order to accommodate multiple pointers in the same declaration more easily and clearly mark a variable as a pointer, we will adhere to the convention of placing an asterisk directly in front of each pointer variable name. This possible error rarely occurs with reference declarations, because references are almost exclusively used as parameters, and single declarations of parameters are mandatory.

Note that the declaration `int *numAddr;` specifies two things: first, that the variable pointed to by `numAddr` is an integer; second, that `numAddr` must be a pointer (because it is used with the indirection operator `*`). Similarly, if the pointer `tabPoint` points to (contains the address of) a floating-point number and `chrPoint` points to a character variable, then the required declarations for these pointers are

```
float *tabPoint;
char *chrPoint;
```

These two declarations can be read, respectively, as *the variable pointed to by* `tabPoint` *is a float* and *the variable pointed to by* `chrPoint` *is a char*. Consider Program 8-3.

Program 8-3

```
#include <iostream.h>

int main()
{
  int *numAddr;          // declare a pointer to an int
  int miles, dist;       // declare two integer variables

  dist = 158;            // store the number 158 into dist
  miles = 22;            // store the number 22 into miles
  numAddr = &miles;      // store the 'address of miles' in numAddr

  cout << "The address stored in numAddr is " << numAddr << endl;
  cout << "The value pointed to by numAddr is " << *numAddr << endl;

  numAddr = &dist;     // now store the address of dist in numAddr
  cout << "\nThe address now stored in numAddr is " << numAddr << endl;
  cout << "The value now pointed to by numAddr is " << *numAddr << endl;

  return 0;
}
```

The output of Program 8-3 is

```
The address stored in numAddr is 0x0064FDF4
The value pointed to by numAddr is 22

The address now stored in numAddr is 0x0064FDF0
The value now pointed to by numAddr is 158
```

The only value of Program 8-3 is in helping us understand "what gets stored where." Let's review the program to see how the output was produced.

The declaration statement `int *numAddr;` declares `numAddr` to be a pointer variable used to store the address of an integer variable. The statement `numAddr = &miles;` stores the address of the variable `miles` into the pointer `numAddr`. The first `cout` statement causes this address to be displayed. The second `cout` statement in Program 8-3 uses the indirection operator to retrieve and print out *the value pointed to by* `numAddr`, which is, of course, the value stored in `miles`.

Because `numAddr` has been declared as a pointer to an integer variable, we can use this pointer to store the address of any integer variable. The statement `numAddr = &dist` illustrates this by storing the address of the variable `dist` in `numAddr`. The last two `cout` statements verify the change in `numAddr`'s value and confirm that the new stored address does point to the variable `dist`. As illustrated in Program 8-3, only addresses should be stored in pointers.

It certainly would have been much simpler if the pointer used in Program 8-3 could have been declared as pointer `numAddr;`. Such a declaration, however, conveys no information about the storage used by the variable whose address is stored in `numAddr`. This information is essential when the pointer is used with the indirection operator, as it is in the second `cout` statement in Program 8-3. For example, if the address of an integer is stored in `numAddr`, then only two bytes of storage are typically retrieved when the address is used. If the address of a character is stored in `numAddr`, only one byte of storage would be retrieved, and a float typically requires the retrieval of four bytes of storage.[4] The declaration of a pointer must therefore include the type of variable being pointed to. Figure 8–7 illustrates this concept.

FIGURE 8–7 Addressing Different Data Types Using Pointers

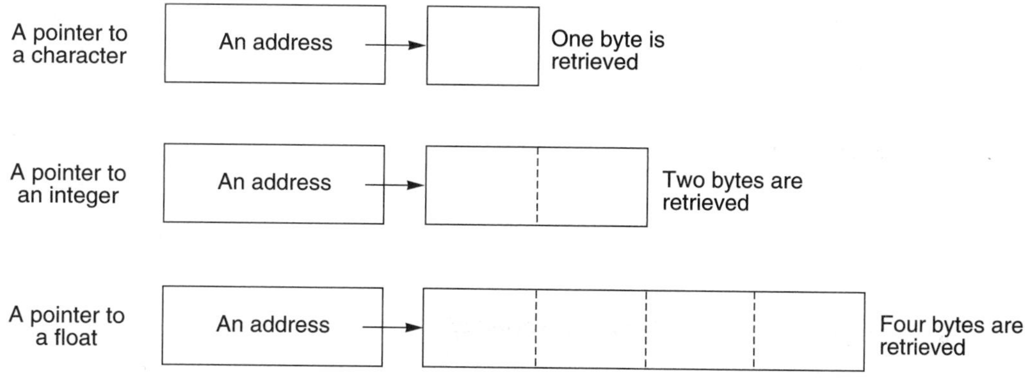

4 The amount of storage used is compiler-dependent.

References and Pointers

At this point you might be asking what the difference is between a pointer and a reference. Essentially, a reference is a pointer with restricted capabilities that has the advantage of hiding a lot of internal pointer manipulations from the programmer. For example, consider these statements:

```
int b;       // b is an integer variable
int &a = b;  // a is a reference variable that stores b's address
a = 10;      // this changes b's value to 10
```

Here a is declared as a reference variable that contains the address of an integer—the address of b, in particular. Because the compiler knows, from the declaration, that a is a reference variable, it automatically assigns the address of b (rather than the contents of b) in the declaration statement. Finally, in the statement `a = 10;` the compiler uses the address stored in a to change the value stored in b to 10. The advantage of using the reference is that it automatically performs an indirect access of b's value without the need for explicitly using the indirection operator symbol, *. This type of access is referred to as an *automatic dereference*.

Implementing this same correspondence between a and b using pointers is done by the following sequence of instructions:

```
int b;        // b is an integer variable
int *a = &b;  // a is a pointer - store b's address in a
*a = 10;      // this changes b's value to 10
```

Here a is defined as a pointer that is initialized to store the address of b. Thus *a, which can be read either as "the variable whose address is in a" or as "the variable pointed to by a," is b, and the expression `*a = 10` changes b's value to 10. Note that in the pointer case, the stored address can be altered to point to another variable; in the reference case, the reference variable cannot be altered to refer to any variable except the one to which it is initialized.

For simple cases, where an alias is required, using references is easier than using pointers and is clearly preferred. The same is true when we consider references to structures, which is the topic of Section 10.3. For other situations, such as dynamically allocating new sections of memory for additional variables as a program is running, or using alternatives to array notation (both topics of the next section), pointers are required. In other situations, such as passing addresses to a function, references provide a simpler notational interface and are usually preferred (see Section 8.4). Pointers are described in the remaining sections of this chapter.

Exercises 8.1

1. If `average` is a variable, what does `&average` mean?

2. For the variables and addresses illustrated in Figure 8–8, determine `&temp`, `&dist`, `&date`, and `&miles`.

3. *a.* Write a C++ program that includes the following declaration statements. Have the program use the address operator and the `cout` object to display the addresses that correspond to each variable.

```
int num, count;
long date;
float yield;
double price;
```

b. After running the program written for Exercise 3a, draw a diagram of how your computer has set aside storage for the variables in the program. On your diagram, fill in the addresses displayed by the program.

c. Modify the program written in Exercise 3a to display the amount of storage your computer reserves for each data type (use the `sizeof()` operator). With this information and the address information provided in Exercise 3b, determine whether your computer set aside storage for the variables in the order in which they were declared.

FIGURE 8–8 Memory Bytes for Exercise 2

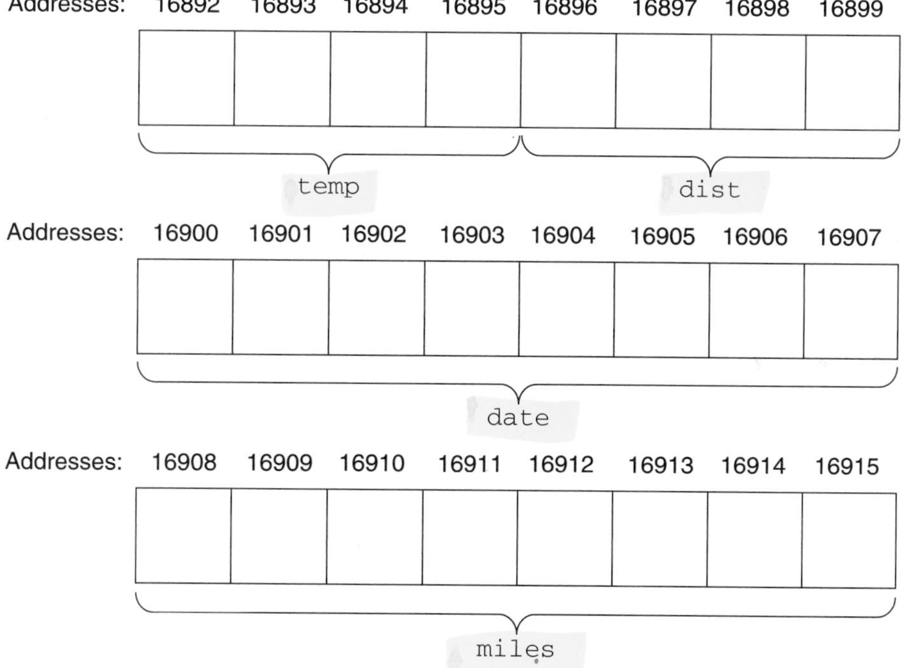

4. If a variable is declared as a pointer, what must be stored in the variable?

5. Using the indirection operator, write expressions for the following:
   a. The variable pointed to by `xAddr`
   b. The variable whose address is in `yAddr`
   c. The variable pointed to by `ptYld`
   d. The variable pointed to by `ptMiles`
   e. The variable pointed to by `mptr`
   f. The variable whose address is in `pdate`
   g. The variable pointed to by `distPtr`
   h. The variable pointed to by `tabPt`
   i. The variable whose address is in `hoursPt`

6. Write declaration statements for the following:
   a. The variable pointed to by `yAddr` is an integer.
   b. The variable pointed to by `chAddr` is a character.
   c. The variable pointed to by `ptYr` is a long integer.
   d. The variable pointed to by `amt` is a double-precision variable.
   e. The variable pointed to by `z` is an integer.
   f. The variable pointed to by `qp` is a floating-point variable.
   g. `datePt` is a pointer to an integer.
   h. `yldAddr` is a pointer to a double-precision variable.
   i. `amtPt` is a pointer to a floating-point variable.
   j. `ptChr` is a pointer to a character.

7. *a.* What are the variables `yAddr`, `chAddr`, `ptYr`, `amt`, `z`, `qp`, `datePtr`, `yldAddr`, `amtPt`, and `ptChr`, used in Exercise 6, called?
   b. Why are the variable names `amt`, `z`, and `qp`, used in Exercise 6, not good choices for pointer variable names?

8. Write English sentences that describe what is contained in the following declared variables.
   a. `char *keyAddr;`
   b. `int *m;`
   c. `double *yldAddr;`
   d. `long *yPtr;`
   e. `float *pCou;`
   f. `int *ptDate;`

9. Which of the following are declarations for pointers?
   a. `long a;`
   b. `char b;`
   c. `char *c;`
   d. `int x;`
   e. `int *p;`
   f. `double w;`
   g. `float *k;`
   h. `float l;`
   i. `double *z;`

10. Consider the following declarations.

```
int *xPt, *yAddr;
long *dtAddr, *ptAddr;
double *ptZ;
int a;
long b;
double c;
```

Given these declarations, determine which of the following statements are valid.

a. `yAddr = &a;`
b. `yAddr = &b;`
c. `yAddr = &c;`
d. `yAddr = a;`
e. `yAddr = b;`
f. `yAddr = c;`
g. `dtAddr = &a;`
h. `dtAddr = &b;`
i. `dtAddr = &c;`
j. `dtAddr = a;`
k. `dtAddr = b;`
l. `dtAddr = c;`
m. `ptZ = &a;`
n. `ptAddr = &b`
o. `ptAddr = &c;`
p. `ptAddr = a;`
q. `ptAddr = b;`
r. `ptAddr = c;`
s. `yAddr = xPt;`
t. `yAddr = dtAddr;`
u. `yAddr = ptAddr;`

11. For the variables and addresses illustrated in Figure 8–9, fill in the appropriate data as determined by the following statements.

a. `ptNum = &m;`
b. `amtAddr = &amt;`
c. `*zAddr = 25;`
d. `k = *numAddr;`
e. `ptDay = zAddr;`
f. `*ptYr = 1987;`
g. `*amtAddr = *numAddr;`

FIGURE 8–9 Memory Locations for Exercise 11

Variable	Address	Contents
`ptNum`	500	
`amtAddr`	564	
`zAddr`	8024	20492
`numAddr`	10132	18938
`ptDay`	14862	
`ptYr`	15010	694
`years`	694	
`m`	8096	
`amt`	16256	
`firstnum`	18938	154
`balance`	20492	
`k`	24608	

12. Using the `sizeof()` operator, determine the number of bytes used by your computer to store the address of an integer, character, and double-precision number. (*Hint:* `sizeof(*int)` can be used to determine the number of memory bytes used for a pointer to an integer.) Would you expect the size of each address to be the same? Why or why not?

8.2 Array Names as Pointers

Although pointers are simply, by definition, variables used to store addresses, there is also a direct and intimate relationship between array names and pointers. In this section, we describe that relationship in detail.

Figure 8–10 illustrates the storage of a single-dimensional array named `grade`, which contains five integers. Assume that each integer requires two bytes of storage.

Using subscripts, the third element in the `grade` array is referred to as `grade[3]`. The use of a subscript, however, conceals the extensive use of addresses by the computer. Internally, the computer immediately uses the subscript to calculate the address of the desired element on the basis of both the starting address of the array and the amount of storage used by each element. Calling the third element `grade[3]` forces the compiler, internally, to make the address computation (assuming two bytes per integer)

```
&grade[3] = &grade[0] + (3 * 2)
```

Remembering that the address operator, `&`, means "the address of," we read this last statement "the address of `grade[3]` equals the address of `grade[0]` plus 6." Figure 8–11 illustrates the address computation used to locate `grade[3]`.

Remember that a pointer is a variable used to store an address. If we create a pointer to store the address of the first element in the `grade` array, we can mimic the operation used by the computer to access the array elements. Before we do this, let us consider Program 8-4.

FIGURE 8–10 The `grade` Array in Storage

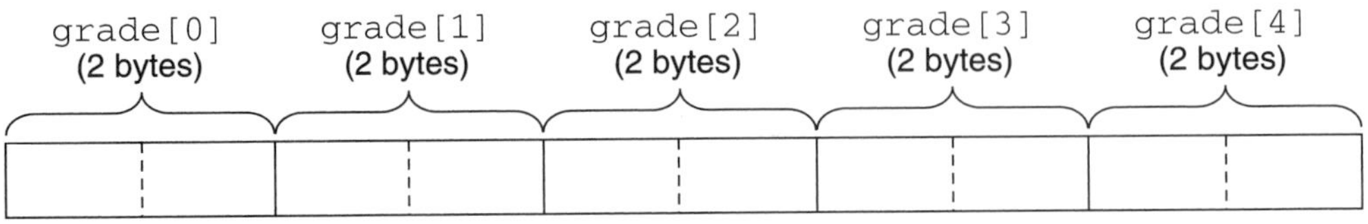

grade[0] (2 bytes)	grade[1] (2 bytes)	grade[2] (2 bytes)	grade[3] (2 bytes)	grade[4] (2 bytes)

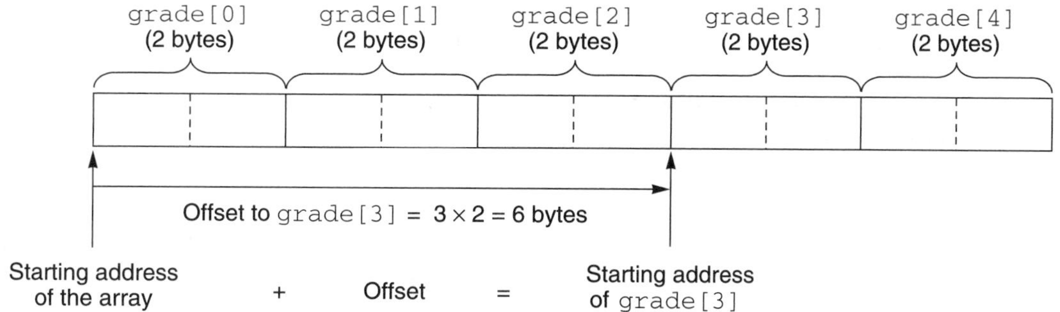

FIGURE 8–11 Using a Subscript to Obtain an Address

Program 8-4

```
#include <iostream.h>
int main()
{
  const int SIZE = 5;
  int i, grade[SIZE] = {98, 87, 92, 79, 85};

  for (i = 0; i < SIZE; i++)
    cout << "Element " << i << " is " << grade[i] << endl;

  return 0;
}
```

When Program 8-4 is run, the following display is obtained:

```
Element 0 is 98
Element 1 is 87
Element 2 is 92
Element 3 is 79
Element 4 is 85
```

Program 8-4 displays the values of the `grade` array using standard subscript notation. Now, let us store the address of array element 0 in a pointer. Then, using the indirection operator, `*`, we can use the address in the pointer to access each array element. For example, if we store the address of `grade[0]` in a pointer variable named `gPtr` (using the assignment statement `gPtr = &grade[0];`), then, as illustrated in Figure 8–12, the expression `*gPtr`, which means "the variable pointed to by `gPtr`," references `grade[0]`.

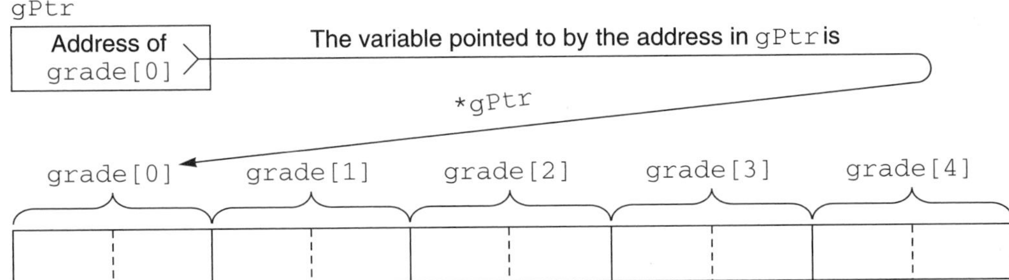

FIGURE 8–12 The Variable Pointed to by `*gPtr` Is `grade[0]`.

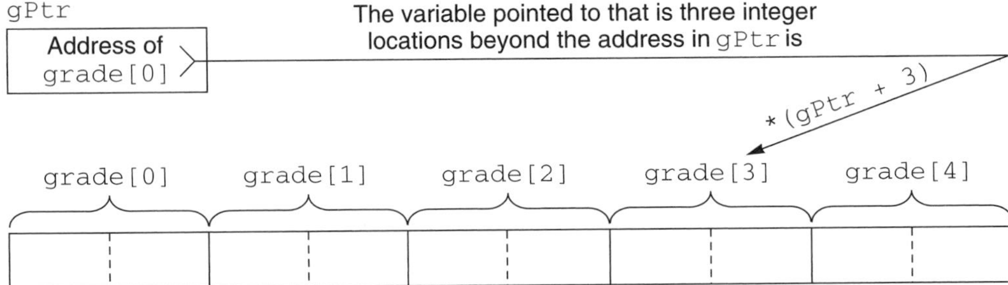

FIGURE 8–13 An Offset of 3 from the Address in `gPtr`

One unique feature of pointers is that offsets may be included in expressions using pointers. For example, the 1 in the expression `*(gPtr + 1)` is an offset. The complete expression references the integer that is one beyond the variable pointed to by `gPtr`. Similarly, as illustrated in Figure 8–13, the expression `*(gPtr + 3)` references the variable that is three integers beyond the variable pointed to by `gPtr`. This is the variable `grade[3]`.

Table 8–1 lists the complete correspondence between elements referenced by subscripts and by pointers and offsets. The relationships listed in Table 8–1 are illustrated in Figure 8–14.

TABLE 8–1 Array Elements May Be Referenced in Two Ways

Array Element	Subscript Notation	Pointer Notation
Element 0	`grade[0]`	`*gPtr`
Element 1	`grade[1]`	`*(gPtr + 1)`
Element 2	`grade[2]`	`*(gPtr + 2)`
Element 3	`grade[3]`	`*(gPtr + 3)`
Element 4	`grade[4]`	`*(gPtr + 4)`

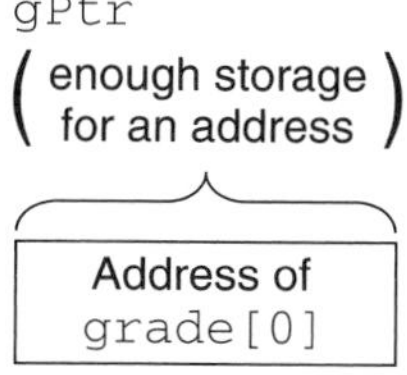

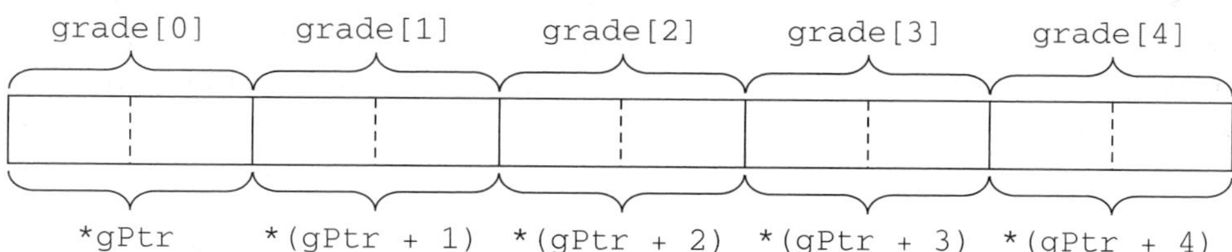

FIGURE 8–14 The Relationship Between Array Elements and Pointers

Using the correspondence between pointers and subscripts illustrated in Figure 8–14, we can now use pointers to access the array elements in Program 8-4 that we previously accessed using subscripts. This is done in Program 8-5.

Program 8-5

```
#include <iostream.h>
int main()
{
  int *gPtr;                // declare a pointer to an int
  const int SIZE = 5;
  int i, grade[SIZE] = {98, 87, 92, 79, 85};

  gPtr = &grade[0];         // store the starting array address
  for (i = 0; i < SIZE; i++)
    cout << "Element " << i << " is " << *(gPtr + i) << endl;

  return 0;
}
```

The following display is obtained when Program 8-5 is run:

```
Element 0 is 98
Element 1 is 87
Element 2 is 92
Element 3 is 79
Element 4 is 85
```

This is the same display that Program 8-4 produced.

The method used in Program 8-5 to access individual array elements simulates the way the compiler internally references all array elements. Any subscript used by a programmer is automatically converted to an equivalent pointer expression by the compiler. In our case, because the declaration of `gPtr` included the information that integers are pointed to, any offset added to the address in `gPtr` is automatically scaled by the size of an integer. Thus `*(gPtr + 3)`, for example, refers to the address of `grade[0]` plus an offset of six bytes (3 * 2). This is the address of `grade[3]` illustrated in Figure 8–11.

The parentheses in the expression `*(gPtr + 3)` are necessary to reference the desired array element correctly. Omitting the parentheses results in the expression `*gPtr + 3`. Because of the precedence of the operators, this expression adds 3 to "the variable pointed to by `gPtr`." Since `gPtr` points to `grade[0]`, this expression adds the value of `grade[0]` and 3 together. Note also that the expression `*(gPtr + 3)` does not change the address stored in `gPtr`. Once the computer uses the offset to locate the correct variable from the starting address in `gPtr`, the offset is discarded, and the address in `gPtr` remains unchanged.

Although the pointer `gPtr` used in Program 8-5 was specifically created to store the starting address of the `grade` array, this was, in fact, unnecessary. When an array is created, the compiler automatically creates an internal pointer constant for it and stores the starting address of the array in this pointer. In almost all respects, a pointer constant is very similar to a pointer variable created by a programmer, but as we shall see, there are some differences.

For each array created, the name of the array becomes the name of the pointer constant created by the compiler for the array, and the starting address of the first location reserved for the array is stored in this pointer. Thus declaring the `grade` array in both Program 8-4 and Program 8-5 actually reserved enough storage for five integers, created an internal pointer named `grade`, and stored the address of `grade[0]` in the pointer. This is illustrated in Figure 8–15.

The implication is that every reference to `grade` using a subscript can be replaced by an equivalent reference using `grade` as a pointer. Thus, wherever the expression `grade[i]` is used, the expression `*(grade + i)` can also be used. This is illustrated in Program 8-6, where `grade` is used as a pointer to reference all of its elements.

grade

&grade[0]

grade[0]	grade[1]	grade[2]	grade[3]	grade[4]
or	or	or	or	or
*grade	*(grade + 1)	*(grade + 2)	*(grade + 3)	*(grade + 4)

FIGURE 8–15 Creating an Array Also Creates a Pointer

Program 8-6

```
#include <iostream.h>
int main()
{
  const int SIZE = 5;
  int i, grade[SIZE] = {98, 87, 92, 79, 85};

  for (i = 0; i < SIZE; i++)
    cout << "Element " << i << " is " << *(grade + i) << endl;

  return 0;
}
```

Executing Program 8-6 produces the same output as that produced by Program 8-4 and Program 8-5. However, using `grade` as a pointer made it unnecessary to declare and initialize the pointer `gPtr` used in Program 8-5.

In most respects, an array name and a pointer can be used interchangeably. *A true pointer is a variable, however, and the address stored in it can be changed. An array name is a pointer constant, and the address stored in the pointer cannot be changed by an assignment statement.* Thus a statement such as `grade = &grade[2];` is invalid. This should come as no surprise. The whole purpose of an array name is to locate the beginning of the array correctly, so allowing a programmer to change the address stored in the array name would defeat this purpose and lead to havoc whenever array elements were referenced. Also, expressions that take the address of an array name are invalid because the pointer created by the compiler is internal to the computer, not stored in memory as are pointer variables. Thus, trying to store the address of `grade` by using the expression `&grade` results in a compiler error.

An interesting sidelight to the observation that elements of an array can be accessed using pointers is that a pointer access can always be replaced using subscript notation. For example, if `numPtr` is declared as a pointer variable, the expression `*(numPtr + i)` can also be written as `numPtr[i]`. This is true even though `numPtr` is not created as an array. As before, when the compiler encounters the subscript notation, it replaces it internally with the pointer notation.

Dynamic Array Allocation

As each variable is defined in a program, sufficient storage for it is assigned from a pool of computer memory locations made available to the compiler. Once specific memory locations have been reserved for a variable, these locations are fixed for the life of that variable, whether they are used or not. For example, if a function requests storage for an array of 500 integers, the storage for the array is allocated and fixed from the point of the array's definition. If the application requires less than 500 integers, the unused allocated storage is not released back to the system until the array goes out of existence. On the other hand, if the application requires more than 500 integers, the size of the integer array must be increased and the function defining the array recompiled.

An alternative to this fixed, or static, allocation of memory storage locations is the dynamic allocation of memory. Under a *dynamic allocation* scheme, the amount of storage to be allocated is determined and adjusted as the program is run, rather than being fixed at compile time.

The dynamic allocation of memory is extremely useful when we are dealing with lists, because it allows the list to expand as new items are added and to contract as items are deleted. For example, in constructing a list of grades, we may not know the exact number of grades ultimately needed. Rather than creating a fixed array to store the grades, it is extremely useful to have a mechanism whereby the array can be enlarged and shrunk as necessary. Two C++ operators that provide this capability, `new` and `delete`, are described in Table 8–2.

TABLE 8–2 Dynamic Allocation and Deallocation Operators

Operator Name	Description
`new`	Reserves the number of bytes requested by the declaration. Returns the address of the first reserved location or returns NULL if sufficient memory is not available.
`delete`	Releases a block of bytes previously reserved. This operator requires the address of the first location of memory to be deallocated.

Explicit dynamic storage requests for scalar variables or arrays are made as part of either a declaration or assignment statement.[5] For example, the declaration statement `int *num = new int;` reserves an area sufficient to hold one integer and places the address of this storage area into the pointer `num`. This same dynamic allocation can be made by first declaring the pointer using the declaration statement `int *num;` and then subsequently assigning the pointer an address with the assignment statement `num = new int;`. In either case, the allocated storage area comes from the computer's free storage area.[6]

A similar (and more useful) process is the dynamic allocation of arrays. For example, the declaration

```
int *grade = new int[200];
```

reserves an area sufficient to store 200 integers and places the address of the first integer into the pointer `grade`. Although we have used the constant 200 in this example declaration, a variable dimension can be used. For example, consider the sequence of instructions

```
cout << "Enter the number of grades to be processed: ";
cin  >> numgrades;
int *grade = new int[numgrades];
```

In this sequence, the actual size of the array that is created depends on the number input by the user. Because pointer and array names are related, each value in the newly created storage area can be accessed using standard array notation, such as `grade[i]`, rather than the equivalent pointer notation `*(grade + i)`. Program 8-7 illustrates this sequence of code in the context of a complete program.

Note in Program 8-7 that the `delete` operator has been used to restore the allocated block of storage to the operating system while the programming is executing.[7] The only address required by `delete` is the starting address of the block of storage that was dynamically allocated. Thus any address returned by `new` can subsequently be used by `delete` to restore the reserved memory to the computer. The `delete` operator does not alter the address passed to it; rather, it simply removes the storage that the address references.

---

[5] Note that the compiler automatically provides this dynamic allocation and deallocation from the stack for all `auto` variables.

[6] The free storage area of a computer is formally referred to as the *heap*. The heap consists of unallocated memory that can be allocated to a program, as requested, while the program is running.

[7] The allocated storage would be returned automatically to the heap when the program completed execution. It is, however, good practice to restore the allocated storage formally to the heap, using `delete`, when the memory is no longer needed. This is especially true for larger programs that make numerous requests for additional storage areas.

Program 8-7

```
#include <iostream.h>
int main()
{
  int numgrades, i;

  cout << "Enter the number of grades to be processed: ";
  cin  >> numgrades;

  int *grade = new int[numgrades];  // create the array

  for(i = 0; i < numgrades; i++)
  {
    cout << "  Enter a grade: ";
    cin  >> grade[i];
  }
  cout << "\nAn array was created for " << numgrades << " integers\n";
  cout << " The values stored in the array are:";
  for (i = 0; i < numgrades; i++)
    cout << "\n   " << grade[i];

  delete grade;   // return the storage to the heap

  return 0;
}
```

Following is a sample run using Program 8-7:

```
Enter the number of grades to be processed: 4
  Enter a grade: 85
  Enter a grade: 96
  Enter a grade: 77
  Enter a grade: 92

An array was created for 4 integers
 The values stored in the array are:
   85
   96
   77
   92
```

Exercises 8.2

1. Replace each of the following references to a subscripted variable with a pointer reference.

a. `prices[5]`	*d.* `dist[9]`	*g.* `celsius[16]`
b. `grades[2]`	*e.* `mile[0]`	*h.* `num[50]`
c. `yield[10]`	*f.* `temp[20]`	*i.* `time[12]`

2. Replace each of the following references using a pointer with a subscript reference.

a. `*(message + 6)`	*c.* `*(yrs + 10)`	*e.* `*(rates + 15)`
b. `*amount`	*d.* `*(stocks + 2)`	*f.* `*(codes + 19)`

3. *a.* List the three things that the declaration statement `double prices[5];` causes the compiler to do.
   b. If each double-precision number uses eight bytes of storage, how much storage is set aside for the `prices` array?
   c. Draw a diagram similar to Figure 8–15 for the `prices` array.
   d. Determine the byte offset relative to the start of the `prices` array, corresponding to the offset in the expression `*(prices + 3)`.

4. *a.* Write a declaration to store the string `"This is a sample"` into an array named `samtest`. Include the declaration in a program that displays the values in `samtest` using a `for` loop that uses a pointer access to each element in the array.
   b. Modify the program written in Exercise 4a to display only array elements 10 through 15 (these are the letters `s`, `a`, `m`, `p`, `l`, and `e`).

5. Write a declaration to store the following values into an array named `rates`: 12.9, 18.6, 11.4, 13.7, 9.5, 15.2, 17.6. Include the declaration in a program that displays the values in the array using pointer notation.

6. Repeat Exercise 6 in Section 7.1, but use pointer references to access all array elements.

7. Repeat Exercise 7 in Section 7.1, but use pointer references to access all array elements.

8. As described in Table 8–2, the `new` operator either returns the address of the first new storage area allocated or returns NULL if insufficient storage is available. Modify Program 8-7 to check that a valid address has been returned before attempting to place values into the `grade` array. Display an appropriate message if sufficient storage is not available.

8.3 Pointer Arithmetic

Pointer variables, like all variables, contain values. The value stored in a pointer is, of course, an address. Thus, by adding numbers to and subtracting numbers from pointers, we can obtain different addresses. Additionally, the addresses in pointers can be compared by using any of the relational operators (==, !=, <, >, etc.) that are valid for comparing other variables. In performing arithmetic on pointers, we must be careful to produce addresses that point to something meaningful. In comparing pointers, we must also make comparisons that make sense. Consider these declarations:

```
int nums[100];
int *nPt;
```

To set the address of `nums[0]` into `nPt`, we can use either of the following two assignment statements:

```
nPt = &nums[0];
nPt = nums;
```

The two assignment statements produce the same result because `nums` is a pointer constant that is the address of the first location in the array. This is, of course, the address of `nums[0]`. Figure 8–16 illustrates the allocation of memory that results from the previous declaration and assignment statements, assuming that each integer requires two bytes of memory and that the location of the beginning of the `nums` array is at address 18934.

Once `nPt` contains a valid address, values can be added to and subtracted from the address to produce new addresses. When adding numbers to or

FIGURE 8–16 The `nums` Array in Memory

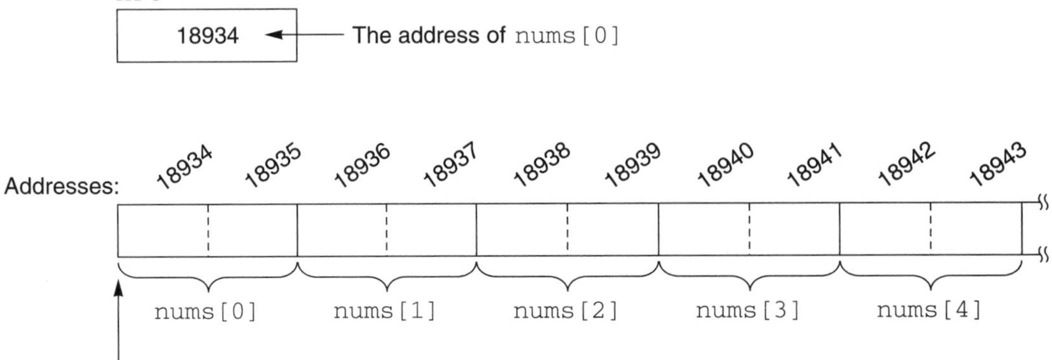

subtracting numbers from pointers, the computer automatically adjusts the number to ensure that the result still "points to" a value of the correct type. For example, the statement `nPt = nPt + 4;` forces the program to scale the 4 by the correct number to ensure that the resulting address is the address of an integer. Assuming that each integer requires two bytes of storage, as illustrated in Figure 8–16, the computer multiplies the 4 by 2 and then adds 8 to the address in `nPt`. The resulting address is 18942, which is the correct address of `nums[4]`.

This automatic scaling by the program ensures that the expression `nPt + i`, where `i` is any positive integer, correctly points to the `i`th element beyond the one currently being pointed to by `nPt`. Thus, if `nPt` initially contains the address of `nums[0]`, then `nPt + 4` is the address of `nums[4]`, `nPt + 50` is the address of `nums[50]`, and `nPt + i` is the address of `nums[i]`. Although we have used actual addresses in Figure 8–16 to illustrate the scaling process, the programmer normally does not know or need to know the actual addresses used by the computer. The manipulation of addresses using pointers generally does not require knowledge of the actual address.

Addresses can also be incremented or decremented using both prefix and postfix increment and decrement operators. Adding 1 to a pointer causes the pointer to point to the next element of the type being pointed to. Decrementing a pointer causes the pointer to point to the previous element. For example, if the pointer variable `p` is a pointer to an integer, the expression `p++` causes the address in the pointer to be incremented to point to the next integer. This is illustrated in Figure 8–17.

In reviewing Figure 8–17, note that the increment added to the pointer is correctly scaled to account for the fact that the pointer is used to point to

FIGURE 8–17 Increments Are Scaled When Used with Pointers

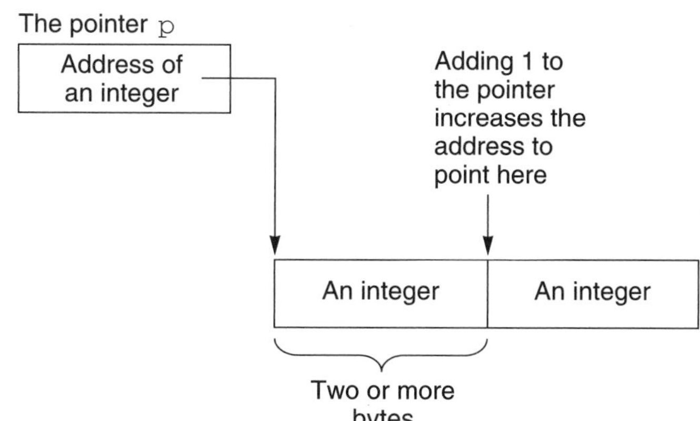

integers. It is, of course, up to the programmer to ensure that the correct type of data is stored in the new address contained in the pointer.

The increment and decrement operators can be applied as both prefix and postfix pointer operators. All of the following combinations using pointers are valid:

```
*ptNum++     // use the pointer and then increment it
*++ptNum     // increment the pointer before using it
*ptNum--     // use the pointer and then decrement it
*--ptNum     // decrement the pointer before using it
```

Of the four possible forms, the most commonly used is the form `*ptNum++`. This is because such an expression allows each element in an array to be accessed as the address is "marched along" from the starting address of the array to the address of the last array element. To see the use of the increment operator, consider Program 8-8. In this program, each element in the `nums` array is retrieved by successively incrementing the address in `nPt`.

Program 8-8

```
#include <iostream.h>
int main()
{
  const int NUMPTS = 5;
  int nums[NUMPTS] = {16, 54, 7, 43, -5};
  int i, total = 0, *nPt;

  nPt = nums;     // store address of nums[0] in nPt
  for (i = 0; i < NUMPTS; i++)
    total = total + *nPt++;

  cout << "The total of the array elements is " << total << endl;

  return 0;
}
```

The output produced by Program 8-8 is

```
The total of the array elements is 115
```

The expression `total = total + *nPt++` used in Program 8-8 is a standard accumulating expression. Within this expression, the term `*nPt++` first causes the compiler to retrieve the integer pointed to by `nPt`. This is done by the `*nPt` part of the term. The postfix increment, `++`, then adds one to the address in `nPt` so that `nPt` now contains the address of the next array element. The increment is, of course, scaled correctly by the computer so that the actual address in `nPt` is the correct address of the next array element.

Pointers may also be compared. This is particularly useful when we are dealing with pointers that point to elements in the same array. For example, rather than using a counter in a `for` loop to access each element in an array correctly, the address in a pointer can be compared to the starting and ending address of the array itself. The expression

```
nPt <= &nums[4]
```

is true (nonzero) as long as the address in `nPt` is less than or equal to the address of `nums[4]`. Since `nums` is a pointer constant that contains the address of `nums[0]`, the term `&nums[4]` can be replaced by the equivalent term `nums + 4`. Using either of these forms, we can rewrite Program 8-8 as Program 8-9 to continue adding array elements while the address in `nPt` is less than or equal to the address of the last array element.

Program 8-9

```
#include <iostream.h>
int main()
{
  const int NUMPTS = 5;
  int nums[NUMPTS] = {16, 54, 7, 43, -5};
  int total = 0, *nPt;

  nPt = nums;     // store address of nums[0] in nPt

  while (nPt < nums + NUMPTS)
    total += *nPt++;

  cout << "The total of the array elements is " << total << endl;

  return 0;
}
```

Note that in Program 8-9 the compact form of the accumulating expression, `total += *nPt++`, was used in place of the longer form, `total = total + *nPt++`. Also, the expression `nums + NUMPTS` does not change the address in `nums`. This expression retrieves the address in `nums`, adds 4 to this address (appropriately scaled), and uses the result for comparison purposes. Expressions such as `*nums++`, which attempt to change the address, are invalid because `nums` is an array name, not a pointer variable; as such, its value cannot be changed. Expressions such as `*nums` and `*(nums + i)`, which use the address without attempting to alter it, are valid.

Pointer Initialization

Like all variables, pointers can be initialized when they are declared. When initializing pointers, however, we must be careful to set an address in the pointer. For example, an initialization such as

```
int *ptNum = &miles;
```

is valid only if `miles` itself was declared as an integer variable prior to `ptNum`. Here we are creating a pointer to an integer and setting the address in the pointer to the address of an integer variable. Note that if the variable `miles` is declared subsequently to `ptNum`, as follows,

```
int *ptNum = &miles;
int miles;
```

an error occurs. This is because the address of `miles` is used before `miles` has even been defined. Because the storage area reserved for `miles` has not been allocated when `ptNum` is declared, the address of `miles` does not yet exist.

Pointers to arrays can be initialized within their declaration statements. For example, if `prices` has been declared as an array of floating-point numbers, either of the following two declarations can be used to initialize the pointer named `zing` to the address of the first element in `prices`:

```
float *zing = &prices[0];
float *zing = prices;
```

The last initialization is correct because `prices` is itself a pointer constant containing an address of the proper type. (The variable name `zing` was selected in this example to reinforce the idea that any variable name can be selected for a pointer.)

Exercises 8.3

1. Replace the `while` statement in Program 8-9 with a `for` statement.

2. a. Write a C++ program that initializes an array named `rates` with the following numbers: 6.25, 6.50, 6.8, 7.2, 7.35, 7.5, 7.65, 7.8, 8.2, 8.4, 8.6, 8.8, 9.0. Display the values in the array by changing the address in a pointer called `dispPt`. Use a `for` statement in your program.

b. Modify the program written in Exercise 2a to use a `while` statement.

3. a. Write a program that stores the string `Hooray for All of Us` into an array named `strng`. Use the declaration `strng[] = "Hooray for All of Us";`, which ensures that the end-of-string escape sequence `\0` is included in the array. Display the characters in the array by changing the address in a pointer called `messPt`. Use a `for` statement in your program.

b. Modify the program written in Exercise 3a to use the `while` statement `while (*messPt++ != '\0')`.

c. Modify the program written in Exercise 3a to start the display with the word `All`.

4. Write a C++ program that stores the following numbers in the array named `miles`: 15, 22, 16, 18, 27, 23, 20. Have your program copy the data stored in `miles` to another array named `dist` and then display the values in the `dist` array.

5. Write a C++ program that stores the following letters in the array named `message`: `This is a test`. Have your program copy the data stored in `message` to another array named `mess2` and then display the letters in the `mess2` array.

6. Write a C++ program that declares three single-dimensional arrays named `miles`, `gallons`, and `mpg`. Each array should be capable of holding ten elements. In the `miles` array store the numbers 240.5, 300.0, 189.6, 310.6, 280.7, 216.9, 199.4, 160.3, 177.4, 192.3. In the `gallons` array store the numbers 10.3, 15.6, 8.7, 14, 16.3, 15.7, 14.9, 10.7, 8.3, 8.4. Each element of the `mpg` array should be calculated as the corresponding element of the `miles` array divided by the equivalent element of the `gallons` array; for example, `mpg[0] = miles[0] / gallons[0]`. Use pointers when calculating and displaying the elements of the `mpg` array.

8.4 Passing Addresses

We have already seen one method of passing addresses to a function. This was accomplished using reference variables, as was described in Section 6.3. Although passing reference variables to a function provides the function with the address of the passed variables, it is an implied use of addresses because the function call does not reveal the fact that reference parameters are being used. For example, the function call `swap(num1, num2);` does not reveal whether num1 or num2 is passed by value or reference. Only when one looks at the function prototype for these variables or examines the function header line for swap() is the type of pass revealed.

In contrast to implicitly passing addresses using references, addresses can be explicitly passed using pointer variables. Let us see how this is accomplished.

To explicitly pass an address to a function, all we need do is place the address operator, &, in front of the variable being passed. For example, the function call

```
swap(&firstnum, &secnum);
```

passes the addresses of the variables firstnum and secnum to swap(), as illustrated in Figure 8–18. Explicitly passing addresses using the address operator effectively is a *pass by reference* because the called function can reference, or access, variables in the calling function using the passed addresses. As we saw in Section 6.3, calls by reference are also accomplished using reference parameters. Here we will use the passed addresses and pointers to directly access the variables firstnum and secnum from within swap() and exchange their values—a procedure that was previously accomplished in Program 6-10 using reference parameters.

One of the first requirements in writing swap() is to construct a function header line that correctly receives and stores the passed values, which in this case are two addresses. As we saw in Section 8.1, addresses are stored in pointers, which means that the parameters of swap() must be declared as pointers. Assuming that firstnum and secnum are double-precision variables and that swap() returns no value, a suitable function header line for swap() is

```
void swap(double *nm1Addr, double *nm2Addr)
```

FIGURE 8–18 Explicitly Passing Addresses to swap()

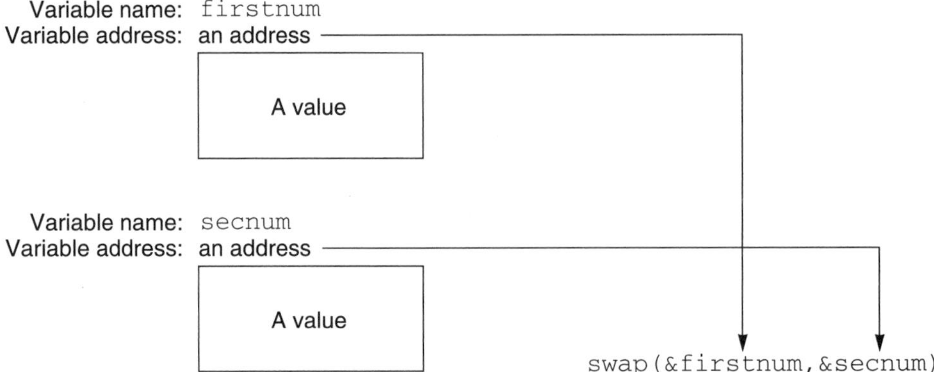

The choice of the parameter names nm1Addr and nm2Addr is, as with all parameter names, up to the programmer. The declaration double *nm1Addr, however, declares that the parameter named nm1Addr will be used to store the address of a double-precision value. Similarly, the declaration double *nm2Addr declares that nm2Addr will also store the address of a double- precision value.

Before writing the body of swap() to exchange the values in firstnum and secnum, let's first check that the values accessed using the addresses in nm1Addr and nm2Addr are correct. This is done in Program 8-10.

Program 8-10

```
#include <iostream.h>
int main()
{
  double firstnum = 20.5, secnum = 6.25;
  void swap(double *, double *);      // function prototype

  swap(&firstnum, &secnum);           // call swap

  return 0;
}

void swap(double *nm1Addr, double *nm2Addr)
{
  cout << "The number whose address is in nm1Addr is "
       << *nm1Addr << endl;
  cout << "The number whose address is in nm2Addr is "
       << *nm2Addr << endl;

  return;
}
```

The output displayed when Program 8-10 is run is

```
The number whose address is in nm1Addr is 20.5
The number whose address is in nm2Addr is 6.25
```

In reviewing Program 8-10, note two things. First, the function prototype for swap(),

```
void swap(double *, double *)
```

declares that `swap()` returns no value directly and that its parameters are two pointers that "point to" double-precision values. Thus, when the function is called, it will require that two addresses be passed and that each address be the address of a double-precision value.

The second item to note is that within `swap()` the indirection operator is used to access the values stored in `firstnum` and `secnum`. `swap()` itself has no knowledge of these variable names, but it does have the address of `firstnum` stored in `nm1Addr` and the address of `secnum` stored in `nm2Addr`. The expression `*nm1Addr` used in the first `cout` statement means "the variable whose address is in `nm1Addr`." This is of course the variable `firstnum`. Similarly, the second `cout` statement obtains the value stored in `secnum` as "the variable whose address is in `nm2Addr`." Thus we have successfully used pointers to allow `swap()` to access variables in `main()`. Figure 8–19 illustrates the concept of storing addresses in parameters.

Having verified that `swap()` can access `main()`'s local variables `firstnum` and `secnum`, we can now expand `swap()` to exchange the values in these variables. The values in `main()`'s variables `firstnum` and `secnum` can be interchanged from within `swap()` using the three-step interchange algorithm described in Section 6.3, which for convenience we repeat here:

1. *Store `firstnum`'s value in a temporary location.*
2. *Store `secnum`'s value in `firstnum`.*
3. *Store the temporary value in `secnum`.*

Using pointers from within `swap()`, this takes the form:

FIGURE 8–19 Storing Addresses in Parameters

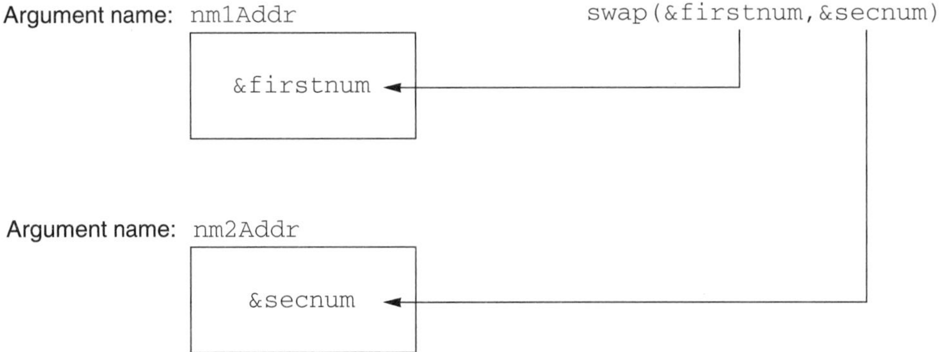

1. Store the value of the variable pointed to by `nm1Addr` in a temporary location. The statement `temp = *nm1Addr;` does this (see Figure 8–20).
2. Store the value of the variable whose address is in `nm2Addr` in the variable whose address is in `nm1Addr`. The statement `*nm1Addr = *nm2Addr;` does this (see Figure 8–21).
3. Move the value in the temporary location into the variable whose address is in `nm2Addr`. The statement `*nm2Addr = temp;` does this (see Figure 8–22).

Program 8-11 contains the final form of `swap()`, written according to our description.

Program 8-11

```
#include <iostream.h>

void swap(double *, double *);     // function prototype

int main()
{
  double firstnum = 20.5, secnum = 6.25;

  cout << "The value stored in firstnum is: " << firstnum << endl;
  cout << "The value stored in secnum is: " << secnum << "\n\n";

  swap(&firstnum, &secnum);          // call swap

  cout << "The value stored in firstnum is now: " << firstnum << endl;
  cout << "The value stored in secnum is now: " << secnum << endl;

  return 0;
}

void swap(double *nm1Addr, double *nm2Addr)
{
  double temp;

  temp = *nm1Addr;              // save firstnum's value
  *nm1Addr = *nm2Addr;          // move secnum's value in firstnum
  *nm2Addr = temp;              // change secnum's value

  return;
}
```

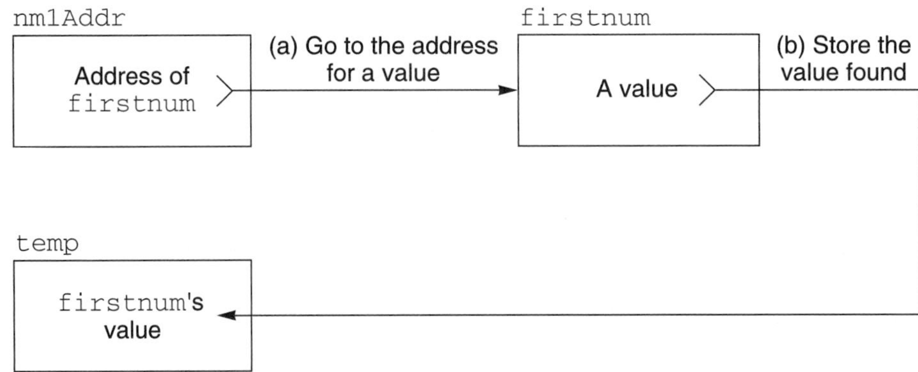

FIGURE 8–20 Indirectly Storing `firstnum`'s value

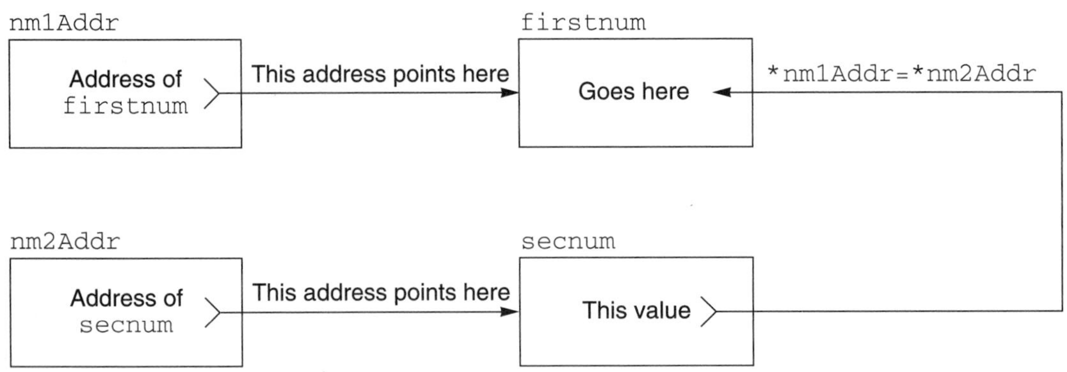

FIGURE 8–21 Indirectly Changing `firstnum`'s Value

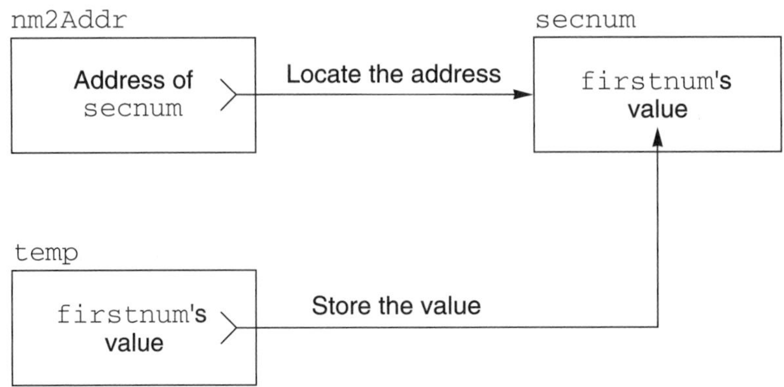

FIGURE 8–22 Indirectly Changing `secnum`'s Value

The following sample run was obtained using Program 8-11:

```
The value stored in firstnum is: 20.5
The value stored in secnum is: 6.25

The value stored in firstnum is now: 6.25
The value stored in secnum is now: 20.5
```

As illustrated in this output, the values stored in `main()`'s variables have been modified from within `swap()`, which was made possible by the use of pointers. The interested reader should compare this version of `swap()` with the version using references that was presented in Program 6-8. The advantage of using pointers rather than references is that the function call itself explicitly designates that addresses are being used, which directly alerts you that the function will probably alter variables of the calling function. The advantage of using references is that the notation is much simpler.

Generally, for functions such as `swap()`, the notational convenience wins out and references are used. In passing arrays to functions, however, which is our next topic, the compiler explicitly passes an address. This dictates that a pointer parameter be used to store the address.

Passing Arrays

When an array is passed to a function, its address is the only item actually passed. By this we mean the address of the first location used to store the array, as illustrated in Figure 8–23. Because the first location reserved for an array corresponds to element 0 of the array, the "address of the array" is also the address of element 0.

For a specific example in which an array is passed to a function, consider Program 8-12. In this program, the `nums` array is passed to the `FindMax()` function using conventional array notation.

FIGURE 8–23 The Address of an Array Is the Address of the First Location Reserved for the Array

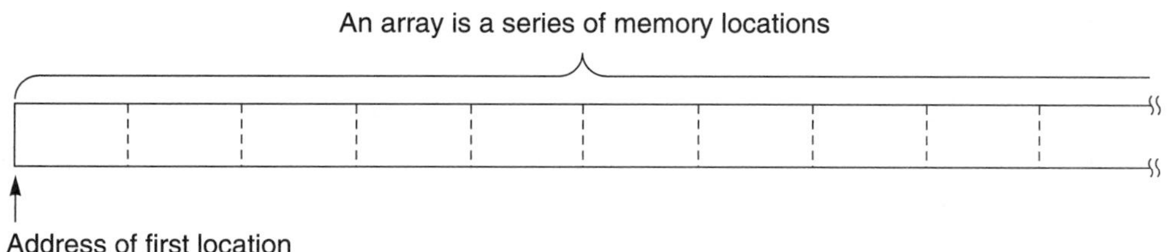
An array is a series of memory locations
Address of first location

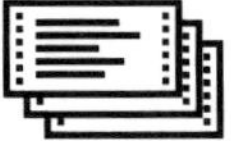

Program 8-12

```
#include <iostream.h>

int FindMax(int [], int);      // function prototype

int main()
{
  const int NUMPTS = 5;
  int nums[NUMPTS] = {2, 18, 1, 27, 16};

  cout << "\nThe maximum value is "
       << FindMax(nums,NUMPTS) << endl;

  return 0;
}

int FindMax(int vals[], int NUMELS)   // find the maximum value
{
  int i, max = vals[0];

  for (i = 1; i < NUMELS; i++)
   if (max < vals[i]) max = vals[i];

  return max;
}
```

The output displayed when Program 8-12 is executed is

```
The maximum value is 27
```

The parameter named `vals` in the header line declaration for `FindMax()` actually receives the address of the array `nums`. Thus, `vals` is really a pointer, because pointers are variables (or parameters) used to store addresses. The address passed into `FindMax()` is the address of an integer, so another suitable header line for `FindMax()` is

```
int FindMax(int *vals, int NUMELS) // here vals is declared as
                                   // a pointer to an integer
```

The declaration `int *vals` in the header line declares that `vals` is used to store an address of an integer. The address stored is, of course, the location of the beginning of an array.

The following rewritten version of the FindMax() function uses a pointer declaration for vals but retains the use of subscripts to refer to individual array elements.

```
int FindMax(int *vals, int NUMELS)    // find the maximum value
{
  int i, max = vals[0];

  for (i = 1; i < NUMELS; i++)
   if (max < vals[i]) max = vals[i];

  return max;
}
```

Regardless of how vals is declared in the function header or how it is used within the function body, it is truly a pointer. Thus the address in vals may be modified. This is not true for the name nums. Because nums is the name of the originally created array, it is a pointer constant. As described in Section 8.2, this means that the address in nums cannot be changed and that the address of nums itself cannot be taken. No such restrictions, however, apply to the pointer variable named vals. All the address arithmetic that we learned in the previous section can be legitimately applied to vals.

We shall write two additional versions of FindMax(), both of which use pointers instead of subscripts. In the first version, we simply substitute pointer notation for subscript notation. In the second version, we use address arithmetic to change the address in the pointer.

As previously stated, access to an array element using the subscript notation array_name[i] can always be replaced by the pointer notation *(array_name + i). In our first modification to FindMax(), we use this correspondence by simply replacing all references to vals[i] with the equivalent expression *(vals + i):

```
int FindMax(int *vals, int NUMELS)    // find the maximum value
{
  int i, max = *vals;

  for (i = 1; i < NUMELS; i++)
   if (max < *(vals + i) )  max = *(vals + i);

  return max;
}
```

Our next version of FindMax() uses the fact that the address stored in vals can be changed. After each array element is retrieved using the address in vals, the address itself is incremented by 1 in the altering list of the for statement. The expression max = *vals previously used to set max to the value of vals[0] is replaced by the expression max = *vals++, which adjusts the address in vals to point to the second element in the array. The element assigned to max by this expression is the array element pointed to by vals before vals is incremented. The postfix increment, ++, does not change the address in vals until after the address has been used to retrieve the array element.

```
int FindMax(int *vals, int NUMELS)    // find the maximum value
{
  int i, max = *vals++;    // get the first element and increment
  for (i = 1; i < NUMELS; i++, vals++)
  {
    if (max < *vals)  max = *vals;
  }

  return max;
}
```

Let us review this version of FindMax(). Initially the maximum value is set to "the thing pointed to by vals." Because vals initially contains the address of the first element in the array passed to FindMax(), the value of this first element is stored in max. The address in vals is then incremented by 1. The 1 that is added to vals is automatically scaled by the number of bytes used to store integers. Thus, after the increment, the address stored in vals is the address of the next array element. This is illustrated in Figure 8–24. The value of this next element is compared to the maximum, and the address is again incremented, this time from within the altering list of the for statement. This process continues until all the array elements have been examined.

Which version of FindMax() appeals to you is a matter of personal style and taste. Generally, beginning programmers feel more at ease using subscripts than using pointers. Also, if the program uses an array as the natural storage structure for the application and data at hand, an array access using subscripts is more appropriate to indicate clearly the intent of the program. However, as we learn about strings and data structures, we will see that the use of pointers becomes an increasingly powerful tool in its own right. In these instances, there is no simple or equivalent way to use subscripts.

One further "neat trick" can be gleaned from our discussion. Because passing an array to a function really involves passing an address, we can just as well pass

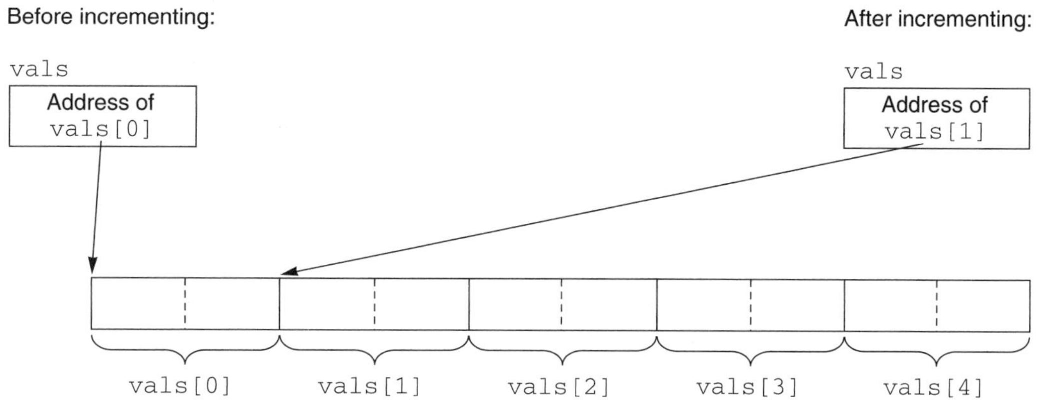

FIGURE 8–24 Pointing to Different Elements

any valid address. For example, the function call `FindMax(&nums[2],3)` passes the address of `nums[2]` to `FindMax()`. Within `FindMax()` the pointer `vals` stores the address, and the function starts the search for a maximum at the element corresponding to this address. Thus, from `FindMax()`'s perspective, it has received an address and proceeds appropriately.

Advanced Pointer Notation[8]

Access to multidimensional arrays can also be made using pointer notation, although the notation becomes more and more cryptic as the array dimensions increase. An extremely useful application of this notation occurs with two-dimensional character arrays, one of the topics of the next chapter. Here we consider pointer notation for two-dimensional numeric arrays. For example, consider the declaration

```
int nums[2][3] = { {16,18,20},
                   {25,26,27} };
```

This declaration creates an array of elements and a set of pointer constants named `nums`, `nums[0]`, and `nums[1]`. The relationship between these pointer constants and the elements of the `nums` array is illustrated in Figure 8–25.

The availability of the pointer constants associated with a two-dimensional array enables us to access array elements in a variety of ways. One way is to consider the two-dimensional array as an array of rows, where each row is itself an array of three elements. Considered in this light, the address of the first element in the first row is provided by `nums[0]`, and the address of the first element in the second row is provided by `nums[1]`. Thus the variable pointed

[8] This topic may be omitted with no loss of subject continuity.

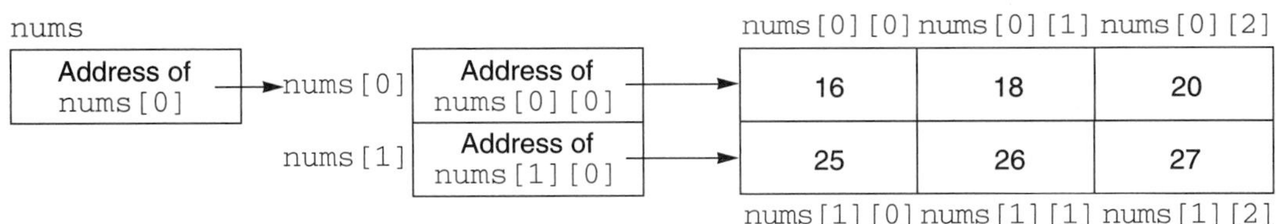

FIGURE 8–25 Storage of the nums Array and Associated Pointer Constants

to by nums[0] is num[0][0], and the variable pointed to by nums[1] is num[1][0]. Once the nature of these constants is understood, each element in the array can be accessed by applying an appropriate offset to the appropriate pointer. Thus the following notations are equivalent:

Pointer Notation	Subscript Notation	Value
*nums[0]	nums[0][0]	16
*(nums[0] + 1)	nums[0][1]	18
*(nums[0] + 2)	nums[0][2]	20
*nums[1]	nums[1][0]	25
*(nums[1] + 1)	nums[1][1]	26
*(nums[1] + 2)	nums[1][2]	27

We can now go even further and replace nums[0] and nums[1] with their respective pointer notations, using the address of nums itself. As illustrated in Figure 8–25, the variable pointed to by nums is nums[0]. That is, *nums is nums[0]. Similarly, *(nums + 1) is nums[1]. Using these relationships leads to the following equivalences:

Pointer Notation	Subscript Notation	Value
*(*nums)	nums[0][0]	16
*(*nums + 1)	nums[0][1]	18
*(*nums + 2)	nums[0][2]	20
((nums + 1))	nums[1][0]	25
((nums + 1) + 1)	nums[1][1]	26
((nums + 1) + 2)	nums[1][2]	27

The same notation applies when a two-dimensional array is passed to a function. For example, assume that the two-dimensional array `nums` is passed to the function `calc()` using the call `calc(nums);`. Here, as with all array passes, an address is passed. A suitable function header line for the function `calc()` is

```
calc(int pt[2][3])
```

As we have already seen, the parameter declaration for `pt` can also be

```
calc(int pt[][3])
```

Using pointer notation, another suitable declaration is

```
calc(int (*pt)[3])
```

In this last declaration, the inner parentheses are required to create a single pointer to objects of three integers. Each object is, of course, equivalent to a single row of the `nums` array. By suitably offsetting the pointer, we can access each element in the array. Note that without the parentheses, the declaration becomes

```
int *pt[3]
```

which creates an array of three pointers, each one pointing to a single integer.

Once the correct declaration for `pt` is made (any of the three valid declarations can be used), the following notations within the function `calc()` are all equivalent:

Pointer Notation	Subscript Notation	Value
`*(*pt)`	`pt[0][0]`	16
`*(*pt+1)`	`pt[0][1]`	18
`*(*pt+2)`	`pt[0][2]`	20
`*(*(pt+1))`	`pt[1][0]`	25
`*(*(pt+1)+1)`	`pt[1][1]`	26
`*(*(pt+1)+2)`	`pt[1][2]`	27

The last two notations using pointers are encountered in more advanced C++ programs. The first of these occurs because functions can return any valid C++ scalar data type, including pointers to any of these data types. If a function returns a pointer, the data type being pointed to must be declared in the function's declaration. For example, the declaration

```
int *calc()
```

declares that `calc()` returns a pointer to an integer value. This means that an address of an integer variable is returned. Similarly, the declaration

```
float *taxes()
```

declares that `taxes()` returns a pointer to a floating-point value. This means that an address of a floating-point variable is returned.

In addition to declaring pointers to integers, floating-point numbers, and C++'s other data types, pointers can also be declared that point to (contain the address of) a function. Pointers to functions are possible because function names, like array names, are themselves pointer constants. For example, the declaration

```
int (*calc)()
```

declares `calc()` to be a pointer to a function that returns an integer. This means that `calc` will contain the address of a function, and the function whose address is in the variable `calc` returns an integer value. If, for example, the function `sum()` returns an integer, the assignment `calc = sum;` is valid.

Exercises 8.4

1. The following declaration was used to create the `prices` array:

```
double prices[500];
```

Write three different header lines for a function named `sortArray()` that accepts the `prices` array as an argument named `inArray` and returns no value.

2. The following declaration was used to create the `keys` array:

```
char keys[256];
```

Write three different header lines for a function named `findKey()` that accepts the `keys` array as an argument named `select` and returns no value.

3. The following declaration was used to create the `rates` array:

```
float rates[256];
```

Write three different header lines for a function named `prime()` that accepts the `rates` array as an argument named `rates` and returns a floating-point value.

4. Modify the `FindMax()` function to locate the minimum value of the passed array. Write the function using only pointers.

5. In the last version of `FindMax()` presented, `vals` was incremented inside the altering list of the `for` statement. Instead, suppose that the incrementing was done within the condition expression of the `if` statement, as follows:

```
int FindMax(int *vals, int NUMELS)     // incorrect version
{
  int i, max = *vals++;    // get the first element and increment
  for (i = 1; i < NUMELS; i++)
  {
    if (max < *vals++)  max = *vals;
  }
  return max;
}
```

This version produces an incorrect result. Determine why.

6. ***a.*** Write a program that has a declaration in `main()` to store the following numbers into an array named `rates`: 6.5, 7.2, 7.5, 8.3, 8.6, 9.4, 9.6, 9.8, 10.0. There should be a function call to `show()` that accepts `rates` in a parameter argument named `rates` and then displays the numbers using the pointer notation `*(rates + i)`.
   b. Modify the `show()` function written in Exercise 6a to alter the address in `rates`. Always use the expression `*rates` rather than `*(rates + i)` to retrieve the correct element.

7. ***a.*** Write a program that has a declaration in `main()` to store the string `Vacation is near` into an array named `message`. There should be a function call to `display()` that accepts `message` in an argument named `strng` and then displays the message using the pointer notation `*(strng + i)`.
   b. Modify the `display()` function written in Exercise 7a to alter the address in `message`. Always use the expression `*strng` rather than `*(strng + i)` to retrieve the correct element.

8. Write a program that declares three single-dimensional arrays named `price`, `quantity`, and `amount`. Each array should be declared in `main()` and should be capable of holding ten double-precision numbers. The numbers to be stored in `price` are 10.62, 14.89, 13.21, 16.55, 18.62, 9.47, 6.58, 18.32, 12.15, 3.98. The numbers to be stored in `quantity` are 4, 8.5, 6, 7.35, 9, 15.3, 3, 5.4, 2.9, 4.8. Have your program pass these three arrays to a function called `extend()`, which calculates the elements in the `amount` array as the product of the equivalent elements in the `price` and `quantity` arrays (for example, `amount[1] = price[1] * quantity[1]`).

After `extend()` has put values into the `amount` array, display the values in the array from within `main()`. Write the `extend()` function using pointers.

9. a. Determine the output of the following program:

```
#include <iostream.h>

const int ROWS = 2;
const int COLS = 3;
void arr(int [][COLS]);   // function prototype
int main()
{
  int nums[ROWS][COLS] = { {33,16,29},
                           {54,67,99}};

  arr(nums);

  return 0;
}

void arr(int (*val)[3])
{
    cout <<  *(*val) << endl;
    cout <<  *(*val + 1) << endl;
    cout <<  *(*(val + 1) + 2) << endl;
    cout <<  *(*val) + 1 << endl;

  return;
}
```

b. Given the declaration for `val` in the `arr()` function, would the notation `val[1][2]` be valid within the function?

8.5 Common Programming Errors

In using the material presented in this chapter, be aware of the following possible errors:

1. Attempting to store an address in a variable that has not been declared as a pointer.
2. Using a pointer to access nonexistent array elements. For example, if `nums` is an array of ten integers, then the expression `*(nums + 10)` points one

integer location beyond the last element of the array. Most C++ compilers do not do any bounds checking on array accesses, so this type of error is not caught by the compiler. This is the same error, disguised in pointer notation form, as using a subscript to access an out-of-bounds array element.

3. Incorrectly applying the address and indirection operators. For example, if `pt` is a pointer variable, the expressions

```
pt = &45
pt = &(miles + 10)
```

are both invalid because they attempt to take the address of a value. Note that the expression `pt = &miles + 10`, however, is valid. Here, 10 is added to the address of `miles`. Again, it is the programmer's responsibility to ensure that the final address "points to" a valid data element.

4. Taking addresses of a register variable. Thus, for the declarations

```
register int total;
int *ptTot;
```

the assignment

```
ptTot = &total;     // INVALID
```

is invalid. The reason is that register variables are stored in a computer's internal registers, and these storage areas do not have standard memory addresses.

5. Taking addresses of pointer constants. For example, given the declarations

```
int nums[25];

int *pt;
```

the assignment

```
pt = &nums;
```

is invalid. `nums` is a pointer constant that is itself equivalent to an address. The correct assignment is `pt = nums`.

6. Initializing pointer variables incorrectly. For example, the initialization

```
int *pt = 5;
```

is invalid. Because `pt` is a pointer to an integer, it must be initialized with a valid address.

7. Becoming confused about whether a variable *contains* an address or *is* an address. Pointer variables and pointer arguments contain addresses. Although a pointer constant is synonymous with an address, it is useful to treat pointer constants as pointer variables with two restrictions:

   - The address of a pointer constant cannot be taken.
   - The address "contained in" the pointer constant cannot be altered.

   Except for these two restrictions, pointer constants and variables can be used almost interchangeably. Therefore, when an address is required, any of the following can be used:

   - a pointer variable name
   - a pointer argument name
   - a pointer constant name
   - a nonpointer variable name preceded by the address operator (such as, `&variable`)
   - a nonpointer argument name preceded by the address operator (such as, `&argument`)

Some of the confusion surrounding pointers is caused by the cavalier use of the word *pointer*. For example, the phrase "a function requires a pointer argument" is more clearly understood when we realize that it really means "a function requires an address as an argument." Similarly, the phrase "a function returns a pointer" really means "a function returns an address."

If you are ever in doubt about what is really contained in a variable or how it should be treated, use the `cout` object to display the contents of the variable, the "thing pointed to," or "the address of the variable." Seeing what is displayed frequently helps sort out what is really in the variable.

8.6 Chapter Summary

1. Every variable has a data type, an address, and a value. In C++ the address of a variable can be obtained by using the address operator, `&`.
2. A pointer is a variable that is used to store the address of another variable. Pointers, like all C++ variables, must be declared. The indirection operator, `*`, is used both to declare a pointer variable and to access the variable whose address is stored in a pointer.

3. An array name is a pointer constant. The value of the pointer constant is the address of the first element in the array. Thus, if `val` is the name of an array, `val` and `&val[0]` can be used interchangeably.
4. Any access to an array element using subscript notation can always be replaced using pointer notation. That is, the notation `a[i]` can always be replaced by the notation `*(a + i)`. This is true whether `a` was initially declared explicitly as an array or as a pointer.
5. Arrays can be dynamically created as a program is executing. For example, the sequence of statements

```
cout << "Enter the array size: ";
cin  >> num;
int *grades = new int[num];
```

   creates an array named `grades` of size `num`. The area allocated for the array can be dynamically destroyed using the `delete` operator. For example, the statement `delete grades;` will return the allocated area for the `grades` array to the computer.
6. Arrays are passed to functions as addresses. The called function always receives direct access to the originally declared array elements.
7. When a single-dimensional array is passed to a function, the parameter declaration for the function can be either an array declaration or a pointer declaration. Thus the following parameter declarations are equivalent:

```
float a[];
float *a;
```

8. Pointers can be incremented, decremented, compared, and assigned. Numbers added to or subtracted from a pointer are automatically scaled. The scale factor used is the number of bytes required to store the data type originally pointed to.

Character Strings

Chapter Nine

Each computer language has its own method of handling strings of characters. Some languages, such as C++, have an extremely rich set of string manipulation functions and capabilities. Other languages, such as FORTRAN, which is predominantly used for numerical calculations, added string-handling capabilities with later versions of the compiler. Languages such as LISP, which are targeted for list-handling applications, provide an exceptional string manipulation capability.

The way strings are stored, accessed, and manipulated is very language-dependent. Because of this, the string-handling methods presented in this chapter are, of necessity, dependent on C++'s string storage structure.

On a fundamental level, strings in C++ are simply arrays of characters. Accordingly, they can be manipulated using standard element-by-element array-processing techniques. On a higher level, string library functions are available for handling strings as complete entities. This chapter explores the input, manipulation, and output of strings using all of these approaches. We also examine the particularly close connection between string-handling functions and pointers.

9.1 String Fundamentals

A string constant, informally referred to as a string, is any sequence of characters enclosed in double quotes. For example, `"This is a string"`, `"Hello World!"`, and `"xyz 123 *!#@&"` are all strings.

A string is stored as an array of characters terminated by a special end-of-string marker called the null character. The null character, represented by the escape sequence `\0`, is the sentinel marking the end of the string. For example, Figure 9–1 illustrates how the string `"Good Morning!"` is stored in memory. The string uses 14 storage locations, the last character in the string being the end-of-string marker `\0`. The double quotes are not stored as part of the string.

Because a string is stored as an array of characters, the individual characters in the array can be input, manipulated, or output using standard array-handling techniques that utilize either subscript or pointer notation. When we are handling strings in this fashion, the end-of-string null character is useful for detecting the end of the string.

FIGURE 9–1 Storing a String in Memory

G	o	o	d		M	o	r	n	i	n	g	!	\0

String Input and Output

Although you have a choice of using either library or user-written functions for processing a string already in memory, inputting a string from a keyboard or displaying a string always requires some reliance on standard library routines. Table 9–1 lists the commonly available library routines for both character-by-character and complete string input/output.

TABLE 9–1 String and Character Library Routines

C++ Routine	Description
`cout`	General-purpose screen output
`cin`	General-purpose keyboard input
`cin.getline()`	Input a string of characters from the keyboard
`cin.get()`	Input a single character from the keyboard

As Table 9–1 shows, in addition to the `cout` and `cin` streams, C++ provides two routines, `cin.getline()` and `cin.get()`, that are especially designed for string and character input. Programs that use any of the routines listed in Table 9-1 must include the `iostream.h` header.

Program 9-1 illustrates the use of `cin.getline()` and `cout` to input and output a string entered at the user's terminal.

Program 9-1

```
#include <iostream.h>
int main()
{
  const int MAXCHARS = 80;
  char message[MAXCHARS];    // enough storage for a complete line

  cout << "Enter a string:\n";
  cin.getline(message, MAXCHARS);
  cout << "The string just entered is:\n";
  cout << message << endl;

  return 0;
}
```

The following is a sample run of Program 9-1:

```
Enter a string:
This is a test input of a string of characters.
The string just entered is:
This is a test input of a string of characters.
```

The `cin.getline()` function (the reason for the period in `cin.getline()` is discussed in Chapter 11) used in Program 9-1 continuously accepts and stores characters typed at the terminal into the character array named `message` until either 79 characters are entered (the 80th character is then used to store the end-of-string null character, `\0`) or the Enter key is detected. Pressing the Enter key at the terminal generates a newline character, `\n`, which is interpreted by `cin.getline()` as the end-of-line entry. All the characters encountered by `cin.getline()`, except the newline character, are stored in the `message` array. Before returning, the `cin.getline()` function appends the null character to the stored set of characters, as illustrated in Figure 9–2. The `cout` statement is then used to display the string.

Although the `cout` object is used in Program 9-1 for string output, `cin` could not be used in place of `cin.getline()` for string input. This is because the `cin` object reads a set of characters up to either a blank space or a newline character. Thus, attempting to enter the characters `This is a string` using the statement `cin >> message;` results in only the word `This` being assigned to the `message` array. Entering the complete line using a `cin` object call requires a statement such as

```
cin >> message1 >> message2 >> message3 >> message4;
```

Here the word `This` is assigned to the string `message1`, the word `is` is assigned to the string `message2`, and so on. The fact that a blank is `cin`'s default delimiter restricts this object's usefulness for entering string data and is the reason for using `cin.getline()`.

In its most general form, the `cin.getline()` function has the syntax

```
cin.getline(str, length, char)
```

where `str` is a string or character pointer variable, `length` is an integer constant or variable that is one more than the maximum number of input characters, and `char` is an optional character constant or variable specifying

FIGURE 9–2 Inputting a String with `cin.getline()`

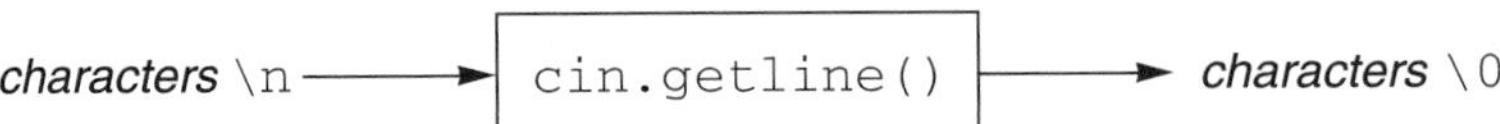

the terminating character. If this optional third argument is omitted, the default terminating character is the newline ('\n') character. Thus the statement `cin.getline(message,80,'\n');` can be used in place of the statement `cin.getline(message,80);` in Program 9-1. Both of these functions stop reading characters when the return key is pressed or when 79 characters have been read, whichever comes first. Because `cin.getline()` permits specification of any terminating character for the input stream, a statement such as `cin.getline(message,80,'x');` is also valid. This particular statement will stop accepting characters whenever the X key is pressed.

String Processing

Strings can be manipulated by using either standard library functions or standard array-processing techniques. The library functions typically available for use are presented in the next section. For now, we will concentrate on processing a string in a character-by-character fashion. This will allow us to understand how the standard library functions are constructed and to create our own library functions. For a specific example, consider the function `strcopy()` that copies the contents of `string2` to `string1`.

```
// copy string2 to string1
void strcopy(char string1[], char string2[])
{
  int i = 0;                      // i will be used as a subscript

  while ( string2[i] != '\0')     // check for the end-of-string
  {
    string1[i] = string2[i];      // copy the element to string1
    i++;
  }
  string1[i] = '\0';              // terminate the first string
  return;
}
```

Although this string copy function can be shortened considerably and written more compactly, which is done in Section 9.2, the function illustrates the main features of string manipulation. The two strings are passed to `strcopy` as arrays. Each element of `string2` is then assigned to the equivalent element of `string1` until the end-of-string marker is encountered. The detection of the null character forces the termination of the `while` loop that controls the copying of elements. Because the null character is not copied from `string2` to `string1`, the last statement in `strcopy()` appends an end-of-string character to `string1`. Before calling `strcopy()`, the programmer must ensure that sufficient space has been allocated for the `string1` array to be able to store the elements of the `string2` array. Program 9-2 includes the `strcopy()` function in a complete program. Note that the function prototype for `strcopy()` in `main()` declares that the function expects to receive the addresses of the beginnings of the two character arrays.

Program 9-2

```
#include <iostream.h>
void strcopy(char [], char []); // function prototype

int main()
{
  const int MAXCHARS = 80;
  char message[MAXCHARS];      // enough storage for a complete line
  char new_message[MAXCHARS];  // enough storage for a copy of message
  int i;

  cout << "Enter a sentence: ";
  cin.getline(message,MAXCHARS);  // get the string
  strcopy(new_message,message);   // pass two array addresses
  cout << new_message << endl;

  return 0;
}

void strcopy(char string1[], char string2[])   // copy string2 to string1
{
  int i = 0;                      // i will be used as a subscript

  while (string2[i] != '\0')      // check for the end-of-string
  {
    string1[i] = string2[i];      // copy the element to string1
    i++;
  }
  string1[i] = '\0';              // terminate the first string

  return;
}
```

The following is a sample run of Program 9-2:

```
Enter a sentence: How much wood could a woodchuck chuck.
How much wood could a woodchuck chuck.
```

Character-by-Character Input

Just as strings can be processed by means of character-by-character techniques, they can also be entered and displayed in this manner. For example, consider Program 9-3, which uses the character input function `cin.get()` to accept a string one character at a time. The shaded portion of Program 9-3 essentially replaces the `cin.getline()` function previously used in Program 9-1.

Program 9-3

```
#include <iostream.h>
int main()
{
  const int MAXCHARS = 80;
  char message[MAXCHARS], c;

  cout << "Enter a sentence:\n";

  int i = 0;
  while(i < MAXCHARS && (c = cin.get()) != '\n')
  {
    message[i] = c;        // store the character entered
    i++;
  }
  message[i] = '\0';       // terminate the string a

  cout << "The sentence just entered is:\n";
  cout << message << endl;

  return 0;
}
```

The following is a sample run of Program 9-3:

```
Enter a sentence:
This is a test input of a string of characters.
The sentence just entered is:
This is a test input of a string of characters.
```

The `while` statement in Program 9-3 causes characters to be read, provided that the number of characters entered is less than 80 and that the character returned by `cin.get()` is not the newline character. The parentheses surrounding the expression `c = cin.get()` are necessary to assign the character returned by `cin.get()` to the variable `c` prior to comparing it to the newline escape sequence. Without the surrounding parentheses, the comparison operator, `!=`, which takes precedence over the assignment operator, causes the entire expression to be equivalent to

```
c = (cin.get() != '\n')
```

which is an invalid application of `cin.get()`.[1]

Program 9-3 also illustrates a useful technique for developing functions. The shaded statements constitute a self-contained unit for entering a complete line of characters from a terminal. These statements can be removed from `main()` and placed together as a new function. Program 9-4 illustrates placing the shaded statements from Program 9-3 in a separate function named `getaline()`. Note that in the process the constant `MAXCHARS` has been placed above the `main()` function. This placement gives this constant a global scope, which makes it available to both the `main()` and the `getaline()` functions.

Program 9-4

```
#include <iostream.h>

const int MAXCHARS = 80; // global named constant
void getaline(char []);  // function prototype

int main()
{
  char message[MAXCHARS];    // enough storage for a complete line
  int i;

  cout << "Enter a sentence:\n";
  getaline(message);
  cout << "The sentence just entered is:\n";
  cout << message << endl;
}
```

[1] The equivalent statement in C is `c= (getchar() != '\n')`, which is a valid expression that produces an unexpected result for most beginning programmers. Here the character returned by `getchar()` is compared to `'\n'`, and the value of the comparison is either 0 or 1, depending on whether or not `getchar()` received the newline character. This value, either 0 or 1, is then assigned to `c`.

```
void getaline(char strng[])
{
  int i = 0;
  char c;
  while(i < MAXCHARS && (c = cin.get()) != '\n')
  {
    strng[i] = c;        // store the character entered
    i++;
  }
  strng[i] = '\0';       // terminate the string

  return;
}
```

Exercises 9.1

1. a. The following function can be used to select and display all vowels contained within a user-input string.

```
void vowels(char strng[])
{
  int i = 0;
  char c;
  while ((c = strng[i++]) != '\0')
    switch(c)
    {
       case 'a':
       case 'e':
       case 'i':
       case 'o':
       case 'u':
         cout << c;
    } // end of switch
  cout << endl;

  return;
}
```

Note that the `switch` statement in `vowels()` uses the fact that selected cases "drop through" in the absence of `break` statements. Thus, all selected cases result in a `cout` object call. Include `vowels()` in a working program that accepts a user-input string and then displays all vowels in the string. In response to the input `How much is the little worth worth?`, your program should display `ouieieoo`.

b. Modify `vowels()` to count and display the total number of vowels contained in the string passed to it.

2. Modify the `vowels()` function given in Exercise 1a to count and display the individual numbers of each vowel contained in the string.

3. *a.* Write a C++ function to count the total number of characters, including blanks, contained in a string. Do not include the end-of-string marker in the count.

b. Include the function written for Exercise 3a in a complete working program.

4. Write a program that accepts a string of characters from a terminal and displays the hexadecimal equivalent of each character.

5. Write a C++ program that accepts a string of characters from a terminal and displays the string one word per line.

6. Write a function that reverses the characters in a string. (*Hint:* This can be considered as a string copy starting from the back end of the first string.)

7. Write a function called `delChar()` that can be used to delete characters from a string. The function should take three arguments: the string name, the number of characters to delete, and the starting position in the string where characters should be deleted. For example, the function call `delChar(strng,13,5)`, when applied to the string `all enthusiastic people`, should result in the string `all people`.

8. Write a function call `addChar()` to insert one string of characters into another string. The function should take three arguments: the string to be inserted, the original string, and the position in the original string where the insertion should begin. For example, the call `addChar("for all",message,6)` should insert the characters `for all` in `message` starting at `message[5]`.

9. *a.* Write a C++ function named `ToUpper()` that converts lowercase letters to uppercase letters. The expression `c - 'a' + 'A'` can be used to make the conversion for any lowercase character stored in `c`.

b. Add a data input check to the function written in Exercise 9a to verify that a valid lowercase letter is passed to the function. A character in ASCII is lowercase if it is greater than or equal to a and less than or equal to z. If the character is not a valid lowercase letter, have the function `ToUpper()` return the passed character unaltered.

c. Write a C++ program that accepts a string from a terminal and converts all lowercase letters in the string to uppercase letters.

10. Write a C++ program that accepts a string from a terminal and converts all uppercase letters in the string to lowercase letters.

11. Write a C++ program that counts the number of words in a string. A word is encountered whenever a transition from a blank space to a nonblank character is encountered. Assume that the string contains only words separated by blank spaces.

9.2 Pointers and Library Functions

Pointers are exceptionally useful in constructing string-handling functions. When pointer notation is used in place of subscripts to access individual characters in a string, the resulting statements are both more compact and more efficient. In this section, we describe the equivalence between subscripts and pointers when accessing individual characters in a string.

Consider the `strcopy()` function introduced in the previous section. This function was used to copy the characters of one string to a second string. For convenience, this function is repeated below.

```
void strcopy(char string1[], char string2[])   // copy string2 to string1
{
  int i = 0;

  while (string2[i] != '\0')       // check for the end-of-string
  {
    string1[i] = string2[i];       // copy the element to string1
    i++;
  }
  string1[i] = '\0';               // terminate the first string

  return;
}
```

The function `strcopy()` is used to copy the characters from one array to another array, one character at a time. As currently written, the subscript `i` in the function is used successively to access each character in the array named `string2` by "marching along" the string one character at a time. Before we write a pointer version of `strcopy()`, we will make two modifications to the function to make it more efficient.

The `while` statement in `strcopy()` tests each character to ensure that the end of the string has not been reached. Like all relational expressions, the tested expression, `string2[i] != '\0'`, is either true or false. To take the string `this is a string` illustrated in Figure 9–3 as an example, as long as `string2[i]` does not access the end-of-string character, the value of the expression is nonzero and is considered to be true. The expression is false only when the value of the expression is zero. This occurs when the last element in the string is accessed.

Recall that C++ defines false as zero and true as anything else. Thus the expression `string2[i] != '\0'` becomes zero, or false, when the end of the string is reached. It is nonzero, or true, everywhere else. The null character has an internal value of zero by itself, so the comparison to `'\0'` is not necessary. When `string2[i]` accesses the end-of-string character, the value of `string2[i]` is zero. When `string2[i]` accesses any other character, the value of `string2[i]` is the value of the code used to store the character and is nonzero. Figure 9–4 lists the ASCII codes for the string `this is a string.` As the figure shows, each element has a nonzero value except for the null character.

Because the expression `string2[i]` is zero only at the end of a string and is nonzero for every other character, the expression `while (string2[i] !=`

Element	String array	Expression	Value
Zeroth element	`t`	`string2[0]!='\0'`	1
First element	`h`	`string2[1]!='\0'`	1
Second element	`i`	`string2[2]!='\0'`	1
	`s`		
	`i`		
	`s`		
.		.	.
.	`a`	.	.
.		.	.
	`s`		
	`t`		
	`r`		
	`i`		
	`n`		
Fifteenth element	`g`	`string2[15]!='\0'`	1
Sixteenth element	`\0`	`string2[16]!='\0'`	0

End-of-string marker

FIGURE 9–3 The `while` Test Becomes False at the End of the String

`'\0')` can be replaced by the simpler expression `while (string2[i])`. Although this may appear confusing at first, the revised test expression is certainly more compact than the longer version. End-of-string tests are frequently written by advanced C++ programmers in this shorter form, so it is worthwhile to be familiar with this expression. Including this expression in `strcopy()` results in the following version of `strcopy()`:

String array	Stored codes	Expression	Value
t	116	string2[0]	116
h	104	string2[1]	104
i	105	string2[2]	105
s	115		
	32		
i	105		
s	115		
	32	.	.
a	97	.	.
	32	.	.
s	115		
t	116		
r	114		
i	105		
n	110		
g	103	string2[15]	113
\0	0	string2[16]	0

FIGURE 9–4 The ASCII Codes Used to Store `this is a string`

```
void strcopy(char string1[], char string2[])   // copy string2 to string1
{
  int i = 0;

  while (string2[i])
  {
    string1[i] = string2[i];     // copy the element to string1
    i++;
  }
  string1[i] = '\0';            // terminate the first string

  return;
}
```

The second modification that can be made to this string copy function is to include the assignment inside the test portion of the while statement. Our new version of the string copy function is

```
void strcopy(char string1[], char string2[])    // copy string2 to string1
{
  int i = 0;

  while (string1[i] = string2[i])
    i++;

  return;
}
```

Note that including the assignment statement within the test part of the while statement eliminates the necessity of separately terminating the copied string with the null character. The assignment within the parentheses ensures that the null character is copied from string2 to string1. The value of the assignment expression becomes zero only after the null character is assigned to string1, at which point the while loop is terminated.

The conversion of strcopy() from subscript notation to pointer notation is now straightforward. Although each subscript version of strcopy() can be rewritten using pointer notation, the following is the equivalent of our last subscript version:

```
void strcopy(char *string1, char *string2)   // copy string2 to string1
{
  while (*string1 = *string2)
  {
    string1++;
    string2++;
  }

  return;
}
```

In both subscript and pointer versions of strcopy(), the function receives the name of the array being passed. Recall that passing an array name to a function actually passes the address of the first location of the array. In our pointer version of strcopy(), the two passed addresses are stored in the pointer parameters string1 and string2, respectively.

The declarations char *string1; and char *string2; used in the pointer version of strcopy() indicate that string1 and string2 are both pointers containing the address of a character, and they stress the treatment of the passed addresses as pointer values rather than array names. These declarations are equivalent to the declarations `char string1[]` and `char string2[]`, respectively.

Internal to `strcopy()`, the pointer expression `*string1`, which refers to "the element whose address is in `string1`," replaces the equivalent subscript expression `string1[i]`. Similarly, the pointer expression `*string2` replaces the equivalent subscript expression `string2[i]`. The expression `*string1 = *string2` causes the element pointed to by `string2` to be assigned to the element pointed to by `string1`. Because the starting addresses of both strings are passed to `strcopy()` and stored in `string1` and `string2`, respectively, the expression `*string1` initially refers to `string1[0]`, and the expression `*string2` initially refers to `string2[0]`.

Consecutively incrementing both pointers in `strcopy()` with the expressions `string1++` and `string2++` simply causes each pointer to "point to" the next consecutive character in the respective string. As with the subscript version, the pointer version of `strcopy()` steps along, copying element by element, until the end of the string is copied. One final change to the string copy function can be made by including the pointer increments as postfix operators within the test part of the `while` statement. The final form of the string copy function is:

```
void strcopy(char *string1, char *string2)    // copy string2 to string1
{
  while (*string1++ = *string2++)
    ;

  return;
}
```

There is no ambiguity in the expression `*string1++ = *string2++` even though the indirection operator, `*`, and the increment operator, `++`, have the same precedence. Here the character pointed to is accessed before the pointer is incremented. Only after completion of the assignment `*string1 = *string2` are the pointers incremented to point correctly to the next characters in the respective strings.

The string copy function included in the standard library supplied with C++ compilers is typically written exactly like our pointer version of `strcopy()`.

Library Functions

C++ does not provide built-in operations for complete arrays, such as array assignment or array comparisons. Because a string is just an array of characters terminated with a `'\0'` character, this means that assignment and relational operations *are not* provided for strings. Extensive collections of string-handling functions and routines, however, that effectively supply string assignment, comparison, and other very useful string operations are included with all C++ compilers. The more commonly used of these are listed in Table 9–2.

TABLE 9–2 String Library Routines (required header file is `string.h`)

Name	Description	Example
`strcpy(string_var, string_exp)`	Copies `string_exp` to `string_var`, including the `'\0'`.	`strcpy(test, "efgh")`
`strcat(string_var, string_exp)`	Appends `str_exp` to the end of the string value contained in `string_var`.	`strcat(test, "there")`
`strlen(string_exp)`	Returns the length of the string. Does not include the `'\0'` in the length count.	`strlen("Hello World!")`
`strcmp(string_exp1, string_exp2)`	Compares `string_exp1` to `string_exp2`. Returns a negative integer if `string_exp1 < string_exp2`, 0 if `string_exp1 == string_exp2`, and a positive integer if `string_exp1 > string_exp2`.	`strcmp("Bebop","Beehive")`
`strncpy(string_var, string_exp, n)`	Copies at most *n* characters of `string_exp` to `string_var`. If `string_exp` has fewer than *n* characters, it will pad `string_var` with `'\0'`s.	`strncpy(str1, str2, 5)`
`strncmp(string_exp1, string_exp2, n)`	Compare at most *n* characters of `string_exp1` to `string_exp2`. Returns the same values as `strcmp()` based on the number of characters compared.	`strncmp("Bebop", "Beehive", 2)`
`strchr(string_exp, character)`	Locates the position of the first occurrence of the character within the string. Returns the address of the character.	`strchr("Hello", 'l')`
`strtok(string_exp, character)`	Parses `string1` into tokens. Returns the next sequence of characters contained in `string1`, up to but not including the delimiter character `ch`.	`strtok("Hello there World!, ' ')`

String library functions are called in the same manner as all C++ functions. This means that the appropriate declarations for these functions, which are contained in the standard header files `<string.h>`, must be included in your program before the function is called.

The most commonly used functions listed in Table 9–2 are the first four. The `strcpy()` function copies a source string expression, which consists of either a string literal or the contents of a string variable, into a destination string variable. For example, in the function call `strcpy(string1, "Hello World!")` the source string literal `"Hello World!"` is copied into the destination string variable `string1`. Similarly, if the source string is a string variable named `src_string`, the function call `strcpy(string1, src_string)` copies the

POINT OF INFORMATION

Initializing and Processing Strings

All of the following declarations produce the same result.

```
char test[5] = "abcd";
char test[] = "abcd";
char test[5] = {'a', 'b', 'c', 'd', '\0'};
char test[] = {'a', 'b', 'c', 'd', '\0'};
```

Each declaration creates storage for exactly five characters and initializes this storage with the characters `'a'`, `'b'`, `'c'`, `'d'`, and `'\0'`. A string literal is used for initialization in the first two declarations, so the compiler automatically supplies the end-of-string null character.

String variables declared in either of these ways preclude the use of any subsequent assignments, such as `test = "efgh";`, to the character array. In place of an assignment, you can use the `strcpy()` function, such as `strcpy(test, "efgh")`. The only restriction on using `strcpy()` is the size of the declared array, which in this case is five elements. Attempting to copy a larger string value into `test` causes the copy to overflow the destination array, beginning with the memory area immediately following the last array element. This overwrites whatever was in these memory locations and typically causes a run-time crash when the overwritten areas are accessed via their legitimate identifier name(s).

The same problem can arise in using the `strcat()` function. It is your responsibility to ensure that the concatenated string will fit into the original string.

An interesting situation arises when string variables are defined using pointers (see the Point of Information in Section 9.3). In this situation, assignments can be made after the declaration statement.

Finally, C++ provides a string class (see Section 9.6) that permits assignment, copy, and concatenation in a manner that checks for sufficient memory space before these operations are performed.

contents of `src_string` into `string1`. In both cases, it is the programmer's responsibility to ensure that `string1` is large enough to contain the source string (see Point of Information above).

The `strcat()` function appends a string expression onto the end of a string variable. For example, if the contents of a string variable named `dest_string` is `"Hello"`, then the function call `strcat(dest_string, " there World!")` results in the string value `"Hello there World!"` being assigned to `dest_string`. As with the `strcpy()` function, it is the programmer's responsibility to ensure that the destination string has been defined as large enough to hold the additional concatenated characters.

The `strlen()` function returns the number of characters in its string parameter but does not include the terminating null character in the count. For example, the value returned by the function call `strlen("Hello World!")` is 12.

Finally, two string expressions may be compared for equality using the `strcmp()` function. Each character in a string is stored in binary using either the ANSI or the UNICODE code. Although these codes are different, they have some characteristics in common: In each of them, a blank precedes (is less than) all letters and numbers; the letters of the alphabet are stored in order from A to Z; and the digits are stored in order from 0 to 9. (It is important to note that ANSI uses 8 bits per character, while UNICODE uses 16 bits per character that supports multilingual characters.)

When two strings are compared, their individual characters are compared a pair at a time (both first characters, then both second characters, and so on). If no differences are found, the strings are equal; if a difference is found, the string with the first lower character is considered the smaller string. Thus,

`"Hello"` is less than `"Good Bye"` because the first `'H'` in `Hello` is less than the first `'G'` in `Good Bye`.
`"Hello"` is less than `"hello"` because the first `'H'` in `Hello` is less than the first `'h'` in `hello`.
`"Hello"` is less than `"Hello"` because the `'\0'` terminating the first string is less than the `' '` in the second string.
`"SMITH"` is greater than `"JONES"` because the first `'S'` in `SMITH` is greater than the first `'J'` in `JONES`.
`"123"` is greater than `"1227"` because the third character, the `'3'`, in `123` is greater than the third character, the `'2'`, in `1227`.
`"1237"` is greater than `"123"` because the fourth character, the `'7'`, in `1237` is greater than the fourth character, the `'\0'`, in `123`.
`"Behop"` is greater than `"Beehive"` because the third character, the `'h'`, in `Behop` is greater than the third character, the `'e'`, in `Beehive`.

Program 9-5 uses these string functions within the context of a complete program. Following is a sample output produced by Program 9-5:

```
Hello is less than Hello there

The length of string1 is 5 characters
The length of string2 is 11 characters

After concatenation, string1 contains the string value
Hello there World!
The length of this string is 18 characters

Type in a sequence of characters for string2: It's a wonderful day
After copying string2 to string1, the string value in string1 is:
It's a wonderful day
The length of this string is 20 characters
```

Program 9-5

```
#include <iostream.h>
#include <string.h>   // required for the string function library
int main()
{
  const int MAXELS = 50;
  char string1[MAXELS] = "Hello";
  char string2[MAXELS] = "Hello there";
  int n;

  n = strcmp(string1, string2);

  if (n < 0)
    cout << string1 << " is less than " << string2 << endl;
  else if (n == 0)
    cout << string1 << " is equal to " << string2 << endl;
  else
    cout << string1 << " is greater than " << string2 << endl;

  cout << "\nThe length of string1 is " << strlen(string1)
       << " characters" << endl;
  cout << "The length of string2 is " << strlen(string2)
       << " characters" << endl;

  strcat(string1," there World!");

  cout << "\nAfter concatenation, string1 contains "
       << "the string value\n" << string1
       << "\nThe length of this string is "
       << strlen(string1) << " characters" << endl;

  cout << "\nType in a sequence of characters for string2: ";
  cin.getline(string2, MAXELS);

  strcpy(string1, string2);

  cout << "After copying string2 to string1, "
       << "the string value in string1 is:\n" << string2
       << "\nThe length of this string is "
       << strlen(string1) << " characters" << endl;

  return 0;
}
```

Character Routines

In addition to string manipulation functions, all C++ compilers include the character-handling routines listed in Table 9–3. The prototypes for each of these routines are contained in the header file `ctype.h`, which should be included in any program that uses these routines.

TABLE 9–3 Character Library Routines (required header file is `ctype.h`)

Prototype	Description	Example
`int isalpha(char)`	Returns a nonzero number if the character is a letter; otherwise, returns a zero.	`isalpha('a')`
`int isupper(char)`	Returns a nonzero number if the character is uppercase; otherwise, returns a zero.	`isupper('a')`
`int islower(char)`	Returns a nonzero number if the character is lowercase; otherwise, returns a zero.	`islower('a')`
`int isdigit(character)`	Returns a nonzero number if the character is a digit (0 through 9); otherwise, returns a zero.	`isdigit('a')`
`int isascii(character)`	Returns a nonzero number if the character is an ASCII character; otherwise, returns a zero.	`isascii('a')`
`int isspace(character)`	Returns a nonzero number if the character is a space; otherwise, returns a zero.	`isspace(' ')`
`int isprint(character)`	Returns a nonzero number if the character is a printable character; otherwise, returns a zero.	`isprint('a')`
`int iscntrl(character)`	Returns a nonzero number if the character is a control character; otherwise, returns a zero.	`iscntrl('a')`
`int ispucnt(character)`	Returns a nonzero number if the character is a punctuation character; otherwise, returns a zero.	`ispucnt('!')`
`int toupper(char)`	Returns the uppercase equivalent if the character is lowercase; otherwise, returns the character unchanged.	`toupper('a')`
`int tolower(char)`	Returns the lowercase equivalent if the character is uppercase; otherwise, returns the character unchanged.	`tolower('A')`

Because all of the functions listed in Table 9–3 return a nonzero integer (that is, a True value) if the character meets the desired condition and a zero integer (that is, a False value) if the condition is not met, these functions can be used directly within an `if` statement. For example, consider the following code segment:

```
char ch;

ch = cin.get();   // get a character from the keyboard

if(isdigit(ch))
  cout << "The character just entered is a digit" << endl;
else if(ispunct(ch))
  cout << "The character just entered is a punctuation mark" << endl;
```

Note that the character function is included as a condition within the `if` statement because the function effectively returns either a True (nonzero) or a False (zero) value.

Program 9-6 illustrates the use of the `toupper()` function within the function `ConvertToUpper()`, which is used to convert all lowercase string characters to their uppercase form.

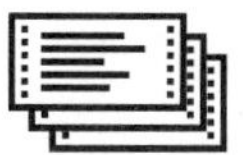

Program 9-6

```
#include <iostream.h>
#include <ctype.h>      // required for the character function library

const int MAXCHARS = 100;

void ConvertToUpper(char []);

int main()
{
  char message[MAXCHARS];

  cout << "\nType in any sequence of characters: ";

  cin.getline(message,MAXCHARS);

  ConvertToUpper(message);

  cout << "The characters just entered, in uppercase are: "
       << message << endl;

  return 0;
}

// this function converts all lowercase characters to uppercase
void ConvertToUpper(char message[])
{
  for(int i = 0; message[i] != '\0'; i++)
    message[i] = toupper(message[i]);

  return;
}
```

The output produced when Program 9-6 is executed is

```
Type in any sequence of characters: this is a test OF 12345.
The characters just entered, in uppercase are: THIS IS A TEST OF 12345.
```

Note that the `touppper()` library function converts only lowercase letters and that all other characters are unaffected.

Conversion Routines

The last group of standard string library routines, which are listed in Table 9–4, are used to convert strings to and from integer and double-precision data types. The prototypes for each of these routines are contained in the header file `stdlib.h`, which should be included in any program that uses these routines.

Program 9-7 illustrates the use of the `atoi()` and `atof()` functions. The output produced when Program 9-7 is executed is

```
The string "12345" as an integer number is: 12345
This number divided by 3 is: 4115
The string "12345.96" as a double number is: 12345.96
This number divided by 3 is: 4115.32
```

As this output illustrates, once a string has been converted to either an integer or a double-precision value, mathematical operations on the numerical value are valid.

TABLE 9–4 String Conversion Routines (required header file is `stdlib.h`)

Prototype	Description	Example
`int atoi(string_exp)`	Convert an ASCII string to an integer. Conversion stops at the first noninteger character.	`atoi("1234")`
`double atof(string_exp)`	Convert an ASCII string to a double-precision number. Conversion stops at the first character that cannot be interpreted as a double.	`atof("12.34")`
`char[] itoa(string_esp)`	Convert an integer to an ASCII string. The space allocated for the returned string must be large enough for the converted value.	`itoa(1234)`

Program 9-7

```
#include <iostream.h>
#include <string.h>
#include <stdlib.h>     // required for string conversion function library

const int MAXELS = 20;

int main()
{
  char string[MAXELS] = "12345";
  int num;
  double dnum;

  num = atoi(string);

  cout << "The string \"" << string << "\" as an integer number is: "
       << num;
  cout << "\nThis number divided by 3 is: " << num / 3 << endl;

  strcat(string, ".96");

  dnum = atof(string);

  cout << "The string \"" << string << "\" as a double number is: "
       << dnum;
  cout << "\nThis number divided by 3 is: " << dnum / 3 << endl;

  return 0;
}
```

Exercises 9.2

1. Determine the value of `*text`, `*(text + 3)`, and `*(text + 10)`, assuming that `text` is an array of characters and that the following has been stored in the array.

a. `now is the time`
b. `rocky raccoon welcomes you`
c. `Happy Holidays`
d. `The good ship`

2. a. The following function, `convert()`, "marches along" the string passed to it and sends each character in the string one at a time to the `ToUpper()` function until the null character is encountered.

```
void convert(char strng[])       // convert a string to uppercase letters
{
  int i = 0;
  while (strng[i] != '\0')
  {
    strng[i] = ToUpper(strng[i]);
    i++;
  }

  return;
}

char ToUpper(char letter)  // convert a character to uppercase
{
  if( (letter >= 'a') && (letter <= 'z') )
    return (letter - 'a' + 'A');
  else
    return (letter);
}
```

The `ToUpper()` function takes each character passed to it and first examines it to determine whether the character is a lowercase letter (a lowercase letter is any character between a and z, inclusive). Assuming that characters are stored using the standard ASCII character codes, the expression `letter - 'a' + 'A'` converts a lowercase letter to its uppercase equivalent. Rewrite the `convert()` function using pointers.

b. Include the `convert()` and `ToUpper()` functions in a working program. The program should prompt the user for a string and echo the string back to the user in uppercase letters.

3. Using pointers, repeat Exercise 1 from Section 9.1.

4. Using pointers, repeat Exercise 2 from Section 9.1.

5. Using pointers, repeat Exercise 3 from Section 9.1.

6. Write a function named `remove()` that returns nothing and deletes all occurrences of a character from a string. The function should take two arguments: the string name and the character to be removed. For example, if `message` contains the string `Happy Holidays`, the function call `remove(message,'H')` should place the string `appy olidays` into `message`.

7. Using pointers, repeat Exercise 6 from Section 9.1.

8. Write a program using the `cin.get()`, and `toupper()` library routines, along with a `cout` stream object to echo back each entered letter in its uppercase form. The program should terminate when the digit 1 key is pressed.

9. Write a function that uses pointers to add a single character at the end of an existing string. The function should replace the existing `\0` character with the new character and append a new `\0` at the end of the string. The function returns nothing.

10. Write a function that uses pointers to delete a single character from the end of a string. This is effectively achieved by moving the `\0` character one position closer to the start of the string. The function returns nothing.

11. Determine what string-handling functions are available with your C++ compiler. For each available function, list the data types of the arguments expected by the function and the data type of any returned value.

12. Write a function named `trimfrnt()` that deletes all leading blanks from a string. Write the function using pointers. The function returns nothing.

13. Write a function named `trimrear()` that deletes all trailing blanks from a string. Write the function using pointers. The function returns nothing.

14. Write a function named `strlen()` that returns the number of characters in a string. Do not include the `\0` character in the returned count.

9.3 String Definitions and Pointer Arrays

The definition of a string automatically involves a pointer. For example, the definition `char message1[80];` both reserves storage for 80 characters and automatically creates a pointer constant, `message1`, that contains the address of `message1[0]`. As a pointer constant, the address associated with the pointer cannot be changed; it must always "point to" the beginning of the created array.

Instead of creating a string as an array, however, it is also possible to create a string using a pointer. For example, the definition `char *message2;` creates a pointer to a character. In this case, `message2` is a true pointer variable. Once a pointer to a character is defined, assignment statements, such as `message2 = "this is a string";`, can be made. In this assignment, `message2`, which is a pointer, receives the address of the first character in the string.

The main difference in the definitions of `message1` as an array and `message2` as a pointer is the way the pointer is created. Defining `message1` using the declaration `char message1[80]` explicitly calls for a fixed amount of storage for the array. This causes the compiler to create a pointer constant. Defining `message2` using the declaration `char *message2` explicitly creates a pointer variable first. This pointer is then used to hold the address of a string when the string is actually specified. This difference in definitions has both storage and programming consequences.

From a programming perspective, defining `message2` as a pointer to a character allows string assignments, such as `message2 = "this is a string";`, to be made within a program. Similar assignments are not allowed for strings defined as arrays. Thus the statement `message1 = "this is a string";` is not valid. Both definitions, however, allow initializations to be made using a string assignment. For example, both of the following initializations are valid:

```
char message1[80] = "this is a string";
char *message2 = "this is a string";
```

From a storage perspective, the allocation of space for `message1` is quite different from that for `message2`. As illustrated in Figure 9–5, both initializations cause the computer to store the same string internally. In the case of `message1`, a specific set of 80 storage locations is reserved, and the first 17 locations are initialized. For `message1`, different strings can be stored, but each string will overwrite the previously stored characters. The same is not true for `message2`.

The definition of `message2` reserves enough storage for one pointer. The initialization then causes the string to be stored in memory and the address of the string's first character, in this case the address of the `t`, to be loaded into the pointer. If a later assignment is made to `message2`, the initial string remains in memory, and new storage locations are allocated to the new string. For example, consider the sequence of instructions

```
char *message2 = "this is a string";
message2 = "A new message";
```

FIGURE 9–5 String Storage Allocation

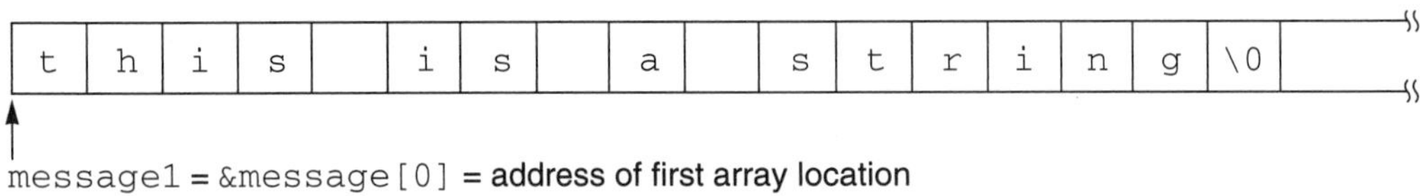

a. Storage allocation for a string defined as an array

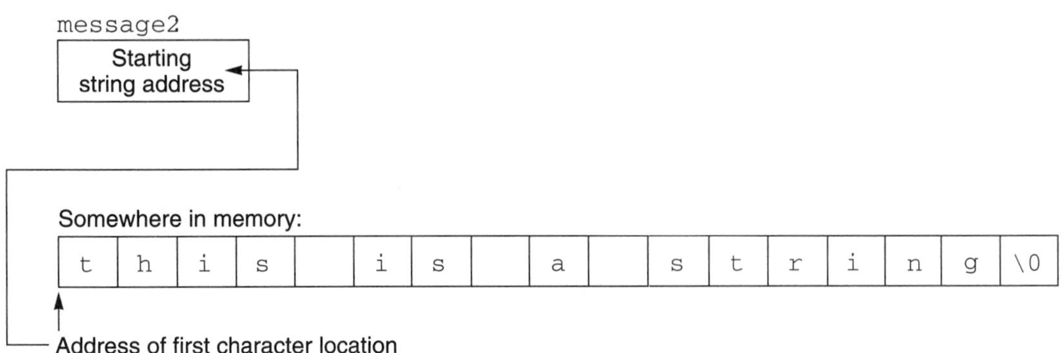

b. Storage of a string using a pointer

The first statement defines `message2` as a pointer variable, stores the initialization string in memory, and loads the starting address of the string (the address of the `t` in `this`) into `message2`. The next assignment statement causes the computer to store the second string and change the address in `message2` to point to the starting location of this new string.

It is important to realize that the second string assigned to `message2` does not overwrite the first string but simply changes the address in `message2` to point to the new string. As Figure 9–6 shows, both strings are stored inside the computer. Any additional string assignment to `message2` would result in the additional storage of the new string and a corresponding change in the address stored in `message2`. Doing so also means that we no longer have access to the original memory location.

Pointer Arrays

The declaration of an array of character pointers is an extremely useful extension to single string pointer declarations. For example, the declaration

```
char *seasons[4];
```

creates an array of four elements, where each element is a pointer to a character. As individual pointers, each pointer can be assigned to point to a string using string assignment statements. Thus the statements

FIGURE 9–6 Storage Allocation for Figure 9–5

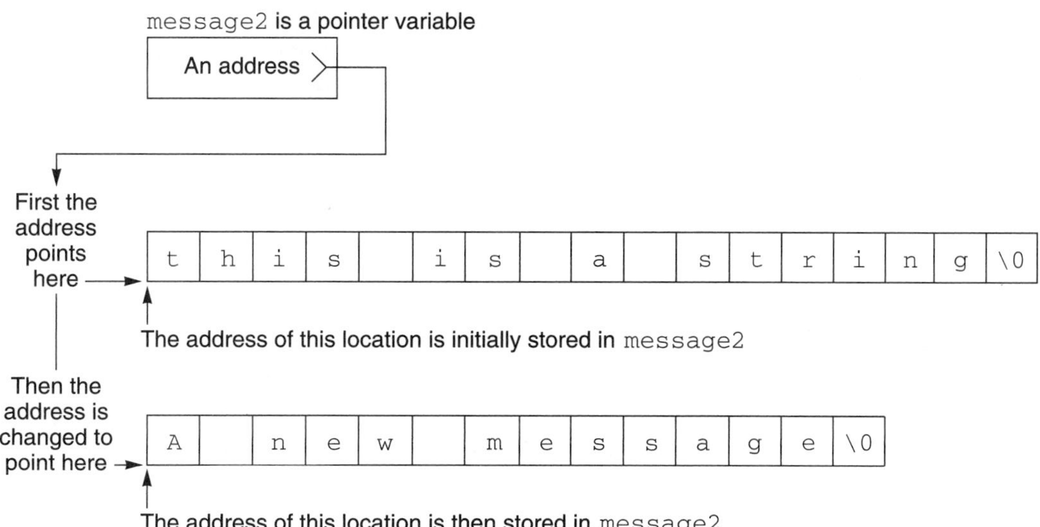

POINT OF INFORMATION

Allocating Space for a String

Although the two declarations

```
char test[5] = "abcd";
```

and

```
char *test = "abcd";
```

both create storage for the characters `'a'`, `'b'`, `'c'`, `'d'`, and `'\0'`, there is a subtle difference between the two declarations and in how values can be assigned to `test`. Except within the declaration, an array declaration, such as `char test[5];`, precludes the use of any subsequent assignment expression, such as `test = "efgh"`, to assign values to the array. The use of a `strcpy`, such as `strcpy(test, "efgh")`, however, is subsequently valid. The only restriction on the `strcpy` is the size of the array, which in this case is five elements. This situation is reversed when a pointer is created. A pointer declaration, such as `char *test;`, precludes the use of a `strcpy` to initialize the memory locations pointed to by the pointer, but it does allow assignments. For example, the following sequence of statements is valid:

```
char *test;
test = "abcd";
test = "here is a longer string";
```

Once a string of characters has been assigned to `test`, a `strcpy` can be used, provided that the copy uses no more elements than are currently contained in the string.

The difference in usage is explained by the fact that the compiler automatically allocates sufficient new memory space for any string pointed to by a pointer variable but does not do so for an array of characters. The array size is fixed by the definition statement.

Formally, any expression that yields a value that can be used on the left side of an assignment expression is said to be an *lvalue.* (Similarly, any expression that yields a value that can be used on the right side of an assignment statement is said to be an *rvalue*). Thus a pointer variable can be an *lvalue,* but an array name cannot.

```
seasons[0] = "Winter";
seasons[1] = "Spring";
seasons[2] = "Summer";
seasons[3] = "Fall";    // note: string lengths may differ
```

set appropriate addresses into the respective pointers. Figure 9–7 illustrates the addresses loaded into the pointers for these assignments.

As shown in Figure 9–7, the `seasons` array does not contain the actual strings assigned to the pointers. These strings are stored elsewhere in the computer in the normal data area allocated to the program. The array of pointers contains only the addresses of the starting location for each string.

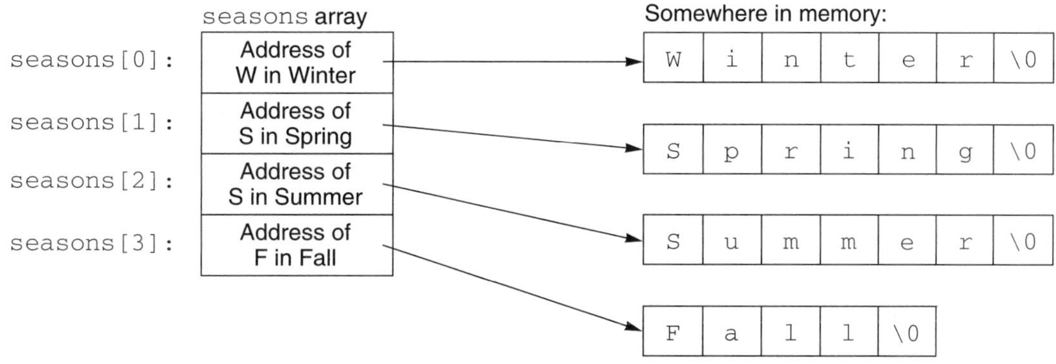

FIGURE 9–7 The Addresses Contained in the `seasons[]` Pointers

The initializations of the `seasons` array can also be incorporated directly within the definition of the array, as follows:

```
char *seasons[4] = {"Winter",
                    "Spring",
                    "Summer",
                    "Fall"};
```

This declaration both creates an array of pointers and initializes the pointers with appropriate addresses. Once addresses have been assigned to the pointers, each pointer can be used to access its corresponding string. Program 9-8 uses the `seasons` array to display each season using a `for` loop.

Program 9-8

```
#include <iostream.h>
int main()
{
  const int NUMSEASONS = 4;
  int n;
  char *seasons[] = {"Winter",
                     "Spring",
                     "Summer",
                     "Fall"};

  for( n = 0; n < NUMSEASONS; n++)
  cout << "\nThe season is " << seasons[n];

  return 0;
}
```

The output obtained for Program 9-8 is

```
The season is Winter
The season is Spring
The season is Summer
The season is Fall
```

The advantage of using a list of pointers is that logical groups of data headings can be collected and accessed with one array name. For example, the months in a year can be collectively grouped in one array called `months`, and the days in a week can be collectively grouped in an array called `days`. The grouping of like headings allows the programmer to access and print an appropriate heading by simply specifying the correct position of the heading in the array. Program 9-9 uses the `seasons` array to correctly identify and display the season corresponding to a user-input month.

Program 9-9

```
#include <iostream.h>
int main()
{
  int n;
  char *seasons[] = {"Winter",
                     "Spring",
                     "Summer",
                     "Fall"};

  cout << "\nEnter a month (use 1 for Jan., 2 for Feb., etc.): ";
  cin  >> n;
  n = (n % 12) / 3;     // create the correct subscript
  cout << "The month entered is a "<< seasons[n] << " month.";

  return 0;
}
```

Except for the expression `n = (n % 12) / 3`, Program 9-9 is rather straightforward. The program requests the user to input a month and accepts the number corresponding to the month using a `cin` object to display the selected month. The expression `n = (n % 12) / 3` uses a common program "trick" to scale a set of numbers into a more useful set. Using subscripts, the four elements of the `seasons` array must be accessed via a subscript from 0 through 3. Thus the months of the year, which correspond to the numbers 1 through 12, must be adjusted to correspond to the correct season subscript. This is done by using the expression `n = (n % 12) / 3`. The expression `n % 12` adjusts the month entered to lie within the range 0 through 11, with 0 corresponding to December, 1 to January, and so on. Dividing by 3 causes the resulting number to range between 0 and 3, corresponding to the possible seasons elements. The result of the division by 3 is assigned to the integer variable `n`. The months 0, 1, and 2, when divided by 3, are set to 0; the months 3, 4, and 5 are set to 1; the months 6, 7, and 8 are set to 2; and the months 9, 10, and 11 are set to 3. This is equivalent to the following assignments:

Months	Season
December, January, February	Winter
March, April, May	Spring
June, July, August	Summer
September, October, November	Fall

The following is a sample output obtained for Program 9-9:

```
Enter a month (use 1 for Jan., 2 for Feb., etc.): 12
The month entered is a Winter month.
```

Exercises 9.3

1. Write two declaration statements that can be used in place of the declaration `char text[] = "Hooray!";`.

2. Determine the value of `*text`, `*(text + 3)`, and `*(text + 7)` for each of the following sections of code.

a.
```
char *text;
char message[] = "the check is in the mail";
text = message;
```
b.
```
char *text;
char formal[] = {'t','h','i','s',' ','i','s',' ','a','n',' ',
                 'i','n','v','i','t','a','t','i','o','n','\0'};
text = &formal[0];
```
c.
```
char *test;
char more[] = "Happy Holidays";
text = &more[4];
```
d.
```
char *text, *second;
char blip[] = "The good ship";
second = blip;
text = ++second;
```

3. Determine the error in the following program:

```
#include <iostream.h>
int main()
{
  int i = 0;
  char message[] = {'H','e','l','l','o','\0'};

  for( ; i < 5; i++)
  {
    cout << *message;
    message++;
  }

  return 0;
}
```

4. ***a.*** Write a C++ function that displays the day of the week corresponding to a user-entered input number between 1 and 7. That is, in response to an input of 2, the program displays the name Monday. Use an array of pointers in the function.
b. Include the function written for Exercise 4a in a complete working program.

5. Modify the function written in Exercise 4a so that the function returns the address of the character string containing the proper day to be displayed.

6. Write a function that will accept ten lines of user-input text and store the entered lines as ten individual strings. Use a pointer array in your function.

9.4 Common Programming Errors

Three errors are frequently made when pointers to strings are used. The most common is using the pointer to "point to" a nonexistent data element. This error is, of course, the same error we have already seen using subscripts. C++ compilers do not perform bounds checking on arrays, so it is the programmer's responsibility to ensure that the address in the pointer is the address of a valid data element.

The second common error lies in not providing sufficient space for the string to be stored. A simple variation of this is not providing space for the end-of-string null character when a string is defined as an array of characters, and not including the `\0` character when the array is initialized. A more complicated variation of this error is declaring a character pointer, such as `char *p`, and then attempting to copy a string with a statement such as `strcpy(p, "Hello")`. Because no space has been allocated for the string, the string will overwrite the memory area pointed to by `p`.

The last commonly encountered error relates to a misunderstanding of terminology. For example, if text is defined as

```
char *text;
```

the variable `text` is sometimes referred to as a string. Thus the terminology "store the characters `Hooray for the Hoosiers` into the `text` string" may be encountered. Strictly speaking, calling `text` a string or a string variable is incorrect. The variable `text` is a pointer that contains the address of the first character in the string. Nevertheless, referring to a character pointer as a string occurs frequently enough that you should be aware of it.

9.5 Chapter Summary

1. A string is an array of characters that is terminated by the null character.
2. Strings can always be processed using standard array-processing techniques. The input and display of a string, however, always require reliance on a standard library function.
3. The `cin`, `cin.get()`, and `cin.getline()` routines can be used to input a string. The `cin` object tends to be of limited usefulness for string input because it terminates input when a blank is encountered.
4. The `cout` object can be used to display strings.
5. In place of subscripts, pointer notation and pointer arithmetic are especially useful for manipulating string elements.
6. Many standard library functions exist for processing strings as a complete unit. Internally, these functions manipulate strings in a character-by-character manner, generally using pointers.
7. String storage can be created by declaring an array of characters. It can also be created by declaring and initializing a pointer to a character.
8. Arrays can be initialized using a string assignment of the form

```
char *arr_name[ ] = "text";
```

This initialization is equivalent to

```
char *arr_name[ ] = {'t','e','x','t','\0'};
```

9. A pointer to a character can be assigned a string. String assignment to an array of characters is invalid except for initialization within a declaration statement.

9.6 Chapter Supplement: A String Data Type[2]

Although strings can be manipulated using both standard element-by-element array operations and string library functions, these techniques do have disadvantages. For example, there are no string assignment operators, and the defined array size inadvertently can be exceeded by both the `strcpy()` function and the `strcat()` function. Additionally, input of a string value terminates at the first blank character. Thus any string with an embedded space cannot be input as a string but requires the `cin.getline()` method.

The underlying cause of all these problems is that strings are not a unique data type. Rather, they are implemented as character arrays whose last value is the null, `'\0'`, character. Because C++ provides for user-defined data types, however, we can remove the disadvantages of processing strings as character arrays by using a suitably defined string data type. Fortunately, such a data type is provided as a template class (see Appendix I). In this section, we show how to access and use the features in this class.

From a user standpoint, we would expect a string data type to provide all of the processing currently available using both array element processing techniques and standard library functions, without any of the disadvantages. Thus, at a minimum, a string class should provide the following features:

1. Creation of a string variable
2. Initialization of a string variable using another string variable
3. Initialization of a string variable using a string literal

[2] Although it can be used here, the material in this section is more easily understood after the material in Chapter 11 is presented.

4. String length determination
5. An assignment operator, `=`, for assignment from a string variable to a string variable
6. An assignment operator, `=`, for assignment from a string literal to a string variable
7. A concatenation operator, `+`, for concatenation from a string variable to a string variable
8. A concatenation operator, `+`, for concatenation from a string literal to a string variable
9. An equality operator, `==`, for comparing two string variables to a string variable
10. An equality operator, `==`, for comparing a string literal to a string variable
11. An extraction operator, `>>`, for extracting strings that have embedded blank spaces from the `cin` standard input stream
12. An insertion operator, `<<`, for inserting strings into the `cout` standard output stream

The string class `basic_string` provides all of these operations. To incorporate this class into a program, we must use the header file `string`. Note that this header file is not appended with a `.h` suffix. (The reason for this is explained in Appendix H.) Program 9-10 uses this string class within the context of a working program. The program illustrates how variables can be declared as a data type of `string` and then how such variables can be copied, compared, concatenated, input, and manipulated in appropriate ways. Except for the initial `#include` statements, which are explained in Appendix H, the program is rather straightforward. The only terminology that may appear unfamiliar is the use of the word `object`, where the word `variable` would be more familiar. In object-oriented terms, a *variable* is an identifier declared using a language's built-in data types, such as `int`, `float`, and so on, whereas the term *object* is used instead for an identifier declared using a language's constructed data types, which is exactly what the string class is. If it makes it easier for you to understand, however, replace the word `object` in Program 9-10 with the word `variable`. Also note that the statement `getline(cin, string4);` is used to input a string into the `string4` object from the standard input stream, `cin`. The `getline()` function is an example of an overloaded function within the string class that permits entry of text data until a newline (`'\n'`) character is detected. Using this function permits entry of a string value with embedded white space.

Program 9-10

```
#include <iostream>   // see Appendix H for an
#include <string>     // explanation of these
using namespace std;  // three lines

int main()
{
  string string1 = "Hello World!";  // initialize with a string literal
  string string2 = string1;         // initialize with a string object
  string string3, string4;

  cout << "\n---- Test of object initializations ----" << endl;
  cout << "  string1, which was initialized by a string literal,\n"
       << "     has the value: " << string1 << endl;
  cout << "  string2, which was initialized by a string object,\n"
       << "     has the value: " << string2 << endl;
  cout << "  The string lengths of string1 through string4 are: "
       << string1.length() << ", " << string2.length() << ", "
       << string3.length() << ", and " << string4.length() << endl;

  cout << "\n---- Test of string input and output ----" << endl;
  cout << "  Enter a string to be assigned to string4: ";
  getline(cin, string4);
  cout << "  string4 is now: " << string4;
  cout << "\n  The length of this string is " << string4.length() << endl;

  cout << "\n---- Test of string assignment ----" << endl;
  string3 = string4;
  cout << "  After assigning string4 to string3, string3 is now:\n    "
       << string3 << endl;
  string4 = "test of a string literal";
  cout << " After assigning a string literal to string4, string4 is now:\n    "
       << string4 << endl;
  cout << "  The length of this string is: " << string4.length() << endl;

  cout << "\n---- Test of string concatenation ----" << endl;
  string3 = string3 + " " + string4;
  cout << "After concatenation, string3 is now: " << string3 << endl;

  cout << "\n---- Test of string comparison ----" << endl;
  if (string1 == string2)
    cout << "  string1 and string2 are equal" << endl;
  else
    cout << "  string1 and string2 are not equal" << endl;
  if (string3 == string4)
    cout << "  string3 and string4 are equal" << endl;
  else
    cout << "  string3 and string4 are not equal" << endl;

  return 0;
}
```

In reviewing Program 9-10, note that the only requirement in using the `basic_string` class is the inclusion of the interface header file `string`. A sample output produced by Program 9-10 is

```
---- Test of variable initializations ----
  string1, which was initialized by a string literal,
     has the value: Hello World!
  string2, which was initialized by a string variable,
     has the value: Hello World!
  The string lengths of string1 through string4 are: 12, 12, 0, and 0

---- Test of string input and output ----
  Enter a string to be assigned to string4: This is a test of
  string4 is now: This is a test of
  The length of this string is 17

---- Test of string assignment ----
  After assigning string4 to string3, string3 is now:
     This is a test of
  After assigning a string literal to string4, string4 is now:
     test of a string literal
  The length of this string is: 24

---- Test of string concatenation ----
After concatenation, string3 is now: This is a test of a string literal

---- Test of string comparison ----
  string1 and string2 are equal
  string3 and string4 are not equal
```

As this output shows, the demonstrated class operations work as expected.

Records as Data Structures

Chapter Ten

Name:
Street Address:
City:
State:
Zip Code:

FIGURE 10–1 Typical Mailing List Components

Name: Rhona Bronson-Karp
Street Address: 614 Freeman Street
City: Orange
State: NJ
Zip Code: 07052

FIGURE 10–2 The Form and Contents of a Record

An array makes it possible to access a list or table of data of the same data type by using a single variable name. At times, however, we may want to store information of varying types, such as a string name, an integer part number, and a real price, together in one structure. A data structure that stores different types of data under a single variable name is called a record.

To make this discussion more tangible, let's consider data items typically used in preparing mailing labels, as illustrated in Figure 10–1. Each of the individual data items listed in Figure 10–1 is an entity by itself that is referred to as a *data field*. Taken together, all the data fields form a single unit that is referred to as a *record*. In C++, a record is referred to as a *structure*.

Although there could be thousands of names and addresses in a complete mailing list, all the mailing labels are identical in form. In dealing with records, then, it is important to distinguish between a record's form and its contents.

A record's form consists of the symbolic names, data types, and arrangement of individual data fields in the record. The record's contents are the actual data stored in the symbolic names. Figure 10–2 shows acceptable contents for the record form illustrated in Figure 10–1.

In this chapter, we describe the C++ statements required to create, fill, use, and pass records between functions.

10.1 Single Records

To use a record, we need to carry out the same two steps needed for using any variable. First the record structure must be declared. Then specific values can be assigned to the individual record elements. Declaring a record requires listing the data types, data names, and arrangement of data items. For example, the definition

```
struct
{
  int month;
  int day;
  int year;
}  birth;
```

gives the form of a record structure called `birth` and reserves storage for the individual data items listed in the structure. The `birth` structure consists of three data items or fields, which are called *structure members.*

Assigning actual data values to the data items of a structure is referred to as *populating the structure,* and it is a relatively straightforward procedure. Each member of a structure is accessed by giving both the structure name and the individual data item name, separated by a period. Thus `birth.month` refers to the first member of the `birth` structure, `birth.day` refers to the second member of the structure, and `birth.year` refers to the third member. The period in each of these variable names is called the *member access operator* or the *dot operator* (the terms are used synonymously). Program 10-1 illustrates assigning values to the individual members of the `birth` structure.

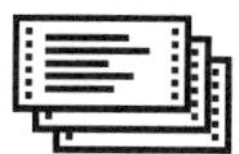

Program 10-1

```
// a program that defines and populates a record
#include <iostream.h>

int main()
{
  struct
  {
    int month;
    int day;
    int year;
  } birth;

  birth.month = 12;
  birth.day = 28;
  birth.year = 82;

  cout << "My birth date is "
       << birth.month << '/'
       << birth.day   << '/'
       << birth.year  << endl;

  return 0;
}
```

The output produced by Program 10-1 is

```
My birth date is 12/28/82
```

As in most C++ statements, the spacing of a structure definition is not rigid. For example, the `birth` structure could just as well have been defined as

```
struct {int month; int day; int year;} birth;
```

Also, as with all C++ definition statements, multiple variables can be defined in the same statement. For example, the definition statement

```
struct
{
  int month;
  int day;
  int year;
} birth, current;
```

creates two structure variables that have the same form. The members of the first structure are referenced by the individual names `birth.month`, `birth.day`, and `birth.year`, whereas the members of the second structure are referenced by the names `current.month`, `current.day`, and `current.year`. Note that the form of this particular structure definition statement is identical to that used in defining any program variable: The data type is followed by a list of variable names.

The most commonly used modification for defining structure types is listing the form of the structure with no following variable names. In this case, however, the list of structure members must be preceded by a user-selected data type name. For example, in the declaration

```
struct Date
{
  int month;
  int day;
  int year;
};
```

the term `Date` is a structure type name: It defines a new data type that is a data structure of the declared form.[1] By convention, the first letter of a user-selected data type name is uppercase, as in the name `Date`; this practice helps us identify them when they are used in subsequent definition statements. Here,

---

[1] For completeness, we should mention that a C++ structure can also be declared as a class with no member functions and all public data members. Similarly, a C++ class can be declared as a structure that has all private data members and all public member functions. Thus C++ provides two syntaxes for both structures and classes. The convention, however, is not to mix notations and always to use structures for creating record types and classes for providing true information and implementation hiding.

the declaration for the Date structure creates a new data type without actually reserving any storage locations. Thus it is not a definition statement. It simply declares a Date structure type and describes how individual data items are arranged within the structure. Actual storage for the members of the structure is reserved only when specific variable names are assigned. For example, the definition statement

```
Date birth, current;
```

reserves storage for two Date structure variables named birth and current, respectively. Each of these individual structures has the form previously declared for the Date structure.[2]

The declaration of a structure data type, like all declarations, may be global or local. Program 10-2 illustrates the global declaration of a Date data type. Internal to main(), the variable birth is defined as a local variable of Date type.

Program 10-2

```
#include <iostream.h>

struct Date  // this is a global declaration
{
  int month;
  int day;
  int year;
};

int main()
{
  Date birth;

  birth.month = 12;
  birth.day = 28;
  birth.year = 82;

  cout << "My birth date is "
       << birth.month << '/'
       << birth.day   << '/'
       << birth.year  << endl;

  return 0;
}
```

[2] The type name in C++ for this declaration is Date. In C, the type name would be struct Date and defining variables, such as birth and current, would be defined as struct Date birth, current;.

The output produced by Program 10-2 is identical to the output produced by Program 10-1.

The initialization of structures follows the same rules as the initialization of arrays: Global and local structures may be initialized by following the definition with a list of initializers. For example, the definition statement

```
Date birth = {12, 28, 82};
```

can be used to replace the first four statements internal to `main()` in Program 10-2. Note that the initializers are separated by commas, not semicolons.

The individual members of a structure are not restricted to integer data types, as in the `Date` structure. Any valid C++ data type can be used. For example, consider an employee record consisting of the following data items:

Name:
Identification Number:
Regular Pay Rate:
Overtime Pay Rate:

A suitable declaration for these data items is

```
struct PayRecord
{
  char name[20];
  int idNum;
  float regRate;
  float otRate;
};
```

Once the `PayRecord` data type is declared, a specific structure variable using this type can be defined and initialized. For example, the definition

```
PayRecord employee = {"H. Price",12387,15.89,25.50};
```

creates a structure named `employee` of the `PayRecord` data type. The individual members of `employee` are initialized with the respective data listed between braces in the definition statement.

Note that a single structure is simply a convenient method for combining and storing related items under a common name. Although a single structure is useful in explicitly identifying the relationship among its members, the individual members could be defined as separate variables. One of the real advantages of using structures is realized only when the same data type is used in a list many times over. Creating lists with the same data type is the topic of the next section.

Before we leave single structures, it is worth noting that the individual members of a structure can be any valid C++ data type, including both arrays and structures. An array of characters was used as a member of the `employee` structure defined previously. Accessing an element of a member array requires giving the structure's name, followed by a period, followed by the array designation. For example, `employee.name[4]` refers to the fifth character in the `employee.name` array.

To include a structure within a structure, we follow the same rules for including any data type in a structure. For example, assume that a structure is to consist of a name and a date of birth, where a `Date` structure has been declared as

```
struct Date
{
  int month;
  int date;
  int year;
};
```

A suitable definition of a structure that includes a name and a `Date` structure is

```
struct
{
  char name[20];
  Date birth;
} person;
```

In declaring the `Date` structure, note that the term `Date` is a data type name; thus it appears before the braces in the declaration statement. In defining the `person` structure variable, we note that `person` is a variable name; thus it is the name of a specific structure. The same is true of the variable named `birth`. This is the name of a specific `Date` structure. Individual members in the `person` structure are accessed by preceding the desired member with the structure name followed by a period. For example, `person.birth.month` refers to the `month` variable in the `birth` structure contained in the `person` structure.

Exercises 10.1

1. Declare a structure data type named `STemp` for each of the following records.
   a. A student record consisting of a student identification number, number of credits completed, and cumulative grade point average
   b. A student record consisting of a student's name, date of birth, number of credits completed, and cumulative grade point average

c. A mailing list consisting of the items illustrated in Figure 10–1
d. A stock record consisting of the stock's name, the price of the stock, and the date of purchase
e. An inventory record consisting of an integer part number, a part description, the number of parts in inventory, and an integer reorder number

2. For the individual data types declared in Exercise 1, define a suitable structure variable name, and initialize each structure with the following data.
   a. Identification Number: 4672
   Number of Credits Completed: 68
   Grade Point Average: 3.01
   b. Name: Rhona Karp
   Date of Birth: 8/4/1960
   Number of Credits Completed: 96
   Grade Point Average: 3.89
   c. Name: Kay Kingsley
   Street Address: 614 Freeman Street
   City: Indianapolis
   State: IN
   Zip Code: 07030
   d. Stock: IBM
   Price Purchased: 134.5
   Date Purchased: 10/1/86
   e. Part Number: 16879
   Description: Battery
   Number in Stock: 10
   Reorder Number: 3

3. *a.* Write a C++ program that prompts a user to input the current month, day, and year. Store the data entered in a suitably defined record, and display the date in an appropriate manner.
   b. Modify the program written in Exercise 3a to use a record that accepts the current time in hours, minutes, and seconds.

4. Write a C++ program that uses a structure for storing the name of a stock, its estimated earnings per share, and its estimated price-to-earnings ratio. Have the program prompt the user to enter these items for five different stocks, each time using the same structure to store the entered data. When the data has been entered for a particular stock, have the program compute and display the stock price anticipated on the basis of the entered earnings and price-per-share values. For example, if a user entered the data `XYZ 1.56 12`, the anticipated price for a share of XYZ stock would be `(1.56)*(12) = $18.72.`

5. Write a C++ program that accepts a user-entered time in hours and minutes. Have the program calculate and display the time 1 minute later.

6. *a.* Write a C++ program that accepts a user-entered date. Have the program calculate and display the date of the next day. For purposes of this exercise, assume that all months consist of 30 days.
   b. Modify the program written in Exercise 6a to account for the actual number of days in each month.

POINT OF INFORMATION

Homogeneous and Heterogeneous Data Structures

Both arrays and records are structured data types. The difference between these two data structures is the types of elements they contain. An array is a *homogeneous* data structure, which means that each of its components must be of the same data type. A record is a *heterogeneous* data structure, which means that its components can be of different data types. Thus an array of records would be a homogeneous data structure whose elements are of the same heterogeneous type.

10.2 Arrays of Records

The real power of structures is realized when the same structure is used for lists of data. For example, assume that the data shown in Figure 10–3 must be processed. Clearly, the employee numbers can be stored together in an array of integers, the names in an array of pointers, and the pay rates in an array of either floating-point or double-precision numbers. In organizing the data in this fashion, we consider each column in Figure 10–3 as a separate list, which is stored in its own array. The correspondence between items for each individual employee is maintained by storing an employee's data in the same array position in each array.

The separation of the complete list into three individual arrays is unfortunate, because all of the items related to a single employee constitute a natural organization of data into records, as illustrated in Figure 10–4. Using a structure, we can make the program maintain and reflect the integrity of the data organization as a record. Under this approach, the list illustrated in Figure 10–4 can be processed as a single array of ten structures.

FIGURE 10–3 A List of Employee Data

Employee Number	Employee Name	Employee Pay Rate
32479	Abrams, B.	6.72
33623	Bohm, P.	7.54
34145	Donaldson, S.	5.56
35987	Ernst, T.	5.43
36203	Gwodz, K.	8.72
36417	Hanson, H.	7.64
37634	Monroe, G.	5.29
38321	Price, S.	9.67
39435	Robbins, L.	8.50
39567	Williams, B.	7.20

	Employee Number	Employee Name	Employee Pay Rate
1st record ⟶	32479	Abrams, B.	6.72
2nd record ⟶	33623	Bohm, P.	7.54
3rd record ⟶	34145	Donaldson, S.	5.56
4th record ⟶	35987	Ernst, T.	5.43
5th record ⟶	36203	Gwodz, K.	8.72
6th record ⟶	36417	Hanson, H.	7.64
7th record ⟶	37634	Monroe, G.	5.29
8th record ⟶	38321	Price, S.	9.67
9th record ⟶	39435	Robbins, L.	8.50
10th record ⟶	39567	Williams, B.	7.20

FIGURE 10–4 A List of Records

Declaring an array of structures is the same as declaring an array of any other variable type. For example, if the data type `PayRecord` is declared as

```
struct PayRecord
{
  int idNum;
  char name[20];
  float rate;
};
```

then an array of ten such structures can be defined as

```
PayRecord employee[10];
```

This definition statement constructs an array of ten elements, each of which is a structure of the data type `PayRecord`. Note that the creation of an array of ten structures has the same form as the creation of any other array. For example, creating an array of ten integers named `employee` requires the declaration

```
int employee[10];
```

In this declaration the data type is integer, whereas in the former declaration for `employee`, the data type is `PayRecord`.

Once an array of structures is declared, a particular data item is referenced by giving the position of the desired structure in the array, followed by a period and the appropriate structure member. For example, the variable `employee[0].rate` refers to the `rate` member of the first `employee` structure in the `employee` array. Including structures as elements of an array makes it possible to process a list of records using standard array programming techniques. Program 10-3 displays the first five employee records illustrated in Figure 10-4.

Program 10-3

```
#include <iostream.h>
#include <iomanip.h>

const int MAXNAME = 20;  // maximum characters in a name
const int NUMRECS = 5;   // maximum number of records

struct PayRecord   // this is a global declaration
{
  long id;
  char name[MAXNAME];
  float rate;
};

int main()
{
  int i;
  PayRecord employee[NUMRECS] = {
                                { 32479, "Abrams, B.", 6.72 },
                                { 33623, "Bohm, P.", 7.54},
                                { 34145, "Donaldson, S.",  5.56},
                                { 35987, "Ernst, T.", 5.43 },
                                { 36203, "Gwodz, K.", 8.72 }
                                };

  cout << endl;   // start on a new line
  cout << setiosflags(ios::left);  // left justify the output
  for ( i = 0; i < NUMRECS; i++)
    cout << setw(7)  << employee[i].id
         << setw(15) << employee[i].name
         << setw(6)  << employee[i].rate << endl;

  return 0;
}
```

The output displayed by Program 10-3 is

```
32479  Abrams, B.       6.72
33623  Bohm, P.         7.54
34145  Donaldson, S.    5.56
35987  Ernst, T.        5.43
36203  Gwodz, K.        8.72
```

In reviewing Program 10-3, note the initialization of the array of structures. Although the initializers for each structure have been enclosed in inner braces, these are not strictly necessary because all members have been initialized. As with all external and static variables, in the absence of explicit initializers, the numeric elements of both static and external arrays or structures are initialized to zero, and their character elements are initialized to nulls. The `setiosflags(ios::left)` manipulator included in the `cout` object stream forces each name to be displayed left-justified in its designated field width.

Exercises 10.2

1. Define arrays of 100 structures for each of the data types described in Exercise 1 of the previous section.

2. ***a.*** Using the data type

```
struct DaysInMonth
{
  char name[10];
  int days;
};
```

define an array of 12 structures of type `DaysInMonth`. Name the array `convert[]`, and initialize the array with the names of the 12 months in a year and the number of days in each month.

b. Include the array created in Exercise 2a in a program that displays the name of, and the number of days in, each month.

3. Using the data type declared in Exercise 2a, write a C++ program that accepts a month from a user in numeric form and displays the name of the month and the number of days in the month. Thus, in response to an input of `3`, the program would display `March has 31 days.`

4. ***a.*** Declare a single-structure data type suitable for an employee record of the type illustrated:

Number	Name	Rate	Hours
3462	Jones	4.62	40
6793	Robbins	5.83	38
6985	Smith	5.22	45
7834	Swain	6.89	40
8867	Timmins	6.43	35
9002	Williams	4.75	42

b. Using the data type declared in Exercise 4a, write a C++ program that interactively accepts the above data into an array of six structures. Once the data have been entered, the program should create a payroll report listing each employee's name, number, and gross pay. Include the total gross pay of all employees at the end of the report.

5. *a.* Declare a single-structure data type suitable for a car record of the type illustrated below:

Car Number	Miles Driven	Gallons Used
25	1,450	62
36	3,240	136
44	1,792	76
52	2,360	105
68	2,114	67

b. Using the data type declared for Exercise 5a, write a C++ program that interactively accepts the above data into an array of five structures. Once the data have been entered, the program should create a report listing each car number and the miles per gallon achieved by the car. At the end of the report include the average miles per gallon achieved by the complete fleet of cars.

10.3 Record Structures as Function Arguments

Individual structure members may be passed to a function in the same manner as any scalar variable. For example, given the structure definition

```
struct
{
  int idNum;
  double payRate;
  double hours;
} emp;
```

the statement

```
display(emp.idNum);
```

passes a copy of the structure member `emp.idNum` to a function named `display()`. Similarly, the statement

```
calcPay(emp.payRate,emp.hours);
```

passes copies of the values stored in structure members `emp.payRate` and `emp.hours` to the function `calcPay()`. Both functions, `display()` and `calcPay`, must declare the correct data types of their respective parameters.

Complete copies of all members of a structure can also be passed to a function by including the name of the structure as an argument to the called function. For example, the function call

```
calcNet(emp);
```

passes a copy of the complete `emp` structure to `calcNet()`. Internal to `calcNet()`, an appropriate declaration must be made to receive the structure. Program 10-4 declares a global data type for an employee record. This type is then used by both the `main()` and the `calcNet()` functions to define specific structures with the names `emp` and `temp`, respectively.

The output produced by Program 10-4 is

```
The net pay for employee 6782 is $361.66
```

In reviewing Program 10-4, observe that both `main()` and `calcNet()` use the same data type to define their individual structure variables. The structure variable defined in `main()` and the structure variable defined in `calcNet()` are two completely different structures. Any changes made to the local `temp` variable in `calcNet()` are not reflected in the `emp` variable of `main()`. In fact, because both structure variables are local to their respective functions, the same structure variable name could have been used in both functions with no ambiguity.

When `calcNet()` is called by `main()`, copies of `emp`'s structure values are passed to the `temp` structure. `calcNet()` then uses two of the passed member values to calculate a number, which is returned to `main()`.

Program 10-4

```
#include <iostream.h>
#include <iomanip.h>

struct Employee        // declare a global type
{
  int idNum;
  double payRate;
  double hours;
};

double calcNet(Employee);    // function prototype

int main()
{
  Employee emp = {6782, 8.93, 40.5};
  double netPay;

  netPay = calcNet(emp);       // pass copies of the values in emp

    // set output formats
  cout << setw(10)
       << setiosflags(ios::fixed)
       << setiosflags(ios::showpoint)
       << setprecision(2);

  cout << "The net pay for employee " << emp.idNum
       << " is $" << netPay << endl;

  return 0;
}

double calcNet(Employee temp) // temp is of data type Employee
{
  return (temp.payRate * temp.hours);
}
```

An alternative to the pass by value function call illustrated in Program 10-4, in which the called function receives a copy of a structure, is a pass by reference that passes a reference to a structure. This permits the called function to directly access and alter values in the calling function's structure variable. For example, referring to Program 10-4, the prototype of `calcNet()` can be modified to

```
double calcNet(Employee &);
```

If this function prototype is used and the `calcNet()` header line is rewritten to conform to it, the `main()` function in Program 10-4 may be used as is. Program 10-4a illustrates these changes within the context of a complete program.

Program 10-4a

```
#include <iostream.h>
#include <iomanip.h>

struct Employee        // declare a global type
{
  int idNum;
  double payRate;
  double hours;
};

double calcNet(Employee &);   // function prototype

int main()
{
  Employee emp = {6782, 8.93, 40.5};
  double netPay;

  netPay = calcNet(emp);        // pass a reference

    // set output formats
  cout << setw(10)
       << setiosflags(ios::fixed)
       << setiosflags(ios::showpoint)
       << setprecision(2);

  cout << "The net pay for employee " << emp.idNum
       << " is $" << netPay << endl;

  return 0;
}

double calcNet(Employee& temp)   // temp is a reference variable
{
  return (temp.payRate * temp.hours);
}
```

Program 10-4a produces the same output as Program 10-4, except that the `calcNet()` function in Program 10-4a receives direct access to the `emp` structure rather than a copy of it. This means that the variable name `temp` within `calcNet()` is an alternative name for the variable `emp` in `main()`, and any changes to `temp` are direct changes to `emp`. Although the same function call, `calcNet(emp)`, is made in both programs, the call in Program 10-4a passes a reference, whereas the call in Program 10-4 passes values.

Passing a Pointer

Instead of passing a reference, we can use a pointer. Using a pointer requires that we modify the function's prototype and header line and also that the call to `calcNet()` in Program 10-4 be modified to

```
calcNet(&emp);
```

Here the function call clearly indicates that an address is being passed (which is not the case in Program 10-4a). The disadvantage, however, is in the dereferencing notation required internal to the function. However, pointers are widely used in practice, so it is worthwhile to become familiar with the notation used.

To store the passed address, `calcNet()` must declare its parameter as a pointer. A suitable function definition for `calcNet()` is

```
calcNet(Employee *pt)
```

Here, the declaration for `pt` declares this parameter as a pointer to a structure of type `Employee`. The pointer `pt` receives the starting address of a structure whenever `calcNet()` is called. Within `calcNet()`, this pointer is used to access any member in the structure. For example, `(*pt).idNum` refers to the `idNum` member of the structure, `(*pt).payRate` refers to the `payRate` member of the structure, and `(*pt).hours` refers to the `hours` member of the structure. These relationships are illustrated in Figure 10–5.

The parentheses around the expression `*pt` in Figure 10–5 are necessary to access initially "the structure whose address is in `pt`." This is followed by an identifier to access the desired member within the structure. In the absence of the parentheses, the structure member operator `.` takes precedence over the indirection operator. Thus the expression `*pt.hours` is another way of writing `*(pt.hours)`, which would refer to "the variable whose address is in the `pt.hours` variable." This last expression clearly makes no sense, because there is no structure named `pt` and `hours` does not contain an address.

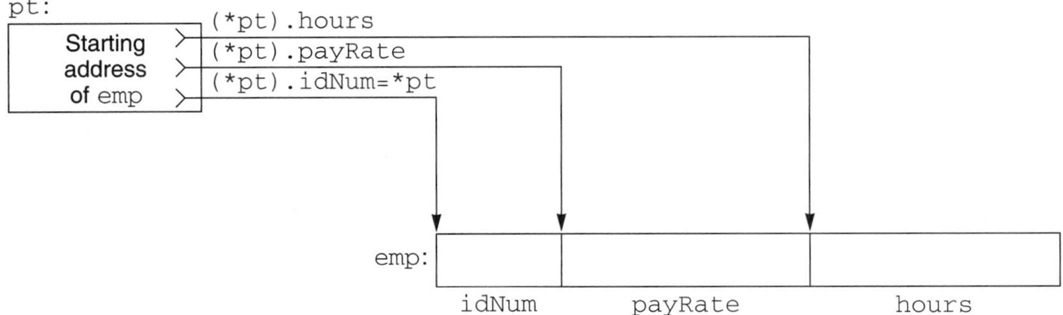

FIGURE 10–5 A Pointer Can Be Used to Access Structure Members

As illustrated in Figure 10–5, the starting address of the `emp` structure is also the address of the first member of the structure.

The use of pointers in this manner is so common that a special notation exists for it. The general expression *`(*pointer).member`* can always be replaced with the notation *`pointer->member`*, where the `->` operator is constructed using a minus sign followed by a right-facing arrow (greater-than symbol). Either expression can be used to locate the desired member. For example, the following expressions are equivalent:

`(*pt).idNum`	can be replaced by	`pt->idNum`
`(*pt).payRate`	can be replaced by	`pt->payRate`
`(*pt).hours`	can be replaced by	`pt->hours`

Program 10-5 illustrates passing a structure's address and using a pointer with the new notation to reference the structure directly.

The name of the pointer parameter declared in Program 10-5 is, of course, selected by the programmer. When `calcNet()` is called, `emp`'s starting address is passed to the function. Using this address as a starting point, individual members of the structure are accessed by including their names with the pointer.

As with all C++ expressions that access a variable, the increment and decrement operators can also be applied to them. For example, the expression

```
++pt->hours
```

adds one to the `hours` member of the `emp` structure. Because the `->` operator has a higher priority than the increment operator, the `hours` member is accessed first and then the increment is applied.

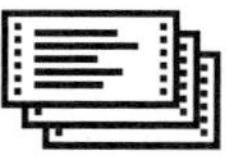

Program 10-5

```
#include <iostream.h>
#include <iomanip.h>

struct Employee    // declare a global type
{
  int idNum;
  double payRate;
  double hours;
};

double calcNet(Employee *);    //function prototype

int main()
{
  Employee emp = {6782, 8.93, 40.5};
  double netPay;

  netPay = calcNet(&emp);        // pass an address

     // set output formats
  cout << setw(10)
       << setiosflags(ios::fixed)
       << setiosflags(ios::showpoint)
       << setprecision(2);

  cout << "The net pay for employee " << emp.idNum
       << " is $" << netPay << endl;

  return 0;
}

double calcNet(Employee *pt)    // pt is a pointer to a
{                               // structure of Employee type
  return (pt->payRate * pt->hours);
}
```

Alternatively, the expression `(++pt)->hours` uses the prefix increment operator to increment the address in `pt` before the `hours` member is accessed. Similarly, the expression `(pt++)->hours` uses the postfix increment operator to increment the address in `pt` after the `hours` member is accessed. In both of these cases, however, there must be enough defined structures to ensure that the incremented pointers actually point to legitimate structures.

As an example, Figure 10–6 illustrates an array of three structures of type `employee`. Assuming that the address of `emp[1]` is stored in the pointer variable `pt`, the expression `++pt` changes the address in `pt` to the starting address of `emp[2]`, whereas the expression `--pt` changes the address to point to `emp[0]`.

Returning Structures

In practice, most structure-handling functions receive direct access to a structure by receiving a structure reference or address. Then any changes to the structure can be made directly from within the function. If you want to have a function return a separate structure, however, you must follow the same procedures for returning complete data structures as for returning scalar values. These procedures include declaring the function appropriately and alerting any calling function to the type of data structure being returned. For example, the function `getValues()` in Program 10-6 returns a complete structure to `main()`.

The following output is displayed when Program 10-6 is run:

```
The employee id number is 6789
The employee pay rate is $16.25
The employee hours are 38
```

FIGURE 10–6 Changing Pointer Addresses

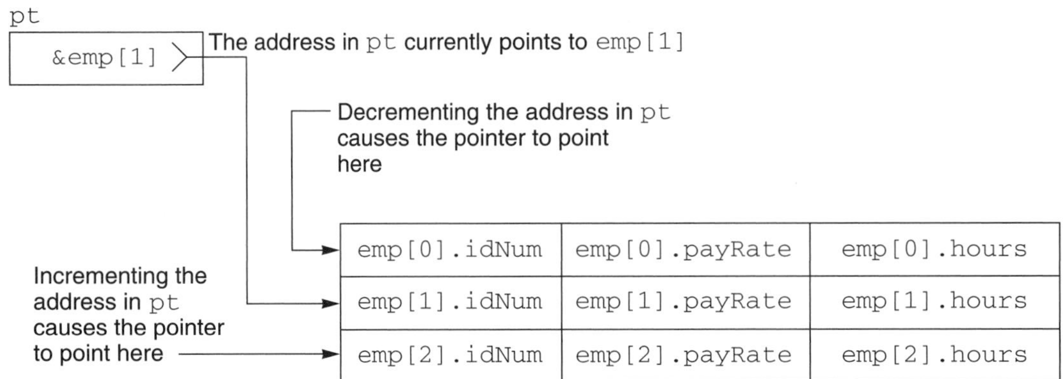

Program 10-6

```
#include <iostream.h>
#include <iomanip.h>

struct Employee       // declare a global type
{
  int idNum;
  double payRate;
  double hours;
};

struct Employee getValues();   // function prototype

int main()
{
  Employee emp;

  emp = getValues();
  cout << "\nThe employee id number is " << emp.idNum
       << "\nThe employee pay rate is $" << emp.payRate
       << "\nThe employee hours are " << emp.hours << endl;

  return 0;
}

struct Employee getValues() // return an employee structure
{
  Employee next;

  next.idNum = 6789;
  next.payRate = 16.25;
  next.hours = 38.0;

  return(next);
}
```

The `getValues()` function returns a structure, so the function header for `getValues()` must specify the type of structure being returned. Because `getValues()` does not receive any arguments, the function header has no parameter declarations and consists of the line

```
Employee getValues();
```

Within `getValues()`, the variable `next` is defined as a structure of the type to be returned. After values have been assigned to the `next` structure, the structure values are returned by including the structure name within the parentheses of the `return` statement.

On the receiving side, `main()` must be alerted that the function `getValues()` will be returning a structure. This is handled by including a function declaration for `getValues()` in `main()`. Note that these steps for returning a structure from a function are identical to the normal procedures, described in Chapter 6, for returning scalar data types.

Exercises 10.3

1. Write a C++ function named `days()` that determines the number of days since January 1, 1900 for any date passed as a structure. Use the `Date` structure

```
struct Date
{
  int month;
  int day;
  int year;
};
```

In writing the `days()` function, use the convention that all years have 360 days and each month consists of 30 days. The function should return the number of days for any `Date` structure passed to it. Make sure you declare the returned variable a long integer to reserve sufficient room for converting dates such as 12/19/2002.

2. Write a C++ function named `difDays()` that calculates and returns the difference between two dates. Each date is passed to the function as a structure using the following global type:

```
struct Date
{
  int month;
  int day;
  int year;
};
```

The `difDays()` function should make two calls to the `days()` function written for Exercise 1.

3. *a.* Rewrite the `days()` function written for Exercise 1 to receive a reference to a `Date` structure, rather than a copy of the complete structure.
   b. Redo Exercise 3a, using a pointer rather than a reference.

4. *a.* Write a C++ function named `larger()` that returns the later of any two dates passed to it. For example, if the dates 10/9/1999 and 11/3/1999 were passed to `larger()`, the second date would be returned.
   b. Include the `larger()` function that was written for Exercise 4a in a complete program. Store the `Date` structure returned by `larger()` in a separate `Date` structure and display the member values of the returned `Date`.
5. *a.* Modify the function `days()` written for Exercise 1 to account for the actual number of days in each month. Assume, however, that each year contains 365 days (that is, do not account for leap years).
   b. Modify the function written for Exercise 5a to account for leap years.

10.4 Linked Lists

A classic data-handling problem is making additions or deletions to existing records that are maintained in a specific order. This is best illustrated by considering the alphabetical telephone list shown in Figure 10–7. Starting with this initial set of names and telephone numbers, we want to add new records to the list in the proper alphabetical sequence and to delete existing records in such a way that the storage for deleted records is eliminated.

Although the insertion or deletion of ordered records can be accomplished by using an array of structures, these arrays are not efficient representations for adding or deleting records internal to the array. Arrays are fixed and prespecified in size.

Deleting a record from an array creates an empty slot that requires either special marking or shifting up of all elements below the deleted record to close

FIGURE 10–7 A Telephone List in Alphabetical Order

Acme, Sam
(555) 898-2392

Dolan, Edith
(555) 682-3104

Lanfrank, John
(555) 718-4581

Mening, Stephen
(555) 382-7070

Zemann, Harold
(555) 219-9912

the empty slot. Similarly, adding a record to the body of an array of structures requires that all elements below the addition be shifted down to make room for the new entry; alternatively, the new element can be added to the bottom of the existing array and the array then resorted to restore the proper order of the records. Thus, either adding records to or deleting records from such a list generally requires restructuring and rewriting the list—a cumbersome, time-consuming, and inefficient practice.

A linked list provides a convenient method for maintaining a constantly changing list without the need to reorder and restructure the complete list continually. A *linked list* is simply a set of structures in which each structure contains at least one member whose value is the address of the next logically ordered structure in the list. Rather than each record having to be physically stored in the proper order, each new record is physically added wherever the computer has free space in its storage area. The records are "linked" together by including the address of the next record in the record immediately preceding it. From a programming standpoint, the record currently being processed contains the address of the next record, no matter where the next record is actu- ally stored.

The concept of a linked list is illustrated in Figure 10–8. Although the actual data for the Lanfrank structure illustrated in the figure may be physically stored anywhere in the computer, the additional member included at the end of the Dolan structure maintains the proper alphabetical order. This member provides the starting address of the location where the Lanfrank record is stored. As you might expect, this member is a pointer.

To see the usefulness of the pointer in the Dolan record, let us add a telephone number for June Hagar into the alphabetical list shown in Figure 10–7. The data for June Hagar is stored in a data structure by using the same type as that used for the existing records. To ensure that the telephone number for Hagar is correctly displayed after the Dolan telephone number, we must alter the address in the Dolan record to point to the Hagar record, and the address in the Hagar record must be set to point to the Lanfrank record. This is illustrated in Figure 10–9. Note that the pointer in each structure simply points to the location of the next ordered structure, even if that structure is not physically located in the correct order.

FIGURE 10–8 Using Pointers to Link Structures

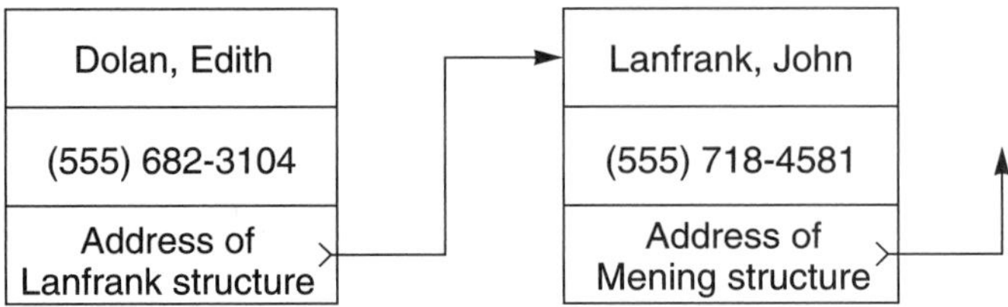

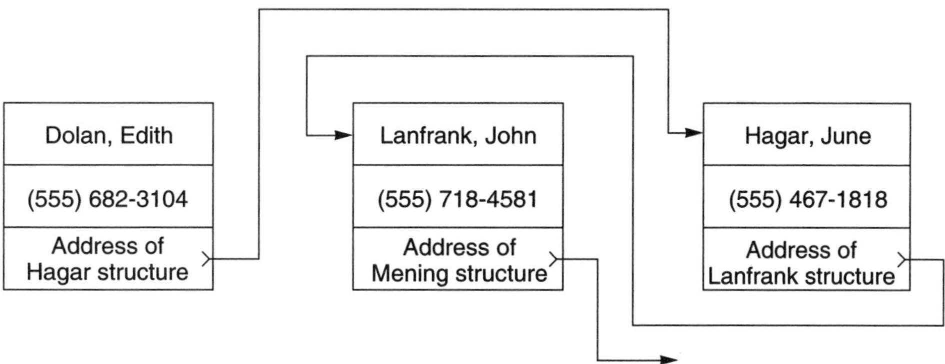

FIGURE 10–9 Adjusting Addresses to Point to Appropriate Records

Removal of a structure from the ordered list is the reverse process of adding a record. The actual record is logically removed from the list by simply changing the address in the structure preceding it to point to the structure that immediately follows the deleted record.

All structures in a linked list have the same format; however, it is clear that the last record cannot have a valid pointer value that points to another record, because there is none. C++ provides a special pointer value called `NULL` that acts as a sentinel, or flag, to indicate when the last record has been processed. The `NULL` pointer value, like its end-of-string counterpart, has a numerical value of zero.

Besides a pointer to act as an end-of-list sentinel value, a special pointer must also be provided for storing the address of the first structure in the list. Figure 10–10 illustrates the complete set of pointers and structures for a list consisting of three names.

The inclusion of a pointer in a structure should not be surprising. As we discovered in Section 10.1, a structure can contain any C++ data type. For example, the structure declaration

FIGURE 10–10 Use of the Initial and Final Pointer Values

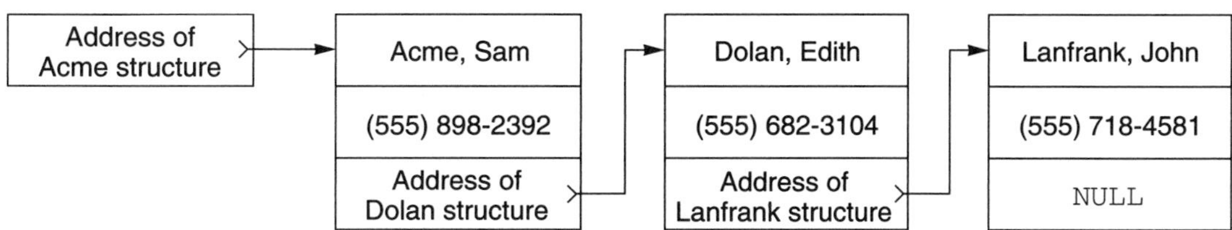

```
struct Test
{
  int idNum;
  double *ptrPay
};
```

declares a structure type that consists of two members. The first member is an integer variable named `idNum`, and the second variable is a pointer named `ptrPay`, which is a pointer to a double-precision number. Program 10-7 illustrates that the pointer member of a structure is used like any other pointer variable.

Program 10-7

```
#include <iostream.h>
#include <iomanip.h>

struct Test
{
  int idNum;
  double *ptrPay;
};

int main()
{
  Test emp;
  double pay = 456.20;

  emp.idNum = 12345;
  emp.ptrPay = &pay;

  // set output formats
cout << setw(6)
     << setiosflags(ios::fixed)
     << setiosflags(ios::showpoint)
     << setprecision(2);

  cout << "\nEmployee number " << emp.idNum << " was paid $"
       << *emp.ptrPay << endl;

  return 0;
}
```

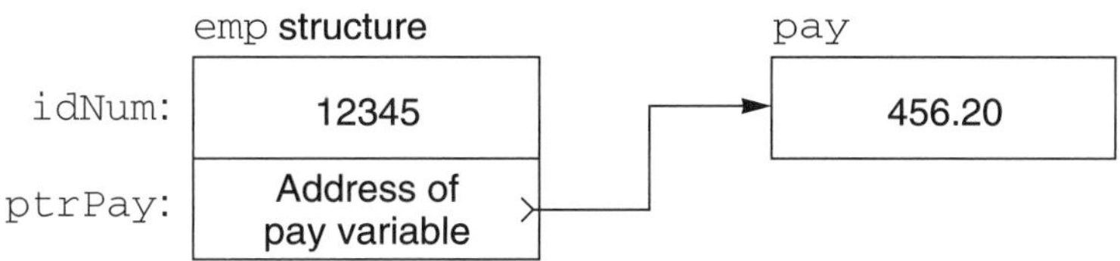

FIGURE 10–11 Storing an Address in a Structure Member

The output produced by executing Program 10-7 is

```
Employee number 12345 was paid $456.20
```

Figure 10–11 illustrates the relationship between the members of the `emp` structure defined in Program 10-7 and the variable named `pay`. The value assigned to `emp.idNum` is the number 12345 and the value assigned to `pay` is 456.20. The address of the `pay` variable is assigned to the structure member `emp.ptrPay`. This member has been defined as a pointer to a double-precision number, so placing the address of the double-precision variable `pay` in it is a correct use of this member. Finally, because the member operator `.` has a higher precedence than the indirection operator `*`, the expression used in the `cout` statement in Program 10-7 is correct. The expression `*emp.ptrPay` is equivalent to the expression `*(emp.ptrPay)`, which is translated as "the variable whose address is contained in the member `emp.ptrPay`."

Although the pointer defined in Program 10-7 has been used in a rather trivial fashion, the program does illustrate the concept of including a pointer in a structure. This concept can be easily extended to create a linked list of structures suitable for storing the names and telephone numbers listed in Figure 10–7. The following declaration creates a type for such a structure:

```
struct TeleType
{
  char name[30];
  char phoneNo[15];
  TeleType *nextaddr;
};
```

The `TeleType` type consists of three members. The first member is an array of 30 characters, suitable for storing names with a maximum of 29 letters and an end-of-string `NULL` marker. The next member is an array of 15 characters, suitable for storing telephone numbers with their respective area codes. The last member is a pointer suitable for storing the address of a structure of the `TeleType` type.

Program 10-8 illustrates the use of the `TeleType` type by specifically defining three structures that have this form. The three structures are named `t1`, `t2`, and `t3`, and the name and telephone members of each of these structures are initialized when the structures are defined, using the data listed in Figure 10–7.

Program 10-8

```
#include <iostream.h>

const int MAXNAME = 30; // maximum no. of characters in a name
const int MAXTEL = 15;  // maximum no. of characters in a telephone number

struct TeleType
{
  char name[MAXNAME];
  char phoneNo[MAXTEL];
  TeleType *nextaddr;
};

int main()
{
  TeleType t1 = {"Acme, Sam","(555) 898-2392"};
  TeleType t2 = {"Dolan, Edith","(555) 682-3104"};
  TeleType t3 = {"Lanfrank, John","(555) 718-4581"};
  TeleType *first;      // create a pointer to a structure

  first = &t1;          // store t1's address in first
  t1.nextaddr = &t2;    // store t2's address in t1.nextaddr
  t2.nextaddr = &t3;    // store t3's address in t2.nextaddr
  t3.nextaddr = NULL;   // store the NULL address in t3.nextaddr

  cout << '\n' << first->name
       << '\n' << t1.nextaddr->name
       << '\n' << t2.nextaddr->name
       << endl;

  return 0;
}
```

The output produced by executing Program 10-8 is

```
Acme, Sam
Dolan, Edith
Lanfrank, John
```

Program 10-8 demonstrates the use of pointers to access successive structure members. As illustrated in Figure 10–12, each structure contains the address of the next structure in the list.

The initialization of the names and telephone numbers for each of the structures defined in Program 10-8 is straightforward. Although each structure consists of three members, only the first two members of each structure are initialized. Both of these members are arrays of characters, so they can be initialized with strings. The remaining member of each structure is a pointer. To

FIGURE 10–12 The Relationship Between Structures in Program 10-8

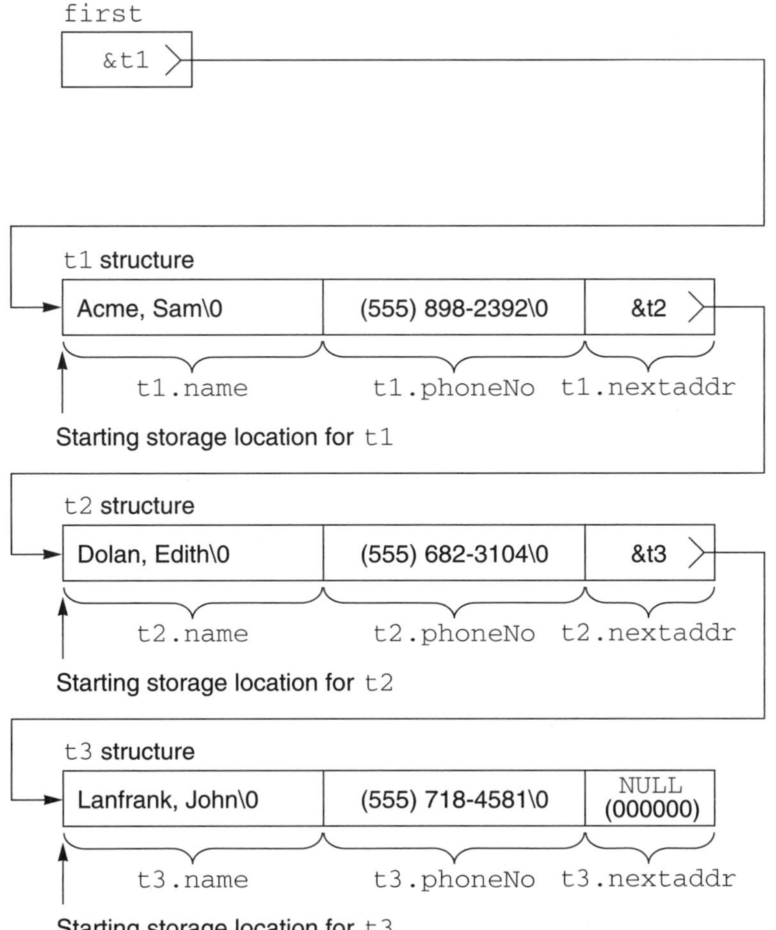

create a linked list, each structure pointer must be assigned the address of the next structure in the list.

The four assignment statements in Program 10-8 perform the correct assignments. The expression `first = &t1` stores the address of the first structure in the list in the pointer variable named `first`. The expression `t1.nextaddr = &t2` stores the starting address of the `t2` structure into the pointer member of the `t1` structure. Similarly, the expression `t2.nextaddr = &t3` stores the starting address of the `t3` structure into the pointer member of the `t2` structure. To end the list, the value of the `NULL` pointer, which is zero, is stored into the pointer member of the `t3` structure.

Once values have been assigned to each structure member and correct addresses have been stored in the appropriate pointers, the addresses in the pointers are used to access each structure's name member. For example, the expression `t1.nextaddr->name` refers to the `name` member of the structure whose address is in the `nextaddr` member of the `t1` structure. The precedence of the member operator `.` and that of the structure pointer operator `->` are equal and are evaluated from left to right. Thus the expression `t1.nextaddr->name` is evaluated as `(t1.nextaddr)->name`. Because `t1.nextaddr` contains the address of the `t2` structure, the proper name is accessed.[3]

The addresses in a linked list of structures can be used to loop through the complete list. As each structure is accessed, it can be either examined to select a specific value or used to print out a complete list. For example, the `display()` function in Program 10-9 illustrates the use of a `while` loop, which uses the address in each structure's pointer member to cycle through the list and successively display data stored in each structure.

The output produced by Program 10-9 is

```
Acme, Sam                (555) 898-2392
Dolan, Edith             (555) 682-3104
Lanfrank, John           (555) 718-4581
```

The important concept illustrated by Program 10-9 is the use of the address in one structure to access members of the next structure in the list. When the `display()` function is called, it is passed the value stored in the variable named `first`. Because `first` is a pointer variable, the actual value passed is an address (the address of the `t1` structure). `display()` accepts the passed value in the argument named `contents`. To store the passed address correctly, `contents` is declared as a pointer to a structure of the `TeleType` type. Within `display()`,

---

[3] The expression `t1.nextaddr->name` can, of course, be replaced by the equivalent expression `(*t1.nextaddr).name`, which uses the more conventional indirection operator. This expression also refers to "the `name` member of the variable whose address is in `t1.nextaddr`."

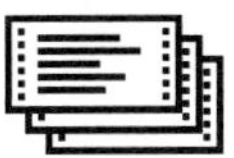

Program 10-9

```
#include <iostream.h>
#include <iomanip.h>

const int MAXNAME = 20; // maximum no. of characters in a name
const int MAXTEL = 15;  // maximum no. of characters in a telephone number

struct TeleType
{
  char name[MAXNAME];
  char phoneNo[MAXTEL];
  TeleType *nextaddr;
};

void display(TeleType *);    // function prototype

int main()
{
  TeleType t1 = {"Acme, Sam","(555) 898-2392"};
  TeleType t2 = {"Dolan, Edith","(555) 682-3104"};
  TeleType t3 = {"Lanfrank, John","(555) 718-4581"};
  TeleType *first;     // create a pointer to a structure

  first = &t1;         // store t1's address in first
  t1.nextaddr = &t2;   // store t2's address in t1.nextaddr
  t2.nextaddr = &t3;   // store t3's address in t2.nextaddr
  t3.nextaddr = NULL;  // store the NULL address in t3.nextaddr

  display(first);      // send the address of the first structure

  return 0;
}

void display(TeleType *contents) // contents is a pointer to a structure
{                                // of type TeleType
  while (contents != NULL)      // display till end of linked list
  {
    cout << '\n' << setiosflags(ios::left)
                 << setw(30) << contents->name
                 << setw(20) << contents->phoneNo ;
    contents = contents->nextaddr;      // get next address
  }
  cout << endl;

  return;
}
```

a `while` loop is used to cycle through the linked structures, starting with the structure whose address is in `contents`. The condition tested in the `while` statement compares the value in `contents`, which is an address, to the `NULL` value. For each valid address, the name and phone number members of the addressed structure are displayed. The address in `contents` is then updated with the address in the pointer member of the current structure. The address in `contents` is then retested, and the process continues while the address in `contents` is not equal to the `NULL` value. `display()` "knows" nothing about the names of the structures declared in `main()` or even how many structures exist. It simply cycles through the linked list, structure by structure, until it encounters the end-of-list `NULL` address. The value of `NULL` is zero, so the tested condition can be replaced by the equivalent expression `contents`.

A disadvantage of Program 10-9 is that exactly three structures are defined in `main()` by name, and storage for them is reserved at compile time. Should a fourth structure be required, the additional structure would have to be declared and the program recompiled. In the next section, we show how to have the program dynamically allocate and release storage for structures at run time, as storage is required. Only when a new structure is to be added to the list, and while the program is running, is storage for the new structure created. Similarly, when a structure is no longer needed and can be deleted from the list, the storage for the deleted record is relinquished and returned to the computer.

Exercises 10.4

1. Modify Program 10-9 to prompt the user for a name. Have the program search the existing list for the entered name. If the name is in the list, display the corresponding phone number; otherwise, display this message: `The name is not in the current phone directory.`

2. Write a C++ program containing a linked list of ten integer numbers. Have the program display the numbers in the list.

3. Using the linked list of structures illustrated in Figure 10–12, write the sequence of steps necessary to delete the record for Edith Dolan from the list.

4. Generalize the description obtained in Exercise 3 to describe the sequence of steps necessary to remove the *n*th structure from a list of linked structures. The *n*th structure is preceded by the $(n - 1)$st structure and followed by the $(n + 1)$st structure. Be sure to store all pointer values correctly.

5. a. A doubly linked list is a list in which each structure contains a pointer to both the following and the previous structures in the list. Define an appropriate type for a doubly linked list of names and telephone numbers.

b. Using the type defined in Exercise 5a, modify Program 10-9 to list the names and phone numbers in reverse order.

10.5 Dynamic Structure Allocation

We have already encountered the concept of explicitly allocating and deallocating memory space using the `new` and `delete` operators (see Section 8.2). For convenience, the descriptions of these operators are repeated in Table 10–1.

TABLE 10–1 Memory Allocation and Deallocation Operators

Operator Name	Description
`new`	Reserves the number of bytes required by the requested data type. Returns the address of the first reserved location or returns `NULL` if sufficient memory is not available.
`delete`	Releases a block of bytes previously reserved. The address of the first reserved location is passed as an argument to the function.

This dynamic allocation of memory is especially useful when we are dealing with a list of structures, because it permits the list to expand as new records are added and to contract as records are deleted.

In requesting additional storage space, the user must provide the new operator with an indication of the amount of storage needed. This is done by requesting enough space for a particular type of data. For example, the expression `new(int)` or `new int` (the two forms may be used interchangeably) requests enough storage to store an integer number. A request for enough storage for a data structure is made in the same fashion. For example, using the declaration

```
struct TeleType
{
  char name[25];
  char phoneNo[15];
};
```

both the expressions `new TeleType` and `new(TeleType)` reserve enough storage for one `TeleType` data structure.

In allocating storage dynamically, we have no advance indication of where the computer system will physically reserve the requested number of bytes, and we have no explicit name to access the newly created storage locations. To provide access to these locations, new returns the address of the first location that has been reserved. This address must, of course, be assigned to a pointer. The return of an address by new is especially useful for creating a linked list of data structures. As each new structure is created, the address returned by new to the structure can be assigned to a member of the previous structure in the list.

Program 10-10 illustrates the use of new to create a structure dynamically in response to a user-input request.

Program 10-10

```
// a program illustrating dynamic structure allocation
#include <iostream.h>
#include <string.h>

const int MAXNAME = 30; // maximum no. of characters in a name
const int MAXTEL = 15;  // maximum no. of characters in a telephone number

struct TeleType
{
  char name[MAXNAME];
  char phoneNo[MAXTEL];
};

void populate(TeleType *);  // function prototype needed by main()
void dispOne(TeleType *);   // function prototype needed by main()

int main()
{
  char key;
  TeleType *recPoint;     // recPoint is a pointer to a
                          // structure of type TeleType

  cout << "Do you wish to create a new record (respond with y or n): ";
  key = cin.get();
  if (key == 'y')
  {
    key = cin.get();       // get the Enter key in buffered input
    recPoint = new TeleType;
    populate(recPoint);
    dispOne(recPoint);
  }
  else
    cout << "\nNo record has been created.";

  return 0;
}
```

```
  // input a name and phone number
void populate(TeleType *record) // record is a pointer to a
  {                             // structure of type TeleType
    cout << "Enter a name: ";
    cin.getline(record->name,MAXNAME);
    cout << "Enter the phone number: ";
    cin.getline(record->phoneNo,MAXTEL);

    return;
  }
  // display the contents of one record
void dispOne(TeleType *contents)  // contents is a pointer to a
{                                 // structure of type TeleType
    cout << "\nThe contents of the record just created is:"
         << "\nName: " << contents->name
         << "\nPhone Number: " << contents->phoneNo << endl;

    return;
}
```

A sample run produced by Program 10-10 is

```
Do you wish to create a new record (respond with y or n): y
Enter a name: Monroe, James
Enter the phone number: (555) 617-1817
The contents of the record just created is:
Name: Monroe, James
Phone Number: (555) 617-1817
```

In reviewing Program 10-10, note that only two variable declarations are made in `main()`. The variable `key` is declared as a character variable, and the variable `recPoint` is declared as being a pointer to a structure of the `TeleType` type. Because the declaration for the type `TeleType` is global, `TeleType` can be used within `main()` to define `recPoint` as a pointer to a structure of the `TeleType` type.

If a user enters `y` in response to the first prompt in `main()`, a call to `new` is made for the required memory to store the designated structure. Once `recPoint` has been loaded with the proper address, this address can be used to access the newly created structure. The function `populate()` is used to prompt the user for data needed in filling the structure and to store the user-entered data in the correct members of the structure. The argument passed to `populate()` in `main()` is the pointer `recPoint`. Like all passed arguments, the value contained in `recPoint` is passed to the function. The value in `recPoint` is an address, so `populate()` receives the address of the newly created structure and can directly access the structure members.

Within `populate()`, the value it receives is stored in the argument named `record`. Because the value to be stored in `record` is the address of a structure, `record` must be declared as a pointer to a structure. This declaration is provided by the statement `TeleType *record;`. The statements within `populate()` use the address in `record` to locate the respective members of the structure.

The `dispOne()` function in Program 10-10 is used to display the contents of the newly created and populated structure. The address passed to `dispOne()` is the same address that was passed to `populate()`. This passed value is the address of a structure, so the parameter name used to store the address is declared as a pointer to the correct structure type.

Once you understand the mechanism of using `new`, you can use this operator to construct a linked list of structures. As described in the previous section, the structures used in a linked list must contain at least one pointer member. The address in the pointer member is the starting address of the next structure in the list. Additionally, a pointer must be reserved for the address of the first structure, and the pointer member of the last structure in the list is given a `NULL` address to indicate that no more members are being pointed to. Program 10-11 illustrates the use of `new` to construct a linked list of names and phone numbers. The `populate()` function used in Program 10-11 is the same function used in Program 10-10, whereas the `display()` function is the same function used in Program 10-9.

Program 10-11

```
#include <iostream.h>
#include <iomanip.h>

const int MAXNAME = 30; // maximum no. of characters in a name
const int MAXTEL = 15;  // maximum no. of characters in a telephone number
const int MAXRECS = 3;  // maximum no. of records

struct TeleType
{
  char name[MAXNAME];
  char phoneNo[MAXTEL];
  TeleType *nextaddr;
};
```

```
void populate(TeleType *);    // function prototype needed by main()
void display(TeleType *);     // function prototype needed by main()

int main()
{
  int i;
  TeleType *list, *current; // two pointers to structures of
                            // type TeleType

    // get a pointer to the first structure in the list
  list = new TeleType;
  current = list;

    // populate the current structure and create the remaining structures
  for(i = 0; i < MAXRECS - 1; i++)
  {
    populate(current);
    current->nextaddr = new TeleType;
    current = current->nextaddr;
  }

  populate(current);          // populate the last structure
  current->nextaddr = NULL;   // set the last address to a NULL address
  cout << "\nThe list consists of the following records:\n";
  display(list);              // display the structures

  return 0;
}

// input a name and phone number
void populate(TeleType *record)  // record is a pointer to a
{                                // structure of type TeleType
  cout << "Enter a name: ";
  cin.getline(record->name,MAXNAME);
  cout << "Enter the phone number: ";
  cin.getline(record->phoneNo,MAXTEL);

  return;
}

void display(TeleType *contents)// contents is a pointer to a
{                               // structure of type TeleType
  while (contents != NULL)      // display till end of linked list
  {
    cout << "\n" << setiosflags(ios::left)
         << setw(30) << contents->name
         << setw(20) << contents->phoneNo;
    contents = contents->nextaddr;
  }
  cout << endl;

  return;
}
```

The first time new is called in Program 10-11, it is used to create the first structure in the linked list. Accordingly, the address returned by new is stored in the pointer variable named list. The address in list is then assigned to the pointer named current. This pointer variable is always used by the program to point to the current structure. Because the current structure is the first structure created, the address in the pointer named list is assigned to the pointer named current.

Within main()'s for loop, the name and phone number members of the newly created structure are populated by calling populate() and passing the address of the current structure to the function. Upon return from populate(), the pointer member of the current structure is assigned an address. This address is the address of the next structure in the list, which is obtained from new. The call to new creates the next structure and returns its address into the pointer member of the current structure. This completes the population of the current member. The final statement in the for loop resets the address in the current pointer to the address of the next structure in the list.

After the last structure has been created, the final statements in main() populate this structure, assign a NULL address to the pointer member, and call display() to display all the structures in the list. A sample run of Program 10-11 is provided below.

```
Enter a name: Acme, Sam
Enter the phone number: (555) 898-2392
Enter a name: Dolan, Edith
Enter the phone number: (555) 682-3104
Enter a name: Lanfrank, John
Enter the phone number: (555) 718-4581
The list consists of the following records:

Acme, Sam                     (555) 898-2392
Dolan, Edith                  (555) 682-3104
Lanfrank, John                (555) 718-4581
```

Just as new dynamically creates storage while a program is executing, the delete function restores a block of storage to the computer while the programming is executing. The only argument required by delete is the starting address of a block of storage that was dynamically allocated. Thus any address returned by new can subsequently be passed to delete to restore the reserved memory to the computer. delete does not alter the address passed to it but simply removes the storage that the address references.

Exercises 10.5

1. As described in Table 10–1, the `new` operator either returns the address of the first new storage area allocated or returns `NULL` if sufficient storage is not available. Modify Program 10-11 to check that a valid address has been returned before a call to `populate()` is made. Display an appropriate message if sufficient storage is not available.

2. Write a C++ function named `remove()` that removes an existing structure from the linked list of structures created by Program 10-11. The algorithm for removing a linked structure should follow the sequence developed for removing a structure in Exercise 4 of Section 10.4. The argument passed to `remove()` should be the address of the structure preceding the record to be removed. In the removal function, make sure that the value of the pointer in the removed structure replaces the value of the pointer member of the preceding structure before the structure is removed.

3. Write a function named `insert()` that inserts a structure into the linked list of structures created in Program 10-11. The algorithm for inserting a structure in a linked list should follow the sequence for inserting a record illustrated in Figure 10–9. The argument passed to `insert()` should be the address of the structure preceding the structure to be inserted. The inserted structure should follow this current structure. The `insert()` function should create a new structure dynamically, call the `populate()` function used in Program 10-11, and adjust all pointer values appropriately.

4. We desire to insert a new structure into the linked list of structures created by Program 10-11. The function developed to do this in Exercise 3 assumed that the address of the preceding structure is known. Write a function called `findRec()` that returns the address of the structure immediately preceding the point at which the new structure is to be inserted. (*Hint:* `findRec()` must request the new name as input and compare the entered name to existing names to determine where to place the new name.)

5. Write a C++ function named `modify()` that can be used to modify the name and phone number members of a structure of the type created in Program 10-11. The argument passed to `modify()` should be the address of the structure to be modified. The `modify()` function should first display the existing name and phone number in the selected structure and then request new data for these members.

6. *a.* Write a C++ program that initially presents a menu of choices for the user. The menu should consist of the following choices:

   A. Create an initial linked list of names and phone numbers.
   B. Insert a new structure into the linked list.
   C. Modify an existing structure in the linked list.
   D. Delete an existing structure from the list.
   E. Exit from the program.

   Upon the user's selection, the program should execute the appropriate functions to satisfy the request.

   b. Why is the original creation of a linked list usually done by one program, and the options to add, modify, or delete a structure in the list provided by a different program?

10.6 Unions[4]

A union is a data type that reserves the same area in memory for two or more variables, each of which can be a different data type. A variable that is declared as a union data type can be used to hold a character variable, an integer variable, a double-precision variable, or any other valid C++ data type. Each of these types—but only one at a time—can actually be assigned to the union variable.

The definition of a union has the same form as a structure definition, with the keyword `union` used in place of the keyword `structure`. For example, the declaration

```
union
{
  char key;
  int num;
  double price;
} val;
```

creates a union variable named `val`. If `val` were a structure, it would consist of three individual members. As a union, however, `val` contains a single member that can be a character variable named `key`, an integer variable named `num`, or a double-precision variable named `price`. In effect, a union reserves sufficient memory locations to accommodate its largest member's data type. This same set of locations is then accessed by different variable names, depending on the data type of the value currently residing in the reserved locations. Each value stored overwrites the previous value, using as many bytes of the reserved memory area as necessary.

Individual union members are accessed using the same notation as structure members. For example, if the `val` union is currently being used to store a character, the correct variable name to access the stored character is `val.key`. Similarly, if the union is used to store an integer, the value is accessed by the name `val.num`, and a double-precision value is accessed by the name `val.price`. In using union members, it is the programmer's responsibility to ensure that the correct member name is used for the data type currently residing in the union.

Typically, a second variable is used to keep track of the current data type stored in the union. For example, the following code could be used to select the appropriate member of `val` for display. Here the value in the variable `uType` determines the currently stored data type in the `val` union.

---

[4] This topic is presented for completeness only and may be omitted on first reading with no loss of subject continuity. Unions are rarely used in practice anymore. Originally, unions provided a means of sharing the same storage between variables, which enabled programmers to conserve storage when memory space was severely limited.

```
switch(uType)
{
  case 'c': cout << val.key;
            break;
  case 'i': cout << val.num;
            break;
  case 'd': cout << val.price;
            break;
  default : cout << "Invalid type in uType :" << uType;
}
```

Just as in structures, a data type can be associated with a union. For example, the declaration

```
union DateTime
{
   long int days;
   double time;
};
```

provides a union data type without actually reserving any storage locations. This data type can then be used to define any number of variables. For example, the definition

```
DateTime first, second, *pt;
```

creates a union variable named `first`, a union variable named `second`, and a pointer that can be used to store the address of any union that has the form of `DateTime`. Once a pointer to a union has been declared, the same notation used to access structure members can be used to access union members. For example, if the assignment `pt = &first;` is made, then `pt->date` references the `date` member of the union named `first`.

Unions may themselves be members of structures or arrays, and structures, arrays, and pointers may be members of unions. In each case, the notation used to access a member must be consistent with the nesting employed. For example, in the structure defined by

```
struct
{
  char uType;
  union
  {
    char *text;
    float rate;
  } uTax;
}  flag;
```

the variable `rate` is referenced as

```
flag.uTax.rate
```

Similarly, the first character of the string whose address is stored in the pointer `text` is referenced as

```
*flag.uTax.text
```

Exercises 10.6

1. Assume that the following definition has been made

```
union
{
  float rate;
  double taxes;
  int num;
} flag;
```

For this union, write appropriate `cout` stream activations to display the various members of the union.

2. Define a union variable named `car` that contains an integer named `year`, an array of ten characters named `name`, and an array of ten characters named `model`.

3. Define a union variable named `lang` that would allow a floating-point number to be referenced by both the variable names `interest` and `rate`.

4. Declare a union data type named `Amt` that contains an integer variable named `intAmt`, a double-precision variable named `dblAmt`, and a pointer to a character named `ptKey`.

5. ***a.*** What do you think will be displayed by the following section of code?

```
union
{
  char ch;
  float btype;
} alt;
alt.ch = 'y';
cout << alt.btype;
```

b. Include the code presented in Exercise 5a in a program and run the program to verify your answer to Exercise 5a.

10.7 Common Programming Errors

There are three errors that are often made when using structures or unions. The first error occurs because structures and unions, as complete entities, cannot be used in relational expressions. For example, even if `TeleType` and `PhoneType` are two structures of the same type, the expression `TeleType == PhoneType` is invalid. Individual members of a structure or union can, of course, be compared, if they are of the same data type, by using any of C++'s relational operators.

The second common error is really an extension of a pointer error as it relates to structures and unions. Whenever a pointer is used to "point to" either of these data types, and whenever a pointer is itself a member of a structure or a union, take care to use the address in the pointer to access the appropriate data type. Should you be confused about just what is being pointed to, remember the saying: "If in doubt, print it out."

The final error is related specifically to unions. Because a union can store only one of its members at a time, you must be sure to keep track of the currently stored variable. Storing one data type in a union and accessing it by the wrong variable name can result in an error that is particularly troublesome to locate.

10.8 Chapter Summary

1. A structure allows individual variables to be grouped under a common variable name. Each variable in a structure is accessed by its structure variable name, followed by a period, followed by its individual variable name. Data structures are also called records. One form for declaring a structure is

```
struct
{
  individual member declarations;
} structure-name;
```

2. A data type can be created from a structure by using the declaration form

```
struct Data-type
{
  individual member declarations;
};
```

Individual structure variables may then be defined as this data type. By convention, the first letter of the `Data-type` name is always capitalized.

3. Structures are particularly useful as elements of arrays. Used in this manner, each structure becomes one record in a list of records.
4. Complete structures can be used as function arguments, in which case the called function receives a copy of each element in the structure. The address of a structure may also be passed, either as a reference or as a pointer, which provides the called function with direct access to the structure.
5. Structure members can be any valid C++ data type, including other structures, unions, arrays, and pointers. When a pointer is included as a structure member, a linked list can be created. Such a list uses the pointer in one structure to "point to" (contain the address of) the next logical structure in the list.
6. Unions are declared in the same manner as structures. The definition of a union creates a memory overlay area, with each union member using the same memory storage locations. Thus only one member of a union can be active at a time.

Object-Oriented Programming

Part III

Introduction to Classes

Chapter Eleven

Besides being an improved version of C, C++ is distinguished by its support of object-oriented programming. Central to this object orientation is the concept of an abstract data type, which is a programmer-defined data type. In this chapter, we explore the implications of permitting programmers to define their own data types and then present C++'s mechanism for constructing abstract data types. As we will see, the construction of a data type is based on both structures and functions; structures provide the means for creating new data configurations, and functions provide the means for performing operations on the structures. What C++ provides is a unique way of combining structures and functions in a self-contained, cohesive unit from which objects can be created.

11.1 Object-Based Programming

We live in a world full of objects—planes, trains, cars, telephones, books, computers, and so on. Until quite recently, however, programming techniques have not reflected this at all. The primary programming paradigm[1] has been procedural, where a program is defined as an algorithm written in a machine-readable language. The reasons for this emphasis on procedural programming are primarily historical.

When computers were developed in the 1940s, they were used by mathematicians for military purposes—for computing bomb trajectories, decoding enemy orders, and diplomatic transmissions. After World War II, computers were still used primarily by mathematicians for mathematical computations. This reality was reflected in the name of the first commercially available high-level language introduced in 1957. The language's name was FORTRAN, which was an acronym for FORmula TRANslation. In the 1960s, nearly all computer courses were taught in either engineering or mathematics departments. The term *computer science* was not yet in common use, and computer science departments were just being formed.

This situation has changed dramatically, primarily for two reasons. One of the reasons for disenchantment with procedural-based programs has been the failure of traditional procedural languages to provide an adequate means of containing software costs. Software costs include all costs associated with initial program development and subsequent program maintenance. As illustrated in Figure 11–1, the major cost of most computer projects today, whether technical or commercial, is for software.

[1] A paradigm is a standard way of thinking about or doing something.

POINT OF INFORMATION

Procedural, Hybrid, and Pure Object-Oriented Languages

Most high-level programming languages can be categorized into one of three main categories: procedural, hybrid, or object-oriented. FORTRAN, which was the first commercially available high-level programming language, is procedural. This makes sense because FORTRAN was designed to perform mathematical calculations that used standard algebraic formulas. Formally, these formulas were described as algorithms, and then the algorithms were coded using function and subroutine procedures. Other procedural languages that followed FORTRAN include BASIC, COBOL, and Pascal.

Currently there are only two pure object-oriented languages: Smalltalk and Eiffel. The first requirement of a pure object-oriented language is that it contain three specific features: classes, inheritance, and polymorphism (each of these features is described in this and the next two chapters). In addition to providing these features, however, a "pure" object-oriented language must always use classes. In a pure object-oriented language, all data types are constructed as classes, all data values are objects, all operators can be overloaded, and every data operation can be executed using only a class member function. *It is impossible, in a pure object-oriented language, not to use object-oriented features* throughout a program. This is not the case in a hybrid language.

In a hybrid language, such as C++, *it is impossible not to use elements of a procedural program.* This is because the use of any built-in data type or operation effectively violates the pure object-oriented paradigm. Although a hybrid language must have the ability to define classes, the distinguishing feature of a hybrid language is that it is possible to write a complete program using only procedural code. Furthermore, hybrid languages need not even provide inheritance and polymorphic features, but they must provide classes. Languages that use classes but do not provide inheritance and polymorphic features are referred to as *object-based* languages rather than *object-oriented.* All versions of Visual Basic prior to Version 4 are examples of object-based hybrid languages.

Software costs contribute so heavily to total project costs because they are directly related to human productivity (they are labor-intensive), whereas the equipment associated with hardware costs is related to manufacturing technologies. For example, microchips that cost over $500 ten years ago can now be purchased for less than $1.

It is far easier, however, to increase manufacturing productivity a thousandfold, with the resulting decrease in hardware costs, than it is for programmers to double either the quantity or the quality of the code they produce. Consequently, as hardware costs have plummeted, software productivity and its associated costs have remained relatively constant. Thus the ratio of software costs to total system costs (hardware plus software) has increased dramatically.

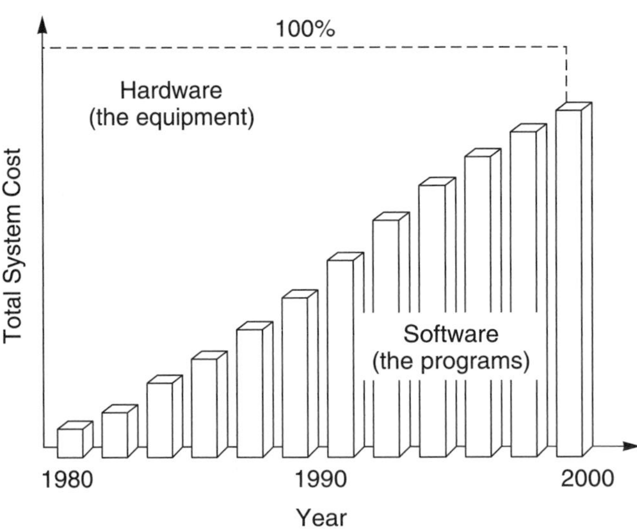

FIGURE 11–1 Software Is the Major Cost of Most Computer Projects

One way to increase programmer productivity significantly is to create code that can be reused without extensive revision, retesting, and revalidation. The inability of procedurally structured code to provide this type of reusability has led to the search for other software approaches.

The second reason for disenchantment with procedural-based programming has been the emergence of graphical screens and the subsequent interest in window applications. Programming multiple windows on the same graphical screen is virtually impossible with standard procedural programming techniques.

The solution to producing programs that efficiently manipulate graphical screens and provide reusable windowing code was found in artificial intelligence–based and simulation programming techniques. The former area, artificial intelligence, contained extensive research on geometrical object specification and recognition. The latter area, simulation, contained considerable background on simulating items as objects with well-defined interactions between them. This object-based paradigm fit well in a graphical windows environment, where each window can be specified as a self-contained object.

An object is also well suited to a programming representation because it can be specified by two basic characteristics: a current *state*, which defines how the object appears at the moment, and a *behavior*, which defines how the object reacts to external inputs.

To make this more concrete, consider a geometric object, such as a rectangle. A rectangle's current state is defined by its shape and location. The shape is traditionally specified by its length and width, whereas its location can be specified in a number of ways. One simple way is to list the values of two corner positions. The behavior we provide a rectangle depends on what we are willing to have our rectangle do. For example, if we intend to display the rectangle on a screen, we might provide it with the ability to move its position and change either its length or its width.

It is worthwhile distinguishing here between an actual rectangle, which might exist on a piece of paper or a computer screen, and our description of it. Our description is more accurately termed a model. By definition, a *model* is only a representation of a real object; it is not the object itself. Very few models are ever complete; that is, a model typically does not reveal every aspect of the object it represents. Each model is defined for a particular purpose that usually requires representing only the part of an object's state or behavior that is of interest to us. To clarify this point further, let's consider another common object, an elevator.

Like all objects, an elevator can be modeled in terms of a state and a behavior. Its state might be given in terms of its size, location, interior decoration, or any number of attributes. Likewise, its behavior might be specified in terms of its reaction when one of its buttons is pushed. Constructing a model of an elevator, however, requires that we select those attributes and behaviors that are of interest to us. For purposes of a simulation, for example, we may be concerned only with the current floor position of the elevator and with how to make it move to another floor location. Other attributes and behaviors of the elevator may be left out of the model because they do not affect the aspects of the elevator that we are interested in studying. At the end of this chapter, we will see how to model an elevator in C++ and make our model elevator "move" using a very simple representation.

It is also important to distinguish between the attributes we choose to include in our model and the values that these attributes can have. The attributes and behavior together define a category, or type, of object out of which many individual objects can be designated. In object-based programming, the category of objects defined by a given set of attributes and behaviors is called a *class*. Only when specific values have been assigned to the attributes is a particular object defined.

For example, the attributes length and width can be used to define a general type of shape called a rectangle. Only when specific values have been assigned to these attributes have we represented a particular rectangle. This distinction carries over into C++: The attributes and behavior we select are said to define a general class, or type, of object. The object itself comes into existence only when we assign specific values to the attributes.

As you might expect, attributes in C++ are defined by variables, and behaviors are constructed from functions. The set of attributes and behavior defining a class is frequently referred to as the class's *interface*. Once the interface has been specified, creating a particular object is achieved by assigning specific values to the appropriate variables. How all of this is constructed is the topic of the remaining sections.

Exercises 11.1

1. Define the following terms.
   a. Attribute
   b. Behavior
   c. State
   d. Model
   e. Class
   f. Object
   g. Interface
2. *a.* Instead of specifying a rectangle's location by listing the position of two corner points, what other attributes could we use?
   b. What other attributes, besides length and width, might be used to describe a rectangle if the rectangle were to be drawn on a color monitor?
   c. Describe a set of attributes that could be used to define circles that are to be drawn on a black-and-white monitor.
   d. What additional attributes would you add to those selected in response to Exercise 2c if the circles were to be drawn on a color monitor?
3. *a.* For each of the following, determine what attributes might be of interest to someone considering buying the item.
   i. A book
   ii. A can of soda
   iii. A pen
   iv. A cassette tape
   v. A cassette tape player
   vi. An elevator
   vii. A car
   b. Do the attributes you used in Exercise 3a model an object or a class of objects?
4. For each of the following items, what behavior might be of interest to someone considering buying the item?
   a. A car
   b. A cassette tape player
5. All of the examples of classes considered in this section have consisted of inanimate objects. Do you think that animate objects such as pets and even human beings could be modeled in terms of attributes and behavior? Why or why not?
6. *a.* The attributes of a class represent how objects of the class appear to the outside world. The behavior represents how an object of a class reacts to an external stimulus. Given this, what do you think is the mechanism by which one object "triggers" the designated behavior in another object? (*Hint:* Consider how one person typically gets another person to do something.)
   b. If behavior in C++ is constructed by defining an appropriate function, how do you think the behavior is activated in C++?

11.2 Classes

A *class* is a programmer-defined data type (more generally, a programmer-defined data type is also referred to as an *abstract data type*). To understand the full implications of this more clearly, consider three of the built-in data types supplied by C++: integers, reals, and characters. In using these data types, we typically declare one or more variables of the desired type, use them in their accepted ways, and avoid using them in ways that are not specified. Thus, for example, we would not use the modulus operator on two floating-point numbers. Because this operation makes no sense, it has not been supplied in C++.

In computer terminology, the combination of data and their associated operations is defined as a class. That is, a class defines *both* the types of data and the types of operations that may be performed on the data. Seen in this light, it is more accurate to speak of the built-in data types provided by C++ as the integer class, the floating-point class, and the character class. Such a definition conveys that both a type of data and specific operational capabilities are being supplied. In a simplified form, this relationship can be described as

```
Class = Allowable Data + Operational Capabilities
```

Before seeing how to construct our own classes, let's take a moment to list some of the operational capabilities supplied with C++'s built-in classes. The reason for this is that we will have to provide the same capabilities as part of our own classes. The minimum set of the capabilities provided by C++'s built-in classes is listed in Table 11–1.

TABLE 11–1 Built-in Data Type Capabilities

Capability	Example
Define one or more variables of the class	`int a, b;`
Initialize a variable at definition	`int a = 5;`
Assign a value to a variable	`a = 10;`
Assign one variable's value to another variable	`a = b;`
Perform mathematical operations	`a + b`
Convert from one data type to another	`a = (int) 7.2;`

Although we don't normally think of these capabilities individually when we use them, the designers of C++ clearly had to when they created the C++ compiler. C++ allows us to create our own classes, so we must now be aware of these capabilities and provide them with the classes that we construct.

Construction of a class is inherently easy, and we already have all the necessary tools in variables and functions. In C++, various combinations of variables provide the means of defining new data types, and functions provide the means of defining operational capabilities. Using this information, we can now extend our equation definition of a class to its C++ representation:

```
C++ Class = Data + Functions
```

Thus, in C++, a class provides a mechanism for packaging a data structure and functions together in a self-contained unit. In this chapter we describe how classes are constructed and how variables are declared and initialized. The assignment and mathematical capabilities listed in Table 11–1, as they apply to classes, are presented in Chapter 12. Type conversions are presented in Chapter 13.

Class Construction

A class defines both data and functions. This is usually accomplished by constructing a class in two parts, consisting of a declaration section and an implementation section. As illustrated in Figure 11–2, the declaration section declares both the data types and the functions of the class. The implementation section is then used to define the functions whose prototypes have been declared in the declaration section.[2]

FIGURE 11–2 Format of a Class Definition

```
// class declaration section
class class-name
{
  data members  // instance variables
    and
  function members  // inline and prototypes
};
// class implementation section
function definitions
```

[2] This separation into two parts is not mandatory; the implementation can be included within the declaration section if inline functions are used.

Both the variables and the functions listed in the class declaration section are collectively referred to as *class members*. Individually, the variables are referred to as both *data members* and *instance variables* (the terms are synonymous), and the functions are referred to as *member functions*. A member function name may not be the same as a data member name.

As a specific example of a class, consider the following definition of a class named Date.

```
//--- class declaration section

class Date
{
  private:
    int month;
    int day;
    int year;
  public:
    Date(int = 7, int = 4, int = 2001); // constructor with defaults
    void setdate(int, int, int);       // member function to copy a date
    void showdate(void);               // member function to display a date
};

//--- class implementation section

Date::Date(int mm, int dd, int yyyy)
{
  month = mm;
  day = dd;
  year = yyyy;
}

void Date::setdate(int mm, int dd, int yyyy)
{
  month = mm;
  day = dd;
  year = yyyy;

  return;
}

void Date::showdate(void)
{
  cout << "The date is ";
  cout << setfill('0')
       << setw(2) << month << '/'
       << setw(2) << day << '/'
       << setw(2) << year % 100; // extract the last 2 year digits
  cout << endl;
  return;
}
```

Because this definition may initially look overwhelming, first simply note that it does consist of two sections—a declaration section and an implementation section. Now let's consider each of these sections individually.

The class declaration section begins with the keyword `class` followed by a class name. Following the class name are the class's variable declarations and function prototypes, enclosed in a brace pair that is terminated with a semicolon. Thus the general structure of the form that we have used is[3]

```
class Name
{
  private:
    a list of variable declarations
  public:
    a list of function prototypes
};
```

Note that this format is followed by our `Date` class, which for convenience we have listed below with no internal comments:

```
//--- class declaration section

class Date
{
  private:
      int month;
      int day;
      int year;
  public:
      Date(int = 7, int = 4, int = 2001);
      void setdate(int, int, int);
      void showdate(void);
};  // this is a declaration - don't forget the semi-colon
```

The name of this class is `Date`. Although the initial capital letter is not required, it is conventionally used to designate a class. The body of the declaration section, which is enclosed within braces, consists of variable and function declarations. In this case the data members `month`, `day`, and `year` are declared as integers, and three functions named `Date()`, `setdate()`, and `showdate()` are declared via prototypes. The keywords `private` and `public` are access specifiers that define access rights. The `private` keyword specifies

---

[3] Other forms are possible. This form is one of the most commonly used and easily understood, so it will serve as our standard model throughout the text.

that the class members that follow—in this case the data members `month`, `day`, and `year`—may be accessed only by using the class functions (or friend functions, as we will see in Section 12.3).[4] The purpose of the `private` designation is to enforce data security by requiring all accesses to private data members through the provided member functions. This type of access, which restricts a user from seeing how the data is actually stored, is referred to as *data hiding*. Once a class category such as `private` is designated, it remains in force until a new category is listed.

Specifically, we have chosen to store a date using three integers: one each for the month, day, and year. We will also always store the year as a four-digit number. Thus, for example, we will store the year 1998 as 1998, not as 98. Being sure to store all years with their correct century designation will eliminate a multitude of problems that can crop up if only the last two digits, such as 98, are stored. For example, the number of years between 2002 and 1999 can be quickly calculated as 2002 – 1999 = 3 years, but this same answer is not so easily obtained if only the year values 02 and 99 are used. Additionally, we are sure of what the year 2000 refers to, whereas a two-digit value such as 00 could refer to either 1900 or 2000.[5]

Following the `private` class data members, the function prototypes listed in the `Date` class have been declared as `public`. This means that these class functions *can* be called by any objects and functions not in the class (outside). In general, all class functions should be public; thus they furnish capabilities to manipulate the class variables from outside of the class. For our `Date` class, we have initially provided three functions named `Date()`, `setdate()`, and `showdate()`. Note that one of these member functions has the same name, `Date`, as the class name. This particular function is referred to as a *constructor* function, and it has a specially defined purpose: It can be used to initialize class data members with values. The default values that are used for this function are the numbers `7`, `4`, and `2001`, which, as we will shortly see, are used as the default month, day, and year values, respectively. The only point to remember now is that the default year is correctly represented as a four-digit integer that retains the century designation. Also note that the constructor function has no return type, which is a requirement for this special function. The two remaining functions declared in our declaration example are `setdate()` and `showdate()`, both of which have been declared as returning no value (`void`). In the implementation section of the class, these three member functions will be written to permit initialization, assignment, and display capabilities, respectively.

---

[4] Note that the default membership category in a class is `private`, which means that this keyword can be omitted. In this text, we will explicitly use the `private` designation to reinforce the idea of access restrictions inherent in class membership.

[5] These problems are all included under the designation "The year 2000 problem."

The *implementation section* of a class is where the member functions declared in the declaration section are written.[6] Figure 11–3 illustrates the general form of functions included in the implementation section. This format is correct for all functions except the constructor, which, as we have stated, has no `return` type.

As shown in Figure 11–3, member functions defined in the implementation section have the same format as all user-written C++ functions, with the addition of the class name and the scope resolution operator, `::`, that identifies the function as a member of a particular class. Let us now reconsider the implementation section of our `Date` class, which is repeated below for convenience.

```
//--- class implementation section
Date::Date(int mm, int dd, int yyyy)
{
  month = mm;
  day = dd;
  year = yyyy;
}
void Date::setdate(int mm, int dd, int yyyy)
{
  month = mm;
  day = dd;
  year = yyyy;

  return;
}
void Date::showdate(void)
{
  cout << "The date is ";
  cout << setfill('0')
       << setw(2) << month << '/'
       << setw(2) << day << '/'
       << setw(2) << year % 100;  // extract the last 2 year digits
  cout << endl;
  return;
}
```

FIGURE 11–3 Format of a Member Function

```
return-type  class-name::function-name(parameter list)
{
  function body
}
```

[6] It is also possible to define these functions within the declaration section by declaring and writing them as inline functions. Examples of inline member functions are presented in Section 11.3.

Note that the first function in this implementation section has the same name as the class, which makes it a constructor function. Accordingly, it has no return type. The `Date::` included at the beginning of the function header line identifies this function as a member of the `Date` class. The rest of the header line,

```
Date(int mm, int dd, int yyyy)
```

defines the function as having three integer parameters. The body of this function simply assigns the data members `month`, `day`, and `year` with the values of the parameters `mm`, `dd`, and `yyyy`, respectively.

The next function header line

```
void Date::setdate(int mm, int dd, int yyyy)
```

defines this as the `setdate()` function belonging to the `Date` class (`Date::`). This function returns no value (`void`) and expects three integer parameters, `mm`, `dd`, and `yyyy`. In a manner similar to the `Date()` function, the body of this function assigns the data members `month`, `day`, and `year` with the values of its parameters. In a moment we will see the difference between `Date()` and `setdate()`.

Finally, the last function header line in the implementation section defines a function named `showdate()`. This function has no parameters, returns no value, and is a member of the `Date` class. The body of this function, however, needs a little more explanation.

Although we have chosen to store all years internally as four-digit values that retain century information, users are accustomed to seeing dates where the year is represented as a two-digit value, such as 12/15/99. To display the last two digits of the `year` value, the expression `year % 100` can be used. For example, if the year is 1999, the expression `1999 % 100` yields the value 99, and if the year is 2001, the expression `2001 % 100` yields the value 1. Note that if we had used an assignment such as `year = year % 100;`, we would actually be altering the stored value of `year` to correspond to the last two digits of the year. Because we want to retain the year as a four-digit number, we must be careful to manipulate only the displayed value using the expression `year % 100` within the `cout` stream. The `setfill` and `setw` manipulators are used to ensure that the displayed values correspond to conventionally accepted dates. For example, the date March 9, 2002 should appear as either 3/9/02 or 03/09/02. The `setw` manipulator forces each value to be displayed in a field width of 2. Because this manipulator remains in effect only for the next insertion, we have included it before the display of each date value. The `setfill` manipulator, however, remains in effect until the `fill` character is changed, so we only have to include it once.[7] We have used the `setfill` manipulator here to change the `fill` character from its default of a blank space to the character `0`. Doing this ensures that a date such as December 9, 2002 will appear as 12/09/02, not as 12/ 9/ 2.

To see how our `Date` class can be used within the context of a complete program, consider Program 11-1. To make the program easier to read, it has been shaded in light and darker areas. The lighter area contains the class declaration and implementation sections that we have already considered. The darker area contains the header and the `main()` function. For convenience, we will retain this shading convention for all programs that use classes.[8]

The declaration and implementation sections contained in the lightly shaded region of Program 11-1 should look familiar to you; they contain the class declaration and implementation sections that we have already discussed. Note, however, that this region only declares the class, it does not create any variables of this class type. This is true of all C++ types, including the built-in types such as integers and floats. Just as a variable of an integer type must be defined, variables of a user-declared class must also be defined. Variables defined to be of a user-declared class are referred to as *objects*.

Using this new terminology, the first statement in Program 11-1's `main()` function, contained in the darker area, defines three objects, named `a`, `b`, and `c`, to be of class type `Date`. In C++, whenever a new object is defined, memory is allocated for the object and its data members are automatically initialized. This is done by an automatic call to the class constructor function. For example, consider the definition `Date a, b, c(4,1,1998);` contained in `main()`. When the object named `a` is defined, the constructor function `Date` is automatically called. Because no parameters have been assigned to `a`, the default values of the constructor function are used, resulting in the initialization

```
a.month = 7
a.day = 4
a.year = 2001
```

[7] This type of information is easily obtained by using the online Help facility, as described in Section 2.8.

[8] This shading is not accidental. In practice, the lightly shaded region containing the class definition would be placed in a separate file. A single `#include` statement would then be used to include this class declaration in the program. Thus the final program would consist of the two darkly shaded regions illustrated in Program 11-1 and one more `#include` statement in the first region.

Program 11-1

```
#include <iostream.h>
#include <iomanip.h>
```

```
// class declaration

class Date
{
  private:
    int month;
    int day;
    int year;
  public:
    Date(int = 7, int = 4, int = 2001); // constructor with defaults
    void setdate(int, int, int);       // member function to copy a date
    void showdate(void);               // member function to display a date
};

// implementation section

Date::Date(int mm, int dd, int yyyy)
{
  month = mm;
  day = dd;
  year = yyyy;
}

void Date::setdate(int mm, int dd, int yyyy)
{
  month = mm;
  day = dd;
  year = yyyy;

  return;
}

void Date::showdate(void)
{
  cout << "The date is ";
  cout << setfill('0')
       << setw(2) << month << '/'
       << setw(2) << day << '/'
       << setw(2) << year % 100; // extract the last 2 year digits
  cout << endl;
  return;
}
```

(continued on next page)

(continued from previous page)

```
int main()
{
  Date a, b, c(4,1,1998);  // declare 3 objects and initialize 1 of them

  b.setdate(12,25,2002);   // assign values to b's data members
  cout << endl;

  a.showdate();            // display object a's values
  b.showdate();            // display object b's values
  c.showdate();            // display object c's values

  cout << endl;

  return 0;
}
```

Note the notation that we have used here. It consists of an object name and an attribute name separated by a period. This is the standard syntax for referring to an object's attribute:

object-name.attribute-name

where *object-name* is the name of a specific object and *attribute-name* is the name of a data member defined for the object's class.

Thus the notation `a.month = 7` refers to the fact that object a's `month` data member has been set to the value `7`. Similarly, the notation `a.day = 4` and `a.year = 2001` refers to the fact that a's `day` and `year` data members have been set to the values `4` and `2001`, respectively. In the same manner, when the object named `b` is defined, the same default parameters are used, resulting in the initialization of b's data members as

```
b.month = 7
b.day = 4
b.year = 2001
```

The object named `c`, however, is defined with the arguments `4`, `1`, and `1998`. These three arguments are passed into the constructor function when the object is defined, resulting in the initialization of c's data members as

```
c.month = 4
c.day = 1
c.year = 1998
```

The next statement in `main()`, which is `b.setdate(12,25,2002)`, calls b's `setdate` function, which assigns the argument values `12`, `25`, and `2002` to b's data members, resulting in the assignment

```
b.month = 12
b.day = 25
b.year = 2002
```

Note the syntax for referring to an object's method. This syntax is

```
object-name.method-name(parameters)
```

where *`object-name`* is the name of a specific object and *`method-name`* is the name of one of the functions defined for the object's class. Because we have defined all class functions as public, a statement such as

```
b.setdate(12,25,2002)
```

is valid inside the `main()` function and is a call to the class's `setdate()` function. This statement tells the `setdate()` function to operate on the `b` object with the arguments `12`, `25`, and `2002`. It is important to understand that because all class data members were specified as private, a statement such as `b.month = 12` would be invalid from within `main()`. We are therefore forced to rely on member functions to access data member values.

The last three statements in `main()` call the `showdate()` function to operate on the `a`, `b`, and `c` objects. The first call results in the display of `a`'s data values, the second call in the display of `b`'s data values, and the third call in the display of `c`'s data values. Thus the output displayed by Program 11-1 is

```
The date is 02/04/10
The date is 12/25/02
The date is 04/01/98
```

Note that a statement such as `cout << a;` is invalid within `main()` because `cout` does not know how to handle an object of class `Date`. Thus we have supplied our class with a function that can be used to access and display an object's internal values.

Terminology

Confusion sometimes arises about the terms associated with object-oriented programming, so we will take a moment to clarify and review this terminology.

POINT OF INFORMATION

Interfaces, Implementations, and Information Hiding

The terms *interface* and *implementation* are used extensively in object-oriented programming literature. Each of these terms can be equated to specific parts of a class's declaration and implementation sections.

An *interface* consists of a class's public member function declarations and any supporting comments. As such, the interface should be all that is required to tell a programmer how to use the class.

The *implementation* consists of both the class's implementation section, which is made up of both private and public member definitions, *and* the class's private data members that are contained in a class declaration section.

The implementation is the essential means of providing information hiding. In its most general context, *information hiding* refers to the principle that *how* a class is internally constructed is not relevant to any programmer who wishes to use the class. That is, the implementation can and should be hidden from all class users precisely to ensure that the class is not altered or compromised in any way. All that a programmer needs know to use the class correctly should be provided by the interface.

A *class* is a programmer-defined data type out of which objects can be created. *Objects* are created from classes; they have the same relationship to classes as variables do to C++'s built-in data types. For example, in the declaration

```
int a;
```

`a` is said to be a variable, whereas in Program 11-1's declaration

```
Date a;
```

`a` is said to be an object. If it initially helps you to think of an object as a variable, do so.

Objects are also referred to as *instances* of a class, and the process of creating a new object is frequently referred to as an *instantiation* of the object. Each time a new object is instantiated (created), a new set of data members belonging to the object is created.[9] The particular values contained in these data members determines the object's *state.*

Seen in this way, a class can be thought of as a blueprint out of which particular instances (objects) can be created. Each instance (object) of a class will have its own set of particular values for the set of data members specified in the class declaration section.

---

[9] Note that only one set of class functions is created. These functions are shared between objects.

In addition to the data types allowed for an object, a class also defines *behavior*—that is, the operations that are permitted to be performed on an object's data members. Users of the object need to know *what* these functions can do and how to activate them through function calls, but unless run time or space implications are relevant, they do not need to know *how* the operation is done. The actual implementation details of an object's operations are contained in the class implementation, which can be hidden from the user. Other names for the operations defined in a class implementation section are *procedures, functions, services,* and *methods*. We will use these terms interchangeably throughout the remainder of the text.

Exercises 11.2

1. Define the following terms.

a. Class
b. Object
c. Declaration section
d. Implementation section
e. Instance variable
f. Member function
g. Data member
h. Constructor
i. Class instance
j. Services
k. Methods
l. Interface

2. Write a class declaration section for each of the following specifications. In each case, include a prototype for a constructor and a member function named `showdata()` that can be used to display member values.

a. A class named `Time` that has integer data members named `secs`, `mins`, and `hours`.
b. A class named `Complex` that has floating-point data members named `real` and `imaginary`.
c. A class named `Circle` that has integer data members named `xcenter` and `ycenter` and a floating-point data member named `radius`.
d. A class named `System` that has character data members named `computer`, `printer`, and `screen`, each capable of holding 30 characters (including the end-of-string `NULL`), and floating-point data members named `comp_price`, `print_price`, and `scrn_price`.

3. *a.* Construct a class implementation section for the constructor and `showdate()` function members corresponding to the class declaration created for Exercise 2a.
b. Construct a class implementation section for the constructor and `showdate()` function members corresponding to the class declaration created for Exercise 2b.
c. Construct a class implementation section for the constructor and `showdate()` function members corresponding to the class declaration created for Exercise 2c.
d. Construct a class implementation section for the constructor and `showdate()` function members corresponding to the class declaration created for Exercise 2d.

4. *a.* Include the class declaration and implementation sections prepared for Exercises 2a and 3a in a complete working program.

b. Include the class declaration and implementation sections prepared for Exercises 2b and 3b in a complete working program.
c. Include the class declaration and implementation sections prepared for Exercises 2c and 3c in a complete working program.
d. Include the class declaration and implementation sections prepared for Exercises 2d and 3d in a complete working program.

5. Determine the errors in the following class declaration section:

```
class Employee
{
public:
  int empnum;
  char code;
private:
  class(int = 0);
  void showemp(int, char);
};
```

6. *a.* Add to Program 11-1 another member function named `convrt()` that does the following: The function should access the `month`, `year`, and `day` data members and should display and then return a long integer that is calculated as *year* * *10000* + *month* * *100* + *day*. For example, if the date is 4/1/1996, the returned value is 19960401 (dates in this form are useful when performing sorts, because placing the numbers in numerical order automatically places the corresponding dates in chronological order).
b. Include the modified `Date` class constructed for Exercise 6a in a complete C++ program.

7. *a.* Add to Program 11-1's class definition an additional member function named `leapyr()` that returns a 1 if the year is a leap year and a 0 if it is not a leap year. A leap year is any year that is evenly divisible by 4 but not evenly divisible by 100, with the exception that all years evenly divisible by 400 are leap years. For example, the year 1996 is a leap year because it is evenly divisible by 4 and not evenly divisible by 100. The year 2000 will be a leap year because it is evenly divisible by 400.
b. Include the class definition constructed for Exercise 7a in a complete C++ program. The `main()` function should display the message `The year is a leap year` or the message `The year is not a leap year`, depending on the `date` object's `year` value.

8. *a.* Add to Program 11-1's class definition a member function named `dayOfWeek()` that determines the day of the week for any `date` object. An algorithm for determining the day of the week, known as Zeller's algorithm, follows.

```
If mm is less than 2
  mm = mm + 12
  yyyy = yyyy - 1
Endif
Set century = Int(yyyy/100)
Set year = yyyy Mod 100
Set T = dd + Int(26*(mm + 1)/10) + year + Int(year/4)
          + Int(century/4) - 2 * century
Set DayofWeek = T Mod 7
If DayofWeek is less than 0 then DayofWeek = DayofWeek + 1
```

Using this algorithm, the variable `Day-of-week` will have a value of 1 if the date is a Sunday, 2 if a Monday, etc.
b. Include the class definition constructed for Exercise 8a in a complete C++ program. The `main()` function should display the name of the day (`Sun`, `Mon`, `Tue`, etc.) for the `Date` object being tested.

9. a. Construct a class named `Rectangle` that has floating-point data members named `length` and `width`. The class should have a member function named `perimeter()` and `area()` to calculate the perimeter and area of a rectangle, a member function named `getdata()` to set a rectangle's length and width, and a member function named `showdata()` that displays a rectangle's length, width, perimeter, and area.
b. Include the `Rectangle` class constructed in Exercise 9a within a working C++ program.

10. a. Modify the `Date` class defined in Program 11-1 to include a `nextDay()` function that increments a date by one day. Test your function to ensure that it correctly increments days into a new month and into a new year.
b. Modify the `Date` class defined in Program 11-1 to include a `priorDay()` function that decrements a date by one day. Test your function to ensure that it correctly decrements days into a prior month and into a prior year.

11. Modify the `Date` class in Program 11-1 to contain a function that compares two `Date` objects and returns the larger of the two. The function should be written according to the following algorithm:

```
Comparison function
   Accept two Date values as parameters
   Determine the later date using the following procedure:
      Convert each date into an integer value having the form yyyymmdd.
      (This can be accomplished using the formula year * 10000 + month * 100 + day)
      Compare the corresponding integers for each date.
      The larger integer corresponds to the later date.
   Return the later date
```

11.3 Constructors

A *constructor* function is any function that has the same name as its class. Multiple constructors can be defined for each class as long as they are distinguishable by the numbers and types of their parameters (which is simply an example of function overloading).

The intended purpose of a constructor is to initialize a new object's data members. Thus, depending on the number and types of supplied arguments, one constructor function is automatically called each time an object is created.

If no constructor function is written, the compiler supplies a default constructor. In addition to its initialization role, a constructor function may perform other tasks when it is called, and it can be written in a variety of ways. In this section we present the possible variations of constructor functions and introduce another function, the destructor, that is automatically called whenever an object goes out of existence.

Figure 11–4 illustrates the general format of a constructor. As shown in this figure, a constructor

- must have the same name as the class to which it belongs
- must have no return type (not even `void`)

If you do not include a constructor in your class definition, the compiler supplies a do-nothing default one for you. For example, consider the following class declaration:

```
class Date
{
  private:
    int month, day, year;
  public:
    void setdate(int, int, int);
    void showdate(void)
};
```

Because no user-defined constructor has been declared here, the compiler creates a default constructor. For our `Date` class, this default constructor is equivalent to the implementation `Date(void){}`—that is, the compiler-supplied default constructor expects no parameters and has an empty body. Clearly, this default constructor is not very useful, but it does exist if no other constructor is declared.

The term *default constructor* is used quite frequently in C++. It refers to any constructor that does not require any arguments when it is called. This can be because no parameters are declared, which is the case for the compiler-supplied default, or because all arguments have been given default values. For example,

FIGURE 11–4 Constructor Format

```
class-name::class-name(parameter list)
{
  function body
}
```

the constructor `Date(int = 7, int = 4, int = 2001)` is a valid prototype for a default constructor. Here, each argument has been given a default value, and an object can be declared as type `Date` without supplying any further arguments. Using such a constructor, the declaration `Date a;` initializes the `a` object with the default values 7, 4, and 2001.

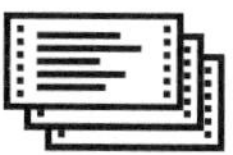

Program 11-2

```
#include <iostream.h>
#include <iomanip.h>

// class declaration section

class Date
{
  private:
    int month;
    int day;
    int year;
  public:
    Date(int = 7, int = 4, int = 2001);     // constructor with defaults
};

// implementation section

Date::Date(int mm, int dd, int yyyy)
{
  month = mm;
  day = dd;
  year = yyyy;
  cout << "Created a new data object with data values "
       << month << ", " << day << ", " << year << endl;
}

int main()
{
  Date a;             // declare an ojbect
  Date b;             // declare an object
  Date c(4,1,2002);   // declare an object

  return 0;
}
```

To verify that a constructor function is automatically called whenever a new object is created, consider Program 11-2. Note that in the implementation section, the constructor function uses `cout` to display the message `Created a new data object with data values`. Thus, whenever the constructor is called, this message is displayed. Because the `main()` function creates three objects, the constructor is called three times, and the message is displayed three times.

The following output is produced when Program 11-2 is executed:

```
Created a new data object with data values 7, 4, 2001
Created a new data object with data values 7, 4, 2001
Created a new data object with data values 4, 1, 2002
```

Although any legitimate C++ statement can be used within a constructor function, such as the `cout` statement used in Program 11-2, it is best to keep constructors simple and to use them only for initializing purposes. One further point needs to be made with respect to the constructor function contained in Program 11-2. According to the rules of C++, object members are initialized in the order in which they are declared in the class declaration section, *not* in the order in which they may appear in the function's definition within the implementation section. Usually this will not be an issue, unless one member is initialized using another data member's value.

Calling Constructors

As we have seen, constructors are called whenever an object is created. The actual declaration, however, can be made in a variety of ways. For example, the declaration

```
Date c(4,1,2002);
```

used in Program 11-2 could also have been written as

```
Date c = Date(4,1,2002);
```

This second form declares `c` as being of type `Date` and then makes a direct call to the constructor function with the arguments `4`, `1`, and `2002`. This second form can be simplified when only one argument is passed to the constructor. For example, if only the `month` data member of the `c` object needed to be initialized with the value 8, and the `day` and `year` members can use the default values, the object can be created using the declaration

```
Date c = 8;
```

Because this resembles declarations in C, it and its complete form using the equals sign are referred to as the C *style of initialization*. The form of declaration used in Program 11-2 is referred to as the C++ *style of initialization,* and this is the form we will use most of the time throughout the remainder of the text.

Regardless of which initialization form you use, in no case should an object be declared with empty parentheses. For example, the declaration `Date a();` is not the same as the declaration `Date a;`. The latter declaration uses the default constructor values, whereas the former declaration results in no object being created.

Overloaded and Inline Constructors

The primary difference between a constructor and other user-written functions is how the constructor is called: Constructors are called automatically each time an object is created, whereas other functions must be explicitly called by name.[10] As a function, however, a constructor must still follow all of the rules applicable to user-written functions that were presented in Chapter 6. This means that constructors may have default arguments, as was illustrated in Programs 11-1 and 11-2, may be overloaded, and may be written as inline functions.

Recall from Section 6.1 that function overloading permits the same function name to be used with different parameter lists. On the basis of the argument types supplied, the compiler determines which function to use when the call is encountered. Let's see how this can be applied to our `Date` class. For convenience, the appropriate class declaration is repeated below:

```
// class declaration section
class Date
{
  private:
    int month;
    int day;
    int year;
  public:
    Date(int = 7, int = 4, int = 2001);    // constructor
};
```

Here, the constructor prototype specifies three integer parameters, which are used to initialize the `month`, `day`, and `year` data members.

An alternative method of specifying a date is to use a long integer in the form *year* * *10000* + *month* * *100* + *day*. For example, the date 12/24/1998 would

---

[10] This is true for all functions except destructors, which are described later in this section. A destructor function is automatically called each time an object is destroyed.

be 19981224, and the date 2/5/2002 would be 20020205.[11] A suitable prototype for a constructor that uses dates of this form is

```
Date(long);    // an overloaded constructor
```

Here, the constructor is declared as receiving one long-integer argument. The code for this new Date function must, of course, correctly convert its single argument into a month, day, and year and would be included within the class implementation section. The actual code for such a constructor is

```
Date::Date(long yyyymmdd)    // a second constructor
{
  year = int(yyyymmdd/10000.0);     // extract the year
  month = int( (yyyymmdd - year * 10000.0) / 100.00 ); // extract the month
  day = int(yyyymmdd - year * 10000.0 - month * 100.0); // extract the day
}
```

Do not be overly concerned with the actual conversion code used within the function's body. The important point here is the concept of overloading the Date() function to provide two constructors. Program 11-3 contains the complete class definition within the context of a working program.

The output provided by Program 11-3 is

```
The date is 07/04/01
The date is 04/01/98
The date is 05/15/02
```

Three objects are created in Program 11-3's main() function. The first object, a, is initialized with the default constructor using its default arguments. Object b is also initialized with the default constructor but uses the arguments 4, 1, and 1998. Finally, object c, which is initialized with a long integer, uses the second constructor in the class implementation section. The compiler "knows" that it should use this second constructor because the argument specified, 20020515L, is clearly designated as a long integer. It is worthwhile pointing out that a compiler error would occur if both Date constructors had default values. In such a case, a declaration such as Date d; would be ambiguous to the compiler, because it would not be able to determine which constructor to use. Thus, in each implementation section, only one constructor can be written as the default.

---

[11] The reasons for specifying dates in this manner are that only one number needs to be used per date and that sorting the numbers automatically puts the corresponding dates into chronological order.

Program 11-3

```
#include <iostream.h>
#include <iomanip.h>

// class declaration

class Date
{
 private:
    int month;
    int day;
    int year;
  public:
    Date(int = 7, int = 4, int = 2001);      // constructor with defaults
    Date(long);                    // another constructor
    void showdate(void);          // member function to display a date
};

// implementation section

Date::Date(int mm, int dd, int yyyy)
{
  month = mm;
  day = dd;
  year = yyyy;
}

Date::Date(long yyyymmdd)
{
  year = int(yyyymmdd/10000.0);     // extract the year
  month = int( (yyyymmdd - year * 10000.0)/100.00 ); // extract the month
  day = int(yyyymmdd - year * 10000.0 - month * 100.0); // extract the day
}

void Date::showdate(void)
{
  cout << "The date is " << setfill('0')
       << setw(2) << month << '/'
       << setw(2) << day << '/'
       << setw(2) << year % 100; // extract the last 2 year digits
  return;
}

int main()
{
  Date a, b(4,1,1998), c(20020515L); // declare three objects

  cout << endl;

  a.showdate();          // display object a's values
  cout << endl;

  b.showdate();          // display object b's values
  cout << endl;

  c.showdate();          // display object c's values
  cout << endl << endl;

  return 0;
}
```

POINT OF INFORMATION

Constructors

A *constructor* is any function that has the same name as its class. The primary purpose of a constructor is to initialize an object's member variables when an object is created. Thus, a constructor is automatically called when an object is declared.

A class can have multiple constructors, provided that each constructor is distinguishable by having a different formal parameter list. A compiler error results when unique identification of a constructor is not possible. If no constructor is provided, the compiler will supply a do-nothing default constructor.

Every constructor function must be declared *with no return type* (not even `void`). Because they are functions, constructors may also be explicitly called in nondeclarative statements. When used in this manner, the function call requires parentheses following the constructor name, even if no parameters are used. However, when the function is used in a declaration, parentheses *must not* be included for a zero parameter constructor. For example, the declaration `Date a();` is incorrect. The correct declaration is `Date a;`. When parameters are used, however, they must be enclosed within parentheses in both declarative and nondeclarative statements. Default parameter values should be included within the constructor's prototype.

Just as constructors may be overloaded, they may also be written as *inline member functions.*[12] Doing so simply means defining the function in the class declaration section. For example, making both of the constructors contained in Program 11-3 inline is accomplished by the declaration section

```
// class declaration

class Date
{
  private:
    int month;
    int day;
    int year;
  public:
    Date(int mm = 7, int dd = 4, int yyyy = 2001)
    {
      month = mm;
      day = dd;
      year = yyyy;
    }
    Date(long yyyymmdd)    // here is the overloaded constructor
    {
      year = int(yyyymmdd/10000.0);     // extract the year
      month = int( (yyyymmdd - year * 10000.0)/100.00 );  // extract the month
      day = int(yyyymmdd - year * 10000.0 - month * 100.0); // extract the day
    }
};
```

[12] A discussion of the advantages and disadvantages of inline functions was presented at the end of Section 6.2.

POINT OF INFORMATION

Accessor Functions

An *accessor function* is any nonconstructor member function that accesses a class's private data members. For example, the function `showdate()` in the `Date` class is an accessor function. Such functions are extremely important because they provide a means of displaying private data members' stored values.

When you construct a class make sure to provide a complete set of accessor functions. Each accessor function does not have to return a data member's exact value, but it should return a useful representation of the value. For example, assume that a date such as 12/25/2002 is stored as a long-integer member variable in the form `20022512`. Although an accessor function could display this value, a more useful representation would typically be either 12/25/02, or December 25, 2002.

Besides being used for output, accessor functions can also provide a means of data input. For example, the `setdate()` function in the `Date` class is an example of an input accessor function. As we will see in Section 13.4, both the extraction and insertion operators can be overloaded to provide another means of object data input and output. Constructor functions, whose primary purpose is to initialize an object's member variables, are not considered as accessor functions.

The keyword `inline` is not required in this declaration, because member functions defined inside the class declaration are inline by default.

Generally, only functions that can be coded on a single line are good candidates for inline functions. This reinforces the convention that inline functions should be small. Thus the first constructor is more conventionally written as

```
Date(int mm = 7, int dd = 4, int yyyy = 2001)
{ month = mm; day = dd; year = yyyy; }
```

The second constructor, which extends over three lines, should not be written as an inline function.

Destructors

The counterparts of constructor functions are destructor functions. Destructors are functions that have the same class name as constructors but are preceded with a tilde (~). Thus, for our `Date` class, the destructor name is `~Date()`. Like constructors, a default do-nothing destructor is provided by the C++ compiler in the absence of an explicit destructor. Unlike constructors, however, there can be only one destructor function per class. This is because destructors take no arguments—they also return no values.

Destructors are automatically called whenever an object goes out of existence and are meant to "clean up" any undesirable effects that might be left by the object. Generally, such effects occur only when an object contains a pointer member, which is the topic of Section 12.2.

Arrays of Objects[13]

The importance of default constructors becomes evident when arrays of objects are created. Because a constructor is called each time an object is created, the default constructor provides an elegant way of initializing all objects to the same state.

Declaring an array of objects is the same as declaring an array of any built-in type. For example, the declaration

```
Date thedate[5];
```

will create five objects named `thedate[0]` through `thedate[4]`. Member functions for each of these objects are called by listing the object name followed by a dot (`.`) and the desired function. An example using an array of objects is provided by Program 11-4, which also includes `cout` statements within both the constructor and the destructor. As illustrated by the output of this program, the constructor is called for each declared object, followed by five member function calls to `showdate()`, followed by five destructor calls. The destructor is called when the objects go out of scope. In this case, the destructor is called when the `main()` function terminates execution.

The output produced by Program 11-4 is

```
*** A Date object is being initialized ***
*** A Date object is being initialized ***
*** A Date object is being initialized ***
*** A Date object is being initialized ***
*** A Date object is being initialized ***
        The date is 01/01/1999
        The date is 01/01/1999
        The date is 01/01/1999
        The date is 01/01/1999
        The date is 01/01/1999
*** A Date object is going out of existence ***
*** A Date object is going out of existence ***
*** A Date object is going out of existence ***
*** A Date object is going out of existence ***
*** A Date object is going out of existence ***
```

[13] This topic can be omitted with no loss of subject continuity.

Program 11-4

```
#include <iostream.h>
#include <iomanip.h>
```

```
// class declaration section
class Date
{
  private:
    int month;
    int day;
    int year;
  public:
    Date();     // constructor
    ~Date();    // destructor
    void showdate(void);
};

// class implementation
Date::Date()        // user-defined default constructor
{
  cout << "*** A Date object is being initialized ***\n";
  month = 1;
  day = 1;
  year = 1999;
}

Date::~Date()       // user-defined default destructor
{
  cout << "*** A Date object is going out of existence ***\n";
}

void Date::showdate(void)
{
  cout << "          The date is " << setfill('0')
       << setw(2) << month << '/'
       << setw(2) << day << '/'
       << setw(2) << year % 100;  // extract the last 2 year digits

  return;
}
```

```
int main()
{
  const int NUMDATES = 5;
  Date thedate[NUMDATES];

  for(int i = 0; i < NUMDATES; i++)
  {
    thedate[i].showdate();
    cout << endl;
  }

  return 0;
}
```

Exercises 11.3

1. Determine whether the following statements are true or false.
   a. A constructor function must have the same name as its class.
   b. A class can have only one constructor function.
   c. A class can have only one default constructor function.
   d. A default constructor can be supplied only by the compiler.
   e. A default constructor can have no parameters or all parameters must have default values.
   f. A constructor must be declared for each class.
   g. A constructor must be declared with a `return` type.
   h. A constructor is automatically called each time an object is created.
   i. A class can have only one destructor function.
   j. A destructor must have the same name as its class, preceded by a tilde (~).
   k. A destructor can have default arguments.
   l. A destructor must be declared for each class.
   m. A destructor must be declared with a `return` type.
   n. A destructor is automatically called each time an object goes out of existence.
   o. Destructors are not useful when the class contains a pointer data member.

2. For Program 11-3, what date would be initialized for object `c` if the declaration `Date c(15);` were used in place of the declaration `Date c(20020515L);`?

3. Modify Program 11-3 so that the only data member of the class is a long integer named `yyyymmdd`. Do this by substituting the declaration

```
long yyyymmdd;
```

for the existing declarations

```
int month;
int day;
int year;
```

Then, using the same constructor function prototypes currently declared in the class declaration section, rewrite them so that the `Date(long)` function becomes the default constructor and the `Date(int, int, int)` function converts a month, day, and year into the proper form for the class data member.

4. *a.* Construct a `Time` class containing integer data members `seconds`, `minutes`, and `hours`. Have the class contain two constructors. The first should be a default constructor having the prototype `time(int, int, int)`, which uses default values of 0 for each data member. The second constructor should accept a long integer representing a total number of seconds and disassemble the long integer into hours, minutes, and seconds. The final function member should display the class data members.
   b. Include the class written for Exercise 4a within the context of a complete program.

5. *a.* Construct a class named `Student` consisting of an integer student identification number, an array of five floating-point grades, and an integer representing the total number of grades entered. The constructor for this class should initialize all `Student`

data members to zero. Included in the class should be member functions to (1) enter a student ID number, (2) enter a single test grade and update the total number of grades entered, and (3) compute an average grade and display the student ID followed by the average grade.

b. Include the class constructed in Exercise 5a within the context of a complete program. Your program should declare two objects of type `Student` and should accept and display data for the two objects to verify operation of the member functions.

6. *a.* In Exercise 4 you were asked to construct a `Time` class. For such a class, include a `tick()` function that increments the time by 1 second. Test your function to ensure that it correctly increments into a new minute and a new hour.

b. Modify the `Time` class written for Exercise 6a to include a `detick()` function that decrements the time by 1 second. Test your function to ensure that it correctly decrements time into a prior hour and into a prior minute.

11.4 Examples

Now that you have an understanding of how classes are constructed and the terminology used in describing them, let's apply this knowledge to construct two new examples using an object-oriented programming approach. In the first example, we construct a single elevator object. We assume that the elevator can travel between the 1st and 15th floors of a building and that the location of the elevator must be known at all times. In the second example, we simulate the operation of a gas pump.

Example 1: Constructing an Elevator Object

In this example we will simulate the operation of an elevator. What is required is an output that describes the current floor that the elevator is either stationed at or passing by and an internal elevator request button that is pushed as a request to move to another floor. The elevator can travel between the 1st and 15th floors of the building it is situated in.

Solution

For this application we have one object, which is an elevator. The only attribute of interest is the location of the elevator. The single requested service is the ability to request a change in the elevator's position (state). Additionally, we must be able to establish the initial floor position when a new elevator is put in service.

The location of the elevator, which corresponds to its current floor position, can be represented by an integer member variable. The value of this variable, which we will name currentFloor, effectively represents the current state of the elevator. The services that we will provide for changing the state of the elevator will be (1) an initialization function to set the initial floor position when a new elevator is put in service and (2) a request function to change the elevator's position (state) to a new floor. Putting an elevator in service is accomplished by declaring a single class instance (declaring an object of type Elevator), and requesting a new floor position is equivalent to pushing an elevator button. To accomplish this, a suitable class declaration is

```
// class declaration section
class Elevator
{
  private:
    int currentFloor;
  public:
    Elevator(int);         // constructor
    void request(int);
};
```

Note that we have declared one data member, currentFloor, and two class functions. The data member, currentFloor, is used to store the current floor position of the elevator. As a private member, it can be accessed only through member functions. The two declared public member functions, Elevator() and request(), will be used to define the external services provided by each Elevator object. The Elevator() function, which has the same name as its class, becomes a constructor function that is automatically called when an object of type Elevator is created. We will use this function to initialize the starting floor position of the elevator. The request() function is used to alter the position of the elevator. To accomplish these services, a suitable class implementation section is

```
// class implementation section

Elevator::Elevator(int cfloor)   // constructor
{
  currentFloor = cfloor;
}

void Elevator::request(int newfloor)  // access function
{
  if (newfloor < 1 || newfloor > MAXFLOOR || newfloor == currentFloor)
    ;  // do nothing
  else if ( newfloor > currentFloor)  // move elevator up
  {
    cout << "\nStarting at floor " << currentFloor << endl;
    while (newfloor > currentFloor)
    {
```

```
      currentFloor++;     // add one to current floor
      cout << "   Going Up - now at floor " << currentFloor << endl;
    }
    cout << "Stopping at floor " << currentFloor << endl;
  }
  else  // move elevator down
  {
    cout << "\nStarting at floor " << currentFloor << endl;
    while (newfloor < currentFloor)
    {
      currentFloor--;    // subtract one from current floor
      cout << "   Going Down - now at floor " << currentFloor << endl;
    }
    cout << "Stopping at floor " << currentFloor << endl;
  }

  return;
}
```

The constructor function is straightforward. When an `Elevator` object is declared, it is initialized to the floor specified; if no floor is explicitly given, the default value of 1 will be used. For example, the declaration

```
Elevator a(7);
```

initializes the variable `a.currentFloor` to 7, whereas the declaration

```
Elevator a;
```

uses the default argument value and initializes the variable `a.currentFloor` to 1.

The `request()` function defined in the implementation section is more complicated and provides the class's primary service. Essentially, this function consists of an `if-else` statement that has three parts: If an incorrect service is requested, no action is taken; if a floor above the current position is selected, the elevator is moved up; and if a floor below the current position is selected, the elevator is moved down. For movement up or down, the function uses a `while` loop to increment the position one floor at a time and reports the elevator's movement using a `cout` object call. Program 11-5 includes this class in a working program.

Testing the `Elevator` class entails testing each class operation. To do this, we first include the `Elevator` class within the context of a working program, which is listed as Program 11-5.

The lightly shaded portion of Program 11-5 contains the class construction that we have already described. To see how this class is used, concentrate on the

Program 11-5

```
#include <iostream.h>
const int MAXFLOOR = 15;

// class declaration
class Elevator
{
  private:
    int currentFloor;
  public:
    Elevator(int = 1);        // constructor
    void request(int);
};

// implementation section
Elevator::Elevator(int cfloor)
{
  currentFloor = cfloor;
}

void Elevator::request(int newfloor)
{
 if (newfloor < 1 || newfloor > MAXFLOOR || newfloor == currentFloor)
    ;  // do nothing
  else if ( newfloor > currentFloor)  // move elevator up
  {
    cout << "\nStarting at floor " << currentFloor << endl;
    while (newfloor > currentFloor)
    {
      currentFloor++;     // add one to current floor
      cout << "   Going Up - now at floor " << currentFloor << endl;
    }
    cout << "Stopping at floor " << currentFloor << endl;
  }
  else  // move elevator down
  {
    cout << "\nStarting at floor " << currentFloor << endl;
    while (newfloor < currentFloor)
    {
      currentFloor--;    // subtract one from current floor
      cout << "   Going Down - now at floor " << currentFloor << endl;
    }
    cout << "Stopping at floor " << currentFloor << endl;
  }
  return;
}

int main()
{
  Elevator a;   // declare 1 object of type Elevator

  a.request(6);
  a.request(3);

  return 0;
}
```

darkly shaded section of the program. At the top of the program, we have included the `iostream.h` header file and declared a named constant `MAXFLOOR`, which corresponds to the highest floor that can be requested.

Three statements are included within the `main()` function. The first statement creates an object named `a` of type `Elevator`. Because no explicit floor has been given, this elevator will begin at floor 1, which is the default constructor argument.

A request is then made to move the elevator to floor 6, which is followed by a request to move to floor 3. The output produced by Program 11-5 is

```
Starting at floor 1
   Going Up - now at floor 2
   Going Up - now at floor 3
   Going Up - now at floor 4
   Going Up - now at floor 5
   Going Up - now at floor 6
Stopping at floor 6

Starting at floor 6
   Going Down - now at floor 5
   Going Down - now at floor 4
   Going Down - now at floor 3
Stopping at floor 3
```

The basic requirements of object-oriented programming are evident in even as simple a program as Program 11-5. Before the `main()` function can be written, a useful class must be constructed. This is typical of programs that use objects. For such programs the design process is front-loaded with the requirement that careful consideration of the class—its declaration and implementation —be given. Code contained in the implementation section effectively removes code that would otherwise be part of `main()`'s responsibility. Thus any program that uses the object does not have to repeat the implementation details within its `main()` function. Rather, the `main()` function and any function called by `main()` is only concerned with sending messages to its objects to activate them appropriately. How the object responds to the messages and how the state of the object is retained is not `main()`'s concern—these details are hidden within the class construction.

One further point should be made concerning Program 11-5, which is the control provided by the `main()` function. Notice that this control is sequential, with two calls made to the same object operation, using different argument values. This control is perfectly correct for testing purposes. However, by incorporating calls to `request()` within a `while` loop and using the random number function `rand()` to generate random floor requests, a continuous simulation of the elevator's operation is possible (see Exercise 3).

Example 2: A Single-Object Gas Pump Simulation

Assume that we have been requested to write a program that simulates the operation of a gas pump. At any time during the simulation, we should be able to determine, from the pump, the price per gallon of gas and the amount remaining in the supply tank from which the gas is being pumped. If a request for gas, in gallons, is less than the amount of gas in the tank, the request should be filled; otherwise, only the amount available in the supply tank should be used. Once the gas is pumped, the total price of the gallons pumped should be displayed, and the amount of gas, in gallons, that was pumped should be subtracted from the amount in the supply tank.

Additionally, for each request for gas, we will want to know how many gallons of gas were pumped and the total price of the transaction. The pump itself must keep track of the price per gallon of gas and the amount of gas remaining in the tank. Typically, the price per gallon is $1.00, but the price used for the simulation should be $1.25. The supply tank has a capacity of 500 gallons but currently contains 300 gallons.

Solution

The model for constructing a gas pump class that meets the specified requirements is easily described in pseudocode as follows:

```
Put Pump in Service
  Initialize the amount of gas in the tank
  Initialize the price per gallon of gas

Display Values
  Display the amount of gas in the tank
  Display the price per gallon

Pump an amount of Gas
  If the amount in the tank = amount to be pumped
    Set pumped amount equal to the amount in the tank
  Else
    Set pumped amount equal to the amount to be pumped
  EndIf
  Subtract the pumped amount from the amount in the tank
  Calculate the total price as (price per gallon * pumped amount)
  Display the pumped amount
  Display the amount remaining in the tank
  Display the total price
```

From this pseudocode description, the implementation of a `Pump` class is rather straightforward. The attributes of interest for the pump are the amount of gallons in the tank and the price per gallon. The required operations include supplying initial values for the pump attributes, interrogating the pump for its attribute values, and satisfying a request for gas.

Because the two attributes, the amount in the tank and the price per gallon, can have fractional values, it is appropriate to make them floating-point values. Additionally, three services need to be provided. The first is to initialize a pump's attributes, which consists of setting values for the amount in the supply tank and the price per gallon. The second is to satisfy a request for gas, and the third service is simply to provide a reading of the pump's current attribute values. To accomplish this, a suitable class declaration is

```
// class declaration

class Pump
{
  private:
    float amtInTank;
    float price;
  public:
    Pump(float = 500.0, float = 1.00);    // constructor
    void values(void);
    void request(float);
};
```

Note that we have declared two data members and three member functions. As private members, the two data attributes can be accessed only through the class's declared member functions: `Pump()`, `values()`, and `request()`. It is these functions that provide the external services available to each `Pump` object.

The `Pump()` function, which has the same name as its class, is the constructor function that is automatically called when an object of type `Pump` is created. The `values()` function simply provides a readout of the current attribute values, and the `request()` function handles the logic for fulfilling a customer's request for gas. To accomplish these services, a suitable class implementation section is

```
// implementation section

Pump::Pump(float start, float todaysPrice)
{
  amtInTank = start;
  price = todaysPrice;
}
```

(continued on next page)

(continued from previous page)

```
void Pump::values(void)
{
  cout << setiosflags(ios::fixed) << setiosflags(ios::showpoint)
       << setprecision(2);
  cout << "The gas tank has " << amtInTank << " gallons of gas." << endl;
  cout << "The price per gallon of gas is $" << price << endl;

  return;
}

void Pump::request(float pumpAmt)
{
  float pumped;

  if (amtInTank >= pumpAmt)
     pumped = pumpAmt;
  else
     pumped = amtInTank;
  amtInTank -= pumped;

  cout << setiosflags(ios::fixed) << setiosflags(ios::showpoint)
       << setprecision(2);
  cout << "     Gallons requested: " << pumpAmt << endl;
  cout << "     Gallons pumped: " << pumped << endl;
  cout << "     Gallons remaining in tank: " << amtInTank << endl;
  cout << "     The price of the sale is $" << (pumped * price) << endl;

  return;
}
```

The constructor function is straightforward. When a `Pump` object is declared, it will be initialized to a given amount of gas in the supply tank and a given price per gallon. If no values are given, the defaults of 500 gallons and $1 per gallon will be used.

The `values()` function defined in the implementation section simply provides a readout of the current attribute values. It is the `request()` function that is the most complicated, because it provides the primary `Pump` service. The code follows the requirements of the pump as described in pseudocode; that is, it provides all of the gas required unless the amount remaining in the supply tank is less than the requested amount. Finally, it subtracts the amount pumped from the amount in the tank and calculates the total dollar value of the transaction.

Testing the `Pump` class entails testing each class operation. To do this, we first include the `Pump` class within the context of a working program, which is listed as Program 11-6.

Program 11-6

```
#include <iostream.h>
#include <iomanip.h>
const float AMT_IN_TANK = 300;  // initial gallons in the tank
const float TODAYS_PRICE = 1.25;  // price-per-gallon
```

```
// class declaration

class Pump
{
  private:
    float amtInTank;
    float price;
  public:
    Pump(float = 500.0, float = 1.00);   // constructor
    void values(void);
    void request(float);
};

// implementation section

Pump::Pump(float start, float todaysPrice)
{
  amtInTank = start;
  price = todaysPrice;
}

void Pump::values(void)
{
  cout << setiosflags(ios::fixed) << setiosflags(ios::showpoint)
       << setprecision(2);
  cout << "The gas tank has " << amtInTank << " gallons of gas." << endl;
  cout << "The price per gallon of gas is $" << price << endl;

  return;
}

void Pump::request(float pumpAmt)
{
  float pumped;

  if (amtInTank >= pumpAmt)
     pumped = pumpAmt;
  else
     pumped = amtInTank;

  amtInTank -= pumped;

  cout << setiosflags(ios::fixed) << setiosflags(ios::showpoint)
            << setprecision(2);
  cout << "    Gallons requested: " << pumpAmt << endl;
  cout << "    Gallons pumped: " << pumped << endl;
  cout << "    Gallons remaining in tank: " << amtInTank << endl;
  cout << "    The price of the sale is $" << (pumped * price) << endl;

  return;
}
```

(continued on next page)

(continued from previous page)

```
int main()
{
  Pump a(AMT_IN_TANK, TODAYS_PRICE);    // declare 1 object of type Pump
  a.values();
  cout << endl;
  a.request(30.0);
  cout << endl;
  a.request(280.0);

  return 0;
}
```

The lightly shaded portion of Program 11-6 contains the class construction that we have already described. To see how this class is used, concentrate on the darkly shaded section of the program. At the top of the program, we have included the required include files and two constants, AMT_IN_TANK and TODAYS_PRICE, which correspond to the data that is to be used in the simulation.

Within the main() function six statements are included. The first statement creates an object named a of type Pump. The supply tank for this pump contains AMT_IN_TANK gallons, and the price per gallon is set to TODAYS_PRICE.

A request is then made to values() to display the pump's attribute values, which are correctly set at 300 gallons and $1.25 per gallon. The next cout statement simply provides a blank line.

The first request for gas is for 30 gallons, followed by a cout statement to provide a blank line again. Finally, the last statement is a request for 280 gallons, which exceeds the available gas in the supply tank.

The output produced by Program 11-6 is

```
The gas tank has 300 gallons of gas.
The price per gallon of gas is $1.25


30.00 gallons were requested
30.00 gallons were pumped
270.00 gallons remain in the tank
The total price is $37.50


280.00 gallons were requested
270.00 gallons were pumped
0.00 gallons remain in the tank
The total price is $337.50
```

Exercises 11.4

1. Enter Program 11-5 in your computer and execute it.

2. *a.* Modify the `main()` function in Program 11-5 to put a second elevator in service starting at the 5th floor. Have this second elevator move to the 1st floor and then move to the 12th floor.
   b. Verify that the constructor function is called by adding, within the constructor, a message that is displayed each time a new object is created. Run your program to ensure its operation.

3. Modify the `main()` function in Program 11-5 to use a `while` loop that calls the `Elevator`'s request function with a random number between 1 and 15. If the random number is the same as the elevator's current floor, generate another request. The `while` loop should terminate after five valid requests have been made and satisfied by movement of the elevator. (*Hint:* Review Section 6.8 for the use of random numbers.)

4. *a.* Modify the `main()` function in Program 11-6 to use a `while` loop that calls the `Pump`'s request function with a random number between 3 and 20. The `while` loop should terminate after five requests have been made.
   b. Modify the `main()` function written for Exercise 4a to provide a 30-minute simulation of the gas pump's operation. To do this, you will have to modify the `while` loop to select a random number between 1 and 15 that represents the idle time between customer requests. Have the simulation stop once the idle time exceeds 30 minutes. (*Hint:* Review Section 6.8 for the use of random numbers.)

5. *a.* Construct a class definition of a `Person` object type. The class is to have no attributes, a single constructor function, and two additional member functions named `arrive()` and `gallons()`. The constructor function should simply call `srand()` with the argument `time(NULL)` to initialize the `rand()` function. The `arrive()` function should provide a random number between 1 and 15 as a `return` value, and the `gallons()` function should provide a random number between 3 and 20. (*Hint:* Review Section 6.8 for the use of random numbers.)
   b. Test the `Person` class functions written for Exercise 5a in a complete working program.
   c. Use the `Person` class function to simulate a random arrival of a `Person` and a random request for gallons of gas within the program written for Exercise 4b.

6. Modify Program 11-6 so that the `Pump` class definition resides in a file named `PUMP.H`. Then have Program 11-5 use a `#include` statement to include the class definition within the program. Be sure to use a full path name in the `include` statement. For example, if `PUMP.H` resides in the directory named `FOO` on the `C` drive, the `include` statement should be `#include <C:\FOO\PUMP.C>`.

7. Construct a class named `Light` that simulates a traffic light. The color attribute of the class should change from `Green` to `Yellow` to `Red` and then back to `Green` by the class's `change()` function. When a new `Light` object is created, its initial color should be `Red`.

8. *a.* Construct a class definition that can be used to represent an employee of a company. Each employee is defined by an integer ID number, a floating-point pay rate, and the maximum number of hours the employee should work each week. The

services provided by the class should be the ability to enter data for a new employee, the ability to change data for a new employee, and the ability to display the existing data for a new employee.

b. Include the class definition created for Exercise 8a in a working C++ program that asks the user to enter data for three employees and displays the entered data.

c. Modify the program written for Exercise 8b to include a menu that offers the user the following choices:

```
1. Add an Employee
2. Modify Employee data
3. Delete an Employee
4. Exit this menu
```

In response to a choice, the program should initiate appropriate action to implement the choice.

9. *a.* Construct a class definition that can be used to represent types of food. A type of food is classified as basic or prepared. Basic foods are further classified as either dairy, meat, fruit, vegetable, or grain. The services provided by the class should be the ability to enter data for a new food, the ability to change data for a new food, and the ability to display the existing data for a new food.

b. Include the class definition created for Exercise 9a in a working C++ program that asks the user to enter data for four food items and displays the entered data.

c. Modify the program written for Exercise 9b to include a menu that offers the user the following choices:

```
1. Add a Food Item
2. Modify a Food Item
3. Delete a Food Item
4. Exit this menu
```

In response to a choice the program should initiate appropriate action to implement the choice.

11.5 Common Programming Errors

The more common programming errors initially associated with the construction of classes are

1. Failing to terminate the class declaration section with a semicolon.
2. Including a return type with the constructor's prototype or failing to include a return type with the other functions' prototypes.

POINT OF INFORMATION

Encapsulation

The term *encapsulation* refers to the packaging of a number of items into a single unit. For example, a function is used to encapsulate the details of an algorithm. Similarly, a class encapsulates both variables and functions together in a single package.

Although the term *encapsulation* is sometimes used to refer to the process of information hiding, this usage is technically not accurate. The term *information hiding* refers to the encapsulation *and* hiding of all implementation details.

3. Using the same name for a data member as for a member function.
4. Defining more than one default constructor for a class.
5. Forgetting to include the class name and scope operator, `::`, in the header line of all member functions defined in the class implementation section.

All of these errors will result in a compiler error message.

11.6 Chapter Summary

1. A *class* is a programmer-defined data type. *Objects* of a class may be defined and have the same relationship to their class as variables do to C++'s built-in data types.
2. A class definition consists of a declaration and an implementation section. The most common form of a class definition is

```
// class declaration section
class name
{
  private:
   a list of variable declarations;
  public:
    a list of function prototypes;
};

// class implementation section
class function definitions
```

The variables and functions declared in the class declaration section are collectively referred to as *class members*. The variables are individually referred to as class data members and the functions as class member functions. The terms `private` and `public` are access specifiers. Once an access specifier is listed, it remains in force until another access specifier is given. The `private` keyword specifies that the class members following it are private to the class and can be accessed only by member functions. The `public` keyword specifies that the class members following may be accessed from outside the class. Generally all data members should be specified as `private` and all member functions as `public`.

3. Class functions listed in the declaration section may either be written inline or their definitions included in the class implementation section. Except for constructor and destructor functions, all class functions defined in the class implementation section have the header line syntax

   ```
   return-type  class-name::function-name(parameter list);
   ```

   Except for the addition of the class name and scope operator, `::`, which are necessary to identify the function name with the class, this header line is identical to the header line used for any user-written function.

4. A *constructor function* is a special function that is automatically called each time an object is declared. It must have the same name as its class and cannot have any `return` type. Its purpose is to initialize each declared object.
5. If no constructor is declared for a class, the compiler will supply a default constructor. This is a do-nothing function that has the definition *`class-name::class-name(void){}`*.
6. The term *default constructor* refers to any constructor that does not require any arguments when it is called. This can be because no parameters are declared (as is the case for the compiler-supplied default constructor) or because all parameters have been given default values.
7. Each class may only have one default constructor. If any constructor is user-defined, the compiler will not create its default constructor. Thus, if any class constructor is user-defined, a default class constructor should also be user-defined.
8. Objects are created using either the C++ or the C style of declaration. The C++ style of declaration has the form

   ```
   class-name list-of-object-names(list of initializers);
   ```

   where the list of initializers is optional. An example of this style of declaration, including initializers, for a class named `Date` is

   ```
   Date a, b, c(12,25,2002);
   ```

Here the objects `a` and `b` are declared to be of type `Date` and are initialized using the default constructor, and the object `c` is initialized with the values 12, 25, and 2002.

The equivalent C style of declaration, including the optional list of initializers, has the form

```
class-name object-name = class-name(list of initializers);
```

An example of this style of declaration for a class named `Date` is

```
Date c = Date(12,25,2002)
```

Here the object `c` is created and initialized with the values 12, 25, and 2002.

9. Constructors may be overloaded in the same manner as any other user-written C++ function.
10. If a constructor is defined for a class, a user-defined default constructor should be written, because the compiler will not supply it.
11. A destructor function is called each time an object goes out of scope. Destructors must have the same name as their class, preceded by a tilde (~). There can be only one destructor per class.
12. A *destructor function* takes no arguments and returns no value. If a user-defined destructor is not included in a class, the compiler will provide a do-nothing destructor.

11.7 Chapter Supplement: Insides and Outsides

Just as the concept of an algorithm is central to procedures, the concept of encapsulation is central to objects. In this section, we present this encapsulation concept using an inside-outside analogy, which should help you understand what object-oriented programming is all about.

In programming terms, an object's attributes are described by data, such as the length and width of a rectangle, and the operations that can be applied to the attributes are described by procedures and functions.

As a practical example of this, assume that we will be writing a program that can deal a hand of cards. From an object-oriented approach, one of the objects that we must model is clearly a deck of cards. For our purposes, the attribute of interest for the card deck is that it contains 52 cards, divided into

4 suits (hearts, diamonds, spades, and clubs), each suit consisting of 13 pip values (ace to ten, Jack, Queen, and King).

Now consider the behavior of our deck of cards, which consists of the operations that can be applied to the deck. At a minimum, we will want the ability to shuffle the deck and to deal single cards. Let's now see how this simple example illustrates encapsulation using an inside-outside concept.

A useful visualization of the inside-outside concept is to consider an object as a boiled egg, such as shown in Figure 11–5. Note that the egg consists of three parts: a very inside yolk, a less inside white surrounding the yolk, and an outside shell, which is the only part of the egg visible to the outside world.

In terms of our boiled egg model, the attributes and behavior of an object correspond to the yolk and white, respectively, which are inside the egg. That is, the innermost protected area of an object, its data attributes, can be compared to the egg yolk.

Surrounding the data attributes, much as an egg's white surrounds its yolk, are the operations that we choose to incorporate within an object. Finally, the interface to the outside world, which is analogous to the shell, represents the means by which a user invokes the object's internal procedures.

The egg model, with its egg shell interface separating the inside of the egg from the outside, is useful precisely because it so clearly depicts the separation between what should be contained inside an object and what should be seen from the outside. This separation is an essential element in object-oriented programming. Let's see why.

From an inside-outside perspective, an object's data attributes, the selected algorithms for the object's operations, and how these algorithms are actually implemented are always "inside" issues that are hidden from the view of an object user. How a user or another object can actually activate an inside procedure, by contrast, is an "outside" issue.

Now let's apply this concept to our deck of cards. First, consider how we might represent cards in the deck. Any of the following attributes (and there are others) could be used to represent a card:

FIGURE 11–5 The Boiled Egg Object Model

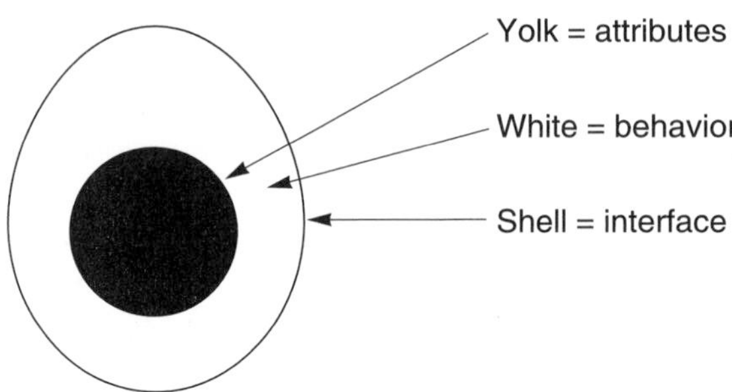

1. Two integer variables, one representing a suit (a number from 1 to 4) and one representing a value (a number from 1 to 13).
2. One character value and one integer value. The character represents a card's suit, and the integer represents a card's value.
3. One integer variable having a value from 0 to 51. The expression `int(number / 13 + 1)` provides a number from 1 to 4, which represents the suit, and the expression (`number Mod 13 + 1`) represents a card value from 1 to 13.

Which attribute we select, however, is not relevant to the outside. The specific way we choose to represent a card is an inside issue to be decided by the designer of the deck object. From the outside, all that is of concern is that we have access to a deck consisting of 52 cards that have the necessary suits and pip values.

The same is true for the operations we decide to provide as part of our card deck object. Consider just the shuffling for now.

There are a number of algorithms for producing a shuffled deck. For example, we could use C++'s random number function, `Rand()`, or we could create our own random number generator. Again, the selected algorithm is an inside issue to be determined by the designer of the deck. Which algorithm is selected and how it is applied to the attributes we have chosen for each card in the deck are not relevant from the object's outside. For purposes of illustration, assume that we decide to use C++'s `Rand()` function to produce a randomly shuffled deck.

If we use the first attribute set previously given, each card in a shuffled deck is produced using `Rand()` at least twice: once to create a random number from 1 to 4 for the suit, and then again to create a random number from 1 to 13 for the card's pip value. This sequence must be done to construct 52 different attribute sets, with no duplicates allowed.

If, on the other hand, we use the second attribute set previously given, a shuffled deck can be produced in exactly the same fashion as above, with one modification: The first random number (from 1 to 4) must be changed into a character to represent the suit.

Finally, if we use the third representation for a card, we need to use `Rand()` once for each card to produce 52 random numbers from 0 to 51, with no duplicates allowed.

The important point here is that the selection of an algorithm and how it will be applied to an object's attributes are implementation issues, *and implementation issues are always inside issues.* A user of the card deck, who is outside, does not need to know how the shuffling is done. All the user of the deck must know is how to produce a shuffled deck. In practice, this means that the user is supplied with sufficient information to invoke the shuffle function correctly. This corresponds to the interface, or the outer shell of the egg.

Abstraction and Encapsulation

The distinction between insides and outsides is directly related to the concepts of abstraction and encapsulation. Abstraction means concentrating on what an object is and does before making any decisions about how the object will be implemented. Thus, abstractly, we define a deck and the operations we want to provide. (Clearly, if our abstraction is to be useful, it had better capture the attributes and operations of a real-world deck.) Once we have decided on the attributes and operations, we can actually implement them.

Encapsulation in general usage means separating the implementation details of the chosen abstract attributes and behavior and hiding them from outside users of the object. The external side of an object should provide, to users of the object, only the interface necessary for activating internal procedures. Imposing a strict inside-outside discipline when creating objects is really another way of saying that the object successfully encapsulates all implementation details. In our deck-of-cards example, encapsulation means that users need never know how we have internally modeled the deck or how an operation, such as shuffling, is performed; they need only know how to activate the given operations.

Code Reuse and Extensibility

A direct advantage of an inside-outside object approach is that it encourages both code reuse and extensibility. This is a direct result of having all interactions between objects centered on the outside interface and hiding all implementation details within the object's inside.

For example, consider the object shown in Figure 11–6. Here, each of the object's two operations can be activated by correctly stimulating either the circle or the square on the outside. In practice, the stimulation is simply a method

FIGURE 11–6 Using an Object's Interface

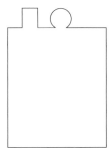

call. We have used a circle and a square to emphasize that two different methods are provided for outside use. In our deck-of-cards example, activation of one method might produce a shuffled deck, whereas activation of another method might result in a card suit and pip value being returned from the object.

Now assume that we want to alter the implementation of an existing operation or add more functionality to our object. *As long as the existing outside interface is maintained, the internal implementation of any and all operations can be changed without the user ever being aware that a change took place.* This is a direct result of encapsulating the attribute data and operations within an object.

Furthermore, as long as the interface to existing operations is not changed, new operations can be added as they are needed. Essentially, from the perspective of the outside world, all that is being added is another function call that accesses the inside attributes and modifies them in a new way.

Additional Class Capabilities

Chapter Twelve

The creation of a class requires that we provide the capability to declare, initialize, assign, manipulate, and display data members. In the previous chapter the declaration, initialization, and display of objects were presented. In this chapter we continue our construction of classes and see how to provide assignment between objects and include pointer members within a class declaration.

12.1 Assignment

In Chapter 3 we saw how C++'s assignment operator, `=`, performs assignment between variables. In this section we shall see how assignment works when it is applied to objects and how to define our own assignment operator to override the default provided for user-defined classes.

For a specific assignment example, consider the `main()` function of Program 12-1.

Note that the implementation section of the `Date` class in Program 12-1 contains no assignment function. Nevertheless, we would expect the assignment statement `a = b;` in `main()` to assign `b`'s data member values to their counterparts in `a`. This is, in fact, the case and it is verified by the output produced when Program 12-1 is executed:

```
The date stored in a is originally 04/01/99
After assignment the date stored in a is 12/18/01
```

This type of assignment is called *memberwise assignment*. In the absence of any specific instructions to the contrary, the C++ compiler builds this type of default assignment operator for each class. If the class *does not* contain any pointer data members, this default assignment operator is adequate and can be used without further consideration. Before considering the problems that can occur with pointer data members, let's see how to construct our own explicit assignment operators.

Assignment operators, like all class members, are declared in the class declaration section and defined in the class implementation section. For the declaration of operators, however, the keyword `operator` must be included in the declaration. When we use this keyword, a simple assignment operator declaration has the form

```
void operator=(class-name& );
```

Here the keyword `void` indicates that the assignment returns no value, the `operator=` indicates that we are overloading the assignment operator with our own version, and the class name and ampersand within the parentheses indicate that the argument to the operator is a class reference. For example, to declare a simple assignment operator for our `Date` class, we can use the declaration

```
void operator=(Date& );
```

Program 12-1

```
#include <iostream.h>
#include <iomanip.h>

// class declaration

class Date
{
  private:
    int month;
    int day;
    int year;
  public:
    Date(int = 7, int = 4, int = 2001); // constructor prototype with defaults
    void showdate(void);       // member function to display a Date
};

// implementation section

Date::Date(int mm, int dd, int yyyy)
{
  month = mm;
  day = dd;
  year = yyyy;
}

void Date::showdate(void)
{
  cout << setfill ('0')
       << setw(2) << month << '/'
       << setw(2) << day << '/'
       << setw(2) << year % 100;
  return;
}

int main()
{
  Date a(4,1,1999), b(12,18,2001); // declare two objects

  cout << "\nThe date stored in a is originally ";
  a.showdate();  // display the original date
  a = b;         // assign b's value to a
  cout << "\nAfter assignment the date stored in a is ";
  a.showdate();  // display a's values
  cout << endl;

  return 0;
}
```

The actual implementation of the assignment operator is defined in the implementation section. For our declaration, a suitable implementation is

```
void Date::operator=(Date& newdate)
{
  day = newdate.day;        // assign the day
  month = newdate.month;    // assign the month
  year = newdate.year;      // assign the year
}
```

The use of the reference parameter in the definition of this operation is not accidental. In fact, one of the primary reasons for adding reference variables to C++ was to facilitate the construction of overloaded operators and make the notation more natural.[1] In this definition, `newdate` is defined as a reference to a `Date` class. Within the body of the definition, the `day` member of the object referenced by `newdate` is assigned to the `day` member of the current object, which is then repeated for the `month` and `year` members. Assignments such as `a.operator=(b);` can then be used to call the overloaded assignment operator and assign `b`'s member values to `a`. For convenience, the expression `a.operator=(b)` can be replaced with `a = b;`. Program 12-2 contains our new assignment operator within the context of a complete program.

Except for the addition of the overloaded assignment operator declaration and definition, Program 12-2 is identical to Program 12-1 and produces the same output. Its usefulness to us is that it illustrates how we can explicitly construct our own assignment definitions. In the next section, when we introduce pointer data members, we will see how C++'s default assignment can cause troublesome errors that are circumvented by constructing our own assignment operators. Before moving on, however, we need to make two simple modifications to our assignment operator.

First, to preclude any inadvertent alteration to the object used on the right-hand side of the assignment, a constant reference parameter should be used. For our `Date` class, this takes the form

```
void Date::operator=(const Date& secdate);
```

The final modification concerns the operation's return value. As constructed, our simple assignment operator returns no value, which precludes our using it in multiple assignments such as `a = b = c`. The reason for this is that overloaded operators retain the same precedence and associativity as their equivalent built-in versions. Thus an expression such as `a = b = c` is evaluated in the order

[1] Passing a reference is preferable to passing an object by value, because it eliminates the overhead required in making a copy of each object's data members.

Program 12-2

```
#include <iostream.h>
#include <iomanip.h>

// class declaration

class Date
{
  private:
    int month;
    int day;
    int year;
  public:
    Date(int = 7, int = 4, int = 2001); // constructor prototype with defaults
    void operator=(Date&);    // define assignment of a date
    void showdate(void);      // member function to display a date
};

// implementation section

Date::Date(int mm, int dd, int yyyy)
{
  month = mm;
  day = dd;
  year = yyyy;
}

void Date::operator=(Date& newdate)
{
  day = newdate.day;        // assign the day
  month = newdate.month;    // assign the month
  year = newdate.year;      // assign the year

  return;
}

void Date::showdate(void)
{
  cout << setfill('0')
       << setw(2) << month << '/'
       << setw(2) << day << '/'
       << setw(2) << year % 100;

  return;
}

int main()
{
  Date a(4,1,1999), b(12,18,2001); // declare two objects

  cout << "\nThe date stored in a is originally ";
  a.showdate();  // display the original date
  a = b;         // assign b's value to a
  cout << "\nAfter assignment the date stored in a is ";
  a.showdate();  // display a's values
  cout << endl;

  return 0;
}
```

`a = (b = c)`. As we have defined assignment, unfortunately, the expression `b = c` returns no value, making subsequent assignment to `a` an error. To provide for multiple assignments, a complete assignment operation would return a reference to its class type. Because the implementation of such an assignment requires a special class pointer, the presentation of this complete assignment operator is deferred until the material presented in the next chapter is introduced. Until then, our simple assignment operator will be more than adequate for our needs.

Copy Constructors

Although assignment looks similar to initialization, it is worthwhile noting that they are two entirely different operations. In C++ an initialization occurs every time a new object is created. In an assignment, no new object is created—the value of an existing object is simply changed. Figure 12–1 illustrates this difference.

One type of initialization that closely resembles assignment occurs in C++ when one object is initialized using another object of the same class. For example, in the declaration

```
Date b = a;
```

or its entirely equivalent form

```
Date b(a);
```

the `b` object is initialized to a previously declared `a` object. The constructor that performs this type of initialization is called a *copy constructor*, and if you do not declare one, the compiler will construct one for you. The compiler's *default copy constructor* performs in a similar manner as the default assignment operator by doing a memberwise copy between objects. Thus, for the declaration `Date b = a;` the default copy constructor sets `b`'s month, day, and year values to their respective counterparts in `a`. Like default assignment operators, default copy constructors work just fine unless the class contains pointer data members. Before considering the complications that can occur with pointer data members and how to handle them, it will be helpful to see how to construct our own copy constructors.

FIGURE 12–1 Initialization and Assignment

```
                      c = a          <—— Assignment
Type definition ——> Date c = a;      <—— Initialization
```

Copy constructors, like all class functions, are declared in the class declaration section and defined in the class implementation section. The declaration of a copy constructor has the general form

```
class-name(const class-name& );
```

As with all constructors, the function name must be the class name. As further illustrated by the declaration, the parameter is a reference to the class, which is a characteristic of all copy constructors.[2] To ensure that the parameter is not inadvertently altered, it is always specified as a `const`. Applying this general form to our `Date` class, a copy constructor can be explicitly declared as

```
Date(const Date& );
```

The actual implementation of this constructor, if it were to perform the same memberwise initialization as the default copy constructor, would take the form

```
Date:: Date(const Date& olddate)
{
  month = olddate.month;
  day = olddate.day;
  year = olddate.year;
}
```

As with the assignment operator, the use of a reference parameter for the copy constructor is no accident: The reference parameter again facilitates a simple notation within the body of the function. Program 12-3 contains this copy constructor within the context of a complete program.

The output produced by Program 12-3 is

```
The date stored in a is 04/01/99
The date stored in b is 12/18/02
The date stored in c is 04/01/99
The date stored in d is 12/18/02
```

As illustrated by this output, `c`'s and `d`'s data members have been initialized by the copy constructor to `a`'s and `b`'s values, respectively. Although the copy constructor defined in Program 12-3 adds nothing to the functionality provided by the compiler's default copy constructor, it does provide us with the fundamentals of defining our own copy constructors. In the next section, we will see how to modify this basic copy constructor to handle cases that are not adequately taken care of by the compiler's default.

---

[2] A copy constructor is frequently defined as a constructor whose first parameter is a reference to its class type, any additional parameters being defaults.

Program 12-3

```
#include <iostream.h>
#include <iomanip.h>

// class declaration
class Date
{
  private:
    int month;
    int day;
    int year;
  public:
    Date(int = 7, int = 4, int = 2001); // constructor with defaults
    Date(const Date&);       // copy constructor
    void showdate(void);     // member function to display a date
};
// implementation section
Date::Date(int mm, int dd, int yyyy)
{
  month = mm;
  day = dd;
  year = yyyy;
}
Date::Date(const Date& olddate)
{
  month = olddate.month;
  day = olddate.day;
  year = olddate.year;
}
void Date::showdate(void)
{
  cout << setfill('0')
       << setw(2) << month << '/'
       << setw(2) << day << '/'
       << setw(2) << year % 100;
  return;
}

int main()
{
  Date a(4,1,1999), b(12,18,2002); // use the constructor
  Date c(a);    // use the copy constructor
  Date d = b;   // use the copy constructor
  cout << "\nThe date stored in a is ";
  a.showdate();
  cout << "The date stored in b is ";
  b.showdate();
  cout << "The date stored in c is ";
  c.showdate();
  cout << "The date stored in d is ";
  d.showdate();
  return 0;
}
```

Base/Member Initialization[3]

Except for the reference names `olddate` and `secdate`, a comparison of Program 12-3's copy constructor to Program 12-2's assignment operator shows them to be essentially the same function. The difference between these functions is that the copy constructor creates an object's data members before the body of the constructor uses assignment to specify member values. Thus the copy constructor does not perform a true initialization, but rather a creation followed by assignment.

A true initialization would have no reliance on assignment whatsoever and is possible in C++ using a *base/member initialization list*. Such a list can be applied only to constructor functions and may be written in two ways.

The first way to construct a base/member initialization list is within a class's declaration section by using the form

```
class-name(parameter list) : list of data members(initializing values) {}
```

For example, when we use this form, a default constructor that performs true initialization is

```
// class declaration section
public:
  Date(int mo = 7, int da = 4, int yr = 2001) : month(mo), day(da), year(yr) {}
```

The second way is to declare a prototype in the class's declaration section followed by the initialization list in the implementation section. For our `Date` constructor, this takes the form

```
// class declaration section

public:
  Date(int = 7, int = 4, int = 2001);  // prototype with defaults

// class implementation section

Date::Date(int mo, int da, int yr) : month(mo), day(da), year(yr) {}
```

Note that in both forms, the body of the constructor function is empty. This is not a requirement, and the body can include any subsequent operations that you would like the constructor to perform. The interesting feature of this type of constructor is that it clearly differentiates among the initialization tasks

3 The material in this section is presented for completeness only and may be omitted without loss of subject continuity.

performed in the member initialization list, contained between the colon and the braces, and any subsequent assignments that might be contained within the function's body. Although we will not be using this type of initialization subsequently, it is required whenever there is a `const` class instance variable.

Exercises 12.1

1. Describe the difference between assignment and initialization.

2. *a.* Construct a class named `Time` that contains three integer data members named `hrs`, `mins`, and `secs`, which will be used to store hours, minutes, and seconds. The function members should include a constructor that provides default values of 0 for each data member, a display function that prints an object's data values, and an assignment operator that performs a memberwise assignment between two `Time` objects.
   b. Include the `Time` class developed in Exercise 2a in a working C++ program that creates and displays two `Time` objects, the second of which is assigned the values of the first object.

3. *a.* Construct a class named `Complex` that contains two floating-point data members named `real` and `imag`, which will be used to store the real and imaginary parts of a complex number. The function members should include a constructor that provides default values of 0 for each member function, a display function that prints an object's data values, and an assignment operator that performs a memberwise assignment between two complex number objects.
   b. Include the class written for Exercise 3a in a working C++ program that creates and displays the values of two complex objects, the second of which is assigned the values of the first object.

4. *a.* Construct a class named `Car` that contains the following four data members: a floating-point variable named `engineSize`, a character variable named `bodyStyle`, an integer variable named `colorCode`. The function members should include a constructor that provides default values of 0 for each numeric data member and an 'X' for each character variable; a display function that prints the engine size, body style, and color code; and an assignment operator that performs a memberwise assignment between two `Car` objects for each instance variable.
   b. Include the class written for Exercise 4a in a working C++ program that creates and displays two `Car` objects, the second of which is assigned the values of the first object, except for the pointer data member.

5. *a.* Construct a class named `Cartesian` that contains two floating-point data members named `x` and `y`, which will be used to store the `x` and `y` values of a point in rectangular coordinates. The function members should include a constructor that initializes the `x` and `y` values of an object to 0, and functions to input and display an object's `x` and `y` values. Additionally, there should be an assignment function that performs a memberwise assignment between two `Cartesian` objects.

b. Include the class written for Exercise 5a in a working C++ program that creates and displays the values of two `Cartesian` objects, the second of which is assigned the values of the first object.

6. *a.* Construct a class named `Savings` that contains three floating-point data members named `balance`, `rate`, and `interest` and a constructor that initializes each of these members to 0. Additionally, there should be a member function that inputs a balance and rate and then calculates an interest. The rate should be stored as a percent, such as 6.5 for 6.5%, and the interest computed as $interest = balance \times rate/100$. Additionally, there should be a member function to display all member values.
b. Include the class written for Exercise 6a in a working C++ program that tests each member function.

12.2 Pointers as Class Members

As we saw in Section 11.2, a class can contain any C++ data type. Thus the inclusion of a pointer variable in a class should not seem surprising. For example, the class declaration

```
// class declaration

class Test
{
  private:
    int idNum;
    double *ptPay;
  public:
    Test(int = 0, double * = NULL); // constructor
    void setvals(int, double *);    // access function
    void display();                 // access function
};
```

declares a class consisting of two member variables and three member functions. The first member variable is an integer variable named `idNum`, and the second instance variable is a pointer named `ptPay`, which is a pointer to a double-precision number. We will use the `setvals()` member function to store values into the private member variables and the `display()` function for output purposes. The implementation of these two functions along with the constructor function `Test()` is contained in the class implementation section:

POINT OF INFORMATION

Values and Identities

Apart from any behavior that an object is supplied with, a characteristic feature of objects that they share with variables is that they always have a unique identity. It is an object's identity that permits distinguishing one object from another. This is not true of a value, such as the number 5, because all occurrences of 5 are indistinguishable from one another. Accordingly, values are not considered objects in object-oriented programming languages such as C++.

Another feature that differentiates an object from a value is that a value can never be a container whose value can change, whereas an object clearly can. A value is simply an entity that stands for itself.

Now consider a string such as `"Chicago"`. As a string, this is a value. However, because `Chicago` could also be a specific and identifiable object of type `City`, the context in which the name is used is important. Note that if the string `"Chicago"` were assigned to an object's `name` attribute, it would revert to being a value.

```
// implementation section

Test::Test(int id, double *pt)
{
  idNum = id;
  ptPay = pt;
}

void Test::setvals(int a, double *b)
{
  idNum = a;
  ptPay = b;

  return;
}

void Test::display()
{
  cout << "\nEmployee number " << idNum << " was paid $"
       << setiosflags(ios::fixed)
       << setiosflags(ios::showpoint)
       << setw(6) << setprecision(2)
       << *ptPay << endl;

  return;
}
```

In this implementation the `Test()` constructor initializes its `idNum` data member to its first parameter and its pointer member to its second parameter; if no parameters are given, these variables are initialized to `0` and `NULL`, respectively. The display function simply outputs the value pointed to by its pointer member. As defined in this implementation, the `setvals()` function is very similar to the constructor and is used to alter member values after the object has been declared: the function's first parameter (an integer) is assigned to `idNum`, and its second parameter (an address) is assigned to `ptPay`.

The `main()` function in Program 12-4 illustrates the use of the `Test` class by first creating one object, named `emp`, which is initialized using the constructor's default arguments. The `setvals()` function is then used to assign the value 12345 and the address of the variable `pay` to the data members of this `emp` object. Finally, the `display()` function is used to display the value whose address is stored in `emp.ptPay`. As illustrated by the program, the pointer member of an object is used like any other pointer variable.

The output produced by executing Program 12-4 is

```
Employee number 12345 was paid $456.20
```

Figure 12–2 illustrates the relationship between the data members of the `emp` object defined in Program 12-4 and the variable named `pay`. The value assigned to `emp.idNum` is the number 12345, and the value assigned to `pay` is 456.20. The address of the `pay` variable is assigned to the object member `emp.ptPay`. Because this member has been defined as a pointer to a double-precision number, placing the address of the double-precision variable `pay` in it is a correct use of this data member.

Although the pointer defined in Program 12-4 has been used in a rather trivial fashion, the program does illustrate the concept of including a pointer in a class.

Clearly, it would be more efficient to include the `pay` variable directly as a data member of the `Test` class, rather than using a pointer to it. In some cases, however, pointers are advantageous. For example, assume we need to store a list of book titles. Rather than use a fixed-length character array as a data member to hold each title, we could include a pointer member to a character array and then allocate the array of the correct size for each book title as it is needed. This arrangement is illustrated in Figure 12–3, which shows two objects,

FIGURE 12–2 Storing an Address in a Data Member

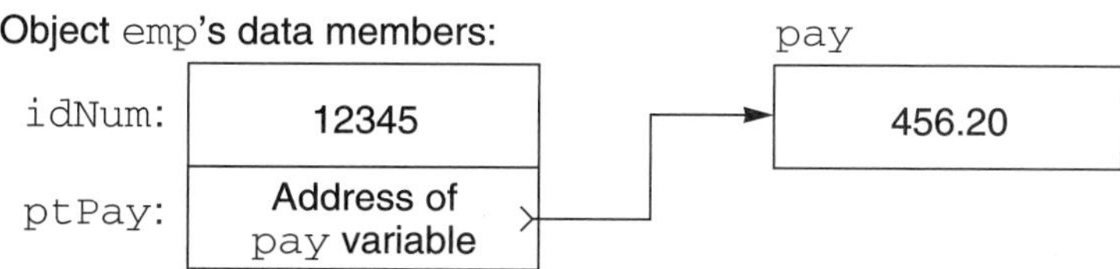

Program 12-4

```
#include <iostream.h>
#include <iomanip.h>
```

```
// class declaration

class Test
{
  private:
    int idNum;
    double *ptPay;
  public:
    Test(int = 0, double * = NULL);     // constructor
    void setvals(int, double *);        // access function
    void display();                     // access function
};

// implementation section

Test::Test(int id, double *pt)
{
  idNum = id;
  ptPay = pt;
}

void Test::setvals(int a, double *b)
{
  idNum = a;
  ptPay = b;

  return;
}

void Test::display()
{
  cout << "\nEmployee number " << idNum << " was paid $"
       << setiosflags(ios::fixed)
       << setiosflags(ios::showpoint)
       << setw(6) << setprecision(2)
       << *ptPay << endl;

  return
}
```

```
int main()
{
  Test emp;
  double pay = 456.20;

  emp.setvals(12345, &pay);
  emp.display();

  return 0;
}
```

a and b, each of which consists of a single pointer data member. As depicted, object a's pointer contains the address of ("points to") a character array containing the characters DOS Primer, while object b's pointer contains the address of a character array containing the characters A Brief History of Western Civilization.

A suitable class declaration section for a list of book titles that are to be accessed as illustrated in Figure 12–3 is

```
// class declaration
class Book
{
  private:
    char *title;    // a pointer to a book title
  public:
    Book(char * = '\0');     // constructor
    void showtitle(void);    // display the title
};
```

FIGURE 12–3 Two Objects That Contain Pointer Data Members

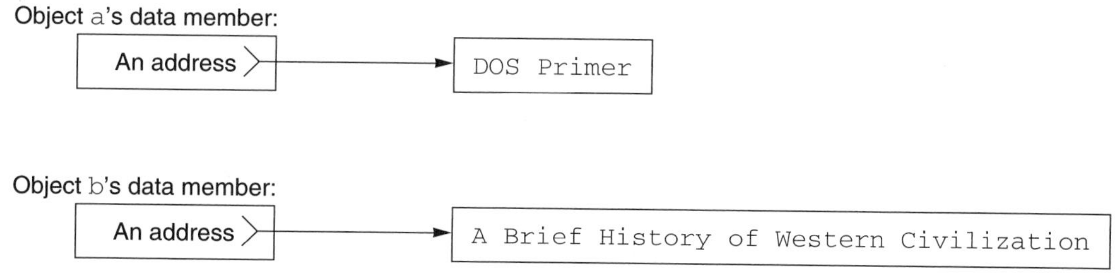

The constructor function, `Book()`, and the display function, `showtitle()`, are defined in the implementation section as follows:

```
// class implementation

Book::Book(char *name)
{
  title = new char[strlen(name)+1];  // allocate memory
  strcpy(title,name);                // store the string
}

void Book::showtitle(void)
{
  cout << title << endl;
}
```

The body of the `Book()` constructor contains two statements. The first statement, `title = new char[strlen(name)+1];`, performs two tasks. First, the right-hand side of the statement allocates enough storage for the length of the `name` parameter plus one, to accommodate the end-of-string null character, `'\0'`. Next, the address of the first allocated character position is assigned to the pointer variable `title`. These operations are illustrated in Figure 12–4. The second statement in the constructor copies the characters in the `name` argument to the newly created memory allocation. If no argument is passed to the constructor, then `title` is set to `NULL`. Program 12-5 uses this class definition within the context of a complete program.

The output produced by Program 12-5 is:

```
DOS Primer
A Brief History of Western Civilization
```

FIGURE 12–4 Allocating Memory for `title = new char[strlen(name)+1]`

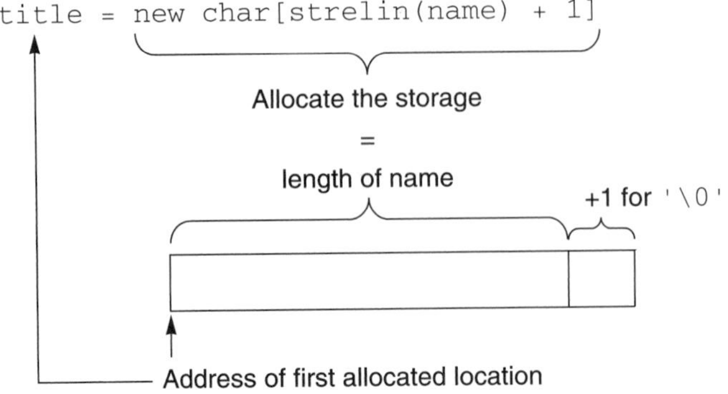

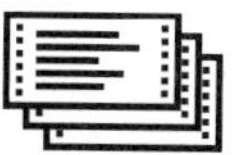

Program 12-5

```
#include <iostream.h>
#include <string.h>

// class declaration

class Book
{
  private:
    char *title;    // a pointer to a book title
  public:
    Book(char * = '\0');     // constructor
    void showtitle(void);    // display the title
};

// class implementation

Book::Book(char *strng)
{
  title = new char[strlen(strng)+1];  // allocate memory
  strcpy(title,strng);                // store the string
}

void Book::showtitle(void)
{
  cout << title << endl;

  return;
}

int main()
{
  Book  book1("DOS Primer");    // create 1st title
  Book  book2("A Brief History of Western Civilization");  // 2nd title

  book1.showtitle();    // display book1's title
  book2.showtitle();    // display book2's title

  return 0;
}
```

Assignment Operators and Copy Constructors Reconsidered[4]

When a class contains no pointer data members, the compiler-provided defaults for the assignment operator and copy constructor adequately perform their intended tasks. Both of these defaults provide a member-by-member operation that produces no adverse side effects. This is not the case when a pointer member is included in the class declaration. Let's see why this is so.

Figure 12–5a illustrates the arrangement of pointers and allocated memory produced by Program 12-5 just before it completes execution. Let's now assume that we insert the assignment statement `book2 = book1;` before the closing brace of the `main()` function. Because we have not defined an assignment operation, the compiler's default assignment is used. As we know, this assignment produces a memberwise copy (that is, `book2.title = book1.title`) and means that the address in `book1`'s pointer is copied into `book2`'s pointer. Thus both pointers now "point to" the character array containing the characters `DOS Primer`, and the address of `A Brief History of Western Civilization` has been lost. This situation is illustrated in Figure 12–5b.

Because the memberwise assignment illustrated in Figure 12–5b results in the loss of the address of `A Brief History of Western Civilization`, there is no way for the program to release this memory storage (it will be cleaned up by the operating system when the program terminates). Worse, however, is the case where a destructor attempts to release the memory. Once the memory pointed to by `book2` is released (again, referring to Figure 12–5b), `book1` points to an undefined memory location. If this memory area is subsequently reallocated before `book1` is deleted, the deletion will release memory that another object is using. The results of this can wreck havoc on a program.

What is typically desired is that the book titles themselves be copied, as shown in Figure 12–5c, and that their pointers be left alone. This situation also removes all of the side effects of a subsequent deletion of any `book` object. To achieve the desired assignment, we must explicitly write our own assignment operator. A suitable definition for this operator is

```
void Book::operator=(Book& oldbook)
{
  if(oldbook.title != NULL)  // check that it exists
    delete(title);           // release existing memory
  title = new char[strlen(oldbook.title) + 1];  // allocate new memory
  strcpy(title, oldbook.title);  // copy the title
}
```

[4] The material in this section pertains to the problems that occur when the default assignment, copy constructor, and destructor functions are used with classes that contain pointer members, and how to overcome these problems. On first reading, this section can be omitted without loss of subject continuity.

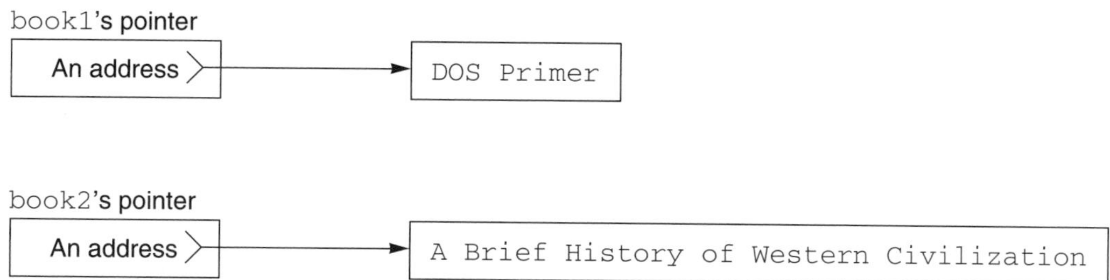

FIGURE 12–5a Before the Assignment `book2 = book1;`

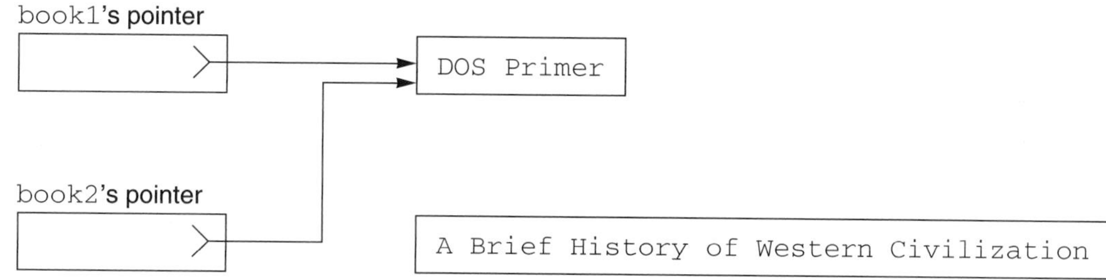

FIGURE 12–5b The Effect Produced by Default Assignment

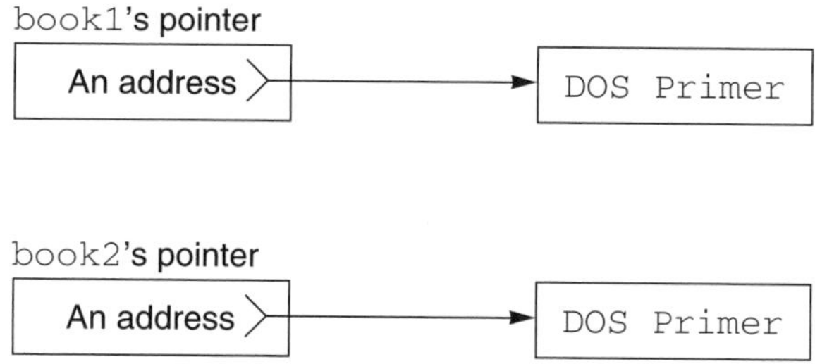

FIGURE 12–5c The Desired Effect

This definition cleanly releases the memory previously allocated for the object and then allocates sufficient memory to store the copied title.

The problems associated with the default assignment operator also exist with the default copy constructor, because it also performs a memberwise copy. As with assignment, we can avoid these problems by writing our own copy constructor. For our `Book` class, such a constructor is

```
Book::Book(Book& oldbook)
{
  title = new char[strlen(oldbook.title) + 1];  // allocate new memory
  strcpy(title, oldbook.title);  // copy the title
}
```

Comparing the body of this copy constructor to the assignment operator's function body reveals they are identical except for the deallocation of memory performed by the assignment operator. This is because the copy constructor does not have to release the existing array before allocating a new one; none exists when the constructor is called.

Exercises 12.2

1. Include the copy constructor and assignment operator presented in this section in Program 12-5 and run the program to verify their operation.

2. Write a suitable destructor function for Program 12-5.

3. *a.* Construct a class named `Car` that contains the following four data members: a floating-point variable named `engineSize`, a character variable named `bodyStyle`, an integer variable named `colorCode`, and a character pointer named `vinPtr` to a vehicle identification code. The function members should include a constructor that provides default values of `0` for each numeric data member, an `'X'` for each character variable, and a `NULL` for each pointer; a display function that prints the engine size, body style, color code, and vehicle identification number; and an assignment operator that performs a memberwise assignment between two `Car` objects that correctly handles the pointer member.
b. Include the class written for Exercise 5a in a working C++ program that creates two `Car` objects, the second of which is assigned the values of the first object.

4. Modify Program 12-5 to include the assignment statement `b = a`, and then run the modified program to assess the error messages, if any, that occur.

5. Using Program 12-5 as a start, write a program that creates five `Book` objects. The program should allow the user to enter the five book titles interactively and then display the titles entered.

6. Modify the program written in Exercise 5 so that the program sorts the entered book titles in alphabetical order before it displays them. (*Hint:* You will have to define a sort routine for the titles.)

12.3 Additional Class Features[5]

This section presents additional features pertaining to classes. These include the scope of a class, creating static class members, and granting access privileges to nonmember functions. Each of these topics may be read independently of the others.

[5] Except for the material on the `this` pointer, which is required for the material in Section 13.1, the topics in this section may be omitted on first reading with no loss of subject continuity.

Class Scope

We have already encountered local and global scope in Sections 6.4 and 6.5. As we saw, the scope of a variable defines the portion of a program where the variable can be accessed.

For local variables, this scope is defined by any block contained within a brace pair, `{ }`. This includes both the complete function body and any internal subblocks. Additionally, all parameters of a function are considered as local function variables.

Global variables are accessible from their point of declaration throughout the remaining portion of the file containing them, with three exceptions:

1. If a local variable has the same name as a global variable, the global variable can only be accessed within the scope of the local variable by using the global resolution operator, `::`.
2. The scope of a global variable can be extended into another file by using the keyword `extern`.
3. The same global name can be reused in another file to define a separate and distinct variable by using the keyword `static`. `Static` global variables are unknown outside of their immediate file.

In addition to local and global scopes, each class also defines an associated *class scope*. That is, the names of the data and function members are local to the scope of their class. Thus, if a global variable name is reused within a class, the global variable is hidden by the class data member in the same manner as a local function variable hides a global variable of the same name. Similarly, member function names are local to the class they are declared in and can be used only by objects declared for the class. Additionally, local function variables hide the names of class data members that have the same name. Figure 12–6 illustrates the scope of the variables and functions for the following declarations:

```
float rate;     // global
// class declaration
class Test
{
  private:
    float amount, price, total;   // class scope
  public:
    float extend(float, float);   // class scope
};
```

`static` Members

As each class object is created, it gets its own block of memory for its data members. In some cases, however, it is convenient for every instantiation of a class to share the *same* memory location for a specific variable. For example,

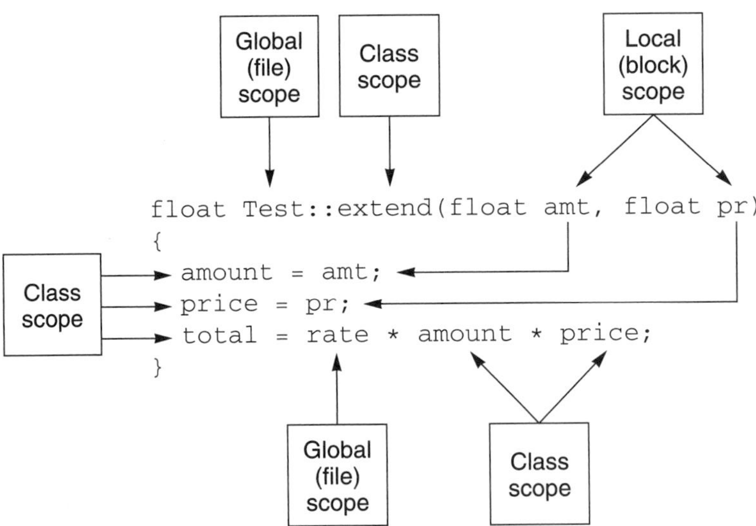

FIGURE 12–6 Example of Scopes

consider a class that consists of employee records, where each employee is subject to the same state sales tax. Clearly, we could make the sales tax a global variable, but this is not very safe. Such data could be modified anywhere in the program, could conflict with an identical variable name within a function, and certainly violates C++'s principle of data hiding.

This type of situation is handled in C++ by declaring a class variable to be `static`. Static data members share the same storage space for all objects of the class; accordingly, they act as global variables for the class and provide a means of communication between objects.

C++ requires that static variables be declared as such within the class's declaration section. Because a static data member requires only a single storage area, regardless of the number of class instantiations, it is defined in a single place outside of the class definition. This is typically done in the global part of the program where the class implementation section is provided. For example, assuming the class declaration

```
// class declaration

class Employee
{
  private:
    static float taxRate;
    int idNum;
  public:
    Employee(int);    //constructor
    void display();
};
```

Program 12-6

```
#include <iostream.h>

// class declaration

class Employee
{
  private:
    static float taxRate;
    int idNum;
  public:
    Employee(int = 0);     // constructor
    void display();        // access function
};

// static member definition
float Employee::taxRate = 0.0025;

// implementation section

Employee::Employee(int num)
{
  idNum = num;
}

void Employee::display()
{
  cout << "\nEmployee number " << idNum
       << " has a tax rate of " << taxRate << endl;

  return;
}

int main()
{
  Employee emp1(11122), emp2(11133);

  emp1.display();
  emp2.display();

  return 0;
}
```

the definition and initialization of the static variable `taxRate` are accomplished using a statement such as

```
float Employee::taxRate = 0.0025;
```

Here the scope resolution operator, `::`, is used to identify `taxRate` as a member of the class `Employee`, and the keyword `static` is not included. Program 12-6 uses this definition within the context of a complete program.

The output produced by Program 12-6 is

```
Employee number 11122 has a tax rate of 0.0025
Employee number 11133 has a tax rate of 0.0025
```

Although it might appear that the initialization of `taxRate` is global, it is not. Once the definition is made, any other definition will result in an error. Thus the actual definition of a static member remains the responsibility of the class creator. The storage sharing produced by the static data member and the objects created in Program 12-6 is illustrated in Figure 12–7.

In addition to static data members, static member functions can also be created. Such functions apply to a class as a whole rather than to individual class objects and can access only static data members and other static member functions of the class.[6] An example of such a function is provided by Program 12-7.

The output produced by Program 12-7 is

```
The static tax rate is 0.0025
Employee number 11122 has a tax rate of 0.0025
Employee number 11133 has a tax rate of 0.0025
```

FIGURE 12–7 Sharing the Static Data Member `taxRate`

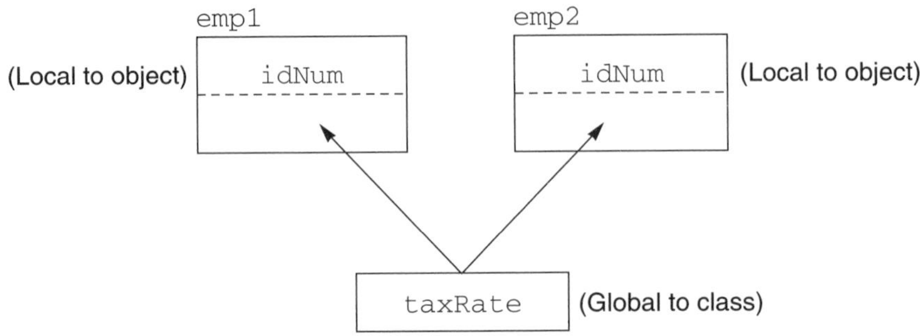

[6] The reason for this is that the `this` pointer, discussed next, is not passed to static member functions.

Program 12-7

```
#include <iostream.h>

// class declaration

class Employee
{
  private:
    static float taxRate;
    int idNum;
  public:
    Employee(int = 0);         // constructor
    void display();            // access function
    static void disp();        // static function
};

// static member definition
float Employee::taxRate = 0.0025;

// implementation section

Employee::Employee(int num)
{
  idNum = num;
}

void Employee::display()
{
  cout << "Employee number " << idNum
       << " has a tax rate of " << taxRate << endl;

  return;
}

void Employee::disp()
{
  cout << "\nThe static tax rate is " << taxRate << endl;

  return;
}

int main()
{
  Employee::disp();   // call the static functions
  Employee emp1(11122), emp2(11133);

  emp1.display();
  emp2.display();

  return 0;
}
```

In reviewing Program 12-7, note that the keyword `static` is used only when static data and function members are declared; it is not included in the definition of these members. Also note that the static member function is called by using the resolution operator with the function's class name. Finally, because static functions access only static variables that are not contained within a specific object, static functions may be called before any instantiations are declared.

The `this` Pointer

Except for static data members, which are shared by all class objects, each object maintains its own set of member variables. This permits each object to have its own clearly defined state as determined by the values stored in its member variables.

For example, consider the `Date` class previously defined in Program 12-1 and repeated here for convenience:

```
#include <iostream.h>

// class declaration

class Date
{
  private:
    int month;
    int day;
    int year;
  public:
    Date(int, int, int);      // constructor
    void showdate(void);      // member function to display a Date
};

// implementation section

Date::Date(int mm = 7, int dd = 4, int yyyy = 2001)
{
  month = mm;
  day = dd;
  year = yyyy;
}

void Date::showdate(void)
{
  cout << "The date is ";
  cout << setfill('0')
       << setw(2) << month << '/'
       << setw(2) << day << '/'
       << setw(2) << year % 100;
  cout << endl;
  return;
}
```

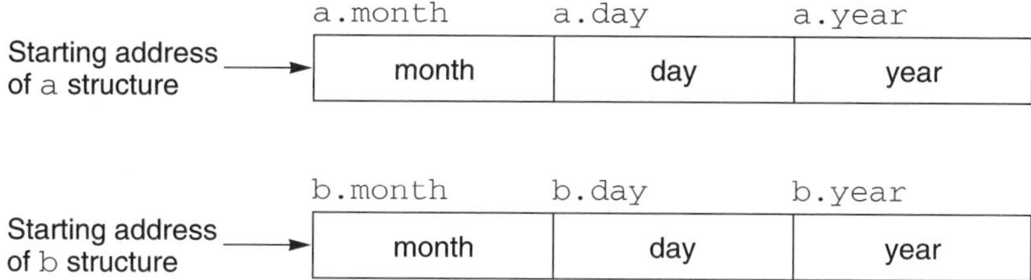

FIGURE 12–8 The Storage of Two `Date` Objects in Memory

Each time an object is created from this class, a distinct area of memory is set aside for its data members. For example, if two objects named `a` and `b` were created from this class, the memory storage for these objects would be as illustrated in Figure 12–8. Note that each set of data members has its own starting address in memory, which corresponds to the address of the first data member for the object.

This replication of data storage is not implemented for member functions. In fact, for each class *only one copy of the member functions is retained in memory,* and each object uses these same functions.

Sharing member functions requires providing a means of identifying which specific data structure a member function should be operating on. This is accomplished by providing address information to the function indicating where in memory the particular data structure, corresponding to a specific object, is located. This address is provided by the name of the object, which is, in fact, a reference name. For example, again using our `Date` class and assuming that `a` is an object of this class, the statement `a.showdate()` passes the address of the `a` object into the `showdate()` member function.

An obvious question at this point is how this address is passed to `showdate()` and where it is stored. The answer is that the address is stored in a special pointer variable named `this`, which is automatically supplied as a hidden argument to each nonstatic member function when the function is called. For our `Date` class, which has two member functions, the actual parameter list of `Date()` is equivalent to

```
Date(Date *this, int mm = 7, int dd = 4, int yyyy = 2001)
```

and the actual parameter list of `showdate()` is equivalent to

```
showdate(Date *this)
```

That is, each member function actually receives an extra argument that is the address of a data structure. Although it is usually not necessary to do so, this pointer data member can be explicitly used in member functions. For example, consider Program 12-8, which incorporates the `this` pointer in each of its member functions to access the appropriate instance variables.

Program 12-8

```
#include <iostream.h>
#include <iomanip.h>
```

```
// class declaration

class Date
{
  private:
    int month;
    int day;
    int year;
  public:
    Date(int, int, int);      // constructor
    void showdate(void);      // member function to display a Date
};

// implementation section

Date::Date(int mm = 7, int dd = 4, int yyyy = 2001)
{
  month = mm;
  day = dd;
  year = yyyy;
}

void Date::showdate(void)
{
  cout << setfill('0')
       << setw(2) << this->month << '/'
       << setw(2) << this->day << '/'
       << setw(2) << this->year % 100;
  return;
}
```

```
int main()
{
  Date a(4,1,1999), b(12,18,2001); // declare two objects

  cout << "\nThe date stored in a is originally ";
  a.showdate();  // display the original date
  a = b;         // assign b's value to a
  cout << "\nAfter assignment the date stored in a is ";
  a.showdate();  // display a's values
  cout << endl;

  return 0;
}
```

The output produced by Program 12-8 is

```
The date stored in a is originally 04/01/99
After assignment the date stored in a is 12/18/01
```

This is the same output produced by Program 12-1, which omits using the `this` pointer to access the data members. Clearly, using the `this` pointer in Program 12-8 is unnecessary and simply clutters up the member function code. There are times, however, when an object must pass its address on to other functions. In these situations, one of which we will see in Section 13.1, the address stored in the `this` pointer must be used explicitly.

`Friend` Functions

The only method we currently have for accessing and manipulating private class data members is through the class's member functions. Conceptually, this arrangement can be viewed as illustrated in Figure 12–9a. There are times,

FIGURE 12–9a Direct Access Is Provided to Member Functions

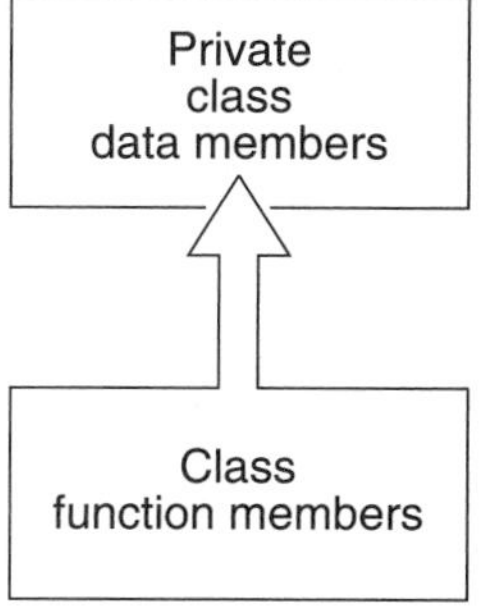

FIGURE 12–9b Access Provided to Nonmember Functions

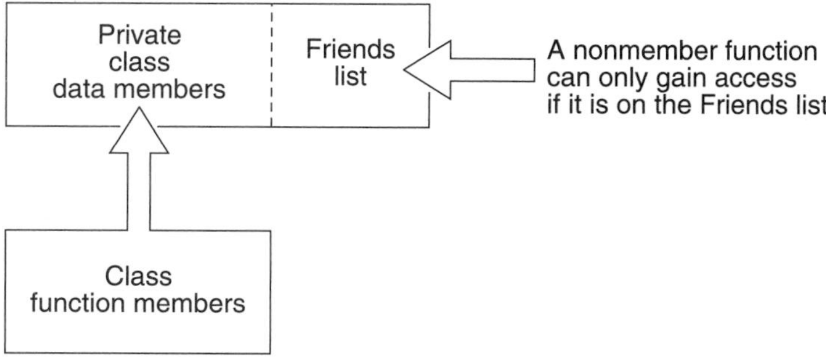

however, when it is useful to provide such access to selected nonmember functions.[7]

The procedure for providing this external access is rather simple—the class maintains its own approved list of nonmember functions that are granted the same privileges as member functions. The nonmember functions on the list are called friend functions, and the list is referred to as a friends list.

Figure 12–9b conceptually illustrates the use of such a list for nonmember access. Any function attempting to get access to an object's private data members is first checked against the friends list. If the function is on the list, access is approved; otherwise, access is denied.

From a coding standpoint, the friends list is simply a series of function prototype declarations that are preceded by the word `friend` and included in the class's declaration section. For example, if the functions named `addreal()` and `addimag()` are to be allowed access to the private members of a class named `Complex`, the following prototypes would be included within `Complex`'s declaration section:

```
friend float addreal(Complex&, Complex&);
friend float addimag(Complex&, Complex&);
```

Here the friends list consists of two declarations. The prototypes indicate that each function returns a floating-point number and expects two references to objects of type `Complex` as arguments. Program 12-9 includes these two friend declarations in a complete program.

The output produced by Program 12-9 is

```
The first complex number is 3.2+5.6i
The second complex number is 1.1-8.4i

The sum of these two complex numbers is 4.3-2.8i
```

In reviewing Program 12-9, note four things. The first is that because friends are not class members, they are unaffected by the access section in which they are declared; *they may be declared anywhere within the declaration section.* The convention we have followed is to include all friend declarations immediately following the class header. The second thing to notice is that the keyword `friend` (like the keyword `static`) is used only within the class declaration and not in the actual function definition. Third, because a friend function is intended to have access to an object's private data members, at least one of the

[7] In practice, this occurs when one class needs access to another class's private data members.

Program 12-9

```
#include <iostream.h>
#include <math.h>
```

```
// class declaration

class Complex
{
  // friends list
  friend float addreal(Complex&, Complex&);
  friend float addimag(Complex&, Complex&);
  private:
    float real;
    float imag;
  public:
    Complex(float = 0, float = 0);  // constructor
    void display();

};

// implementation section

Complex::Complex(float rl, float im)
{
  real = rl;
  imag = im;
}

void Complex::display()
{
  char sign = '+';

  if(imag < 0) sign = '-';
  cout << real << sign << fabs(imag) << 'i';

  return;
}

// friend implementations

float addreal(Complex &a, Complex &b)
{
  return(a.real + b.real);
}

float addimag(Complex &a, Complex &b)
{
  return(a.imag + b.imag);
}
```

(continued on next page)

(continued from previous page)

```
int main()
{
  Complex a(3.2, 5.6), b(1.1, -8.4);
  float re, im;

  cout << "\nThe first complex number is ";
  a.display();
  cout << "\nThe second complex number is ";
  b.display();

  re = addreal(a,b);
  im = addimag(a,b);
  Complex c(re,im);  // create a new Complex object
  cout << "\n\nThe sum of these two complex numbers is ";
  c.display();
  cout << endl;

  return 0;
}
```

friend's parameters should be a reference to an object of the class that has made it a friend. Finally, as illustrated by Program 12-9, it is the class that grants friend status to a function, not the other way around. The function can never confer friend status on itself, because to do so would violate the concepts of data hiding and access provided by a class.

Exercises 12.3

1. *a.* Rewrite Program 12-7 to include an integer static data member named `numemps`. This variable should act as a counter that is initialized to zero and is incremented by the class constructor each time a new object is declared. Rewrite the static function `disp()` to display the value of this counter.
   b. Test the program written for Exercise 1a. Have the `main()` function call `disp()` after each `Employee` object is created.
2. *a.* Construct a class named `Circle` that contains two integer data members named `xCenter` and `yCenter` and a floating-point data member named `radius`. The class should also contain a static data member named `scaleFactor`. Here the `xCenter` and `yCenter` values represent the center point of a circle, `radius` represents the circle's actual radius, and `scaleFactor` represents a scale factor that will be used to scale the circle to fit on a variety of display devices.
   b. Include the class written for Exercise 2a in a working C++ program.

3. Rewrite the `Date()`, `setdate()`, and `showdate()` member functions in Program 11-1 to explicitly use the `this` pointer when referencing all data members. Run your program and verify that the same output as produced by Program 11-1 is achieved.

4. *a.* Indicate whether the following three statements in Program 12-9,

```
re = addreal(a,b);
im = addimag(a,b);
Complex c(re,im);   // create a new complex object
```

could be replaced by the single statement

```
Complex c(addreal(a,b), addimag(a,b));
```

b. Verify your answer to Exercise 4a by running Program 12-9 with the suggested replacement statement.

5. Rewrite Program 12-9 to have only one `friend` function named `addcomplex()`. This function should accept two complex objects and return a `Complex` object. The real and imaginary parts of the returned object should be the sum of the real and imaginary parts, respectively, of the two objects passed to `Complex()`.

6. *a.* Rewrite the program written for Exercise 2a, but include a `friend` function that multiplies an object's radius by the `static` scale factor and then displays the actual radius value and the scaled value.
b. Include the class written for Exercise 6a in a working C++ program.

7. *a.* Construct a class named `Coord` that contains two floating-point data members named `xval` and `yval`, which will be used to store the `x` and `y` values of a point in rectangular coordinates. The function members should include appropriate constructor and display functions and a `friend` function named `convPol()`. The `convPol()` function should accept two floating-point numbers that represent a point in polar coordinates and convert them into rectangular coordinates. For conversion from polar to rectangular coordinates, use the formulas

$$x = r \cos \theta$$
$$y = r \sin \theta$$

b. Include the class written for Exercise 7a in a working C++ program.

8. *a.* Construct two classes named `RecCoord` and `PolCoord`. The class named `RecCoord` should contain two floating-point data members named `xval` and `yval`, which will be used to store the `x` and `y` values of a point in rectangular coordinates. The function members should include appropriate constructor and display functions and a `friend` function named `convPol()`.

The class named `PolCoord` should contain two floating-point data members named `dist` and `theta`, which will be used to store the distance and angle values of a point represented in polar coordinates. The function members should include appropriate constructor and display functions and a `friend` function named `convPol()`.

The `friend` function should accept an integer argument named `dir`; two floating-point arguments named `val1` and `val2`; and two reference arguments named `recref` and `polref`, the first of which should be a reference to an object of type `RecCoord` and the second to an object of type `PolCoord`. If the value of `dir` is 1, `val1` and `val2` are to be considered as `x` and `y` rectangular coordinates that are to be converted to polar coordinates; if the value of `dir` is any other value, `val1` and `val2` are to be considered as distance and angle values that are to be converted to rectangular coordinates. For conversion from rectangular to polar coordinates, use the formulas

$$r = \sqrt{x^2 + y^2}$$
$$\theta = tan^{-1}(y/x)$$

For conversion from polar to rectangular coordinates, use the formulas

$$x = r \cos \theta$$
$$y = r \sin \theta$$

b. Include the class written for Exercise 8a in a working C++ program.

12.4 Common Programming Errors

1. Using the default copy constructor and default assignment operators with classes that contain pointer members. These default functions do a memberwise copy, so the address in the source pointer is copied to the destination pointer. Typically, this is not what is wanted with both pointer members, because both pointers end up pointing to the same memory area.
2. Using a user-defined assignment operator in a multiple assignment expression when the operator has not been defined to return an object.
3. Using the keyword `static` when defining either a static data or function member. Here, the `static` keyword should be used only within the class declaration section.
4. Using the keyword `friend` when defining a friend function. The `friend` keyword should be used only within the class declaration section.
5. Failing to instantiate static data members before creating class objects that must access these data members.
6. Forgetting that `this` is a pointer that must be dereferenced using either `*this` or `this->`.

12.5 Chapter Summary

1. An *assignment operator* may be declared for a class with the function prototype

   ```
   void operator=(class-name& );
   ```

   Here, the argument is a reference to the class name. The `return` type of `void` precludes using this operator in multiple assignment expressions such as `a = b = c`.
2. A type of initialization that closely resembles assignment occurs in C++ when one object is initialized using another object of the same class. The constructor that performs this type of initialization is called a *copy constructor* and has the function prototype

   ```
   class-name(const class-name& );
   ```

   This is frequently represented using the notation `X(X&)`.
3. Pointers may be included as class data members. A pointer member adheres to the same rules as a pointer variable.
4. The default copy constructor and default assignment operators are typically not useful with classes that contain pointer members. This is because these default functions do a memberwise copy in which the address in the source pointer is copied to the destination pointer, resulting in both pointers "pointing to" the same memory area. For these situations, you must define your own copy constructor and assignment operator.
5. Each class has an associated class scope, which is defined by the brace pair, `{}`, containing the class declaration. Data and function members are local to the scope of their class and can be used only by objects declared for the class. If a global variable name is reused within a class, the global variable is hidden by the class variable. Within the scope of the class variable, the global variable may be accessed using the scope resolution operator, `::`.
6. For each class object, a separate set of memory locations is reserved for all data members, except those declared as `static`. A static data member is shared by all class objects and provides a means of communication between objects. Static data members must be declared as such within the class declaration section and are defined outside of the declaration section.
7. Static function members apply to the class as a whole, rather than individual objects. Thus a static function member can access only static data members and other static function members. Static function members must be declared

as such within the class declaration section and are defined outside of the declaration section.

8. For each class, only one copy of the member functions is retained in memory, and each object uses the same function. The address of the object's data members is provided to the member function by passing a hidden argument reference, corresponding to the memory address of the selected object, to the member function. The address is passed in a special pointer argument named `this`. The `this` pointer may be used explicitly by a member function to access a data member.
9. A nonmember function may access a class's private data members if it is granted friend status by the class. This is accomplished by declaring the function as a `friend` within the class's declaration section. Thus it is always the class that determines which nonmember functions are `friends`; a function can never confer friend status on itself.

Class Functions, Conversions, and Inheritance

Chapter Thirteen

This chapter completes our introduction to classes. First we will see how to create operator and conversion capabilities similar to those inherent in C++'s built-in types. With these additions, our user-defined types will have all the functionality of built-in types.

This functionality is then extended by showing how a class designed by one programmer can be altered by another in a way that retains the integrity and design of the original class. This is accomplished using inheritance, a new feature that is central to object-oriented programming. Inheritance permits reusing and extending existing code in a way that ensures that the new code does not adversely affect what has already been written. It is the driving force behind the move to object-oriented programming.

13.1 Operator Functions

A simple assignment operator was constructed in Section 12.1. In this section we extend this capability and show how to broaden C++'s built-in operators to work with class objects. As we will discover, class operators are themselves either member or friend functions.

The only symbols permitted for user-defined purposes are the subset of C++'s built-in symbols listed in Table 13–1. Each of these symbols may be adopted for class use with no limitation as to its meaning.[1] This is done by making each operation a function that can be overloaded like any other function.

The operation of the symbols listed in Table 13-1 can be redefined as we see fit for our classes, subject to the following restrictions:

- Symbols that do not appear in Table 13–1 cannot be redefined. For example, the `.`, `::`, and `?:` symbols cannot be redefined.
- New operator symbols cannot be created. For example, because `%%` is not an operator in C++, it cannot be defined as a class operator.
- Neither the precedence nor the associativity of C++'s operators can be modified. Thus you cannot give the addition operator a higher precedence than the multiplication operator.

[1] The only limitation is that the syntax of the operator cannot be changed. Thus a binary operator must remain binary, and a unary operator must remain unary. Within this syntax restriction, an operator symbol can be used to produce any operation, whether or not the operation is consistent with the symbol's accepted usage. For example, we could redefine the addition symbol to provide multiplication. This, however, would violate the intent and spirit of making these symbols available to us. We shall be very careful to redefine each symbol in a manner consistent with its accepted usage.

- Operators cannot be redefined for C++'s built-in types.
- A C++ operator that is unary cannot be changed to a binary operator, and a binary operator cannot be changed to a unary operator.
- The operator must either be a member of a class or be defined to take at least one class member as an operand.

TABLE 13–1 Operators Available for Class Use

Operator	Description
`()`	Function call
`[]`	Array element
`->`	Structure member pointer reference
`new`	Dynamically allocate memory
`delete`	Dynamically deallocate memory
`++`	Increment
`--`	Decrement
`-`	Unary minus
`!`	Logical negation
`~`	One's complement
`*`	Indirection
`*`	Multiplication
`/`	Division
`%`	Modulus (remainder)
`+`	Addition
`-`	Subtraction
`<<`	Left shift
`>>`	Right shift
`<`	Less than
`<=`	Less than or equal to
`>`	Greater than
`>=`	Greater than or equal to
`==`	Equal to
`!=`	Not equal to
`&&`	Logical AND
`||`	Logical OR
`&`	Bitwise AND
`^`	Bitwise exclusive OR
`|`	Bitwise inclusive OR
`=`	Assignment
`+=  -=  *=`	Assignment
`/=  %=  &=`	Assignment
`^=  |=`	Assignment
`<<=  >>=`	Assignment
`,`	Comma

The first step in providing a class with operators from Table 13–1 is to decide which operations make sense for the class and how they should be defined. As a specific example, we continue to build on the Date class introduced in Chapter 11. For this class a small, meaningful set of class operations is defined.

Clearly, the addition of two dates is not meaningful. The addition of a date with an integer, however, does make sense if the integer is taken as the number of days to be added to the date. Likewise, the subtraction of an integer from a date makes sense. Also, the subtraction of two dates is meaningful if we define the difference to mean the number of days between the two dates. Similarly, it makes sense to compare two dates and determine whether the dates are equal or one date occurs before or after another date. Let's now see how these operations can be implemented using C++'s operator symbols.

A user-defined operation is created as a function that redefines C++'s built-in operator symbols for class use. Functions that define operations on class objects and use C++'s built-in operator symbols are referred to as *operator functions*.

Operator functions are declared and implemented in the same manner as all member functions, with one exception: It is the function's name that connects the appropriate operator symbol to the operation defined by the function. An operator function's name is always of the form operator<symbol>, where <symbol> is one of the operators listed in Table 13–1. For example, the function name operator+ is the name of the addition function, and the function name operator== is the name of the "equal to" comparison function.

Once the appropriate function name is selected, the process of writing the function amounts simply to having it accept the desired inputs and produce the correct returned value.[2] For example, in comparing two Date objects for equality, we would select C++'s equality operator. Thus the name of our function becomes operator==. We would want our comparison operation to accept two Date objects, internally compare them, and return an integer value indicating the result of the comparison, for example, 1 for equality and 0 for inequality. As a member function, a suitable prototype that could be included in the class declaration section is

```
int operator==(const Date& );
```

This prototype indicates that the function is named operator==, that it returns an integer, and that it accepts a reference to a Date object.[3] Only one

---

[2] As previously noted, this implies that the specified operator can be redefined to perform any operation. Good programming practice, however, dictates avoiding such redefinitions.

[3] The prototype int operator==(const Date) also works. Passing a reference, however, is preferable to passing an object, because it reduces the function call's overhead. This is because passing an object means that a copy of the object must be made for the called function, whereas passing a reference gives the function direct access to the object whose address is passed.

Date object is required here because the second Date object will be the object that calls the function. Let's now write the function definition to be included in the class implementation section. The const keyword ensures that the referenced Date object cannot be changed within the function. Assuming that our class is named Date, a suitable definition is

```
int Date::operator==(const Date& Date2)
{
  if( day == date2.day && month == date2.month && year == date2.year)
    return 1;
  else
    return 0;
}
```

Once this function has been defined, it may be called by using the same syntax as for C++'s built-in types. For example, if a and b are objects of type Date, the expression if (a == b) is valid. Program 13-1 includes the if statement as well as the declaration and definition of this operator function within the context of a complete program.

The output produced by Program 13-1 is

```
Dates a and b are not the same.
Dates a and c are the same.
```

The first new feature to be illustrated in Program 13-1 is the declaration and implementation of the function named operator==(). Except for its name, this operator function is constructed in the same manner as any other member function: It is declared in the declaration section and defined in the implementation section. The second new feature is how the function is called. Operator functions may be called by using their associated symbols rather than in the way other functions are called. Because operator functions are true functions, however, the traditional method of calling them can also be used—specifying their name and including appropriate arguments. Thus, rather than calling the function using the expression a == b in Program 13-1, we could have used the call a.operator==(b).

Let's now create another operator for our Date class, an addition operator. As before, creating this operator requires that we specify three items:

1. The name of the operator function
2. The processing that the function is to perform
3. The data type, if any, that the function is to return

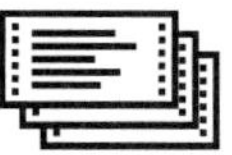

Program 13-1

```
#include <iostream.h>

// class declaration

class Date
{
  private:
    int month;
    int day;
    int year;
  public:
    Date(int = 7, int = 4, int = 2001);      // constructor
    int operator==(const Date &);  // declare the operator== function
};

// implementation section

Date::Date(int mm, int dd, int yyyy)
{
  month = mm;
  day = dd;
  year = yyyy;
}

int Date::operator==(const Date &date2)
{
  if(day == date2.day && month == date2.month && year == date2.year)
    return 1;
  else
    return 0;
}

int main()
{
  Date a(4,1,1999), b(12,18,2001), c(4,1,1999); // declare 3 objects

  if (a == b)
    cout << "\nDates a and b are the same." << endl;
  else
    cout << "\nDates a and b are not the same." << endl;

  if (a == c)
    cout << "Dates a and c are the same.\n" << endl;
  else
    cout << "Dates a and c are not the same.\n" << endl;

  return 0;
}
```

Clearly, for addition we will use the operator function named `operator+`. Having selected the function's name, we must now determine what we want this function to do, as it specifically relates to `Date` objects. As we noted previously, the sum of two dates makes no sense. Adding an integer to a date is meaningful, however, when the integer represents the number of days either before or after the given date. Here the sum of an integer to a `Date` object is simply another `Date` object, which should be returned by the addition operation. Thus a suitable prototype for our addition function is

```
Date operator+(int);
```

This prototype would be included in the class declaration section. It specifies that an integer is to be added to a class object and that the operation returns a `Date` object. Thus, if `a` is a `Date` object, the function call `a.operator+(284)`, or its more commonly used alternative, `a + 284`, should cause the number 284 to be correctly added to `a`'s date value. We must now construct the function to accomplish this.

Constructing the function requires that we first select a specific date convention. For simplicity, we will adopt the financial date convention that considers each month to consist of 30 days and each year to consist of 360 days. Thus our function will first add the integer number of days to the `Date` object's `day` value and then adjust the resulting `day` value to lie within the range 1 to 30 and the `month` value to lie within the range 1 to 12. A function that accomplishes this is

```
Date Date::operator+(int days)
{
  Date temp;  // a temporary Date to store the result

  temp.day = day + days;  // add the days
  temp.month = month;
  temp.year = year;
  while (temp.day > 30)    // now adjust the months
  {
    temp.month++;
    temp.day -= 30;
  }
  while (temp.month > 12)  // adjust the years
  {
    temp.year++;
    temp.month -= 12;
  }
  return temp;      // the values in temp are returned
}
```

Program 13-2

```
#include <iostream.h>
#include <iomanip.h>

// class declaration

class Date
{
  private:
    int month;
    int day;
    int year;
  public:
    Date(int = 7, int = 4, int = 2001);     // constructor
    Date operator+(int);     // overload the + operator
    void showdate(void);     // member function to display a date
};

// implementation section

Date::Date(int mm, int dd, int yyyy)
{
  month = mm;
  day = dd;
  year = yyyy;
}

Date Date::operator+(int days)
{
  Date temp;  // a temporary date to store the result

  temp.day = day + days;  // add the days
  temp.month = month;
  temp.year = year;
  while (temp.day > 30)    // now adjust the months
  {
    temp.month++;
    temp.day -= 30;
  }
  while (temp.month > 12)  // adjust the years
  {
    temp.year++;
    temp.month -= 12;
  }
  return temp;     // the values in temp are returned
}

void Date::showdate(void)
{
  cout << setfill('0')
       << setw(2) << month << '/'
       << setw(2) << day << '/'
       << setw(2) << year % 100;

  return;
}
```

```
int main()
{
  Date a(4,1,1999), b; // declare two objects

  cout << "\nThe initial date is ";
  a.showdate();
  b = a + 284;    // add in 284 days = 9 months and 14 days
  cout << "\nThe new date is ";
  b.showdate();
  cout << endl;

  return 0;
}
```

The important feature to note here is the use of the `temp` object. The purpose of this object is to ensure that none of the function's arguments, which become the operator's operands, are altered. To understand this, consider a statement such as `b = a + 284;` that uses this operator function, where `a` and `b` are `Date` objects. This statement should never modify `a`'s value. Rather, the expression `a + 284` should yield a `Date` value that is then assigned to `b`. The result of the expression is, of course, the `temp Date` object returned by the `operator+()` function. Program 13-2 uses this function within the context of a complete program.

The output produced by Program 13-2 is

```
The initial date is 04/01/99
The new date is 01/15/00
```

We can actually improve on the `operator+()` function contained in Program 13-2 by initializing the `temp` object with the value of its calling `Date` object. This is accomplished by using either of the following declarations:

```
Date temp(*this);
Date temp = *this;
```

Both of these declarations initialize the `temp` object with the object pointed to by the `this` pointer, which is the calling `Date` object. If the initialization is done, the first assignment statement in the function can be altered to

```
temp.day += days;
```

Operator Functions as Friends

The operator functions in both Programs 13-1 and 13-2 have been constructed as class members. An interesting feature of operator functions is that except for the operator functions `=`, `()`, `[]`, and `->`, they may also be written as friend functions. For example, if the `operator+()` function used in Program 13-2 were written as a friend, a suitable declaration section prototype would be

```
friend Date operator+(Date& , int);
```

Notice that the friend version contains a reference to a `Date` object that is not contained in the member function version. In all cases, the equivalent friend version of a member operator function *must* contain an additional class reference that is not required by the member function.[4] This equivalence is listed in Table 13–2 for both unary and binary operators.

Program 13-2's `operator+()` function, written as a friend function, is

```
Date Date::operator+(Date& op1, int days)
{
  Date temp;  // a temporary Date to store the result

  temp.day = op1.day + days;  // add the days
  temp.month = op1.month;
  temp.year = op1.year;
  while (temp.day > 30)    // now adjust the months
  {
    temp.month++;
    temp.day -= 30;
  }
  while (temp.month > 12)  // adjust the years
  {
    temp.year++;
    temp.month -= 12;
  }
  return temp;     // the values in temp are returned
}
```

TABLE 13–2 Operator Function Argument Requirements

	Member Function	Friend Function
Unary operator	1 implicit	1 explicit
Binary operator	1 implicit and 1 explicit	2 explicit

[4] This extra parameter is necessary to identify the correct object. This parameter is not needed when a member function is used, because the member function "knows" which object it is operating on. The mechanism of this "knowing" is supplied by an implied member function argument named `this`, which was presented in Section 12.3.

The only difference between this version and the member version is the explicit use of a `Date` argument named `op1` (the choice of this name is entirely arbitrary) in the friend version. This means that within the body of the friend function, the first three assignment statements explicitly reference `op1`'s data members as `op1.day`, `op1.month`, and `op1.year`, whereas the member function simply refers to its parameters as `day`, `month`, and `year`.

In making the determination to overload a binary operator as either a friend or a member operator function, the following convention can be applied: *friend functions are more appropriate for binary functions that modify neither of their operands, such as `==`, `+`, and `-`, whereas member functions are more appropriate for binary functions, such as `=`, `+=`, and `-=` that are used to modify one of their operands.*

The Assignment Operator Revisited

In Section 12.1 a simple assignment operator function was presented. It is repeated here for convenience.

```
void Date::operator=(Date &newdate)
{
  day = newdate.day;        // assign the day
  month = newdate.month;    // assign the month
  year = newdate.year;      // assign the year
}
```

The drawback of this function is that it returns no value, which makes multiple assignments such as `a = b = c` impossible. Now that we have introduced operator functions with return types and have the `this` pointer at our disposal, we can fix our simple assignment operator function to provide an appropriate return type. In this case, the return value should be a `Date`. Thus an appropriate prototype for our operator is

```
Date operator=(const Date &);
```

Note that we have declared the function's parameter to be a `const` to ensure that this operand will not be altered by the function. A suitable function for this prototype is

```
Date Date::operator=(const Date &newdate)
{

  day = newdate.day;        // assign the day
  month = newdate.month;    // assign the month
  year = newdate.year;      // assign the year

  return *this;
}
```

In the case of an assignment such as `b = c`, or its equivalent form `b.operator=(c)`, the function first alters `b`'s member values from within the function and then returns the value of this object, which may be used in a subsequent assignment. Thus a multiple assignment expression such as `a = b = c` is possible; it is illustrated in Program 13-3.

Program 13-3

```
#include <iostream.h>
#include <iomanip.h>
```

```
// class declaration
class Date
{
  private:
    int month;
    int day;
    int year;
  public:
    Date(int, int, int);       // constructor
    Date operator=(const Date &);  // define assignment of a date
    void showdate(void);       // member function to display a date
};

// implementation section
Date::Date(int mm = 7, int dd = 4, int yyyy = 2001)
{
  month = mm;
  day = dd;
  year = yyyy;
}
Date Date::operator=(const Date &newdate)
{
  day = newdate.day;         // assign the day
  month = newdate.month;     // assign the month
  year = newdate.year;       // assign the year

  return *this;
}
void Date::showdate(void)
{
  cout << setfill('0')
       << setw(2) << month << '/'
       << setw(2) << day << '/'
       << setw(2) << year % 100;

  return;
}
```

```
int main()
{
  Date a(4,1,99), b(12,18,2002), c(1,1,2004); // declare three objects

  cout << "Before assignment a's date value is ";
  a.showdate();
  cout << "\nBefore assignment b's date value is ";
  b.showdate();
  cout << "\nBefore assignment c's date value is ";
  c.showdate();

  a = b = c;  // multiple assignment

  cout << "\n\nAfter assignment a's date value is ";
  a.showdate();
  cout << "\nAfter assignment b's date value is ";
  b.showdate();
  cout << "\nAfter assignment c's date value is ";
  c.showdate();

  return 0;
}
```

The output produced by Program 13-3 is

```
Before assignment a's date value is 04/01/99
Before assignment b's date value is 12/18/02
Before assignment c's date value is 01/01/04

After assignment a's date value is 01/01/04
After assignment b's date value is 01/01/04
After assignment c's date value is 01/01/04
```

As we noted previously, the only restriction on the assignment operator function is that it can be overloaded only as a member function. It cannot be overloaded as a friend.

Exercises 13.1

1. *a.* Define a *greater than* relational operator function named `operator>()` that can be used with the `Date` class declared in Program 13-1.
   b. Define a *less than* operator function named `operator<()` that can be used with the `Date` class declared in Program 13-1.
   c. Include the operator functions written for Exercises 1a and 1b in a working C++ program.

2. *a.* Define a subtraction operator function named `operator-()` that can be used with the `Date` class defined in Program 13-1. The subtraction should accept a long-integer argument that represents the number of days to be subtracted from an object's date and should return a date. In doing the subtraction, use the financial assumption that all months consist of 30 days and all years of 360 days. Additionally, an end-of-month adjustment should be made, if necessary, that converts any resulting day of 31 to a day of 30, except if the month is February. If the resulting month is February and the day is either 29, 30, or 31, it should be changed to 28.
   b. Define another subtraction operator function named `operator-()` that can be used with the `Date` class defined in Program 13-1. The subtraction should yield a long integer that represents the difference in days between two dates. In calculating the day difference, use the financial assumption that all months have 30 days and all years have 360 days.
   c. Include the overloaded operators written for Exercises 2a and 2b in a working C++ program.
3. *a.* Determine whether the following addition operator function provides the same result as the function used in Program 13-2:

```
Date Date::operator+(int days)    // return a date object
{
  Date temp;

  temp.day = day + days;    // add the days in
  temp.month = month + int(temp.day/30);   // determine total months
  temp.day = temp.day % 30;                // determine actual day
  temp.year = year + int(temp.month/12);   // determine total years
  temp.month = temp.month % 12;            // determine actual month

  return temp;
}
```

   b. Verify your answer to Exercise 3a by including the function in a working C++ program.
4. *a.* Rewrite the equality relational operator function in Program 13-1 as a friend function.
   b. Verify the operation of the friend operator function written for Exercise 4a by including it in a working C++ program.
5. *a.* Rewrite the addition operator function in Program 13-2 to account for the actual days in a month, neglecting leap years.
   b. Verify the operation of the operator function written for Exercise 5a by including it in a working C++ program.
6. *a.* Construct an addition operator for the `Complex` class declared in Program 12-9. This should be a member function that adds two complex numbers and returns a complex number.

POINT OF INFORMATION

Program and Class Libraries

The concept of a program library began with FORTRAN, introduced in 1954 as the first commercial high-level language. The FORTRAN library consisted of a group of completely tested and debugged mathematical routines that were provided with the compiler. Since that time, every programming language has provided its own library of functions. In both C and C++, this library is referred to as the standard program library and includes more than 100 functions declared in 15 different header files. Examples of standard library functions include `sqrt()`, `pow()`, `abs()`, `rand()`, `srand()`, and `time()`. The advantage of library functions is that they significantly enhance program development and design by providing code that is known to work correctly without the need for additional testing and debugging.

With the introduction of object-oriented languages, the concept of a program library has been extended to include class libraries. A *class library* is a library of tested and debugged classes that includes both interfaces and implementations. Generally, the interface portion is placed in a header file and the implementation in a separate implementation file.

One of the key practical features of class libraries is that they help realize the goal of code reuse in a significant way. By providing tested and debugged code that consists of both data and function members, class libraries furnish large sections of prewritten and reusable code ready for incorporation within new applications. This shifts the focus of writing application programs from the creation of new code to understanding how to use predefined objects and stitch them together in a cohesive and useful way. A prime example of this is the visual object classes consisting of check boxes, list boxes, dialogs, command buttons, and option buttons provided in both Visual C++ and Visual Basic.

b. Add a member multiplication operator function to the class used in Exercise 6a that multiplies two complex numbers and returns a complex number.
c. Verify the operation of the operator functions written for Exercises 6a and 6b by including them in a working C++ program.

7. *a.* Create a class named `String` and include an addition operator function that concatenates two strings. The function should return a string.
b. Include the overloaded operator written for Exercise 7a in a working C++ program.

13.2 Two Useful Alternatives—`operator()` and `operator[]`

There are times when it is convenient to define an operation having more than two arguments, which is the limit imposed on all binary operator functions. For example, each of our `Date` objects contains three integer data members: `month`, day, and year. For such an object, we might want to add an integer value to any of these three members, instead of just the day member as was done in Program 13-2. C++ provides for this possibility by supplying the parentheses operator function, operator(), which has no limits on the number of arguments that may be passed to it.

On the other end of the spectrum, the case illustrated by Program 13-2, where only a single nonobject argument is required, occurs so frequently that C++ also provides an alternative means of achieving it. For this special case, C++ supplies the subscript operator function, operator[], which permits a maximum of one argument. The only restriction imposed by C++ on the operator() and operator[] functions is that they must be defined as member (not friend) functions. For simplicity, we consider the operator[] function first.

The subscript operator function, operator[], is declared and defined in the same manner as any other operator function, but it is called differently from the normal function and operator call. For example, if we want to use this operator function to accept an integer argument and return a Date object, the following prototype is valid:

```
Date operator[](int);   // declare the subscript operator
```

Except for the operator function's name, this is similar in construction to any other operator function prototype. Assuming that we want this function to add its integer argument to a Date object, a suitable function implementation is

```
Date Date::operator[](int days)
{
  Date temp;  // a temporary date to store the result

  temp.day = day + days;  // add the days
  temp.month = month;
  temp.year = year;
  while (temp.day > 30)    // now adjust the months
  {
    temp.month++;
    temp.day -= 30;
  }
  while (temp.month > 12)  // adjust the years
  {
    temp.year++;
    temp.month -= 12;
  }
  return temp;     // the values in temp are returned
}
```

Again, except for the initial header line, this is similar in construction to other operator function definitions. Once the function is created, however, it can only be called by passing the required argument through the subscript brackets. For example, if a is a Date object, the function call a[284] calls the subscript operator function and causes the function to operate on the a object using the integer value 284. This call is illustrated in Program 13-4.

Program 13-4

```
#include <iostream.h>
#include <iomanip.h>
```

```
// class declaration

class Date
{
  private:
    int month;
    int day;
    int year;
  public:
    Date(int = 7, int = 4, int = 2001);     // constructor
    Date operator[](int);     // overload the subscript operator
    void showdate(void);      // member function to display a date
};

// implementation section

Date::Date(int mm, int dd, int yyyy)
{
  month = mm;
  day = dd;
  year = yyyy;
}

Date Date::operator[](int days)
{
  Date temp;  // a temporary date to store the result
```

(continued on next page)

(continued from previous page)

```
  temp.day = day + days;   // add the days
  temp.month = month;
  temp.year = year;
  while (temp.day > 30)     // now adjust the months
  {
    temp.month++;
    temp.day -= 30;
  }
  while (temp.month > 12)  // adjust the years
  {
    temp.year++;
    temp.month -= 12;
  }
  return temp;      // the values in temp are returned
}

void Date::showdate(void)
{
  cout << setfill('0')
       << setw(2) << month << '/'
       << setw(2) << day << '/'
       << setw(2) << year % 100;

  return;
}
```

```
int main()
{
  Date a(4,1,1999), b; // declare two objects

  cout << "\nThe initial date is ";
  a.showdate();
  b = a[284];  // add in 284 days = 9 months and 14 days
  cout << "\nThe new date is ";
  b.showdate();
  cout << endl;

  return 0;
}
```

Program 13-4 is identical in every way to Program 13-2, except that we have used an overloaded subscript operator function in place of an overloaded addition operator function. Programs 13-4 and 13-2 produce identical output.

Although the expression a[284] used in Program 13-2 *appears* to indicate that a is an array, it is not. It is simply the notation that is required to call an overloaded subscript function.

The parentheses operator function, operator()(), is almost identical in construction and calling to the subscript function, operator[](), with the substitution of the parentheses, (), for the brackets, []. The difference between these two operator functions is in the number of allowable arguments. Whereas the subscript operator permits passing zero or one argument, the parentheses operator has no limit on the number of its arguments. For example, a suitable operator prototype to add an integer number of months, days, or years to a Date object is

```
Date operator()(int, int, int);
```

Once such a function is implemented (which is left as an exercise) a call such as a(2,4,3) can be used to add 2 months, 4 days, and 3 years to the Date object named a.

These two extra functions provide a great deal of programming flexibility. In the case where only one argument is needed, they permit two different overloaded functions to be written, both of which have the same argument type. For example, we could use operator[] to add an integer number of days to a Date object and operator() to add an integer number of months. Because both functions have the same argument type, one function name could not be overloaded for both of these cases.

These two functions also permit us the flexibility to restrict the other operator functions to class member arguments and use these two functions for any other argument types or operations, such as adding an integer to a Date object.

Exercises 13.2

1. Replace the subscript operator[] function in Program 13-4 with the parentheses operator() function.

2. *a.* Replace the subscript operator[] function in Program 13-4 with a member operator() function that accepts an integer month, day, and year count. Have the function add the input days, months, and years to the object's date and return the resulting date. For example, if the input is 3,2,1 and the object's date is 7/16/1997, the function should return the date 10/18/1998. Make sure that your function correctly handles an input such as 37 days and 15 months and that it adjusts the calculated day to be within the range 1 to 30 and the month to be within the range 1 to 12.

b. Include the operator function written for Exercise 2a in a working C++ program and verify its operation.

3. *a.* Construct a class named `Student` consisting of the following private data members: an integer ID number, an integer count, and an array of four floating-point grades. The constructor for this class should set all data member values to zero. The class should also include a member function that displays all valid member grades, as determined by the grade count, and calculates and displays the average of the grades. Include the class in a working C++ program that declares three class objects named `a`, `b`, and `c`.
   b. Include, in the class constructed for Exercise 3a, a member `operator[]` function that has a floating-point grade argument. The function should check the `count` data member, and if fewer than four grades have been entered, the function should store its argument into the `grade` array using the count as an index value. If four grades have already been entered, the function should return an error message indicating that the new grade cannot be accepted. Additionally, a new grade should force an increment to the `count` data member.
   c. Include, in the class constructed for Exercise 3a, a member `operator()` function that has a grade index and grade value as arguments. The function should force a change to the grade corresponding to the index value and should update the count if necessary. For example, an argument list of 4,98.5 should change the fourth test grade value to 98.5.
4. *a.* Add to Program 12-9 a member `operator[]` function that multiples an object's complex number (both the real and the imaginary parts) by a real number and returns a complex number. For example, if the real number is 2 and the complex number is 3 + 4i, the result is 6 + 8i.
   b. Verify the operation of the operator function written for Exercise 4a by including it in a working C++ program.

13.3 Data Type Conversions

In Chapter 3, we discussed the conversion from one built-in data type to another. The introduction of user-defined data types expands the possibilities for conversion between data types to the following cases:

- Conversion from built-in type to built-in type
- Conversion from built-in type to user-defined type
- Conversion from user-defined type to built-in type
- Conversion from user-defined type to user-defined type

The first conversion is handled either by C++'s built-in implicit conversion rules or by its explicit cast operator. The second conversion type is made using a *type conversion constructor*. The third and fourth conversion types are made using a *conversion operator function*. In this section, we will examine the specific means of performing each of these conversions.

Conversion from Built-in to Built-in

The conversion from one built-in data type to another was presented in Section 3.2. To review this case briefly, recall that this type of conversion is either implicit or explicit.

An implicit conversion occurs in the context of one of C++'s operations. For example, when a floating-point value is assigned to an integer variable, only the integer portion of the value is stored. The conversion is implied by the operation and is performed automatically by the compiler.

An explicit conversion occurs whenever a cast is used. Two cast notations exist in C++. Using the older C notation, a cast has the form `(data-type)expression`; the newer C++ notation has the function-like form `data-type(expression)`. For example, both of the expressions `(int)24.32` and `int(24.32)` cause the floating-point value 24.32 to be truncated to the integer value 24.

Conversion from Built-in to Class

User-defined casts for converting a built-in to a user-defined data type are created by using constructor functions. A constructor whose first argument is not a member of its class and whose remaining arguments, if any, have default values is a *type conversion constructor*. If the first argument of a type conversion constructor is a built-in data type, the constructor can be used to cast the built-in data type to a class object. Clearly, one restriction of such functions is that, as constructors, they must be member functions.

Although this type of cast occurs when the constructor is invoked to initialize an object, it is actually a more general cast than might be evident at first glance. This is because a constructor function can be explicitly invoked after all objects have been declared, whether or not it was invoked previously as part of an object's declaration. Before exploring this further, let's construct a type conversion constructor. We will then see how to use it as a cast independent of its initialization purpose.

The cast we will construct will convert a long integer into a `Date` object. Our `Date` object will consist of dates in the form month/day/year and will use our now familiar `Date` class. The long integer will be used to represent dates in the form year * 10000 + month * 100 + day. For example, using this representation, the date 12/31/2001 becomes the long integer 20011231. Representing dates in this fashion is very useful for two reasons: First, it permits a date to be stored as a single integer, and second, such dates are in numerically increasing date order, which makes sorting extremely easy. For example, the date 01/03/2002, which occurs after 12/31/2001, becomes the integer 20020103, which is larger than 20011231. Because the integers that represent dates can exceed the size of a normal integer, the integers are always declared as longs.

A suitable constructor function for converting from a long-integer date to a date stored as a month, day, and year is

```
// type conversion constructor from long to Date

Date::Date(long findate)
{
  year = int(findate/10000.0);
  month = int((findate - year * 10000.0)/100.0);
  day = int(findate - year * 10000.0 - month * 100.0);
}
```

Program 13-5 uses this type conversion constructor both as an initialization function at declaration time and as an explicit cast later on in the program.

Program 13-5

```
#include <iostream.h>
#include <iomanip.h>

// class declaration

class Date
{
  private:
    int month, day, year;
  public:
    Date(int = 7, int = 4, int = 2001);  // constructor
    Date(long);              // type conversion constructor
    void showdate(void);
};

// implementation section

// constructor
Date::Date(int mm, int dd, int yyyy)
{
  month = mm;
  day = dd;
  year = yyyy;
}

// type conversion constructor from long to date
Date::Date(long findate)
{
  year = int(findate/10000.0);
  month = int((findate - year * 10000.0)/100.0);
  day = int(findate - year * 10000.0 - month * 100.0);
}
```

```
// member function to display a date
void Date::showdate(void)
{
  cout << setfill('0')
       << setw(2) << month << '/'
       << setw(2) << day << '/'
       << setw(2) << year % 100;

  return;
}
```

```
int main()
{
  Date a, b(20011225L), c(4,1,1999); // declare 3 objects--initialize 2 of them

  cout << "\nDates a, b, and c are \n  ";
  a.showdate();
  cout << ", ";
  b.showdate();
  cout << ", and ";
  c.showdate();
  cout << ".\n";

  a = Date(20020101L);  // cast a long to a date

  cout << "Date a is now ";
  a.showdate();
  cout << ".\n\n";

  return 0;
}
```

The output produced by Program 13-5 is

```
Dates a, b, and c are 07/04/01, 12/25/01, and 04/01/99.
Date a is now 01/03/02.
```

The change in `a`'s date value illustrated by this output is produced by the assignment expression `a = Date(20020101L)`, which uses a type conversion constructor to perform the cast from long to `Date`.

Conversion from Class to Built-in

Conversion from a user-defined data type to a built-in data type is accomplished using a conversion operator function. A *conversion operator function* is a member operator function that has the name of a built-in data type or class. When the operator function has a built-in data type name, it is used to convert from a class to a built-in data type. For example, a conversion operator function for casting a class object to a long integer would have the name `operator long()`. Here the name of the operator function indicates that a conversion to a long will take place. If this function were part of a `Date` class, it would be used to cast a `Date` object to a long integer. This usage is illustrated by Program 13-6.

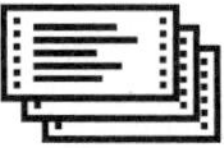

Program 13-6

```
#include <iostream.h>
#include <iomanip.h>

// class declaration

class Date
{
  private:
    int month, day, year;
  public:
    Date(int = 7, int = 4, int = 2001);     // constructor
    operator long();         // conversion operator function
    void showdate(void);
};

// implementation section

// constructor
Date::Date(int mm, int dd, int yyyy)
{
  month = mm;
  day = dd;
  year = yyyy;
}

// conversion operator function converting from Date to long
Date::operator long()    // must return a long
{
  long yyyymmdd;

  yyyymmdd = year * 10000.0 + month * 100.0 + day;

  return(yyyymmdd);
}

// member function to display a date
void Date::showdate(void)
{
  cout << setfill('0')
       << setw(2) << month << '/'
       << setw(2) << day << '/'
       << setw(2) << year % 100;

  return;
}
```

```
int main()
{
  Date a(4,1,1999); // declare and initialize one object of type date
  long b;           // declare an object of type long

  b = a;            // a conversion takes place here

  cout << "\n a's date is ";
  a.showdate();
  cout << "\n This date, as a long integer, is " << b << "\n\n";

  return 0;
}
```

The output produced by Program 13-6 is

```
a's date is 04/01/99
This date, as a long integer, is 19990401
```

The change in `a`'s `date` value to a long integer illustrated by this output is produced by the assignment expression `b = a`. This assignment, which also could have been written as `b = long(a)`, calls the conversion operator function `long()` to perform the cast from `Date` to `long`. In general, because explicit conversion more clearly documents what is happening, its use is preferred to implicit conversion.

Note that the conversion operator has no explicit argument and no explicit return type. This is true of all conversion operators: Its implicit argument will always be an object of the class being cast from, and the return type is implied by the name of the function. Additionally, as previously indicated, a conversion operator function *must be* a member function.

Conversion from Class to Class

Converting from a user-defined data type to a user-defined data type is performed in the same manner as a cast from a user-defined to a built-in data type—it is done using a member conversion operator function. In this case, however, the operator function uses the class name being converted to rather than a built-in data name. For example, if two classes named `Date` and `Intdate` exist, the operator function named `operator Intdate()` could be placed in the `Date` class to convert from a `Date` object to an `Intdate` object. Similarly, the operator function named `Date()` could be placed in the `Intdate` class to convert from an `Intdate` to a `Date`.

Note that as before, in converting from a user-defined data type to a built-in data type, *the operator function's name determines the result of the conversion*; the class containing the operator function determines the data type being converted from.

Before we look at a specific example of a class-to-class conversion, we must note one additional point. Converting between classes clearly implies that we have two classes, one of which is always defined first and one of which is defined second. Having, within the second class, a conversion operator function with the name of the first class poses no problem, because the compiler knows of the first class's existence. However, including in the first class a conversion operator function with the second class's name does pose a problem, because the second class has not yet been defined. This is remedied by including a declaration for the second class prior to the first class's definition. This declaration, which is formally referred to as a *forward declaration,* is illustrated in Program 13-7, which also includes conversion operators between the two defined classes.

Program 13-7

```
#include <iostream.h>
#include <iomanip.h>
```

```
// forward declaration of class Intdate
class Intdate;

// class declaration for Date
class Date
{
  private:
    int month, day, year;
  public:
    Date(int = 7, int = 4, int = 2001);     // constructor
    operator Intdate();     // conversion operator Date to Intdate
    void showdate(void);
};
// class declaration for Intdate
class Intdate
{
  private:
    long yyyymmdd;
  public:
    Intdate(long = 0);    // constructor
    operator Date();  // conversion operator Intdate to Date
    void showint(void);
};
```

```
implementation section for Date
Date::Date(int mm, int dd, int yyyy)  // constructor
{
  month = mm;
  day = dd;
  year = yyyy;
}
// conversion operator function converting from Date to Intdate class
Date::operator Intdate()   // must return an Intdate object
{
  long temp;

  temp = year * 10000.0 + month * 100.0 + day;
  return(Intdate(temp));
}
// member function to display a Date
void Date::showdate(void)
{

  cout << setfill('0')
       << setw(2) << month << '/'
       << setw(2) << day << '/'
       << setw(2) << year % 100;
  return;
}

// implementation section for Intdate
Intdate::Intdate(long ymd)  // constructor
{
  yyyymmdd = ymd;
}
// conversion operator function converting from Intdate to Date class
Intdate::operator Date()    // must return a Date object
{
  int mo, da, yr;

  yr = int(yyyymmdd/10000.0);
  mo = int((yyyymmdd - yr * 10000.0)/100.0);
  da = int(yyyymmdd - yr * 10000.0 - mo * 100.0);
  return(Date(mo,da,yr));
}
// member function to display an Intdate
void Intdate::showint(void)
{
  cout << yyyymmdd;
  return;
}
```

(continued on next page)

(continued from previous page)

```
int main()
{
  Date a(4,1,1999), b;       // declare two Date objects
  Intdate c(20011215L), d;   // declare two Intdate objects

  b = Date(c);       // cast c into a Date object
  d = Intdate(a);    // cast a into an Intdate object

  cout << "\n a's date is ";
  a.showdate();
  cout << "\n   as an Intdate object this date is ";
  d.showint();

  cout << "\n c's date is ";
  c.showint();
  cout << "\n   as a Date object this date is ";
  b.showdate();
  cout << "\n\n";

  return 0;
}
```

The output produced by Program 13-7 is

```
a's date is 04/01/99
  as an Intdate object this date is 19990401
c's date is 20011215
  as a Date object this date is 12/15/01
```

As illustrated by Program 13-7, the cast from `Date` to `Intdate` is produced by the assignment `b = Date(c)`, and the cast from `Intdate` to `Date` is produced by the assignment `d = Intdate(a)`. Alternatively, the assignments `b = c` and `d = a` would produce the same results. Note also the forward declaration of the `Intdate` class prior to the `Date` class's declaration. This is required so that the `Date` class can reference `Intdate` in its operator conversion function.

Exercises 13.3

1. *a.* Define the four data type conversions available in C++ and the method of accomplishing each conversion.
   b. Define the terms *type conversion constructor* and *conversion operator function,* and describe how they are used in user-defined conversions.

2. Write a C++ program that declares a class named `Time` having integer data members named `hours`, `minutes`, and `seconds`. Include in the program a type conversion constructor that converts a long integer, representing the elapsed seconds from midnight, into an equivalent representation as `hours:minutes:seconds`. For example, the long integer 30336 should convert to the time 8:25:36. Use a military representation of time so that 2:30 p.m. is represented as 14:30:00. The relationship between time representations is

$$elapsed\ seconds = hours * 3600 + minutes * 60 + seconds$$

3. A Julian date is a date represented as the number of days from a known base date. One algorithm for converting from a Gregorian date, in the form month/day/year, to a Julian date with a base date of 0/0/0 follows. All of the calculations in this algorithm use integer arithmetic, which means that the fractional part of all divisions must be discarded. In this algorithm, M = month, D = day, and Y = 4-digit year.

```
If M is less than or equal to 2
  set the variable MP = 0 and YP = Y-1
Else
  set MP = int(0.4 * M + 2.3) and YP = Y

T = int(YP/4) - int(YP/100) + int(YP/400)

Julian date = 365 * Y + 31 * (M - 1) + D + T - MP
```

Using this algorithm, modify Program 13-6 to cast from a Gregorian date object to its corresponding Julian representation as a long integer. Test your program by using the Gregorian dates 1/31/1985 and 3/16/1986, which correspond to the Julian dates 725037 and 725446, respectively.

4. Modify the program written for Exercise 2 to include a member conversion operator function that converts an object of type `time` into a long integer representing the number of seconds from twelve midnight.

5. Write a C++ program that has a `Date` class and a `Julian` class. The `Date` class should be the same `Date` class as that used in Program 13-7, whereas the `Julian` class should represent a date as a long integer. For this program, include a member conversion operator function within the `Date` class that converts a `Date` object to a `Julian` object, using the algorithm presented in Exercise 3. Test your program by converting the dates 1/31/1995 and 3/16/1996, which correspond to the Julian dates 728689 and 729099, respectively.

6. Write a C++ program that has a `Time` class and an `Ltime` class. The `Time` class should have integer data members named `hours`, `minutes`, and `seconds`, whereas the `Ltime` class should have a long data member named `elsecs`, which represents the number of elapsed seconds since midnight. For the `Time` class, include a member conversion operator function named `Ltime()` that converts a `Time` object to an `Ltime` object. For the `Ltime` class, include a member conversion operator function named `Time()` that converts an `Ltime` object to a `Time` object.

13.4 Class Inheritance and Polymorphism

The ability to create new classes from existing ones is the underlying motivation and power behind class and object-oriented programming techniques. Doing so facilitates reusing existing code in new ways without the need for retesting and validation. It permits the designers of a class to make it available to others for additions and extensions without relinquishing control over the existing class features.

Constructing one class from another is accomplished by using a capability called inheritance. Related to this capability is an equally important feature named polymorphism. Polymorphism provides the ability to redefine, on the basis of the class object being referenced, how member functions of related classes operate. In fact, for a programming language to be classified as an object-oriented language, it must provide the features of classes, inheritance, and polymorphism. In this section we describe the inheritance and polymorphism features provided in C++.

Inheritance

Inheritance is the capability of deriving one class from another class. The initial class that is used as the basis for the derived class is referred to as the *base class, parent class,* or *superclass*. The derived class is referred to as the *derived class, child class,* or *subclass*.

A derived class is a completely new class that incorporates all of the data and member functions of its base class. It can (and usually does), however, add its own additional new data and function members, and it can override any base class function.

FIGURE 13–1 Relating Object Types

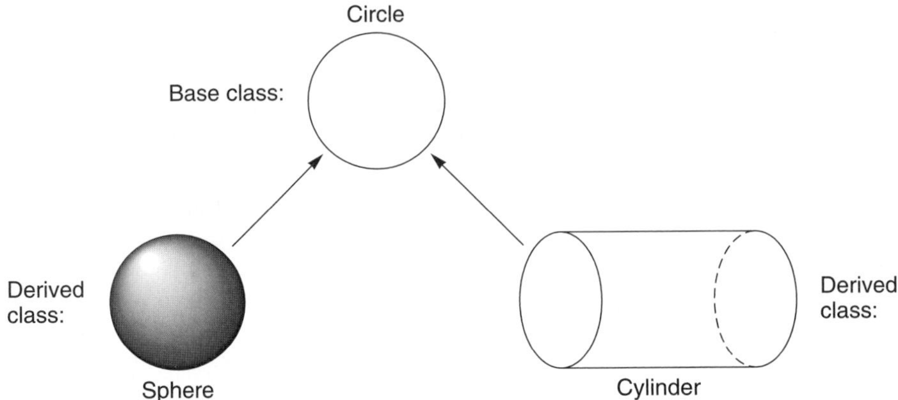

Object-Based versus Object-Oriented Languages

An *object-based* language is one in which data and operations can be incorporated together in such a way that data values can be isolated and accessed through the specified class functions. The ability to bind the data members with operations in a single unit is referred to as *encapsulation*. In C++, encapsulation is provided by its class capability.

For a language to be classified as *object-oriented*, it must also provide inheritance and polymorphism. *Inheritance* is the capability to derive one class from another. A derived class is a completely new data type that incorporates all of the data members and member functions of the original class with any new data and function members unique to itself. The class used as the basis for the derived type is referred to as the *base* or *parent* class, and the derived data type is referred to as the derived or child class.

Polymorphism permits the same method name to invoke one operation in objects of a parent class and a different operation in objects of a derived class.

As an example of inheritance, consider three geometric shapes: a circle, cylinder, and sphere. All of these shapes share a common characteristic, a radius. Thus, for these shapes, we can make the circle a base type for the other two shapes, as illustrated in Figure 13–1. By convention, arrows always point from the derived class to the base class. Reformulating these shapes as class types we would make the circle the base class and derive the cylinder and sphere classes from it.

The relationships illustrated in Figure 13–1 are examples of simple inheritance. In *simple inheritance,* each derived type has only one immediate base type. The complement to simple inheritance is multiple inheritance. In *multiple inheritance,* a derived type has two or more base types. Figure 13–2 gives an example of multiple inheritance. In this text we will only consider simple inheritance.

The class derivations illustrated in both Figure 13–1 and Figure 13–2 are formally referred to as *class hierarchies,* because they illustrate the hierarchy, or

FIGURE 13–2 An Example of Multiple Inheritance

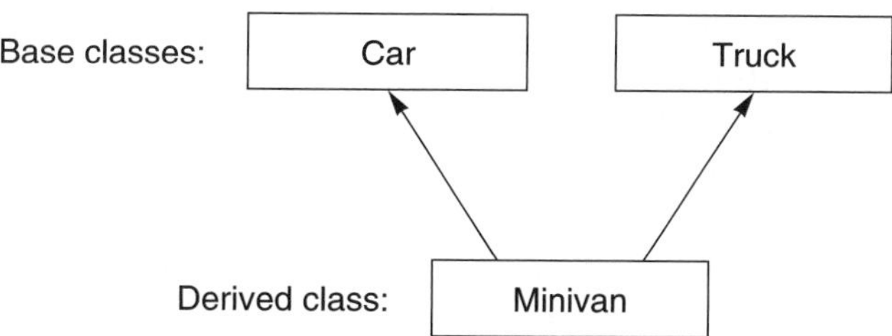

order, in which one class is derived from another. Let's now see how to derive one class from another.

A derived class has the same form as any other class in that it consists of both a declaration and an implementation. The only difference is in the first line of the declaration section. For a derived class, this line is extended to include an access specification and a base class name and has the form

```
class  derived-class-name : class-access  base-class-name
```

For example, if `Circle` is the name of an existing class, a new class named `Cylinder` can be derived as follows:

```
class Cylinder : public Circle
{
   // add any additional data and
   // function members in here
}; // end of Cylinder class declaration
```

Except for the class-access specifier after the colon and the base class name, there is nothing inherently new or complicated about the construction of the `Cylinder` class. Before providing a description of the `Circle` class and adding data and function members to the derived `Cylinder` class, we will need to reexamine access specifiers and how they are related to derived classes.

Access Specifications

Until now we have used only private and public access specifiers within a class. Giving all data members private status ensured that they could be accessed only by class member functions or friends. This restricted access prevents access by any nonclass functions (except friends), *which also precludes access by any derived class functions.* This is a sensible restriction. If it did not exist, anyone could "jump around" the private restriction by simply deriving a class.

To retain a restricted type of access across derived classes, C++ provides a third access specification—protected. Protected access behaves identically to private access in that it permits only member or friend function access, but it permits this restriction to be inherited by any derived class. The derived class then defines the type of inheritance it is willing to take on, subject to the base class's access restrictions. This is done by the class-access specifier, which is listed after the colon at the start of its declaration section. Table 13–3 lists the resulting derived class member access based on the base class member specifications and the derived class-access specifier.

TABLE 13–3 Inherited Access Restrictions

Base Class Member	Derived Class Access	Derived Class Member
private →	: private →	inaccessible
protected →	: private →	private
public →	: private →	private
private →	: public →	inaccessible
protected →	: public →	protected
public →	: public →	public
private →	: protected →	inaccessible
protected →	: protected →	protected
public →	: protected →	protected

Table 13–3 shows (shaded region) that if the base class member has a protected access and the derived class specifier is public, then the derived class member will be protected to its class. Similarly, if the base class has a public access and the derived class specifier is public, then the derived class member will be public. Because this is the most commonly used type of specification for base class data and function members, respectively, it is the one we will use. This means that for all classes intended for use as a base class, we will use a protected data member access in place of a private designation.

An Example

To illustrate the process of deriving one class from another, we will derive a `Cylinder` class from a base `Circle` class. The definition of the `Circle` class is

```
// class declaration

class Circle
{
  protected:
    double radius;
  public:
    Circle(double);   // constructor
    double calcval();
};

// class implementation

// constructor
Circle::Circle(double r = 1.0)   // constructor
{
  radius = r;
}
```

(continued on next page)

(continued from previous page)

```
// calculate the area of a circle
double Circle::calcval(void)
{
  return(PI * radius * radius);
}
```

Except for the substitution of the access specifier `protected` in place of the usual private specifier for the data member, this is a standard class definition. The only identifier not defined is PI, which is used in the `calcval()` function. We will define this as

```
const double PI = 2.0 * asin(1.0);
```

This is simply a "trick" that forces the computer to return the value of pi accurate to as many decimal places as allowed by your computer. This value is obtained by taking the arcsin of 1.0, which is $\pi/2$, and multiplying the result by 2.

Having defined our base class, we can now extend it to a derived class. The definition of the derived class is

```
// class declaration where
// Cylinder is derived from Circle

class Cylinder : public Circle
{
  protected:
    double length;   // add one additional data member and
  public:            // two additional function members
    Cylinder(double r = 1.0, double l = 1.0) : Circle(r), length(l) {}
    double calcval();
};

// class implementation

double Cylinder::calcval(void)    // this calculates a volume
{
  return (length * Circle::calcval()); // note the base function call
}
```

This definition encompasses several important concepts related to derived classes. First, as a derived class, `Cylinder` contains all of the data and function members of its base class, `Circle`, plus any additional members that it may add. In this particular case, the `Cylinder` class consists of a `radius` data member, inherited from the `Circle` class, plus an additional `length` member. Thus each `Cylinder` object contains *two* data members, as is illustrated in Figure 13–3.

In addition to having two data members, the `Cylinder` class also inherits `Circle`'s function members. This is illustrated in the `Cylinder` constructor, which uses a base member initialization list (see Section 12.1) that specifically calls the `Circle` constructor. It is also illustrated in `Cylinder`'s `calcval()` function, which makes a call to `Circle::calcval()`.

In both classes the same function name, `calcval()`, has been specifically used to illustrate the overriding of a base function by a derived function. When a `Cylinder` object calls `calcval()`, it is a request to use the `Cylinder` version of the function, and a `Circle` object call to `calcval()` is a request to use the `Circle` version. In this case the `Cylinder` class can only access the `Circle` class version of `calcval()` using the `scope` resolution operator, as is done in the call `Circle::calcval()`. Program 13-8 uses these two classes within the context of a complete program.

The output produced by Program 13-8 is

```
The area of circle_1 is 3.141593
The area of circle_2 is 12.566371
The volume of cylinder_1 is 113.099336

The area of circle_1 is now 28.274334
```

The first three output lines are all straightforward and are produced by the first three `cout` statements in the program. As the output shows, a call to `calcval()` using a `Circle` object activates the `Circle` version of this function, whereas a call to `calcval()` using a `Cylinder` object activates the `Cylinder` version.

The assignment statement `circle_1 = cylinder_1;` introduces another important relationship between a base and derived class: *A derived class object can be assigned to a base class object.* This should not be surprising, because both

FIGURE 13–3 Relationship Between `Circle` and `Cylinder` Data Members

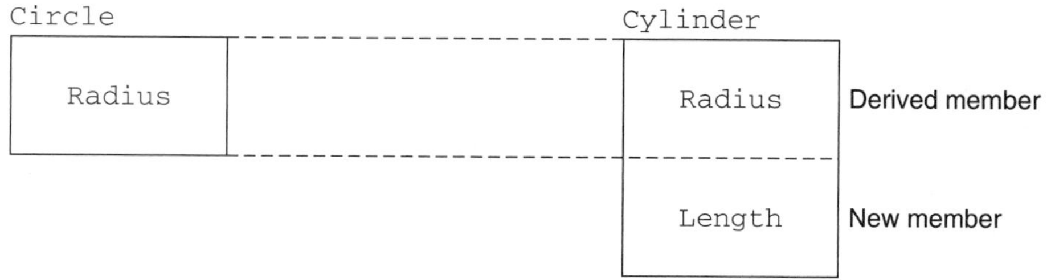

Program 13-8

```
#include <iostream.h>
#include <math.h>

const double PI = 2.0 * asin(1.0);

// class declaration

class Circle
{
  protected:
    double radius;
  public:
    Circle(double r = 1);  // constructor
    double calcval();
};

// implementation section for Circle

// constructor
Circle::Circle(double r)
{
  radius = r;
}

// calculate the area of a circle
double Circle::calcval(void)
{
  return(PI * radius * radius);
}

// class declaration for the derived class
// Cylinder which is derived from Circle
class Cylinder : public Circle
{
  protected:
    double length;  // add one additional data member and
  public:           // two additional function members
    Cylinder(double r = 1.0, double l = 1.0) : Circle(r), length(l) {}
    double calcval();
};

// implementation section for Cylinder

double Cylinder::calcval(void)   // this calculates a volume
{
  return (length * Circle::calcval()); // note the base function call
}
```

```
int main()
{
  Circle circle_1, circle_2(2);  // create two Circle objects
  Cylinder cylinder_1(3,4);      // create one Cylinder object

  cout << "\nThe area of circle_1 is " << circle_1.calcval() << endl;
  cout << "The area of circle_2 is " << circle_2.calcval() << endl;
  cout << "The volume of cylinder_1 is " << cylinder_1.calcval() << endl;

  circle_1 = cylinder_1;  // assign a cylinder to a Circle

  cout << "\nThe area of circle_1 is now "
       << circle_1.calcval() << endl;

  return 0;
}
```

base and derived classes share a common set of data member types. In this type of assignment, it is only this set of data members, which consists of all the base class data members, that are assigned. Thus, as illustrated in Figure 13–4, our `Cylinder` to `Circle` assignment results in the following memberwise assignment:

```
circle_1.radius = cylinder_1.radius;
```

The `length` member of the `Cylinder` object is not used in the assignment because it has no equivalent variable in the `Circle` class. The reverse cast, from base to derived class, is not as simple and requires a constructor to correctly initialize the additional derived class members not in the base class.

Before leaving Program 13-8, we need to make one additional point. Although the `Circle` constructor was explicitly called using a base/member initialization list for the `Cylinder` constructor, an implicit call could also have been made. In the absence of an explicitly derived class constructor, the compiler will automatically call the default base class constructor first, before the derived class

FIGURE 13–4 Assignment from Derived to Base Class

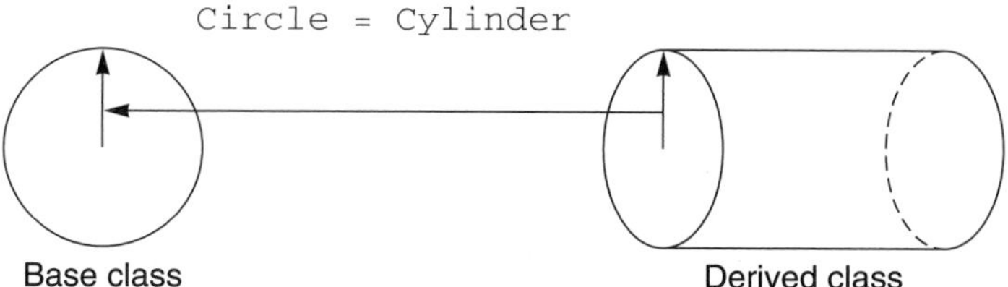

constructor is called. This works because the derived class contains all of the base class data members. In a similar fashion, the destructor functions are called in the reverse order—first derived class and then base class.

Polymorphism

The overriding of a base member function using an overloaded derived member function, as illustrated by the `calcval()` function in Program 13-8, is an example of polymorphism. *Polymorphism* permits the same function name to invoke one response in objects of a base class and another response in objects of a derived class. In some cases, however, this method of overriding does not work as one might desire. To understand why this is so, consider Program 13-9.

Program 13-9

```
#include <iostream.h>
#include <math.h>

// class declaration for the base class

class One
{
  protected:
    float a;
  public:
    One(float = 2);     // constructor
    float f1(float);    // a member function
    float f2(float);    // another member function
};

// class implementation for One

One::One(float val)   // constructor
{
  a = val;
}

float One::f1(float num)   // a member function
{
  return(num/2);
}
float One::f2(float num)   // another member function
{
  return( pow(f1(num),2) );  // square the result of f1()
}
```

```
// class declaration for the derived class

class Two : public One
{
  public:
    float f1(float);    // this overrides class One's f1()
};

// class implementation for Two

float Two::f1(float num)
{
  return(num/3);
}
```

```
int main()
{
  One object_1;  // object_1 is an object of the base class
  Two object_2;  // object_2 is an object of the derived class

     // call f2() using a base class object call
  cout << "The computed value using a base class object call is "
       << object_1.f2(12) << endl;

    // call f2() using a derived class object call
  cout << "The computed value using a derived class object call is "
       << object_2.f2(12) << endl;

  return 0;
}
```

The output produced by Program 13-9 is

```
The computed value using a base class object call is 36
The computed value using a derived class object call is 36
```

As this output shows, the same result is obtained no matter which object type calls the `f2()` function. This result is produced because the derived class does not have an override to the base class `f2()` function. Thus both calls to `f2()` result in the base class `f2()` function being called.

Once invoked, the base class `f2()` function will always call the base class version of `f1()` rather than the derived class override version. This behavior is due to a process referred to as *function binding*. In normal function calls, static binding is used. In *static binding*, the determination of which function is called is made at compile time. Thus, when the compiler first encounters the `f1()`

function in the base class, it makes the determination that whenever `f2()` is called, either from a base class or a derived class object, it will subsequently call the base class `f1()` function.

In place of static binding, we would like a binding method that is capable of determining which function should be invoked at run time, on the basis of the object type making the call. This type of binding is referred to as *dynamic binding*. To achieve dynamic binding, C++ provides virtual functions.

A *virtual function* specification tells the compiler to create a pointer to a function but not to fill in the value of the pointer until the function is actually called. Then, at run time, *and on the basis of the object making the call,* the appropriate function address is used. Creating a virtual function is extremely easy—all that is required is that the keyword `virtual` be placed before the function's return type in the declaration section. For example, consider Program 13-10, which is identical to Program 13-9 except for the virtual declaration of the `f1()` function.

Program 13-10

```
#include <iostream.h>
#include <math.h>

// class declaration for the base class

class One
{
  protected:
    float a;
  public:
    One(float = 2);    // constructor
    virtual float f1(float);   // a member function
    float f2(float);   // another member function
};

// class implementation for One

One::One(float val)   // constructor
{
  a = val;
}

float One::f1(float num)  // a member function
{
  return(num/2);
}
```

```
float One::f2(float num)   // another member function
{
  return( pow(f1(num),2) );  // square the result of f1()
}

// class declaration for the derived class

class Two : public One
{
  public:
    virtual float f1(float);     // this overrides class One's f1()
};

// class implementation for Two

float Two::f1(float num)
{
  return(num/3);
}
```

```
int main()
{
  One object_1;  // object_1 is an object of the base class
  Two object_2;  // object_2 is an object of the derived class

     // call f2() using a base class object call
  cout << "The computed value using a base class object call is "
       << object_1.f2(12) << endl;

    // call f2() using a derived class object call
  cout << "The computed value using a derived class object call is "
       << object_2.f2(12) << endl;

  return 0;
}
```

The output produced by Program 13-10 is

```
The computed value using a base class object call is 36
The computed value using a derived class object call is 16
```

As illustrated by this output, the `f2()` function now calls different versions of the overloaded `f1()` function on the basis of the object type making the call. This selection, which is based on the object making the call, is the classic definition of polymorphic function behavior and is caused by the dynamic binding imposed on `f1()` because it is a virtual function.

Once a function is declared as `virtual`, *it remains virtual for the next derived class with or without a virtual declaration in the derived class*. Thus the second `virtual` declaration in the derived class is not strictly needed, but it should be included both for clarity and to ensure that any subsequently derived classes correctly inherit the function. To understand why, consider the inheritance diagram illustrated in Figure 13-5, where class C is derived from class B and class B is derived from class A.[5] In this situation, if function `f1()` is virtual in class A but is not declared in class B, it will not be virtual in class C. The only other requirement is that once a function has been declared as virtual, the return type and parameter list of all subsequent derived class override versions *must be* the same.

Exercises 13.4

1. Define the following terms:

a. inheritance
b. base class
c. derived class
d. simple inheritance
e. multiple inheritance
f. class hierarchy
g. polymorphism
h. static binding
i. dynamic binding
j. virtual function

FIGURE 13–5 Inheritance Diagram

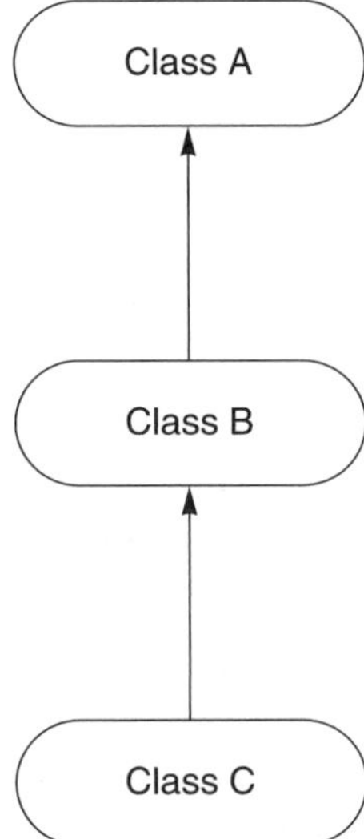

5 By convention, as previously noted, arrows always point from the derived class to the base class.

2. Describe the two methods that C++ provides for implementing polymorphism.

3. What three features must a programming language provide for it to be classified as an object-oriented language?

4. Describe the difference between a private and a protected class member.

5. *a.* Modify Program 13-8 to include a derived class named `Sphere` from the base `Circle` class. The only additional class members of `Sphere` should be a constructor and a `calcval()` function that returns the volume of the sphere. (*Note:* volume = $4/3\pi$ radius^3)
b. Include the class constructed for Exercise 5a in a working C++ program. Have your program call all of the member functions in the `Sphere` class.

6. *a.* Create a base class named `Point` that consists of an `x` and a `y` coordinate. From this class, derive a class named `Circle` that has an additional data member named `radius`. For this derived class, the `x` and `y` data members represent the center coordinates of a circle. The function members of the first class should consist of a constructor, an area function named `area` that returns zero, and a `distance` function that returns the distance between two points, where

$$\text{distance} = \sqrt{(x_2 - x_1)^2 + (y_2 - y_1)^2}$$

Additionally, the derived class should have a constructor and an override function named `area` that returns the area of a circle.
b. Include the classes constructed for Exercise 6a in a working C++ program. Have your program call all of the member functions in each class. In addition, call the base class `distance` function with two `Circle` objects, and explain the result returned by the function.

7. *a.* Using the classes constructed for Exercise 6a, derive a class named `Cylinder` from the derived `Circle` class. The `Cylinder` class should have a constructor and a member function named `area` that determines the surface area of the cylinder. For this function, use the algorithm

$$\textit{surface area} = 2\pi r\,(l + r)$$

where r is the radius of the cylinder and l is the length.
b. Include the classes constructed for Exercise 7a in a working C++ program. Have your program call all of the member functions in the `Cylinder` class.
c. What do you think might be the result if the base class `distance` function were called with two `Cylinder` objects?

8. *a.* Create a base class named `Rectangle` that contains `length` and `width` data members. From this class derive a class named `Box` that has an additional data member named `depth`. The function members of the base `Rectangle` class should consist of a constructor and an `area` function. The derived `Box` class should have a constructor and an override function named `area` that returns the surface area of the `box` and a `volume` function.
b. Include the classes constructed for Exercise 8a in a working C++ program. Have your program call all of the member functions in each class and explain the result when the `distance` function is called using a `Box` object.

13.5 Common Programming Errors

The common programming errors associated with operator functions, conversions, and inheritance are the following:

1. Attempting to redefine an operator's meaning as it applies to C++'s built-in data types.
2. Redefining an overloaded operator to perform a function not indicated by its conventional meaning. Although this will work, it is extremely bad programming practice.
3. Attempting to make a conversion operator function a friend, rather than a member function.
4. Attempting to specify a return type for a member conversion operator function.
5. Attempting to override a virtual function without using the same type and number of parameters as the original function.
6. Using the keyword `virtual` in the class implementation section. Functions are declared as `virtual` only in the class declaration section.

13.6 Chapter Summary

1. User-defined operators can be constructed for classes by using member operator functions. An operator function has the form `operator<symbol>`, where `<symbol>` is one of the following:

```
()   []   ->   new   delete   ++   --   !   ~   *   /   %   +   -
<<   >>   <    <=    >    >=   ++   !=   &&   ||   &   ^   |   =   +=
-=   *=   /=   %=   &=   ^=   |=   <<=   >>=   ,
```

   For example, the function prototype `Date operator+(int);` declares that the addition operator will be defined to accept an integer and return a `Date` object.

2. User-defined operators may be called in either of two ways—as a conventional function with arguments or as an operator expression. For example, for an operator that has the header line

```
Date Date::operator+(int)
```

if `dte` is an object of type `Date`, the following two calls produce the same effect:

```
dte.operator+(284)

dte + 284
```

3. Operator functions may also be written as friend functions. The equivalent friend version of a member operator function will always contain an additional class reference that is not required by the member function.
4. The subscript operator function, `operator[]`, permits a maximum of one nonclass argument. This function can be defined only as a member function.
5. The parentheses operator function, `operator()`, has no limits on the number of arguments. This function can be defined only as a member function.
6. There are four categories of data type conversions. They are conversions from

   - Built-in types to built-in types
   - Built-in types to user-defined (class) types
   - User-defined (class) types to built-in types
   - User-defined (class) types to user-defined (class) types

   Conversions from built-in to built-in type are done by using C++'s implicit conversion rules or by explicitly using casts. Conversions from built-in to user-defined type are done using type conversion constructors. Conversions from user-defined types to either built-in or other user-defined types are done using conversion operator functions.
7. A *type conversion constructor* is a constructor whose first argument is not a member of its class and whose remaining arguments, if any, have default values.
8. A *conversion operator function* is a member operator function that has the name of a built-in data type or class. It has no explicit arguments or return type; rather, the return type is the name of the function.
9. *Inheritance* is the capability of deriving one class from another class. The initial class used as the basis for the derived class is referred to as the base class, parent class, or superclass. The derived class is referred to as the derived class, child class, or subclass.
10. Base member functions can be overridden by derived member functions with the same name. The override function is simply an overloaded version of the base member function defined in the derived class.

11. *Polymorphism* is the capability of having the same function name invoke different responses on the basis of the object making the function call. It can be accomplished by using either override functions or virtual functions.
12. In *static binding,* the determination of which function actually is invoked is made at compile time. In *dynamic binding,* the determination is made at run time.
13. A *virtual function* specification designates that dynamic binding should take place. The specification is made in the function's prototype by placing the keyword `virtual` before the function's return type. Once a function has been declared as `virtual` it remains so for all derived classes, so long as there is a continuous trail of function declarations through the derived chain of classes.

I/O File Streams and Data Files

Chapter Fourteen

14.1 I/O File Stream Objects and Methods
14.2 Reading from and Writing to Files
14.3 Random File Access
14.4 File Streams as Function Arguments
14.5 Common Programming Errors
14.6 Chapter Summary
14.7 Chapter Supplement: The `iostream` Class Library

The data for the programs we have seen so far has either been assigned internally within the programs or entered interactively during program execution. This type of data entry is fine for small amounts of data.

In this chapter, we learn how to store data outside of a program using C++'s object-oriented capabilities. This external data storage permits a program to use the data without the user having to recreate it interactively each time the program is executed. This provides the basis for sharing data between programs, so that the data that is output by one program can be input directly to another program. Additionally, it serves as an introduction to the stream objects used in delivering data to and from a program. Accordingly, this chapter can also be used as an introduction to the more general topic of object-oriented programming formally presented in Chapter 11.

14.1 I/O File Stream Objects and Methods

To store and retrieve data on a file in C++ three items are required:

- A file
- A file stream object
- A mode

Files

Any collection of data that is stored together under a common name on a storage medium other than the computer's main memory is called a *data file*. Typically, data files are stored on a disk, magnetic tape, or CD-ROM. For example, the C++ programs that you store on disk are examples of files. The stored data in this particular form of a file is referred to as a *program file* and consists of the program code that becomes input data to the C++ compiler.

A file is physically stored on an external medium such as a disk, using a unique file name referred to as the external file name. The *external file name* is the name of the file as it is known by the operating system. It is the external name that is displayed when you use an operating command such as `dir` or `ls` or display the contents of a directory.

Each computer operating system has its own specification as to the maximum number of characters permitted for an external file name. Table 14–1 lists these specifications for the more commonly used operating systems.

TABLE 14–1 Maximum Allowable File Name Characters

Operating System	Maximum Length
DOS	8 characters plus an optional period and 3-character extension
VMX	8 characters plus an optional period and 3-character extension
Windows 3.1[1]	8 characters plus an optional period and 3-character extension
Windows 95	255 characters
Windows 98	255 characters
UNIX	
Early Versions	14 characters
Current Versions	255 characters

To ensure that the examples presented in this text are compatible with all of the operating systems listed in Table 14–1, we will adhere to the more restrictive DOS and VMX specifications. If you are using one of the other operating systems, however, you should take advantage of the increased length specification to create descriptive file names within the context of a manageable length (generally considered to be no more than 12 to 14 characters). Very long file names should be avoided. Although such names can be extremely descriptive, they take more time to type and are prone to typing errors.

Using the DOS convention then, the following are all valid computer data file names:

```
bessel.dat    records      info.txt
exper1.dat    volts.dat    math.mem
```

Computer file names should be chosen to indicate both the type of data in the file and the application for which it is used. Frequently, the first eight characters are used to describe the data itself, and an extension (the three characters after the decimal point) is used to describe the application. For example, the Lotus 123 spreadsheet program automatically applies an extension of `wk3` to all spreadsheet files, Microsoft's Word and the WordPerfect word

[1] Because Windows 3.1 runs under DOS, it has the same restrictions as DOS. Technically, Windows 3.1 is not an operating system at all but an application that runs under DOS. Thus, it more properly should be referred to as a dynamic linker and file-managing application.

processing programs use the extensions `doc` and `wpx` (where `x` refers to the version number), respectively, and most C++ compilers require a program file to have the extension `cpp`. When creating your own file names, you should adhere to this practice. For example, the name `exper1.dat` is appropriate in describing a file of data corresponding to experiment number 1.

File Stream Objects and Modes

A *file stream* is a one-way transmission path that is used to connect a file stored on a physical device, such as a disk or CD-ROM, to a program. Associated with every file stream is a *mode,* which determines the direction of data on the transmission path—that is, whether the path will be used for moving data from a file into a program, or whether the path will be used for moving data from a program to a file. A file stream with a mode designated as *input* is referred to as an *input file stream* and is used to receive or read data from a file. A file stream with an *output* mode designation is referred to as an *output file stream* and is used to send or write data to a file.

Figure 14–1 illustrates the data flow from and to a file using input and output streams.

For each file that your program uses, a distinct file stream object must be created. If you are going to both read and write to a file, both an input and an output file stream object is required. Input file stream objects are declared to be of type `ifstream`, and output file streams are declared to be of type `ofstream`. For example, the declaration

```
ifstream inStream;
```

declares an input file stream object named `inStream` that is of type `ifstream`. Similarly, the declaration

```
ofstream outStream;
```

FIGURE 14–1 Input and Output File Streams

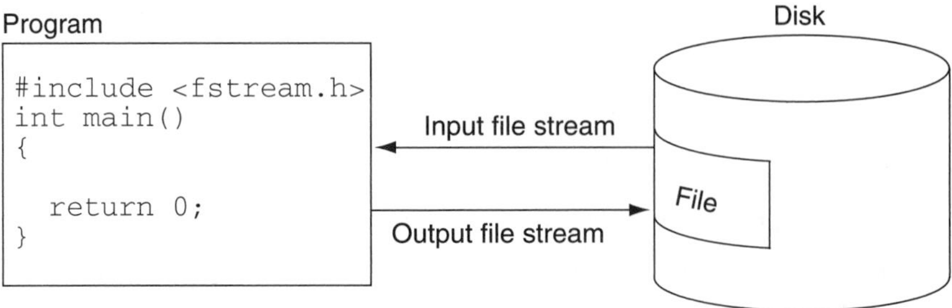

declares an output file stream object named `outStream` that is of type `ofstream`. Within a C++ program, a file stream is always accessed by its appropriate stream object name, one name for reading the file and one name for writing to the file. Object names, such as `inStream` and `outStream`, can be any programmer-chosen names that conform to C++'s identifier rules.

File Stream Methods

Each file stream object has access to prewritten functions defined for its respective `ifstream` or `ofstream` class. These functions include connecting a stream to an external file name (called *opening a file*), determining whether a successful connection has been made, closing a connection (called *closing a file*), getting the next data item into the program from an input stream, putting a new data item from the program onto an output stream, and detecting when the end of a file has been reached.

Opening a file connects each file stream object to a specific external file name. This is accomplished by using a file stream's `open()` function, which is a "cookbook" procedure that accomplishes two purposes. First, opening a file establishes the physical connecting link between a program and a file. Because details of this link are handled by the computer's operating system and are transparent to the program, the programmer normally need not consider them.

From a coding perspective, the second purpose of opening a file is more relevant. Besides establishing the actual physical connection between a program and a data file, opening a file equates the file's external computer name to the stream object name used internally by the program. The function that performs this task is named `open()` and is provided by both the `ifstream` and `ofstream` classes.

In using the `open()` function to connect a file's external name to its internal object stream name, only one argument is required, which is the external file name. For example, the statement

```
inFile.open("test.dat");
```

connects the external file named `test.dat` to the internal program file stream object named `inFile`. This assumes, of course, that `inFile` has been declared as either an `ifstream` or an `ofstream` object. Although this statement may look a little strange for a function call, there is a good reason for it. The name to the left of the required period identifies a specific object, and the name to the right of the period identifies the function being called. This notation is used because, when we are dealing with objects, such as a file stream, more than one function with the same name typically exists. For example, there is more than one `open()` function.

POINT OF INFORMATION

Input and Output Streams

A *stream* is a one-way transmission path between a source and a destination. What gets sent down this transmission path is a stream of bytes. A good analogy to this "stream of bytes" is a stream of water that provides a one-way transmission path of water from a source to a destination.

Two stream objects that we have already used extensively are the input stream object named `cin` and the output stream object named `cout`. The `cin` object provides a transmission path from keyboard to program, whereas the `cout` object provides a transmission path from program to terminal screen. These two objects are created from the stream classes named `istream` and `ostream`, respectively. When the `iostream.h` header file is included in a program using the `#include <iostream.h>` directive, the `cin` and `cout` stream objects are automatically declared as belonging to these streams and are opened by the C++ compiler for use by the compiled program.

File stream objects provide the same capabilities as the `cin` and `cout` objects, except that they connect a program to a file rather than the keyboard or terminal screen. Also, file stream objects must be explicitly declared. File stream objects that will be used for input must be declared as type `ifstream`, and file stream objects that will be used for output must be declared as type `ofstream`. These two classes, as well as the capability for automatically constructing the `cin` and `cout` objects, are made available to a program by inclusion of the `fstream.h` header file using the directive `#include <fstream.h>`.

Specifically, there is a function named `open()` that is used for opening input streams, and there is a different function, also named `open()`, that is used for opening output streams. Although both functions clearly perform a similar "opening" task, one effectively opens a file for input, whereas the other is used to open a file for output. The compiler correctly determines which `open()` function to use by the name that appears to the left of the period. Functions, such as `open()`, that are associated with objects are referred to as both *member functions* and *methods* (the terms are used interchangeably), and using such functions requires that the function name be preceded by a period and an object name.

Once an input stream has been opened with the above statement, the program accesses the file by using the internal object name `inFile`, whereas the computer saves the file under the external name `test.dat`. Note that the external file name argument passed to `open()` is a string contained between double quotes.

When an existing file is connecting to an input file stream, the file's data is made available for input, starting at the first data item in the file. Similarly, a file connected to an output file stream creates a new file and makes the file available for output. If a file exists with the same name as a file opened in output mode, the old file is erased and all its data is lost.

When you are opening a file, for input or output, good programming practice requires that you check that the connection has been established before attempting to use the file in any way. The check can be made by using the `fail()` method. This method will return a true value, which is a 1, if the open was successful, or a false value, which is a 0, if the open failed. To use the `fail()` method correctly, however, you must open the file in `ios::nocreate` mode, as is shown below and explained more fully in the following two "Point of Information" boxes. Doing this sets a fail bit when the file is not found, which is the bit used by `fail()` to determine whether a successful open occurred. Typically, the `fail()` method is used in code similar to the following, which attempts to open a file named `test.dat`, checks that a valid connection was made, and reports an error message if the file was not successfully opened for input.[2]

```
ifstream inFile;   // any object name can be used here

inFile.open("test.dat", ios::nocreate);   // open the file

// check that the connection was successfully opened
if (inFile.fail())
{
  cout << "\nThe file was not successfully opened"
       << "\n Please check that the file currently exists."
       << endl;
  exit(1);
}
```

If the `fail()` method returns a true, which indicates that the open failed, a message is displayed by this code, and the `exit()` function, which is a request to the operating system to end program execution immediately, is called. The `exit()` function requires inclusion of the `stdlib.h` header function in any program that uses this function, and `exit()`'s single-integer argument is passed directly to the operating system for possible further operating system program action or user inspection. Throughout the remainder of the text, we will include this type of error checking whenever a file is opened.

Program 14-1 illustrates the statements required to open a file in read mode, including an error checking routine to ensure that a successful open was obtained.

---

[2] To use the `fail()` method correctly on some compilers, you must open input files by using the `ios::nocreate` mode; for example, as `inFile("test.dat", ios::nocreate)`. This prevents a new file from being created if the named file does not exist and correctly sets the bit tested by `fail()` to indicate that the file was not opened.

Program 14-1

```
#include <fstream.h>
#include <stdlib.h>   // needed for exit()

int main()
{
  ifstream inFile;

  inFile.open("test.dat",ios::nocreate); // open the file with the
                                         // external name test.dat
  if (inFile.fail())  // check for a successful open
  {
    cout << "\nThe file was not successfully opened"
         << "\n Please check that the file currently exists."
         << endl;
    exit(1);
  }

  cout << "\nThe file has been successfully opened for reading."
       << endl;

  return 0;
}
```

Assuming that a file named `test.dat` is available on the current directory, a sample run using Program 14-1 will display the following output line:

```
The file has been successfully opened for reading.
```

Although Program 14-1 can be used to open an existing file in read mode, it clearly lacks statements either to read the file's data or to close the file. These topics are discussed shortly. Before leaving Program 14-1, however, we should note two items. First, we did not have to include the `iostream.h` header file in the program to use the `cout` object, because its definition is incorporated within the `fstream.h` header file. Next, it is possible to combine the declaration of an `ifstream` object and its associated open statement into one statement. For example, the two statements in Program 14-1

```
ifstream inFile;
inFile.open("test.dat", ios::nocreate);   // open the file
```

Checking for a Successful Connection

It is important to check that the `open()` method successfully established a connection between a file stream and an external file. This is because the `open()` call is really a request to the operating system that can fail for a variety of reasons. (Chief among these reasons is a request to open an existing file for reading that the operating system cannot locate.) If the operating system cannot satisfy the open request, you need to know about it and gracefully terminate your program. Failure to do so almost always results in some abnormal program behavior or a subsequent program crash. There are two styles of coding for checking the return value.

The most common method for checking that a fail did not occur is the one coded in Program 14-1. It is used to distinguish clearly the `open()` request from the check made via the `fail()` call and is repeated below for convenience:

```
inFile.open("test.dat",ios::nocreate);  // request to open the file

if (inFile.fail())   // check for a failed connection
{
  cout << "\nThe file was not successfully opened"
       << "\n Please check that the file currently exists."
       << endl;
  exit(1);
}
```

Alternatively, you may encounter programs that use `fstream` objects in place of both `ifstream` and `ofstream` objects. When you are using `fstream`'s `open()` method, two arguments are required: a file's external name and an explicit mode indication. If the `open()` function is not successful, the `fstream` stream object is assigned the named constant `NULL`. When this named constant is used, the open request and check typically appear as follows:

```
fstream inFile;

infile.open("external file name", ios::in | ios::nocreate);
if (inFile == NULL)
{
  cout << "\nThe file was not successfully opened"
       << "\n Please check that the file currently exists."
       << endl;
  exit(1);
}
```

Note that the `ios::nocreate` mode is ORed with the `ios::in` mode. The definitions for these modes are presented in the next "Point of Information" box. Many times, the conditional expression `inFile == NULL` is replaced by the equivalent expression `!inFile`. Although we will always use `ifstream` and `ofstream` objects, be prepared to encounter the styles that use `fstream` objects.

can be combined into the single statement

```
ifstream inFile("test.dat", ios::nocreate);
```

In this text, we will continue to declare all `ifstream` and `ofstream` objects at the top of the program and explicitly call the `open()` method in a separate statement. You may, however, choose to use the alternative single-statement form.

Embedded and Interactive File Names

There are two practical problems with Program 14-1:

1. The external file name is embedded within the program code.
2. There is no provision for a user to enter the desired file name while the program is executing.

As Program 14-1 is written, if the file name is to change, a programmer must modify the external file name in the call to `open()` and recompile the program. Both of these problems can be alleviated by assigning the file name to a string variable.

A *string variable* is a variable that can hold a string value, which is any sequence of zero or more characters enclosed within double quotes. For example, `"Hello World"`, `"test.dat"`, and `""` are all strings. Note that strings are always written with double quotes that delimit the beginning and end of a string but are not stored as part of the string. The declaration of a string variable is extremely simple.[3] For example, whereas the declaration

```
char filename = 'a';
```

declares a character variable named `filename` and initializes this character variable to the single letter `a`, the declaration

```
char filename[21] = "test.dat";
```

declares a string variable capable of holding 21 characters in total and initializes the string variable with the string value `test.dat`.

In declaring and initializing a string variable, three items must be considered. First, the maximum length of the string must be specified within brackets

[3] For a complete description of string variables, which are stored as character arrays in C++, refer to Chapter 9.

POINT OF INFORMATION

Using fstream Objects

In the use of both `ifstream` and `ofstream` objects, the mode—input or output—is implied by the object. Thus `ifstream` objects can be used only for input, and `ofstream` objects only for output.

Another means of creating file streams is to use `fstream` objects, which can be used for input or output but require an explicit mode assignment. An `fstream` object is declared using the syntax

```
fstream object-name;
```

When the `fstream` class's `open()` member function is used, two arguments are required: a file's external name and a mode indicator. Permissible mode indicators are

Indicator	Description
`ios::in`	Open in input mode
`ios::out`	Open in output mode
`ios::app`	Open in append mode
`ios::ate`	Go to the end of the opened file
`ios::binary`	Open in binary mode (default is text)
`ios::trunc`	Delete file contents if it exists
`ios::nocreate`	If file does not exist, open fails
`ios::noreplace`	If file exists, open for output fails

As with `ofstream` objects, an `fstream` object in output mode creates a new file and makes the file available for writing. If a file exists with the same name as a file opened for output, the old file is erased. For example, assuming that `file1` has been declared as an object of type `fstream` using the statement

```
fstream file1;
```

then the statement

```
file1.open("test.dat",ios::out);
```

attempts to open the file named `test.dat` for output. Once this file has been opened, the program accesses the file using the internal object name `file1`, and the computer saves the file under the external name `test.dat`.

An `fstream` file object opened in append mode means that an existing file is available for data to be added to the end of the file. If the file opened for appending does not exist, a new file with the designated name is created and made available to receive output from the program. For example, again assuming that `file1` has been declared to be of type `fstream`, the statement

```
file1.open("test.dat",ios::app);
```

attempts to open a file named `test.dat` and makes it available for data to be appended to the end of the file.

Finally, an `fstream` object opened in input mode means that an existing external file has been connected and its data is available as input. For example, assuming that `file1` has been declared to be of type `fstream`, the statement

```
file1.open("test.dat",ios::in);
```

attempts to open a file named `test.dat` for input.

immediately after the variable's name. This is the function of the [21] in the foregoing declaration. Second, *the number in brackets always represents one more than* the maximum number of characters that you can assign to the variable. This is because the compiler always adds a final end-of-string character to terminate the string. Thus the string value test.dat, which consists of eight characters, is actually stored as nine characters. The extra character is an end-of-string marker supplied by the compiler. Finally, each initializing string value can be any sequence of characters from zero to one less than the maximum length specifier in brackets. Thus the maximum string value assignable to the string variable filename is a string value consisting of 20 characters.

Once a string variable is declared to store a file name, it can be used in one of two ways. First, as shown in Program 14-1a, it can be placed at the top of a program, rather than embedded within an open() method call, to identify a file's external name clearly.

Program 14-1a

```
#include <fstream.h>
#include <stdlib.h>

int main()
{
  const int MAXLENGTH = 21;  // maximum file name length
  char file1[MAXLENGTH] = "test.dat";    // place the file name up front
  ifstream inFile;

  inFile.open(file1, ios::nocreate);  // open the file

  if (inFile.fail())  // check for successful open
  {
    cout << "\nThe file named " << file1 << " was not successfully opened"
         << "\n Please check that the file currently exists." << endl;
    exit(1);
  }

  cout << "\nThe file has been successfully opened for reading.\n";

  return 0;
}
```

POINT OF INFORMATION

Character and String Variables

The primary difference between character and string variables is that a character variable can store only a single character value, whereas a string variable can store a string value of zero or more characters. The stored value, however, always contains an additional end-of-string symbolic constant named `NULL`. For example, consider the declarations

```
char nameOne = 'x';
char nameTwo[2] = "x";
```

First note that the initializing character value is enclosed within single quotes and the initializing string value is enclosed in double quotes. In the first case, only one character, an `x`, is stored in the character variable `nameOne`. In the second case, two characters are stored: the `x` character and an end-of-string termination character supplied by the compiler. For all string variables, this character is the named constant `NULL`, which has the value `'\0'`. As we saw in Chapter 9, this end-of-string `NULL` constant is extremely useful in processing strings. This is because it provides a relatively easy method of always determining where a string ends without knowing, beforehand, the actual string length.

Because of this terminating `NULL`, a string value such as `""` is not stored as an empty string but consists of the single `NULL` terminating character.

One other very important difference between character and string variables is that assignment to a string variable is always invalid except within a declaration statement. Assignment in nondeclarative statements is accomplished using the `strcopy()` function, which was described in Chapter 9.

In reviewing Program 14-1a, note that we have used a symbolic constant named `MAXLENGTH` to define the length of the string variable `file1` and that we have declared and initialized this string variable at the top of the program for easy file identification. Next note that when a string variable is used, as opposed to a string value, the variable name is *not* enclosed within double quotes in the `open()` method call. Finally, note that in the `fail()` method code, we can display the file's external name by inserting the string variable name in the `cout` standard output stream. For all of these reasons, we will continue to identify the external names of files in this manner.

Another extremely useful role played by string variables is to permit the user to enter the file name as the program is executing. For example, the code

```
const int MAXLENGTH = 21;
char file1[MAXLENGTH];

cout << "Please enter the name of the file you wish to open: ";
cin  >> file1;
```

allows a user to enter a file's external name at run time. The only restriction in this code is that the user must not enclose the entered string value in double quotes, which is a plus, and that the entered string value cannot contain any blanks. The reason for this is that the compiler will terminate the string when it encounters a blank.

Program 14-1b uses this code in the context of a complete program.

Program 14-1b

```
#include <fstream.h>
#include <stdlib.h>

int main()
{
  const int MAXLENGTH = 21;    // maximum file name length
  char file1[MAXLENGTH];
  ifstream inFile;

  cout << "Please enter the name of the file you wish to open: ";
  cin  >> file1;

  inFile.open(file1, ios::nocreate);  // open the file

  if (inFile.fail())  // check for successful open
  {
    cout << "\nThe file named " << file1 << " was not successfully opened"
         << "\n Please check that the file currently exists." << endl;
    exit(1);
  }

  cout << "\nThe file has been successfully opened for reading.\n";

  return 0;
}
```

A sample run using Program 14-1b produced the following output

```
Please enter the name of the file you wish to open: foobar

The file named foobar was not successfully opened
 Please check that the file currently exists.
```

Closing a File

A file is closed using the `close()` method. This method breaks the connection between the file's external name and the file stream object, which can then be used for another file. For example, the statement

```
inFile.close();
```

closes the `inFile` stream's connection to its current file. As indicated, the `close()` method takes no argument.

Because all computers have a limit on the number of files that can be open at one time, closing files that are no longer needed makes good sense. Any open files that exist at the end of normal program execution will be automatically closed by the operating system.

Exercises 14.1

1. *a.* Enter and execute Program 14-1 on your computer.
   b. Add a `close()` method to Program 14-1 and then execute the program.

2. *a.* Enter and execute Program 14-1b on your computer.
   b. Add a `close()` method to Program 14-1b and then execute the program.

3. Using the reference manuals provided with your computer's operating system, determine:
   a. The maximum number of characters that can be used to name a file for storage by the computer system.
   b. The maximum number of data files that can be open at the same time.

4. Would it be appropriate to call a saved C++ program a file? Why or why not?

5. *a.* Write a suitable declaration statement for each of the following `ifstream` objects: `inData`, `prices`, `coupons`, and `file1`.
   b. Write a suitable declaration statement for each of the following `ofstream` objects: `outData`, `rates`, `distance`, and `file2`.

6. Write individual declaration and open statements to link the following external data file names to their corresponding internal object names:

External Name	Object Name	Mode
`coba.mem`	`memo`	output
`book.let`	`letter`	output
`coupons.bnd`	`coups`	append
`yield.bnd`	`ptYield`	append
`test.dat`	`priFile`	input
`rates.dat`	`rates`	input

7. Write close statements for each of the files opened in Exercise 6.

14.2 Reading from and Writing to Files

Reading from and writing to an open file involve almost exactly the same operations as reading input from a terminal and writing data to a display screen. For writing to a file, the `cout` object is replaced by the `ofstream` object declared in the program. For example, if `outFile` is declared as an object of type `ofstream`, the following output statements are valid:

```
outFile << 'a';
outFile << "Hello World!";
outFile << descrip << ' ' << price;
```

The file name in each of these statements, in place of `cout`, simply directs the output stream to a specific file instead of to the standard display device. Program 14-2 illustrates the use of a file write function to write a list of descriptions and prices to a file.

Note that in Program 14-2, we have not used the `ios::nocreate` mode in the `open()` function call. The reason for this is that we want to create the file for writing even if it does not currently exist. Here, we only want to know that a fail has occurred for any reason except that the file doesn't already exist. Thus, when Program 14-2 is executed, a file named `test.dat` will be created and saved by the computer. The file is a sequential file that, after it is opened, is written with the following data:

```
Batteries 39.95
Bulbs 3.22
Fuses 1.00
```

The actual storage of characters in the file depends on the character codes used by the computer. Although only 35 characters appear to be stored in the file, corresponding to the descriptions, blanks, and prices written to the file, the file actually contains 38 characters. The extra characters consist of the newline escape sequence at the end of the first two lines and the special end-of-file marker placed as the last item in the file when the file is closed. Assuming that characters are stored using either the ASCII or ANSI codes, the `test.dat` file is physically stored as illustrated in Figure 14–2. For convenience, the character corresponding to each hexadecimal code is listed below the code. A code of 20 represents the blank character. Although the actual code used for the end-of-file marker depends on the system you are using, the hexadecimal code 26, corresponding to Control-Z, is common for DOS and Windows operating systems.

Program 14-2

```
#include <fstream.h>
#include <stdlib.h>
#include <iomanip.h>

int main()
{
  const int MAXLENGTH = 21;  // maximum file name length
  char filename[MAXLENGTH] = "test.dat";  // put the filename up front
  ofstream outFile;

  outFile.open(filename);

  if (outFile.fail())
  {
    cout << "The file was not successfully opened" << endl;
    exit(1);
  }

     // set the output file stream formats
   outFile << setiosflags(ios::fixed)
           << setiosflags(ios::showpoint)
           << setprecision(2);

     // send data to the file
   outFile << "Batteries " << 39.95 << endl
           << "Bulbs " << 3.22 << endl
           << "Fuses " << 1.00;

   outFile.close();

   return 0;
}
```

FIGURE 14–2 The `test.dat` File as Stored by the Computer

```
 42 61 74 74 65 72 69 65 73 20 33 39 2e 32 35 0A 42 75 6c 62 73
  B  a  t  t  e  r  i  e  s     3  9  .  2  5 \n  B  u  l  b  s

20 33 2e 32 32 0A 46 75 73 65 73 20 31 2e 30 30 26
    3  .  2  2 \n  F  u  s  e  s     1  .  0  0 ^Z
```

POINT OF INFORMATION

Formatting Output File Stream Data

Output file streams can be formatted in the same manner as the `cout` standard output stream. For example, if an output stream named `fileOut` has been declared, the statement

```
fileOut << setiosflags(ios::fixed)
        << setiosflags(ios::showpoint)
        << setprecision(2);
```

formats all data inserted in the `fileOut` stream in the same way that these parameterized manipulators work for the `cout` stream. The first manipulator parameter, `ios::fixed`, causes the stream to output all numbers in conventional fixed-point notation (not exponential). The next parameter, `ios::showpoint`, tells the stream always to provide a decimal point. Thus a value such as 1.0 will appear as 1.0, not 1. Finally, the `setprecision` manipulator tells the stream always to display two decimal values after the decimal point. Thus the number 1.0, for example, will appear as 1.00.

Instead of using manipulators, you can also use the stream methods `setf()` and `precision()`. For example, the previous formatting can also be accomplished using the code

```
fileOut.setf(ios::fixed);
fileOut.setf(ios::showpoint);
file.out.precision(2);
```

Which style you select is a matter of preference. In both cases, the formats need only be specified once and remain in effect for every number subsequently inserted into the file stream.

Reading data from a file is almost identical to reading data from a standard keyboard, except that the `cin` object is replaced by the `fstream` object declared in the program. For example, if `inFile` is declared as an object of type `ifstream` that is opened for input, the input statement

```
inFile >> descrip >> price;
```

will read the next two items in the file and store them in the variables `descrip` and `price`.

The file stream name in this statement, in place of `cin`, simply directs the input to come from the file stream rather than the standard input device stream. Other methods that can be used for stream I/O are listed in Table 14–2. Each of these methods must, of course, be preceded by a stream object name.

TABLE 14–2 **`fstream` Methods**

Method Name	Description
`get(character-variable)`	Extract the next character from the input stream.
`getline(string var, int n, '\n')`	Extract characters from the input stream until either $n - 1$ characters are read or a newline is encountered (terminates the input with a `'\0'`).
`peek(character-variable)`	Return the next character in the input stream without extracting it from the stream.
`put(character-expression)`	Put a character on the output stream.
`putback(character-expression)`	Push a character back onto the input stream (does not alter the data in the file).
`eof(void)`	Returns a True if a read has been attempted past the EOF (end of file).
`ignore(int n)`	Skip over the next *n* characters; if *n* is omitted, the default is to skip over the next single character.

Reading data from a file requires that the programmer know how the data appears in the file. This is necessary for correct "stripping" of the data from the file into appropriate variables for storage. All files are read sequentially, so once an item is read, the next item in the file becomes available for reading.

Program 14-3 illustrates reading the `test.dat` file that was created in Program 14-2. The program also illustrates how the `EOF` marker, which is the `NULL` character, can be detected by the `peek()` function. As long as the `EOF` has not been detected, the program will continue to read characters from the file.

Program 14-3 continues to read the file until the `EOF` marker has been detected. Each time the file is read, a string and a floating-point number are input to the program. The display produced by Program 14-3 is

```
Batteries 39.95
Bulbs 3.22
Fuses 1.00
```

In place of the `inFile` extraction, `>>`, used in Program 14-3, a `getline()` function call can be used. The `getline()` requires three arguments: a string variable where the characters read from the file will be stored, the maximum number of characters to be input in a single read, and a terminating character. For example, the function call

```
inFile.getline(line,80,'\n');
```

Program 14-3

```
#include <fstream.h>
#include <stdlib.h>
#include <iomanip.h>

int main()
{
  const int MAXLENGTH = 21;  // maximum file name length
  const int MAXCHARS = 31;   // maximum description length

  char filename[MAXLENGTH] = "test.dat";
  char descrip[MAXCHARS];
  int ch;
  float price;
  ifstream inFile;

  inFile.open(filename, ios::nocreate);

  if (inFile.fail())  // check for successful open
  {
    cout << "\nThe file was not successfully opened"
         << "\n Please check that the file currently exists."
         << endl;
    exit(1);
  }

    // set the format for the standard output stream
  cout << setiosflags(ios::fixed)
       << setiosflags(ios::showpoint)
       << setprecision(2);

  cout << endl;  // start on a new line

    // read and display the file's contents
  while ( (ch = inFile.peek()) != EOF ) // check next character
  {
    inFile >> descrip >> price;  // input the data
    cout << descrip << ' ' << price << endl;
  }

  inFile.close();
  cout << endl;

  return 0;
}
```

POINT OF INFORMATION

The `istream get()` and `putback()` Methods

All input streams have a `get()` method that permits character-by-character input from the stream. This method works in a similar manner to character extraction using the `>>` operator, with two important differences: If a newline character, `'\n'`, or a blank character, `' '`, is encountered, these characters are read in the same manner as any other alphanumeric character. The syntax of this method call is

```
istream-name.get(character-variable);
```

For example, the following code can be used to read the next character from the standard input stream and store the character into the variable `ch`:

```
char ch;
cin.get(ch);
```

In a similar manner, if `inFile` is an `istream` object that has been opened to a file, the following code reads the next character in the stream and assigns it to the character `keycode`:

```
char keycode;
inFile.get(keycode);
```

In addition to the `get()` method, all input streams have a `putback()` method that can be used to put the last character read from an input stream back on the stream. This method has the syntax

```
istream-name.putback(character-expression);
```

where `character-expression` can be any character variable or character value.

The `putback()` method provides an output capability to an input stream. It should be noted that the `putback` character need not be the last character read; rather, it can be any character. All `putback` characters, however, have no effect on the data file, but only on the open input stream. Thus the data file characters remain unchanged, although the characters subsequently read from the input stream can change. For this reason, `putback()` is typically used to permit prescanning a character from an input stream using `get()` followed by an immediate return of the same character to the stream.

causes a maximum of 79 characters (one less than the specified number) to be read from the file named `inFile` and stored starting in the string variable named `line`. The `getline()` function continues reading characters until 79 characters have been read or a newline character has been encountered. If a newline character is encountered, it is included with the other entered characters before the string is terminated with the end-of-string `NULL` marker, `\0`. Program 14-4 illustrates the use of `getline()` in a working program.

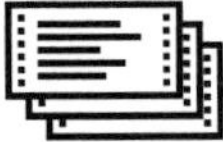

Program 14-4

```
#include <fstream.h>
#include <stdlib.h>
#include <iomanip.h>

int main()
{
  const int MAXLENGTH = 21;  // maximum file name length
  const int MAXCHARS = 80;   // maximum line length
  char file1[MAXLENGTH] = "test.dat";
  char line[MAXCHARS];
  int ch;
  ifstream inFile;

  inFile.open(file1, ios::nocreate);

  if (inFile.fail())   // check for successful open
  {
    cout << "\nThe file was not successfully opened"
         << "\n Please check that the file currently exists."
         << endl;
    exit(1);
  }

  cout << endl;   // start on a new line

    // now read the file
  while( (ch = inFile.peek()) != EOF )
  {
    inFile.getline(line,MAXCHARS,'\n');
    cout << line << endl;
  }

  inFile.close();
  cout << endl;

  return 0;
}
```

Program 14-4 is really a line-by-line text-copying program, reading a line of text from the file and then displaying it on the terminal. The display produced by Program 14-4 is the same as that produced by Program 14-3.

POINT OF INFORMATION

The `ostream put()` Method

All output streams have a `put()` method that permits character-by-character output to a stream. This method works in the same manner as the character insertion operator, <<. The syntax of this method call is

```
ostream-name.put(character-expression);
```

where the character expression can be either a character variable or a character value.

For example, the following code can be used to output an `'a'` to the standard output stream:

```
cin.put('a');
```

In a similar manner, if `outFile` is an `ostream` object that has been opened to a file, the following code outputs the character value in the character variable named `keycode` to this output.

```
char keycode;
   .
   .
   .
outFile.put(keycode);
```

If it were necessary to obtain the description and price as individual variables, either Program 14-3 should be used or the string returned by `getline()` in Program 14-4 must be processed further to extract the individual data items.

Standard Device Files

The file stream objects we have used have all been logical file objects. A *logical file object* is a stream that connects a file of logically related data such as a data file to a program. In addition to logical file objects, C++ also supports physical file objects. A *physical file object* is a stream that connects to a hardware device, such as a keyboard, screen, or printer.

The actual physical device assigned to your program for data entry is formally called the *standard input file.* Usually this is a keyboard. When a `cin` object method call is encountered in a C++ program, a request goes to the operating system to this standard input file for the expected input. Similarly, when a `cout` object method call is encountered, the output is automatically displayed or "written to" a device that has been assigned as the *standard output file.* For most systems this is a terminal screen, although it can be a printer.

When a program is executed, the standard input stream `cin` is automatically connected to the standard input device. Similarly, the standard output stream `cout` is automatically connected to the standard output device. These two object streams are always available for programmer use.

Other Devices

The keyboard, display, and error-reporting devices are automatically connected to the internal stream objects named `cin`, `cout`, and `cerr`, respectively, by a C++ program using either the `iostream.h` or the `fstream.h` header file. Additionally, other devices can be used for input or output if the name assigned by the system is known. For example, most IBM and IBM-compatible personal computers assign the name `prn` to the printer connected to the computer. For these computers, a statement such as `outFile.open("prn")` connects the printer to the `ofstream` object named `outFile`. A subsequent statement, such as `outFile << "Hello World!";`, would then cause the string `Hello World!` to be printed directly on the printer. Note that as the name of an actual file, `prn` must be enclosed in double quotes in the `open()` function call.

Exercises 14.2

1. *a.* Write a C++ program that accepts lines of text from the keyboard and writes each line to a file named `text.dat` until an empty line is entered. An empty line is a line with no text—just a new line caused by pressing the Enter (or Return) key.
   b. Modify Program 14-4 to read and display the data stored in the `text.dat` file created in Exercise 1a.

2. Determine the operating system command provided by your computer to display the contents of a saved file. Compare its operation with the program developed for Exercise 1b. (*Hint:* Typically, the operating system command is called `LIST`, `TYPE`, or `CAT`.)

3. Write, compile, and run a C++ program that writes the four real numbers 92.65, 88.72, 77.46, and 82.93 to a text file named `result`. After writing the data to the file, your program should read the data from the file, determine the average of the four numbers read, and display the average. Verify the output produced by your program by manually calculating the average of the four input numbers.

4. *a.* Write, compile, and execute a C++ program that creates a text file named `points` and writes the following numbers to the file:

6.3	8.2	18.25	24.32
4.0	4.0	10.0	–5.0
–2.0	5.0	4.0	5.0

b. Using the data in the `points` file created in Exercise 4a, write, compile, and run a C++ program that reads each record and interprets the first and second numbers in each record as the coordinates of one point and the third and fourth numbers as the coordinates of a second point. Have your program compute and display the slope and midpoint of the two points entered.

5. *a.* Write, compile, and run a C++ program that creates a text file named `volts` and writes the following five records to the file:

120.3	122.7	90.3	99.8
95.3	120.5	127.3	120.8
123.2	118.4	123.8	115.6
122.4	95.6	118.2	120.0
123.5	130.2	123.9	124.4

b. Using the data in the `volts` file created in Exercise 5a, write, compile, and run a C++ program that reads each record in the file, computes the average for each record, and displays the average.

6. *a.* Create a file that contains the following car numbers, numbers of miles driven, and numbers of gallons of gas used by each car.

Car Number	Miles Driven	Gallons Used
54	250	19
62	525	38
71	123	6
85	1,322	86
97	235	14

b. Write a C++ program that reads the data in the file created in Exercise 6a and displays the car number, the miles driven, the gallons used, and the miles per gallon for each car. The output should also contain the total miles driven, the total gallons used, and the average miles per gallon for all the cars. These totals should be displayed at the end of the output report.

7. *a.* A file named `polar.dat` contains the polar coordinates needed in a graphics program. Currently this file contains the following data:

DISTANCE (inches)	ANGLE (degrees)
2.0	45.0
6.0	30.0
10.0	45.0
4.0	60.0
12.0	55.0
8.0	15.0

Write a C++ program to create this file on your computer system.

b. Using the `polar.dat` file created in Exercise 7a, write a C++ program that accepts distance and angle data from the user and adds the data to the end of the file.
c. Using the `polar.dat` file created in Exercise 7a, write a C++ program that reads this file and creates a second file named `xycord.dat`. The entries in the new file should contain the rectangular coordinates that correspond to the polar coordinates in the `polar.dat` file. Polar coordinates are converted to rectangular coordinates using the equations

$$x = r \cos \theta$$
$$y = r \sin \theta$$

where r is the distance coordinate and θ is the radian equivalent of the angle coordinate in the `polar.dat` file.

9. a. Store the following data in a file:

5 96 87 78 93 21 4 92 82 85 87 6 72 69 85 75 81 73

b. Write a C++ program to calculate and display the average of each group of numbers in the file created in Exercise 9a. The data is arranged in the file so that each group of numbers is preceded by the number of data items in the group. Thus the first number in the file, 5, indicates that the next five numbers should be grouped together. The number 4 indicates that the following four numbers are a group, and the 6 indicates that the last six numbers are a group. (*Hint:* Use a nested loop. The outer loop should terminate when the `EOF` marker is encountered.)

14.3 Random File Access

File organization refers to the way data is stored in a file. All the files we have used have *sequential organization.* This means that the characters in the file are stored in a sequential manner, one after another. We have also read the files in a sequential manner. The way data is retrieved from the file is called *file access.* The fact that the characters in the file are stored sequentially, however, does not force us to access the file sequentially.

In *random access* any character in the file can be read directly, without our first having to read all the characters stored ahead of it. To provide random access to files, each `ifstream` object establishes a file position marker. This marker is a long integer that represents an offset from the beginning of each file and keeps track of where the next character is to be read from or written to. The member functions that are used to access and change the file position marker are listed in Table 14–3 on page 632.

A Way to Identify a File's Name and Location Clearly

During program development, test files are usually placed in the same directory as the program. Therefore, a method call such as `inFile.open("exper.dat")` causes the operating system no problems. In production systems, however, it is not uncommon for data files to reside in one directory while program files reside in another. For this reason, it is always a good idea to include the full path name of any file opened.

For example, if the `exper.dat` file resides in the directory /test/files, the `open()` call should include the full path name, `inFile.open("/test/files/exper.dat")`. Then, no matter where the program is run from, the operating system will know where to locate the file.

Another important convention is to list all file names at the top of a program instead of embedding the names deep within the code. This can easily be accomplished by using string variables to store each file name.

For example, if the statements

```
const int MAXLENGTH = 31;
char file1[MAXLENGTH] = "\test\files\exper.dat";
```

are placed at the top of a program file, the declaration statement clearly lists both the name of the desired file and its location. Then, if some other file is to be tested, all that is required is a simple one-line change at the top of the program.

Using a string variable for the file's name is also useful for the `fail()` method check. For example, consider the following code:

```
ifstream infile;

inFile.open(file1);

if (inFile.fail())
{
  cout << "\n The file named " << file1
       << was not successfully opened"
       <<\n Please check that this file currently exists."
       exit(1);
}
```

In this code, the name of the file that failed to open is directly displayed within the error message, without the name being embedded as a string value.

The `seek()` functions allow the programmer to move to any position in the file. In order to understand this function, you must first clearly understand how data is referenced in the file by using the file position marker.

Each character in a data file is located by its position in the file. The first character in the file is located at position 0, the next character at position 1, and so on. A character's position is also referred to as its offset from the start of the file. Thus the first character has a 0 offset, the second character has an offset of 1, and so on for each character in the file.

The `seek()` functions require two arguments: the offset, as a long integer, into the file; and where the offset is to be calculated from, as determined by the mode. The three possible alternatives for the mode are `ios::beg`, `ios::cur`, and `ios::end`, which denote the beginning, the current position, and the end of the file, respectively. Thus a mode of `ios::beg` means the offset is the true offset from the start of the file. A mode of `ios::cur` means the offset is relative to the current position in the file, and an `ios::end` mode means the offset is relative to the end of the file. A positive offset means move forward in the file, and a negative offset means move backward. Examples of `seek()` function calls follow. In these examples, assume that `inFile` has been opened as an input file and `outFile` as an output file.

```
inFile.seekg(4L,ios::beg);     // go to the fifth character in the input file
outFile.seekp(4L,ios::beg);    // go to the fifth character in the output file
inFile.seekg(4L,ios::cur);     // move ahead five characters in the input file
outFile.seekp(4L,ios::cur);    // move ahead five characters in the output file
inFile.seekg(-4L,ios::end);    // move back five characters in the input file
outFile.seekp(-4L,ios::end);   // move back five characters in the output file
inFile.seekg(0L,ios::beg);     // go to start of the input file
outFile.seekp(0L,ios::beg);    // go to start of the output file
inFile.seekg(0L,ios::end);     // go to end of the input file
outFile.seekp(0L,ios::end);    // go to end of the output file
inFile.seekg(-10L,ios::end);   // go to 10 characters before the input file's end
outFile.seekp(-10L,ios::end);  // go to 10 characters before the output file's end
```

Note, in these examples, that the offset passed to `seekg()` and `seekp()` must be a long integer.

TABLE 14–3 File Position Marker Functions

Name[4]	Description
`seekg(offset, mode)`	For input files, move to the offset position as indicated by the mode
`seekp(offset, mode)`	For output files, move to the offset position as indicated by the mode
`tellg(void)`	For input files, return the current value of the file position marker
`tellp(void)`	For output files, return the current value of the file position marker

[4] The suffixes `g` and `p` denote `get` and `put`, respectively, where `get` refers to an input (get from) file and `put` refers to an output (put to) file.

Unlike the `seek()` functions that move the file position marker, the `tell()` functions simply return the offset value of the file position marker. For example, if 10 characters have already been read from an input file named `inFile`, the function call

```
inFile.tellg();
```

returns the long integer 10. This means that the next character to be read is offset 10 byte positions from the start of the file, and is the 11th character in the file.

Program 14-5 illustrates the use of `seekg()` and `tellg()` to read a file in reverse order, from last character to first. As each character is read, it is also displayed.

Program 14-5

```
#include <fstream.h>
#include <stdlib.h>

int main()
{
  const int MAXLENGTH = 31;
  char filename[MAXLENGTH] = "test.dat";
  char ch;
  long offset, last;

  ifstream inFile(filename);

  if (inFile.fail())    // check for successful open
  {
    cout << "\nThe file was not successfully opened"
         << "\n Please check that the file currently exists"
         << endl;
    exit(1);
  }

  inFile.seekg(0L,ios::end);    // move to the end of the file
  last = inFile.tellg();        // save the offset of the last character

  for(offset = 1L; offset <= last; offset++)
  {
    inFile.seekg(-offset, ios::end);
    ch = inFile.get();
    cout << ch << " : ";
  }

  inFile.close()

  return 0;
}
```

Assuming that the file `test.dat` contains the following data,

```
The grade was 92.5
```

the output line displayed by Program 14-5 is

```
5 : . : 2 : 9 :   : s : a : w :   : e : d : a : r : g :   : e : h : T:
```

Program 14-5 initially goes to the last character in the file. The offset of this character, which is the end-of-file character, is saved in the variable `last`. Because `tellg()` returns a long integer, `last` has been declared as long integer.

Starting from the end of the file, `seekg()` is used to position the next character to be read, referenced from the end of the file. As each character is read, the character is displayed and the offset adjusted in order to access the next character. It should be noted that the first offset used is –1, which represents the character immediately preceding the end-of-file marker.

Exercises 14.3

1. ***a.*** Either using a text editor or copying the file `test.dat` from **http//www.brookscole.com/compsci/bronson/cpp** create a file named `test.dat` on the directory that contains your program files.
b. Enter and execute Program 14-5 on your computer.

2. Rewrite Program 14-5 so that the origin for the `seekg()` function used in the `for` loop is the start of the file rather than the end.

3. The `seek()` functions return 0 if the position specified has been reached or return 1 if the position specified was beyond the file's boundaries. Modify Program 14-5 to display an error message if `seekg()` returns 1.

4. Write a program that will read and display every second character in a file named `test.dat`.

5. ***a.*** Write a function named `r_bytes()` that reads and displays *n* characters starting from any position in a file. The function should accept three arguments: a file object name, the offset of the first character to be read, and the number of characters to be read. (*Note:* The prototype for `r_bytes` should be `void r_bytes(fstream&, long, long)`.)
b. Modify the `r_bytes()` function written in Exercise 5a to store the characters read into a string or an array. The function should accept the address of the storage area as a fourth argument.

6. Using the `seek()` and `tell()` functions, write a function named `f_chars()` that returns the total number of characters in a file.

14.4 File Streams as Function Arguments

A file stream object can be a function argument. The only requirement is that the function's formal parameter be a reference to the appropriate stream, either as `ifstream&` or as `ofstream&`. For example, in Program 14-6 an `ofstream` object named `outFile` is opened in `main()`, and this stream object is passed to the function `inOut()`. Note that the function prototype and header line for `inOut()` both declare the formal parameter as a reference to an `ostream` object type. The `inOut()` function is then used to write five lines of user-entered text to the file.

Program 14-6

```
#include <fstream.h>
#include <stdlib.h>

const int MAXCHARS = 21;
char fname[MAXCHARS] = "list.dat";  // here is the file we are working with

void inOut(ofstream&);  // function prototype

int main()
{
  ofstream outFile;

  outFile.open(fname);
  if (outFile.fail())    // check for a successful open
  {
    cout << "\nThe output file " << fname << " was not successfully opened"
         << endl;
    exit(1);
  }

  inOut(outFile);  // call the function

  return 0;
}

void inOut(ofstream& fileOut)
{
  const int LINELEN = 80;  // longest length of a line of text
  const int NUMLINES = 5;  // number of lines of text
  int count;
  char line[LINELEN];  // enough storage for one line of text

  cout << "Please enter five lines of text:" << endl;
  for (count = 0; count < NUMLINES; count++)
  {
    cin.getline(line,LINELEN, '\n');
    fileOut << line << endl;
  }

  return;
}
```

Within main() the file ostream object is named outFile. This object is passed to the inOut() function and is accepted as the formal parameter named fileOut, which is declared to be a reference to an ostream object type. The function inOut() then uses its reference parameter fileOut as an output file stream name exactly as main() would use the outFile stream object. Note also that Program 14-6 uses the getline() method introduced in Section 14.2 (see Table 14-2). Although we have explicitly included the newline character as the third argument passed to getline(), this argument can be omitted. This is because the '\n' is a default value for the third formal parameter.

In Program 14-7 we have expanded on Program 14-6 by adding a getOpen() function to perform the open. Note that getOpen(), like inOut(), accepts a reference argument to an ofstream object. After the getOpen() function completes execution, this reference is passed to inOut(), as it was in Program 14-6. Although you might be tempted to write getOpen() to return a reference to an fstream, this will not work because it ultimately results in an attempt to assign a returned reference to an existing one.

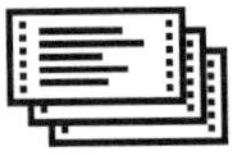

Program 14-7

```
#include <fstream.h>
#include <stdlib.h>

int getOpen(ofstream&);   // pass a reference to an fstream
void inOut(ofstream&);    // pass a reference to an fstream

int main()
{

  ofstream outFile;     // file1 is an fstream object

  getOpen(outFile);    // open the file
  inOut(outFile);      // write to it
}

int getOpen(ofstream& fileOut)
{
  const int MAXCHARS = 13;
  char name[MAXCHARS];

  cout << "\nEnter a file name: " << endl;
  cin.getline(name,MAXCHARS, '\n');
```

```
  fileOut.open(name);     // open the file

  if (fileOut.fail())     // check for successful open
  {
    cout << "Cannot open the file" << endl;
    exit(1);
  }
  else
    return 0;
}

void inOut(ofstream& fileOut)
{
  const int NUMLINES = 5;     // number of lines
  const int LINELEN = 80;     // maximum line length
  int count;
  char line[LINELEN];    // enough storage for one line of text

  cout << "Please enter five lines of text:" << endl;
  for (count = 0; count < NUMLINES; ++count)
  {
    cin.getline(line,LINELEN, '\n');
    fileOut << line << endl;
  }

  return;
}
```

Program 14-7 is simply a modified version of Program 14-6 that allows the user to enter a file name from the standard input device and then opens the `ostream` connection to the external file. If the name of an existing data file is entered, the file will be destroyed when it is opened for output. A useful "trick" that you may encounter to prevent this type of mishap is to open the entered file using an input file stream. Then, if the file exists, the `fail()` method will indicate a successful open (that is, the open does not fail), which indicates that the file is available for input. This can be used to alert the user that a file with the entered name currently exists in the system and to request confirmation that the data in the file can be destroyed and the file reopened for output. Before the file is reopened for output, the input file stream should be closed. The implementation of this algorithm is left as an exercise.

Exercises 14.4

1. A function named `p_file()` is to receive a file name as a reference to an `ifstream` object. What declarations are required to pass a file name to `p_file()`?

2. Write a function named `fcheck()` that checks whether a file exists. The function should accept an `ifstream` object as a reference parameter. If the file exists, the function should return a value of 1; otherwise, the function should return a value of zero.

3. Rewrite the function `getOpen()` used in Program 14-7 to incorporate the file-checking procedures described in this section. Specifically, if the entered file name exists, an appropriate message should be displayed. The user should then be presented with the option of entering a new file name or allowing the program to overwrite the existing file. Use the function written for Exercise 2 in your program.

4. Assume that a data file consisting of a group of individual lines has been created. Write a function named `printLine()` that will read and display any desired line of the file. For example, the function call `printLine(fstream& f_name,5);` should display the fifth line of the passed object stream.

14.5 Common Programming Errors

Three programming errors are often made in the use of files. The most common error is to use the file's external name, in place of the internal file stream object name, when accessing the file. The only stream method that uses the data file's external name is the `open()` function. As always, all stream methods presented in this chapter must be preceded by a stream object name and the dot operator.

A second error occurs when using the `EOF` marker to detect the end of a file. Any variable used to accept the `EOF` must be declared as an integer variable. For example, if `ch` is declared as a character variable, the expression

```
while ( (ch = in.file.peek()) != EOF )
```

produces an infinite loop.[5] This occurs because a character variable can never take on an `EOF` code. `EOF` is an integer value (usually –1) that has no character representation. This ensures that the `EOF` code can never be confused with any legitimate character encountered as normal data in the file. To terminate the loop created by the foregoing expression, the variable `ch` must be declared as an integer variable.

[5] This will not occur on UNIX systems where characters are stored as signed integers.

The last error concerns the offset argument sent to the `seekg()` and `seekp()` functions. This offset must be a long-integer constant or variable. Any other value passed to these functions can result in an unpredictable effect.

14.6 Chapter Summary

1. A data file is any collection of data stored together in an external storage medium under a common name.
2. A data file is connected to a file stream using `fstream`'s `open()` method. This function connects a file's external name with an internal object name. After the file is opened, all subsequent accesses to the file require the internal object name.
3. A file can be opened in input or output mode. An opened output file stream either creates a new data file or erases the data in an existing opened file. An opened input file stream makes an existing file's data available for input. An error condition results if the file does not exist. This error can be detected using the `fail()` method.
4. All file streams must be declared as objects of either the `fstream` or the `ofstream` class. This means that a declaration similar to either of the following,

```
ifstream inFile;
ofstream outFile;
```

   must be included with the declarations in which the file is opened. The stream object names `inFile` and `outFile` can be replaced with any user-selected object name.
5. In addition to any files opened within a function, the stream objects `cin`, `cout`, and `cerr` are automatically declared and opened when a program is run. `cin` is the object name of an input file stream used for data entry (usually from the keyboard), `cout` is the object name of an output file stream used for default data display (usually the terminal screen), and `cerr` is the object name of an output file stream used for displaying system error messages (usually the terminal screen).
6. Data files can be accessed randomly using the `seekg()`, `seekp()`, `tellg()`, and `tellp()` methods. The `g` versions of these functions are used to alter and query the file position marker for input file streams, and the `p` versions do the same for output file streams.

TABLE 14–4 `fstream` Methods

Method Name	Description
`get(character-variable)`	Extract the next character from the input stream.
`getline(string var,int n,'\n')`	Extract characters from the input stream until either *n* – 1 characters are read or a newline is encountered (terminates the input with a `'\0'`).
`peek(character-variable)`	Return the next character in the input stream without extracting it from the stream.
`put(character-expression)`	Put a character on the output stream.
`putback(character-expression)`	Push a character back onto the input stream (does not alter the data in the file).
`eof(void)`	Returns a True if a read has been attempted past the EOF (end of file).
`ignore(int n)`	Skip over the next *n* characters; if *n* is omitted, the default is to skip over the next single character.

7. Table 14–4 lists the methods supplied by the `fstream` class for file manipulation.

14.7 Chapter Supplement: The `iostream` Class Library[6]

The `iostream` class library provided as part of each C++ compiler is not part of the C++ language. By convention, each C++ compiler provides an input/output library named `iostream` that contains a number of classes that adhere to a common ANSI specification.

As we have already seen, the classes contained within the `iostream` class library access files using entities called streams. For most systems, the data bytes transferred on a stream represent either ASCII characters or binary numbers.

[6] Although this supplement contains material directly relating to file stream, understanding it requires familiarity with the material presented in Chapter 9. Therefore, this section should not be read until Chapter 13 has been completed.

When the data transfer between a computer and an external data file modifies the data, so that the data stored in the file *is not* an exact representation of the data as it is stored internally within the computer, the file is referred to as a *formatted file*. Examples of this include files that store their data using ASCII codes. Such files are also referred to as text files, and the terms *text* and *formatted* are sometimes used interchangeably.

When the data transfer between a computer and an external data file is done without modification, so that the data stored in the file *is* an exact representation of the data as it is stored internally within the computer, the file is referred to as a *binary file* or *unformatted file*.

The mechanism for reading a byte stream from a file or writing a byte stream to a file, with or without formatting, is always hidden when a high-level language such as C++ is used. Nevertheless, it is useful to understand this mechanism so that we can place the services provided by the `iostream` class library in their appropriate context.

File Stream Transfer Mechanism

The mechanism for transferring data between a program and a data file is illustrated in Figure 14–3.

As illustrated in Figure 14–3, transferring data between a program and a file involves an intermediate file buffer contained in the computer's memory. Each opened file is assigned its own file buffer, which is simply a storage area that is used by the data as it is transferred between the program and the file.

For its part, the program either writes a set of data bytes to the file buffer or reads a set of data bytes from the file buffer using a stream object.

On the other side of the buffer, the transfer of data between the device storing the actual data file (usually a tape, disk, or CD-ROM drive) and the file buffer is handled by special operating system programs that are referred to as *device*

FIGURE 14–3 The Data Transfer Mechanism

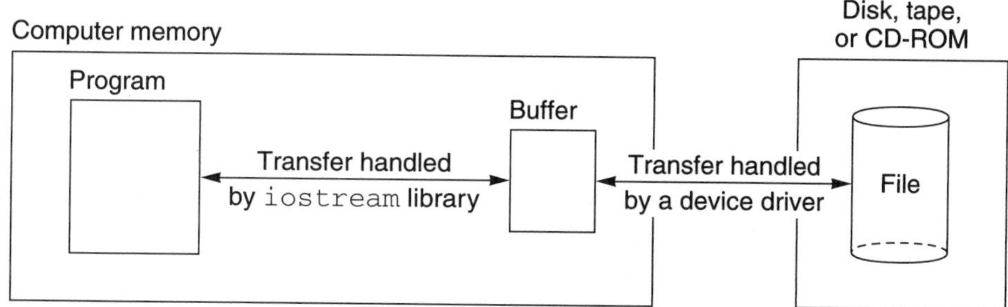

drivers.[7] Typically, a disk device driver will transfer data between the disk and file buffer only in fixed sizes, such as 1024 bytes at a time. Thus the file buffer provides a convenient means of permitting a device driver to transfer data in blocks of one size, whereas the program can access them using a different size (typically as individual characters or as a fixed number of characters per line).

Components of the `iostream` Class Library

The `iostream` class library consists of two primary base classes, the `streambuf` class and the `ios` class. The `streambuf` class provides the file buffer illustrated in Figure 14–3 and a number of general routines for transferring data when little or no formatting is required. The `ios` class contains a pointer to the file buffers provided by the `streambuf` class and a number of general routines for transferring data with formatting. From these two base classes, a number of other classes are derived and included in the `iostream` class library.

Figure 14–4 illustrates an inheritance diagram for the `ios` family of classes as it is related to the `ifstream`, `ofstream`, and `fstream` classes. The inheritance diagram for the `streambuf` family of classes is shown in Figure 14–5. As described in the previous chapter, the convention adopted for inheritance diagrams is that the arrows point from a derived class to a base class.

The correspondence between the classes illustrated in Figures 14–4 and 14–5, including the header files that define these classes, is shown in Table 14–5.

Thus the `ifstream`, `ofstream`, and `fstream` classes that we have used for file access all use a buffer provided by the `filebuf` class and is defined in the `fstream.h` header file. Similarly, the `cin`, `cout`, and `cerr` `iostream` objects that we have been using throughout the text use a buffer provided by the `streambuf` class and defined in both the `iostream.h` and `fstream` header files.

TABLE 14–5

`ios` Class	`streambuf` Class	Header File

`istream`
`ostream`
`iostream`
	`streambuf`	`iostream.h`
		or
		`fstream.h`

`ifstream`
`ofstream`
`fstream`
	`filebuf`	`fstream.h`

[7] Device drivers are not stand-alone programs but, rather, are an integral part of the operating system. Essentially, the device driver is a section of operating system code that accesses a hardware device, such as a disk unit, and handles the data transfer between the device and the computer's memory. Thus it must correctly synchronize the speed of the data transfer between the computer and the device sending or receiving the data. This is because the computer's internal data transfer rate is generally much faster than any device connected to it.

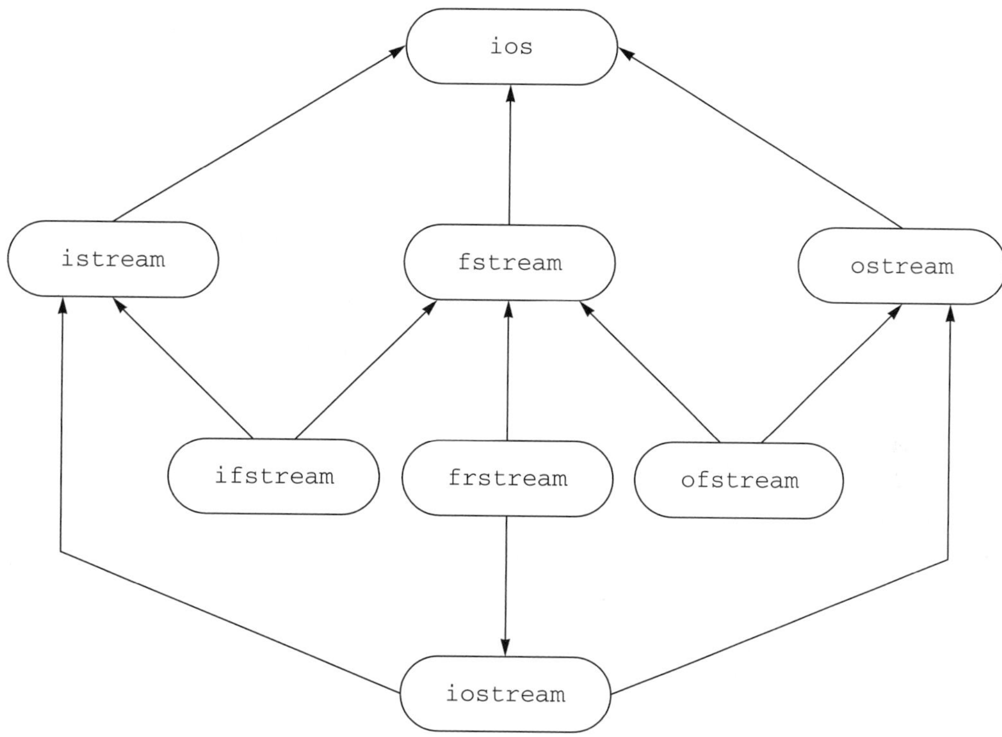

FIGURE 14–4 The Base Class `ios` and Its Derived Classes (not all derived classes are shown)

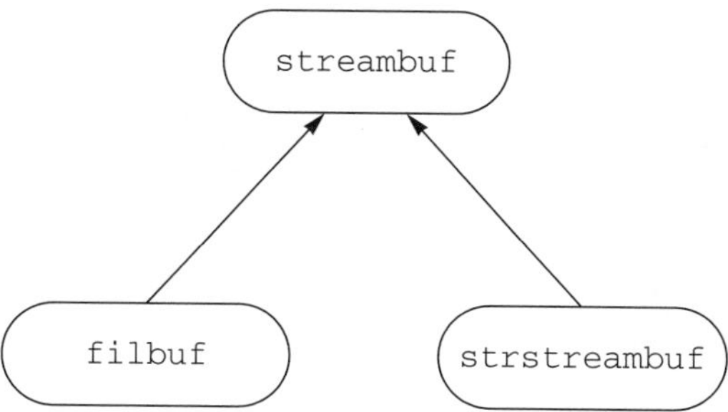

FIGURE 14–5 The Base Class `streambuf` and Its Derived Classes (not all derived classes are shown)

In-Memory Formatting

In addition to the classes illustrated in Figure 14–4, a class named `strstream` is also derived from the `ios` class. This class uses the `strstreambuf` class illustrated in Figure 14–5, requires the `strstream.h` header file, and provides capabilities for writing and reading strings to and from in-memory defined streams.

As an output stream, such streams are typically used to "assemble" a string from smaller pieces until a complete line of characters is ready to be written, either to `cout` or to a file. Attaching a `strstream` object to a buffer for this purpose is done in a similar manner as attaching an `fstream` object to an output file. For example, the statement

```
strstream inmem(buf, 72, ios::out);
```

attaches a `strstream` object to an existing buffer of 72 bytes in output mode. Program 14-8 illustrates using this statement within the context of a complete program.

Program 14-8

```
#include <strstream.h>
#include <iomanip.h>

int main()
{
  const int MAXCHARS = 81;  // one more than the maximum
                            // characters in a line
  int units = 10;
  float price = 36.85;
  char buf[MAXCHARS];

  strstream inmem(buf, MAXCHARS, ios::out);  // open an in-memory stream

    // write to the buffer through the stream
  inmem << "No. of units = "
        << setw(3) << units
        << "  Price per unit = $"
        << setw(8) << setprecision(2) << price << '\0';

  cout << '|' << buf << '|';

  return 0;
}
```

The output produced by Program 14-8 is

```
|No. of units =  10  Price per unit = $   36.85|
```

As illustrated by this output, the character buffer has been correctly filled in by insertions to the `inmem` stream (note that the end-of-string `NULL`, `\0`, which is the last insertion to the stream, is required to close off the string correctly). Once the `buf` string variable has been filled, it would typically be written to a file as a single string.

In a similar manner, a `strstream` object can be opened in input mode. Typically, such a stream would be used as a working storage area, or buffer, for storing a complete line of text from either a file or standard input. Once the buffer has been filled, the extraction operator would be used to "disassemble" the string into component parts and convert each data item into its designated data type. Doing this permits inputting data from a file on a line-by-line basis before assigning individual data items to their respective variables.

Appendixes

Appendix A Operator Precedence Table

Table A–1 presents the symbols, precedence, descriptions, and associativity of C++'s operators. Operators toward the top of the table have a higher precedence than those toward the bottom. Operators within each box have the same precedence and associativity.

TABLE A–1 Summary of C++ Operators

Operator	Description	Associativity
()	Function call	Left to right
[]	Array element	
->	Structure member pointer reference	
.	Structure member reference	
++	Increment	Right to left
--	Decrement	
-	Unary minus	
!	Logical negation	
~	One's complement	
(type)	Type conversion (cast)	
sizeof	Storage size	
&	Address of	
*	Indirection	
*	Multiplication	Left to right
/	Division	
%	Modulus (remainder)	
+	Addition	Left to right
-	Subtraction	
<<	Left shift	Left to right
>>	Right shift	
<	Less than	Left to right
<=	Less than or equal to	
>	Greater than	
>=	Greater than or equal to	
==	Equal to	Left to right
!=	Not equal to	
&	Bitwise AND	Left to right
^	Bitwise exclusive OR	Left to right
|	Bitwise inclusive OR	Left to right
&&	Logical AND	Left to right
||	Logical OR	Left to right
?:	Conditional expression	Right to left
=	Assignment	Right to left
+= -= *=	Assignment	
/= %= &=	Assignment	
^= |=	Assignment	
<<= >>=	Assignment	
,	Comma	Left to right

Appendix B ASCII Character Codes

Key(s)	Dec	Oct	Hex	Key	Dec	Oct	Hex	Key	Dec	Oct	Hex
Ctrl 1	0	0	0	+	43	53	2B	V	86	126	56
Ctrl A	1	1	1	,	44	54	2C	W	87	127	57
Ctrl B	2	2	2	-	45	55	2D	X	88	130	58
Ctrl C	3	3	3	.	46	56	2E	Y	89	131	59
Ctrl D	4	4	4	/	47	57	2F	Z	90	132	5A
Ctrl E	5	5	5	0	48	60	30	[	91	133	5B
Ctrl F	6	6	6	1	49	61	31	\	92	134	5C
Ctrl G	7	7	7	2	50	62	32	]	93	135	5D
Ctrl H	8	10	8	3	51	63	33	^	94	136	5E
Ctrl I	9	11	9	4	52	64	34	_	95	137	5F
\n	10	12	A	5	53	65	35	‘	96	140	60
Ctrl K	11	13	B	6	54	66	36	a	97	141	61
Ctrl L	12	14	C	7	55	67	37	b	98	142	62
RETURN	13	15	D	8	56	70	38	c	99	143	63
Ctrl N	14	16	E	9	57	71	39	d	100	144	64
Ctrl O	15	17	F	:	58	72	3A	e	101	145	65
Ctrl P	16	20	10	;	59	73	3B	f	102	146	66
Ctrl Q	17	21	11	<	60	74	3C	g	103	147	67
Ctrl R	18	22	12	=	61	75	3D	h	104	150	68
Ctrl S	19	23	13	>	62	76	3E	i	105	151	69
Ctrl T	20	24	14	?	63	77	3F	j	106	152	6A
Ctrl U	21	25	15	@	64	100	40	k	107	153	6B
Ctrl V	22	26	16	A	65	101	41	l	108	154	6C
Ctrl W	23	27	17	B	66	102	42	m	109	155	6D
Ctrl X	24	30	18	C	67	103	43	n	110	156	6E
Ctrl Y	25	31	19	D	68	104	44	o	111	157	6F
Ctrl Z	26	32	1A	E	69	105	45	p	112	160	70
Esc	27	33	1B	F	70	106	46	q	113	161	71
Ctrl <	28	34	1C	G	71	107	47	r	114	162	72
Ctrl /	29	35	1D	H	72	110	48	s	115	163	73
Ctrl =	30	36	1E	I	73	111	49	t	116	164	74
Ctrl -	31	37	1F	J	74	112	4A	u	117	165	75
Space	32	40	20	K	75	113	4B	v	118	166	76
!	33	41	21	L	76	114	4C	w	119	167	77
"	34	42	22	M	77	115	4D	x	120	170	78
#	35	43	23	N	78	116	4E	y	121	171	79
$	36	44	24	O	79	117	4F	z	122	172	7A
%	37	45	25	P	80	120	50	{	123	173	7B
&	38	46	26	Q	81	121	51	|	124	174	7C
'	39	47	27	R	82	122	52	}	125	175	7D
(	40	50	28	S	83	123	53	~	126	176	7E
)	41	51	29	T	84	124	54	del	127	177	7F
*	42	52	2A	U	85	125	55				

Appendix C Using Visual C++, Version 5.0

All C++ programs presented in the text can be created as *console applications* in Visual C++, Version 5.0. These types of applications hide all of the visual components that can be created using Visual C++ and permit concentration on the basic syntax of C++ programming. The steps necessary to create console applications in Visual C++, Version 5.0, are presented in this appendix.

To create C++ programs successfully using Visual C++, you must first understand the development environment provided by a product known as Microsoft® Developer Studio.® *Developer Studio* is the coordinating program under which many of Microsoft's programming languages, such as Visual C++ and JAVA, are developed, compiled, and executed.[1] When you start Visual C++, the screen shown in Figure C–1 is presented. This initial screen is referred to

FIGURE C–1 Developer Studio's Integrated Development Environment (IDE)

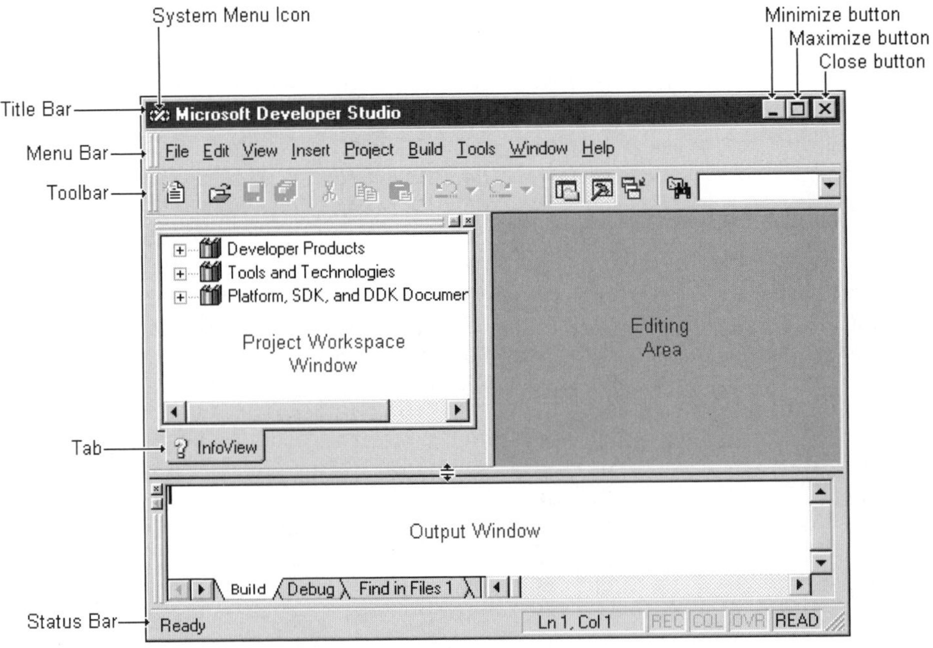

[1] Developer Studio currently supports the following development products: Visual C++, Visual J++,® Visual InterDev,™ Visual SourceSafe,™ and Microsoft Development Library (MSDN™). Visual Basic® has its own development system.

as the integrated development environment (IDE, pronounced as both I-D-E and IDEE). As a practical matter, the IDE simply provides a single, centralized screen from which all program development tools, from editing source code to compilation and production of an executable program, are accessible.[2]

As Figure C–1 shows, the IDE consists of a standard Microsoft window, where the conventional window components, such as the Title Bar, Menu Bar, and various toolbars, have been labeled around the window's outside border. Table C–1 gives the purpose of each of these components.

The complete process, from providing an editor for creating a source code file to building an executable program from one or more object files, can be controlled from Developer Studio's integrated development environment. Keeping track of when the executable program is out of date because one or more of the source files have been modified, maintaining all graphical components

TABLE C–1 IDE Window Components

Component	Description
Title Bar	The colored bar at the top edge of a window that contains the window's name.
Menu Bar	Contains the names of the menus that can be used with the currently active window. The Menu Bar can be modified but cannot be deleted from the window.
Toolbars	The IDE contains 10 toolbars, all of which can be visible at the same time. A toolbar contains icons, also referred to as buttons, that provide quick access to commonly used Menu Bar commands. Clicking a Toolbar button initiates the designated action represented by the button.
Status Bar	The Status Bar provides indicators about the window and its current status.
System Menu Icon	Clicking on this icon causes a pop-up menu to appear. The pop-up menu contains options to set the window's size, to set its position, or to close the window.
Minimize Box	Clicking on this icon causes the Windows operating system to reduce the window to the size of an icon.
Resize Box	Clicking on this icon causes the Windows operating system to reduce the size of the window and replaces the Resize Box with a Maximize Box.
Maximize Box	Clicking on this icon causes the Windows operating system to enlarge the window to the size of the screen and replaces the Maximize Box with a Resize Box.
Close Box	Clicking on this icon causes the Windows operating system to close the window.

[2] Historically, the concept of an IDE was introduced with Borland's Turbo Pascal product.

used by a program, and handling other details required in the building of an executable file are accomplished by Developer Studio via a number of internal files that it also automatically maintains. The complete set of files needed to build a Visual C++ program, including all user-entered source code files and all graphical resources, is referred to as a *project.*

Another term used in relation to all Windows operating systems is the term *application.* This term is frequently used in preference to the word *program,* for two reasons: It is the term selected by Microsoft to designate any program that can be run under a Windows operating system, and it can be used to avoid confusion with older procedural programs that had no graphical capabilities. In practice, the terms *program* and *application* are often used interchangeably. Formally, though, it is more accurate to say that each Visual C++ application is developed and stored as a project.

For each Visual C++ application that you create, Developer Studio uses a project workspace to store all of the files needed for a project, where a *project workspace,* or *workspace* for short, is simply a folder under which files related to a specific project are stored.[3] With the understanding that a project consists of a number of files, one of which must be a source code file if an executable application is to be created, and all of which are typically stored in the same workspace folder,[4] we now show how Developer Studio's integrated development environment can be used to construct a C++ console application.

To begin a new program, choose the File item from the Menu Bar shown in Figure C–1, which will bring up the File submenu illustrated in Figure C–2. As seen in this figure, the File submenu provides a number of file options, which we will use for creating a new program, as well as for saving and recalling existing programs. For now, select the New option from within this submenu, which will bring up the New dialog box shown in Figure C–3.

As shown in Figure C–3, Visual C++'s Professional Edition provides a choice of 12 project types, the most common of which are listed in Table C–2.[5] When starting a new project, first make sure that the Projects tab is active. From within the Projects tab, there are three items that must be provided. First, you must select the project type. To create the programs presented in this text, always select a `Win32 Console Application` type. This type provides character-mode support for creating a C++ program that can run either within a DOS window

---

3 The files need not all reside in the same workspace folder, although for convenience they typically do.

4 There will also be a number of subfolders contained within the main project folder.

5 The number of project types displayed depends on the number of installed Developer Studio products. For example, if you have installed Visual J++ (Microsoft's JAVA product), the options appropriate to this language will also appear.

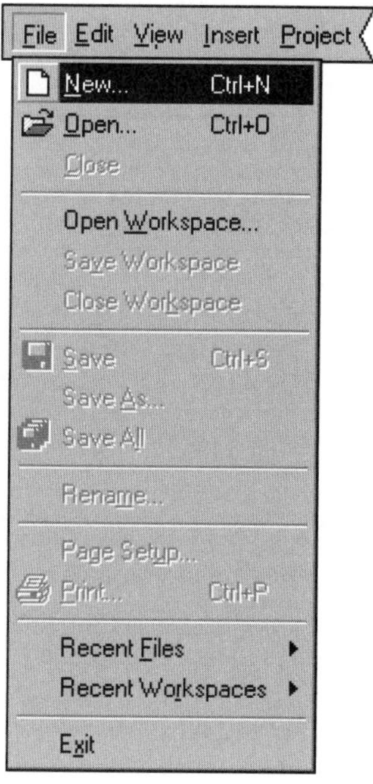

FIGURE C–2 The File Submenu

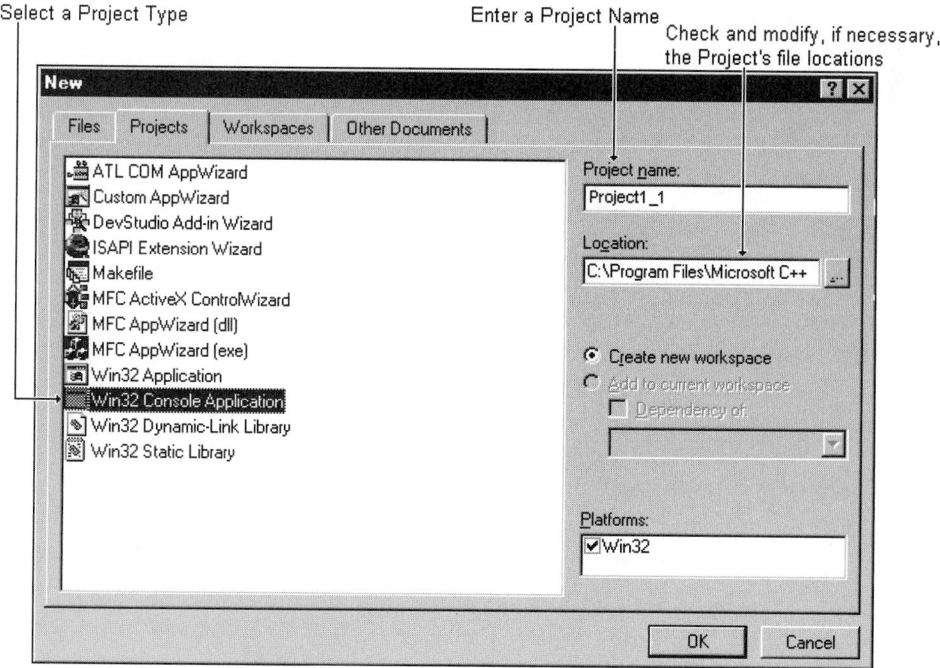

FIGURE C–3 The New Dialog Box

TABLE C–2 The Professional Edition's Available Project Types

Project Type	Description
ATL COM AppWizard	Use an applications wizard to develop a COM object.
Custom AppWizard	Use an applications wizard to develop a complete customized application.
ISAPI Extension Wizard	Use an applications wizard to create modules that extend Internet web servers.
Makefile	Create your own makefile that automatically compiles source code and create an executable application.
MFC ActiveX Control Wizard	Use an applications wizard to create an ActiveX control.
MFC AppWizard (DLL)	Use an applications wizard to create a dynamic link library (DLL) Microsoft Foundation Classes (MFC)-based module.
MFC AppWizard (exe)	Use an applications wizard to create an executable MFC-based application.
Win32 Application	Create a Windows-based application that does not have to use the MFC. The MFC also can be used in these applications.
Win32 Console Application	Create an empty project file with options correctly set to build a character-mode application.
Win32 Dynamic Link Library	Create an empty project file with options correctly set to build a DLL.
Win32 Static Library	Create a static library file.

under the Windows operating system or as a stand-alone DOS-executable program.

The second item that must be provided is the name of the project. This project name must be entered in the Project name Text box shown in Figure C–3. In this text, each individual application will be constructed in its own project workspace, using project names such as `Project1_1`. Specifically, what this does for new projects is create a new folder, which in this case is named `Project1_1`. As shown in Figure C–3, the location of this folder is within the path listed in the Location drop-down List box, which is the third item that must be provided. Typically, the initial path for all project workspaces (again, this means directories) that you create is a default selectable from within the Options submenu of Developer Studio's Tools menu. For the project named `Project1_1`, a folder by this name will be created that has the drive and full path name `C:\Program Files\Microsoft C++\Project1_1`.

Once you have provided the information required by the dialog shown in Figure C–3 and have selected the OK Command button, two things will happen. The first is that a number of files will be automatically created and placed in

TABLE C–3 File Types Provided within a Workspace Folder

File Extension	Description
.dsw	A project workspace file used to store information at the workspace level, such as the number of projects stored in the workspace.
.dsp	A project file that contains information about how the executable version of a single project is to be built. This is equivalent to the makefile used in earlier versions of Visual C++ that had the extension .mak.
.opt	The workspace options file, which is used to store project workspace settings. This file contains local settings, such as the appearance of the project workspace using your hardware configuration. A new options file is created automatically whenever a workspace is opened and no workspace options file is found.

the workspace folder for the new project. A list of the file types that are created is provided in Table C–3. Next, Developer Studio's IDE will appear as shown in Figure C–4. In this figure, pay particular attention to the Project Workspace Window. This window, which is also referred to as the Workspace window, displays a hierarchical list of projects in the current workspace and shows all

FIGURE C–4 The IDE Containing an Active Workspace

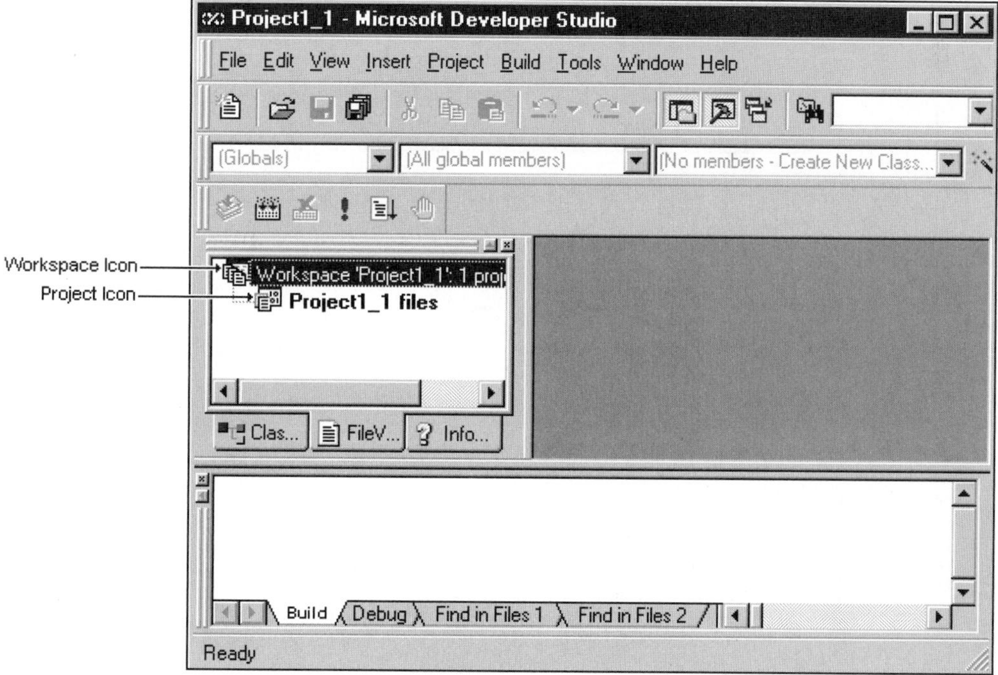

of the items contained within each project. Note that only one workspace can be open at one time but that a single workspace can contain multiple projects. Also note that the icon used to represent a workspace is slightly different from the icon used to represent the project. And finally, note that two additional tabs have been added to the Workspace window: the ClassView and FileView tabs. As files are now added or removed from a project, Visual C++ will reflect all of these changes within the displayed hierarchical tree.

The hierarchical tree shown in Figure C–4 is a standard Windows folder tree, which means that you can expand and contract tree sections by clicking on plus (+) and minus (–) symbols, respectively. As always, sections of the tree that are hidden from view because of the size of the window can be displayed by using the attached scroll bars.

Also, double-clicking on any file icon (none are shown in Figure C–4) will automatically invoke the proper editor for the file and bring up the file in the Editing area. Now, however, lets add a single C++ source file to our project.

The procedure for creating a C++ source code file is almost identical to the one used in creating a new project. To create the source code file, select the New option from within the Menu Bar's File menu. This will bring up the New dialog, which we previously used in creating a new project (see Figure C–3).

FIGURE C–5 Creating a C++ Source Code File

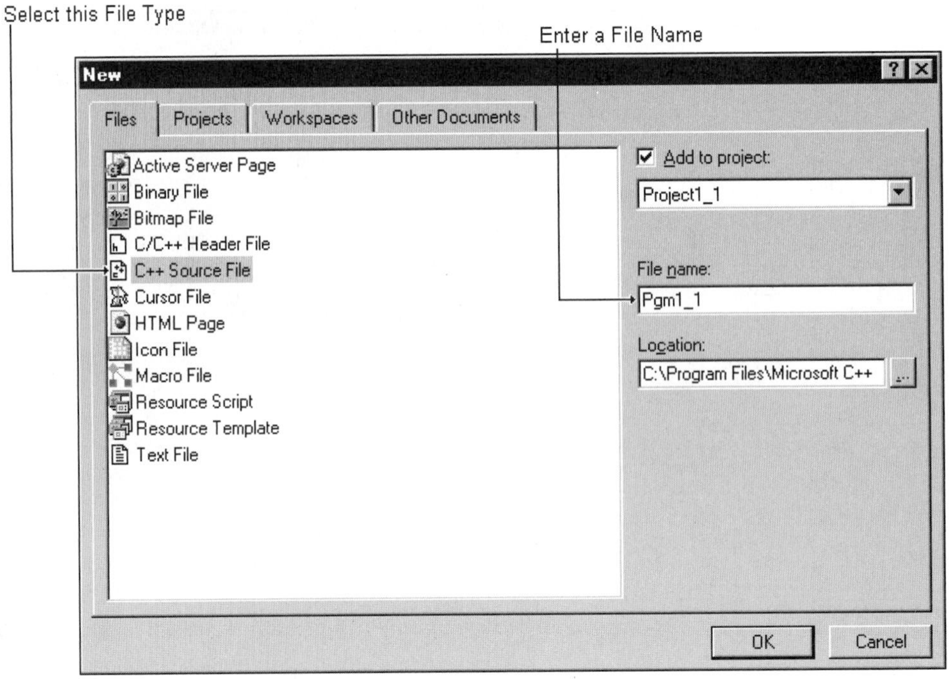

POINT OF INFORMATION

Creating a Console Application

To create a console application:

1. Select the File Menu and select New (or use the accelerator key sequence Ctrl+N), which will bring up a New dialog box.
2. Click on the Projects tab.
3. Select `Win32 Console Application` as the project type.
4. Enter a project name, which becomes the name of the workspace folder for the project.
5. Modify, if necessary, the workspace folder's path.
6. Click the OK Command button.

In this case, however, activate the Files tab, as illustrated in Figure C–5. Within this dialog, you will see that the check box to add a file to the existing project has been checked, and the active project workspace name has been inserted within the first drop-down List box. Additionally, the drive and path for this current project workspace folder will automatically be provided in the file `Location` Text box. Your responsibility is now to select a file type and provide the file with a name.

From the list of file types provided in the New dialog shown in Figure C–5, select the `C++ Source File` choice, and then provide a name for the file. As shown in Figure C–5, the name we have given to the source file is `Pgm1_1`. When you provide this information and press the dialog's OK Command button, Developer Studio will create a file named `Pgm1_1.cpp` within the `Project1_1` folder. Note that the `cpp` extension to the file name is automatically appended by Developer Studio, because Visual C++ requires that all source code files have this extension. After this is done, the IDE will appear as shown in Figure C–6.

In reviewing Figure C–6, pay particular attention to the Workspace window. Note that the FileView tab is active and that a file named `Pgm1_1.cpp` has been added to the hierarchy tree. Also note the icon used for a source code file. The arrow within the icon indicates that this file is an active part of the project (for example, it is not part of some other project that is being stored in the current workspace folder) and that it will be used when an executable file is ultimately built.

At this stage the Visual C++ text editor has been loaded, and you can now enter C++ source code in the Editing area. For now, however, we will simply save the existing project, including the empty file named `Pgm1_1`, and show how to recall this project for further additions and modifications. Once your source code has been entered, select the `Build` menu's `Execute` to compile and run

Adding Source Code to a Project

To add a new source code file to a currently active project:

1. Select the File Menu and select New (or use the accelerator key sequence Ctrl+N), which will bring up a New dialog box.
2. Click on the Files tab.
3. Select `C++ Source File` as the file type.
4. Enter a File name.
5. Modify, if necessary, the file's folder path.
6. Click the OK Command button.

your program. Alternatively, you can press the Control and F5 Function keys together to activate the accelerator keys for compiling and running an application.

Saving and Recalling a Project

To save a project, first select the File menu and then select either the Save Workspace or the Save All option from the File menu shown in Figure C–2. Doing so will save all of the files in the current workspace.

FIGURE C–6 The IDE after Addition of a Source File

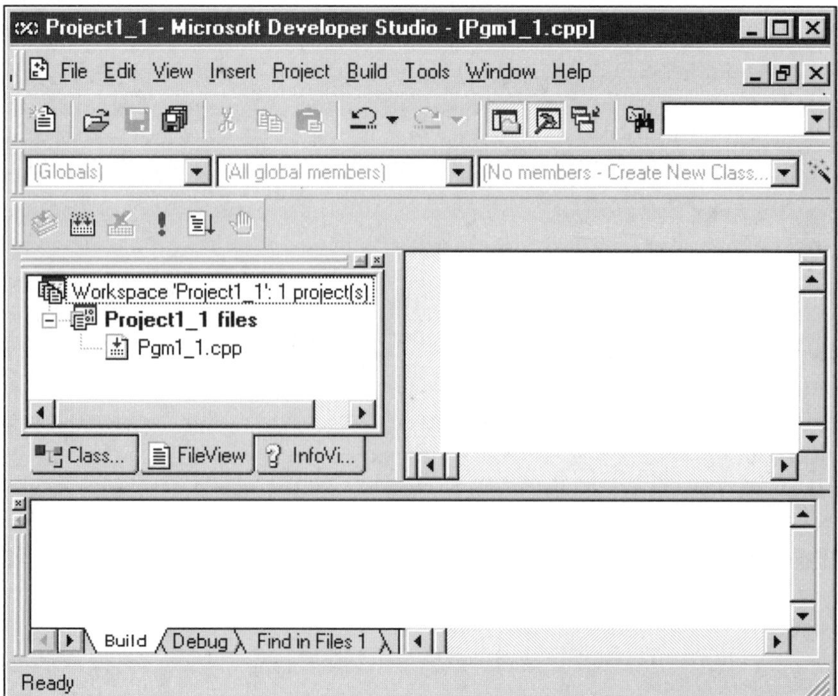

To retrieve a project, either select the Open Workspace option from the File submenu or select the Recent Workspaces option from this same submenu (see Figure C–2). If you select the Open Workspace option, you will be presented with a standard Windows Open dialog, which requires that you select a disk, folder, and file name. If you select the Recent Workspaces option, you will be presented with a number of recently used workspaces, from which you can select the desired workspace (the maximum number of recently used workspaces that is displayed can be set using the Workspace tab under the Options selection of the Tools submenu).

Using the Toolbar

Once you have become comfortable with the Menu bar items and have seen how they operate and interconnect, you should take a closer look at the standard Toolbar (see Figure C–1). For the most commonly used features of Visual C++, a click on the appropriate Toolbar icon performs the desired operation. To make sure the standard Toolbar is visible, simply right-click the mouse on the Menu bar, and make sure that a check mark (✓) appears to the left of the Standard item. For your immediate use, the most useful standard Toolbar button is the Save All icon, which is the fourth icon from the left. It is the icon that appears as a stacked set of three diskettes.

Important Settings

Once a program has been opened, an important setting that you need to know about is the Settings option provided by the Project submenu, shown in Figure C–7. Selecting this option brings up the Project Settings dialog box shown in Figure C–8. The most important setting in this dialog is for the Microsoft Foundation Classes drop-down list box contained within the General tab. As shown in Figure C–8, you can select among three choices for this box.[6] To create C++ programs for this text, make sure that this selection is "Not Using MFC." Any other selection will cause linking errors when the executable application is being built.

A Potential Problem

One annoying problem that people often encounter when using Version 5.0's Help facilities occurs because all online documentation, including Help topics, provided by Developer Studio is written using hypertext markup language (HTML). As a practical matter, this means that when any documentation or

---

6 This is true for the Professional and Enterprise editions. In the Learning edition, the option of using the MFC as a Static Library is not available.

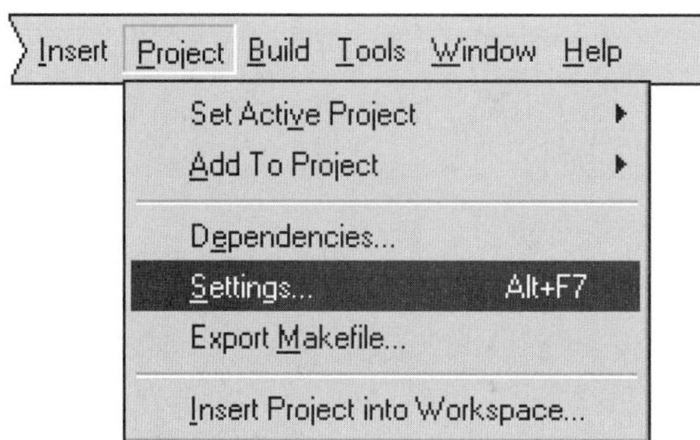

FIGURE C–7 The Project Submenu

Help topic is requested, a browser, such as Microsoft® Internet Explorer may be automatically invoked to read and display the information. The browser, however, is a distinct program, separate from Developer Studio, and has its own set of options. One of these options is to automatically initiate a connection to your Internet provider when the browser is started. If this option is set, which is the case for most systems, each time you request any documentation or Help topic, you will notice that your system seems to interrupt your work and begins the dial-up procedure that connects you to the Internet. To prevent this from happening, when the dial-up procedure begins, locate the connect option that

FIGURE C–8 The MFC Drop-Down List

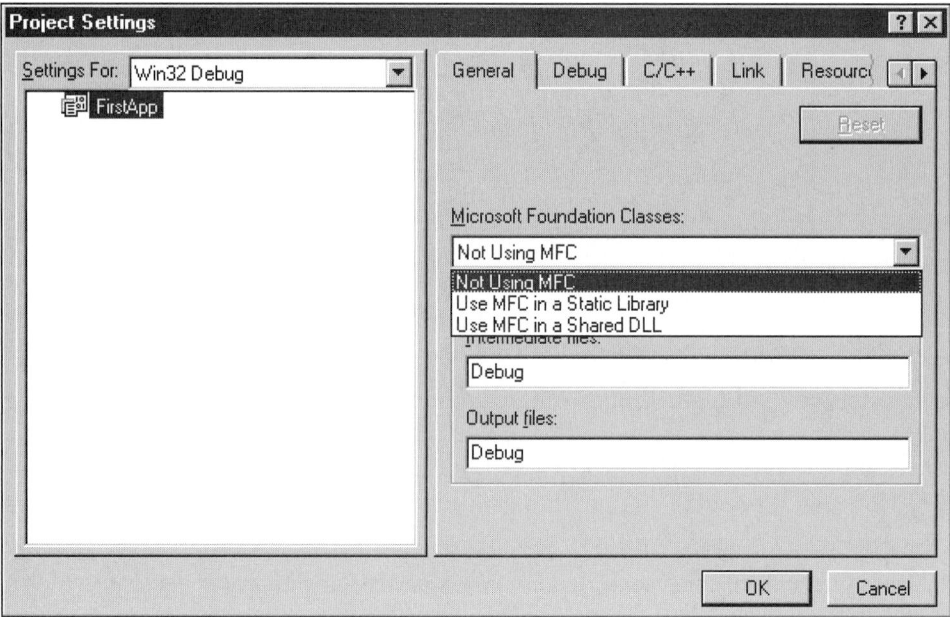

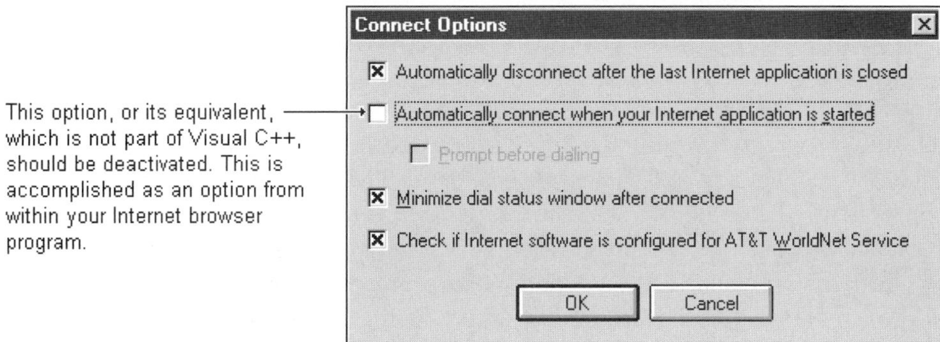

FIGURE C–9 Deselecting the Automatic Internet Connection Option

permits you to connect automatically to the Internet when the browser is activated, and deselect this option. Figure C–9 illustrates how this option appears for the Microsoft browser supplied by AT&T's WorldNet® Service.

Appendix D Using Visual C++, Version 6.0

All C++ programs presented in the text can be created as *console applications* in Visual C++, Version 6.0. These types of applications hide all of the visual components that can be created using Visual C++ and permit concentration on the basic syntax of C++ programming. The steps necessary to create console applications in Visual C++, Version 6.0, are presented in this appendix.

To create C++ programs successfully using Visual C++, you must first understand the development environment provided by a product known as Developer Studio. *Developer Studio* is the coordinating program under which many of Microsoft's programming languages, such as Visual C++ and JAVA, are developed, compiled, and executed.[1] When you start Visual C++, the screen shown in Figure D–1 is presented. This initial screen is referred to as the *integrated development environment* (IDE—pronounced as both I-D-E and IDEE). As a practical matter, the IDE simply provides a single, centralized screen from which all program development tools, from editing source code to compilation and production of an executable program, are accessible.[2]

FIGURE D–1 Developer Studio's Integrated Development Environment (IDE)

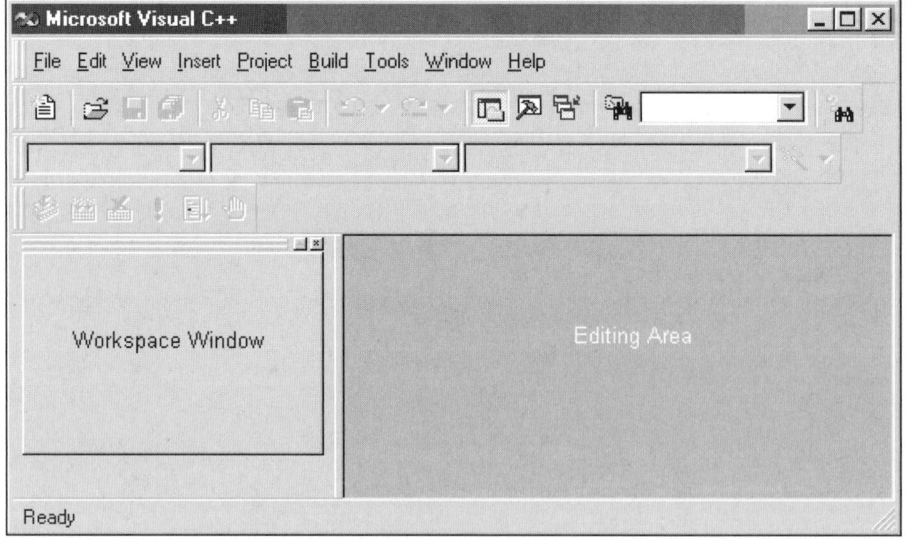

[1] Developer Studio currently supports the following development products: Visual C++, Visual J++, Visual InterDev, Visual SourceSafe, and Microsoft Development Library (MSDN). Visual Basic has its own development system.

[2] Historically, the concept of an IDE was introduced with Borland's Turbo Pascal product.

As Figure D–1 shows, the IDE consists of a standard Microsoft window, where the conventional window components, such as the Title Bar, Menu Bar, and various toolbars, have been labeled around the window's outside border. Table D–1 gives the purpose of each of these components.

The complete process, from providing an editor for creating a source code file to building an executable program from one or more object files, can be controlled from Developer Studio's integrated development environment. Keeping track of when the executable program is out of date because one or more of the source files have been modified, maintaining all graphical components used by a program, and handling other details required in the building of an executable file are accomplished by Developer Studio via a number of internal files that it also automatically maintains. The complete set of files needed to build a Visual C++ program, including all user-entered source code files and all graphical resources, is referred to as a *project.*

Another term used in relation to all Windows operating systems is the term *application.* This term is frequently used in preference to the word *program,* for

TABLE D–1 IDE Window Components

Component	Description
Title Bar	The colored bar at the top edge of a window that contains the window's name.
Menu Bar	Contains the names of the menus that can be used with the currently active window. The Menu Bar can be modified but cannot be deleted from the window.
Toolbars	The IDE contains 10 toolbars, all of which can be visible at the same time. A toolbar contains icons, also referred to as buttons, that provide quick access to commonly used Menu Bar commands. Clicking a Toolbar button initiates the designated action represented by the button.
Status Bar	The Status Bar provides indicators about the window and its current status.
System Menu Icon	Clicking on this icon causes a pop-up menu to appear. The pop-up menu contains options to set the window's size, to set its position, or to close the window.
Minimize Box	Clicking on this icon causes the Windows operating system to reduce the window to the size of an icon.
Resize Box	Clicking on this icon causes the Windows operating system to reduce the size of the window and replaces the Resize Box with a Maximize Box.
Maximize Box	Clicking on this icon causes the Windows operating system to enlarge the window to the size of the screen and replaces the Maximize Box with a Resize Box.
Close Box	Clicking on this icon causes the Windows operating system to close the window.

two reasons: It is the term selected by Microsoft to designate any program that can be run under a Windows operating system, and it can be used to avoid confusion with older procedural programs that had no graphical capabilities. In practice, the terms *program* and *application* are often used interchangeably. Formally, though, it is more correct to say that each Visual C++ application is developed and stored as a project.

For each Visual C++ application that you create, Developer Studio uses a project workspace to store all of the files needed for a project, where a *project workspace,* or *workspace* for short, is simply a folder under which files related to a specific project are stored.[3] With the understanding that a project consists of a number of files, one of which must be a source code file if an executable application is to be created, and all of which are typically stored under the same workspace folder,[4] we now proceed to use Developer Studio to select a project type.

The first step in creating a new C++ console application is to choose the File item from the Menu Bar, which will bring up the File submenu illustrated in

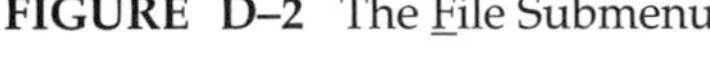

FIGURE D–2 The File Submenu

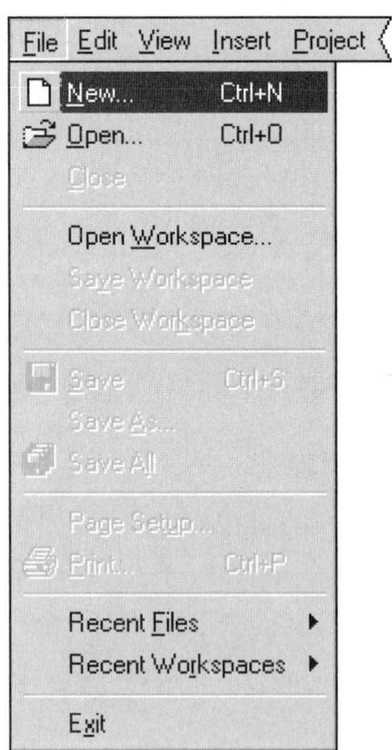

---

[3] The files need not all reside in the same workspace folder, although for convenience they typically do.

[4] There will also be a number of subfolders contained within the main project folder.

Figure D–2. As seen in this figure, the File submenu provides a number of file options, which we will use for creating a new program, as well as for saving and recalling existing programs. For now, select the New option from within this submenu, which will bring up the New dialog box shown in Figure D–3.

As shown in Figure D–3, Visual C++'s Professional Edition provides a choice of 15 project types, the most commonly used of which are listed in Table D–2.[5] When starting a new project, first make sure that the Projects tab is active. From within the Projects tab, you must actively designate three items. First, you must select the project type. The second item that must be provided is the name of the project. This project name must be entered in the Project name Text box shown in Figure D–3. In this text, each individual application will be constructed in its own project workspace, using project names such as `pgm1_1`. Specifically, what this does for new projects is create a new folder, which in this case is named `pgm1_1`. As shown in Figure D–3, the location of this folder is within the path listed in the Location drop-down List box, which is the third item that must be provided. Typically, the initial path for all project workspaces (again,

FIGURE D–3 The New Dialog Box

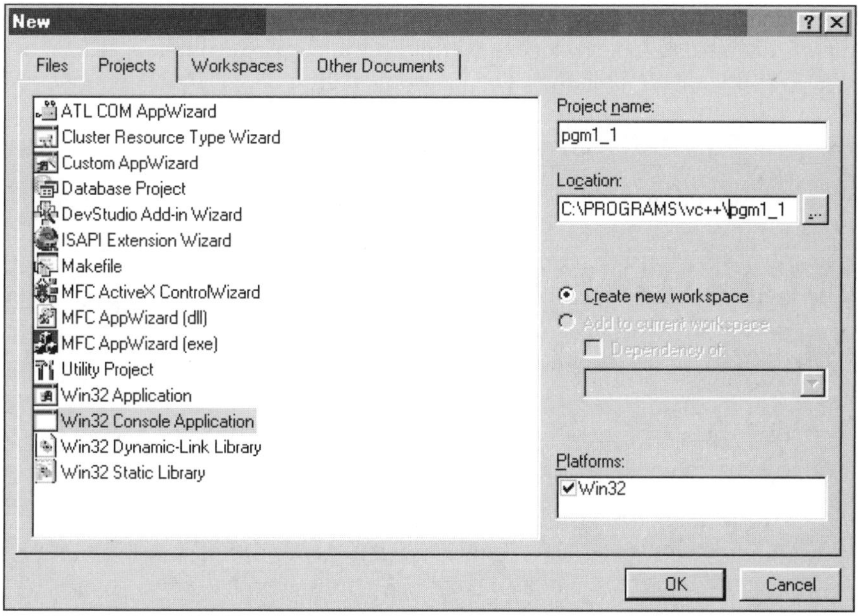

[5] The number of project types displayed depends on the number of installed Developer Studio products. For example, if you have installed Visual J++ (Microsoft's JAVA product), the options appropriate to this language will also appear.

TABLE D–2 The Professional Edition's Available Project Types

Project Type	Description
ATL COM AppWizard	Use an applications wizard to develop a COM object.
Custom AppWizard	Use an applications wizard to develop a complete customized application.
ISAPI Extension Wizard	Use an applications wizard to create modules that extend Internet web servers.
Makefile	Create your own makefile that automatically compiles source code and create an executable application.
MFC ActiveX Control Wizard	Use an applications wizard to create an ActiveX control.
MFC AppWizard (DLL)	Use an applications wizard to create a dynamic link library (DLL) Microsoft Foundation Classes (MFC)-based module.
MFC AppWizard (exe)	Use an applications wizard to create an executable MFC-based application.
Win32 Application	Create a Windows-based application that does not have to use the MFC. The MFC also can be used in these applications.
Win32 Console Application	Create an empty project file with options correctly set to build a character-mode application.
Win32 Dynamic Link Library	Create an empty project file with options correctly set to build a DLL.
Win32 Static Library	Create a static library file.

this means folders) that you create is a default selectable from within the Options submenu of Developer Studio's Tools menu.

Once you have provided the information required by the dialog shown in Figure D–3 and have selected the OK Command button, the dialog shown in Figure D–4 will appear. From this dialog select the first radio button option labeled `An empty project`. This selection will bring up the information dialog shown in Figure D–5.

Pressing the OK button on the dialog box shown in Figure D–5 causes two things to happen. The first is that a number of files are automatically created and placed in the workspace folder for the new project. A list of the file types that are created is provided in Table D–3. Next, Developer Studio's IDE will appear as shown in Figure D–6. In this figure, pay particular attention to the Workspace Window. This window, which is also referred to as the Project Workspace window, displays a hierarchical list of projects in the current workspace and shows all of the items contained within each project.

Although only one workspace can be open at one time, a single workspace can contain multiple projects. Also note that two additional tabs have been

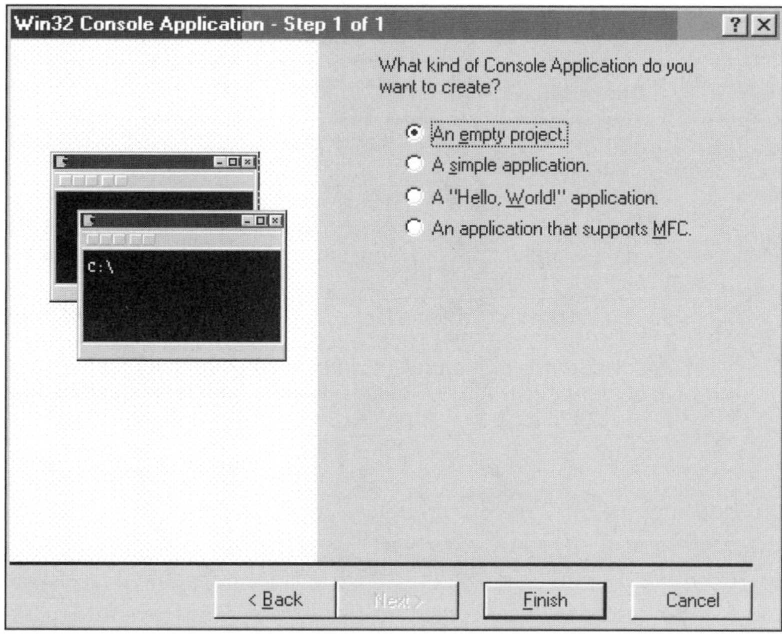

FIGURE D–4 Selecting the Type of Console Application

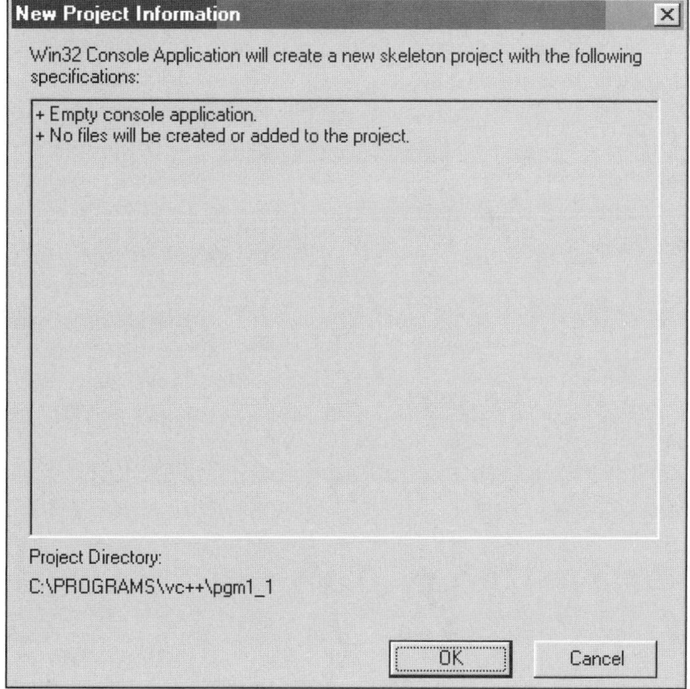

FIGURE D–5 The Application's Information Dialog

TABLE D–3 File Types Provided within a Workspace Folder

File Extension	Description
`.dsw`	A project workspace file used to store information at the workspace level, such as the number of projects stored in the workspace.
`.dsp`	A project file that contains information about how the executable version of a single project is to be built. This is equivalent to the makefile used in earlier versions of Visual C++ that had the extension `.mak`.
`.opt`	The workspace options file, which is used to store project workspace settings. This file contains local settings, such as the appearance of the project workspace using your hardware configuration. A new options file is automatically created whenever a workspace is opened and no workspace options file is found.

added to the Workspace window: the ClassView and FileView tabs. As files are now added or removed from a project, Visual C++ will reflect all of these changes within the displayed hierarchical tree. The hierarchical tree used in both the ClassView tab and the FileView tab is a standard Windows folder tree, which

FIGURE D–6 The IDE Containing an Active Workspace

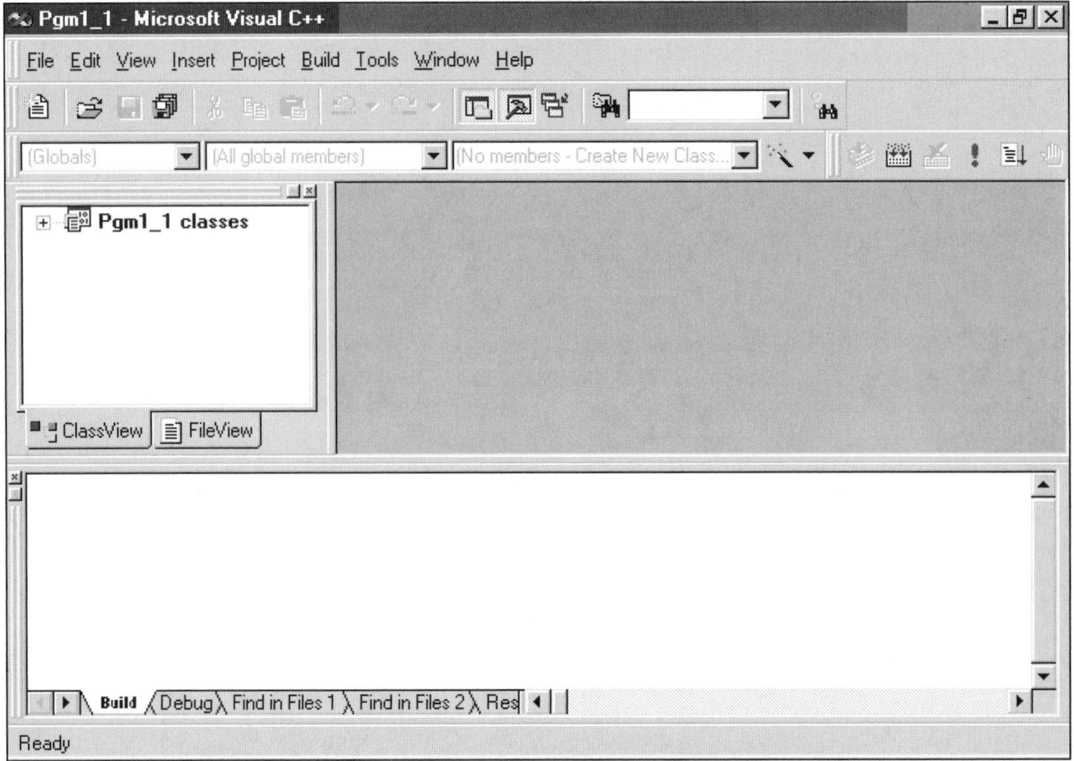

POINT OF INFORMATION

Creating a Console Application

To create a console application:

1. Select the File Menu and select New (or use the accelerator key sequence Ctrl+N), which will bring up a New dialog box.
2. Click on the Projects tab.
3. Select `Win32 Console Application` as the project type.
4. Enter a project name, which becomes the name of the workspace folder for the project.
5. Modify, if necessary, the workspace folder's path.
6. Click the OK Command button.

means that you can expand and contract tree sections by clicking on plus (+) and minus (–) symbols, respectively. As always, sections of the tree that are hidden from view because of the size of the window can be displayed by using the attached scroll bars.

The procedure for creating a C++ source code file is almost identical to the one used in creating a new project. To create the source code file, select the New option from within the Menu Bar's File menu. This will bring up the New dialog, which we previously used in creating a new project (see Figure D–3). In this case, however, activate the Files tab, as illustrated in Figure D–7. Within

FIGURE D–7 Creating a C++ Source Code File

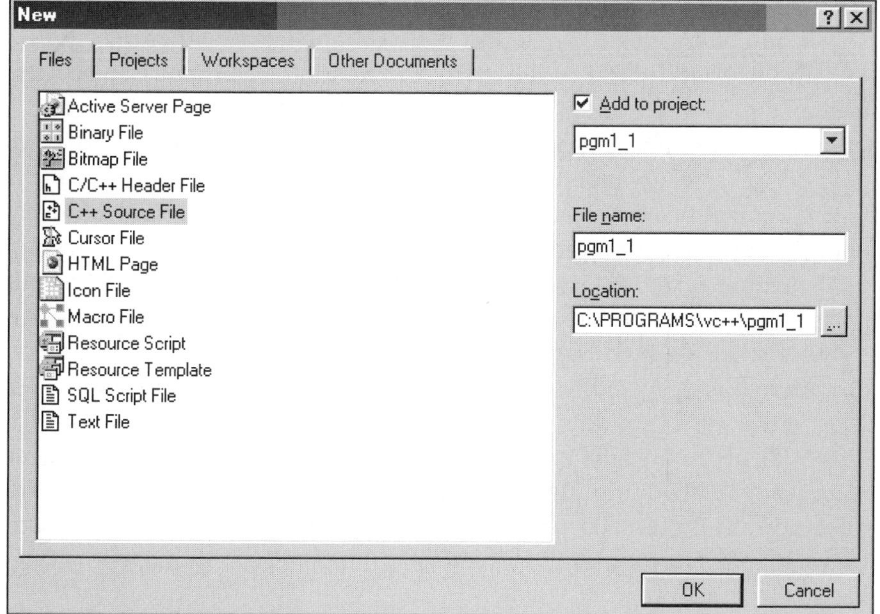

POINT OF INFORMATION

Adding Source Code to a Project

To add a new source code file to a currently active project:

1. Select the File Menu and select New (or use the accelerator key sequence Ctrl+N), which will bring up a New dialog box.
2. Click on the Files tab.
3. Select `C++ Source File` as the file type.
4. Enter a File name.
5. Modify, if necessary, the file's folder path.
6. Click the OK Command button.

this dialog, you will see that the check box to add a file to the existing project has been checked, and the active project workspace name has been inserted within the first drop-down List box. Additionally, the drive and path for this current project workspace folder will automatically be provided in the file `Location` Text box. Your responsibility is now to select a file type and provide the file with a name.

From the list of file types provided in the New dialog shown in Figure D–7, select the `C++ Source File` choice, and then provide a name for the file. As shown in Figure D–7, the name we have given to the source file is `pgm1_1`. When you provide this information and press the dialog's OK Command button, Developer Studio will create a file named `pgm1_1.cpp` within the `pgm1_1` folder. Note that the `cpp` extension to the file name is automatically appended by Developer Studio, because Visual C++ requires that all source code files have this extension. After this is done, the IDE will appear as shown in Figure D–8.

In reviewing Figure D–8, pay particular attention to the Workspace window. Note that the ClassView tab is active. Activating the FileView tab and then expanding the tree, as shown in Figure D–9, will reveal that a file named `pgm1_1.cpp` has been added to the hierarchy tree. The arrow that is displayed within the icon indicates that this file is an active part of the project (for example, it is not part of some other project that is being stored in the current workspace folder) and that it will be used when an executable file is ultimately built. At this stage the Visual C++ text editor has been loaded, and you can now enter C++ source code in the Editing area that would be saved as the file `pgm1_1.cpp`.

An alternative to creating a new source file, as illustrated in Figure D–7, is to select either of the middle two options shown in Figure D–4. Both of these choices will automatically create a source code file and display the editor window shown in Figure D–9, with a number of code lines already added. Because not all of the code provided is needed, you can delete it and type in the desired code, starting with the line `#include <iostream.h>`

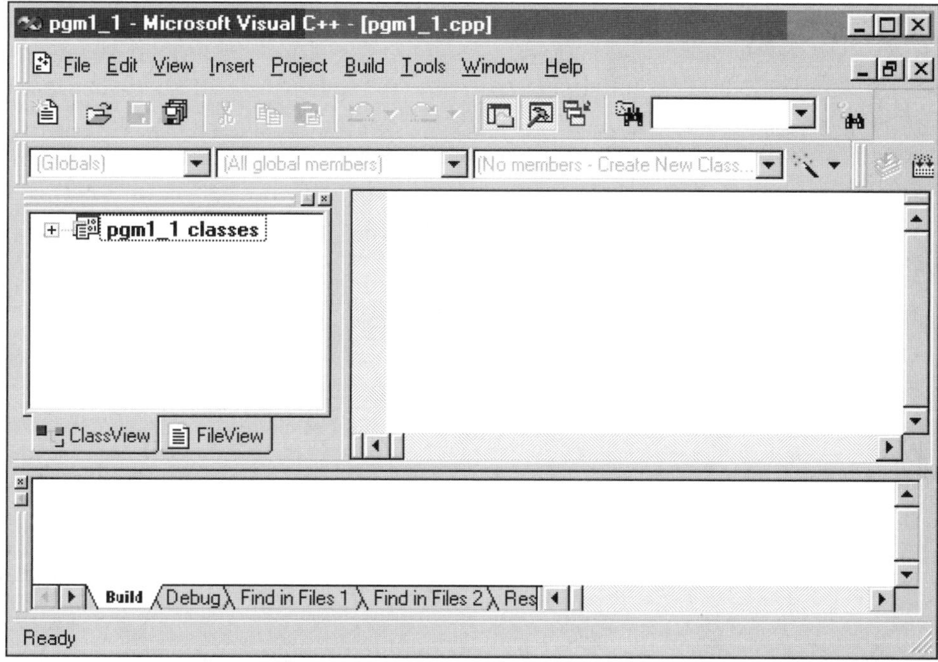

FIGURE D–8 The IDE after Addition of an Active Project

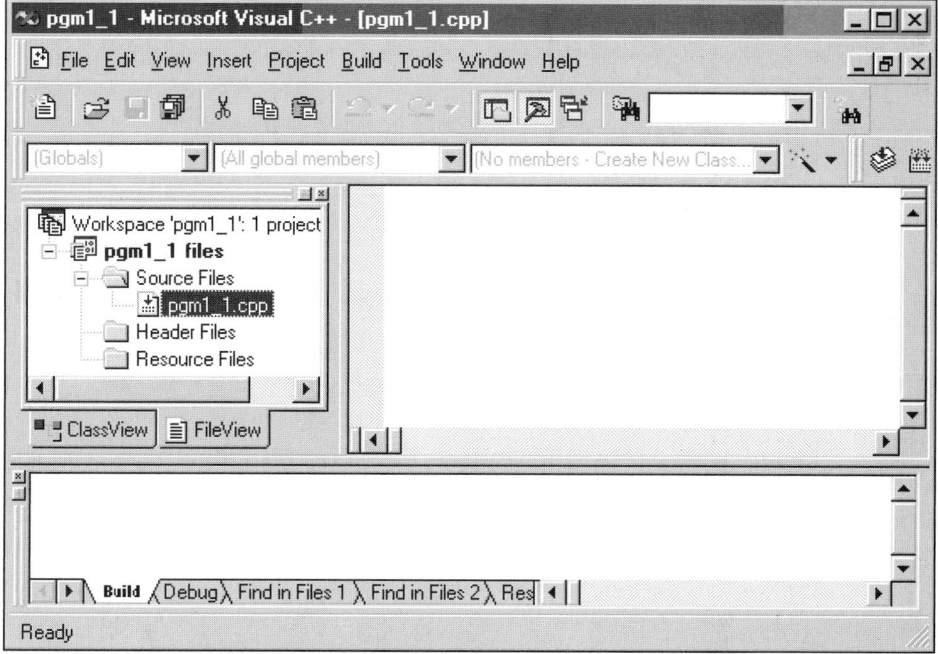

FIGURE D–9 Activating a Source Code File

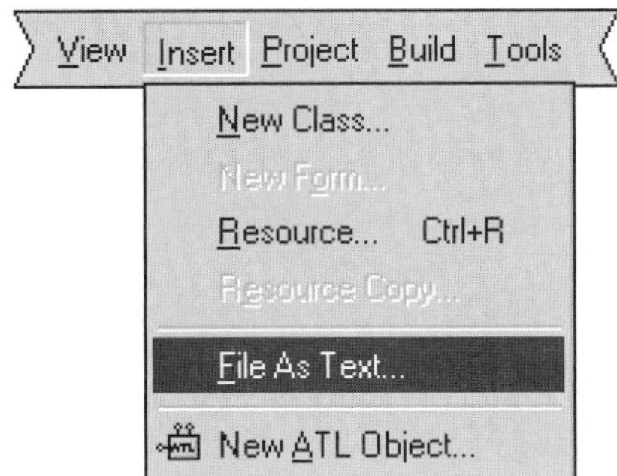

FIGURE D–10 Inserting a Source Code File

An alternative to entering source code manually is to insert an existing source code file into the current project. For example, if you wanted to run one of the programs contained in this text, you could insert the desired source code into the editing area. To do this, you would first select the `File As Text` option from the `Insert` menu, as shown in Figure D–10, and then provide the correct path and file name in the next displayed dialog.

Once your source code has been entered, select the `Build` menu's `Execute` to compile and run your program. Alternatively, you can press the Control and F5 Function keys together to activate the accelerator keys for compiling and running an application.

Saving and Recalling a Project

To save a project, first select the File menu and then select either the Save Workspace or the Save All option from the File menu shown in Figure D–2. Doing so will save all of the files in the current workspace.

To retrieve a project, either select the Open Workspace option from the File submenu or select the Recent Workspaces option from this same submenu (see Figure D–2). If you select the Open Workspace option, you will be presented with a standard Windows Open dialog, which requires that you select a disk, folder, and file name. If you select the Recent Workspace option, you will be presented with a number of recently used workspaces, from which you can select the desired workspace (the maximum number of recently used workspaces that is displayed can be set by using the Workspace tab under the Options selection of the Tools submenu).

Using the Toolbar

Once you have become comfortable with the Menu bar items and have seen how they operate and interconnect, you should take a closer look at the standard Toolbar. For the most commonly used features of Visual C++, a click on the appropriate Toolbar icon performs the desired operation. To make sure the standard Toolbar is visible, simply right-click the mouse on the Menu bar and make sure that a check mark (✓) appears to the left of the Standard item. For your immediate use, the most useful standard Toolbar button is the Save All icon, which is the fourth icon from the left. It is the icon that appears as a stacked set of three diskettes.

Appendix E Using Borland's C++ Builder

All of the C++ programs presented in this text can be created as *console applications* in C++ Builder. These types of applications hide all of the visual components that can be created using C++ Builder and make it possible to concentrate on the basic syntax of C++ programming. The steps necessary to create console applications in C++ Builder are presented in this appendix.

When you start C++ Builder, the screen shown in Figure E–1 is presented. This initial screen is referred to as the *integrated development environment* (IDE, pronounced as both I-D-E and IDEE). As a practical matter, the IDE simply provides a single, centralized screen from which all program development tools, from editing source code to compilation and production of an executable program, are accessible.

The first step in creating a new C++ console application is to choose the File item from the Menu Bar, which will bring up the File submenu illustrated in Figure E–2. As this figure shows, the File submenu provides a number of file

FIGURE E–1 The C++ Builder's IDE

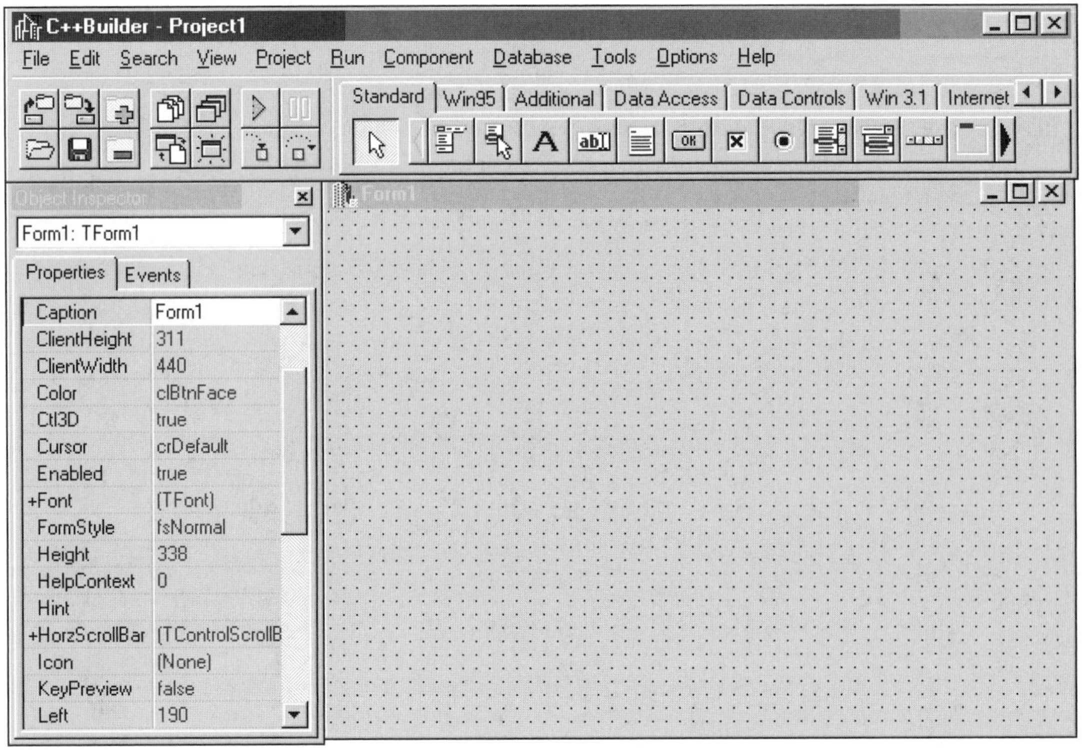

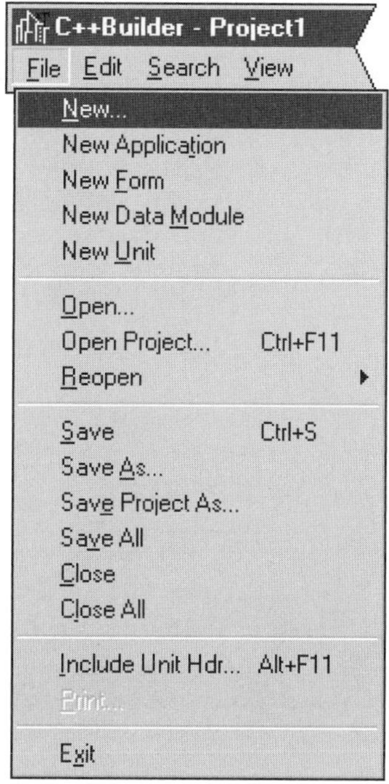

FIGURE E–2 The File Submenu

options, which we will use for creating a new program, as well as for saving and recalling existing programs. For now, select the New option from within this submenu, which will bring up the New Items dialog box shown in Figure E–3.

As shown in Figure E–3, Borland's Professional Edition of C++ Builder provides a choice of 10 new item types. To create C++ console programs for this text, always select the `Console App` icon contained within the New tab shown in Figure E–3. This will bring up the editor window shown in Figure E–4, which includes a number of code lines already added. Because these lines are not needed, you can delete them all and type in the desired code, starting with the line `#include <iostream.h>`. To compile and run your program, you can either click the Toolbar's arrowhead icon (the one shown in Figure E–1, directly under the Main menu's Project option) or use the Main menu's Run option. Similarly, a program can be saved and recalled using the File menu's Save and Open options, as previously shown in Figure E–1.

A Potential Problem

One annoying problem that users typically encounter when executing a C++ Builder console application is the immediate closing of the DOS window under

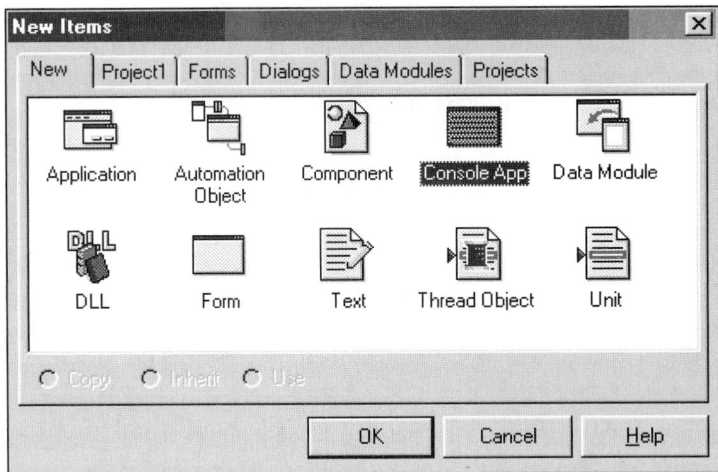

FIGURE E–3 The New Items Dialog Box

C:\Program Files\Borland\CBuilder\BIN\Project1.cpp

Project1.cpp

```
//-------------------------------------------
#include <vcl\condefs.h>
#include <stdio.h>
#include <stdlib.h>
#include <string.h>

#pragma hdrstop
//-------------------------------------------
USERES("Project1.res");
//-------------------------------------------
int main(int argc, char **argv)
{
    return 0;
}
```

1: 1 Modified Insert

FIGURE E–4 The Initial Editor Window

which the program is run. To keep this DOS window from closing immediately, you can use code similar to the following:

```
int i;      // place this after the opening brace {
cin >> i;   // place this before the return statement
```

This code will hold the window open, waiting for the user to input a value. Pressing any digit key will then cause the program to terminate.

Appendix F Bit Operations

C++ operates with data entities that are stored as one or more bytes, such as character, integer, and double-precision constants and variables. In addition, C++ provides for the manipulation of individual bits of character and integer constants and variables. Generally, these bit manipulations are used in engineering and computer science applications and are not required in commercial applications.

The operators that are used to perform bit manipulations are called *bit operators.* They are listed in Table F–1.

TABLE F–1 Bit Operators

Operator	Description
&	Bitwise AND
|	Bitwise inclusive OR
^	Bitwise exclusive OR
~	Bitwise one's complement
<<	Left shift
>>	Right shift

All the operators listed in Table F–1, except ~, are binary operators, requiring two operands. Each operand is treated as a binary number consisting of a series of individual 1s and 0s. The respective bits in each operand are then compared on a bit-by-bit basis, and the result is determined on the basis of the selected operation.

The AND Operator

The AND operator causes a bit-by-bit AND comparison between its two operands. *The result of each bit-by-bit comparison is a 1 only when both bits being compared are 1s; otherwise, the result of the AND operation is a 0.* For example, assume that the following two eight-bit numbers are to be ANDed:

```
1 0 1 1 0 0 1 1
1 1 0 1 0 1 0 1
---------------
```

To perform an AND operation, each bit in one operand is compared to the bit occupying the same position in the other operand. Figure F–1 illustrates the correspondence between bits for these two operands. As shown in the figure, when both bits being compared are 1s, the result is a 1; otherwise, the result is a 0. The result of each comparison is, of course, independent of any other bit comparison.

Program F-1 illustrates the use of an AND operation. In this program, the variable `op1` is initialized to the octal value 325, which is the octal equivalent of the binary number `1 1 0 1 0 1 0 1`, and the variable `op2` is initialized to the octal value 263, which is the octal representation of the binary number `1 0 1 1 0 0 1 1`. These are the same two binary numbers illustrated in Figure F–1.

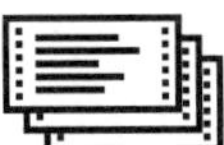

Program F-1

```
#include <iostream.h>
int main()
{
  int op1 = 0325, op2 = 0263;

  int op3 = op1 & op2;
  cout << oct << op1 << " ANDed with "<< op2 << " is " << op3 << endl;

  return 0;
}
```

Program F-1 produces the following output

```
325 ANDed with 263 is 221
```

The result of ANDing the octal numbers 325 and 263 is the octal number 221. The binary equivalent of 221 is the binary number `1 0 0 1 0 0 0 1`, which is the result of the AND operation illustrated in Figure F–1.

FIGURE F–1 A Sample AND Operation

```
  1 0 1 1 0 0 1 1
& 1 1 0 1 0 1 0 1
-----------------
  1 0 0 1 0 0 0 1
```

AND operations are extremely useful in *masking*, or eliminating, selected bits from an operand. This is a direct result of the fact that ANDing any bit (1 or 0) with a 0 forces the resulting bit to be a 0, whereas ANDing any bit (1 or 0) with a 1 leaves the original bit unchanged. For example, assume that the variable `op1` has the arbitrary bit pattern `x x x x x x x x`, where each `x` can be either 1 or 0, independent of any other `x` in the number. The result of ANDing this binary number with the binary number `0 0 0 0 1 1 1 1` is

```
   op1 =   x x x x x x x x
   op2 =   0 0 0 0 1 1 1 1
           ---------------
Result =   0 0 0 0 x x x x
```

As can be seen from this example, the 0s in `op2` effectively mask, or eliminate, the respective bits in `op1`, whereas the 1s in `op2` filter the respective bits in `op1`, or pass them through, with no change in their values. In this example, the variable `op2` is called a *mask*. By choosing the mask appropriately, any individual bit in an operand can be selected and filtered from an operand for inspection. For example, ANDing the variable `op1` with the mask `0 0 0 0 0 1 0 0` forces all the bits of the result to be a 0, except for the third bit. The third bit of the result will be a copy of the third bit of `op1`. Thus, if the result of the AND is a 0, the third bit of `op1` must have been a 0, and if the result of the AND is a nonzero number, the third bit must have been a 1.

Program F-2 uses this masking property to convert lowercase letters in a word into their uppercase form, assuming that the letters are stored using the ASCII code. The algorithm for converting letters is based on the fact that the binary codes for lowercase and uppercase letters in ASCII are the same except for bit five, which is a 1 for lowercase letters and a 0 for uppercase letters.[1] For example, the binary code for the letter a is `01100001` (hex 61), whereas the binary code for the letter A is `01000001` (hex 41). Similarly, the binary code for the letter z is `01111010` (hex 7A), whereas the binary code for the letter Z is `01011010` (hex 5A). (See Appendix B for the hexadecimal values of the uppercase and lowercase letters.) Thus, given a lowercase letter, it can be converted into its uppercase form by forcing the fifth bit to 0. This is accomplished in Program F-2 by masking the letter's code with the binary value `11011111`, which has the hexadecimal value DF.

---

[1] This assumes the conventional numbering scheme starting with bit zero as the rightmost bit. Using this convention, the rightmost bit (or bit zero) is referred to as the least significant bit (LSB), and the leftmost bit is referred to as the most significant bit (MSB). Here the MSB is bit seven.

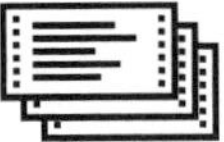

Program F-2

```
#include <iostream.h>
const int TO_UP = 0xDF;
const int max = 80;
int main()
{
  char word[MAX];          // enough storage for a complete line
  void upper(char *);      // function prototype

  cout << "Enter a string of both upper and lowercase letters:\n";
  cin.getline(word,MAX,'\n');
  cout << "\nThe string of letters just entered is:\n"
       << word << endl;
  upper(word);
  cout << "\nThis string, in uppercase letters is:\n"
       << word << endl;

  return 0;
}
void upper(char *word)
{
  while (*word != '\0')
    *word++ &= TO_UP;
  return;
}
```

A sample run using Program F-2 follows.

```
Enter a string of both upper and lowercase letters:
abcdefgHIJKLMNOPqrstuvwxyz

The string of letters just entered is:
abcdefgHIJKLMNOPqrstuvwxyz

This string, in uppercase letters is:
ABCDEFGHIJKLMNOPQRSTUVWXYZ
```

Note that the lowercase letters are converted to uppercase form, whereas uppercase letters are unaltered. This is because bit five of all uppercase letters is a 0 to begin with, so forcing this bit to 0 using the mask has no effect. Only when bit five is a 1, as it is for lowercase letters, is the input character altered.

The Inclusive OR Operator

The inclusive OR operator, |, performs a bit-by-bit comparison of its two operands in a similar fashion to the bit-by-bit AND. The result of the OR comparison, however, is determined by the following rule:

The result of the comparison is a 1 if either bit being compared is a 1; otherwise, the result is a 0.

Figure F–2 illustrates an OR operation. As shown in the figure, when either of the two bits being compared is a 1, the result is a 1; otherwise the result is a 0. As with all bit operations, the result of each comparison is independent of any other comparison.

Program F-3 illustrates an OR operation, using the octal values of the operands illustrated in Figure F–2.

Program F-3

```
#include <iostream.h>
int main()
{
  int op1 = 0325, op2 = 0263;

  int op3 = op1 | op2;
  cout << oct << op1 << " ORed with " << op2 << " is " << op3 << endl;

  return 0;
}
```

Program F-3 produces the following output:

```
325 ORed with 263 is 367
```

FIGURE F–2 A Sample OR Operation

```
  1 0 1 1 0 0 1 1
| 1 1 0 1 0 1 0 1
-----------------
  1 1 1 1 0 1 1 1
```

The result of ORing the octal numbers 325 and 263 is the octal number 367. The binary equivalent of 367 is `1 1 1 1 0 1 1 1`, which is the result of the OR operation illustrated in Figure F–2.

Inclusive OR operations are extremely useful in forcing selected bits to take on a 1 value or for passing through other bit values unchanged. This is a direct result of the fact that ORing any bit (1 or 0) with a 1 forces the resulting bit to be a 1, whereas ORing any bit (1 or 0) with a 0 leaves the original bit unchanged. For example, assume that the variable `op1` has the arbitrary bit pattern `x x x x x x x x`, where each `x` can be either 1 or 0, independent of any other `x` in the number. The result of ORing this binary number with the binary number `1 1 1 1 0 0 0 0` is

```
   op1  =   x x x x x x x x
   op2  =   1 1 1 1 0 0 0 0
            ---------------
Result  =   1 1 1 1 x x x x
```

As this example illustrates, the 1s in `op2` force the resulting bits to 1, whereas the 0s in `op2` filter the respective bits in `op1`, or pass them through, with no change in their values. Thus, using an OR operation, we can produce a masking operation similar to that produced with an AND operation, except the masked bits are set to 1s rather than cleared to 0s. Another way of looking at this is to say that ORing with a 0 has the same effect as ANDing with a 1.

Program F-4 uses this masking property to convert uppercase letters in a word into their respective lowercase form, assuming the letters are stored using the ASCII code. The algorithm for converting letters is similar to that used in Program F-2 and converts uppercase letters into their lowercase form by forcing the fifth bit in each letter to a 1. This is accomplished in Program F-4 by masking the letter's code with the binary value `00100000`, which has the hexadecimal value 20.

A sample run using Program F-4 follows.

```
Enter a string of both upper and lowercase letters:
abcdefgHIJKLMNOPqrstuvwxyz

The string of letters just entered is:
abcdefgHIJKLMNOPqrstuvwxyz

This string, in lowercase letters is:
abcdefghijklmnopqrstuvwxyz
```

Program F-4

```
#include <iostream.h>
const int max = 80;
const int TO_LOW = 0x20;
int main()
{
  char word[MAX];           // enough storage for a complete line
  void lower (char *);      // function prototype
  cout << "Enter a string of both upper and lowercase letters:\n";
  cin.getline(word,MAX,'\n');
  cout << "\nThe string of letters just entered is:\n"
       << word << endl;
  lower(word);
  cout << "\nThis string, in lowercase letters is:\n"
       << word << endl;

  return 0;
}
void lower(char *word)
{
  while (*word != '\0')
    *word++ |= TO_LOW;
  return;
}
```

Note that the uppercase letters are converted to lowercase form, whereas lowercase letters are unaltered. This is because bit five of all lowercase letters is a 1 to begin with, so forcing this bit to 1 using the mask has no effect. Only when bit five is a 0, as it is for uppercase letters, is the input character altered.

The Exclusive OR Operator

The exclusive OR operator, `^`, performs a bit-by-bit comparison of its two operands. The result of the comparison is determined by the following rule:

> *The result of the comparison is 1 if one and only one of the bits being compared is a 1; otherwise, the result is 0.*

Figure F–3 illustrates an exclusive OR operation. As shown in the figure, when both bits being compared are the same value (both 1 or both 0), the result is a 0. Only when both bits have different values (one bit a 1 and the other a 0) is the result a 1. Again, each pair or bit comparison is independent of any other bit comparison.

```
   1 0 1 1 0 0 1 1
 ^ 1 1 0 1 0 1 0 1
 -----------------
   0 1 1 0 0 1 1 0
```

FIGURE F–3 A Sample Exclusive OR Operation

An exclusive OR operation can be used to create the opposite value, or complement, of any individual bit in a variable. This is a direct result of the fact that exclusive ORing any bit (1 or 0) with a 1 forces the resulting bit to be of the value opposite that of its original state, whereas exclusive ORing any bit (1 or 0) with a 0 leaves the original bit unchanged. For example, assume that the variable `op1` has the arbitrary bit pattern `x x x x x x x x`, where each `x` can be either 1 or 0, independent of any other `x` in the number. Using the notation that $\bar{x}$ is the complement (opposite) value of `x`, the result of exclusive ORing this binary number with the binary number `0 1 0 1 0 1 0 1` is

$$
\begin{array}{rcl}
\texttt{op1} & = & x\ x\ x\ x\ x\ x\ x\ x \\
\texttt{op2} & = & 0\ 1\ 0\ 1\ 0\ 1\ 0\ 1 \\
\hline
\text{Result} & = & x\ \bar{x}\ x\ \bar{x}\ x\ \bar{x}\ x\ \bar{x}
\end{array}
$$

As can be seen from this example, the 1s in `op2` force the resulting bits to be the complement of their original bit values, whereas the 0s in `op2` filter the respective bits in `op1`, or pass through, with no change in their values.

Many encryption methods use the exclusive OR operation to code data. For example, the string `Hello there world!` initially used in Program F-1 can be encrypted by exclusive ORing each character in the string with a mask value of 52. The choice of the mask value, which is referred to as the *encryption key*, is arbitrary, and any key value can be used.

Program F-5 uses an encryption key of 52 to code a user-entered message. A sample run using Program F-5 follows.

```
Enter a sentence:
Good morning

The sentence just entered is:
Good morning

The encrypted version of this sentence is:
s[[P¶Y[FZ]ZS
```

Program F-5

```
#include <iostream.h>
const int max = 80;
int main()
{
  char message[MAX];      // enough storage for a complete line
  void encrypt(char *); // function prototype
  cout << "\nEnter a sentence:\n";
  cin.getline(message,MAX,'\n');
  cout << "\nThe sentence just entered is:\n"
       << message << endl;
  encrypt(message);
  cout << "\nThe encrypted version of this sentence is:\n"
       << message << endl;

  return 0;
}

void encrypt(char *message)
{
  while (*message != '\0')
    *message++ ^= 52;
  return;
}
```

Decoding an encrypted message requires exclusive ORing the coded message using the original encryption key.

The Complement Operator

The complement operator, ~, is a unary operator that changes each 1 bit in its operand to 0 and each 0 bit to 1. For example, if the variable `op1` contains the binary number `11001010`, `~op1` replaces this binary number with the number `00110101`. The complement operator is used to force any bit in an operand to 0, independent of the actual number of bits used to store the number. For example, the statement

```
op1 = op1 & ~07;    // 07 is an octal number
```

and its shorter form,

```
op1 &= ~07;     // 07 is an octal number
```

both set the last three bits of `op1` to 0, regardless of how `op1` is stored within the computer. Either of these two statements can, of course, be replaced by ANDing the last three bits of `op1` with 0s, if the number of bits used to store `op1` is known. In a computer that uses 16 bits to store integers, the appropriate AND operation is

```
op1 = op1 & 0177770;     // in octal
```

or

```
op1 = op1 & 0xFFF8;     // in hexadecimal
```

For a computer that uses 32 bits to store integers, the above AND sets the leftmost or higher-order 16 bits to 0 also, which is an unintended result. The correct statement for 32 bits is

```
op1 = op1 & 027777777770;     // in octal
```

or

```
op1 = op1 & 0xFFFFFFF8;     // in hexadecimal
```

Using the complement operator in this situation frees the programmer from having to determine the storage size of the operand and, more important, makes the program portable between machines that use different integer storage sizes.

Different-Sized Data Items

When the bit operators `&`, `|`, and `^` are used with operands of different sizes, the shorter operand is always increased in bit size to match the size of the larger operand. Figure F–4 illustrates the extension of a 16-bit unsigned integer into a 32-bit number.

FIGURE F–4 Extending 16-Bit Unsigned Data to 32 Bits

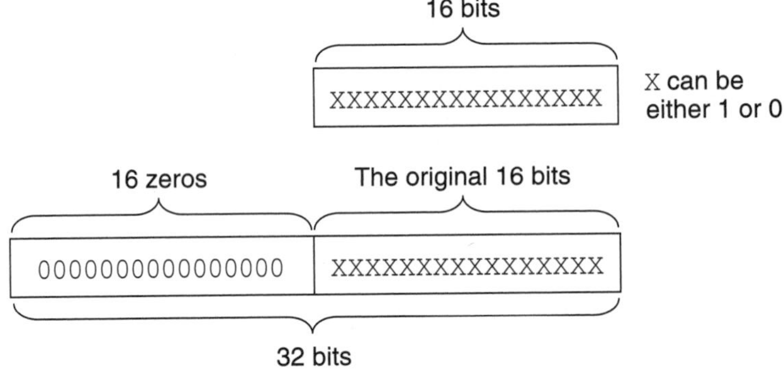

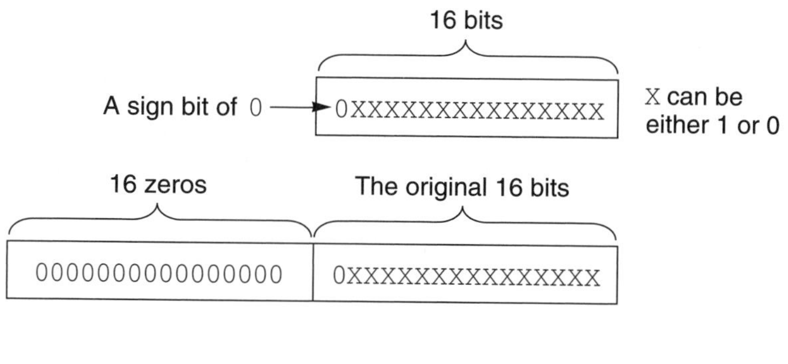

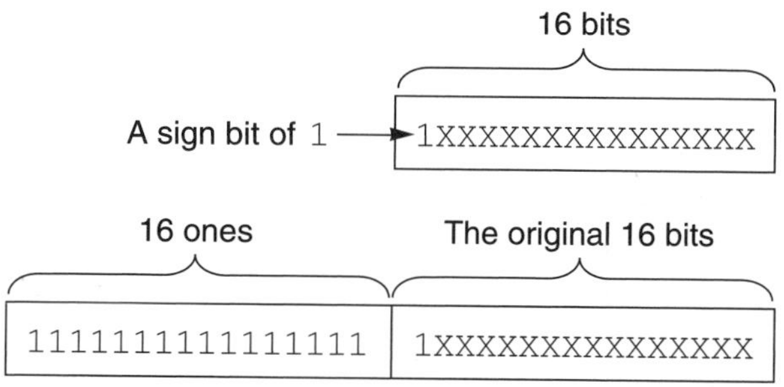

FIGURE F–5 Extending 16-Bit Signed Data to 32 Bits

As the figure shows, the additional bits are added to the left of the original number and filled with 0s. This is the equivalent of adding leading 0s to the number, which has no effect on the number's value.

When extending signed numbers, the original leftmost bit is reproduced in the additional bits that are added to the number. As illustrated in Figure F–5, if the original leftmost bit is 0, corresponding to a positive number, 0 is placed in each of the additional bit positions. If the leftmost bit is 1, which corresponds to a negative number, 1 is placed in the additional bit positions. In either case, the resulting binary number has the same sign and magnitude as the original number.

The Shift Operators

The left shift operator, <<, causes the bits in an operand to be shifted to the left by a given amount. For example, the statement

```
op1 = op1 << 4;
```

causes the bits in `op1` to be shifted four bits to the left, filling any vacated bits with a 0. Figure F–6 illustrates the effect of shifting the binary number `1111100010101011` to the left by four bit positions.

For unsigned integers, each left shift corresponds to multiplication by two. This is also true for signed numbers using twos complement representation, as long as the leftmost bit does not switch values. Because a change in the leftmost bit of a twos complement number represents a change in both the sign and the magnitude represented by the bit, such a shift does not represent a simple multiplication by two.

The right shift operator, >>, causes the bits in an operand to be shifted to the right by a given amount. For example, the statement

```
op2 = op1 >> 3;
```

causes the bits in `op1` to be shifted to the right by three bit positions. Figure F–7a illustrates the right shift of the unsigned binary number `1111100010101011` by three bit positions. As illustrated, the three rightmost bits are shifted "off the end" and are lost.

For unsigned numbers, the leftmost bit is not used as a sign bit. For this type of number, the vacated leftmost bits are always filled with 0s. This is the case that is illustrated in Figure F–7a.

For signed numbers, what is filled in the vacated bits depends on the compiler. Most compilers reproduce the original sign bit of the number. Figure F–7b illustrates the right shift of a negative binary number by four bit positions, where the sign bit is reproduced in the vacated bits. Figure F–7c illustrates the equivalent right shift of a positive signed binary number.

The type of fill illustrated in Figures F–7b and F–7c, where the sign bit is reproduced in vacated bit positions, is called an *arithmetic right shift*. In an arithmetic right shift, each single shift to the right corresponds to a division by two.

FIGURE F–6 An Example of a Left Shift

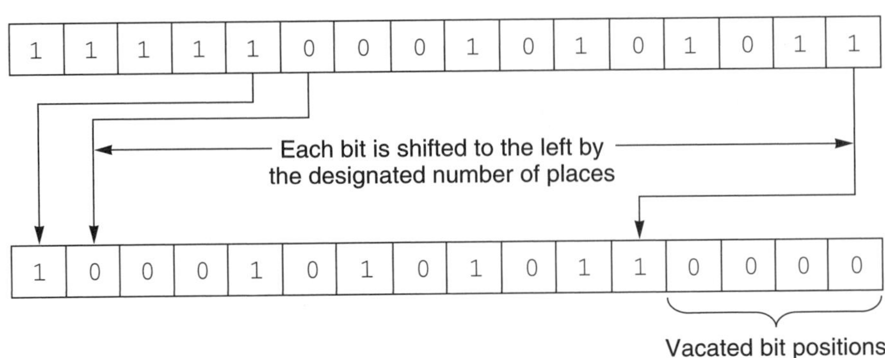

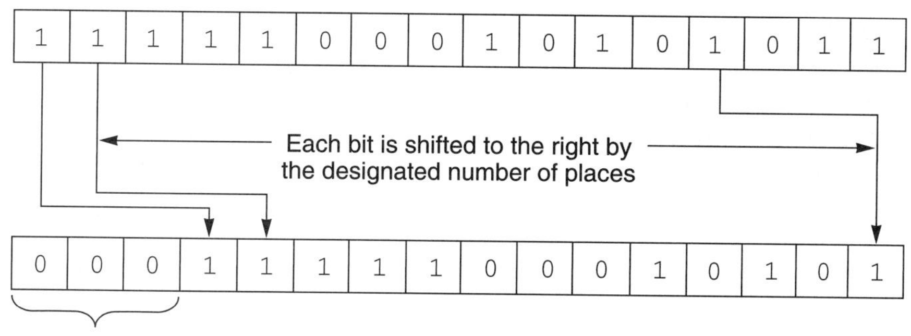

FIGURE F–7a An Unsigned Arithmetic Right Shift

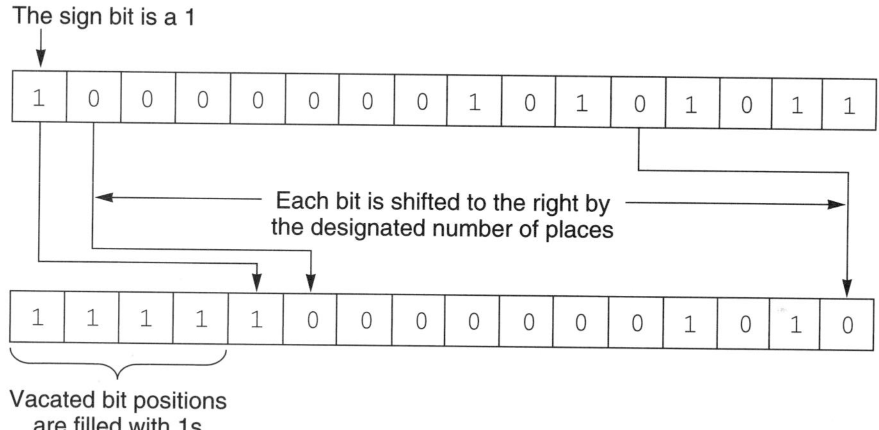

FIGURE F–7b The Right Shift of a Negative Binary Number

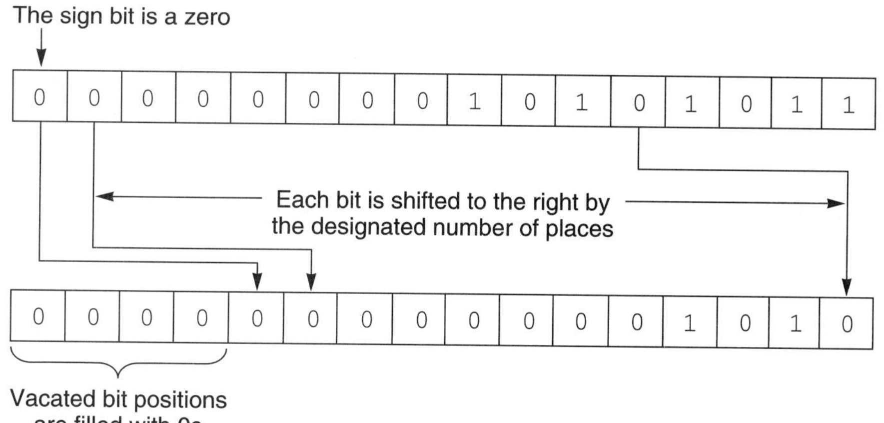

FIGURE F–7c The Right Shift of a Positive Binary Number

Instead of reproducing the sign bit in right-shifted signed numbers, some compilers automatically fill the vacated bits with 0s. This type of shift is called a *logical shift.* For positive signed numbers, where the leftmost bit is 0, both arithmetic and logical right shifts produce the same result. The results of these two shifts are different only when negative numbers are involved.

Appendix G Linked Lists Using Classes

Linked lists provide a convenient method for maintaining lists of items, without the need to reorder and restructure a list continually as items are added or deleted. For example, consider the list of names and phone numbers previously introduced in Section 10.4 and reproduced here as Figure G–1.[1]

Constructing a linked list for this case requires that each record have the same format, which includes an address that points to the next record in the list. Clearly, the last record cannot have a valid address pointing to another record, because there is none. Thus, for this last record we will use a `NULL` address that will act as a sentinel or flag to indicate when the last record has been processed. The `NULL` address value, like its end-of-string counterpart, has a numerical value of zero.

Besides an end-of-list sentinel value, either a pointer or a reference variable must also be provided to store the address of the first record in the list. Figure G–2 illustrates the complete set of addresses and records for the first three names and addresses shown in Figure G–1.

This concept can be easily extended to create a linked list of objects suitable for storing any number of names and telephone numbers. The following interface is suitable for such a class:

FIGURE G–1 A Telephone List in Alphabetical Order

Acme, Sam
(555) 898-2392

Dolan, Edith
(555) 682-3104

Lanfrank, John
(555) 718-4581

Mening, Stephen
(555) 382-7070

Zemann, Harold
(555) 219-9912

[1] Before reading this appendix, the interested reader should be familiar with the introductory material on linked lists provided in Section 10.4.

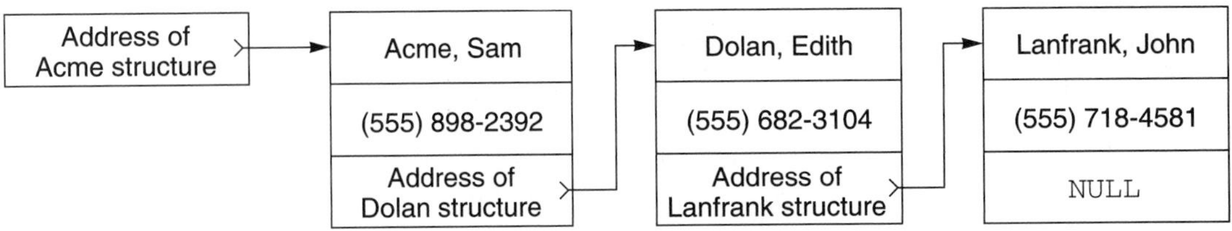

FIGURE G–2 Use of the Initial and Final Address Values

```
// class declaration (interface)
class TeleType
{
  private:
    char name[30];
    char phone[15];
    TeleType *nextaddr;
  public:
    TeleType(char *, char *);  // a constructor
    TeleType *getAddr(); // function returns a pointer to an object of type TeleType
    void setAddr(TeleType *);
    void display();
};
```

This interface declares three data and four function members. The first data member is an array of 30 characters, suitable for storing names with a maximum of 29 letters and an end-of-string `NULL` marker. The next data member is an array of 15 characters, suitable for storing telephone numbers with their respective area codes. The last data member is a pointer suitable for storing the address of an object of the class `TeleType`. The member functions consist of a constructor and three access functions. We will define these functions using the implementation section

```
// class implementation

TeleType::TeleType(char *newName, char *newPhone)
{
  strcpy(name, newName);
  strcpy(phone, newPhone);
  nextaddr = NULL;
}
TeleType *TeleType::getAddr()
{
  return nextaddr;
}
```

```
void TeleType::setAddr(TeleType *nextad)
{
  nextaddr = nextad;
}
void TeleType::display()
{
   cout << "\n" << setiosflags(ios::left)
        << setw(30) << name
        << setw(20) << phone;
}
```

The constructor and display functions are rather straightforward. The constructor copies its first string parameter to the `name` data member and its second string parameter to the `phone` data member. Finally, it initializes its pointer data member with a `NULL` address. The display function simply outputs the values contained in the `name` and `phone` variables. The remaining two access functions, `getAddr()` and `setAddr()`, are used to retrieve and set addresses, respectively, into the pointer data member of an object.

As defined in the implementation, `setAddr()` expects to receive the address of a `TeleType` object and assigns this address to its pointer member. Similarly, `getAddr()` simply returns the address stored in its pointer member—that is, it returns a pointer to an object of type `TeleType`.

Program G-1 illustrates the use of the `TeleType` class by specifically creating three objects of this class. The three objects are named `t1`, `t2`, and `t3`, and each object is initialized with a name and telephone number when the objects are defined, using the data listed in Figure G–1.

The output produced by executing Program G-1 is

```
Acme, Sam                     (555) 898-2392
Dolan, Edith                  (555) 682-3104
Lanfrank, John                (555) 718-4581
```

Because we have already described the class construction, let us now concentrate on the `main()` function in Program G-1 and see how it creates this output. Figure G–3 illustrates the relationship between the three objects created by the program.

From within `main()`, the three objects illustrated in Figure G–3, `t1`, `t2`, and `t3`, are defined. Each of these objects is of class type `TeleType`. Although each object consists of three members, only the first two members of each object are explicitly initialized by the user. Because both of these members are arrays of characters, they can be initialized with strings. The remaining member of each object is a pointer, which is initialized to a `NULL` address by the constructor.

Program G-1

```
#include <iostream.h>
#include <iomanip.h>
#include <string.h>
```

```
// class declaration (interface)
class TeleType
{
  private:
    char name[30];
    char phone[16];
    TeleType *nextaddr;
  public:
    TeleType(char *, char *);  // a constructor
    TeleType *getAddr();  // function returns a pointer to an object of type TeleType
    void setAddr(TeleType *);
    void display();
};

// class implementation
TeleType::TeleType(char *newName, char *newPhone)
{
  strcpy(name, newName);
  strcpy(phone, newPhone);
  nextaddr = NULL;
}
TeleType *TeleType::getAddr()
{
  return nextaddr;
}
void TeleType::setAddr(TeleType *nextad)
{
  nextaddr = nextad;
}
void TeleType::display()
{
   cout << "\n" << setiosflags(ios::left)
        << setw(30) << name
        << setw(20) << phone;
}
```

```
int main()
{
  int i;
  TeleType t1("Acme, Sam", "(555) 898-2392");
  TeleType t2("Dolan, Edith", "(555) 682-3104");
  TeleType t3("Lanfrank, John", "(555) 718-4581");
  TeleType *first, *current;

  first = &t1;            // store t1's address in first
  t1.setAddr(&t2);        // store t2's address in t1.nextaddr
  t2.setAddr(&t3);        // store t3's address in t2.nextaddr

  current = first;         // set current to first
  while (current != NULL)
  {
    (*current).display();              // same as current->display()
    current = (*current).getAddr();    // same as current->getAddr()
  }

  return 0;
}
```

To create a linked list from these three objects, each pointer member must be assigned the address of the next object in the list. The three assignment statements in Program G-1 perform the correct assignments. The expression `first = &t1` stores the address of the `t1` object in the pointer variable named `first`. The function call `t1.setAddr(&t2)` uses `t1`'s `setAddr()` function to store the address of `t2` in `t1`'s pointer variable. The result of this call is `t1.nextaddr = &t2`. Similarly, the function call `t2.setAddr(&t3)` stores the starting address of the `t3` object into the pointer member of the `t2` object (that is, `t2.next = &t3`). The list is automatically terminated by the `NULL` address placed in `t3.next` when the `t3` object was initialized.

Once values have been assigned to each object member and correct addresses have been stored in the appropriate pointers, the addresses can be used to loop through the complete list for display purposes. As each object is accessed, it can be either examined to select a specific value or used to print out a complete list. This is done by `main()`'s `while` loop.

The expression `(*current).display()` in the `while` loop calls the `display()` function of the object pointed to by `current`. Because `current` is initially set to the address of the `t1` object, the function that is called is `t1.display()`. This display function, as defined in the class implementation

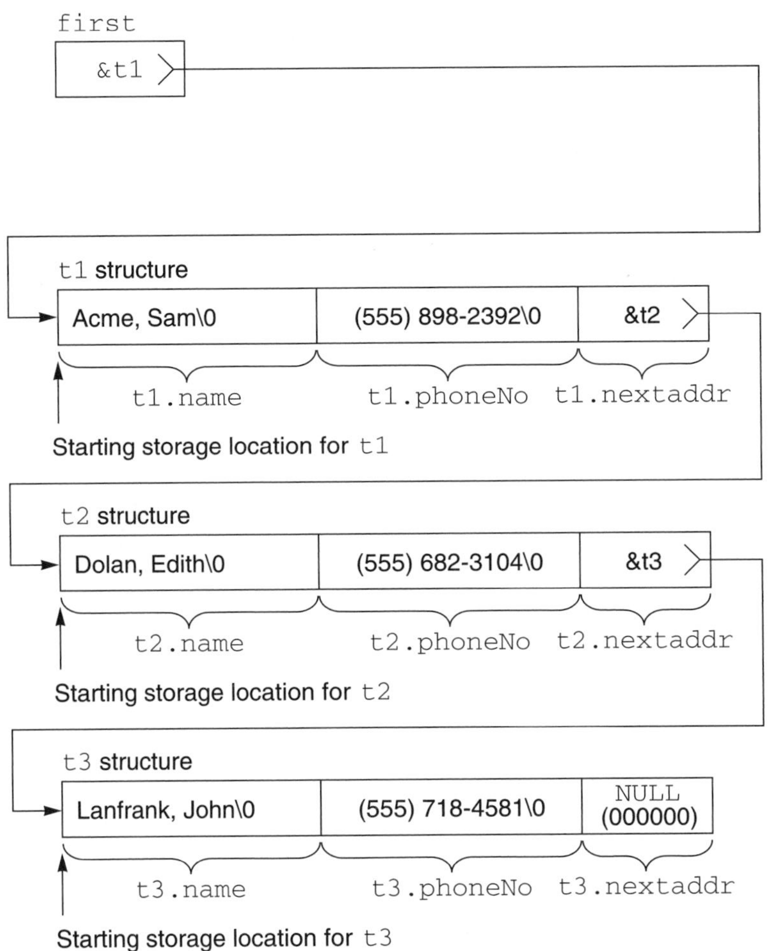

FIGURE G–3 The Relationship Between Objects in Program G-1

section, outputs its object's name and phone number values. `t1`'s `getAddr()` function is then called, which assigns the address in `t1.nextaddr` to `current`. Because `t1.nextaddr` contains the address of the `t2` object, the second time through the loop the `t2.display()` function is called. This process is repeated until the `NULL` address in `t3.nextaddr` is encountered. Note that the expression `(*current).display()` in the `while` loop can be replaced by the equivalent expression `current->display()`.

The important concept illustrated by Program G-1 is the use of the address in one object to access members of the next object in the list. Within `main()`, the `while` loop is used to cycle through the linked objects, starting with the object whose address is in `next`. The condition tested in the `while` statement compares the value in `next`, which is an address, to the `NULL` value. For each valid address, the name and phone number members of the addressed object are displayed. The address in `next` is then updated with the address in the pointer member of the current object. The address in `next` is then retested, and the process continues while the address in `next` is not equal to the `NULL` value. The loop "knows" nothing about the names of the objects declared in `main()` or even how many objects exist. It simply cycles through the linked list, object by object, until it encounters the end-of-list `NULL` address. The value of `NULL` is zero, so the tested condition can be replaced by the equivalent expression `!next`.

A disadvantage of Program G-1 is that exactly three objects are defined in `main()` by name, and storage for them is reserved at compile time. Should a fourth object be required, the additional object would have to be declared and the program recompiled. This limitation is removed by dynamically allocating and freeing storage for objects at run time, as storage is required. Only when a new object is to be added to the list, and while the program is running, is storage for the new object created. Similarly, when an object is no longer needed and can be deleted from the list, the storage for the deleted record is relinquished and returned to the computer.

Program G-2 illustrates using dynamic storage allocation, using the `new` operator, which was described in Sections 8.2 and 10.5, to create an object dynamically in response to a user-input request.

A sample session produced by Program G-2 is

```
Do you wish to create a new record (respond with y or n): y
Enter a name: Monroe, James
Enter a phone number: (617) 555-1817
The contents of the record just created is:
Name: Monroe, James
Phone Number: (617) 555-1817
```

In reviewing Program G-2, note the statement

```
recPoint = new TeleType(newName, newPhone);
```

in `main()`. This statement calls the `new` function to create an object of type `TeleType`, initializes the newly created object with the strings contained in the character arrays `newName` and `newPhone` (via the constructor), and stores the address returned by `new` in the pointer variable `recPoint`. The complete operation of `main()` is as follows:

If a user enters `y` in response to the first prompt in `main()`, the user is requested to enter a name and telephone number. A call is then made to `new`, as just described.

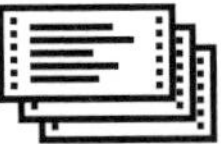

Program G-2

```
#include <iostream.h>
#include <iomanip.h>
#include <string.h>

class TeleType
{
  private:
    char name[30];
    char phone[16];
  public:
    TeleType(char *, char *);  // a constructor
    void display();
};

// class implementation
TeleType::TeleType(char *newName, char *newPhone)
{
  strcpy(name, newName);
  strcpy(phone, newPhone);
}
void TeleType::display()
{
   cout << "\n" << setiosflags(ios::left)
        << setw(30) << name
        << setw(20) << phone;
}

int main()
{
  char key, newName[30], newPhone[16];
  TeleType *recPoint; // a pointer to an object of type TeleType

  cout << "\nDo you wish to create a new record (respond with y or n): ";
  key = cin.get();
  if (key == 'y')
  {
    key = cin.get();  // get the Enter key in buffered input
    cout << "\nEnter a name: ";
    cin.getline(newName,30);
    cout << "Enter a phone number: ";
    cin.getline(newPhone,16);
    recPoint = new TeleType(newName, newPhone);
    (*recPoint).display();    // same as recPoint->display()
  }
  else
    cout << "\nNo record has been created";

  return 0;
}
```

The newly created object's `display()` function is then called to display the contents of the newly created and initialized object. The mechanism for calling `display()` is identical to that previously described for Program G-2.

Once you understand the mechanism of calling `new`, you can use this function to construct a linked list of objects. The address in the pointer member of each object in the list must be the starting address of the next object in the list. Additionally, a pointer must be reserved for the address of the first object, and the pointer member of the last object in the list is given a `NULL` address to indicate that no more members are being pointed to.

Program G-3 illustrates the use of `new` to construct a linked list of names and phone numbers. The `display()` function used in Program G-3 is the same function used in Program G-1.

The first time `new` is called in Program G-3, it is used to create the first object in the linked list. Thus the address returned by `new` is stored in the pointer variable named `newpoint`. The address in `newpoint` is then assigned to the pointer named `current`. This pointer variable is always used by the program to point to the current object. Because the current object is the first object created, the address in the pointer named `list` is assigned to the pointer named `current`.

Within `main()`'s `for` loop, the name and phone number members of the newly created object are populated and the pointer member of the current object is assigned an address. This address is the address of the next object in the list, which is obtained from `new`. The call to `new` creates the next object and returns its address into the pointer member of the current object. This completes the population of the current member. The final statement in the `for` loop resets the address in the current pointer to the address of the next object in the list.

After the last object has been created, the `while` loop in `main()` displays all the objects in the list. A sample run of Program G-3 is provided below:

```
Enter a name: Acme, Sam
Enter a phone number: (555) 898-2392
Enter a name: Dolan, Edith
Enter a phone number: (555) 682-3104
Enter a name: Lanfrank, John
Enter a phone number: (555) 718-4581
The list consists of the following records:


Acme, Sam                    (555) 898-2392
Dolan, Edith                 (555) 682-3104
Lanfrank, John               (555) 718-4581
```

Program G-3

```
#include <iostream.h>
#include <iomanip.h>
#include <string.h>
```

```
// class declaration (interface)
class TeleType
{
  private:
    char name[30];
    char phone[16];
    TeleType *nextaddr;
  public:
    TeleType(char *, char *); // a constructor
    TeleType *getAddr(); // function returns a pointer
                         // to an object of type TeleType
    void setAddr(TeleType *);
    void display();
};

// class implementation
TeleType::TeleType(char *newName, char *newPhone)
{
  strcpy(name, newName);
  strcpy(phone, newPhone);
  nextaddr = NULL;
}
TeleType *TeleType::getAddr()
{
  return nextaddr;
}
void TeleType::setAddr(TeleType *nextad)
{
  nextaddr = nextad;
}
void TeleType::display()
{
   cout << "\n" << setiosflags(ios::left)
        << setw(30) << name
        << setw(20) << phone;
}
```

```
int main()
{
  char newName[30], newPhone[16];
  TeleType *first, *current, *newpoint;

  // create the first object in the list
    cout << "\nEnter a name: ";
    cin.getline(newName,30);
    cout << "Enter a phone number: ";
    cin.getline(newPhone,16);
    current = new TeleType(newName, newPhone);
    first = current;   // save the first address

    for(int i = 1; i <= 2; i++)  // create 2 more objects
    {
      cout << "\nEnter a name: ";
      cin.getline(newName,30);
      cout << "Enter a phone number: ";
      cin.getline(newPhone,16);
      newpoint = new TeleType(newName, newPhone);
      (*current).setAddr(newpoint);
      current = newpoint;
    }

    current = first;
    while (current != NULL)
    {
      (*current).display();
      current = (*current).getAddr();
    }

  return 0;
}
```

Just as `new` dynamically creates storage while a program is executing, the `delete` function restores a block of storage to the computer while the programming is executing. The only argument required by `delete` is the starting address of a block of storage that was dynamically allocated. Thus any address returned by `new` can subsequently be passed to `delete` to restore the reserved memory to the computer. `delete` does not alter the address passed to it but simply removes the storage that the address references.

Appendix H Namespaces

A new feature introduced as part of the ANSI/ISO draft C++ standard is the concept of namespaces, which essentially is a rather simple principle. A *namespace* is a space of code (that is, a section of code) that must be enclosed in braces, can include only definitions or other namespaces, and is given an explicit name. For example, the following section of code consists of two namespaces named `screen` and `printer`, respectively, where each namespace consists of a single definition statement.

```
namespace screen   // the keyword namespace is required
{
  int lines = 5;
}  // end of screen namespace

namespace printer  // the keyword namespace is required
{
  int lines = 10;
}  // end of printer namespace
```

Note that the namespace concept simply provides a means of explicitly naming a blocked section of definition statements. Namespaces are really scoping mechanisms that are used to clearly identify variables within different blocks of code. The only restriction on a namespace is that it can consist only of definition statements and additional internally nested namespaces. The naming of the blocked code provides a means of identifying different variables that may have the same name but reside in different namespaces. This identification is accomplished by prefixing every variable name with its namespace name and the scope resolution operator, `::`. To illustrate how this is accomplished, consider Program H-1.

In reviewing Program H-1, note first that we have used the new style C++ header without the `.h` suffix. All of these new C++ headers are members of a namespace named `std`, which is short for standard. Thus, whenever an identifier defined in this header is used, such as `cout` or `endl`, it must also be preceded by its namespace name and the scope resolution operator, as in `std::cout` and `std::endl`. This is the case also for the variables named `lines` defined in the namespaces `screen` and `printer`. To identify clearly which `line` variable is being accessed, it must be preceded by its namespace name and the scope resolution operator. The output produced when Program H-1 is executed is

```
The screen lines are: 5
The printer lines are: 10
```

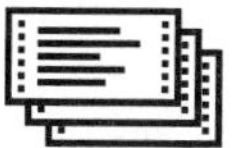

Program H-1

```
#include <iostream>

namespace screen
{
      int lines = 5;
}  // end of screen namespace

namespace printer
{
      int lines = 10;
}  // end of printer namespace

int main()
{
  std::cout << "\nThe screen lines are: "
            << screen::lines << std::endl;
  std::cout << "\nThe printer lines are: "
            << printer::lines;
  std::cout << std::endl;

    return 0;
}
```

The need to append `std::` to each standard library identifier can be quite annoying, although it may someday become the conventional programming style, for a reason that we will explain shortly. To avoid constantly including the `std::` prefix, however, you can either use the old-style `.h` header files, as we have done throughout the text, or include the following statement after the `#include <iostream>` header:

```
using namespace std;
```

This statement declares the namespace `std` as a default, and any variables in this namespace can now be used without the `std::` prefix. Note that we can also use the statement `using namespace screen;` at any point after the `screen` namespace has been defined. Then, whenever the variable `lines` is encountered, it will refer to the `screens::lines` variable. However, if the statement `using namespace printer;` was also used, a conflict would arise when the variable `lines` was used. The compiler would flag this with a `"using ambiguous symbol"` error message.

Clearly, the `using` statement effectively defeats the explicit scope naming provided by namespaces. Because the primary motivation for namespaces was to avoid the possibility of scoping conflicts, especially as more and more third-party libraries become available, the convention for writing C++ programs may eventually be always to include the namespace name when a Standard Library component is used. Finally, all namespaces must appear at file scope or immediately within another namespace. C++ now considers file scope as effectively another namespace, so the terms *file scope* and *global namespace scope* are synonymous.

Appendix I The Standard Template Library

A driving force behind object-oriented programming was the desire to create easily reusable source code. For example, recreating source code each time an array or queue is needed wastes both time and programming effort, to say nothing of the additional time required for fully testing and verifying code that may be only minimally modified. Suppose, for example, that a single program needs to use three arrays: an array of characters, an array of integers, and an array of double-precision numbers. Rather than coding three different arrays, it makes more sense to implement each array from a single, fully tested generic array class that comes complete with methods and algorithms for processing the array, such as sorting, inserting, finding maximum and minimum values, locating values, randomly shuffling values, copying arrays, comparing arrays, and dynamically expanding and contracting the array, as needed. This generic type of data structure, which is referred to as a *container,* forms the basis of the Standard Template Library (STL). In addition to providing seven types of generic data structures, one of which is the array container class (which is formally referred to as the vector container class), the STL provides methods and algorithms for appropriately operating on each of its generic data structures.

This generic programming approach for the STL was initially provided by Hewlett-Packard Corporation in 1994 and has subsequently been incorporated as part of the ANSI/ISO recommendations for inclusion into C++'s Standard Library.[1] In addition to the STL, the Standard Library provides two other major sections:

- **Input/Output headers.** These provide support for conversions between text and encoded data, and for input and output to external files. More specifically, these headers consist of `<fstream>`, `<iomanip>`, `<ios>`, `<iosfwd>`, `<iostream>`, `<istream>`, `<ostream>`, `<stream>`, `<streambuf>`, and `<strstream>`.

- **Other Standard C++ headers.** These include language support for common type definitions, such as `<limits>`; diagnostic components for reporting exceptional conditions, such as `<stdexcept>`; string components for string classes, which are provided by `<string>`; and the 18 additional Standard C Library headers.

---

[1] The initial Hewlett-Packard STL developers were Alexander Stepanov and Meng Lee, with major contributions made by David Musser.

The *Standard Template Library,* which is the third major section of the Standard Library, is divided into the following three categories:

- **Containers,** which are the template classes from which individual data structures can be constructed. By definition, a *container* is an STL template class that manages a sequence of elements. There are currently seven container classes that are used to construct vector, list, deque, stack, queue, set, and map data structures, respectively.

- **Algorithms,** which are template functions (see Section 6.1) that provide useful search, sort, location, and other numeric functions that can be applied to the various data structures created from the container classes.

- **Iterators,** which can be considered generalized pointers for keeping track of the beginning, ending, and other positions within a data structure. Specifically, iterators are used to keep track of the first and last positions in a data structure and to establish the boundaries of sequences of elements to which an algorithm is applied.

Table I–1 lists the 13 headers provided by the Standard Template Library. Seven of the headers are container types, which are used to create data structures; three of the headers are concerned with providing algorithmic capabilities; and three of the headers are concerned with providing iterator capabilities.

In its most general usage, one or more container classes are first used to create the desired data structures. Once these desired data structures have been created, class methods and algorithms, both of which are always constructed as functions, can be applied to them. Iterators, which act like generalized pointers, are used as arguments by all of the algorithms to determine and keep track of which elements in the data structure are to be operated upon.

To make this more tangible and provide a meaningful introduction to using the STL, we will use the vector container class to create two vectors: one for holding integers and one for holding characters. A vector is similar to a C++ array, except that it can automatically expand and contract as needed. We will then use two vector methods and two algorithms to operate on the instantiated vectors. Specifically, one method is used to change an existing element value and another to insert an element within each vector. The first algorithm is next used to sort the elements in each vector, and the second algorithm is used to randomly reshuffle each vector's elements. After each method and algorithm is applied, a `cout` object is employed to display the results. To see how this is accomplished, consider Program I-1.

TABLE I–1 Standard Template Headers

Name	Type	Description
<algorithm>	algorithm	Defines numerous function templates that implement algorithms
<functional>	algorithm	Defines templates required by <algorithm> and <numeric>
<numeric>	algorithm	Defines several function templates that implement numeric functions
<deque>	container	Defines a template class that implements a deque container
<list>	container	Defines a template class for implementing a list container
<map>	container	Defines template classes for implementing associative containers
<queue>	container	Defines a template class for implementing a queue container
<set>	container	Defines template classes for implementing associative containers that have unique elements
<stack>	container	Defines a template class for implementing a stack container
<vector>	container	Defines a template class for implementing a vector container
<iterators>	iterator	Defines templates for defining and manipulating iterators
<memory>	iterator	Defines templates for allocating and freeing container class memory storage
<utility>	iterator	Defines several general-utility templates

In reviewing Program I-1, first note the inclusion of the three header files `<iostream>`, `<vector>`, and `<algorithm>` with the `using namespace std;` statement.[2] Here we need the `<iostream>` header to create and use the `cout` stream; the `<vector>` header to create one or more vector objects; and the `<algorithm>` header for the two algorithms we will be using, named `sort()` and `random_shuffle()`, respectively.

[2] Review Appendix H for the purpose of the `using namespace std;` statement.

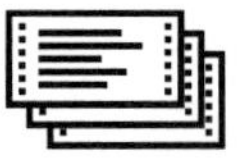

Program I-1

```
#include <iostream>
#include <vector>
#include <algorithm>
using namespace std;

int main()
{
  const int NUMELS = 5;
  int a[NUMELS] = {1,2,3,4,5};
  char b[NUMELS] = {'a','b','c','d','e'};
  int i;

    // instantiate an integer and character vector
    // using a constructor to set the size of each vector
    // and initialize each vector with values
  vector<int> x(a, a + NUMELS);
  vector<char> y(b, b + NUMELS);

  cout << "\nThe vector x initially contains the elements: "  << endl;
  for (i = 0; i < NUMELS; i++)
    cout << x[i] << "  ";
  cout << "\nThe vector y initially contains the elements: " << endl;
  for (i = 0; i < NUMELS; i++)
    cout << y[i] << "  ";

    // instantiate two ostream objects
  ostream_iterator<int> outint(cout, "  ");
  ostream_iterator<char> outchar(cout, "  ");

    // modify elements in the existing list
  x.at(3) = 6;    //set element at position 3 to a 6
  y.at(3) = 'f'; // set element at position 3 to an 'e'
    // add elements to the end of the list
  x.insert(x.begin() + 2,7);  // insert a 7 at position 2
  y.insert(y.begin() + 2,'g'); // insert an 'f' at position 2

  cout << "\n\nThe vector x now contains the elements: "  << endl;
  copy(x.begin(), x.end(), outint);
  cout << "\nThe vector y now contains the elements: " << endl;
  copy(y.begin(), y.end(), outchar);

    //sort both vectors
  sort(x.begin(), x.end());
  sort(y.begin(), y.end());

  cout << "\n\nAfter sorting, vector x's elements are: "  << endl;
  copy(x.begin(), x.end(), outint);
  cout << "\nAfter sorting, vector y's elements are:" << endl;
  copy(y.begin(), y.end(), outchar);
```

```
    // random shuffle the existing elements
  random_shuffle(x.begin(), x.end());
  random_shuffle(y.begin(), y.end());

  cout << "\n\nAfter random shuffling, vector x's elements are:"  << endl;
  copy(x.begin(), x.end(), outint);
  cout << "\nAfter random shuffling, vector y's elements are:" << endl;
  copy(y.begin(), y.end(), outchar);

  cout << endl;
  return 0;
}
```

The two statements in Program I-1 that are used to create and initialize each vector are

```
vector<int> x(a, a + NUMELS);
vector<char> y(b, b + NUMELS);
```

Here, the vector `x` is declared as a vector of type `int` and is initialized with elements from array `a` starting with the first element of the array, located at address `a`, which contains the element `a[0]`, and ending with the element at location `a + NUMELS`, which contains the element `a[NUMELS - 1]`. Thus the vector `x` now has a size sufficient for five integers and has been initialized with the values 1, 2, 3, 4, and 5. Similarly, vector `y` now has an exact size for five characters and has been initialized with the values a, b, c, d, and e. The next set of statements in Program I-1 display the initial values in each vector, using standard subscripted vector notation that is identical to the notation used for accessing array elements. Displaying the vector values in this manner, however, requires knowing how many elements each vector contains. As we insert and remove elements, we would like the vector class itself to keep track of where the first and last elements are; this capability is, in fact, automatically provided by two iterator methods furnished for each vector, named `begin()` and `end()`. Before using these two functions, we will construct two iterator-dependent output objects for making the output display of elements rather simple, using the statements

```
ostream_iterator<int> outint(cout, "  ");
ostream_iterator<char> outchar(cout, "  ");
```

As we will see momentarily, the `outint` and `outchar` objects (the two names are programmer-selected) can be used to display all vector values contained between two iterators with two spaces provided between values, before the value is placed on the cout stream.

The next major set of statements,

```
 // modify elements in the existing list
x.at(3) = 6;    //set element at position 3 to a 6
y.at(3) = 'f'; // set element at position 3 to an 'e'
  // add elements to the end of the list
x.insert(x.begin() + 2,7);    // insert a 7 at position 2
y.insert(y.begin() + 2,'g'); // insert an 'f' at position 2
```

is used both to modify existing vector values and to insert a new value into each vector. Specifically, the `at()` method requires an integer value for its argument, whereas the `insert()` method requires as arguments an iterator and the value to be inserted. Specifically, the `at()` argument of `3` indicates that the fourth element in each vector will be changed (remember that vectors, like arrays, begin at index position 0). This means that the value `4`, which is in the fourth position in the integer array, will be changed to a `6`, and the value `'d'` in the character array will be changed to an `'f'`. The `insert()` method is then used to insert values of `7` and `'g'` in the third position for both vectors. Note that, as for pointers, iterator arithmetic is allowed. Because the `begin()` method returns the iterator value corresponding to the start of the vector, adding 2 to it points to the third position in the array. It is at this position that the new value is inserted with all subsequent values moved up by one position in the vector, the vector automatically expanding to accept the inserted value. At this point in the program, the vector `x` now contains the elements

```
1  2  7  3  6  5
```

and the vector `y` now contains the elements

```
a  b  g  c  f  e
```

For vector `x`, this arrangement was obtained by replacing the original value of `4` with a `6` and then inserting a `7` in the third position, which moved all subsequent elements up by one position and increased the total vector size to accommodate six integers. A similar process resulted in the arrangement shown for vector `y`'s elements. To have the program display these elements, the statements

```
cout << "\n\nThe vector x now contains the elements: "  << endl;
copy(x.begin(), x.end(), outint);
cout << "\nThe vector y now contains the elements: " << endl;
copy(y.begin(), y.end(), outchar);
```

were used. The `copy()` algorithm uses two iterators, which are the values returned by the `begin()` and `end()` methods to delimit the beginning and ending positions to copy. In this case, a copy of each complete vector is made to the `outint` and `outchar` objects, respectively. Because these objects are standard output objects, the values placed on them are displayed on the screen, suitably interspaced with two spaces between elements.

Finally, the last section of code used in Program I-1 uses the `sort()` and `random_shuffle()` algorithms first to sort the elements in each vector and then to shuffle them randomly. Note that both of these algorithms use iterator values to determine the sequence of elements to be operated upon. After each algorithm is applied, the `copy()` algorithm is once again used to force an output display. Following is the complete output produced by Program I-1:

```
The vector x initially contains the elements:
1  2  3  4  5
The vector y initially contains the elements:
a  b  c  d  e

The vector x now contains the elements:
1  2  7  3  6  5
The vector y now contains the elements:
a  b  g  c  f  e

After sorting, vector x's elements are:
1  2  3  5  6  7
After sorting, vector y's elements are:
a  b  c  e  f  g

After random shuffling, vector x's elements are:
6  5  1  3  7  2
After random shuffling, vector y's elements are:
e  a  f  c  g  b
```

Appendix J Solutions to Selected Odd-Numbered Exercises

Section 1.1

1. A computer program is a structured combination of data and instructions that is used to operate a computer.

A programming language is the set of instructions, data, and rules that can be used to construct a program.

Programming is the process of using a programming language to produce a computer program.

An algorithm is a step-by-step sequence of instructions that describes how a computation is to be performed.

Pseudocode is a description of an algorithm using short, English-like statements.

A flowchart is a description of an algorithm that uses specifically defined graphical symbols.

A procedure is a logically consistent set of instructions that produces a specific result.

An object is a self-contained unit that consists of both data and the specific procedures that can be applied to the data.

A method is another term for the procedures contained within an object.

A message is the means used to activate a particular method within an object.

A response is what is produced by an object in reaction to receiving a message.

A class defines a general set of data and procedural characteristics from which specific objects are created.

A source program consists of the program statements comprising a C++ or other programming language program.

An object program is the result of compiling a source program.

An executable program is a program that can be executed by a computer.

A compiler is a program that translates a source program into an object program.

An interpreter is a program that translates individual source program statements, one at a time, into executable statements. Each statement is executed immediately after translation.

3. Step 1: Pour the contents of the first cup into the third cup.
Step 2: Rinse out the first cup.
Step 3: Pour the contents of the second cup into the first cup.
Step 4: Rinse out the second cup.
Step 5: Pour the contents of the third cup into the second cup.

5. Step 1: Compare the first number with the second number and use the smallest of these numbers for the next step
Step 2: Compare the smallest number found in step 1 with the third number. The smallest of these two numbers is the smallest of all three numbers.

7. a. Step 1: Compare the first name in the list with the name JEANS. If the names match, stop the search; else go to step 2.
Step 2: Compare the next name in the list with the name JEANS. If the names match, stop the search; else repeat this step.

Section 1.2

1.
`m1234`	Valid. Not a mnemonic.
`newBal`	Valid. A mnemonic.
`abcd`	Valid. Not a mnemonic.
`A12345`	Valid. Not a mnemonic.
`1A2345`	Invalid. Violates Rule 1; starts with a number.
`power`	Valid. A mnemonic.
`absVal`	Valid. A mnemonic.
`invoices`	Valid. A mnemonic.
`do`	Invalid. Violates Rule 3; is a keyword.
`while`	Invalid. Violates Rule 3; is a keyword.
`add5`	Valid. Could be a mnemonic.
`taxes`	Valid. A mnemonic.
`netPay`	Valid. A mnemonic.
`12345`	Invalid. Violates Rule 1; starts with a number.
`int`	Invalid. Violates Rule 3; a keyword.
`newBalance`	Valid. A mnemonic.
`a2b3c4d5`	Valid. Not a mnemonic.
`salestax`	Valid. A mnemonic.
`amount`	Valid. A mnemonic.
`$taxes`	Invalid. Violates Rule 1; starts with a special character.

3. a.
```
inputBill()      // input the items purchased
calcSalestax()   // compute required salestax
calcBalance()    // determine balance owed
```

Section 1.3

1. a.
```
#include <iostream.h>
int main()
{
  cout << "Joe Smith";
  cout << "\n99 Somewhere Street";
  cout << "\nNonesuch, N.J., 07030";

  return 0;
}
```

3. a. Six `cout` statements would be used.

b. One would work by including newline escape sequences between each two items displayed.

c.
```
#include <iostream.h>
int main()
{
  cout << "PART NO.                    PRICE\n\n";
  cout << "T1267                       $6.34\n";
  cout << "T1300                       $8.92\n";
  cout << "T2401                      $65.40\n";
  cout << "T4482                      $36.99\n";

  return 0;
}
```

Section 1.4

1. ***a.*** Yes.

b. It is not in standard form. To make programs more readable and easier to debug, the standard form presented in Section 1.4 of the textbook should be used.

3. ***a.*** Two backslashes in a row causes one backslash to be displayed.

b. `cout << "\\ is a backslash.\n";`

Section 2.1

1. ***a.*** float or double

b. integer

c. float or double

d. integer

e. float or double

3. 1.23e2 6.5623e2 3.42695e3 4.8932e3 3.21e–1 1.23e–2 6.789e–3

9. ***a.*** $8 \times 1{,}048{,}576 = 8{,}388{,}608$ bytes

b. $16 \times 1{,}048{,}576 = 16{,}777{,}216$ bytes

c. $32 \times 1{,}048{,}576 = 33{,}554{,}432$ bytes

d. $96 \times 1{,}048{,}576 = 100{,}663{,}296$ bytes

e. $8 \times 1{,}048{,}576 = 8{,}388{,}608$ words $\times$ 2 bytes/word $= 16{,}777{,}216$ bytes

f. $16 \times 1{,}048{,}576 = 16{,}777{,}216$ words $\times$ 4 bytes/word $= 67{,}108{,}864$ bytes

g. $1.44 \times 1{,}048{,}576 = 1{,}509{,}949$ bytes

Section 2.2

1. ***a.*** 2 * 3 + 4 * 5

b. (6 + 18) / 2

c. 4.5 / (12.2 – 3.1)

d. 4.6 * (3.0 + 14.9)

e. (12.1 + 18.9) * (15.3 – 3.8)

3. Since all of the operands given are floating-point numbers, the result of each valid expression is a floating-point number.

a. 5
b. 10
c. 24.0
d. 0.2
e. 3.6
f. Invalid expression
g. –50
h. –2.5
i. Invalid expression
j. 10
k. 53

5. *a.* 27.0
b. 8.0
c. 1.0
d. 220.0
e. 22.67
f. 19.78
g. 6.0
h. 2.0

Section 2.3

1. `answer1` is the integer 2
`answer2` is the integer 5

5. *a.* The double quote after the 2nd insertion symbol should come before the symbol and the parentheses at the end of the statement should be a semicolon.
b. The `setw(4)` manipulator should not be enclosed in double quotes.
c. The `setprecision(5)` manipulator should not be enclosed in double quotes.
d. The statement should be `cout << "Hello World!";`
e. The `setw(6)` manipulator should appear before the insertion of the number 47.
f. The `setprecision(2)` manipulator should appear before the insertion of the number 526.768.

Section 2.4

1. The following are not valid:

`12345`	does not begin with either a letter or underscore
`while`	keyword
`$total`	does not begin with either a letter or underscore
`new bal`	cannot contain a space
`9ab6`	does not begin with either a letter or underscore
`sum.of`	contains a special character

3. *a.* `int count;`
b. `float grade;`
c. `double yield;`
d. `char initial;`

7. *a.*

```
#include <iostream.h>
int main()
{
  int num1, num2, total;  // declare the integer variables num1
                          // num2, and num3

  num1 = 25;              // assign the integer 25 to num1
  num2 = 30;              // assign the integer 30 to num2
  total = num1 + num2;  // assign the sum of num1 and num2 to total
  cout << "The total of " << num1 << " and "
       ,, num2 << " is " << total;    // displays the line:
                              // The total of 25 and 30 is 55.

  return 0;
}
```

9.

```
#include <iostream.h>
int main()
{
  int length, width, perim;

  length = 16;
  width = 18;
  perim = 2 * length + 2 * width;
  cout << "The perimeter is " << perim;

  return 0;
}
```

13. Every variable has a type (e.g., int, float, etc.), a value, and an address in memory where it is stored.

15. *a.*

Address:	159	160	161	162	163	164	165	166
					W	O	W	!
	rate				ch1	ch2	ch3	ch4

Address:	167	168	169	170	171	172	173	174
	taxes							

Address:	175	176	177	178	179	180	181	182
			0	0				
	num		count					

The empty addresses preceding are usually filled with *garbage* values, meaning their contents are whatever happened to be placed there by the computer or by the previously run program.

Section 2.5

1. *a.* For an IBM® PC or compatible computer using an Intel Pentium II processor, the storage size of a character is1 byte and an integer is 4 bytes.

b. For an IBM PC or compatible computer using an Intel Pentium II processor, 2 bytes are reserved for short integers, 4 bytes for unsigned integers, and 4 bytes for long integers.

3. All that is required to set aside the right amount of storage space for a variable is a definition statement.

Section 3.1

1. *a.*

```
#include <iostream.h>
int main()
{
                // missing declaration for all variables
  width = 15                  // missing semicolon
  area = length * width;      // no value assigned to length
  cout << "The area is " << area   // missing ;

  return 0;
 }
```

The corrected program is:

```
#include <iostream.h>
int main()
{
  int length, width, area;

  width = 15;
  length = 20;               // must be assigned some value
  area = length * width;
  cout << "The area is " << area;

  return 0;
}
```

b.
```
#include <iostream.h>
int main()
{
  int length, width, area;

  area = length * width; // this should come after the
                         // assignment of values to
  length = 20;           // length and width
  width = 15;
  cout << "The area is " << area;

  return 0;
}
```

The corrected program is:

```
#include <iostream.h>
int main()
{
  int length, width, area;

  length = 20;
  width = 15;
  area = length * width;
  cout << "The area is " << area;

  return 0;
}
```

c.
```
#include <iostream.h>
int main()
{
  int length = 20; width = 15, area; // semicolon after 20
                                     // should be a comma

  length * width = area;  // incorrect assignment statement
  cout << "The area is " << area;

  return 0;
}
```

The corrected program is:

```
#include <iostream.h>
int main()
{
  int length = 20, width = 15, area;

  area = length * width;
  cout << "The area is " << area;

  return 0;
}
```

3. *a.*

```
#include <iostream.h>
int main()
{
  float radius, circum;

  radius = 3.3;    // could have been done in the declaration
  circum = 2 * 3.1416 * radius;
  cout << "The circumference is " << circum << "inches";

  return 0;
}
```

5. *a.*

```
#include <iostream.h>
int main()
{
  float length, width, depth, volume;

  length = 25.0;
  width = 10.0;
  depth = 6.0;
  volume = length * width * depth;
  cout << "The volume of the pool is " << volume;

  return 0;
}
```

7. *a.*

```
#include <iostream.h>
int main()
{
  float  total;

  total = 12*.50 + 20*.25 + 32*.10 + 45*.05 + 27*.01;
  cout << "The total amount is $ " << total << endl;

  return 0;
}
```

9. *c.*

```
#include <iostream.h>
int main()
{
  float speed = 58.0, dist = 183.67, time;

  time = dist/speed;
  cout << "The elapsed time for the trip is " << time " hours";

  return 0;
}
```

11. The second expression is correct because the assignment of 25 to b is done before the subtraction. Without the parentheses the subtraction has the higher precedence and the expression a – b is calculated, yielding a value, assume 10. The subsequent attempt to assign the value of 25 to this value is incorrect and is equivalent to the expression 10 = 25. Values can only be assigned to variables.

Section 3.2

1. a. sqrt(6.37)
b. sqrt(x – y)
c. sin(30.0 * 3.1416 / 180.0)
d. sin(60.0 * 3.1416 / 180.0)
e. abs(pow(a,2.0) – pow(b,2.0)) or abs(a*a + b*b)
f. exp(3.0)

5.
```
#include <iostream.h>
#include <math.h>
int main()
{
  float dist, x1 = 7.0, y1 = 12.0 , x2 = 3.0 , y2 = 9.0;

  dist = sqrt(pow((x1-x2),2.0) + pow((y1-y2),2.0));
  cout << "The distance is " << dist << endl;

  return 0;
}
```

Section 3.3

1. a. `cin >> firstnum;`
b. `cin >> grade;`
c. `cin >> secnum;`
d. `cin >> keyval;`
e. `cin >> month >> years >> average;`
f. `cin >> num1 >> num2 >> grade1 >> grade2`
g. `cin >> interest >> principal >> capital >> price >> yield;`
h. `cin >> ch >> letter1 >> letter2 >> num1 >> num2 >> num3;`
i. `cin >> temp1 >> temp2 >> temp3 >> volts1 >> volts2;`

3. a.
```
#include <iostream.h>
int main()
{
  float fahr, cel;
  cout << "Enter the temperature in degrees Fahrenheit: ";
  cin  >> fahr;
  cel = (5.0/9.0)*(fahr - 32.0;
  cout << fahr << " degrees Fahrenheit is "
       << cel << " degrees Celsius\n";

  return 0;
}
```

5. a.
```
#include <iostream.h>
int main()
{
  float miles, gallons, mpg;

  cout << "Enter the miles driven: ";
  cin  >> miles;
  cout << "Enter the gallons of gas used: ";
  cin  >> gallons;
  mpg = miles/gallons;
  cout << "The miles/gallon is " << mpg << endl;

  return 0;
}
```

7. a.
```
#include <iostream.h>
int main()
{
  float num1, num2, num3, num4, avg;

  cout << "Enter a number: ";
  cin  >> num1;
  cout << "\nEnter a second number: ";
  cin  >> num2;
  cout << "\nEnter a third number: ";
  cin  >> num3;
  cout << "\nEnter a fourth number: ";
  cin  >> num4;
  avg = (num1 + num2 + num3 + num4) / 4.0;
  cout << "\nThe average of the four numbers is "
       << avg << endl;

  return 0;
}
```

c.
```
#include <iostream.h>
int main()
{
  float number, avg, sum = 0;

  cout << "Enter a number: ";
  cin  >> number;
  sum = sum + number;
  cout << "\nEnter a second number: ";
  cin  >> number;
  sum = sum + number;
```

(continued on next page)

(continued from previous page)

```
    cout << "\Enter a third number: ";
    cin  >> number;
    sum = sum + number;
    cout << "\nEnter a fourth number: ";
    cin  >> number;
    sum = sum + number;
    avg = sum / 4.0;
    cout << "\nThe average of the four numbers is "
         << avg << endl;

    return 0;
}
```

11. a. It is easy for a user to enter incorrect data. If wrong or unexpected data is given by the user, either incorrect results will be obtained or the program will *crash*. A crash is an unexpected and premature program termination.

b. In a *data type check* the input is checked to ensure that the values entered are of the correct type for the declared variables. This includes checking that integer values are entered for integer variables, and so on. A *data reasonableness check* determines that the value entered is reasonable for the particular program. Such a check would determine if a large number was entered when a very small number was expected, if a small number was entered when a large number was expected, or if a zero (which could cause problems if the number was the denominator in a division) or a negative number was entered when a positive number was expected, and so on.

c. Data type checks would ensure that the month, day, and year were all entered as integers. Some simple reasonableness checks would ensure that a month was between 1 and 12, a day between 1 and 31, and a year between reasonable limits for the application. More complex reasonableness checks might check that days in months 1, 3, 5, 7, 8, 10, and 12 were between 1 and 31; days in months 4, 6, 9, and 11 were between 1 and 30, and days in month 2 were between 1 and 28 (except for a leap year, in which case the day must be between 1 and 29).

Section 3.4

1.

```
#include <iostream.h>
int main()
{
  const float PI = 3.1416;
  float radius,circum;

  cout << "\nEnter a radius: ";
  cin  >> radius;
  circum = 2.0 * PI * radius;
  cout << "\nThe circumference of the circle is "
       << circum << endl;

  return 0;
}
```

3.
```
#include <iostream.h>
int main()
{
  const float FREEZING = 32.0;
  const float CONVERT = 5.0/9.0;
  float fahren,celsius;

  cout << "\nEnter a temperature in degrees Fahrenheit: ";
  cin  >> fahren;
  celsius = CONVERT * (fahren - FREEZING);
  cout << "\nThe equivalent Celsius temperature is "
       << celsius << endl;

  return 0;
}
```

Section 4.1

1. ***a.*** The relational expression is true. Therefore its value is 1.
b. The relational expression is true. Therefore its value is 1.
c. The final relational expression is true. Therefore its value is 1.
d. The final relational expression is true. Therefore its value is 1.
e. The final relational expression is true. Therefore its value is 1.
f. The arithmetic expression has a value of 10.
g. The arithmetic expression has a value of 4.
h. The arithmetic expression has a value of 0.
i. The arithmetic expression has a value of 10.

3. ***a.*** `age == 30`
b. `temp  98.6`
c. `ht < 6.00`
d. `month == 12`
e. `let_in == 'm'`
f. `age == 30  ht > 6.00`
g. `day == 15  month == 1`
h. `age > 50 || employ >= 5`
i. `id < 500  age > 55`
j. `len > 2.00  len < 3.00`

Section 4.2

1.
```
#include <iostream.h>
int main()
{
  const int LIMIT = 20000;
  const float REGRATE = .02;
  const float HIGHRATE = .025;
  const int FIXED = 400;
  float taxable, taxes;
```

(continued on next page)

(continued from previous page)

```
  cout << "Please type in the taxable income: ";
  cin  >> taxable;
  if (taxable <= LIMIT)
    taxes = REGRATE * taxable;
  else
    taxes = HIGHRATE * (taxable - LIMIT) + FIXED;
  cout << "\n\nTaxes are $ " << taxes << endl;

  return 0;
}
```

3. a.

```
#include <iostream.h>
int main()
{
  float grade;

  cout << "Enter a grade: " ;
  cin  >> grade;

  if (grade >= 70.0)
    cout << "A passing grade\n";
  else
    cout << "A failing grade\n";

  return 0;
}
```

5. a.

```
#include <iostream.h>
int main()
{
  char status;

  cout << "Enter the status: " ;
  cin  >> status;

  if (status == 's')
    cout << "The senior person's salary is $400.00\n";
  else
    cout << "The junior person's salary is $275.00\n";

  return 0;
}
```

7. a.
```
#include <iostream.h>
int main()
{
  int month, day;

  cout << "Enter a month (use a 1 for Jan, 2 for Feb, etc.): ";
  cin  >> month;
  cout << "Enter a day of the month: ";
  cin  >> day;

  if (month > 12 || month < 1)
    cout << "\nAn incorrect month was entered.";

  if (day < 1 || day > 31)
    cout << "\nAn incorrect day was entered.";

  return 0;
}
```

b. If a user enters a floating-point number, the integer part of the number will be assigned to the integer variable `month`. The month will be correct. The program uses the remaining fractional value for the day input. Since the variable `day` is declared as an integer, a value of zero will be assigned to `day`. A possible solution is to accept the `month` variable as a floating-point number, then reassign it to an integer variable to correctly truncate it. No harm is done then if an integer is entered for the month (`scanf()` will first convert it to a floating-point number) or if a floating-point number is entered. More correctly, a cast should be used, as described in Section 3.2.

9.
```
#include <iostream.h>
int main()
{
  char in_key;
  int position;

  cout << "Enter a lowercase letter: ";
  cin  >> in_key;
  if (in_key >= 'a' && in_key <= 'z')
  {
    position = in_key - 'a' + 1;
    cout << "The character's position is " << position;
  }
  else
    cout << "The character just entered is not a lowercase letter";

  return 0;
}
```

13. The error is that the intended relational expression `letter == 'm'` has been written as the assignment expression `letter = 'm'`. When the expression is evaluated the character `m` is assigned to the variable `letter` and the value of the expression itself is the value of `'m'`. Since this is a nonzero value, it is taken as true and the message is displayed.

Realize that, as written in the program, the `if` statement is equivalent to the following two statements:

```
letter = 'm';
if(letter) cout << "Hello there!";
```

A correct version of the program is:

```
#include <iostream.h>
int main()
{
  char letter;

  cout << "Enter a letter:  ";
  cin  >> letter;
  if (letter == 'm')
    cout << "Hello there!" << endl;

  return 0;
}
```

Section 4.3

1.
```
#include <iostream.h>
int main()
{
  float grade;
  char letter;

  cout << "Enter the student's numerical grade:  ";
  cin  >> grade;
  if (grade >= 90.0) letter = 'A';
  else if (grade >= 80.0) letter = 'B';
  else if (grade >= 70.0) letter = 'C';
  else if (grade >= 60.0) letter = 'D';
  else letter = 'F';
  cout << "\nThe student receives a grade of " << letter << endl;

  return 0;
}
```

Notice that an `if-else` chain is used. If simple `if` statements were used, a grade entered as 75.5, for example, would be assigned a 'C' because it was greater than 60.0. But the grade would then be reassigned to 'D' because it is also greater than 60.0.

3.
```
#include <iostream.h>
int main()
{
  float fahr, cels, in_temp;
  char letter;

  cout << "Enter a temperature followed by"
       << " one space and the temperature's type\n"
       << " (an f designates a fahrenheit temperature\n"
       << " and a c designates a celsius temperature): ";
  cin  >> in_temp >> letter;
  if (letter == 'f' || letter == 'F')
  {
    cels = (5.0/9.0)*(in_temp - 32.0);
    cout << in_temp << " degrees Fahrenheit = "
         << cels << " degrees Celsius\n";
  }
  else if (letter == 'c' || letter == 'C')
  {
    fahr = (9.0/5.0)*in_temp - 32.0;
    cout << in_temp << " degrees Celsius = "
         << fahr << " degrees Fahrenheit\n";
  }
  else cout << "The data entered is invalid.\n";

  return 0;
}
```

5. ***a.*** This program will run. It will not, however, produce the correct result.
b and c. This program evaluates correct incomes for `mon_sales` less than 20000.00 only. If 20000.00 or more were entered, the first `else-if` statement would be executed and all others would be ignored. That is, for 20000.00 or more, the income for >= 10000.00 would be calculated and displayed.

Had `if` statements been used in place of the `else-if` statements, the program would have worked correctly, but inefficiently.

Section 4.4

1.
```
switch (letGrad)
{
  case 'A':
    cout << "The numerical grade is between 90 and 100";
    break;
  case 'B':
    cout << "The numerical grade is between 80 and 89.9";
    break;
```

(continued on next page)

(continued from previous page)

```
    case 'C':
      cout << "The numerical grade is between 70 and 79.9";
      break;
    case 'D':
      cout << "How are you going to explain this one" << endl;
      break;
    default:
      cout << "Of course I had nothing to do with the grade." << endl;
      cout << "\nThe professor was really off the wall." << endl;
  }
```

3.
```
#include <iostream.h>
int main()
{
  char marcode;

  cout << "Enter a marital code: " << endl;
  cin  >> marcode;

  switch(marcode)
  {
    case 'M':
      cout << "\nIndividual is married." << endl;
      break;
    case 'S':
      cout << "\nIndividual is single." << endl;
      break;
    case 'D':
      cout << "\nIndividual is divorced." << endl;
      break;
    case 'W':
      cout << "\nIndividual is widowed." << endl;
      break;
    default:
      cout << "\nAn invalid code was entered." << endl;
  }  // end of switch

  return 0;
}
```

Section 5.1

1.
```
#include <iostream.h>
int main()
{
  int count = 2;

  while (count <= 10)
  {
    cout << count;
    count += 2;
  }
}
```

3. *a.* 21 items are displayed, which are the integers from 1 to 21.
   c. 21 items are still displayed, but they would be the integers from 0 to 20 because the `cout` stream is now activated before the increment.

5.
```
#include <iostream.h>
#include <iomanip.h>
int main()
{
  int feet = 3;
  float meters;

  cout << "\n";    // start on a new line
  cout << "  Feet     Meters\n";
  cout << "----------------\n";
  while (feet <= 30)
  {
    meters = feet / 3.28;
    cout << setw(5) << feet
         << setiosflags(ios::showpoint) << setw(10)
         << setprecision(2) << meters << endl;
    feet += 3;

  return 0;
  }
}
```

Section 5.2

1.
```
#include <iostream.h>
#include <iomanip.h>
int main()
{
  int count;
  float num, total;
  const int MAXCOUNT = 8;

  cout << "\nthis program will ask you to enter"
       << " eight numbers.\n";
  count = 1;
  total = 0;

  while (count <= MAXCOUNT)
  {
    cout << "\nenter a number: ";
    cin  >> num;
    total = total + num;
    cout << "The total is now " << total;
    count++;
  }
  cout << "\n\nthe final total is " << total << endl;

  return 0;
}
```

3. *a.*
```
#include <iostream.h>
#include <iomanip.h>
int main()
{
  int num;
  float cels, fahr, incr;

  cout << "Enter the starting temperature in degrees Celsius: ";
  cin  >> cels;
  cout << "\n\nEnter the number of conversions to be made: ";
  cin  >> num;
  cout << "\n\nNow enter the increment between conversions ";
  cout << "in degrees Celsius: ";
  cin  >> incr;
  cout << "\n\n\n";
  cout << "Celsius    Fahrenheit\n";
  cout << "---------------------\n";
  while (count <= num)
  {
```

```
        fahr = (9.0/5.0) * cels + 32.0;
        cout << setiosflags(ios::showpoint) << setw(7)
             << setprecision(2) << cels
             << setiosflags(ios::showpoint) << setw(15)
             << setprecision(2) << fahr;
        cels = cels + incr;
      }

      return 0;
    }
```

7. This program still calculates the correct values, but the average is now calculated four times. Since only the final average is desired, it is better to calculate the average once outside of the while loop.

9. *a.*

```
#include <iostream.h>
int main()
{
  int id, inven, income, outgo, bal, count;

  count = 1;
  while (count <= 3)
  {
    cout << "\nEnter book ID: ";
    cin  >> id;
    cout << "\nEnter inventory at the beginning of the month: ";
    cin  >> inven;
    cout << "\nEnter the number of copies received during the month: ";
    cin  >> income;
    cout << "\nNow enter the number of copies sold during the month: ";
    cin  >> outgo;
    bal = inven + income - outgo;
    cout << "\n\nBook #" << id << " new balance is " << bal << endl;
    count++;
  }

  return 0;
}
```

Section 5.3

1. 20 16 12 8 4 0

5.
```
#include <iostream.h>
#include <iomanip.h>
int main()
{
  int conv, count;
  float f, c;

  cout << "Enter the number of temperature conversions"
       << "\nfrom Fahrenheit to Celsius to be performed: ";
  cin  >> conv;
  cout << endl;
  cout << "Fahrenheit      Celsius\n";
  cout << "----------      -------\n";
  for (f = 20.0, count = 1; count <= conv; count++)
  {
    c = (f - 32.0) * (5.0/9.0);
    cout << setiosflags(ios::showpoint) << setw(4)
         << setprecision(1) << f
         << "       "
         << setiosflags(ios::showpoint) << setw(5)
         << setprecision(2) << c << endl;
    f += 4.0;
  }
  return 0;
}
```

7.
```
#include <iostream.h>
#include <iomanip.h>
int main()
{
  int count;
  float fahren, celsius;

  for(count = 1; count <= 6; ++count)
  {
    cout << "\nEnter a fahrenheit temperature: ";
    cin  >> fahren;
    celsius = (5.0/9.0)*(fahren - 32.0);
    cout << "\nThe corresponding celsius temperature is "
         << setiosflags(ios::showpoint) << setw(5)
         << setprecision(2) << celsius;
  }

  return 0;
}
```

11.
```
#include <iostream.h>
#include <iomanip.h>
int main()
{
  int yr;
  float total;

  for (total = 1000.00, yr = 1; yr <= 10; yr++)
  {
    total = total * 1.08;
    cout << "The balance at the end of " << n
         << " years is $" << setiosflags(ios::showpoint)
         << setw(8) << setprecision(2) << total << endl;
  }

  return 0;
}
```

15.
```
#include <iostream.h>
#include <iomanip.h>
int main()
{
  int i, j;
  float total, avg, data;
  const int EXPERS = 4;
  const int RESULTS = 6;

  for (i = 1; i <= EXPERS; i++)
  {
    cout << endl;
    cout << "Enter 6 results for experiment # " << i << ": ";
    for (j = 1, total = 0.0; j <= RESULTS; j++)
    {
      cin  >> data;
      total += data;
    }
    avg = total/RESULTS;
    cout << "   The average for experiment #" << i
         << " is " << setiosflags(ios::showpoint)
         << setw(6) << setprecision(2) << avg << endl;
  }

  return 0;
}
```

17.
```
#include <iostream.h>
#include <iomanip.h>
int main()
{
  int bowler, game;
  float score, plyr_tot, plyr_avg, team_tot, team_avg;

  const int BOWLERS = 5;
  const int GAMES = 3;

  for(bowler = 1, team_tot = 0; bowler <= BOWLERS; bowler++)
  {
    for(game = 1, plyr_tot = 0; game <= GAMES; game++)
    {
      cout << endl;
      cout << "Enter the score for bowler " << bowler << " game "<< game << ": ";
      cin  >> score;
      plyr_tot = plyr_tot + score;
    }
    team_tot = team_tot + plyr_tot;
    plyr_avg = plyr_tot/3.0;
    cout << "   The average for bowler " << bowler << " is "
         << setiosflags(ios::showpoint) << setw(5)
         << setprecision(2) << plyr_avg << endl;
  }
  team_avg = team_tot/15.0;
  cout << "The average for the whole team is "
       << setiosflags(ios::showpoint) << setw(5)
       << setprecision(2) << team_avg << endl;

  return 0;
}
```

Section 5.4

3. a.
```
#include <iostream.h>
int main()
{
  int num, digit;

  cout << "Enter an integer: ";
  cin  >> num;
  cout << "\nThe number reversed is: ";
  do
  {
    digit = num % 10;
    num /= 10;
    cout << digit;
  } while (num > 0);

  return 0;
}
```

Section 6.1

1. *a.* `factorial()` expects to receive one integer value.

b. `price()` expects to receive one integer and two double-precision values, in that order.

c. An int and two double-precision values, in that order, must be passed to `yield()`.

d. A character and two floating-point values, in that order, must be passed to `interest()`.

e. Two floating-point values must be passed to `total()`.

f. Two integers, two characters, and two floating-point values, in that order, are expected by `roi()`.

g. Two integers and two character values, in that order, are expected by `getVal()`.

3. *a.* The `FindAbs()` function is included in the program written for Exercise 3b.

b.
```
#include <iostream.h>
int main()
{
  double dnum;
  void FindAbs(double);   // function prototype

  cout << "Enter a number: ";
  cin  >> dnum;
  FindAbs(dnum);

  return 0;
}

void FindAbs(double num)
{
  double val;

  if (num < 0)
    val = -num;
  else
    val = num;
  cout << "The absolute value of " << num << " is " << val << endl;

  return;
}
```

5. *a.* The `square()` function is included in the program written for Exercise 5b.

b.
```
#include <iostream.h>
int main()
{
  double first;
  void square(double);   // function prototype

  cout << "\nEnter a number: ";
  cin  >> first;
  square(first);

  return 0;
}
void square(double num)
{
  cout << "The square of " << num << " is " << (num*num) << endl;

  return;
}
```

7. *a.* The function for producing the required table is included in the larger program written for Exercise 7b.

b.
```
#include <iostream.h>
#include <iomanip.h>
int main()
{
  void table();     // function prototype

  table();          // call the function

  return 0;
}

void table()
{
  int num;

  cout << endl
       << "NUMBER    SQUARE    CUBE\n"
       << "------    ------    ----\n";

  for (num = 1; num <= 10; num++)
    cout << setw(3) << num << "         "
         << setw(3) << num * num << "        "
         << setw(4) << num * num * num << endl;

  return;
}
```

Section 6.2

1.
```
#include <iostream.h>
int main()
{
  float firstnum, secnum, max;
  float FindMax(float, float);  // the function prototype

  cout << "\nEnter a number: ";
  cin  >> firstnum;
  cout << "Great! Please enter a second number: ";
  cin  >> secnum;

  max = FindMax(firstnum, secnum); // the function is called here

  cout << "\nThe maximum of the two numbers is " << max << endl;

  return 0;
}
```

```
float FindMax(float x, float y)
{                        // start of function body
  float maxnum;          // variable declaration

  if (x >= y)            // find the maximum number
    maxnum = x;
  else
    maxnum = y;

  return maxnum;         // return statement
}
```

3. *a.* `void check(int num1, float num2, double num3)`
b. `double FindAbs(double x);`
c. `float mult(float first, float second)`
d. `int square(int number)`
e. `int powfun(int num, int exponent)`
f. `void table(void)`

5. *a.* The `mult()` function is included in the program written for Exercise 5b.
b.

```
#include <iostream.h>
int main()
{
  double mult(double, double);     // function prototype
  double first, second;

  cout << "Please enter a number: ";
  cin  >> first;
  cout << "Please enter another number: ";
  cin  >> second;
  cout << "The product of these numbers is "
       << mult(first,second) << endl;

  return 0;
}

  double mult(double num1, double num2)
  {
    return (num1*num2);
  }
```

7. The polynomial function is included in the following working program.

```
#include <iostream.h>
int main()
{
  float a, b, c, x, result;
  float polyTwo(float, float, float, float); // prototype

  cout << "Enter the coefficient for the x squared term : ";
  cin  >> a;
  cout << "\nEnter the coefficient for x : ";
  cin  >> b;
  cout << "\nEnter the constant: ";
  cin  >> c;
  cout << "\nEnter the value for x: ";
  cin  >> x;
  result = polyTwo(a, b, c, x);
  cout << "\n\n\nThe result is " << result << endl;

  return 0;
}

float polyTwo(float c1, float c2, float c3, float x)
{
  return (c1*x*x + c2*x + c3);
}
```

13. *c.* The `fracpart()` function is included in the program written for Exercise 13d.

d.

```
#include <iostream.h>
int main()
{
  double num;
  double fracpart(double);   // function prototype

  cout << "Enter a number: ";
  cin  >> num;
  cout << "\nThe fraction part of " << num
       << " is " << fracpart(num) << endl;

  return 0;
}

double fracpart(double x)
{
  int whole(double);    // function prototype
```

```
  return (x - whole(x));
}
int whole(double n)
{
  int a;

  a = n;   // a = int (n) is preferred - see Section 3.2
  return a;
}
```

Section 6.3

1. a. `float &amount;`
b. `double &price`
c. `int &minutes;`
d. `char &key;`
e. `double &yield;`

3.
```
#include <iostream.h>
int main()
{
  int firstnum, secnum, max;
  void FindMax(int, int, int &);  // function prototype

  cout << "Enter a number: ";
  cin  >>  firstnum;
  cout << "\nGreat! Please enter a second number: ";
  cin  >> secnum;

  FindMax(firstnum, secnum, max); // call the function

  cout << "\nThe maximum of the two numbers is " << max << endl;

  return 0;
}
void FindMax(int x, int y, int &maxval)
{
  if (x >= y)
     maxval = x;
  else
     maxval = y;
  return;
}
```

5.
```
void time(int tot_sec, int &hrs, int &mins, int &secs)
{
  hrs = tot_sec/3600;   // 3600 seconds = 1 hour
                        //  Integer division yields the whole
                        //  number of times 3600 goes into
                        //  tot_sec
  tot_sec -= hrs * 3600;
  mins = tot_sec/60;
  tot_sec -= mins * 60;
  secs = tot_sec;

  return;
}
```

Section 6.4

1. *a.*

Variable Name	Data Type	Scope
`PRICE`	integer	global to `int main()`, `roi()`, and `step()`
`YEARS`	long integer	global to `int main()`, `roi()`, and `step()`
`YIELD`	double precision	global to `int main()`, `roi()`, and `step()`
`bondtype`	integer	local to `int main()` only
`interest`	double precision	local to `int main()` only
`coupon`	double precision	local to `int main()` only
`count`	integer	local to `roi()` only
`effectiveRate`	double precision	local to `roi()` only
`numofyrs`	integer	local to `step()` only
`fracpart`	float	local to `step()` only

Note that although arguments of each function assume a value that is dependent on the calling function, these arguments can change values within their respective functions. This makes them behave as if they were local variables within the called function.

3. All function arguments have local scope with respect to their defined function.

Section 6.5

1. *a.* Local variables may be automatic, static, or register. It is important to realize that not all variables declared inside functions are necessarily local. An example of this is an external variable.

   b. Global variables may be static or external.

3. The first function declares `yrs` to be a static variable and assigns a value of 1 to it only once when the function is compiled. Each time the function is called thereafter, the value in `yrs` is increased by 2. The second function also declares `yrs` to be static, but assigns it the value 1 every time it is called, and the value of `yrs` after the function is finished will always be 3. By resetting the value of `yrs` to 1 each time it is called, the second function defeats the purpose of declaring the variable to be static.

5. The *scope of a variable* tells where the variable is recognized in the program and can be used within an expression. If, for example, the variable `years` is declared inside a function, it is local and its scope is inside that function only. If the variable is declared outside of any function, it is global and its scope is anywhere below the declaration but within that file, unless another file of the same program extends the scope of the variable by declaring the variable to be external.

Section 7.1

1. *a.* `int grades[100];`
b. `float temp[50];`
c. `int code[30];`
d. `int year[100];`
e. `float velocity[32];`
f. `float dist[1000];`
g. `int code_num[6];`

3. *a.* `cin >> grades[0] >> grades[2] >> grades[6];`
b. `cin >> prices[0] >> prices[2] >> prices[6];`
c. `cin >> amps[0] >> amps[2] >> amps[6];`
d. `cin >> dist[0] >> dist[2] >> dist[6];`
e. `cin >> velocity[0] >> velocity[2] >> velocity[6];`
f. `cin >> time[0] >> time[2] >> time[6];`

5. *a.* `a[1] a[2] a[3] a[4] a[5]`
b. `a[1] a[3] a[5]`
c. `b[3] b[4] b[5] b[6] b[7] b[8] b[9] b[10]`
d. `b[3] b[6] b[9] b[12]`
e. `c[2] c[4] c[6] c[8] c[10]`

7.
```
#include <iostream.h>
int main()
{
  const int NUMELS = 8;
  int grade[NUMELS], sum, i;
  float average;

  sum = 0;    // initialize here or in the declaration
  for( i = 0; i < NUMELS; i++)
  {
    cout << "Enter a value for element number " << i << " : ";
    cin  >> grade[i];
    sum = sum + grade[i];
  }
  cout << "\nThe values stored in the array are:\n";
  for (i = 0; i < NUMELS; i++)
    cout << grade[i] << "   ";
  average = sum / NUMELS;

  cout << "\nThe average of these values is "
       << average << endl;

  return 0;
}
```

9. a.
```
#include <iostream.h>
#include <iomanip.h>
int main()
{
  const int NUMELS = 14;
  int grades[NUMELS], total, i;
  float avg, deviation[14];

  total = 0;
  for(i = 0; i < NUMELS; i++)
  {
    cout << "Enter grade # " << (i + 1) << " : ";
    cin  >> grades[i];
    total += grades[i];
  }
  avg = total/NUMELS;
  cout << "\n The average of the grades is " << avg << endl
       << "Element     Element      Deviation\n"
       << "Number       Value        from Avg.\n"
       << "-------     -------      ----------\n";
  for(i = 0; i < NUMELS; i++)
  {
    deviation[i] = grades[i] - avg;
    cout << setw(4) << i << "    "
         << setw(10) << grades[i] << "     "
         << setiosflags(ios::showpoint) << setw(10)
         << setprecision(2) << deviation[i] << endl;
  }

  return 0;
}
```

11. a.
```
#include <iostream.h>
int main()
{
  const int NUMELS = 10;
  double raw[NUMELS], sorted[NUMELS], min = 1.e5;
  int i, j, index;

  for(i = 0; i < NUMELS; i++)
  {
    cout << "Enter value # " << (i+1) << " : ";
    cin  >> raw[i];
  }
  for(i = 0; i < NUMELS; i++)
  {
```

```
      for(j = 0; j < NUMELS; j++)  // find the minimum for this pass
      {
        if(raw[j] < min) // look for next min
        {
          min = raw[j];
          index = j;
        }
      }
      sorted[i] = min;       // put min in next sorted element
      min = 1.e5;            // reset min for start of search
      raw[index] = 1.e7;     // don't select this element again
    }
    cout << "The elements in sorted order are:\n";
    for( i = 0; i < NUMELS; i++)
      cout << sorted[i] << endl;

    return 0;
  }
```

b. To locate each minimum, make a complete pass through the array and find the first minimum. Now only nine numbers need be searched since one has been used. After the second lowest element has been selected, only the remaining eight need be searched. Instead of 10 squared passes through the loop, only 10 factorial passes are needed. The number of passes can be reduced using a shell sort rather than a bubble sort.

Section 7.2

1. *a.* `int grades[10] = {89, 75, 82, 93, 78, 95, 81, 88, 77, 82};`

b. `double amount[5] = {10.62, 13.98, 18.45, 12.68, 14.76};`

c. `double rates[100] = {6.29, 6.95, 7.25, 7.35, 7.40, 7.42};`

d.
```
float temp[64] = {78.2, 69.6, 68.5, 83.9, 55.4, 67.0, 49.8,
                                58.3, 62.5, 71.6};
```

e. `char code[15] = {'f', 'j', 'm', 'q', 't', 'w', 'z'};`

3.
```
#include <iostream.h>
int main()
{
  const int NUMELS = 9;
  float slopes[NUMELS] = {17.24, 25.63,  5.94,
                          33.92,  3.71, 32.84,
                          35.93, 18.24,  6.92};
  int i;
  float max = 0.0, min = 999.9;

  for(i = 0; i < NUMELS; i++)
  {
    if (slopes[i] < min) min = slopes[i];
    if (slopes[i] > max) max = slopes[i];
  }
  cout << "\nThe minimum array value is " << min;
  cout << "\nThe maximum array value is " << max << endl;

  return 0;
}
```

5.
```
char goodstr1[12] = {'G', 'o', 'o', 'd', ' ',
                     'M', 'o', 'r', 'n', 'i', 'n', 'g'};

char goodstr1[] = {'G', 'o', 'o', 'd', ' ',
                   'M', 'o', 'r', 'n','i', 'n', 'g'};
char goodstr1[] = "Good Morning";
```

Note: The last declaration creates an array having one more character than the first two. The extra character is the null character.

Section 7.3

1.
```
void sort_arr(double in_array[500])
               or
void sort_arr(double in_array[])
```

5.
```
#include <iostream.h>
const int NUMELS = 9;
int main()
{
  float rates[NUMELS] = {6.5, 7.2, 7.5, 8.3, 8.6,
                         9.4, 9.6, 9.8, 10.0};
  void show(float []);  // function prototype
  show(rates);
  return 0;
}
void show(float rates[])
{
  int i;
  cout << "\nThe elements stored in the array are:\n";
  for(i = 0; i < NUMELS; i++)
    cout << rates[i] << "  \n";
  return;
}
```

7.
```
#include <iostream.h>
#include <iomanip.h>
const int NUMELS = 10;
int main()
{
  double price[NUMELS] = {10.62, 14.89, 13.21, 16.55, 18.62,
                          9.47, 6.58, 18.32, 12.15, 3.98};
  double quantity[NUMELS] = {4.0, 8.5, 6.0, 7.35, 9.0,
                             15.3, 3.0, 5.4, 2.9, 4.8};
  double amount[NUMELS];
  int i;
  void extend(double [[], double [], double []); // prototype
  extend(price, quantity, amount);
  cout << "The elements in the amount array are:";
  for(i = 0; i < NUMELS; i++)
    cout << setiosflags(ios::showpoint)
         << setw(17) << setprecision(3)
         << amount[i] << endl;
  return 0;
}
void extend(double prc[], double qnty[], double amt[])
{
  int i;
  for(i = 0; i <= 9; i++)
    amt[i] = prc[i] * qnty[i];
  return;
}
```

Section 7.4

1. *a.* `int array[6][10];`
b. `int codes[2][5];`
c. `char keys[7][12];`
d. `char letter[15][7];`
e. `double vals[10][25];`
f. `double test[16][8];`

3.
```
#include <iostream.h>
int main()
{

  const int ROW = 3;
  const int COL = 4;

  int i, j, total = 0;
  int val[ROW][COL] = {8,16,9,52,3,15,27,6,14,25,2,10};

  for (i = 0; i < ROW; i++)
    for (j = 0; j < COL; j++)
      total = total + val[i][j];
  cout << "\nThe total of the values is " << total << endl;

  return 0;
}
```

5. *a.*
```
#include <iostream.h>
int main()
{

  const int NROWS = 4;
  const int NCOLS = 5;

  int i, j, total = 0;
  int max = -999;
  int val[NROWS][NCOLS] = {16, 22,  99, 4, 18,
                         -258,  4, 101, 5, 98,
                          105,  6,  15, 2, 45,
                           33, 88,  72, 16, 3};

  for (i = 0; i < NROWS; i++)
    for (j = 0; j < NCOLS; j++)
   if (val[i][j] > max)
    max = val[i][j];
  cout << "\nThe maximum array value is " << max << endl;

  return 0;
}
```

Section 8.1

1. `&average` means "the address of the variable named average"

3. a.
```
#include <iostream.h>
int main()
{
  int num, count;
  long date;
  float yield;
  double price;

  cout << "The address of the variable num is "
       << &num << endl;
  cout << "The address of the variable count is "
       << &count << endl;
  cout << "The address of the variable date is "
       << &date << endl;
  cout << "The address of the variable yield is "
       << &yield << endl;
  cout << "The address of the variable price is "
       << &price << endl;

  return 0;
}
```

5. a. `*xAddr`
b. `*yAddr`
c. `*ptYld`
d. `*ptMiles`
e. `*mptr`
f. `*pdate`
g. `*distPtr`
h. `*tabPt`
i. `*hoursPt`

7. a. Each of these variables are pointers. This means that addresses will be stored in each of these variables.
b. They are not very descriptive names and do not give an indication that they are pointers.

9. All pointer variable declarations must have an asterisk. Therefore, `c`, `e`, `g`, and `i` are pointer declarations.

11.

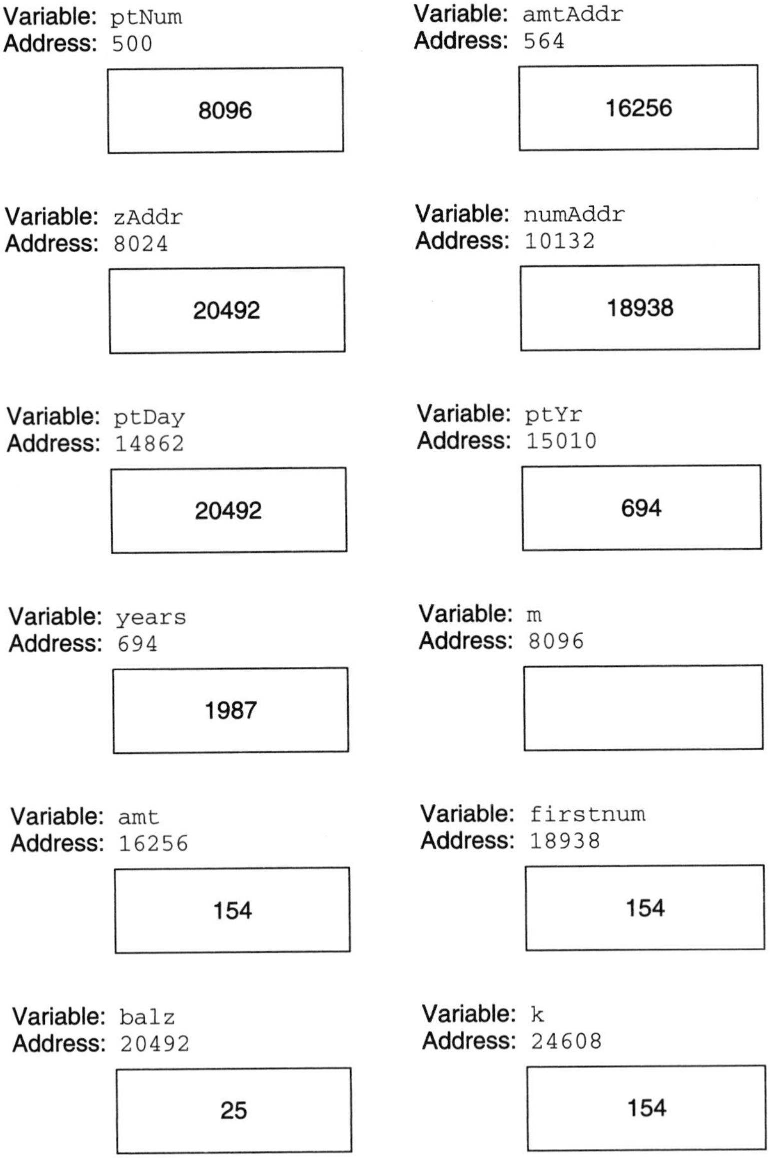

Variable: `ptNum`
Address: `500`

8096

Variable: `amtAddr`
Address: `564`

16256

Variable: `zAddr`
Address: `8024`

20492

Variable: `numAddr`
Address: `10132`

18938

Variable: `ptDay`
Address: `14862`

20492

Variable: `ptYr`
Address: `15010`

694

Variable: `years`
Address: `694`

1987

Variable: `m`
Address: `8096`

Variable: `amt`
Address: `16256`

154

Variable: `firstnum`
Address: `18938`

154

Variable: `balz`
Address: `20492`

25

Variable: `k`
Address: `24608`

154

Section 8.2

1. *a.* `*(prices + 5)`
b. `*(grades + 2)`
c. `*(yield + 10)`
d. `*(dist + 9)`
e. `*mile`
f. `*(temp + 20)`
g. `*(celsius + 16)`
h. `*(num + 50)`
i. `*(time + 12)`

3. *a.* The declaration `double prices [5];` causes storage space for five double precisionnumbers, creates a pointer constant named `prices`, and equates the pointer constant to the address of the first element (`&prices[0]`).
b. Each element in prices contains eight bytes, and there are five elements for a total of 40 bytes.
c.

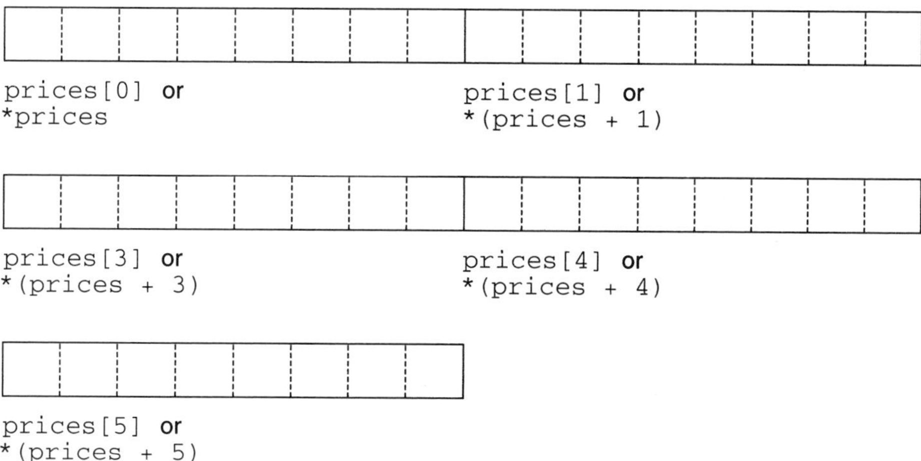

d. The byte offset for this element, from the beginning of the array, is 3 * 8 = 24 bytes.

5.
```
#include <iostream.h>
int main()
{
  const int NUMS = 7;
  float rates[] = {12.9, 18.6, 11.4, 13.7, 9.5, 15.2, 17.6};
  int i;

  cout << "The elements of the array are:\n";
  for(i = 0; i < NUMS; i++)
    cout << "    " << *(rates + i);    // The variable pointed
                                       // to by rates offset by i
  return 0;
}
```

Section 8.3

3. *a.*
```
#include <iostream.h>
int main()
{
  char strng[] = "Hooray for all of us";
  char *mess_pt;

  mess_pt = &strng[0];    // mess_pt = strng; is equivalent
  cout << "\nThe elements in the array are: ";
  for(  ; *mess_pt != '\0'; mess_pt++)
    cout << *mess_pt;
  cout << endl;

  return 0;
}
```

b.
```
#include <iostream.h>
int main()
{
  char strng[] = "Hooray for all of us";
  char *mess_pt;

  mess_pt = &strng[0];    // mess_pt = strng; is equivalent
  cout << "\nThe elements in the array are: ";
  while (*mess_pt != '\0')  // search for the null character
    cout << *mess_pt++;
  cout << endl;

  return 0;
}
```

Section 8.4

1.
```
void sort_arr(double in_array[500])

void sort_arr(double in_array[])

void sort_arr(double *in_array)
```

5. The problem with this method of finding the maximum value lies in the line

```
if(max < *vals++)  max = *vals;
```

This statement compares the correct value to `max`, but then increments the address in the pointer before any assignment is made. Thus, the element assigned to `max` by the expression `max = *vals` is one element beyond the element pointed to within the parentheses.

9. a. The following output is obtained:

```
33
16
99
34
```

This is why:

```
*(*val) = *(val[0]) = val[0][0] = 33;
*(*val + 1) = *(val[1]) = val[0][1] = 16;
*(*(val + 1) + 2) = *(*(val[1]) + 2) = *(val[1][2]) = 99;
*(*val) + 1 = *(val[0]) + 1 = val[0][0] + 1 = 33 + 1 = 34.
```

In other words, for any two-dimensional array, `arr[x][y]`, what we really have is two levels of pointers. What is meant by `*(arr + x)` is that there are x number of pointers, each successively pointing to `arr[1][0], arr[2][0], arr[3][0],...,` `arr[x][0]`. So an expression such as `*(*(arr + x) + y)` translates to `arr[x][y]`.

Section 9.1

1. b.

```
#include <iostream.h>
int main()
{
  char line[80];
  void vowels(char []); // function prototype

  cout << "Enter a string.\n";
  cin.getline(line,80);
  vowels(line);

  return 0;
}

void vowels(char strng[])
{
  int i = 0, v = 0; // Array element number and vowel counter
  char c;

  while((c = strng[i++]) != '\0')
  switch(c)
  {
    case 'a':
    case 'e':
    case 'i':
    case 'o':
    case 'u':
   cout << c;
   v++;
  }
  cout << endl;
  cout << "There were " << v << " vowels.\n";

  return;
}
```

3. *a.* The function is included in the program written for Exercise 3b.

b.
```
#include <iostream.h>
int main()
{
  const int NUMCHARS = 80;
  char strng[NUMCHARS];
  void countStr(char []);  // function prototype

  cout << "Enter a line of text\n";
  cin.getline(strng,NUMCHARS);
  countStr(strng);

  return 0;
}
void countStr(char message[])
{
  int i;
  for(i = 0; message[i] != '\0'; i++);  // The semicolon at
                                        // the end of this
                                        // statement is the
                                        // null statement
  cout << "\nThere number of total characters, "
       << "including blanks,\nin the line just entered is "
       << i << ".\n";

  return;
}
```

7.
```
#include <iostream.h>
int main()
{
  const int NUMCHARS = 80;
  char word[NUMCHARS];
  void delChar(char [], int, int);   // function prototype

  cout << "Enter a string\n";
  cin.getline(word,NUMCHARS);
  cout << "The word just entered is: " << word << endl;
  delChar(word, 13, 5); // string, how many to delete, starting position
  cout << word << endl;  // display the edited string

  return 0;
}
void delChar(char strng[], int x, int pos)
{
  int i, j;

  i = pos-1;   // first element to be deleted (actually, overwritten)
  j = i + x;   // first element beyond delete range
  while (strng[j] != '\0')
    strng[i++] = strng[j++];  // copy over an element
  strng[i] = '\0';   // close off the edited string
  return;
}
```

This program assumes the number of characters to be deleted actually exists. Otherwise the `while` loop would not terminate (unless it just happened to encounter another `null` character somewhere in memory beyond the original string).

9. a. The `ToUpper()` function is included in the program written for Exercise 9c.

c.
```
#include <iostream.h>
int main()
{
  const int NUMCHARS = 80;
  char strng[NUMCHARS];
  int i = 0;
  char ToUpper(char ch);    // function prototype
  cout << "Enter a line of text\n";
  cin.getline(strng,NUMCHARS);
  while (strng[i] != '\0')  // get the character
  {
    strng[i] = ToUpper(strng[i]);  // send it to the function
    i++;                           // move to next character
  }
  cout << "The string, with all lowercase letters"
       << " converted is:\n";
  cout << strng << endl;
  return 0;
}
char ToUpper(char ch)
{
  if ( ch >= 'a' && ch <= 'z')     // test it
    return(ch - 'a' + 'A');        // change it, if necessary
   else
     return(ch);
}
```

11.
```
#include <iostream.h>
int main()
{
  const int NUMCHARS = 80;
  char strng[NUMCHARS];
  int i = 0, count = 1;
  cout << "Enter a line of text\n";
  cin.getline(strng,NUMCHARS);
  if(strng[i] == ' ' || strng[i] == '\0')
    count--;
  while(strng[i] != '\0')
  {
    if(strng[i] == ' ' && (strng[i + 1] != ' ' && strng[i + 1] != '\0'))
      count++;      // encountered a new word
    i++;            // move to the next character
  }
  cout << "\nThe number of words in the line just entered is " << count << endl;
  return 0;
}
```

The program increases the word count whenever a transition from a blank to a nonblank character occurs. Thus, even if words are separated by more than one space the word count will be incremented correctly. Initially the program assumes the text starts with a word (`count = 1`). If the first character is either a blank or an end-of-string `Null`, this assumption is incorrect and the `count` is decremented to zero.

Section 9.2

1. *a.*
```
*text = 'n'
*(text + 3) = ' '
*(text + 10) = ' '
```
b.
```
*text = 'r'
*(text + 3) = 'k'
*(text + 10) = 'o'
```
c.
```
*text = 'H'
*(text + 3) = 'p'
*(text + 10) = 'd'
```
d.
```
*text = 'T'
*(text + 3) = ' '
*(text + 10) = 'h'
```

3.
```
#include <iostream.h>
int main()
{
  const int NUMCHARS = 80;
  char line[NUMCHARS];
  void vowels(char *);    // function prototype

  cout << "Enter a string.\n";
  cin.getline(line,NUMCHARS);
  vowels(line);

  return 0;
}
void vowels(char *strng)   // strng treated as a pointer variable

{
  int v = 0;     // v = vowel counter
  char c;

  while((c = *strng++) != '\0')   // an address is incremented
  switch(c)
  {
    case 'a':
    case 'e':
    case 'i':
    case 'o':
    case 'u':
      cout << c;
      v++;
  }
  cout << "\nThere were " << v << " vowels.\n";

  return;
}
```

5.
```
#include <iostream.h>
int main()
{
  const int NUMCHARS = 80;
  char strng[NUMCHARS];
  void count_str(char *);    // function prototype

  cout << "Enter a line of text\n";
  cin.getline(strng,NUMCHARS);
  count_str(strng);

  return 0;
}

void count_str(char *message)    // message as a pointer variable
{
  int count;

  for(count = 0; *message++ != '\0'; ++count) ; // The semicolon at the
                                // end of this statement is the null statement
  cout << "\nThe number of total characters, including blanks,"
       << "\nin the line just entered is " << count << ".\n";

  return;
}
```

7.
```
#include <iostream.h>
int main()
{
  const int NUMCHARS = 80;
  char forward[NUMCHARS], rever[NUMCHARS];
  void reverse(char *, char *); // function prototype

  cout << "\nEnter a line of text:\n";
  cin.getline(forward,NUMCHARS);
  reverse(forward,rever);
  cout << "\nThe text: " << forward;
  cout << "\nspelled backwards is: " << rever << endl;

  return 0;
}

void reverse(char *forw, char *rev)
{
  int i = 0, j = 0;

  while(*(forw + i) != '\0')          // count the elements
    i++;                              // in the string
  for(i--; i >= 0; i--)
    *rev++ = *(forw + i);
  *rev = '\0';                    // close off reverse string
  return;
}
```

9. The function is included within a complete program.

```
#include <iostream.h>
int main()
{
  const int NUMCHARS = 80;
  char ch, line[NUMCHARS];
  void append_c(char, char *);  // function prototype

  cout << "\nEnter a line of text: ";
  cin.getline(line,NUMCHARS);
  cout << "Enter a single character: ";
  ch = cin.get();
  append_c(ch,line);
  cout << "The new line of text with the appended "
       << "last character is:\n";
  cout << line;

  return 0;
}

void append_c(char c, char *strng)
{

  while(*strng++ != '\0')     // this advances the pointer
    ;                         // one character beyond '\0 '
  strng--;                    // point to the '\0')
  *strng++ = c;               // replace it with the new char
  *strng = '\0';              // close the new string

  return;
}
```

13.
```
void trimrear(char *strng)
  {

    while(*strng != '\0') strng++;    // move to end of string
    strng--;                          // move to char before '\0'
    while(*strng == ' ') strng--;     // skip over blank characters

    *(++strng) = '\0';                // close off string
    return;
  }
```

Section 9.3

1.
```
char *text = "Hooray!";
char text[] = {'H','o','o','r','a','y','!','\0'};
```

3. `message` is a pointer constant. Therefore, the statement `++message`, which attempts to alter its address, is invalid. A correct statement is

```
cout << *(message + i);
```

Here the address in `message` is unaltered and the character pointed to is the character offset `i` bytes from the address corresponding to `message`.

Section 10.1

1. a.
```
struct sTemp
{
  int idNum;
  int credits;
  float avg;
};
```
b.
```
struct sTemp
{
  char name[40];
  int month;
  int day;
  int year;
  int credits;
  float avg;
};
```
c.
```
struct sTemp
{
  char name[40];
  char street[80];
  char city[40];
  char state[2];
  int zip;              // or char zip[5];
};
```
d.
```
struct sTemp
{
  char name[40];
  float price;
  char date[10];    // assumes a date in the form XX/XX/XXXX
};
```
e.
```
struct sTemp
{
  int partNo;
  char desc[100];
  int quant;
  int reorder;
};
```

3\. *a.*
```
#include <iostream.h>
int main()
{
  struct
  {
    int month;
    int day;
    int year;
  }  date;     // define a structure variable named date

   cout << "\nEnter the current month: ";
   cin  >> date.month;
   cout << "Enter the current day: ";
   cin  >> date.day;
   cout << "Enter the current year: ";
   cin  >> date.year;
   cout << "\nThe date entered is : "
        << date.month << '/' << date.day
        << '/' << date.year << endl;

  return 0;
}
```
b.
```
#include <iostream.h>
#include <iomanip.h>
int main()
{
  struct Clock
  {
    int hours;
    int minutes;
    int seconds;
  } time;    // define a structure variable named time

  cout << "\nEnter the current hour: ";
  cin  >> time.hours;
  cout << "Enter the current minute: ";
  cin  >> time.minutes;
  cout << "Enter the current second: ";
  cin  >> time.seconds;
  cout << "\nThe time entered is: "
       << setw(2) << setfill('0') << time.hours << ':'
       << setw(2) << time.minutes << ':'
       << setw(2) << time.seconds << endl;

return 0;
}
```

Note the use of the setw and setfill manipulators. The fill character of 0 forces the field of 2 to be filled with leading zeros.

5.
```
#include <iostream.h>
#include <iomanip.h>
int main()
{
  struct
  {
    int hours;
    int minutes;
  } time;
   cout << "Enter the current hour: ";
   cin  >> time.hours;
   cout << "Enter the current minute: ";
   cin  >> time.minutes;
   if(time.minutes != 59)
     time.minutes += 1;
   else
   {
     time.minutes = 0;
     if(time.hours != 12)
    time.hours += 1;
     else
    time.hours = 1;
  }
  cout << "\nThe time in one minute will be "
       << setiosflags(ios::showpoint) << setfill('0')
       << setw(2) << time.hours << ':'
       << setw(2) << time.minutes << endl;

  return 0;
}
```

Note the use of the setw and setfill manipulators. The fill character of 0 forces the field of 2 to be filled with leading zeros.

Section 10.2

1. *a.*
```
struct sTemp
{
  int idNum;
  int credits;
  float avg;
};

#include <iostream.h>
int main()
{
  sTemp student[100];
```

b.
```
struct sTemp
{
  char name[40];
  int month;
  int day;
  int year;
  int credits;
  float avg;
};

#include <iostream.h>
int main()
{
  sTemp student[100];
```

c.
```
struct sTemp
{
  char name[40];
  char street[80];
  char city[40];
  char state[2];
  int zip;            // or char zip[5];
};

#include <iostream.h>
int main()
{
  sTemp address[100];
```

d.
```
struct sTemp
{
  char name[40];
  float price;
  char date[10]; // Assumes a date in the form XX/XX/XXXX
};

#include <iostream.h>
int main()
{
  sTemp stock[100];
```

e.
```
struct sTemp
{
  int partNo;
  char desc[100];
  int quant;
  int reorder;
};

#include <iostream.h>
int main()
{
  sTemp inven[100];
```

3.
```
struct DaysInMonth
{
  char name[10];
  int days;
};

#include <iostream.h>
int main()
{
  DaysInMonth convert[12] = {"January", 31, "February", 28, "March", 31,
                             "April", 30, "May", 31, "June", 30,
                             "July", 31, "August", 31, "September", 30,
                             "October", 31, "November", 30, "December", 31};
    int i;

    cout << "\nEnter the number of a month: ";
    cin  >> i;
    cout << convert[i-1].name << " has "
         << convert[i-1].days << " days\n";

  return 0;
}
```

Section 10.3

1.
```
struct Date
{
  int month;
  int day;
  int year;
};

#include <iostream.h>
int main()
{
  Date present;
  long num;
  long days(Date);  // function prototype

  cout << "Enter the month: ";
  cin  >> present.month;
  cout << "Enter the day: ";
  cin  >> present.day;
  cout << "Enter the year: ";
  cin  >> present.year;
  num = days(present);
  cout << "The number of days since the turn"
       << " of the century is " << num << endl;

  return 0;
}
```

(continued on next page)

(continued from previous page)

```
long days(Date temp)
{
  return (temp.day + 30*(temp.month - 1) + 360*temp.year);
}
```

Note: The reference version of the function `long days()` is written for Exercise 3a, and the pointer version for Exercise 3b.

3. *a.*
```
struct Date
{
  int month;
  int day;
  int year;
};

#include <iostream.h>
int main()
{
  Date present;
  long num;
  long days(Date &);   // function prototype

cout << "Enter the month: ";
cin  >> present.month;
cout << "Enter the day: ";
cin  >> present.day;
cout << "Enter the year: ";
cin  >> present.year;
num = days(present);
cout << "The number of days since the turn"
     << " of the century is " << num << endl;

return 0;
}

long days(Date &temp)
{
  return (temp.day + 30*(temp.month - 1) + 360*temp.year);
}
```

b.
```
struct Date
{
  int month;
  int day;
  int year;
};

#include <iostream.h>
int main()
{
  Date present;
  long num;
  long days(Date *);    // function prototype

  cout << "Enter the month: ";
  cin  >> present.month;
  cout << "Enter the day: ";
  cin  >> present.day;
  cout << "Enter the year: ";
  cin  >> present.year;
  num = days(&present);
  cout << "The number of days since the turn"
       << " of the century is " << num << endl;

  return 0;
}

long days(Date *temp)
{
  return(temp->day + 30*(temp->month - 1) + 360*temp->year);
}
```

5.
```
struct Date
{
  int month;
  int day;
  int year;
};

#include <iostream.h>
int main()
{
  char ch;
  Date present;
  long num;
  long days(Date);  // function prototype
```

(continued on next page)

(continued from previous page)

```
  cout << "Enter the date as mm/dd/yy: ";
  cin  >> present.month >> ch >> present.day >> ch >> present.year;
  num = days(present);
  cout << "The number of days since the turn of the century is "
       << num << endl;

  return 0;
}

long days(Date temp)
{
  long actualDays;
  int daycount[12] = { 0, 31, 59, 90, 120, 151,
                       180, 211, 241, 271, 302, 333};

  actualDays = temp.day + daycount[temp.month-1] + 364*temp.year;
  return (actualDays);
}
```

Section 10.4

1.
```
#include <iostream.h>
#include <string.h>
const int MAXNAME = 20;
const int MAXTEL = 16;
struct TeleType
{
  char name[MAXNAME];
  char phoneNo[MAXTEL];
   TeleType *nextaddr;
};

#include <iostream.h>
int main()
{

  TeleType t1 = {"Acme, Sam", "(555) 898-2392"};
  TeleType t2 = {"Dolan, Edith", "(555) 682-3104"};
  TeleType t3 = {"Lanfrank, John", "(555) 718-4518"};
  TeleType *first;
  char strng[30];
  void search(TeleType *, char *); // function prototype
```

```
    first = &t1;
    t1.nextaddr = &t2;
    t2.nextaddr = &t3;
    t3.nextaddr = NULL;
    cout << "Enter a name: ";
    cin.getline(strng,MAXNAME);
    search(first, strng);
    cout << endl;

    return 0;
  }

   void search(TeleType *contents, char *strng)
   {
    cout << strng;
    while(contents != NULL)
    {
      if(strcmp(contents->name,strng) == 0)
      {
     cout << "\nFound. The number is " << contents->phoneNo;
     return;
      }
      else
      {
     contents = contents->nextaddr;
      }
    }
    cout << "\nThe name is not in the current phone directory.";

    return;
  }
```

3. To delete the second record, the pointer in the first record must be changed to point to the third record.

5. ***a.***

```
struct PhoneBook
{
  char name[30];
  char phoneNum[15];
    PhoneBook *previous;
    PhoneBook *next;
};
```

Section 10.5

1. The `check()` function is included below in a complete program used to verify that `check()` works correctly.

```
struct TeleType
{
  char name[25];
  char phoneNo[15];
  TeleType *nextaddr;
};

#include <iostream.h>
#include <iomanip.h>
#include <stdlib.h>   // need this for the exit() funciton
int main()
{
  int i;
  TeleType *list, *current;
  int check(TeleType *);        // function prototype
  void populate(TeleType *);    // function prototype
  void display(TeleType *);     // function prototype

  list = new (TeleType);
  check(list);
  current = list;
  for(i = 0; i < 2; i++)
  {
    populate(current);
    current->nextaddr = new (TeleType);

    if (check(current->nextaddr) == 0)
    {
   cout << "No available memory remains. Program terminating";
   exit(0); // terminate program and return to operating system
    }
    current = current->nextaddr;

    return 0;
  }
  populate(current);
  current->nextaddr = NULL;
  cout << "\nThe list consists of the following records:\n";
  display(list);

  return;
}
```

```
int check( TeleType *addr)
{

  if(addr == NULL)
    return 0;
  else
    return 1;
}

void populate( TeleType *record)
{
  cout << "\nEnter a name: ";
  cin.getline(record->name, 30);
  cout << "Enter the phone number: ";
  cin.getline(record->phoneNo,16);
  return;
}

void display( TeleType *contents)
{
  while(contents != NULL)
  {
    cout << endl << setiosflags(ios::left)
         << setw(30) << contents->name
         << setw(20) << contents->phoneNo;
    contents = contents->nextaddr;
  }
  cout << endl;
  return;
}
```

3. The `insert()` function in the complete program below is used to verify that `insert()` works correctly. As written, the function will insert a structure after the structure whose address is passed to it. Since the address of the first structure is passed to it, the new structure is inserted between the first and second structures.

```
struct TeleType
{
  char name[25];
  char phoneNo[15];
  TeleType *nextaddr;
};
```

(continued on next page)

(continued from previous page)

```
#include <iostream.h>
#include <iomanip.h>
int main()
{
  int i;
  TeleType *list, *current;
  void insert(TeleType *);     // function prototype
  void populate(TeleType *);   // function prototype
  void display(TeleType *);    // function prototype

  list = new (TeleType);
  populate(list); // populate the first structure
  list->nextaddr = new (TeleType);
  current = list->nextaddr;
  populate(current); // populate the second structure
  current->nextaddr = NULL;
  cout << "\nThe list initially consists of the following records:";
  display(list);
  insert(list);   // insert between first and second structures
  cout << "\nThe new list now consists of the following records:";
  display(list);
}
void insert(TeleType *addr)
{
  TeleType *temp;
  void populate(TeleType *);  // function prototype

  temp = addr->nextaddr;      // save pointer to next structure
    // now change address to point to inserted structure
  addr->nextaddr = new (TeleType);
  populate(addr->nextaddr);   // populate the new structure
    // set address member of new structure to saved addr
  addr->nextaddr->nextaddr = temp;
  return;
}

void populate(TeleType *record)
{
  cout << "\nEnter a name: ";
  cin.getline(record->name,30);
  cout << "Enter the phone number: ";
  cin.getline(record->phoneNo,16);
  return;
}
```

```
void display( TeleType *contents)
{
  while(contents != NULL)
  {
    cout << endl << setiosflags(ios::left)
         << setw(30) << contents->name
         << setw(20) << contents->phoneNo;
    contents = contents->nextaddr;
  }
cout << endl;

return;
}
```

Notice that if the `populate` function call is removed from the insert function, then `insert()` becomes a general insertion program that simply creates a structure and correctly adjusts the address members of each structure. Also, notice the notation used in `insert()`. The expression

```
addr->nextaddr->nextaddr
```

is equivalent to

```
(addr->nextaddr)->nextaddr
```

This notation was not used in `main()` because the pointer variable `current` is first used to store the address in `list->nextaddr` using the statement

```
current = list->nextaddr;
```

The statement

```
current->nextaddr = NULL;
```

in `int main()`, however, could have been written as:

```
list->nextaddr->nextaddr = NULL;
```

An interesting exercise is to rewrite `main()` so that the pointer variable named `current` is removed entirely from the function.

5. The `modify()` function in the complete program below is used to verify that `modify()` works correctly. The driver function creates a single structure, populates it, and then calls `modify()`. `modify()` itself calls the function `repop()`. An interesting extension is to write `repop()` so that an Enter key response retains the original structure member value.

```
struct TeleType
{
  char name[25];
  char phoneNo[15];
  TeleType *nextaddr;
};

#include <iostream.h>
#include <iomanip.h>
int main()
{
  int i;
  TeleType *list;
  void populate(TeleType *);  // function prototype
  void modify(TeleType *);    // function prototype

  list = new (TeleType);
  populate(list); // populate the first structure
  list->nextaddr = NULL;
  modify(list);   // modify the structure members

  return 0;
}

void modify(TeleType *addr)
{
  void display(TeleType *);   // function prototype
  void repop(TeleType *);  // function prototype

  cout << "\nThe current structure members are:";
  display(addr);
  repop(addr);
  cout << "\nThe structure members are now:";
  display(addr);
  return;
}
```

```
void populate(TeleType *record)
{
  cout << "\nEnter a name: ";
  cin.getline(record->name,30);
  cout << "Enter the phone number: ";
  cin.getline(record->phoneNo,16);
  return;
}
void repop(TeleType *record)
{
  cout << "\n\nEnter a new name: ";
  cin.getline(record->name,30);
  cout << "Enter a new phone number: ";
  cin.getline(record->phoneNo,16);
  return;
}
void display(TeleType *contents)
{
  while(contents != NULL)
  {
    cout << endl << setiosflags(ios::left)
         << setw(30) << contents->name
         << setw(20) << contents->phoneNo;
    contents = contents->nextaddr;
  }
cout << endl;
return;
}
```

Section 10.6

1. `cout` **stream activations are contained within the following program.**

```
union
{
  float rate;
  double taxes;
  int num;
} flag;
#include <iostream.h>
int main()
{
  flag.rate = 22.5;
  cout << "\nThe rate is " << flag.rate;
  flag.taxes = 44.7;
  cout << "\ntaxes are " << flag.taxes;
  flag.num = 6;
  cout << "\nnum is " << flag.num;

  return 0;
}
```

5. Since a value has not been assigned to `alt.btype`, the display produced is unpredictable (the code for a `'y'` resides in the storage locations overlapped by the variables `alt.ch` and `alt.btype`). Thus, either a garbage value will be displayed or the program could crash.

Section 11.1

1. *a.* An attribute represents a characteristic of an object; specifically, it is a data member of the object.

b. The behavior of an object defines how the object can be activated and the response that will be produced. It is specified by the object's member and friend functions.

c. The state of an object defines how the object appears at the moment. It is specified by the values assigned to the object's data member variables.

d. A model is a representation of a real object.

e. A class defines the attributes and behavior of a category or set of objects. As such it is a general representation from which specific objects can be created.

f. An object is a specific instance of a class. As such, values have been assigned to its data members.

g. The set of attributes and behaviors defining a class is frequently referred to as the class's *interface*.

3. *a.* ***i.*** the title, author, subject, publisher, and date of publication

ii. the type, size, and cost

iii. the type (ballpoint, ink cartridge, or ink refillable), the manufacturer, the color, the cost

iv. the manufacturer of the tape, its length, type, and contents

v. the manufacturer, cost, size, and capabilities (such as rewind, fast forward, record, etc.)

vi. its speed, capacity, cost of installation, cost of operation, cost of maintenance, manufacturer

vii. its manufacturer, overall size, color, cost, engine size, seating capacity, model type, estimated miles per gallon

b. These attributes model a class of objects. Only when specific values are assigned to these attributes is a specific object identified.

5. Animate objects can also be modeled and classified by classes. For example, dogs and cats can be grouped under the category pets, with an attribute of type. In general the attributes included in the class represent characteristics that are of concern for those using the class. For a veterinarian, a more useful attribute might consist of whether the animal has been inoculated or not.

Section 11.2

1. *a.* A class is a programmer-defined data type. The class specifies both the types of data and the types of operations that may be performed on the data.

b. An object is a specific instance of a class.

c. The declaration section declares both the data types and function prototypes of a class.

d. The implementation section defines the class's functions.

e. An instance variable is another name for a class data member.

f. A member function is a function declared in the class declaration section.

g. A data member is a variable declared in the class declaration section.
h. A member function that has the same name as the class and is used to initialize an object's data members.
i. Class instance is synonymous with an object.
j. Services are synonyms for the functions defined in a class implementation section.
k. Methods are synonyms for the functions defined in a class implementation section.

3. *a.* The class implementation section is included within the complete program written for Exercise 4a.
b. The class implementation section is included within the complete program written for Exercise 4b.
c. The class implementation section is included within the complete program written for Exercise 4c.

5. The class name should begin with a capital letter (e.g., Employee). The data members should be declared as private and the function members should be declared as public. Additionally, the declaration for the constructor prototype should be `class(int, char *)`.

7.
```
#include <iostream.h>
// class declaration
class Date
{
  private:
    int month;
    int day;
    int year;
  public:
    Date(int = 7, int = 4, int = 2001);  // constructor
    void setdate(int, int, int);     // member function to assign a date
    void showdate(void);             // member function to display a date
    int leapyr(void);                // the additional member function
};

// implementation section
Date::Date(int mm, int dd, int yyyy)
{
  month = mm;
  day = dd;
  year = yyyy;
}
void Date::setdate(int mm, int dd, int yyyy)
{
  month = mm;
  day = dd;
  year = yyyy;
}
```

(continued on next page)

(continued from previous page)

```
void Date::showdate(void)
{
  cout << setfill('0')
       << setw(2) << month << '/'
       << setw(2) << day << '/'
       << setw(2) << year % 100;

  return;
}
int Date::leapyr(void)
{
  int fullyr;

  fullyr = year + 1900;
  if( (fullyr % 4 == 0 && fullyr % 100 != 0) || (fullyr % 400 == 0) )
    return 1;   // is a leap year
  else
    return 0;   // is not a leap year
}

int main()
{
   Date a, b, c(4,1,96);  // declare 3 objects

   b.setdate(12,25,95);  // assign values to b's data members
   a.showdate();
   cout << "  The leap year indicator is " << a.leapyr() << endl;
   b.showdate();
   cout << "  The leap year indicator is " << b.leapyr() << endl;
   c.showdate();
   cout << "  The leap year indicator is " << c.leapyr() << endl;

   return 0;
}
```

Section 11.3

1. *a.* true
   b. false
   c. true
   d. false
   e. true
   f. false
   g. false
   h. true
   i. true
   j. true
   k. false
   l. false
   m. false
   n. true
   o. false

3.
```
#include <iostream.h>

// class declaration
class Date
{
  private:
    long yyyymmdd;
  public:
    Date(int = 7, int = 4, int = 2001);      // constructor
    Date(long);                          // default constructor
    void showdate(void);                 // member function to display a Date
};

// implementation section
Date::Date(int mm, int dd, int yyyy)
{
  yyyymmdd = yyyy * 10000L + mm * 100L + dd;
}
Date::Date(long ymd = 940704)
{
  yyyymmdd = ymd;
}
void Date::showdate(void)
{
  int year, month, day;

  year = (int)(yyyymmdd/10000.0);     // extract the year
  month = (int)( (yyyymmdd - year * 10000.0)/100.00 ); // extract the month
  day = (int)(yyyymmdd - year * 10000.0 - month * 100.0); // extract the day
  cout << "The Date is " << month << "/" << day << "/" << year << endl;
}

int main()
{
   Date a, b(4,1,1998), c(20020515L); // declare three objects

   a.showdate();          // display object a's values
   b.showdate();          // display object b's values
   c.showdate();          // display object c's values

  return 0;
}
```

Section 12.1

1. Assignment stores a value into an existing variable or object; that is, it occurs after the variable or object has been created by a definition statement. Initialization occurs at the time a new variable or object is created and is part of the creation process.

3. a. The required class is contained within the program solution to Exercise 3b.

b.
```
#include <iostream.h>
#include <iomanip.h>
// declaration section
class Complex
{
  private:
    float real;
    float imaginary;
  public:
   Complex(float, float);     // constructor
   void operator=(Complex &); // overloaded assignment operator function
   void showdata(void);       // display member function
};

// implementation section
Complex::Complex(float re = 0, float im = 0)
{
  real = re;
  imaginary = im;
}
void Complex::operator=(Complex &oldnum)
{
  real = oldnum.real;
  imaginary = oldnum.imaginary;
}
void Complex::showdata(void)
{
  float c;
  char sign = '+';

  c = imaginary;
  if (c < 0)
  {
    sign = '-';
    c = -c;
  }
  cout << "The complex number is "
       << setiosflags(ios::fixed)
       << real << ' ' << sign << ' ' << c << "i\n";

}

int main()
{
   Complex a(4.2, 3.6), b;  // declare 2 objects

   a.showdata();        // display object a's values
   b.showdata();        // display object b's values
   b = a;               // assign a to b
   b.showdata();        // display object b's values

  return 0;
}
```

5. A copy of the pointer from object one to object two results in the loss of the address initially stored in object two. The memory space originally pointed to will, however, still contain data. An additional problem results when a destructor is called for object one. The destruction of object one causes the memory space pointed to by object one to be released. Since object two points to the same memory area, this results in object two's pointer member having the address of unallocated memory.

Section 12.2

1.
```
#include <iostream.h>
#include <string.h>

// class declaration
class Book
{
  private:
    char *title;    // a pointer to a book title
  public:
    Book(char *);   // constructor
    Book(Book &);   // copy constructor
    void operator=(Book &);  // overloaded assignment operator
    void showtitle(void);    // display the title
};
// class implementation

Book::Book(char *strng = NULL)    // constructor
{
  title = new char[strlen(strng)+1];  // allocate memory
  strcpy(title,strng);                // store the string
}

Book::Book(Book &oldbook)    // copy constructor
{
  title = new char[strlen(oldbook.title) + 1];  // allocate new memory
  strcpy(title, oldbook.title);  // copy the title
}

void Book::operator=(Book &oldbook)
{
  if(title != NULL)  // check that it exists
    delete(title);   // release existing memory
  title = new char[strlen(oldbook.title) + 1];  // allocate new memory
  strcpy(title, oldbook.title);  // copy the title
}
```

(continued on next page)

(continued from previous page)

```
void Book::showtitle(void)
{
  cout << title << endl;

return;
}
int main()
{
  Book book1("DOS Primer");    // create 1st title
  Book book2 = book1;          // create a copy
  Book book3("A Brief History of Western Civilization");  // 2nd title

  book1.showtitle();    // display book1's title
  book2.showtitle();    // check the copy worked
  book3.showtitle();    // display the third book title
  book2 = book3;        // assign book3 to book2
  book2.showtitle();    // check the assignment worked

  return 0;
}
```

3. *a.* The required class is contained within the program solution to Exercise 3b.

b.

```
#include <iostream.h>
#include <iomanip.h>
#include <string.h>
// declaration section
class Car
{
  private:
    float engineSize;
    char bodyStyle;
    int colorCode;
    char *vinPtr;
  public:
    Car(float, char, int, char *);  // constructor
    void operator=(Car &);        // overloaded assignment operator
    void showdata(void);          // member function to display a time
};

// implementation section

Car::Car(float eng = 0.0, char styl = 'X', int cd = 0, char *pt = NULL)
{
  engineSize = eng;
  bodyStyle = styl;
  colorCode = cd;
  vinPtr = new char[strlen(pt) + 1];    // allocate memory
  strcpy(vinPtr, pt);                   // store the string
}
```

```
void Car::operator=(Car &oldcar)
{
  engineSize = oldcar.engineSize;
  bodyStyle = oldcar.bodyStyle;
  colorCode = oldcar.colorCode;
  if(vinPtr != NULL)    // check that it exists
    delete(vinPtr);     // release existing memory
  vinPtr = new char[strlen(oldcar.vinPtr) + 1];  // allocate new memory
  strcpy(vinPtr, oldcar.vinPtr);  // copy the vin
}

void Car::showdata(void)
{
  cout << "\nThe values for this object are \n"
       << "  Engine size: " << engineSize << endl
       << "  Body style:  " << bodyStyle << endl
       << "  Color code:  " << colorCode << endl
       << "  VIN: " << vinPtr << endl;
}

int main()
{
   Car a(250.0, 'S', 52, "ABC567YYY"), b;  // declare 2 objects

   a.showdata();    // display object a's values
   b.showdata();    // display object b's values
   b = a;           // assign a to b
   b.showdata();    // display object a's values

  return 0;
}
```

Section 12.3

1. a.

```
#include <iostream.h>
// class declaration
class Employee
{
  private:
    static float taxRate;
    static int numemps;
    int idNum;
  public:
    Employee(int);     // constructor
    void display();    // access function
};
```

(continued on next page)

(continued from previous page)

```
// static member definition
float Employee::taxRate = 0.0025;
int Employee::numemps = 0;
// class implementation
Employee::Employee(int num = 0)
{
  idNum = num;
  numemps++;
}
void Employee::display()
{
  cout << "Employee number " << idNum
       << " has a tax rate of " << taxRate << endl;
  cout << "There are currently " << numemps
       << " Employee objects" << endl;
}

int main()
{
  Employee emp1(11122);

  emp1.display();

  Employee emp2(11133);  // create a second object

  emp2.display();

  return 0;
}
```

3.
```
// implementation section
Date::Date(int mm, int dd, int yyyy)
{
  this->month = mm;
  this->day = dd;
  this->year = yyyy;
}

void Date::setdate(int mm, int dd, int yyyy)
{
  this->month = mm;
  this->day = dd;
  this->year = yyyy;
}
```

```
void Date::showdate(void)
{
  cout << "The date is ";
  cout << setfill('0')
       << setw(2) << this->month << '/'
       << setw(2) << this->day << '/'
       << setw(2) << this->year % 100
  cout << endl;
  return;
}
```

Section 13.1

1. a. The required function is included within the following working program:

```
#include <iostream.h>
// class declaration
class Date
{
  private:
     int month;
     int day;
     int year;

  public:
    Date(int = 7, int = 4, int = 2001);       // constructor
    int operator>(Date &);  // declare the operator> function
};

// implementation section
Date::Date(int mm, int dd, int yyyy)
{
  month = mm;
  day = dd;
  year = yyyy;
}
int Date::operator>(Date &date2)
{
  long dt1, dt2;

  dt1 = year*10000L + month*100 + day;
  dt2 = date2.year*10000L + date2.month*100 + date2.day;
  if (dt1 > dt2)
    return (1);
  else
    return (0);
}
```

(continued on next page)

(continued from previous page)

```
int main()
{
   Date a(4,1,1999), b(12,18,2001), c(4,1,1999); // declare 3 objects

   if (a > b)
     cout << "Date a greater than b \n";
   else
     cout << "Date a less than or equal to b \n";

   if (a > c)
     cout << "Date a greater than c \n";
   else
     cout << "Date a less than or equal to c \n";

  return 0;
}
```

3. *a.* This operator function provides the same result as the `operator()` function used in Program 13-2.

5. *a.* The required function is incorporated within the complete program written for Exercise 5b.

   b.

```
#include <iostream.h>
// class declaration
class Date
{
  private:
    int month;
    int day;
    int year;
  public:
    Date(int = 7, int = 4, int = 2001);     // constructor
    Date operator+(int);       // overload the + operator
    void showdate();           // member function to display a Date
};

// implementation section
Date::Date(int mm, int dd, int yyyy)
{
  month = mm;
  day = dd;
  year = yyyy;
}
Date Date::operator+(int days)
{
  int daysrem;    // days remaining in the month
  int ds[] = {0,31,28,31,30,31,30,31,31,30,31,30,31};
  Date temp;  // a temporary Date to store the result
  temp.day = day;
  temp.month = month;
  temp.year = year;
```

```
  daysrem = ds[month] - temp.day;
  while(daysrem < days)
  {
    temp.month++;
    if(temp.month > 12)
    {
      temp.month = 1;
      temp.year++;
    }
    temp.day = 1;
    days -= (daysrem + 1);
    daysrem = ds[month] - temp.day;
  }
  // now the days remaining is within the current month
  temp.day = temp.day + days;
  return temp;      // the values in temp are returned
}

void Date::showdate(void)
{
  cout << setfill('0')
       << setw(2) << month << '/'
       << setw(2) << day << '/'
       << setw(2) << year % 100;

  return;
}

int main()
{
   Date a(4,1,1999), b; // declare two objects

   cout << "The initial Date is ";
   a.showdate();
   b = a + 284;    // add in 284 days
   cout << "\nThe new Date is ";
   b.showdate();
  cout << endl;

  return 0;
}
```

Section 13.2

1. The function's prototype is:

```
Date operator()(int);     // overload the () operator
```

The function's definition is:

```
Date Date::operator()(int days)
{
  Date temp;  // a temporary Date to store the result

  temp.day = day + days;  // add the days
  temp.month = month;
  temp.year = year;
  while (temp.day > 30)     // now adjust the months
  {
    temp.month++;
    temp.day -= 30;
  }
  while (temp.month > 12)   // adjust the years
  {
    temp.year++;
    temp.month -= 12;
  }
  return temp;      // the values in temp are returned
}
```

Section 13.3

1. ***a.*** Conversion from a built-in type to a built-in type is accomplished by C++'s implicit conversion rules or by explicit casting.

Conversion from a built-in type to a user-defined type is accomplished by a type conversion constructor.

Conversion from a user-defined type to a built-in type is accomplished by a conversion operator function.

Conversion from a user-defined type to a built-in type is accomplished by a conversion operator function.

b. A type conversion constructor is a constructor whose first argument is not a member of its class and whose remaining arguments, if any, have default values.

A conversion operator function is a class member operator function having the name of a built-in data type or class.

3.
```
#include <iostream.h>

// class declaration for Date
class Date
{
  private:
    int month, day, year;
  public:
    Date(int = 7, int = 4, int = 2001);    // constructor
    operator long();          // conversion operator function
    void showdate(void);
};
// constructor
Date::Date(int mm, int dd, int yyyy)
{
  month = mm;
  day = dd;
  year = yyyy;
}
// conversion operator function converting from Date to long
Date::operator long()   // must return a long
{
  int mp, yp, t;
  long julian;

  if (month <= 2)
  {
    mp = 0;
    yp = year - 1;
  }
  else
  {
    mp = int(0.4 * month + 2.3);
    yp = year;
  }

  t = int(yp/4) - int(yp/100) + int(yp/400);
  julian = 365L * year + 31L * (month - 1) + day + t - mp;
  return (julian);
}

// member function to display a Date
void Date::showdate(void)
{
  cout << setfill('0')
       << setw(2) << month << '/'
       << setw(2) << day << '/'
       << setw(2) << year % 100;

  return;
}
```

(continued on next page)

(continued from previous page)

```
int main()
{
   Date a(1,31,1985);  // declare and initialize one object of type Date
   long b;             // declare an object of type long

   b = a;              // a conversion takes place here

   cout << "a's date is ";
   a.showdate();
   cout << "\nThis Date, as a long integer, is " << b << endl;

  return 0;
}
```

5.
```
#include <iostream.h>

// forward declaration of class Julian
class Julian;

// class declaration for Date
class Date
{
  private:
    int month, day, year;
  public:
    Date(int = 7, int = 4, int = 2001);     // constructor
    operator Julian();       // conversion operator to Julian
    void showdate(void);
};

// class declaration for Julian
class Julian
{
  private:
    long yyyymmdd;
  public:
    Julian(long);     // constructor
    void showjulian(void);
};

// class implementation for Date
Date::Date(int mm, int dd, int yyyy)  // constructor
{
  month = mm;
  day = dd;
  year = yyyy;
}
```

```
// conversion operator function converting from Date to Julian class
Date::operator Julian()    // must return a Julian object
{
  int mp, yp, t;
  long temp;

  if (month <= 2)
  {
    mp = 0;
    yp = year - 1;
  }
  else
  {
    mp = int(0.4 * month + 2.3);
    yp = year;
  }
  t = int(yp/4) - int(yp/100) + int(yp/400);
  temp = 365L * year + 31L *s (month - 1) + day + t - mp;
  return (temp);
}

// member function to display a Date
void Date::showdate(void)
{
  cout << setfill('0')
       << setw(2) << month << '/'
       << setw(2) << day << '/'
       << setw(2) << year % 100;

  return;
}
// class implementation for Julian
Julian::Julian(long ymd = 0)  // constructor
{
  yyyymmdd = ymd;
}

// member function to display a Julian
void Julian::showjulian(void)
{
  cout << yyyymmdd;
}

int main()
{
   Date a(1,31,1995), b(3,16,1996);  // declare two Date objects
   Julian c, d;                      // declare two Julian objects

   c = Julian(a);     // cast a into a Julian object
   d = Julian(b);     // cast b into a Julian object
   cout << " a's date is ";
   a.showdate();
   cout << "\n  as a Julian object this date is ";
   c.showjulian();
```

(continued on next page)

(continued from previous page)

```
    cout << "\n b's date is ";
    b.showdate();
    cout << "\n   as a Julian object this date is ";
    d.showjulian();

  return 0;
}
```

Note: There is no conversion operator from `Julian` to `Date`. In general the `Julian` objects are extremely useful for determining actual day count differences between two dates, and for sorting dates. In practice, the `Julian` date would be incorporated as a data member of the `Date` class. Also note that the forward reference to the `Julian` class could be omitted in this program if the `Julian` class were declared prior to the `Date` class.

Section 13.4

1. *a.* Inheritance is the capability of deriving one class from another class.
   b. A base class is the class that is used as the basis for deriving subsequent classes.
   c. A derived class is the class that inherits the characteristics of a base class,
   d. Simple inheritance is a type of inheritance where the parent of each derived class is a single base class.
   e. Multiple inheritance is a type of inheritance where a derived class has two or more parent base classes.
   f. Class hierarchies are the order in which classes are derived.
   g. Polymorphism is the ability of a function or operator to have multiple forms. The particular form that will be invoked is determined at run time and depends on the object being used.
   h. In static binding the determination of which function will be called is made at compile time.
   i. In dynamic binding the determination of which function will be called is made at run time.
   j. A virtual function is a function that is called by a pointer whose value is determined at run time depending on the object making the call.

3. The three features that must be provided for a programming language to be classified as object-oriented are classes, inheritance, and polymorphism. Object-based languages are languages that support objects but do not provide inheritance features.

5.
```
#include <iostream.h>
#include <math.h>

const double PI = 2.0 * asin(1.0);

class Circle
{
  protected:
    double radius;
  public:
    Circle(double);  // constructor
    double calcval();
};
```

```
// class implementation
Circle::Circle(double r= 1.0)  // constructor
{
  radius = r;
}
double Circle::calcval(void)   // this calculates an area
{
  return(PI * radius * radius);
}

class Cylinder : public Circle  // Cylinder is derived from Circle
{
  protected:
    double length;  // add one additional data member and
  public:           // two additional function members
    Cylinder(double r = 1.0, double l = 1.0) : Circle(r), length(l) {}
    double calcval();
};

class Sphere : public Circle  // Sphere is derived from Circle
{
  public:           // two additional function members
    Sphere(double r = 1.0) : Circle(r) {} // base member initialization
    double calcval();
};

// class implementation
double Cylinder::calcval(void)   // this calculates a volume for a cylinder
{
  return (length * Circle::calcval()); // note the base function call
}

double Sphere::calcval(void)   // this calculates a volume for a sphere
{
  return (4.0/3.0 * radius * Circle::calcval()); // note the base function call
}
int main()
{
  Circle circle_1, circle_2(2);  // create two Circle objects
  Cylinder cylinder_1(3,4);      // create one Cylinder object
  Sphere sphere_1(4);            // create one Sphere object

  cout << "The area of circle_1 is " << circle_1.calcval() << endl;
  cout << "The area of circle_2 is " << circle_2.calcval() << endl;
  cout << "The volume of cylinder_1 is " << cylinder_1.calcval() << endl;
  cout << "The volume of sphere_1 is " << sphere_1.calcval() << endl;
  circle_1 = sphere_1;  // assign a Sphere to a Circle

  cout << "\nThe area of circle_1 is now " << circle_1.calcval() << endl;

  return 0;
}
```

Section 14.1

3. *a.* On an IBM PC or compatible, a file name may have up to eight characters, and optionally a decimal point followed by three more characters. If a string is used to hold the file name, an extra character should be provided for the NULL, for a total of 13 characters.

5. *a.*
```
ifstream inData;
ifstream prices;
ifstream coupons;
ifstream inData;
```

Section 14.2

1. *a.*
```
#include <fstream.h>
int main()
{
  const int MAX = 80;
  fstream out;
  char strng[MAX];

  out.open("text.dat", ios::out);
  cout << "Enter lines of text to be stored in the file.\n";
  cout << "Enter a carriage return only to terminate input.\n\n";
  cin.getline(strng, MAX + 1, '\n');
  while(*strng != '\0')
  {
    out << strng << endl;
    cin.getline(strng, MAX + 1, '\n');
  }
  out.close();
  cout << "End of data input.\n";
  cout << "The file has been written.\n";

  return 0;
}
```

Section 14.3

1. The following program displays the data in `test.dat`, in reverse order (as does Program 14-5), but moves the offset relative to the start of the file.

```
#include <fstream.h>
int main()
{
  char ch;
  long offset, last;
  fstream inFile;
```

```
  inFile.open("test.dat", ios::in);
  if (!inFile)    // check for successful open
  {
    cout << "\nThe file was not successfully opened"
         << "\n Please check that the file currently exits."
         << endl;
    return 0;
  }

  inFile.seekg(0L, ios::end);   // move to the end of the file
  last = inFile.tellg();  // determine the length of the file
  cout << "file length = " << last;
  inFile.seekg(0L,ios::beg);    // move to the start of the file
  cout << "\nThe characters in the file, in reverse order, are:" << endl;
  for(offset = (last-1); offset = 0; offset--)
  {
    inFile.seekg(offset, ios::beg);
    ch = inFile.get();
    cout << ch << " : ";
  }
  inFile.close();
}
```

5. ***a.*** The required function is included within the working program listed below. Note that the function does not check that sufficient characters remain in the file for reading.

```
#include <fstream.h>
int main()
{
  const int MCHARS = 13;
  fstream in;
  char name[MCHARS];
  long start, len;
  void r_bytes(fstream &, long, long);  // function prototype

  cout << "\nEnter file name: ";
  cin  >> name;
  in.open(name, ios::in);
  cout << "Enter starting position for reading: ";
  cin  >> start;
  cout << "Enter number of characters to read: ";
  cin  >> len;
  cout << "The characters are: \n";
  r_bytes(in, start, len);
  cout << endl;
  in.close();

  return 0;
}
```

(continued on next page)

(continued from previous page)

```
void r_bytes(fstream &fname, long begin, long num)
{
  char ch;
  long i;
  --begin;        // the offset is one less than position
  fname.seekg(begin, ios::beg);  // move to the starting char
  for(i = 1; i <= num; i++)
  {
    ch = fname.get();
    cout << ch;
  }
  return;
}
```

Section 14.4

1. The filename referred to in the exercise is a reference to an object of type `fstream`. The header line for `p_file()` is:

```
p_file(fstream &fname)
```

3. The `getOpen()` function is included below with a driver function used to test it.

```
#include <fstream.h>
int main()  // driver function to test getOpen() function
{
   void getOpen(fstream &);     // function prototype
   fstream outFile;

   getOpen(outFile);
   if (outFile != NULL)
   {
     cout << "\nThe file has been opened.";
     outFile.close();
   }
   else
     cout << "\nThe file has not been opened.";
}
void getOpen(fstream &fname)
{
  const int MAXCHARS = 13;
  char name[MAXCHARS], key;
```

```
  cout << "Enter a file name: ";
  cin.getline(name, MAXCHARS, '\n');
   // check if the file exists before opening it for writing
  fname.open(name,ios::in);
  if( fname )    // the file exists
  {
    fname.close();
    cout << "\nThe file currently exists. Do you want to"
         << "\nappend to it, overwrite it, or exit."
         << "\nEnter an a, o, or e: ";
    cin  >> key;
    switch(key)
    {
  case 'a':
  case 'A': fname.open(name,ios::app);  // append open
         break;
  case 'o':
  case 'O': fname.open(name,ios::out);  // write open
         break;
  default: fname.close();
   }
 }
 else   // the file doesn't exist - create it for writing
    fname.open(name,ios::out);

 return 0;
}
```

Index

Operators

A

T

U

V

W

QUICK REFERENCE

Function and Header File Reference

Standard I/O — Requires iostream.h header file

cin	Standard input stream
cin.get()	Input a single character
cin.getline(str, ln, chr)	Input a string of length ln or terminate if chr is detected
cout	Standard output stream

I/O Manipulators — Requires iomanip.h header file

setfill(ch)	Set the fill character to ch
setw(n)	Set the field width to n
setprecision(n)	Set the floating-point precision to n places
setiosflags(flags)	Set the format flags
dec	Set output for decimal display
hex	Set output for hexadecimal display
oct	Set output for octal display
endl	Insert newline and flush stream
flush	Flush an ostream

Format Flags for setiosflags( )

ios::showpoint	Always show the decimal point (default of 6 decimal digits)
ios::showpos	Display a leading + sign when the number is positive
ios::fixed	Display up to 3 integer digits and 2 digits after the decimal point For larger integer values revert to exponential notation
ios::scientific	Use exponential display on output
ios::showbase	Show base indicator on output
ios::dec	Display in decimal format
ios::oct	Display in octal format
ios::hex	Display in hexadecimal format
ios::left	Left-justify output
ios::right	Right-justify output
ios::stdio	Flush stdout and stderr after insertion
ios::skipws	Skip whitespace on input

Note: These flags may be combined by OR operators. For example, setiosflags(ios::showpoint | ios::left) sets the showpoint and left flags together.

Function and Header File Reference *(continued)*

Conversion Routines — Requires stdlib.h header file

atof(string	Convert ASCII string to floating point
atio(string)	Convert ASCII string to an integer
itoa(num,string)	Convert integer to ASCII string

Character Routines — Requires ctype.h header file

isalpha(character)	Is the character an alphanumeric
isascii(character)	Is the character an ASCII character
islower(character)	Is the character lowercase
isupper(character)	Is the character uppercase
isdigit(character)	Is the character a digit
isspace(character)	Is the character a whitespace
isprint(character)	Is this a printable character
ispunct(character)	Is this a punctuation character
iscntrl(character)	Is this a control character
toupper(character)	Convert character to uppercase
tolower(character)	Convert character to lowercase

String Routines — Requires string.h header file

strcat(string1, string2)	Concatenate two strings
strcpy(tostring, fromstring)	Copy fromstring to tostring
strlen(string)	Determine the length of a string
strchr(string, character)	Find a character in a string
strcmp(string1, string2)	Compare two strings

File I/O — Requires the fstream.h header file

file.open(char*, mode)	Open an fstream with given mode
file.close()	Close an fstream
file.get()	Extract the next character from the file
file.getline(str, ln, ch)	Extract a string from the file
file.peak()	Return the next file character without changing file position
file.putback(ch)	Push back a character to the file
file.eof()	Return a 1 if end-of-file has been reached

Permissible File Modes

ios::in	Open in input mode
ios::out	Open in output mode
ios::app	Open in append mode
ios::ate	Go to end of file when opened
ios::binary	Open in binary mode (default is text)
ios::trunc	Delete file contents if it exists
ios::nocreate	If file does not exist, an open will fail
ios::noreplace	If file exists, an open for output will fail

C++ REFERENCE *(continued)*

Statements

A *null* statement consists of a semicolon only.

```
;          // the null statement
```

A *simple* statement is either a null statement, declaration, expression, or function statement.

Examples:

```
double a;                       // declaration statement
taxes = rate * income;          // an expression statement
void display(4.875);            // function statement
```

A *compound* statement consists of one or more statements enclosed within braces.

Example:

```
{                               // start of compound statement */
   taxes = rate * income;
   count++;
}                               // end of compound statement
```

Flow control statements are structured statements consisting of a keyword (if, while, for, do, switch) followed by an expression within parentheses and a simple or compound statement.

```
if (expression)
   statement;

if (expression)
   statement1;
else
   statement2;
```

```
if (expression)
   statement1;
else if (expression)
   statement_2;
      .
      .
      .
else
   statement_n;
```

```
switch (expression)
{
   case value_1:
      statement_1;
      break;
   case value_2:
      statement_2;
      break;
         .
         .
         .
   default:
   statement_n;
}
```

```
for (init; expression; alter)
   statement;

while (expression)
   statement;

do
   statement;
while (expression);
```

Classes

A *class* is a user-defined data type that has both data and function members. An *object* is a variable created from a class.

Example:

```
// declaration section
class Date
{
   private:
      int month;
      int day;
      int year;
   public:
      Date(int = 7, int = 4, int = 2001 );       // a constructor prototype with default
arguments
   void showdate(void);    // another member function prototype
}; // this is a declaration — don't forget the semicolon

// implementation section
Date::Date(int mm, int dd, int yyyy)  // a constructor
{
   month = mm;
   day = dd;
   year = yyyy;
}
void showdate(void)
{
   cout << "The date is" << month << '/' << day << '/' << year << endl;
}

Date startdate, enddate;  // create two Date objects
```

Note: Default arguments may be placed within the declarations section prototype. The function definition may also be included within the declaration section. Structures may also be extended to include member functions and define a class.

C++ REFERENCE

A FIRST BOOK OF C++, Second Edition by Gary Bronson

Keywords

auto	default	goto	public	this
break	do	if	register	template
case	double	inline	return	typedef
catch	else	int	short	union
char	enum	long	signed	unsigned
class	extern	new	sizeof	virtual
const	float	overload	static	void
continue	for	private	struct	volatile
delete	friend	protected	switch	while

Operators

Type	Symbols	Associativity
Global resolution	::	right to left
Local resolution	::	left to right
Primary	( ) [ ] . ->	left to right
Unary	sizeof ++ -- ~ !+ - * & () new delete	right to left
Arithmetic	* / %	left to right
Arithmetic	+ -	left to right
Shift	<< >>	left to right
Relational	< <= > >=	left to right
Relational	== !=	left to right
Bitwise AND	&	left to right
Bitwise XOR	^	left to right
Bitwise OR	|	left to right
Logical AND	&&	left to right
Logical OR	||	left to right
Conditional	?:	right to left
Assignment	= += -= /= %= etc.	right to left
Comma	,	left to right

Scalar Data Types

char
int
float
double

Examples:

```
char key;
int num = 10;
float sum, average, factor = 2.5;
double first, second, third;
```

Note: Additionally, long, short, and unsigned qualifiers may be used with these data types.

Arrays

An *array* is a list of elements, all of which are the same data type. The first element in an array is referred to as the zeroth element.

Examples:

```
int prices[5];
char name[20];
float rates [4][15];
```

Structures

A *structure* (or record) is a data type whose elements need not be of the same data type.

Example:

```
struct telRec      // telRec is an optional tag name
{
  char name[20];
  int id;
  double rate;
} phone;           // phone is a structure variable
```

Comments

Line comments begin with a // and are terminated by the end of the line.

Example: // this is a sample line comment

Block comments can span multiple lines and are enclosed within a /* and */.

Example: /* this is a sample block comment */